Second Edition

CHILDREN

John W. Santrock

University of Texas at Dallas

WCB

Wm. C. Brown Publishers

Book Team

Editor *Michael Lange*
Developmental Editor *Carla J. Aspelmeier*
Production Editor *Gloria G. Schiesl*
Designer *Laurie J. Entringer*
Art Editor *Gayle A. Salow*
Photo Editor *Michelle Oberhoffer*
Permissions Editor *Mavis M. Oeth*
Visuals Processor *Joyce E. Watters*

 Wm. C. Brown Publishers

President *G. Franklin Lewis*
Vice President, Publisher *George Wm. Bergquist*
Vice President, Publisher *Thomas E. Doran*
Vice President, Operations and Production *Beverly Kolz*
National Sales Manager *Virginia S. Moffat*
Advertising Manager *Ann M. Knepper*
Marketing Manager *Kathy Law Laube*
Production Editorial Manager *Colleen A. Yonda*
Production Editorial Manager *Julie A. Kennedy*
Publishing Services Manager *Karen J. Slaght*
Manager of Visuals and Design *Faye M. Schilling*

Cover photo © Joe Devenney/The Image Bank.

Cover and interior design by Terri Webb Ellerbach.

The credits section for this book begins on page 603, and is considered an extension of the copyright page.

Printed in the United States of America by Wm. C. Brown Publishers, 2460 Kerper Boulevard, Dubuque, IA 52001

10 9 8 7 6 5 4 3 2

To my family:
Mary Jo, Tracy, and Jennifer

Brief Contents

Contents

Cognitive Development 166

Social Development 198

IV
Early Childhood

Physical Development 238

9

Cognitive Development 264

10

Social Development 298

V

Middle and Late Childhood

11

Physical Development 344

CHAPTER

12

Cognitive Development 374

CHAPTER

13

Social Development 414

SECTION

VI

Adolescence

CHAPTER

14

Physical Development 454

Children

Following is a list of Children boxes that appear in the text.

Cultural Worlds of Children

Following is a list of Cultural Worlds of Children boxes that appear in the text.

Preface

When I undertook the task of writing this second edition of *Children,* I asked myself what I could do to make it truly special—a book that students would not want to put down once they started reading it. How did I try to accomplish this goal? First, I evaluated which themes needed to be given more emphasis.

New Themes of Children's Second Edition

Three content themes merit increased coverage in child development texts as we approach the twenty-first century: cultural worlds of children, education, and health.

Cultural Worlds of Children

Children develop in a culturally diverse world. Both research studies and examples from the real world of children in different cultural and ethnic groups appear in every chapter of this book. An important feature, The Cultural Worlds of Children, was added to each chapter to further emphasize the diversity of children's cultural and ethnic worlds. Examples of these features are how Soviet children view war, an international perspective on abortion trends, mobile day-care units in India, oral rehydration therapy in Bangladesh, kindergarten in Japan, the family ties of Mexican children, the only child policy in China, "Sesame Street" around the world, adolescent sexuality in Holland and Sweden, a black student's view of schools, and literacy and secondary school attendance around the world.

Education

Children's education is another new theme of the second edition of this book. Children are our nation's greatest resource and the future of any society. The issues involved in their education deserve special consideration. Expanded coverage of education appears at each level of development—infancy, early childhood, middle and late childhood, and adolescence. Among the topics given increased attention are day care, especially quality day care; early childhood education, especially whether it matters if children attend preschool before kindergarten; elementary school education, especially the atmosphere of the early elementary school grades and comparison of Japanese and American education; and secondary school education, especially school dropouts and the transition from school to work.

Health

A third new theme of *Children* is health. An extensive amount of new material on children's health practices, nutrition, exercise, stress, and coping has been added. The emphasis on children's health appears throughout the book. Areas where health is discussed extensively include *Children* boxes, a new section of the book called Beginnings, and two new chapters on physical development. Examples of the increased coverage of children's health are expanded coverage of prenatal development and birth, including information about massaging and exercising premature infants, nutrition in infancy, early childhood, and middle and late childhood, including an entire section on malnutrition and illness around the world, as well as an up-to-date discussion of children's stress and coping.

Research, Teaching, and Learning

A book on children's development should include not only considerable information about cultural worlds, education, and health; it should also provide very up-to-date coverage of the scientific knowledge base about children's development, it should be written extremely well, it should include extensive examples of the real lives of children, it should be motivating to students, and it should facilitate learning.

Science and Research Orientation

Children is above all else an extremely up-to-date presentation of research in three domains of children's development: physical, cognitive, and social. Research continues to represent the core of *Children*. This core includes both classic and leading-edge research. *Children* includes more than 580 references from 1986 to 1990, with more than 440 coming from 1988, 1989, 1990, and in press sources. Research on children's development is expanding on many frontiers, and in each chapter I have attempted to capture the excitement of these new discoveries as well as the classic studies that are the foundation of the discipline.

The second edition of *Children* continues to provide balanced coverage of all periods of children's development. This edition contains sixteen chapters, six sections, and an epilogue, "Children: The Future of Society." The first edition contained fourteen chapters and five sections. The new section is called Beginnings. The new chapters are about physical development in early childhood (Chapter 8) and physical development in middle and late childhood (Chapter 11).

Writing

I asked myself what else I could do to improve the second edition of *Children* in addition to providing extensive research updating and coverage of leading-edge research. The most dramatic change in the second edition of *Children* is the improved writing style. Those familiar with the first edition of *Children* will notice this change after only a few minutes. I went over the book thoroughly, adding, subtracting, integrating, and simplifying. I examined alternative ways of presenting ideas and asked college students to give me feedback on which strategies were the most effective. With their suggestions uppermost in my mind, I rewrote every sentence, every paragraph, every section of the book.

The Lives of Real Children

Another noticeable change in the second edition of *Children* is the increased number of examples from the lives of real children. When a concept is introduced, it is often followed by a personal example, a research example, or both. Experiences from the lives of real children often open a chapter or a part of a chapter, and they also are freely used in boxed inserts called The Cultural Worlds of Children. Examples from the real lives of children include discussions of security blankets, children's drawings of "cat-humans" or "human-cats," a 4-year-old child's written version of *The Three Bears,* a story of danger in Bianca's life, an 8-year-old girl's poem about Montlake School, and Josh Maisel's account of his bar mitzvah.

Motivation

In writing *Children,* I have tried to convey the excitement of research and children's lives in each developmental period. I have tried to communicate the discoveries about children's development and children's own discoveries about life, with enthusiasm, with energy, and with constant awareness of the relevance of these subjects to the reader. When a concept is introduced, lively examples and applications of the concept are provided. At the beginning of each chapter, an imaginative piece focuses on a topic related to the chapter's contents. For example, "Biological Beginnings" opens with a discussion of identical twins who were separated at 4 weeks of age and did not see each other again until they were 39 years old. Chapter 10 begins with a description of three black preschool children's dramatic play. "Children" boxes appear several times in each chapter, and a brief glimpse through any chapter reveals their special appeal. For example, they include discussions of ethics and the medical use of fetal tissue, what's good food for an adult can be bad food for a baby, Swedish fathers, Chinese fathers, and Pygmy fathers, shattered innocence, rough-and-tumble play and laughing faces, superhero play, three adolescent mothers, and the dreams and struggles of a young Mexican-American youth.

Learning

Children incorporates an effective and challenging learning system. Two special features of the learning system are Concept Tables and Critical-Thinking Skills. **Concept tables** in the first edition of the book were extremely well received; in the second edition, they have been made briefer and more focused. They are designed to activate the student's memory of and comprehension of major topics or key concepts that have been discussed to that point. This allows the student to get a handle on many ideas and to understand how they are interrelated. Concept tables provide a visual picture of the most important information in each section.

The second special feature of the learning system is the emphasis on **critical-thinking skills,** which has been built into the book in a systematic fashion for the first time. To encourage the student's critical thinking, this textbook asks the student many questions, that require them to challenge the material and to ask questions that go beyond the text and into the real world. Several critical-thinking questions titled "Thinking Critically" appear in the margins of each chapter. It is important for students to see things about children's development from different points of view. Throughout this book, students are encouraged to think about all sides of an issue.

In addition, **Chapter Outlines** at the beginning of each chapter show the overall organization of the material. At the end of each chapter, a detailed **Summary** in outline form provides a helpful review. **Key Terms** are boldfaced in the text, listed with page references at the end of each chapter, and defined in a page-referenced **Glossary** at the end of the book. An annotated list of **Suggested Readings** also appears at the end of each chapter.

Teaching

An important goal I kept in mind while putting together the second edition of *Children* was to write a *teachable* text. The publisher and the ancillary team have worked together to produce an outstanding, integrated package to accompany *Children*. The authors of the teaching supplements are all experienced teachers of child development courses. The supplements have been designed to make it as easy as possible to customize the entire package to meet the unique needs of individual professors and their students.

A key feature of this package is the **Instructor's Binder.** This is a conveniently packaged three-ring binder containing *Children's* pages. The flexible binder allows lecture notes, transparencies, or classroom material to be integrated with the unbound text to create separate teaching units for each chapter.

In addition, a very helpful Instructor's Manual and Test Item File have been prepared by Melvyn B. King and Debra E. Clark. The **Instructor's Manual** includes chapter summaries, learning objectives, key terms, lecture suggestions, research projects, suggested classroom activities and essay questions. All or part of the instructor's manual can be placed in the Instructor's Binder. The **Test Item File** consists of two test banks containing over 1500 multiple-choice items. Each test item is referenced to the proper learning objective and text page and coded as conceptual, analytical, empirical or applied.

A **Transparency Package,** in full color, includes graphics and tables from both the text and outside sources and can be used as lecture outlines. These acetate transparencies have been designed to help in classroom teaching and lecture organization. Also, a set of **Videotapes,** especially designed for *Children,* is available to qualified adopters of the book.

A **Student Study Guide** has been prepared by Debra E. Clark and Melvyn B. King. Each study guide chapter includes learning objectives, a chapter summary, a guided review, key terms matching exercise, self-tests, questions to stimulate thought, and suggested research projects.

Acknowledgments

I would like to thank my editor, Michael Lange, who has given special attention to this book. I value his editorial expertise and knowledge of what it takes to make an outstanding text in children's development. I also value his friendship. I would also like to thank Carla Aspelmeier, the developmental editor of *Children,* for her competent management and hard work. Gloria Schiesl spent long hours overseeing the production of *Children*—I appreciate her careful work with the manuscript. Carol Danielson copyedited the book with competence and care. Terri Ellerback, designer, provided creative touches that make the book very attractive. Janet George went the extra mile in tracking down elusive and effective photos. Mavis Oeth efficiently obtained permissions. Jenny McCauley did an excellent job preparing the glossary. Special thanks go to Debra E. Clark and Melvyn B. King, who prepared the Instructor's Manual and Student Study Guide.

I benefited enoromously from the ideas and insights of many colleagues who reviewed *Children.* I would like to thank the following individuals for providing helpful suggestions:

Harry H. Avis
Sierra College

Patricia J. Bence
Tompkins Cortland Community College

Michael Bergmire
Jefferson College

Ruth Brinkman
St. Louis Community College, Florissant Valley

Dan W. Brunworth
Kishwaukee College

Thomas Gerry
Columbia Greene Community College

Alice S. Honig
Syracuse University

Sally Hoppstetter
Palo Alto College

Diane Carlson Jones
Texas A & M University

Ellen Junn
Indiana University

Claire B. Kopp
UCLA

Mary Ann McLaughlin
Clarion University

Karla Miley
Black Hawk College

Richard Riggle
Coe College

Jane A. Rysberg
California State University, Chico

Ross A. Thompson
University of Nebraska, Lincoln

Dorothy A. Wedge
Faimont State College

William H. Zachry
University of Tennessee, Martin

I

The Nature of Children's Development

In every child who is born, under no matter what circumstances, and of no matter what parents, the potentiality of the human race is born again.

James Agee

◆

Examining the shape of childhood allows us to understand it better. Every childhood is distinct, the first chapter of a new biography in the world. This book is about children's development—its universal features, its individual variations, its nature as we move ever closer to the twenty-first century. *Children* is about the rhythm and meaning of children's lives, about turning mystery into understanding, and about weaving together a portrait of who each of us was, is, and will be.

In this first section of the book, you will read two chapters. Among Chapter 1's contents are ideas about

—How today's world is both the best of times and the worst of times for children
—Child development today and yesterday
—The changing world of children's gender roles
—Whether children's development is like a seedling growing into a giant oak or more like a caterpillar suddenly becoming a butterfly

—How the approach to studying children's development is no different than the approach to studying Saturn's moons
—The ingenious strategies developmentalists use to study children's lives

Among Chapter 2's contents is information about

—Major theories of children's development
—Dreams of bird-headed creatures and bathtubs

—Comparison of a child's mind to a computer
—A boy who learns to control his teacher's behavior
—Children's ability to burst the cocoon and become a butterfly
—Goslings who adopt a researcher as their "mother"   ◆

◇

We reach backward to our parents and forward to our children and through their children to a future we will never see, but about which we need to care.

Carl Jung

1

Introduction

I t is both the best of times and the worst of times for today's children. Their world possesses powers and perspectives inconceivable 50 years ago: computers, longer life expectancies, the ability to reach out to the entire planet through television, satellites, air travel. So much knowledge, though, can be chaotic, even dangerous. School curricula have been adapted to teach students new topics—AIDS, suicide, drug and alcohol abuse, incest. Children want to trust, but the world has become an untrustworthy place. The sometimes-fatal temptations of the adult world sometimes descend upon children so early that their ideals become tarnished. Crack cocaine is a far more addictive and deadly substance than marijuana, the drug of an earlier generation. Strange depictions of violence and sex come flashing out of the television set and lodge in the minds of children. The messages are powerful and contradictory: Rock videos suggest orgiastic sex. Public health officials counsel safe sex. Oprah Winfrey and Phil Donahue conduct seminars on lesbian nuns, exotic drugs, transsexual surgery, serial murders. Television pours a bizarre version of reality into children's imaginations. In New York City, two 5-year-olds argue about whether there is a Santa Claus and what Liberace died of. In New Orleans, a first-grader shaves a piece of chalk and passes the dust around the classroom, acting as if it is cocaine.

Every stable society transmits values from one generation to the next. That is civilization's work. In today's world, the transmission of values is not easy. Parents are raising children in a world far removed from Ozzie and Harriet's era of the 1950s, when two of three American families consisted of a breadwinner (the father), a caregiver (the mother), and the children they were raising. Today fewer than one in five families fits that description. Phrases like "quality time" have found their way into the American vocabulary. A motif of absence plays in the lives of many children. It may be an absence of authority and limits or an absence of emotional commitment (Morrow, 1988).

By examining the shape of childhood, we can understand it better. This book is a window into the nature of children's development—your own and every other child of the human species. In this first chapter, you will be introduced to some ideas about why we should study children, contemporary concerns about child development, and a historical perspective on children's development. You will learn what development is, what issues are raised by a developmental perspective on children, and what it means to study children from a scientific perspective.

Why Study Children?

Why study children? Perhaps you are or will be a parent or teacher. Responsibility for children is or will be a part of your everyday life. The more you learn about children, the better you can deal with them. Perhaps you hope to gain some insight into your own history as an infant, as a child, and as an adolescent. Or perhaps you just stumbled onto this course, thinking that it sounded interesting and that the topic of child development would raise some provocative and intriguing issues about how human beings grow and develop. Whatever your reasons, you will discover that the study of child development *is* provocative, *is* intriguing, and *is* filled with information about who we are and how we grew to be the way we are.

How Soviet Children View Nuclear War

How do Soviet children feel about the threat of nuclear war? Researchers went to the Soviet and questioned 347 boys and girls from 9 to 17 years of age to find out (Chivian & others, 1985). They had been told before they went to Russia that Soviet youth would know little about nuclear war. But the opposite was true. Soviet children were very aware of the consequences of nuclear war. One 13-year-old Russian boy said, "The entire Earth will become a wasteland. All buildings will be destroyed. All living things will perish—no grass, no trees, no greenery." The Soviet youths were pessimistic about the chances of surviving a nuclear war. Only 3 percent thought that they and their families would survive one, compared to about 16 percent of a similar group of American youth. But Soviet youth were more optimistic than American youth about the possibility of avoiding nuclear war. Only 12 percent of the Soviet youth thought a nuclear war would occur in their lifetime, compared to 38 percent of the American youth. Soviet children are active in trying to prevent nuclear war. They sign petitions to send to NATO, and they belong to international friendship clubs. The researchers asked the Soviet youth at the end of the interview if they had any messages for American children. One said, "I wish that they would struggle and fight against nuclear war." Another commented, "We are the same type of people they are. We also want peace." ♦

Shown above are Soviet schoolchildren on a holiday visiting Red Square in Moscow. How do Soviet children and adolescents view nuclear war?

As you might imagine, understanding children's development and taking your own personal journey through childhood are rich and complicated undertakings. You will discover that different experts approach the study of children in many different ways and ask many different questions. Amid this richness and complexity, we seek simple understanding: to know how children change as they grow up and what forces contribute to this change.

What are some of the changes children go through? Children grow in size and weight. They learn to stand and walk and run. They learn language, picking up new words as pigeons pick up peas. They learn to read, to write, and to solve math problems. They learn behaviors and roles that society considers acceptable for boys and girls and for men and women. They learn to juggle the necessity of curbing their will with becoming what they can will freely, developing an understanding of what is morally acceptable and unacceptable. They learn how to communicate and how to get along with many different people. Their parents and siblings are important influences in their lives, but their growth is also shaped by successive groups of friends, teachers, and strangers. In their most pimply and awkward moments as adolescents, they become acquainted with sex and try on one face after another, searching for an identity they can call their own. These are but a few of the fascinating changes that take place as children develop. Many more await you in the remainder of the book.

In some sense, then, the modern study of child development is unexotic. It is concerned with the same matters that you and I, as ordinary, everyday people, might want to understand as we raise children of our own, teach other people's children in school, or try to get along with them as brothers and sisters or nieces and nephews. Whatever the context, it will help us immensely to know and understand precisely how children change in the ways just mentioned.

. . . One's children's children's children. Look back to us as we look to you; we are related by our imaginations. If we are able to touch, it is because we have imagined each other's existence, our dreams running back and forth along a cable from age to age.

Roger Rosenblatt, 1986

Child Development Today and Yesterday

Everywhere a person turns, the development and well-being of children capture public attention, the interest of scientists, and the concern of policymakers. This has not always been so, however; throughout history, interest in the development of children has been uneven.

Some Contemporary Concerns

Consider some of the topics you read about in newspapers and magazines every day: educational reform, contemporary changes in family structure and work, the effect of computers on children, and caring for mentally retarded children. The discoveries the experts are making in each of these areas are having direct and significant consequences for our understanding of children, and our new knowledge is affecting our decisions about how children are to be treated. Let's examine these issues further.

In recent years our nation's educational system has come under attack (Cuban, 1988; Kearns, 1988). A national commission appointed by the Office of Education concluded that our children are being poorly prepared for the increasingly complex future they will face. The problems are legion: declining skills of persons entering the teaching profession, adolescents graduating from high school with grade school level reading and math skills, a shortage of math and science teachers, too little time spent by students in engaging academic work in their classrooms, an absence of any real signs of challenge and thinking required by school curricula, and an unfortunately high dropout rate during the high school years. The solutions to these problems will not be easy. However, in searching for solutions, policymakers will repeatedly find themselves turning to experts in the field of child development, because to design a competent curriculum, a planner must know what engages and motivates children. To improve the national effort in teaching thinking skills, any planner must know what thinking is and how it changes across the school years (Baron & Sternberg, 1987; Belmont, 1989). To improve adolescents' ability to cope with the social difficulties that lead many of them to drop out of school, the planner needs to understand the social transition to adolescence and the ways in which schools fail to address this important change (William T. Grant Foundation, 1988).

We hear a great deal from experts and popular writers about pressures on the contemporary family. Mothers and fathers are increasingly becoming dual-income earners. Masses of children are growing up in divorced and stepparent families. The time parents are able to spend with their children is lessening, and the quality of care they give their children is of concern to many. Are working parents effectively using the time they have with their children? Are day-care arrangements adequate to provide alternatives for parents? How troubled should we be that large numbers of children today are latchkey children—at home after school, often without adult supervision? Answers to these questions can be found through different kinds of information obtained by child development experts. This includes studies of the way working parents use their time with their children, of the nature of their parenting behaviors, of the way various day-care arrangements influence children's social and intellectual growth, and of the consequences of being raised without adult supervision several hours a day after school and all day during the summer months (Belsky, 1989; Ianni, 1989; Scarr, Lande, & McCartney, 1989).

We are now in the information age. Increasingly our nation's economy and our lives depend on the quality, speed, and availability of information. Advances in the area of computing have made more information available. Nowhere is this more apparent than in the greatly increased use of microcomputers in business, at home, and in schools. Computing power—available only to large corporations in the 1960s— is now in the hands of 4- and 5-year-olds. How will the use of computers change the nature of children's learning and development? No one really knows for sure, but futurists have many opinions about this.

The nature of the change must be reckoned with on several fronts at once. Developmentalists have several issues to consider. How do family members interact with each other now that extensive time is spent with the computer? How are television time and school work influenced? How do children's social interaction patterns with other children change because of exposure to computing, the tendency to associate with other computer "hackers," and the discovery of the computer as a companion, babysitter, or mentor? Finally, how will exposure to computing and programming change the very nature of learning, reasoning, and thinking? Will the changes be as dramatic as when human beings first learned to read, write, and use mathematics to understand the world? Developmentalists are beginning to address these questions now, but as you might expect, their findings are still in the formative stages (Glasser & Bassok, 1989; Lehrer & Yussen, 1988; Lepper & Gurtner, 1989).

Parents and educators must face the challenging task of helping mentally retarded children grow and adapt in a world that, for them, is beyond easy comprehension. How are they to do this effectively? What experiences and social grouping

Child development experts are conducting studies about the consequences of being raised without adult supervision after school and all day during the summer months.

The Changing Tapestry of American Culture

Nowhere are environmental and social changes in American life more profound than in the rapidly increasing cultural diversity of America's citizens (Miller, 1989). Ethnic minority groups—Blacks, Hispanics, Native Americans (American Indians), and Asians—make up 20 percent of all children and adolescents under the age of 17. By the year 2000, projections indicate that one-third of all school-age children will fall into this category. This changing demographic tapestry promises not only the richness diversity produces but also difficult challenges in extending the American dream to children of all ethnic minority and social class groups. Historically, minority group children all too often have found themselves at the bottom of the economic and social order. They are disproportionately represented among the poor and the inadequately educated. Half of all black children and one-third of all Hispanic children live in poverty. School dropout rates for minority youth reach the alarming figure of 60 percent in some urban areas.

These population trends and our nation's inability to prepare ethnic minority children for full participation in American life have produced an imperative for the social institutions that serve children (Gibbs & Huang, 1989). Schools, social services, health and mental health agencies, juvenile probation services, and other family- and child-oriented programs need to become more sensitive to race and ethnic origin, and to provide improved services to ethnic minority children and children from low-income families (Solberg, 1989; Thompson, 1989).

An important theme of this textbook is to provide a wide-ranging portrait of cultural and ethnic diversity in children's lives. Throughout the remaining chapters, you will encounter a number of ideas and examples related to this increasingly important topic. An especially important idea in considering the nature of ethnic minority groups is that not only is there ethnic diversity within a culture, such as the United States, but there is also considerable diversity within each ethnic group. All Black children do not come from low-income families. All Hispanic children are not members of the Catholic church. All Asian children are not geniuses. All American Indian children do not drop out of school. It is easy to make the mistake of thinking about an ethnic minority group and stereotyping its members as all being the same. Keep in mind that as we describe children from ethnic minority groups, throughout the text, each group is heterogeneous (Bronstein & Quina, 1988; Jones, 1989; Trimble, 1989).
♦

Educational reform, contemporary changes in family structure and work, the effect of computers on children, and caring for mentally retarded children are some contemporary concerns related to children's development. What other contemporary concerns related to children's development can you generate?

arrangements will have the greatest payoff? Should children be on separate academic tracks at school, or should they be mainstreamed (joined with their nonretarded peers in school)? The answers are not easy. They depend upon the type of retardation, our knowledge of children's learning and thinking, and the results of our practical efforts to train retarded children to master intellectual and practical living skills (Menolascino, in press; Zigler, 1987).

This survey of contemporary issues is deliberately brief. You will learn more about these issues in later chapters of the book. In the meantime, I hope your appetite has been whetted for the exciting field of study you have just begun. Now we turn back the clock and study a brief history of child development.

FIGURE 1.1 These artistic impressions show how children were viewed as miniature adults earlier in history. Artists' renditions of children as miniature adults may have been too stereotypical.
Maria Teresa de Borbon by *Francisco Goya.* Don Manuel Osorio de Zuniga *by Francisco Goya. Courtesy Scala/Art Resource Inc., NY.*

Child Development and History

> At first, the infant,
> Mewling and puking in the nurse's arms,
> Then the whining schoolboy, with his satchel
> And shining morning face, creeping like a snail.

Shakespeare often defined children in terms of such qualities as foolishness, emotionality, innocence, impotence, and need for discipline from adults (Borstelmann, 1983). But the history of interest in children goes back much farther than Shakespeare's late sixteenth- and early seventeenth-century portrayals.

Historical Accounts of Childhood

Childhood has come to be regarded as such a distinct period that it is hard to imagine it was not always thought of in that way. Philip Aries (1962) has suggested that, during much of history, childhood was not considered a distinctive period. Aries presents samples of art along with some available publications to conclude that development was once divided into infancy, which lasted for many years, and adulthood, which extended from what we now call middle childhood to postadolescence (see Figure 1.1 to observe artist's depiction of children as miniature adults in earlier centuries).

New interest in the study of children throughout history casts doubt on Aries' conclusions, which seem to be overdrawn, reflecting artistic style, aristocratic subjects and artists, and an idealization of society at the time. The societies of ancient Egypt, Greece, and Rome, held rich conceptions of children's development (Borstelmann, 1983).

During the Renaissance, from the fourteenth to the seventeenth centuries, philosophers speculated at length about the nature of children and how they should be reared. During the Middle Ages, the goal of child rearing was salvation; the purpose of parenting was to remove sin from a child's life. This perspective, called **original sin,** argued that all children are born bad and that only through the constraints of parenting or through salvation do children become competent adults.

Two contrasting views about the nature of the child emerged during the Renaissance: **tabula rasa** and **innate goodness.** Near the end of the seventeenth century, John Locke argued that children are not innately bad but instead are like a "blank tablet," a tabula rasa. Locke believed that childhood experiences are important determinants of adult characteristics; he advised parents to spend time with their children and to help them become contributing members of society. During the eighteenth century, Jean-Jacques Rousseau agreed with Locke that children are not basically bad, but Rousseau did not consider them blank tablets. Rousseau said children are inherently good and that because of their innate goodness, they should be permitted to grow naturally with little parental monitoring or constraint.

In the past 150 years, our views of children have changed dramatically. We now consider childhood a highly eventful and unique period of life that is the foundation for adulthood. In most approaches to the study of childhood, distinct periods are identified in which special skills are mastered and new life tasks are confronted. Childhood is no longer seen as simply a convenient "waiting" period during which adults must suffer the incompetencies of the young. We now value childhood as a special time of growth and change, and we invest great energy and resources into caring for and educating our children. Through child labor laws, we protect them from the excesses of the adult work world. Under a special system of juvenile justice, we treat their crimes against society. When ordinary family support systems fail or when families seriously interfere with the child's well-being, we have governmental provisions for helping children.

The Modern Study of Child Development

The modern era of studying children has a history spanning just a little more than a century (Cairns, 1983). Modern study began with some important developments in the late 1800s and has extended to the current period. Why has the past century been considered so special? During that time, the study of child development has developed into a sophisticated science. We have a number of major theories that help us organize our thinking about children's development. We have many elegant techniques and methods for studying children. And new knowledge about children—based on direct observation and testing—is accumulating at a breathtaking pace.

During the last quarter of the nineteenth century, a major shift in thinking took place. Whereas matters of human psychology were once treated from a strictly philosophical perspective, they have come to be treated from a perspective that includes direct observation and experimentation. Most of the influential early psychologists were trained either in the natural sciences (like biology or medicine) or in philosophy. In child development, this was true of such influential thinkers as Charles Darwin, G. Stanley Hall, James Mark Baldwin, and Sigmund Freud. Natural scientists of that time understood the importance of conducting experiments and collecting reliable observations of things they were interested in studying. This approach had increased the body of knowledge in fields like physics, chemistry, and biology. However, the scientists were not at all sure that people, much less children or infants, could be profitably studied scientifically. Part of the hesitation was that an established tradition with children did not exist. Another part of the problem is that the philosophers of the time debated, on both intellectual and ethical grounds, whether the methods of science were appropriate for studying people.

The deadlock was broken as some daring and entrepreneurial thinkers began to study infants, children, and adolescents using whatever means they could think of and continually trying out new methods. For example, near the turn of the century, French psychologist Alfred Binet invented many tasks to study attention and memory. With them, he studied normal children, retarded children, extremely gifted children, and adults. He even studied his own daughters. Eventually he collaborated in the development of the first modern test of intelligence, which was named after him (the Binet). Around the same time, G. Stanley Hall pioneered the use of questionnaires with large groups of children and popularized the findings of earlier psychologists whom he encouraged to do likewise. In one investigation, Hall tested 400 children in the Boston schools to find out how much they knew about themselves and the world, asking them such questions as, Where are your ribs?

Later, during the 1920s, a large number of child development research centers were created (Cairns, 1983; Senn, 1975) and the professional staffs at these centers began to chart and observe the myriad behaviors of infants and children. The universities of Minnesota, Iowa, California at Berkeley, and Columbia, at which these centers were located, became famous for their investigations of children's play, friendship patterns, fears, aggression and conflict, and sociability. This work became closely associated with the so-called Child Study Movement. A new organization, The Society for Research in Child Development, was formed at about the same time.

Another ardent observer of children was Arnold Gesell. With his photographic dome, Gessel (1928) could systematically observe children's behavior without interrupting them (see Figure 1.2). The direct study of children, in which investigators directly observe children's behavior, conduct experiments, or obtain information about children by questioning their parents and teachers, had a favorable start in the work of these child study experts. The flow of information about children, based on the direct study of them, has not slowed since that time.

Gesell not only developed sophisticated observational strategies for studying children, but he also had some provocative views on children's development. He theorized that certain characteristics of children simply "bloom" with age because of a biological, maturational blueprint. Gesell strived for precision in charting what a child is like at a specific age. Gesell's views, as well as G. Stanley Hall's, were strongly influenced by Charles Darwin's evolutionary theory. Darwin had made the scientific study of children respectable when he developed a baby journal for recording systematic observations of children. Hall (1904) believed that child development follows a natural evolutionary course that can be revealed by child study. He also theorized that child development unfolds in a stagelike fashion, with distinct motives and capabilities emerging at each stage. Hall had much to say about adolescence, arguing that it is full of "storm and stress."

Sigmund Freud's psychoanalytic theory was prominent in the early part of the twentieth century. Freud believed that children are rarely aware of the motives and reasons for their behavior, the bulk of their mental life being unconscious. His ideas were compatible with Hall's, emphasizing conflict and biological influences on development, although Freud did stress that children's experiences with parents in

FIGURE 1.2 Gesell's photographic dome. Gesell is the man inside the dome with the infant. Cameras rode on metal tracks at the top of the dome and were moved as needed to record the child's activities. Other people, such as the woman in this photo, could observe from outside the dome without being seen by the child.

the first five years of the child's life are important determinants of later personality development. Freud envisioned the child as moving through a series of psychosexual urges, filled with conflict between the child's biological urges and the environmental demands made by society. Freud's theory has had a profound influence on the study of children's personality development and socialization, especially in the areas of gender roles, morality, family processes, and disturbances.

During the 1920s and 1930s, John Watson's (1928) theory of behaviorism influenced thinking about children. Watson proposed a view of children very different from that of Freud, arguing that, by examining and changing the environment, children can be shaped into whatever society wishes. One element of Watson's view, and behaviorism in general, was a strong belief in the systematic observation of children's behavior under controlled conditions. Watson also had some controversial views about child rearing. He stressed that parents were too soft on children and advised parents to cuddle and smile at babies less often.

While John Watson was observing the environment's influence on children's behavior and Sigmund Freud was probing the depths of our unconscious mind to discover the importance of our early experiences with our parents, others were more concerned about the development of children's conscious thoughts (the thoughts they are aware of). Even as early as the 1880s, James Mark Baldwin proposed his theory of **genetic epistemology.** The term *genetic* at the time was a synonym for *development,* and the term *epistemology* means "the nature or study of knowledge." Taken together, then, the terms refer to how knowledge changes over the course of the child's development. Later, in the twentieth century, the Swiss psychologist Jean Piaget picked up many of Baldwin's themes, elaborating on them, keenly observing the development of thought in his own children, and devising clever experiments to investigate how children think. Piaget became a giant in developmental psychology. Many of you may already be familiar with his view that children pass through a series of cognitive or thought stages from infancy through adolescence. For Piaget, children think in a qualitatively different manner than adults do.

Our brief introduction to several influential and diverse theories of children's development was designed to give you a glimpse of some of the different ways children have been viewed as the study of children's development unfolded. Much more about these theoretical perspectives is discussed in Chapter 2.

Sociopolitical events and issues (Karr-Kaiten, 1989; Scarr, 1989; White, 1985) have spurred further research interest in children. Research on children flourishes when there is substantial national activity on behalf of children and families. The War on Poverty in the 1960s led to the formation of Project Head Start, designed to give children from low-income families an opportunity to learn. In the 1980s, the changing nature of society has motivated research interest in the effects of divorce on children, working mothers and day care, and gender roles. (More about the changing nature of gender roles—of cultural standards for males and females—appears in Children 1.1.)

The Nature of Development

In certain ways, each of us develops like all other individuals, like some other individuals, and like no other individuals. Child developmentalists are drawn to children's commonalities as well as to their idiosyncrasies. As children, each of us traveled some common paths. Each of us—Leonardo da Vinci, Joan of Arc, George Washington, Martin Luther King, Jr., the authors of this book, and you, yourself, walked at about the age of 1, talked at about the age of 2, engaged in fantasy play as a young child, and became much more independent as an adolescent.

Just what do we mean when we speak of a child's development? We use the term **development** to mean a pattern of movement or change that begins at conception and continues throughout the life cycle. Most development involves growth, although it can consist of decay (as in death). The pattern of movement is complex because it is the product of several processes: biological, cognitive, and social.

Biological, Cognitive, and Social Processes

Biological processes involve changes in one's physical nature. Genes inherited from parents, the development of the brain, height and weight gains, motor skills, and the hormonal changes of puberty all reflect the role of biological processes in development. Chapters 3, 4, 7, 9, and 12 provide extensive coverage of biological processes in children's development.

The chess-board is the world. The pieces are the phenomena of the universe. The rules of the game are what we call laws of nature.

Thomas Henry Huxley, 1868

Cognitive processes involve changes in children's thought, intelligence, and language. Watching a colorful mobile swinging above the crib, putting together a two-word sentence, memorizing a poem, solving a math problem, and imagining what it would be like to be a movie star all reflect the role of cognitive processes in children's development. Cognitive processes are highlighted in Chapters 5, 7, 9, 10, and 12.

How the Gender Times Have Changed!

The year is 1965. Two 4-year-olds, Barbara and John, are playing together at kindergarten. John tells Barbara, "You stay here with the baby while I go fishing." As John walks away, Barbara calls to him, "I want to go fishing, too." John replies, "Girls don't go fishing."

Three other boys sit around a table in a play kitchen. The boys begin issuing orders: "I want a cup of coffee," "More jelly on the toast over here." Girls run back and forth between the stove and the table as they cook and serve breakfast. The boys begin demanding cups of coffee, one after the other, as one 4-year-old girl, Ann, races around frantically. Finally, Ann gains some control over the situation by announcing that the coffee is all gone. It doesn't seem to occur to Ann to sit down at the table and demand coffee from the boys.

Three-year-old William accompanies his mother to the doctor's office. A man in a white coat walks by and William says, "Hi, Doc." Then a woman in a white coat walks by and William greets her, "Hi, Nurse." William's mother asks the boy how he knew which person was the doctor and which was the nurse. William replies, "Because doctors are daddies and nurses are mommies."

The year is now 1990, some 25 years later. John and Barbara were married five years ago. Their daughter, Tracy, now 4 years old, is interacting with a friend, Todd, at kindergarten. Todd says to Tracy, "What are we going to do this weekend? Why don't we play racquetball?"

In another 1990s kindergarten class, two boys and two girls are trying to decide what to do. Ann, the former 4-year-old "waitress," also is now married, and has a 4-year-old son Tony. Carrie, a member of Tony's play group, asks Tony if he will make some coffee. He says, "Sure" and goes about pretending to make coffee and serve it to the group.

We also find that William—the traditional preschool gender-role enthusiast of the 1960s—now has a son, Robbie, who is 3 years old. William's wife takes Robbie to the doctor's office. Robbie makes no comments about the gender roles of nurses and doctors.

How the gender times have changed! Nowhere in children's development have more sweeping changes occurred in recent years than in the area of gender roles. At different points in the book—especially in Chapters 9 and 12—we will explore further the fascinating world of children's gender roles. ◆

The gender times have changed dramatically in the United States. The two black boys shown playing together here are less likely to stereotype occupations as male or female than their counterparts from earlier decades.

Social processes involve changes in children's relationships with other people, their emotions, and their personalities. An infant's smile in response to her mother's touch, a young boy's aggressive attack on a playmate, a girl's development of assertiveness, and an adolescent's joy at the senior prom all reflect the role of the social processes in children's development. Social processes are emphasized in Chapters 6, 8, 11, 13, and 14.

Remember as you read about biological, cognitive, and social processes that they are intricately interwoven. You will read about how social processes shape cognitive processes, how cognitive processes promote or restrict social processes, and how biological processes influence cognitive processes, for example. While it is helpful to study the different processes involved in children's development in separate sections of the book, keep in mind that you are studying the development of an integrated human child who has only one mind and one body (see Figure 1.3).

Periods of Development

For organization and understanding, we often describe children's development in terms of periods. The most widely used classifications of children's developmental periods include the following sequence: prenatal period, infancy, early childhood, middle and late childhood, and adolescence. Approximate age ranges are given to provide a general idea of when the periods begin and end.

The **prenatal period** is the time from conception to birth. It is a time of tremendous growth. From a single cell, an organism complete with brain and behavioral capabilities is produced in approximately nine months. Chapter 4 provides a detailed biological timetable of the prenatal period along with information about environmental hazards that can significantly alter the entire course of the life cycle.

Infancy extends from birth to 18 or 24 months. Infancy is a time of extreme dependence on adults. Many psychological activities are just beginning—language, symbolic thought, sensorimotor coordination, and social learning, for example. The birth process is described in Chapter 4 and all of Section 3 is devoted to infancy.

Early childhood, which extends from the end of infancy to about 5 or 6 years, corresponds roughly to the period in which the child prepares for formal schooling. The early childhood years sometimes are referred to as the preschool years. During this time, young children learn to become more self-sufficient and to care for themselves, develop school readiness skills (following instructions, identifying letters), and spend many hours in play and with peers. First grade typically marks the end of this period. Section 4 focuses on early childhood.

Middle and late childhood extends from about 6 years to 11 years of age, corresponding approximately to the elementary school years; sometimes the period is called the elementary school years. The fundamental skills of reading, writing, and arithmetic are mastered at this time. Formal exposure to the larger world and its culture takes place. Achievement becomes a more prominent theme of the child's world, and self-control increases. Middle and late childhood is discussed in Section 5.

Adolescence is the period of transition from childhood to early adulthood, entered at approximately 10 to 12 years of age and ending at 18 to 22 years of age. Adolescence begins with rapid physical change—dramatic gains in height, weight, changes in body contours, and the development of sexual characteristics such as enlargement of the breasts, development of pubic and facial hair, and deepening of the voice. At this point in development, the individual pushes for independence and pursues an identity. Thought is more logical, abstract, and idealistic. More and more time is spent outside the family. Section 6 describes adolescent development.

Man is by nature a social animal.

Aristotle

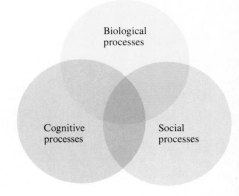

FIGURE 1.3   Changes in development are the result of biological, cognitive, and social processes. These processes are interwoven as the child develops.

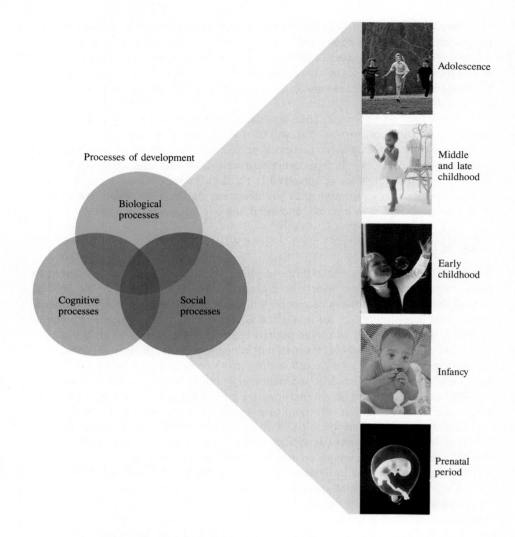

FIGURE 1.4 Development moves through prenatal, infancy, early childhood, middle and late childhood, and adolescence periods. Development is a continuous creation of increasingly complex forms.

Developmentalists today do not believe that change ends with adolescence (Hetherington, Lerner, & Perlmutter, 1988; Santrock 1989). In our definition of development, we described development as a lifelong process. However, the purpose of this book is to describe the changes of development that take place from conception through adolescence.

The periods of development from conception through adolescence are shown in Figure 1.4, along with the processes of biological, cognitive, and social development. As shown in Figure 1.4, the interplay of biological, cognitive, and social processes produces the periods of development.

Maturation and Experience

We can think of development as produced not only by the interplay of biological, cognitive, and social processes, but also by the interplay of maturation and experience. **Maturation** is the orderly sequence of changes dictated by the genetic blueprint each of us has. Just as a sunflower grows in an orderly way, unless flattened by an unfriendly environment, so does the human being grow. The range of one's environments can be vast, but the maturational approach argues that the genetic blueprint produces commonalities in our growth and development. We walk before we talk; we speak one word before two words; we grow rapidly in infancy and less so in early childhood; we experience a rush of sexual hormones in puberty after a lull in childhood; we reach the peak of our physical strength in late adolescence and early adulthood and then decline; and so on. Maturationists acknowledge that extreme environments (those that are psychologically barren or hostile) can depress development, but they believe that basic growth tendencies are genetically wired into each human being.

By contrast, other psychologists emphasize the importance of experiences in development. Experiences run the gamut from the individual's biological environment of nutrition, medical care, drugs, and physical accidents, to the social environment of family, peers, schools, community, media, and culture.

The debate about whether development is influenced primarily by maturation or by experience is another version of the **nature-nurture controversy** that has been a part of psychology throughout its history. The "nature" proponents claim that biological and genetic factors are the most important determinants of development; the "nurture" proponents claim that environment and experience are most important.

Ideas about the nature of child development have been like a pendulum, swinging between nature and nurture. Today we are witnessing a surge of interest in the biological underpinnings of development, probably because the pendulum had swung too far in the direction of thinking that development is due exclusively to environmental experiences (Hinde & Groebel, 1989). But while nature has grown in popularity recently, all psychologists today believe that both nature *and* nurture are responsible for development. The key to development is the interaction of nature and nurture rather than either factor alone (Plomin, 1989). For example, an individual's cognitive development is the result of heredity-environment interaction, not heredity or environment alone. Much more about the importance of heredity-environment interaction appears in Chapter 3.

Continuity and Discontinuity

Think about your development for a moment. Did you gradually grow to become the person you are, not unlike the slow, cumulative growth of a seedling into a giant oak? Or did you experience sudden, distinct changes in your growth, not unlike the way a caterpillar changes into a butterfly? (See Figure 1.5.) For the most part, developmentalists who emphasize experience have described development as a gradual, continuous process; those who emphasize maturation have described development as a series of distinct stages.

Some developmentalists emphasize the **continuity of development,** stressing a gradual, cumulative change from conception to death. A child's first word, while seemingly an abrupt, discontinuous event, is viewed as the result of weeks and months of growth and practice. Puberty, while also seemingly an abrupt, discontinuous occurrence, is viewed as a gradual process occurring over several years.

Other developmentalists emphasize the **discontinuity of development,** stressing distinct stages in the life span. Each of us is described as passing through a sequence of stages in which change is qualitatively rather than quantitatively different. As the oak moves from seedling to giant oak, it is *more* oak; its development is continuous. As the caterpillar changes to a butterfly, it is not just more caterpillar—it is a *different kind* of organism; its development is discontinuous. At some point, a

FIGURE 1.5   Continuity and discontinuity in development. Is development like a seedling gradually growing into a giant oak? Or is it more like a catepillar suddenly becoming a butterfly?

Drawing by Lorenz; © 1988 The New Yorker Magazine, Inc.

"If you ask me, he's come too far too fast."

child moves from not being able to think abstractly about the world to being able to. This is a qualitative, discontinuous change in development, not a quantitative, continuous change.

Another form of the continuity-discontinuity issue is whether development is best described by *stability* or *change*. Will the shy child who hides behind the sofa when visitors arrive be the wallflower at high school dances? Or will this child become a sociable, talkative adult? Will the fun-loving, carefree adolescent have difficulty holding down a 9-to-5 job as an adult or become a serious, straight-laced conformist? The **stability-change issue** addresses the degree to which we become older renditions of our early existence or whether we can develop into someone different than we were at an earlier point in development. Most developmentalists today believe that some change is possible throughout the life cycle, although scholars disagree, sometimes vehemently, about just how much change can take place and how much stability there is (Bornstein & Krasnegor, 1989).

At this point, you should be getting a feel for a developmental perspective in studying children. You have read about some contemporary interests, historical background, and the nature of development. To help you remember the main points of our discussion so far turn to Concept Table 1.1.

History and Issues in Child Development

Concept	Processes and Related Ideas	Characteristics and Description
Why Study Children?	Explanations	Responsibility for children is or will be a part of our everyday lives. The more we learn about children, the more we can better deal with them and assist them in becoming competent human beings.
Child Development Today and Yesterday	Contemporary concerns	Today, the well-being of children is a prominent concern in our culture. Four such concerns are educational reform, changes in family structure and work, the impact of computers on children, and caring for mentally retarded children.
	Child development and history	The history of interest in children is long and rich. In the Renaissance, philosophical views were important, including original sin, *tabula rasa,* and innate goodness. We now conceive of childhood as highly eventful. The modern era of studying children spans a little more than a century, an era in which the study of child development has developed into a sophisticated science. Methodological advances in observation and theoretical views—among them psychoanalytic, behavioral, and cognitive-developmental—characterized this scientific theme in the study of children's development. Sociopolitical events and issues also have spurred research interest in children.
The Nature of Development	What is development?	Development is the pattern of movement or change that occurs throughout the life cycle.
	Biological, cognitive, and social processes	Development is influenced by an interplay of biological, cognitive, and social processes.
	Periods of development	Development is commonly divided into the following periods from conception through adolescence: prenatal, infancy, early childhood, middle and late childhood, and adolescence.
	Maturation and experience	Development is influenced by the interaction of maturation and experience. The debate of whether development is due primarily to maturation or to environment is another version of the nature-nurture controversy.
	Continuity-discontinuity	Some psychologists describe development as continuous (gradual, cumulative); others describe it as discontinuous (abrupt; sequence of stages). Another form of the continuity-discontinuity issue is whether development is better described by stability or by change.

The Science Base of Child Development

Some people have difficulty thinking of child development as a science in the same way that physics, chemistry, and biology are sciences. Can a discipline that studies how babies develop, parents nurture children, peers interact, and children think be equated with disciplines that investigate gravity and the molecular structure of a compound? Science is not defined by *what* it investigates but by *how* it investigates. Whether you are studying photosynthesis, butterflies, Saturn's moons, or human development, it is the way you study that makes the approach scientific or not (see Figure 1.6).

FIGURE 1.6   Science is not defined by *what* it studies but by *how* it investigates it. Photosynthesis, butterflies, Saturn's moons, or family relationships can all be studied in a scientific manner.

Thinking Critically
Theories help us make predictions about how children develop and behave. Do you believe we can predict the course of a child's development? Explain your answer.

Theory and the Scientific Method

In the words of Henri Poincaré, "Science is built of facts the way a house is built of bricks, but an accumulation of facts is no more a science than a pile of bricks a house." Science does depend on the raw material of data or facts, but as Poincaré indicated, science is more than just facts. The nature of theory and the scientific method illustrates Poincaré's point.

Theories are general beliefs that help us to explain the data or facts we have observed and to make predictions. A good theory has **hypotheses,** which are assumptions that can be tested to determine their accuracy. For example, a good theory of children's aggression would explain our observations of aggressive children and help us determine why children become aggressive. We might predict that children become aggressive because of the coercive interchanges they experience and observe in their families. This prediction would help to direct our observations by telling us to look for coercive interchanges in families.

To obtain accurate information about development, it is important to adopt the **scientific method.** To do this, we must follow a number of steps: Identify and analyze the problem, collect data, draw conclusions, and revise theories. For example, you may decide that you want to help aggressive children control their aggression. You have identified a problem, which does not seem like a difficult task. But as part of the first step, you need to go beyond a general description of the problem by isolating, analyzing, narrowing, and focusing on what you hope to investigate. What specific strategies do you want to use to reduce children's aggression? Do you want to look at only one strategy, or at several strategies? What aspect of aggression do you want to study—its biological, cognitive, or social characteristics? Gerald Patterson and his colleagues (Patterson, 1986; Patterson, DeBarsyshe & Ramsey, 1989) argue that parents' failure to teach reasonable levels of compliance sets in motion coercive interchanges with family members. In this first step in the scientific method, a problem was identified and analyzed.

After we identify and analyze a problem, the next step is to collect data (information). Psychologists observe behavior and draw inferences about thoughts and emotions. For example, in the investigation of children's aggression, we might observe how effectively parents teach reasonable compliance levels to their children and the extent to which coercive exchanges occur among family members.

After data have been collected, psychologists use statistical procedures to understand the meaning of quantitative data. They then try to draw conclusions. In the investigation of children's aggression, statistics would help the researchers determine whether or not their observations were due to chance. After data have been collected, psychologists compare their findings with what others have discovered about the same issue.

The final step in the scientific method is revising theory. Psychologists have developed several theories about children's development; they have also developed many theories about why children become aggressive. Data such as those collected by Patterson and his colleagues force us to study existing theories of aggression to see if they are accurate. Over the years, some theories of children's development have been discarded and others revised. Theories are an integral part of understanding the nature of children's development. They will be woven through our discussion of children's development throughout the remainder of the book.

Collecting Information about Children's Development

Systematic observations can be conducted in a number of ways. For example, we can watch behavior in the laboratory or in a more natural setting such as a school, a home, or a neighborhood playground. We can question children by using interviews and surveys, develop and administer standardized tests, conduct case studies, or do physiological research. To help you understand how developmentalists use these methods, we will continue our theme of drawing examples from the study of children's aggression.

Observation

Sherlock Holmes once chided Watson, "You see, but you do not observe." We look at things all the time, but casually watching a mother and her infant is not scientific observation. Unless you are a trained observer and you practice your skills regularly, you may not know what to look for, you may not remember what you saw, what you are looking for may change from one moment to the next, and you may not communicate your observations effectively.

For observations to be effective, we have to know what we are looking for, who we are observing, when and where we will observe, how the observations will be made, and in what form they will be recorded. That is, our observations have to be made in some *systematic* way. Consider aggression. Do we want to study verbal aggression, physical aggression, or both? Do we want to study younger children, older children, or both? Do we want to evelute them in a university laboratory, at school, at home, at a playground, or at all of these locations? A common way to record our observations is to write them down, using shorthand or symbols. However, tape recorders, video cameras, special coding sheets, and one-way mirrors are used increasingly to make observations more efficient.

When we observe, frequently it is necessary to *control* certain factors that determine children's behavior but are not the focus of our inquiry. For this reason, much research on children's development is conducted in a **laboratory,** a controlled setting in which many of the complex factors of the outside world are removed. For example, Albert Bandura (1965) brought children into a laboratory, where he had them observe an adult repeatedly hit a plastic, inflated Bobo doll about 3 feet tall. Bandura wondered to what extent the children would imitate the adult's aggressive behavior. The children's imitation of the adult model's aggressive actions was pervasive.

(a)

(b)

FIGURE 1.7 Observation of a child's aggressive behavior under controlled laboratory and naturalistic conditions. (*a*) The child's aggressive behavior is being observed through a one-way mirror. This allows the observer to exercise control over the observation of aggression. (*b*) The child's aggressive behavior is being observed in a naturalistic situation. This allows the observer to obtain information about the everyday occurrence of behavior.

Conducting laboratory research, though, can be costly. First, it is nearly impossible to conduct without the participants knowing that they are being studied. Second, the laboratory setting may be *unnatural* and therefore cause unnatural behavior on the part of the children. Children usually show less aggressive behavior in the laboratory than in a more familiar, natural setting, such as in a park or at home. They also show less aggression when they are aware that they are being observed. Third, some aspects of children's lives are difficult, if not impossible, to produce in the laboratory. Certain types of stress are difficult (and unethical) to investigate in the laboratory; examples are recreating the circumstances that stimulate marital conflict or physically punishing the child. In **naturalistic observation,** then, developmentalists observe behavior in real-world settings and make no effort to manipulate or control the situation. Naturalistic observations have been conducted at hospitals, day-care centers, schools, parks, homes, malls, dances, and other places where children and families live and frequent (Bronfenbrenner, 1989; Cairns, & Cairns, in press). Figure 1.7 compares aggression in the laboratory and aggression in a more naturalistic context.

Interviews and Questionnaires

Sometimes the best and quickest way to get information from children is to ask them for it. Psychologists use interviews and questionnaires to find out about the experiences and attitudes of children. Most **interviews** are conducted face to face, although they may take place over the telephone. An experienced interviewer knows how to put children at ease and get them to open up. A competent interviewer is sensitive to the way children respond to questions and often probes for more information. Interviewers need to be careful to ask questions at a level the child can understand.

Just as observations can take place in different settings, so can interviews. An interview might occur at a university, in a child's home, or at a child's school. For example, Brenda Bryant (1985) developed "The Neighborhood Walk," an interview conducted with a child while walking through the child's neighborhood. Bryant has found the interview especially worthwhile in generating information about the support systems available to children.

Interviews are not without their problems. Perhaps the most critical of these problems is the response set of "social desirability," in which children or adults tell the interviewer what they think is most socially desirable rather than what they truly think or feel. When asked about conflict in their families, children and their parents may not want to disclose that arguments have been frequent in recent months. Skilled interviewing techniques and questions to eliminate such defenses are critical in obtaining accurate information.

Psychologists also question children and adults using questionnaires or surveys. A **questionnaire** is similar to a highly structured interview, except that children read the questions and mark their answers on the paper rather than verbally responding to the interviewer. One major advantage of questionnaires is that they can be given to large numbers of individuals easily. Questions on surveys should be concrete, specific, and unambiguous, and an assessment of the authenticity of the replies should be made (Agnew & Pyke, 1987; Sax, 1989). Of course, questionnaires are inappropriate for young children because of their lack of reading skills; even with older children and adolescents, researchers need to monitor whether the individuals have the language and cognitive skills to understand the questions.

Case Studies

A **case study** is an in-depth look at an individual. Case studies are used when the unique aspects of a person's life cannot be duplicated, either for practical or ethical reasons, yet they have implications for understanding development. A case study provides information about a person's hopes, fears, fantasies, traumatic experiences, family relationships, health, or anything else that will help the psychologist understand children's development. Some vivid case studies appear at different points in the book. Children 1.2 describes fascinating case study information about the role of social experiences in children's development.

Standardized Tests

Standardized tests require that the child answer a series of written or oral questions. Two distinctive features of standardized tests are that the child's answers usually are tallied to yield a single score or a set of scores that reflect something about the child, and that the child's score is compared to a large group of similar children to determine how the child responded *relative* to the others. Scores often are described in percentiles. For example, perhaps a child scored in the ninety-second percentile of the Stanford-Binet Intelligence Test. This method informs us how much lower or higher the child scored than the large group of children who had taken the test previously.

To continue our look at how different measures are used to evaluate aggression, consider the Minnesota Multiphasic Personality Inventory (MMPI), which includes a scale to assess delinquency or antisocial tendencies. The items on this scale ask you to respond whether or not you are rebellious, impulsive, and have trouble with authority figures. This part of the MMPI might be given to adolescents to determine their delinquent and antisocial tendencies.

Physiological Research

Psychologists also can use physiological methods to obtain information about children's development. Increased research into the biological basis of children's development has produced remarkable insights. For example, researchers recently discovered that an infant's sex seems to be fixed by a single gene in the seventh week of prenatal development (Page & others, 1987). (More about this fascinating discovery appears in Chapter 3.) And researchers recently discovered that higher concentrations of some hormones are associated with delinquent behavior in male adolescents (Inhoff-Germain & others, 1988). (More about this research appears in Chapter 13.)

Multimeasure, Multisource, Multicontext Approach

Methods have their strengths and weaknesses. Direct observations are extremely valuable tools for obtaining information about children. But there are some things we cannot observe in children—their moral thoughts, their inner feelings, the arguments of their parents, how they acquire information about sex, and so on. In such instances, other measures, such as interviews, questionnaires, and case studies may be valuable. Because every method has limitations, many investigators have turned to the use of multiple measures for assessing children's development. For example, a researcher might ask children about their aggressive behavior, check with their friends, observe them carefully at home and in the neighborhood, interview their parents, observe the children at school during recess, and ask teachers to

The Wolf Girls and Victor

The year is 1940. You are living in a rural village in India. You are walking in an isolated area and are feeling peaceful. Suddenly, you hear several howling sounds. You look behind the bushes and see two strange-looking animals—or are they children? Their eyes glint like blue lights in the darkened area of the bushes. One of the girls is about 1½ years old, the other about 8 years old. They are the wolf girls, so called because they appear to have been reared by wolves. A missionary had heard reports of small, naked children running around on all fours and decided to go and observe the wolf children. In *Wolf Children and Feral Men* (*feral* means "wild"), the missionary Singh told the story of the two girls who had been reared by wolves. The younger girl learned to walk upright, but she died about a year after she was taken to an orphanage. The older girl never learned to walk upright, although she eventually stopped howling like a wolf and learned to use about 50 words. She died after eight years at the orphanage.

Another famous case of social isolation involves the Wild Boy of Aveyron. In 1799, a nude boy was observed running through the woods in France. The boy was eventually captured when he was believed to be about 11 years old. It was thought that he had lived in the woods with no human contact for at least six years. Like the wolf girls, he seemed to be more animal than person. Experts examined the boy and proclaimed him an incurable idiot. However, a young French physician, Jean Itard, believed differently, thinking that the boy's bizarre behavior was a result of his social isolation. Itard named the boy Victor, and over a period of five years, he tried to socialize him. When Victor was first found, he walked more like an animal than a human being. When alone, he sat and rocked back and forth. He was unable to focus his eyes on anything for more than a few seconds, and he made no effort to communicate. After five years with Itard, Victor had not changed much. He did learn to eat with silverware, to wear clothes, to focus his eyes, and to sleep in a bed, but he never did learn how to communicate effectively. His social development was impoverished. Although he seemed to develop some affection for Itard and the woman who cared for him, he never learned to interact with others.

Developmentalists have long wondered what people would be like if they were brought up in isolation from other people from the time they were born. Though case studies focused on circumstances such as those experienced by the wolf girls and Victor provide some indication of the outcome, to truly find the answers we would have to randomly assign some children to live in isolation from other people for a number of years and assign other children to live a normal life with parents or care givers. Of course, we cannot ethically do such a thing, so we try to get some sense of the importance of social experiences through naturally occurring situations as those of the wolf girls and Victor, as well as a modern-day socially isolated child, Genie, whose impoverished language and social skills you will read about in Chapter 6.

The experiences of these children provide information about the importance of social conditions in children's development. In impoverished social circumstances, the wolf girls and Victor were able to develop some human competencies, but their desolate experiences seemed to have lasting effects on their development. ◆

Victor

rate the children's aggression. Researchers hope that the convergence of multimeasure (observations, interviews, tests), multisource (parents, peers, teacher), and multicontext (home, playground, school) information provides a more comprehensive and valid assessment of children's development.

Strategies for Setting Up Research Studies

How can we determine if a pregnant mother's smoking of cigarettes affects her offspring's attentional skills? How can we determine if responding nurturantly to an infant's cries increases attachment to the caregiver? How can we determine if day care is damaging to the child's development? How can we determine if listening to rock music lowers an adolescent's grades in school? When designing a research study to answer such questions, the investigator must decide whether to use a correlational or an experimental strategy.

Correlational Strategy

One goal of child development research is to describe how strongly two or more events or characteristics are related. When a researcher has this goal, a **correlational strategy** is used. This is a beneficial strategy because the more strongly two events are correlated (related, associated), the more we can predict one from the other. For example, if we find that as parents use more permissive ways to deal with their children and the children's self-control decreases, it does not mean that the parenting style caused the lack of self-control. It could mean that, but it also could mean that the children's lack of self-control stimulated the parents to simply throw up their arms in despair and give up trying to control the children's behavior. And it also could mean that other factors might be causing this correlation, such as genetic background, poverty, and sociohistorical conditions. (Several decades ago a permissive parenting strategy was widely advocated, but today it no longer is in vogue.) Figure 1.8 portrays these possible interpretations of correlational data.

Researchers often use a **correlation coefficient** to describe the degree of association between two variables. The correlation coefficient ranges from -1.00 to $+1.00$. A negative number means an inverse relation. For example, today we often do find a *negative* correlation between permissive parenting and children's self-control. And we often find a *positive* correlation between a parent's involvement and monitoring of a child's life and the child's self-control. The higher the correlation coefficient (whether positive or negative), the stronger the association between the two variables. A correlation of 0 means that there is no association between the variables. A correlation of $-.40$ is a stronger correlation than $+.20$ because we disregard the negative or positive nature of the correlation in determining the correlation's magnitude.

Experimental Strategy

The **experimental strategy** allows us to determine the causes of behavior precisely. The psychologist accomplishes this task by performing an *experiment,* which is a carefully regulated setting in which one or more of the factors believed to influence the behavior being studied is manipulated and all others are held constant. If the behavior study changes when a factor is manipulated, we say that the manipulated factor causes the behavior to change. Experiments are used to establish cause and effect between events, something correlational studies cannot do. *Cause* is the event being manipulated, and *effect* is the behavior that changes because of the manipulation. Remember that in testing correlation, nothing is manipulated; in an experiment, the researcher actively changes an event to see the effect on behavior.

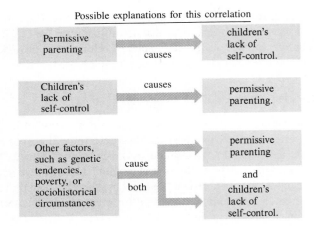

Observed correlation	Possible explanations for this correlation

As permissive parenting increases, children's self-control decreases.

Permissive parenting — causes → children's lack of self-control.

Children's lack of self-control — causes → permissive parenting.

Other factors, such as genetic tendencies, poverty, or sociohistorical circumstances — cause both → permissive parenting and children's lack of self-control.

FIGURE 1.8   The correlation between permissive parenting and children's self-control. An observed correlation between two events does not mean that one event causes a second event. The second event could cause the first, or a third event could cause the correlation between the first two events.

If you wanted to study the effects of aerobic exercise during pregnancy on the infant's development using an experimental design, how would you set up the experiment?

The following example illustrates the nature of an experiment. The problem to be studied is whether aerobic exercise during pregnancy affects the infant's development. To conduct our experiment, we need one group of pregnant women who will participate in aerobic exercise and another group that will not. We randomly assign our subjects to these two groups. *Random assignment* reduces the likelihood that the experiment's results will be a result of some preexisting differences between the two groups. For example, random assignment greatly reduces the probability that the two groups will differ on such factors as prior aerobic exercise, health problems, intelligence, alertness, social class, age, and so forth.

The subjects who participate in the aerobic exercise are called the **experimental group**—that is, the group whose experience is manipulated. The subjects who do not participate in the aerobic exercise are called the **control group**—that is, a comparison group treated in every way like the experimental group except for the manipulated factor. The control group serves as a baseline against which the effects found in the manipulated condition can be compared.

After the subjects in the experimental group have participated in aerobic exercise during their pregnancy and their offspring are born, the behavior of the infants in the two groups is compared. We choose to study the breathing and sleeping patterns of the infants. When we analyze the results, we discover that the experimental group infants have more regular breathing and sleeping patterns than their control group counterparts. We conclude that aerobic exercise by pregnant women promotes more regular breathing and sleeping patterns in infants.

In an experiment, the manipulated, or influential, factor is called the **independent variable.** The label *independent* is used because this variable can be changed independently of other factors. In the aerobic exercise experiment, the amount of aerobic exercise was the independent variable. The experimenter manipulated how much aerobic exercise pregnant women engaged in independently of all other factors. In an experiment, the researcher determines what effect the independent variable has on the **dependent variable.** The label *dependent* is used because this variable depends on what happens to the subjects in the experiment. In the aerobic exercise experiment, the dependent variable was the breathing and sleeping patterns of the infants. The infants' responses on these measures depended on the influence of the independent variable (whether or not aerobic exercise was performed). An illustration of the nature of the experimental strategy, applied to the aerobic exercise study, is shown in Figure 1.9.

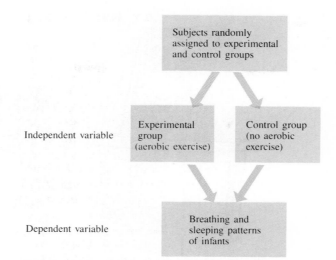

FIGURE 1.9   Principles of experimental strategy applied to a study of the effects of aerobic exercise by pregnant women on infants' breathing and sleeping patterns.

It might seem as if we should always choose an experimental strategy over a correlational strategy, since the experimental strategy gives us a better sense of one variable's influence over another. Are there instances when a correlational strategy might be preferred? Three such instances are (1) when the focus of the investigation is so new that we have little knowledge of which factors to manipulate (for example, factors associated with AIDS); (2) when it is physically impossible to manipulate the variables (for example, suicide); and (3) when it is impractical or unethical to manipulate the variables (for example, determining the link between parenting strategies and children's competence).

Time Span of Inquiry

A special concern of developmentalists is the time span of a research investigation. Studies that focus on the relation of age to some other variable are common in the field of child development. We have several options: We can study different children of different ages and compare them, we can study the same individuals as they grow older over time, or we can use some combination of these two approaches.

Cross-Sectional Approach

In the **cross-sectional approach,** children of different ages are compared all at one time. In a typical study of children's memory, learning, or peer group interaction, we might test a group of 4-year-olds, a group of 8-year-olds, and a group of 12-year-olds with some procedure designed to elicit information about each of these topics. Notice that the children tested are of different ages, different groups, were born at different times, may have experienced different types of parenting and schooling, and been influenced by different trends and fads in dress, television, and play materials.

A cross-sectional design is valuable because it can be conducted in a relatively short period of time. This enables us to get an answer to an important question quickly. Most research in child development that contrasts children of different ages is cross-sectional in nature. However, you may already have anticipated some problems with cross-sectional research: (1) Since different groups of children are tested, it is not "logical" to talk about how "individual children" have changed over time. We can only draw inferences about how the groups of children differed. (2) Group

© 1986; Reprinted courtesy of William Hoest and Parade Magazine.

"That's my dad when he was 10...He was in some sort of cult."

differences may have many sources, only some of which are due to normative features of their development over the age periods in question. For example, the different parenting and school practices that might have been in effect when each group of children was very young could explain some of the differences. Such differences, linked to when the children were born and grew up, are commonly called **cohort effects**—that is, those effects due to a child's time of birth or generation, but not to age.

Longitudinal Approach

The second option is to examine the same group of children repeatedly over some extended period of time. This option is called the **longitudinal approach.** In a typical longitudinal study of the same topics discussed earlier under the cross-sectional approach, we might structure a test that we administer to children once a year when they are 4, 8, and 12 years old. In this example, the same children would be studied over an eight-year time span, allowing us to examine patterns of change within each individual child. One of the great values of the longitudinal approach is its evaluation of how individual children change as they grow up.

Fewer longitudinal than cross-sectional studies are conducted because they are so time consuming and costly. A close examination of the longitudinal approach reveals some additional problems: (1) Since children are examined over a long period of time, some of them drop out because they lose interest or move away and cannot be contacted by the investigator. Quite often, the remaining children represent a slightly biased sample, in that they tend to be psychologically better or superior (in intelligence, motivation, and cooperativeness, for example) to those who have dropped out on almost every dimension the investigator thinks to check out. (2) With repeated testing, individual children may become more "testwise," which may increase their ability to perform "better" or "more mature" the next time the investigator interacts with them. (3) Finally, although cohort effects may not be obvious in a longitudinal approach, they may exist. A group of children born at a particular time may look like they are changing and developing as a result of general maturation. But, in fact, some of the change may be due to special experiences the children encountered during this period of time that were not encountered by children a decade earlier.

The mark of the historic is the nonchalance with which it picks up an individual and deposits him in a trend, like a house playfully moved in a tornado.

Mary McCarthy, On the Contrary, 1961

The Nature of Children's Development

	Cohort		
	1982	1984	1986
Time of testing 1986	4 years old	2 years old	Newborn
1988	6 years old	4 years old	2 years old
1990	8 years old	6 years old	4 years old

FIGURE 1.10   This sequential design includes three cohorts (born in 1982, 1984, and 1986) tested at three different times (1986, 1988, and 1990) plus new independent samples of cohorts.

Sequential Approach

Developmentalists also combine the cross-sectional and longitudinal approaches in their effort to learn more about development; the combined cross-sectional, longitudinal design is called the **sequential approach.** In most instances, this approach starts off with a cross-sectional study that includes children of different ages. A number of months or years after the initial assessment, the same children are tested again; this is the longitudinal aspect of the design. At this later time, a new group of children is assessed at each age level. The new groups at each level are added at a later time to control for changes that might have taken place in the original group of children; some may have dropped out of the study, or retesting might improve their performance, for example. The sequential approach is complex, time consuming, and expensive, but it does provide information that is not possible to obtain from the cross-sectional or longitudinal approaches alone. The sequential approach has been especially beneficial in calling attention to cohort effects in development (Baltes, 1973; Kertzer & Schaie, 1989; Schaie, 1965, 1988). Figure 1.10 shows an example of a sequential design.

Ethics in Research on Child Development

Child developmentalists increasingly recognize that considerable caution needs to be taken to ensure the well-being of children when they are involved in a research study. Today colleges and universities have review boards that evaluate the ethical nature of research conducted at their institutions. Proposed research plans must pass the scrutiny of an ethics research committee before the research can be initiated. In addition, the American Psychological Association (APA) has developed guidelines for its members' ethics.

The code of ethics adopted by APA instructs researchers to protect their subjects from mental and physical harm. The best interests of the subjects need to be kept foremost in the researcher's mind. All subjects, if they are old enough, must give their informed consent to participate in the research study. This consent requires that subjects know what their participation will entail and any risks that might develop. For example, subjects in an investigation of the effects of divorce on children should be told beforehand that interview questions might stimulate them to think about issues they might not anticipate. The subjects should also be informed that, in some instances, a discussion of the family's experiences might improve family relationships, while in other instances it might bring up issues that bring the child unwanted stress. After informed consent is given, the subjects reserve the right to withdraw from the study at any time while it is being conducted.

Thinking Critically
You are faced with designing a study of children's changing gender roles. What specific problem do you want to study? What measures would you use? What strategy would you follow—experimental or correlational? What would be the time span of your inquiry?

Special ethical concerns govern the conduct of research with children. First, if children are to be studied, informed consent from parents or legal guardians must be obtained. Parents have the right to a complete and accurate description of what will be done with their children and may refuse to let them participate. Second, children have rights. The psychologist is obliged to explain precisely what the child will experience. The child may refuse to participate, even after parental permission has been given. If so, the researcher must not test the child. Also, if a child becomes upset during the research study, it is the psychologist's obligation to calm the child. If the psychologist fails to do so, the activity must be discontinued. Third, the psychologist must always weigh the potential for harming children against the prospects of contributing some clear benefits to them. If there is the chance of harm, as when drugs are used, when social deception takes place, or when the child is treated aversively (that is, punished or reprimanded), the psychologist must convince a group of peers that the benefits of the experience clearly outweigh any chance of harm. Fourth, since children are in a vulnerable position and lack power and control when facing an adult, the psychologist should always strive to make the professional encounter a positive and supportive experience.

We have discussed several ideas about the scientific base of children's development. A summary of these ideas is presented in Concept Table 1.2. In the next chapter, we will discuss the major theories of development.

Summary

I. **Why Study Children?**
Responsibility for children is or will be part of our everyday lives. The more we learn about children, the better we can deal with them and help them to become competent human beings.

II. **Child Development Today and Yesterday**
Today, the well-being of children is a prominent concern in our culture. Four such concerns are educational reform, changes in family structure and work, the effect of computers on children, and caring for mentally retarded children. The history of interest in children is long and rich. In the Renaissance, philosophical views were important, including original sin, tabula rasa, and innate goodness. We now conceive of childhood as highly eventful. The modern era of studying children spans a little more than a century, an era in which the study of child development has developed into a sophisticated science. Methodological advances in observation and theoretical views—among them psychoanalytic, behavioral, and cognitive-developmental—characterized this scientific theme in the study of children's development. Sociopolitical events and issues also have spurred research interest on children.

III. **The Nature of Development**
Development is the pattern of movement or change that occurs throughout the life cycle. Development is influenced by an interplay of biological, cognitive, and social processes. Development is commonly divided into the following periods from conception through adolescence: prenatal, infancy, early childhood, middle and late childhood, and adolescence. Development is influenced by the interaction of maturation and experience. The debate of whether development is primarily the result of maturation or of environment is another version of the nature-nurture controversy. Some psychologists describe development as continuous (gradual, cumulative change); others describe it as discontinuous (abrupt, sequence of stages). Another form of the continuity-discontinuity issue is best described by stability or change.

The Science Base of Child Development

Concept	Processes and Related Ideas	Characteristics and Description
Theory and the Scientific Method	Theory	General beliefs that help us to explain what we observe and make predictions. A good theory has hypotheses, which are assumptions that can be tested.
	Scientific method	A series of procedures (identifying and analyzing a problem, collecting data, drawing conclusions, and revising theory) to obtain accurate information.
Ways of Collecting Information—Measures	Observation	A key ingredient in child development research that includes laboratory and naturalistic observation.
	Interviews and questionnaires	Used to assess perceptions and attitudes. Social desirability is a special problem with their use.
	Case studies	Provides an in-depth look at an individual. Caution in generalizing is warranted.
	Standardized tests	Designed to assess a person's characteristics relative to those of a large group of similar people.
	Physiological research	Focus is on the biological dimensions of the child.
	Multimeasure, multisource, multicontext approach	Researchers increasingly are studying children using different measures, obtaining information from different sources, and observing children in different contexts.
Strategies for Setting Up Research Studies	Correlational strategy	Describes how strongly two or more events or characteristics are related. It does not allow causal statements.
	Experimental strategy	Involves manipulation of influential factors, the independent variables, and measurement of their effect on the dependent variables. Subjects are randomly assigned to experimental and control groups in many studies. The experimental strategy can reveal the causes of behavior and tell us how one event influenced another.
Time Span of Inquiry	Cross-sectional approach	People of different ages are compared all at one time.
	Longitudinal approach	The same people are studied over a period of time, usually several years or more.
	Sequential approach	A combined cross-sectional, longitudinal approach that highlights the importance of cohort effects in development.
Ethics in Research on Child Development	Its nature	Researchers must ensure the well-being of subjects in child development research. The risk of mental or physical harm must be reduced, and informed consent should occur. Special ethical considerations are involved when research on children is conducted.

IV. **Theory and the Scientific Method**

Theories are general beliefs that help us explain what we observe and to make good predictions. A good theory has hypotheses, which are assumptions that can be tested. The scientific method is a series of procedures (identifying and analyzing a problem, collecting data, drawing conclusions, and revising theory) to obtain information.

V. **Ways of Collecting Information—Measures**

Observation is a key ingredient in research on child development. It includes laboratory and naturalistic observation. Interviews and questionnaires are used to assess perceptions and attitudes. Social desirability of responses is a special problem with their use. Case studies provide an in-depth look at an individual. Caution in generalizing is necessary. Standardized tests are designed to assess an individual's characteristics relative to those of a large group of similar individuals. Physiological research focuses on the biological dimensions of the child. Researchers increasingly are studying children using different measures, obtaining information from different sources, and observing children in different contexts.

VI. **Strategies for Setting Up Research Studies**

The correlational strategy involves describing how strongly two or more events or characteristics are related. It does not allow causal statements to be made. The experimental strategy involves manipulation of influential factors, the independent variables, and measurement of their effect on the dependent variables. Subjects are randomly assigned to experimental and control groups in many studies. The experimental strategy can reveal the causes of behavior and tell us how one event influenced another.

VII. **Time Span of Inquiry**

In the cross-sectional approach, individual people are compared all at one time. In the longitudinal approach, the same people are studied over a period of time, usually several years or more. In the sequential approach, a combined cross-sectional, longitudinal approach is followed. Cohort effects are a special concern in developmental research.

VIII. **Ethics in Research on Child Development**

Researchers must ensure the well-being of subjects in child development research. The risk of mental and physical harm must be reduced, and informed consent should occur. Special ethical considerations are involved when research on children is conducted.

Key Terms

original sin 14
tabula rasa 14
innate goodness 14
genetic epistemology 16
development 17
biological processes 17
cognitive processes 17
social processes 19
prenatal period 19
infancy 19
early childhood 19
middle and late
   childhood 19
adolescence 19

maturation 20
nature-nurture
   controversy 21
continuity in
   development 21
discontinuity in
   development 21
stability-change issue 22
theories 24
hypotheses 24
scientific method 24
laboratory 25
naturalistic observation 26
interviews 26

questionnaires 26
case study 27
standardized tests 27
correlational strategy 29
correlation coefficient 29
experimental strategy 29
experimental group 30
control group 30
independent variable 30
dependent variable 30
cross-sectional approach 31
cohort effects 32
longitudinal approach 32
sequential approach 33

Suggested Readings

Borstelmann, L. J. (1983). Children before psychology: Ideas about children from antiquity to the late 1800s. In P. H. Mussen (Ed.), *Handbook of Child Psychology* (4th ed., Vol. 1). New York: Wiley.
A comprehensive treatment of the historical conception of children from ancient times up to the twentieth century.

Brim, O. G., & Kagan, J. (Eds.) (1980). *Constancy and change in human development.* Cambridge, MA: Harvard University Press.
Several developmental experts contributed articles to this book, which focuses on how stable or changeable children's lives are.

Child Development and *Developmental Psychology*
These are two of the leading research journals in the field of children's development. Go to your library and leaf through issues from the last several years to get a feel for the research interests of developmentalists.

Kessen, W. (1979). The American child and other cultural inventions. *American Psychologist, 34,* 815–820.
An intriguing essay describing how childhood has come to be understood and viewed in contemporary America. Contrasts this conception with conceptions of children at other times in history.

◇
_____

There is nothing quite so practical as a good theory.

_____

Kurt Lewin, Psychologist, 1890–1947

2

Theories of Development

S igmund Freud and Carl Rogers, whose theories we will address in this chapter, are giants in the field of psychological theorizing. The lives of theorists and their experiences have a major effect on the content of their theories. As with each of us, the search for understanding human behavior begins by examining our own.

Sigmund Freud's theory emphasizes the sexual basis of development. What were Freud's sexual interests like as he was growing up? History shows that Freud repressed most of his sexual desires while busily pursuing intellectual matters. In all of the writings about Freud's life, only one incident during his youth reveals something about his sexual desires:

> The story relates to his first love experience at the age of sixteen when—for the first time in his life—he revisited his birthplace. He stayed there with the Fluss family . . . with their daughter, Gisela, a year or two younger than himself, a companion of his early childhood, he fell in love with her on the spot. He was too shy to communicate his feelings or even to address a single word to her, and she went away to her school after a few days. The disconsolate youth had to content himself with the fantasy of how pleasant life would have been had his parents not left that happy spot where he could have grown up a stout country lad, like the girl's brothers, and married the maiden. So it was all his father's fault. (Jones, 1953, pp. 25–26)

Carl Rogers' theory stresses the importance of developing positive conceptions of ourselves and sensitivity to others' feelings. What was Rogers' youth like? He had virtually no social life outside his family, although he does not remember that this bothered him (Rogers, 1967). At the age of 12, his family moved to a farm; apparently his mother wanted to shield her children from the evils of city life. Even though he was saddled with extensive chores at home, such as milking the cows every morning at 5:00, Rogers managed to make straight A's in school. He had little time for friendships and dating and never had what could be called a real date in high school. Once, as a matter of custom, Carl had to take a girl to a class dinner. He vividly remembered the anxiety of having to ask her to the dinner. She agreed to go, but Rogers said he does not know what he would have done if she had turned him down.

These experiences of Freud and Rogers are examples of how theorists' own experiences and behavior influence their thinking. Perhaps Freud's own sexual repression in adolescence contributed to his theory that human behavior has a sexual basis. And perhaps Rogers' anxieties about social contact as a youth fostered his theoretical emphasis on warmth in social relationships.

Freud's and Rogers' theories are but two of many theories you will read about in this chapter. The diversity of theories make understanding children's development a challenging undertaking. Just when you think one theory correctly explains children's development, another theory will crop up and make you rethink your earlier conclusion. To keep from getting frustrated, remember that life-span development is a complex, multifaceted topic, and no single theory has been able to account for all aspects of children's development. Each theory has contributed an important piece to the developmental puzzle. While theories sometimes disagree about certain aspects of children's development, much of their information is *complementary* rather than contradictory. Together they let us see the total landscape of development in all its richness.

Thinking Critically
What personal experiences in your own life might influence the kind of developmental theory you would construct?

The Nature of Children's Development

Psychoanalytic Theories

For psychoanalytic theorists, children's development is primarily unconscious, beyond awareness, and made up of structures of thought heavily colored by emotion. Psychoanalytic theorists believe that behavior is merely a surface characteristic and that, to truly understand someone's development, we have to look at the symbolic meanings of behavior and the deep inner workings of the mind. Psychoanalytic theorists also stress that early experiences with parents and underlying sexual tension shape our development. These characteristics are highlighted in the main psychoanalytic theory, that of Sigmund Freud (Looney & Blotcky, 1989; Nichtern, 1989).

Freud's Theory

Loved and hated, respected and despised, for some the master, for others misdirected, Sigmund Freud has been one of the most influential thinkers of the twentieth century. Freud was a medical doctor who specialized in neurology. He developed his ideas about psychoanalytic theory from his work with patients with mental problems. He was born in 1856 in Austria, and he died in London at the age of 83. Most of his years were spent in Vienna, though he left the city near the end of his career because of Nazi anti-Semitism.

Sigmund Freud

The Structure of Personality

Freud (1924) believed that personality has three structures: the id, the ego, and the superego. One way to understand the three structures is to consider them as three rulers of a country (Singer, 1984). The id is king or queen, the ego is prime minister, and the superego is high priest. The id is an absolute monarch, owed complete obedience; it is spoiled, willful, and self-centered. The id wants what it wants right now, not later. The ego as prime minister has the job of getting things done right; it is tuned into reality and is responsive to society's demands. The superego as high priest is concerned with right and wrong; the id may be greedy and needs to be told that nobler purposes should be pursued.

The **id** is the reservoir of psychic energy and instincts that perpetually press us to satisfy our basic needs—food, sex, and avoidance of pain, for example. In Freud's view, the id is completely unconscious, beyond our awareness; it has no contact with reality. The id works according to the **pleasure principle;** that is, it *always* seeks pleasure and avoids pain. Freud believed that the id is the only part of personality present at birth. Even in adults, the id acts like a selfish infant, demanding immediate gratification.

It would be a dangerous and scary world if our personalities were all id and nothing else. As young children develop, they learn they cannot eat 26 popsicles. Sometimes they are not allowed to eat even one. They also learn that they have to use the toilet instead of their diapers. As children experience the demands and constraints of reality, a new structure of personality is being formed—the **ego.** The ego abides by the **reality principle,** which tries to bring the individual pleasure within the boundaries of reality. Few of us are cold-blooded killers or wild wheeler-dealers. We take into account obstacles to our satisfaction that exist in our world. We recognize that our sexual and aggressive impulses cannot go unrestrained. The ego helps us to test reality to see how far we can go without getting into trouble and hurting ourselves.

They cannot escape me with their empty empty spaces
Between stars—on stars where
no human race is.
I have it in me so much nearer home
To scare myself with my own
Desert places.

Robert Frost

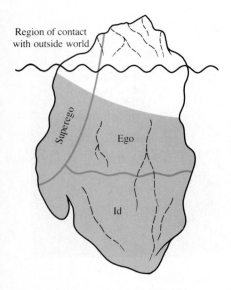

FIGURE 2.1 This rather odd-looking diagram illustrates Freud's belief that most of personality's important thoughts occur beneath the level of conscious awareness. Whereas the ego and superego are partly conscious and partly unconscious, the id is completely unconscious, just like the large, submerged part of an iceberg.

Thinking Critically
Examine your own life for a moment. How frequently do you call on defense mechanisms to help you cope with stress? Can you think of an example in the last week when you used a defense mechanism?

While the id is completely unconscious, the ego is partly conscious. It houses children's higher mental functions—reasoning, problem solving, and decision making, for example. For this reason, the ego is referred to as the executive branch of personality. It functions much like the executive in a company, making the rational decisions that helps the company succeed.

The id and the ego have no morality. They do not take into account whether something is right or wrong. This is left to the third structure of personality, the **superego,** which is referred to as the moral branch of personality. Think of the superego as that entity we refer to as our "conscience." Like the id, the superego does not consider reality. It does not deal with what is realistic, only with whether the id's sexual and aggressive impulses can be satisfied in moral terms. You probably are beginning to sense that both the id and the superego make life rough for the ego. Your ego might say, "I will have sex only occasionally and be sure to take the proper precautions because I don't want the intrusion of a child in the development of my career." But your id is saying, "I want to be satisfied. Sex is pleasurable." And your superego is at work too: "I feel guilty about having sex."

Freud considered personality to be like an iceberg. Most of personality exists below children's level of awareness, just as the massive part of the iceberg is beneath the surface of the water. Figure 2.1 illustrates this analogy.

Defense Mechanisms

How does the ego resolve the conflict between its demands for reality, the wishes of the id, and the constraints of the superego? In Freud's view, the conflicting demands of the personality structures produce anxiety. For example, when the ego blocks the pleasurable pursuits of the id, an inner anxiety is felt. This diffuse, distressed state develops when the ego senses that the id is going to let harm come to the child. The anxiety alerts the ego to resolve the conflict by means of **defense mechanisms,** which protect the ego and reduce the anxiety produced by the conflict.

Freud thought that the most powerful and pervasive defense mechansim is **repression,** which works to push unacceptable id impulses out of awareness and back into the unconscious mind. Repression is the foundation from which all other defense mechanisms work. The goal of every defense mechanism is to *repress* or push threatening impulses out of awareness. Freud said that early childhood experiences, many of which he believed are sexually laden, are too threatening and fraught with conflict to deal with consciously. The child reduces the anxiety of this conflict through the defense mechanisms of repression.

Among the other defense mechanisms children use to protect the ego and reduce anxiety are sublimation, reaction formation, and regression. **Sublimation** occurs when a socially useful course of action replaces a distasteful one. For example, an adolescent with strong sexual urges may turn them into socially approved behavior by painting abstract nudes. **Reaction formation** occurs when the child expresses an unacceable impulse by transforming it into its opposite. For example, a child who hates a particular teacher may act very nice to her, repressing his violent urges. **Regression** occurs when the child behaves in a way that characterizes a previous developmental level. When anxiety overwhelms children, they revert to an early behavior that gave them pleasure. For example, when first-grade children become anxious in a learning situation, they may suck their thumb or want to stay home the next day and not even go to school.

Two final points about defense mechanisms need to be understood. First, they are unconscious. Children are not aware that they are using them to protect their ego. Second, when used in moderation or on a temporary basis, defense mechanisms

The Nature of Children's Development

are not necessarily unhealthy. For example, the defense mechanism of denial can help a child cope with impending death. For the most part, though, it is not psychologically healthy when defense mechanisms dominate a child's life.

The Development of Personality

As Freud listened to, probed, and analyzed his patients, he became convinced that their problems were the result of their early life experiences. Freud believed that individuals go through five stages of psychosexual development and that at each stage of development, pleasure is experienced in one part of the body more than others. He called these body parts **erogenous zones** because of their pleasure-giving qualities.

Freud said that we go through five stages of psychosexual development. In the oral stage (a), pleasure centers around the mouth. In the anal stage (b), pleasure focuses on the anus; the nature of toilet training is important. In the phallic stage (c), pleasure involves the genitals; the opposite-sex parent becomes a love object. In the latency stage (d), the child represses sexual urges; same-sex friendship is prominent. In the genital stage (e), sexual reawakening takes place; the source of pleasure now becomes someone outside the family.

(a)

(b)

(c)

(d)

(e)

Theories of Development

Freud thought that personality was determined by the way conflicts between these early sources of pleasure—the mouth, the anus, and then the genitals—and the demands of reality were resolved. When these conflicts are not resolved, individuals may become fixated at a particular stage of development. **Fixation** is closely related to the defense mechanism of regression. Fixation occurs when the individual's needs are under- or overgratified. For example, a parent may wean a child too early, be too strict in toilet training the child, punish the child for masturbation, or smother the child with attention. We will return to the concept of fixation and how it might be reflected in personality, but first we need to learn more about the early stage of personality development.

During the first 12 to 18 months of life, the activities that bring the greatest amount of pleasure center on the mouth. In the **oral stage** of development, chewing, sucking, and biting are chief sources of pleasure. These actions reduce the infant's tension.

The period from about 1½ years to 3 years of life is called the **anal stage** because the child's greatest pleasure involves the anus or the eliminative functions associated with it. In Freud's view, exercising the anal muscle reduces tension.

The **phallic stage** of development occurs between the ages of about 3 and 6. Its name comes from the word *phallus,* a label for "penis." During the phallic stage, pleasure focuses on the genitals as the child discovers that self-manipulation is enjoyable.

In Freud's view, the phallic stage has special importance because it is during this period that the **Oedipus complex** appears. This name comes from Greek mythology, in which Oedipus, the son of the King of Thebes, unwittingly killed his father and married his mother. In the Oedipus complex, the young child develops an intense desire to replace the parent of the same sex and enjoy the affections of the opposite-sexed parent. How is the Oedipus complex resolved? At about 5 to 6 years of age, children recognize that their same-sex parents might punish them for their incestuous wishes. To reduce this conflict, the child identifies with the same-sex parent, striving to be like him or her. If the conflict is not resolved, though, the individual may become fixated at the phallic stage. Table 2.1 reveals some possible links between adult personality characteristics and fixation, sublimation, and reaction formation involving the phallic stage, as well as the oral and anal stages.

In the **latency stage,** occurring between approximately 6 years of age and puberty, the child represses all interest in sexual urges, showing more interest in developing intellectual and social skills. This activity channels much of the child's energy into emotionally safe areas and aids the child in forgetting the highly stressful conflicts of the phallic stage.

The **genital stage,** which occurs from puberty on, is a time of sexual reawakening. The source of sexual pleasure now becomes someone outside the family. Freud believed that unresolved conflicts with parents reemerge during adolescence. When resolved, the individual was capable of developing a mature love relationship and functioning independently as an adult.

Because Freud explored so many new and uncharted regions of personality and development, it is not surprising that many people thought his views needed to be replaced or revised. One of these people, whose theory has become one of the most prominent perspectives on development, was Erik Erikson.

The passions are at once temptors and chastisers. As temptors, they come with garlands of flowers on the brows of youth; as chastisers, they appear with wreaths of snakes on the forehead of deformity. They are angels of light in their delusion; they are fiends of torment in their inflictions.

Henry Giles

TABLE 2.1 *Possible Links Between Adult Personality Characteristics and Fixation at Oral, Anal, and Phallic Stages*

Stage	Adult Extensions	Sublimations	Reaction Formations
Oral	Smoking, eating, kissing, oral hygiene, drinking, chewing gum	Seeking knowledge, humor, wit, sarcasm, being a food or wine expert	Speech purist, food faddist, prohibitionist, dislike of milk
Anal	Notable interest in one's bowel movements, love of bathroom humor, extreme messiness	Interest in painting or sculpture, being overly giving, great interest in statistics	Extreme disgust for feces, fear of dirt, prudishness, irritability
Phallic	Heavy reliance on masturbation, flirtatiousness, expressions of virility	Interest in poetry, love of love, interest in acting, striving for success	Puritanical attitude toward sex, excessive modesty

From *Introduction to Personality,* by E. J. Phares. Copyright © 1984 by Scott, Foresman and Company.
Reprinted by permission.

Erik Erikson

Erikson's Theory

Erik Erikson spent his childhood and adolescence in Europe. After working as a young adult under Freud's direction, Erikson came to the United States in 1933. He became a United States citizen and taught at Harvard University.

Erikson recognized Freud's contributions but he believed Freud misjudged some important dimensions of human development. For one, Erikson (1950, 1968) says that Freud placed too much emphasis on the sexual basis of development. Erikson thinks that psychosocial development holds the key to understanding life-span development. For another, Erikson says that Freud was wrong in thinking that developmental change does not occur in adulthood. And for yet another, Erikson says that human beings have the potential to solve their conflicts and anxieties as they develop, painting a more optimistic picture of development than Freud's pessimistic view of the id's dominance.

For Erikson, the **epigenetic principle** guides our development through the life cycle. This principle states that anything that grows has a ground plan, out of which the parts arise, each having a special time of ascendency, until all of the parts have arisen to form a functioning whole.

In Erikson's theory, eight stages of development unfold as we go through the life cycle. He called these *psychosocial* stages (in contrast to Freud's *psychosexual* stages). The eight stages are shown in Figure 2.2. Each stage consists of a unique developmental task that confronts the individual with a crisis that must be faced. For Erikson, the crisis is not a catastrophe, but a turning point of increased vulnerability and enhanced potential. The more the individual resolves the crises successfully, the healthier development will be.

The first stage, **trust versus mistrust,** corresponds to the oral stage in Freud's theory. An infant depends almost exclusively on parents, especially the mother, for food, sustenance, and comfort. Parents are the primary representative of society to the child. If parents discharge their infant-related duties with warmth, regularity, and affection, the infant will develop a feeling of trust toward the world, a trust that someone will always be around to care for his or her needs. Alternatively, a sense of mistrust develops if parents, as caregivers, fail to provide for the infant's needs.

The second stage, **autonomy versus shame and doubt,** corresponds to Freud's anal stage. The infant begins to gain control over eliminative functions and motor abilities. At this point, children show a strong push for exploring their world and asserting their will. Parents who are encouraging and patient allow the child to develop a sense of autonomy, but parents who are highly restrictive and impatient promote a sense of shame and doubt.

The third stage, **initiative versus guilt,** corresponds to Freud's phallic stage and the preschool years. The child's motor abilities continue to expand, and mental abilities also become more expansive and imaginative. Parents who allow the child to continue to explore the world's unknowns and encourage symbolic thought and fantasy play promote initiative in their child. Restrictive, punitive parents promote guilt and a passive recipience of whatever the environment brings.

The fourth stage, **industry versus inferiority,** corresponds to Freud's latency stage and the elementary school years. At this time, the child becomes interested in how things work and how they are made. Achievement becomes a more salient part of the child's life. If parents and teachers make work and achievement an exciting and rewarding effort, the child develops a sense of industry; if not, the child develops a sense of inferiority.

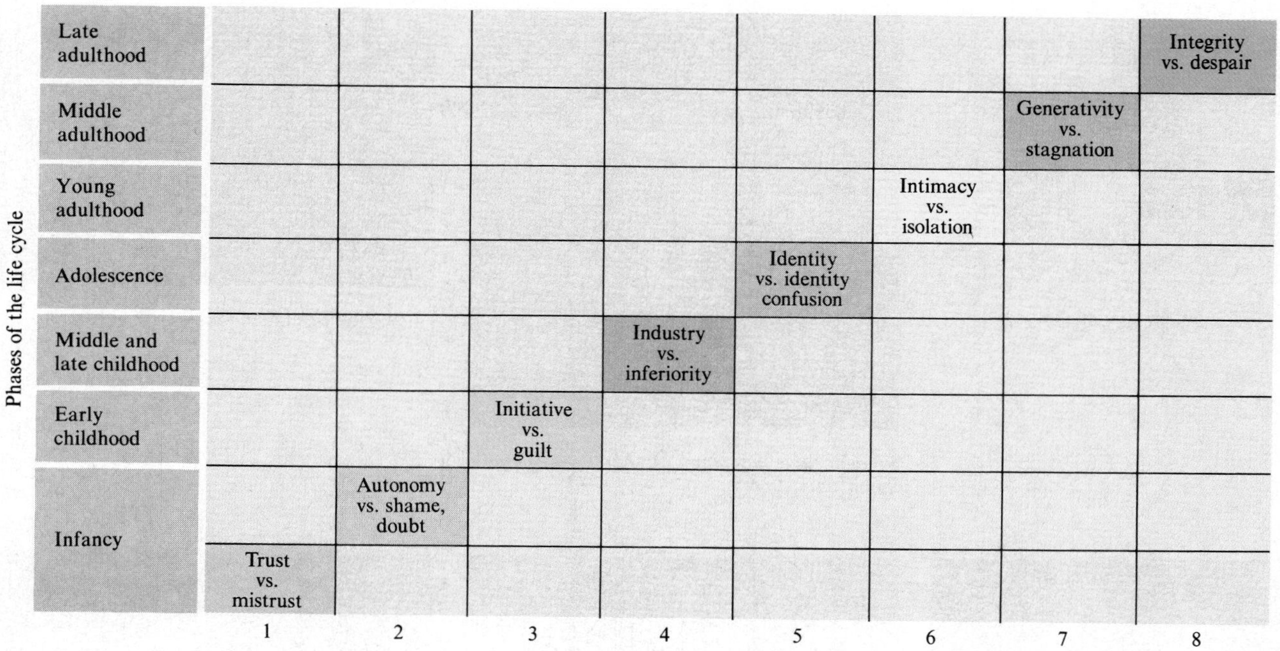

Phases of the life cycle

	1	2	3	4	5	6	7	8
Late adulthood								Integrity vs. despair
Middle adulthood							Generativity vs. stagnation	
Young adulthood						Intimacy vs. isolation		
Adolescence					Identity vs. identity confusion			
Middle and late childhood				Industry vs. inferiority				
Early childhood			Initiative vs. guilt					
Infancy	Trust vs. mistrust	Autonomy vs. shame, doubt						

FIGURE 2.2 Erikson's eight stages of the life cycle.

The fifth stage, **identity versus identity confusion,** corresponds to the adolescent years. At this time, individuals are faced with finding out who they are, what they are all about, and where they are headed in life. Adolescents are confronted with many new roles and adult statuses—vocational and romantic, for example. Parents need to allow the adolescent to explore many different roles and different paths within a particular role. If the adolescent explores such roles in a healthy manner and arrives at a positive path to follow in life, then he or she will achieve a positive identity. If an identity is pushed on the adolescent by parents, if the adolescent does not adequately explore many roles, and if a positive future path is not defined, then identity confusion reigns.

The sixth stage, **intimacy versus isolation,** corresponds to the early adulthood years. Early adulthood brings a stronger commitment to an occupation and the opportunity to form intimate relationships with others. Erikson described intimacy as finding oneself yet losing oneself in another. If the young adult forms healthy friendships and an intimate close relationship with another person, intimacy will be achieved; if not, then isolation will result.

The seventh stage, **generativity versus stagnation,** corresponds to the middle adulthood years. A chief concern of adults is to assist the younger generation in developing and leading useful lives; this is what Erikson meant by *generativity.* The feeling of having done nothing to help the next generation is *stagnation.*

The eighth and final stage, **integrity versus despair,** corresponds to late adulthood. In the later years of life, we look back and evaluate what we have done with our lives. Through many different routes, older persons may have developed a positive outlook in each of the previous stages of development. If so, the restrospective glances will reveal a picture of a life well spent, and the person will feel a sense of satisfaction; integrity will be achieved. If the older adult resolved one or more of the earlier stages negatively, the retrospective glances may yield doubt or gloom—the despair Erikson talks about.

Each of us stands at the heart of the earth pierced through by a ray of sunlight:
and suddenly it is evening.

Salvatore Quasimodo

Erikson's first psychosocial stage: trust vs. mistrust

Second stage: autonomy vs. shame and doubt

Third stage: initiative vs. guilt

Fourth stage: industry vs. inferiority

Fifth stage: identity vs. identity confusion

Sixth stage: intimacy vs. isolation

Seventh stage: generativity vs. stagnation

Eighth stage: integrity vs. despair

The Nature of Children's Development

An Eskimo Girl's Search for Cultural Identity

Mary is an Eskimo girl who has just turned 13. She lives in a small Arctic village. She sympathizes with those who yearn for the old days and ways, but she wants more. She is an expert on rock music, has a stereo, and wonders when she will go to the city and dance in a dance hall. At school one day, she challenged the teacher to describe what "culture" means. The teacher began describing what the Eskimo culture is like. Mary didn't like the teacher's response. According to Mary, "she was talking like she *thought* an Eskimo talks, or like she thought that we all *should* talk. Even my grandfather doesn't talk like that. He likes the electricity the white people brought to our village, he likes to listen to my stereo, and he likes to go on a ride in a snowmobile. He says that if he was younger he'd learn how to ride a motorcycle. . . . The teachers are white and they come here from Chicago and New York. They all say the same things to us. . . . My parents and my grandfather and my aunts and uncles keep telling me that I shouldn't speak my mind to people; instead, I should ask them what they believe and what they want, and be friendly with them. But it's hard for me to pretend I like a person if I don't really like her. . . . My grandfather says a lot of white people who come here would like to see us living in igloos. He jokes that he is going to build an igloo and go live in it, and then he will be the teacher's hero. I'm not sure he would know how to build one!" (Coles, 1977). ◆

Erikson does not believe the proper solution to a stage crisis is always completely positive. Some exposure or commitment to the negative end of the individual's bipolar conflict is sometimes inevitable; you cannot trust all people under all circumstances and survive, for example. Nonetheless, in the healthy solution to a stage crisis, the positive resolution dominates.

Evaluating the Psychoanalytic Theories

Although psychoanalytic theories have become heterogeneous, nonetheless, they share some core principles. Our development is determined not only by current experiences, but by those from early in our life as well. The principles that early experiences are important determinants of personality and that we can better understand personality by examining it developmentally have withstood the test of time. The belief that environmental experiences are mentally transformed and represented in the mind likewise continues to receive considerable attention. Psychoanalytic theorists forced psychologists to recognize that the mind is not all consciousness. Children's minds have an unconscious dimension that influences their behavior. Psychoanalytic theorists' emphasis on the importance of conflict and anxiety requires us to consider the dark side of human nature, not just its bright side. Adjustment is not always easy, and the child's inner world often conflicts with the outer demands of reality (Blos, 1989).

However, the main concepts of psychoanalytic theories have been difficult to test. Inference and interpretation are required to determine whether psychoanalytic ideas are accurate. Researchers have not successfully investigated in the laboratory such key concepts as repression. Much of the data used to support psychoanalytic theories come from patients' reconstruction of the past, often the distant past, and are of doubtful accuracy. Other data come from clinicians' subjective evaluations of clients. In such cases, it is easy for the clinician to see what she expects because of the theory she holds. Many developmentalists object that Freud overemphasized sexuality and the unconscious mind. The psychoanalytic theories also provide a model of the child that is too negative and pessimistic. Children are not born into the world with only a bundle of sexual and aggressive impulses. Their compliance with the external demands of reality does not always conflict with their biological needs.

Cognitive Theories

Exploring the human mind has been regarded with a kind of mystical awe throughout most of human history. Now, 10,000 years after the dawn of civilization, a new understanding of the mind is flourishing. *Mind* is a complex term, but primarily the mind is cognitive activity—perception, attention, memory, language, reasoning, thinking, and the like. Whereas psychoanalytic theorists emphasize unconscious thought, cognitive theorists emphasize *conscious* thoughts. The developing individual is perceived as rational and logical, capable of using the mind to effectively interact with and control the environment. The cognitive theory that has dominated the study of children's development is the masterpiece of Swiss psychologist Jean Piaget. A second important cognitive approach is information processing.

Piaget's Theory

Jean Piaget

Jean Piaget was born in 1896 in Switzerland. Piaget was a child genius. At the age of 10, he wrote an article about a rare albino sparrow, which was published in the *Journal of the Natural History of Neuchatel*. The article was so brilliant that the curators of the Geneva Museum of Natural History, who had no idea that the article had been written by a 10-year-old, offered young Piaget the job of museum curator. The museum heads quickly rescinded their offer when they realized Piaget was only a child. Piaget continued to live in Switzerland as an adult and became one of the most influential forces in child development in the twentieth century. In a eulogy to Piaget following his death at the age of 84 in 1980, it was said that we owe him the present field of cognitive development. What was the theory of this giant in developmental psychology like?

Piaget's theory will be covered in greater detail as we discuss cognitive development in infancy, early childhood, middle and late childhood, and adolescence later in the book. Here we briefly present the main ideas of his theory. Piaget stressed that the child actively constructs his own cognitive world; information is not just poured into his mind from the environment. Two processes underlie the individual's construction of the world: organization and adaptation. To make sense of our world, we organize our experiences. For example, we separate important ideas from less important ideas. We connect one idea to another. But we not only organize our observations and experiences, we also *adapt* our thinking to include new ideas because additional information furthers understanding. Piaget (1954) believed that we adapt in two ways: assimilation and accommodation.

(a)

(b)

(c)

(d)

For Piaget, development is a continuous creation of more complex forms. Piaget described development as occurring in four stages: (a) sensorimotor, (b) preoperational, (c) concrete operational, and (d) formal operational.

Assimilation occurs when we incorporate new information into our existing knowledge. **Accommodation** occurs when we adjust to new information. Consider a circumstance in which a 5-year-old girl is given a hammer and nails to hang a picture on the wall. She has never used a hammer, but from experience and observation she realizes that a hammer is an object to be held, that it is swung by the handle to hit the nail, and that it is usually swung several times. Recognizing each of these things, she fits her behavior into information she already has (assimilation). However, the hammer is too heavy, so she holds it near the top. She swings too hard and the nail bends, so she adjusts the pressure of her strikes. These adjustments reflect her ability to slightly alter her conception of the world (accommodation).

Piaget thought that assimilation and accommodation operate even in the young infant's life. Newborns reflexively suck everything that touches their lips (assimilation), but after several months of experience, they construct their understanding of the world differently. Some objects, such as fingers and the mother's breast, can be sucked, and others, such as fuzzy blankets, should not be sucked (accommodation).

Piaget also believed that we go through four stages in understanding the world. Each of the stages is age related and consists of distinct ways of thinking. It is the *different* way of understanding the world that makes one stage more advanced than another; knowing *more* information does not make the child's thinking more advanced in the Piagetian view. This is what Piaget meant when he said that the child's cognition is *qualitatively* different in one stage compared to another. What are Piaget's four stages of cognitive development?

In the **sensorimotor stage,** which lasts from birth to about 2 years of age, the infant constructs an understanding of the world by coordinating sensory experiences (such as seeing and hearing) with physical, motoric actions—hence the term *sensorimotor.* At the beginning of this stage, the newborn has little more than reflexive patterns with which to work; at the end of the stage, the 2-year-old has complex sensorimotor patterns and is beginning to operate with primitive symbols.

Thinking Critically
What experiences in your own life provide examples of Piaget's concepts of assimilation and accommodation?

TABLE 2.2	*Piaget's Stages of Cognitive Development*	
Stage	**Description**	**Age Range**
Sensorimotor	The infant progresses from reflexive, instinctual action at birth to the beginning of symbolic thought. The infant constructs an understanding of the world by coordinating sensory experiences with physical actions.	Birth to 2
Preoperational	The child begins to represent the world with words and images; these words and images reflect increased symbolic thinking and go beyond the connection of sensory information and physical action.	2 to 7
Concrete operational	The child now can reason logically about concrete events and can mentally reverse information.	7 to 11
Formal operational	The adolescent reasons in more abstract, idealistic, and logical ways.	11 to 15

In the **preoperational stage,** which lasts from approximately 2 to 7 years of age, the child begins to represent the world with words, images, and drawings. Symbolic thought goes beyond simple connections of sensory information and physical action. But while the preschool child can symbolically represent the world, according to Piaget, she still cannot perform *operations*—that is, mental operations that are reversible. This is why Piaget (1967) said that children 2 to 7 years of age are in the preoperational stage of thought.

In the **concrete operational stage,** which lasts approximately from 7 to 11 years of age, the child can use operations; she can mentally pour a liquid from one beaker into a second beaker of a different size and shape, and understand that the volume of liquid is still the same even though the beakers are different. Logical reasoning replaces intuitive thought as long as the principles can be applied to specific or *concrete* examples. For example, the concrete operational thinker cannot imagine the steps necessary to complete an algebraic equation, which is far too abstract for someone at this stage of development.

In the **formal operational stage,** which appears between the ages of 11 and 15, the adolescent moves beyond the world of actual, concrete experiences and thinks in abstract and more logical terms. As part of thinking more abstractly, the adolescent develops images of ideal circumstances. He may think about what an ideal parent is like and compare his parents with this ideal standard. He begins to entertain possibilities for the future and is fascinated with what he might become. In solving problems, the adolescent is more systematic, developing hypotheses about why something is happening the way it is; then he may test these hypotheses in a deductive fashion.

Piaget's stages are summarized in Table 2.2. A comparison of Piaget's stages with Freud's and Erikson's stages is presented in Figure 2.3. Notice that only Erikson's theory describes changes during the adult years. And remember that Piaget's theory stresses conscious thought, while the psychoanalytic theories of Freud and Erikson stress unconscious thought. In particular, Freud was intrigued by the nature of our dreams and saw them as completely unconscious. Recently, the possibility that dreams are much closer to conscious thinking than had been assumed has been explored. Children 2.1 provides a discussion of Freud's ideas on dreaming and some recent Piaget-inspired research on children's dreams.

The Nature of Children's Development

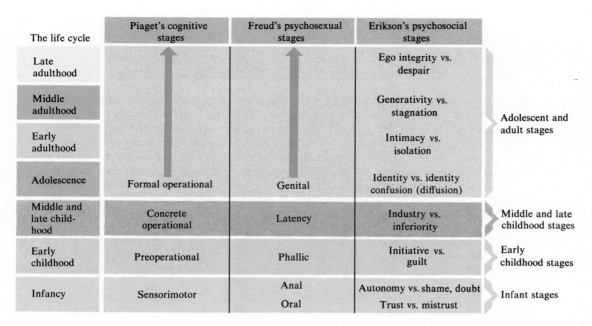

The life cycle	Piaget's cognitive stages	Freud's psychosexual stages	Erikson's psychosocial stages	
Late adulthood			Ego integrity vs. despair	
Middle adulthood			Generativity vs. stagnation	Adolescent and adult stages
Early adulthood			Intimacy vs. isolation	
Adolescence	Formal operational	Genital	Identity vs. identity confusion (diffusion)	
Middle and late childhood	Concrete operational	Latency	Industry vs. inferiority	Middle and late childhood stages
Early childhood	Preoperational	Phallic	Initiative vs. guilt	Early childhood stages
Infancy	Sensorimotor	Anal / Oral	Autonomy vs. shame, doubt / Trust vs. mistrust	Infant stages

FIGURE 2.3   A comparison of Piaget's, Freud's, and Erikson's stages.

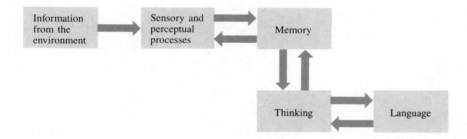

FIGURE 2.4   A simple model of cognition.

Information-Processing Theory

Information-processing theory is concerned with how individuals process information about their world—how information enters the mind, how it is stored and transformed, and how it is retrieved to perform such complex activities as problem solving and reasoning. A simple model of cognition is shown in Figure 2.4. Cognition begins when a child detects information from the world through his or her sensory and perceptual processes. Then the child stores, transforms, and retrieves the information through the processes of memory. Notice in our model that information can flow back and forth between memory and perceptual processes. For example, children are good at remembering the faces they see, yet at the same time, their memory of a person's face may differ from the way the person actually looks. Keep in mind that our information-processing model is a simple one, designed to illustrate the main cognitive processes and their interrelations. We could have drawn other arrows—between memory and language, between thinking and perception, and between language and perception, for example. Also, it is important to know that the boxes in Figure 2.4 do not represent sharp, distinct stages in processing information. There is continuity and flow between the cognitive processes, as well as overlap.

Dreams, Freud, and Piaget: From Bird-Headed Creatures to Bathtubs

Many of us dismiss the nightly excursion into the world of dreams as a second-rate mental activity not worthy of our rational selves. In focusing on the less mysterious waking world, we deny ourselves the opportunity of chance encounters with distant friends, remote places, dead relatives, gods and demons, and reworked childhood experiences. Aren't you curious about this remarkable ability of our minds and the minds of children to escape the limits of time and space?

Do you dream about pits, caves, bottles, apples, and airplanes? Do you dream about reptiles, serpents, umbrellas, and poles? If so, psychoanalytic theorists would argue that your dreams have a strong sexual symbolic content. They believe that dreams conceal but that they can be made to reveal the dreamer's conception of the world.

Freud viewed dreaming as completely unconscious and thought that it reflects sexual and aggressive impulses that cannot be expressed during waking hours. These impulses are always pressing for activation, he said, and dreaming allows these tensions to be relieved. Freud argued that the dream is a distorted and symbolic version of the impulses that triggered it, and that the raw materials for dreams are traces of past perceptual experiences, including both recent and distant encounters. He believed that dreams are highly unorganized, with the pattern of elements often bizarre.

Not all psychologists believe that dreams are a clash between sexual and aggressive instincts and the constraints of reality. Increasingly, psychologists describe both sleep and dreams as closer to conscious thought than had been believed in the past. For example, David Foulkes (1982) followed 42 children from the time they were 3 years old until they were 15. Each child spent nine nights per year in Foulkes' sleep laboratory, where dream reports were obtained. Foulkes' findings about dreams at different ages closely parallel Piaget's stages of conscious cognitive development. A sample of the simple dream of a preoperational child is, "I was asleep in the bathtub." There was no evidence of fantastic characters in the young children's dreams. The 5-, 6-, and 7-year-olds began to tell more concrete stories when reporting their dreams, and the adolescents' dreams were much more abstract, reflecting the formal operational quality of their mental excursions during the night. ◆

A pictorial representation of one of Freud's boyhood dreams. As a young boy, Freud dreamed that his mother was being carried off by two creatures. The bird-headed creatures in the dream closely resembled illustrations from a Bible Freud had seen.

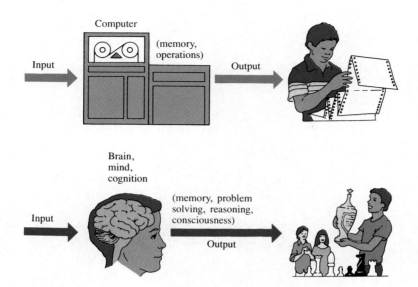

FIGURE 2.5 Computers and cognition: an analogy.

By the 1940s, the behaviorists' claim that children learn primarily through environment-behavior connections was being challenged. The first successful computer suggested that machines could perform logical operations. This indicated that some mental operations might be modeled by computers, and possibly computers could tell us something about how cognition works. Cognitive psychologists often use the computer to help explain the relation between cognition and the brain. The physical brain is described as the computer's hardware and cognition as its software (Figure 2.5). The ability to process information has highlighted psychology's cognitive revolution since the 1950s.

The information-processing approach raises important questions about changes in cognition during children's development. One of these questions is: Does processing speed increase as children grow older? The idea of speed of processing is an important aspect of the information-processing approach. Many cognitive tasks are performed under real time pressure. For example, at school, children have a limited amount of time to add and subtract and take tests; they also have deadlines for completing a project. There is a good deal of evidence that processing speed is slower in younger children than in older children, but the cause of this difference has not been determined. Although some of the difference might be biological in origin, the faster information-processing speed of older children might reflect differences in knowledge about a task or practice on the task (Santrock & Bartlett, 1986).

Evaluating the Cognitive Theories

Piaget's cognitive-developmental and information-processing theories both contribute in important ways to our knowledge about children's development. Today, researchers enthusiastically evaluate the accuracy of Piaget's theory, with the result that some of his ideas remain unscathed while others are requiring extensive modification (Beilin, 1989). The information-processing approach has opened up many avenues of research, offering detailed descriptions of cognitive processes and sophisticated methods for studying cognition (Klahr, 1989). The cognitive theories provide an optimistic view of human development, ascribing to children the ability and motivation to know their world and to cope with it in constructive ways.

"I Feel Pretty Silly Putting Pegs In Holes When I Have A Personal Computer At Home."

Like all theories, the cognitive theories have their weaknesses. There is skepticism about the pureness of Piaget's stages, and his concepts are somewhat loosely defined. The information-processing approach has not yet produced an overall perspective on development. Both the Piagetian and information-processing approaches may have underestimated the importance of the unconscious mind and environmental experiences—especially those involving families—in determining behavior.

So far, we have discussed two main theories of children's development: psychoanalytic and cognitive. A summary of the main ideas in these two theories is presented in Concept Table 2.1. The psychoanalytic and cognitive-developmental theories are stage theories, each highlighting the ascendance of certain characteristics at particular points in development. The remaining theories we will discuss do not specify stages in children's development.

Behavioral and Social Learning Theories

Fifteen-year-old Tom is going steady with 14-year-old Ann. Both have warm, friendly personalities, and they enjoy being together. Psychoanalytic theorists would say that their warm, friendly personalities are derived from longstanding relationships with their parents, especially their early child experiences. They also would argue that the reason for their attraction to each other is unconscious. They are unaware of how their biological heritage and early life experiences have been carried forward to influence their personalities in adolescence.

Psychologists from the behavioral and social learning perspective would observe Tom and Ann and see something quite different. They would examine their experiences, especially their most recent ones, to understand the reason for their attraction. Tom would be described as rewarding Ann's behavior, and vice versa, for example. No reference would be made to unconscious thoughts, the Oedipus complex, defense mechanisms, and so on.

The Nature of Children's Development

The Psychoanalytic and Cognitive Theories

Concept	Processes and Related Ideas	Characteristics and Description
Psychoanalytic Theories	Freud's theory	Freud said that personality is made up of three structures—id, ego, and superego—which conflict with each other. In Freud's view, most of children's thoughts are unconscious, and the id is completely unconscious. The conflicting demands of children's personality structures produce anxiety. Defense mechanisms, especially repression, protect the child's ego and reduce anxiety. Freud was convinced that problems develop because of early childhood experiences. He said individuals go through five psychosexual stages: oral, anal, phallic, latency, and genital. During the phallic stage, the Oedipus complex is a main source of conflict.
	Erikson's theory	Erikson developed a theory that emphasizes eight psychosocial stages of development: trust vs. mistrust, autonomy vs. shame, doubt, initiative vs. guilt, industry vs. inferiority, identity vs. identity confusion, intimacy vs. isolation, generativity vs. stagnation, and integrity vs. despair.
	Evaluating the psychoanalytic theories	Strengths of the theory are an emphasis on the past, the developmental course of personality, mental representation of the environment, unconscious mind, and emphasis on conflict. Weaknesses are the difficulty in testing main concepts, lack of an empirical data base and overreliance on reports of the past, too much emphasis on sexuality and the unconscious mind, and a negative view of human nature.
Cognitive Theories	Piaget's theory	Piaget's theory is responsible for the field of cognitive development. He believes that children are motivated to understand their world and use the processes of organization and adaptation (i.e., assimilation, accommodation) to do so. Piaget says that children go through four cognitive stages: sensorimotor, preoperational, concrete operational, and formal operational.
	Information-processing approach	Is concerned with how individuals process information about their world. Includes how information gets into the child's mind, how it is solved and transformed, and how it is retrieved to allow persons to think and solve problems. The development of the computer promoted this approach. The mind as an information-processing system was compared to how a computer processes information. The information-processing approach raises questions about the nature of development, among them the increased speed of processing information as children grow older.
	Evaluating the cognitive theories	Both the Piagetian and information-processing approachs have made important contributions to our understanding of children's development. They have provided a positive, rational portrayal of how children develop, although they may have underestimated the importance of unconscious thought and environmental experiences, especially in the family. The purity of Piaget's stages has been questioned, and the information-processing approach has not yet produced an overall perspective on development.

Behaviorists believe that we should examine only what can be directly observed and measured (Baer, 1989; Bijou, 1989). At approximately the same time that Freud was interpreting his patients' unconscious minds through early childhood experiences, behaviorists such as Ivan Pavlov and John B. Watson were conducting detailed observations of behavior in controlled laboratory circumstances. Out of the behavioral tradition grew the belief that development is observable behavior, learned through experience with the environment. The two versions of the behavioral approach that are prominent today are the view of B. F. Skinner and social learning theory.

Skinner's Behaviorism

B. F. Skinner

During World War II, B. F. Skinner constructed a rather strange project: a pigeon-guided missile. A pigeon in the warhead of the missile operated the flaps on the missile and guided it home by pecking at an image of a target. How could this possibly work? When the missile was in flight, the pigeon pecked the moving image on the screen. This produced corrective signals to keep the missile on its course. The pigeons did their job well in trial runs, but top Navy officials just could not accept pigeons piloting their missiles during a war. Skinner, however, congratulated himself on the degree of control he was able to exercise over the pigeons.

Following the pigeon experiment, Skinner (1948) wrote *Walden Two,* a novel in which he presented his ideas about building a scientifically managed society. Skinner envisioned a utopian society that could be engineered through behavioral control. Skinner viewed existing societies as poorly managed because individuals believe in myths such as free will. He pointed out that humans are no more free than pigeons; denying that our behavior is controlled by environmental forces is to ignore science and reality, he argued. In the long run, Skinner said we would be much happier when we recognized such truths, especially his concept that we could live in a prosperous life under the control of positive reinforcement.

Skinner did not need the mind, conscious or unconscious, to explain development. For him, development was the individual's behavior. For example, observations of Sam reveal that his behavior is shy, achievement oriented, and caring. Why is Sam's behavior this way? For Skinner, rewards and punishments in Sam's environment have shaped him into a shy, achievement oriented, caring child. Because of interactions with family members, friends, teachers, and others, Sam has *learned* to behave in this fashion.

Because behaviorists believe that development is learned and often changes according to environmental experiences, it follows that rearranging experiences can change the child's development. For the behaviorist, shy behavior can be changed into outgoing behavior; aggressive behavior can be shaped into docile behavior; lethargic, boring behavior can be turned into enthusiastic, interesting behavior.

Skinner describes the way in which behavior is controlled in the following way. The child *operates* on the environment to produce a change that will lead to a reward (Skinner, 1938). Skinner chose the term *operants* to describe the responses that are actively emitted because of the consequences for the child. The consequences—rewards and punishments—are *contingent,* or depend on the child's behavior. For example, an operant might be pressing a lever on a machine that delivers a candy bar; the delivery of the candy bar is contingent on pressing the lever. In sum, **operant conditioning** is a form of learning in which the consequences of behavior lead to changes in the probability of that behavior's occurrence.

Jess and His Teachers

Jess is an eighth grader at a junior high school in California. At 14 years old, he already weighs 185 pounds. He is the school's best athlete, but he used to get some of his biggest thrills out of fighting. Jess knocked out several fellow students with bottles and chairs and once hit the principal with a stick, for which he received a 40-day suspension from school.

Jess's teachers unanimously agreed that he was an impossible case. No one was able to control him. But one week, his teachers began to notice a complete turnabout in Jess's behavior. His math teacher was one of the first to notice the strange but improved behavior. Jess looked at her one day and said, "When you are nice, you help me learn a lot." The teacher was shocked. Not knowing what to say, she finally smiled. Jess continued, "I feel really good when you praise me." Jess continued a consistent pattern of such statements to his teachers and even came to class early or sometimes stayed late just to chat with them.

What was responsible for Jess's turnabout? Some teachers said he attended a mysterious class every day that might provide some clues to his behavior change. In that "mysterious" class, a teacher was training students in behavior modification, which emphasizes that behavior is determined by its consequences. Those consequences weaken some behaviors and strengthen others.

In an experiment, Paul Graubard and Henry Rosenberg (1974) selected seven of the most incorrigible students at a junior high school—Jess was one of them—and had a teacher give them instruction and practice in behavior modification in one 43-minute class period each day. In their daily training sessions, the students were taught a number of rewards to use to shape a teacher's behavior. Rewards included eye contact, smiling, sitting up straight, and being attentive. The students also practiced ways to praise the teacher, saying such things as, "I like working in this class where there is a good teacher." And they worked on ways to discourage certain teacher behaviors by saying such things as, "I just have a rough time working well when you get mad at me." Jess had the hardest time learning how to smile. He was shown a videotape of his behavior and observed that he actually leered at people when he was told to smile. Although it was somewhat hilarious, Jess practiced in front of a camera until he eventually developed a charming smile.

During the five weeks in which the students implemented their behavior-change tactics, observations indicated that teacher-student interchanges were becoming much more positive. Informal observations and comments after the program ended suggested that positive student-teacher interchanges were continuing. But what happened in the long run? In the case of this experiment, we do not know, but in many cases such behavior modification interventions do not result in long-lasting changes once the consequences for behavior are removed (Masters & others, 1988). ◆

More needs to be said about reinforcement and punishment. **Reinforcement** (or reward) is a consequence that increases the probability that a behavior will occur. By contrast, **punishment** is a consequence that decreases the probability that a behavior will occur. For example, consider the situation when a boy starts talking with a girl and she then smiles. Later he strikes up a conversation with another girl, who frowns at him. He subsequently approaches the first girl and talks to her again but doesn't approach the second girl. The first girl's smile has reinforced the boy's talking; the second girl's frown has punished it. More about reinforcement and how a boy named Jess learned to control his teachers' behavior appears in Children 2.2.

Social Learning Theory

Some psychologists believe the behaviorists are right when they say development is learned and is influenced strongly by environmental experiences. But they believe Skinner went too far in declaring that cognition is unimportant in understanding children's development. **Social learning theory** is the view of psychologists who emphasize behavior, environment, *and* cognition as the key factors in children's development.

Thinking Critically
Consider your life during the last 24 hours. How did rewards and punishments influence the way you behaved during this time frame?

Albert Bandura
Reprinted with permission from
PSYCHOLOGY TODAY Magazine © 1986.
(PT Partners, L.P.)

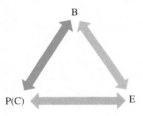

FIGURE 2.6   Bandura's model of the
reciprocal influence of behavior, personal
and cognitive factors, and environment.
P(C) stands for personal and cognitive
factors, *B* for behavior, and *E* for
environment. The arrows reflect how
relations between these factors are
reciprocal rather than unidirectional.
Examples of personal factors include
intelligence, skills, and self-control.
Albert Bandura, Social Foundations of Thought
and Action: A Social Cognitive Theory, *© 1986,*
p. 24. Reprinted by permission of Prentice-
Hall, Inc., Englewood Cliffs, NJ.

The social learning theorists say that children are not like mindless robots, responding mechanically to others in their environment. And they are not like weathervanes, always behaving nicely in the presence of a nice person and nasty in the presence of a nasty person. Rather, children think, reason, imagine, plan, expect, interpret, believe, value, and compare. As they develop, their social skills, strategies, values, and beliefs may enable them to resist others' efforts to control them, or they may exercise the control of others in return.

Albert Bandura (1977, 1989) and Walter Mischel (1973, 1984) are the main architects of social learning theory. Bandura believes that much of children's learning occurs by observing what others do. Through observational learning (also called modeling or imitation), children cognitively represent the behavior of others and then possibly adopt this behavior themselves. For example, a young boy may observe his father's aggressive outbursts and hostile interchanges with people. When observed with his peers, the young boy's style of interaction is highly aggressive, showing the same characteristics as his father's behavior. Or, a girl may adopt the dominant and sarcastic style of her teacher. When observed interacting with her younger brother, she says, "You are so slow. How can you do this work so slow?" Social learning theorists believe children acquire a wide range of such behaviors, thoughts, and feelings through observing others' behavior. These observations form an important part of children's development.

Social learning theorists also differ from Skinner's behavioral view by emphasizing that children can regulate and control their own behavior. For example, another girl who observed her teacher behaving in a dominant and sarcastic way toward her students found the behavior distasteful and went out of her way to be encouraging and supportive toward her younger brother. Someone tries to perusade an adolescent to join a particular club at school. The adolescent thinks about the offer to join the club, considers her own interests and beliefs, and makes the decision not to join. The adolescent's *cognition* (thoughts) led her to control her own behavior and resist environmental influence in this instance.

Bandura's (1986, 1989) most recent model of social learning involves behavior, the person, and the environment. As shown in Figure 2.6, behavior, environment, and cognitive or personal factors operate interactively. Behavior can influence cognition and vice versa, the child's cognitive activities can influence the environment, environmental influences can change the child's thought processes, and so on.

Let's consider how Bandura's model might work in the case of a student's behavior. As the student diligently studies and gets good grades, her behavior produces positive thoughts about her abilities. As part of her effort to make good grades, she plans and develops a number of strategies to make her studying more efficient. In these ways, her behavior has influenced her thought, and her thought has influenced her behavior. At the beginning of the school year, her counselor made a special effort to involve students in a study-skills program. She decided to join. Her success, along with that of other students who attended the program, has led her school to expand the program. In these ways, environment influenced behavior, and behavior influenced environment. And the expectations of the school's counselor and principal that the program would work made it possible in the first place. The program's success has spurred expectations that this type of program could work in other schools. In these ways, cognition changed the environment, and the environment changed cognition. Expectations are important in Bandura's model.

Like the behavioral approach of Skinner, the social learning approach emphasizes the importance of empirical research in studying children's development. This research focuses on the processes that explain children's development—the social and cognitive factors that influence what children are like.

Evaluating the Behavioral and Social Learning Theories

The behavioral and social learning theories emphasize that environmental experiences determine children's development. These approaches have fostered a scientific climate for understanding children's development that highlights the observations of children's behavior. Social learning theory emphasizes that both environmental influences and cognitive processes are involved in understanding children's development. This view also suggests that as children develop, they acquire the ability to control their own behavior and exercise control over their social world.

The criticisms of the behavioral and social learning theories sometimes are directed at the behavioral view alone, and at other times are directed toward both approaches. The behavioral view has been criticized for ignoring the importance of cognition in children's development and placing too much importance on environmental experiences. Both approaches have been described as being too concerned with change and situational influences on children's development, and as not paying tribute to the enduring qualities of children. Both views are said to ignore the biological determinants of children's development. Both are labeled reductionistic, which means that they look at only one or two components of children's development instead of how all of the pieces fit together. Critics have charged that the behavioral and social learning theorists are too mechanical. By being overly concerned with several minute pieces of children's development, the most exciting and rich dimensions of their development is missed, say the detractors. This latter criticism—that the creative, spontaneous, human characteristics of children's development are missing from the behavioral and social learning theories—had been made on numerous occasions by adherents of the humanistic approach, which we consider next.

Phenomenological and Humanistic Theories

Recall the adolescent couple, Tom and Ann, who were described as having warm, friendly personalities. Phenomenological and humanistic psychologists would describe their warm, friendly personalities as reflecting their inner selves. They would emphasize that the key to understanding their attraction is their positive perception of each other. Tom and Ann are not viewed as controlling each other's behavior. Instead, each has determined a course of action, and each has freely chosen to like the other. No recourse to biological instincts or unconscious thoughts as determinants of their attraction occurs in phenomenological and humanistic theories.

Phenomenological theory stresses the importance of children's perceptions of themselves and their world in understanding their development. The approach centers on the belief that for each child, reality is what is *perceived*. The most widely adopted phenomenological theories are the **humanistic theories,** which stress the importance of self-perceptions, inner experiences, self-determination, and self-confidence. Humanistic psychologists emphasize the positive qualities of children, believing they have the ability to handle stress, control their lives, and achieve what they desire. All children have the ability to break through and understand themselves and their world. Each child can burst the cocoon and become a butterfly, say the humanists.

You may sense that the phenomenological and humanistic approaches provide stark contrasts to the psychoanalytic approach to development, which is based on conflict and has little faith in children's ability to understand their development, and to the behavioral view, which emphasizes that the child's behavior is determined by rewards and punishments from others. The leading architect of the phenomenological and humanistic approaches is Carl Rogers.

Carl Rogers

Rogers' Theory

Like Freud, Rogers (1961) began his inquiry about human nature with troubled personalities. Rogers explored the human potential for change. In the knotted, anxious, defensive verbal stream of his clients, Rogers concluded that individuals are prevented from becoming what they are capable of.

Rogers believed that most individuals have considerable difficulty accepting their own true feelings, which are innately positive. As children grow up, significant others condition them to move away from these positive feelings. Children's parents, siblings, teachers, and peers place constraints and contingencies on their behavior. Too often children hear, "Don't do that," "You didn't do that right," "How could you be so stupid?" and "You didn't try hard enough." When children don't do something right, they often get punished. And parents may even threaten to withdraw or withhold their love. Thus, Rogers believed that each child is a victim of **conditional positive regard,** meaning that love and praise are not given unless children conform to parental or social standards. The result is that children's self-esteem is lowered.

These constraints and negative feedback continue throughout our lives. The result is that human relationships carry either the dark cloud of conflict or conformity to what others want. Neither children nor adults are allowed to adequately express their positive nature. As children and adults strive to live up to society's standards, they distort and devalue their true selves. And they may even completely lose their sense of self by mirroring what others want (Rogers, 1961).

Through the child's experiences with the world, a self emerges, this is the "I" or "me" of the child's existence. Rogers did not believe that all aspects of the child's self are conscious, but he did believe that they are accessible to consciousness. The self is construed as a whole. It consists of self-perceptions (how attractive I am, how well I get along with others, how good an athlete I am) and the values attached to those perceptions (good-bad or worthy-unworthy, for example).

Rogers also considered the congruence between the child's real self—that is, the child's self as it really is because of the child's experiences—and the ideal self, which is the self the child would like to be. The greater the discrepancy between the real self and the ideal self, the more maladjusted the child will be, said Rogers. To improve children's adjustment, children can be encouraged to develop more positive perceptions of their real selves, not worry so much about what others want, and increase their positive experiences in the world. In such ways, the child's real self and ideal self will be closer.

Rogers thinks that all children should be valued regardless of their behavior. Even when children's behavior is obnoxious, below acceptable standards, or inappropriate, they need the respect, comfort, and love of others. When these positive behaviors are given without contingency, this is known as **unconditional positive regard.** Rogers believed strongly that unconditional positive regard elevates the child's self-worth and positive self-regard. Unconditional positive regard is directed to the child as a person of worth and dignity, not to his behavior, which may not deserve regard (Rogers, 1974).

Rogers (1980) also stressed the importance of becoming a fully functioning person. What is a fully functioning person? She is open to experience, is not very defensive, is aware of and sensitive to the self and the external world, and for the most part has a harmonious relationship with others. A discrepancy between our real self and our ideal self may occur; others may try to control us; and our world may have too little unconditional positive regard; but Rogers believed that we are highly resilient and capable of becoming a fully functioning person. He believed that our good side could not be kept down.

Half-naked, half-clothed, Picasso's 1932 Girl before a Mirror, *reflects the twin images of Carl Rogers' ideal and real self.*

Pablo Picasso. Girl before a Mirror. *1932, March 14. Oil on canvas, 64" × 51½". Collection, The Museum of Modern Art, New York. Gift of Mrs. Simon Guggenheim.*

The Nature of Children's Development

The Struggles and Triumphs of Black Children and Their Families

The 1985 Children's Defense Fund Study, "Black and White Children in America: Key Facts," found that black children are twice as likely as white children to

—have neither parent employed
—live in institutions

three times as likely to

—be poor
—live with a parent who has separated from a spouse
—live in a female-headed family
—be in foster care
—die of child abuse

four times as likely to

—live with neither parent and be supervised by a child welfare agency

five times as likely to

—be dependent on welfare

twelve times as likely to

—live with a parent who never married

Nonetheless, it is important to keep in mind that millions of black American families are not on welfare, have children who stay in school and out of trouble, and do not get pregnant, and, if they experience difficult times, they find a way to overcome their problems. In 1967, Martin Luther King reflected on the black family and gave the following caution: As public awareness of the predicament of the black family increases, there will be danger and opportunity. The opportunity will be to deal fully rather than haphazardly with the problem as a whole, as a social catastrophe brought on by long years of oppression. We need to develop resources to combat the oppression. The danger is that the problems will be attributed to innate black weaknesses and used to justify further neglect and to rationalize continued oppression. In today's world, Dr. King's words still ring true. ◆

This tendency of ours toward **self-actualization** is reflected in Rogers' comparison of a person with a plant he once observed on the coastline of northern California. Rogers was looking out at the waves beating furiously against the jagged rocks, shooting mountains of spray into the air. Rogers noticed a tiny tree on the rocks, no more than 2 or 3 feet high, taking the pounding of the breakers. The plant was fragile and top-heavy; it seemed clear that the waves would crush the tiny specimen. A wave would crunch the plant, bending its slender trunk almost flat and whipping its leaves in a torrent of spray. Yet the moment the wave passed, the plant was erect, tough, and resilient once again. It was amazing that the plant could take this incessant pounding hour after hour, week after week, year after year, all the time nourishing itself, maintaining its position, and growing. In this tiny plant, Rogers saw the tenacity of life, the forward thrust of development, and the ability of a living thing to push into a hostile environment and not only hold its own, but adapt, develop, and become itself. So it is with each of us as we develop, in Rogers' view (Rogers, 1963).

Evaluating the Phenomenological and Humanistic Theories

The phenomenological and humanistic theories made us sensitive to the importance of phenomenological experience. Children's perceptions of themselves and their world are key ingredients of their development. The emphasis on consciousness likewise has had a significant impact on how we view development. The humanistic psychologists remind us that we need to consider the whole child and the child's positive nature. The contribution of these approaches has been felt in human relationships. Many persons believe that the humanistic approach has helped them to understand both themselves and others. And the approaches have facilitated our ability to effectively communicate with others.

One weakness of these approaches is that they are very hard to test scientifically. Self-actualization, for instance, is not clearly defined. Psychologists are not certain how to study this concept empirically. Some humanistic psychologists even scorn the scientific approach, preferring clinical interpretation as a data base. Verification of humanistic concepts has come mainly from clinical experiences rather than from controlled scientific efforts. Some critics also believe that these approaches are too optimistic about human nature. They possibly overestimate the freedom and rationality of humans. And some critics say that these approaches encourage self-love and narcissism.

Ethological Theories

Sensitivity to different kinds of experience varies over the individual's life cycle. The presence or absence of certain experiences at particular times in the life span influences the individual well beyond the time that they first occur. Ethologists believe that most psychologists underestimate the importance of these special time frames in development and the contribution biology makes to development.

Lorenz's Classical Ethological Theory

Ethology emerged as an important view because of the work of European zoologists, especially Konrad Lorenz. **Ethology** stresses that behavior is biologically determined. Ethologists believe that we can only fully appreciate a child's behavior if we recognize that the behavior is tied to evolution. Ethologists also remind us that early experience plays an important part in development and potentially is irreversible.

Working mostly with graylag geese, Lorenz (1965) studied a behavior pattern that was considered to be programmed within the genes of the animals. A gosling newly hatched from the egg seemed to be born with the instinct for following its mother. Lorenz proved that it was incorrect to assume that such behavior was programmed in the animal.

The tide of evolution carries everything before it, thoughts no less than bodies, and persons no less than nations.

George Santayana, Little Essays, *1920*

The Nature of Children's Development

FIGURE 2.7   Konrad Lorenz, a pioneering student of animal behavior, is followed through the water by three imprinted graylag geese.

In a remarkable set of experiments, Lorenz separated the eggs laid by one female goose into two groups. One group he returned to the female goose to be hatched by her; the other group was hatched in an incubator. The goslings in the first group performed as predicted; they followed their mother as soon as they were hatched. But those in the second group, who saw Lorenz when they were first hatched, followed him everywhere, just as though he was their mother. Lorenz marked the goslings and then placed both groups under a box. Mother goose and "mother" Lorenz stood aside as the box was lifted. Each group of goslings went directly to its "mother" (Figure 2.7). Lorenz called this process **imprinting**—rapid, innate learning within a limited critical period of time that involves attachment to the first moving object seen.

The ethological view of Lorenz and the European zoologists forced American developmental psychologists to recognize the importance of the biological basis of behavior. But the research and theorizing of ethology still seemed to lack some ingredients that would elevate it to the ranks of the other theories discussed so far in this chapter. In particular, there was little or nothing in the classical ethological view about the nature of social relationships across the human life cycle, something that any major theory of development must explain. And too much importance seemed to be attached to the concept of **critical period**—a fixed time period very early in development during which certain behaviors optimally emerge. Classical ethological theory had been weak in stimulating studies with human beings. Recent expansion of the ethological view has improved its status as a viable developmental perspective.

Hinde's Neo-Ethological Theory

Ethologist Robert Hinde (1983, 1989) developed a view that goes beyond classical ethological theory by emphasizing the importance of social relationships, describing sensitive periods of development rather than critical periods, and presenting a framework that is beginning to stimulate research with human children. Insight into Hinde's neo-ethological theory appears in the form of his discussion of selected issues of interest to ethologists.

Robert Hinde, professor of psychology at Cambridge University, England.

Like behaviorists, ethologists are careful observers of behavior. Unlike behaviorists, ethologists believe that laboratories are not good settings for observing behavior. Instead, they observe behavior in its natural surroundings. Behavior should be meticulously observed in homes, playgrounds, neighborhoods, schools, hospitals, and so on.

Ethologists also point out that children's development is studied by adults, who see the end point of development being mature adulthood. However, ethologists believe that an infant's or child's behavior should not always be considered in terms of its importance for mature adulthood. Instead, a behavior may be adaptive at an early stage of development only. For example, caterpillars are excellent leaf eaters, but they do not pretend to be butterflies. Ethologists believe that the word *development* too often diverts attention away from viewing each stage of development in its own right.

Ethologists emphasize sensitive periods. Hinde distinguishes between critical and sensitive periods. Classical ethologists, such as Lorenz, argued for the importance of critical periods in development. The more recently developed concept of **sensitive period** emphasizes a more flexible band of time for a behavior to optimally emerge; sensitive periods occur on the order of months and even years, rather than days or weeks. With human children, there seem to be some flexible sensitive periods for processes such as language, vision, and attachment (Bornstein, 1987).

Ethologists also are becoming interested in social relationships and personality. Hinde argues that certain properties of relationships, such as synchrony and competitiveness, do not describe individuals in isolation. Relationships have properties that emerge from the frequency and patterning of interactions over time. For example if the mother-infant relationship is studied at some point in development, researchers may not be able to describe it as rejecting, controlling, or permissive. But through detailed observations over a period of time, such categorization may be possible.

Evaluating the Ethological Theories

Ethological theory emphasizes the biological and evolutionary basis of behavior, giving biology an appropriate, prominent role in development. Ethologists use careful observations in naturalistic surroundings to obtain information about development. And ethologists believe development involves sensitive periods.

However, like other theories we have discussed, ethology has its weaknesses. At times, even the emphasis on sensitive periods seems to be too rigid; the critical period concept is too rigid for human development. The emphasis still slants more toward biological-evolutionary explanations of behavior rather than a biological-environmental mix. The theory has been slow in generating research about human life-span development. The theory is better at explaining behavior retrospectively than prospectively. That is, ethology is better at explaining what happened to cause a child's behavior after it happens than predicting its occurrence in the future.

An Eclectic Theoretical Orientation

No single indomitable theory is capable of explaining the rich complexity of development (Miller, 1989). Each theory described in this chapter has made important contributions to our understanding of development, but none provides a complete description and explanation. Psychoanalytic theory best explains the unconscious mind. Erikson's theory best describes the changes that occur in adult development. Piaget's theory is the most complete description of children's cognitive development. The behavioral and social learning theories have been the most adept at examining the environmental determinants of development. The phenomenological and humanistic theories have given us the most insight about self-conception. And the ethological theories have made us aware of biology's role and the importance of sensitive periods in development. It is important to recognize that, while theories are helpful guides in understanding development, relying on a single theory to explain development probably is a mistake.

In this chapter, five theoretical perspectives were presented objectively. The same eclectic orientation will be maintained throughout the book. In this way, you can view the study of development as it actually exists—with different theorists making different assumptions about development, stressing different empirical problems, and using different strategies to discover information about development.

These theoretical perspectives, along with the research issues and methods described in Chapter 1, provide a sense of development's scientific nature. Table 2.3 compares the five main theoretical perspectives in terms of how they view some of the issues we have discussed thus far. By studying Table 2.3, you should be able to integrate some of the most important ideas about issues and methods described in Chapter 1 with the main theories described in Chapter 2.

Thus far, we have discussed several ideas about behavioral and social learning theories, phenomenological and humanistic theories, and ethological theories. We also have described an eclectic theoretical orientation and seen how different theories handle various issues in development. A summary of these ideas is presented in Concept Table 2.2.

This chapter concludes the discussion of the book's first section, "The Nature of Children's Development." In the next section, we turn to the beginnings of children's development.

TABLE 2.3 *Theoretical Comparisons and Issues and Methods in Children's Development*

	Theories				
Issues and Methods	**Psychoanalytic**	**Cognitive**	**Behavioral and Social Learning**	**Phenomenological and Humanistic**	**Ethological**
Continuity and Discontinuity	Discontinuity between stages, but continuity between early experiences and later development; later changes in development emphasized in Erikson's theory.	Discontinuity between stages, but continuity between early experiences and later development in Piaget's theory; this has not been an important issue to information processing psychologists.	Continuity (no stages). Experience at all points of development important.	Continuity (no stages). Experience at all points in development important, especially immediate experience.	Discontinuity but no stages are given; critical or sensitive periods are emphasized.
Biological and Environmental Factors	Freud stressed biological determination interacting with early experiences in the family; Erikson provides a more balanced biological-cultural interaction perspective.	Piaget emphasizes biological adaptation. Environment provides the setting for cognitive structures to unfold. Information-processing perspective has not addressed this issue extensively, but hardware-software metaphor emphasizes biological-environmental interaction.	Environment viewed as the cause of behavior in both the behavioral and social learning views.	Environmental influences emphasized, especially warmth and nurturance.	Strong biological view.
Importance of Cognition	Cognition is emphasized, but in the form of unconscious thought.	Cognition is the primary development of behavior.	Cognition is strongly deemphasized in the behavioral approach but plays an important mediating role in the social learning approach.	Cognition is important, especially in the form of self-perception.	Cognition is not emphasized.
Research Methods	Clinical interviews, unstructured personality tests, and psychohistorical analyses of lives.	Interviews and observations.	Observation, especially laboratory observation.	The scientific approach is deemphasized; self-report measures and interviews are used.	Observation in natural settings.

The Behavioral and Social Learning Theories, Phenomenological and Humanistic Theories, Ethological Theories, and an Eclectic Theoretical Orientation

Concept	Processes and Related Ideas	Characteristics and Description
Behavioral and Social Learning Theories	Skinner's behaviorism	Emphasizes that cognition is unimportant in development; development is observed behavior, which is influenced by the rewards and punishments in the environment.
	Social learning theory	The environment is an important determinant of development, but so are cognitive processes. We have the capability of controlling our own behavior through thoughts, beliefs, and values. Bandura's emphasis on observational learning the social learning approach, as does his model of the reciprocal influences of behavior, person (cognition) and environment. The contemporary version of social learning theory is called cognitive social learning theory.
	Evaluating the behavioral social learning	The strengths of both theories include emphases on environmental determinants and a scientific climate for investigating development, as well as the focus on cognitive processes and self-control in social learning theory. The behavioral view has been criticized for taking the person out of development and for ignoring cognition. These approaches have not given adequate attention to biological factors and to development as a whole.
Phenomenological and Humanistic Theories	Their nature	The phenomenological approach emphasizes our perceptions of ourselves and our world and centers on the belief that reality is what is perceived. The humanistic approach is the most widely known phenomenological approach.
	Rogers' theory	Each of us is a victim of conditional positive regard. The result is that our real self is not valued. The self is the core of development; it includes the real self and the ideal self. Rogers advocates unconditional positive regard to enhance our self-concept. Each of us has the innate, inner capacity of becoming a fully functioning person.
	Evaluating the phenomenological and humanistic approaches	These approaches sensitize us to the importance of subjective experience, consciousness, self-conception, the whole child, and children's innate positive nature. Their weaknesses focus on the absence of a scientific orientation, a tendency to be too optimistic, and an inclination to encourage self-love.
Ethological Theories	Lorenz's classical ethological theory	The biological and evolutionary basis of development needs to be emphasized. Critical periods, at which time a characteristic has an optimal time of emergence, occur in development.
	Hinde's neo-ethological theory	Emphasizes sensitive rather than critical periods. Places a premium on naturalistic observation and biological/evolutionary ties but also focuses on social relationships and personality.
	Evaluating the ethological theories	Strengths include the emphasis on the biological and evolutionary basis of behavior, naturalistic observation, and sensitive periods. Weaknesses include the rigidity of the critical period concept, an overemphasis on biology and evolution, a failure to generate studies of human development, and the inability to predict behavior prospectively.
Eclectic Theoretical Orientation	Its nature	No single theory can explain the rich, awesome complexity of children's development. Each of the theories has made a different contribution, and it is probably a wise strategy to adopt an eclectic theoretical perspective as we attempt to understand children's development. The different theoretical perspectives often take different stands on the main issues in children's development.

Summary

I. Freud's Theory

Freud said that personality has three structures—id, ego, and superego—that conflict with each other. In Freud's view, most thoughts are unconscious, and the id is completely unconscious. The conflicting demands of personality structures produce anxiety, defense mechanisms (especially repression), protect the ego, and reduce anxiety. Freud was convinced that problems develop because of childhood experiences. He said that we go through five psychosexual stages: oral, anal, phallic, latency, and genital. During the phallic stage, the Oedipus complex is a main source of conflict.

II. Erikson's Theory and Evaluation of the Psychoanalytic Theories

Erikson developed a theory that emphasizes eight psychosocial stages of development: trust vs. mistrust, autonomy vs. shame and doubt, initiative vs. guilt, industry vs. inferiority, identity vs. identity confusion, intimacy vs. isolation, generativity vs. stagnation, and integrity vs. despair. Strengths of the psychoanalytic theories are an emphasis on the past, the developmental course of personality, mental representation of the environment, unconscious mind, and emphasis on conflict. Weaknesses are the difficulty in testing main concepts, lack of an empirical data base and overreliance on past reports, too much emphasis on sexuality and the unconscious mind, and a negative view of human nature.

III. Piaget's Theory

Piaget's theory is responsible for the field of cognitive development. He believed that children are motivated to understand our world and use the processes of organization and adaptation (assimilation and accommodation) to do so. Piaget said that children go through four cognitive stages: sensorimotor, preoperational, concrete ornamental, and formal operational.

IV. Information-Processing Theory and Evaluation of the Cognitive Theories

The information-processing approach is concerned with how people process information about the world. It includes how information gets into the mind, how it is stored and transformed, and how it is retrieved for thinking and solving problems. The development of the computer promoted this approach; the mind as an information-processing system was compared to the way a computer processes information. The information-processing approach raises questions about children's development, among them developmental changes in the speed of processing information. Both the Piagetian and information-processing approaches have made important contributions to children's development. They have provided a positive, rational portrayal of children as they develop, although they may have underestimated the importance of unconscious thought and environmental experiences, especially family processes. The purity of Piaget's stages has been questioned, and the information-processing approach has not yet produced an overall perspective on development.

V. The Behavioral and Social Learning Theories

Skinner's behaviorism emphasizes that cognition is unimportant in development; development is observed behavior, which is influenced by the rewards and punishments in the environment. In social learning theory, the environment is an important determinant of development, but so are cognitive processes. Children develop the ability to control their own behavior through thoughts, beliefs, values, and social skills. Bandura's emphasis on observational learning and model of the reciprocal influences of behavior, person (cognition), and environment exemplify social learning theory. The contemporary version of social learning theory is called cognitive social learning theory.

VI. Evaluating the Behavioral and Social Learning Theories

The strengths of both theories include emphases on environmental determinants and a scientific climate for investigating development, as well as a focus on cognitive processes and self-control in social learning theory. The behavioral view has been criticized for taking the person out of development and for ignoring cognition. These approaches have not adequately considered biological factors and development as a whole.

VII. **The Phenomenological and Humanistic Theories**

The phenomenological approach emphasizes children's perceptions of themselves and their world, and centers on the belief that reality is what is perceived. The humanistic approach is the most widely known phenomenological approach. In Rogers' theory, every child is a victim of conditional positive regard. The result is that the child's real self is not valued. The self is the core of development; it includes the real self and the ideal self. Rogers advocates unconditional positive regard to enhance children's self-concept. Every child has the innate, inner capacity to become a fully functioning person. The phenomenological and humanistic approaches have sensitized us to the importance of subjective experiences, consciousness, self-conception, the whole child, and children's innate positive nature. Their weaknesses focus on the absence of a scientific orientation, a tendency to be too optimistic, and an inclination to encourage self-love.

VIII. **The Ethological Theories**

Ethological theories emphasize the biological and evolutionary basis of development. In Lorenz's classical ethological theory, critical periods—at which time a characteristic has an optimal time of emergence—are emphasized. In Hinde's neo-ethological theory, sensitive periods rather than critical periods are stressed, along with naturalistic observation, and social relationships and personality. Strengths include the emphasis on biological and evolutionary bases of behavior, naturalistic observation, and sensitive periods. Weaknesses include the rigidity of critical periods, an overemphasis on biology and evolution, a failure to generate studies of human development, and the inability to predict behavior prospectively.

IX. **An Eclectic Theoretical Orientation**

No single theory can explain the rich, awesome complexity of children's development. Each of the theories has made a different contribution, and it is probably a wise strategy to adopt an eclectic theoretical orientation as we attempt to understand children's development. The different theoretical perspectives often take different stands on the main issues in children's development.

Key Terms

id 41
pleasure principle 41
ego 41
reality principle 41
superego 42
defense mechanisms 42
repression 42
sublimation 42
reaction formation 42
regression 42
erogenous zones 43
fixation 44
oral stage 44
anal stage 44
phallic stage 44
Oedipus complex 44
latency stage 44
genital stage 44
epigenetic principle 46

trust versus mistrust 46
autonomy versus shame and
doubt 46
initiative versus guilt 46
industry versus
inferiority 46
identity versus identity
confusion 47
intimacy versus isolation 47
generativity versus
stagnation 47
integrity versus despair 47
assimilation 51
accommodation 51
sensorimotor stage 51
preoperational stage 52
concrete operational
stage 52
formal operational stage 52

information-processing
theory 53
operant conditioning 58
reinforcement 59
punishment 59
social learning theory 59
phenomenological
theory 61
humanistic theory 61
conditional positive
regard 62
unconditional positive
regard 62
self-actualization 63
ethology 64
imprinting 65
critical period 65
sensitive period 66

Suggested Readings

Bandura, A. (1986). *Social foundations of thought and action.* Englewood Cliffs, NJ: Prentice-Hall.

This book presents Bandura's cognitive social learning view of development, including an emphasis on reciprocal connections between behavior, environment, and person.

Cowan, P. (1978). *Piaget with feeling.* New York: Holt, Rinehart & Winston.

Provides a well-written overview of Piaget's theory and draws implications for understanding children's emotional development.

Erikson, E. H. (1968). *Identity: Youth and crisis.* New York: Norton.

Must reading for anyone interested in developmental psychology. Erikson outlines his eight stages of the life cycle and talks extensively about identity.

Hinde, R. (1983). Ethology and child development. In P. H. Mussen (Ed.), *Handbook of Child Psychology* (4th ed., Vol. 2). New York: Wiley.

Hinde's views are strongly influencing thinking about child development. Here he outlines the questions ethologists ask and the issues they research.

Shostrum, E. (1967). *Man, the manipulator.* New York: Bantam Books.

Shostrum presents an intriguing humanistic perspective on development, including many helpful ideas about adjustment and self-evaluation.

II

Beginnings

*What endless questions vex the
thought, of whence and whither,
when and how.*

Sir Richard Burton, Kasidah

The rhythm and meaning of life involve beginnings. Questions are raised about how from so simple a beginning endless forms develop and grow and mature. What was this organism, what is this organism, what will this organism be?

Section 2 consists of two chapters. Chapter 3's contents include ideas about

—Genetics
—Heredity-environmental interaction
—Genetic counseling
—Two identical twins separated from birth who behave in remarkably similar ways when reunited as adults
—Test-tube babies
—A Nobel Prize sperm bank for once-childless couples
—Whether or not we are born to be shy

Among Chapter 4's contents is information on

—The remarkable course of prenatal development
—The hazards of prenatal development
—Ethics and the medical use of fetal tissue
—The stunning events of birth
—Fathers in the delivery room
—Kilogram kids
—Exercising and massaging preterm babies
—Bonding

The frightening part about heredity and environment is that we parents provide both.

Notebook of a Printer

3

Biological Beginnings

J im Springer and Jim Lewis are identical twins. They were separated at the age of 4 weeks and did not see each other again until they were 39 years old. Both worked as part-time deputy sheriffs, both vacationed in Florida, both drove Chevrolets, both had dogs named Toy, and both married and divorced women named Betty. One twin named his son James Allan, and the other named his son James Alan. Both liked math but not spelling, enjoyed carpentry and mechanical drawing, chewed their fingernails down to the nubs, had almost identical drinking and smoking habits, had hemorrhoids, put on 10 pounds at about the same point in development, first suffered headaches at the age of 18, and had similar sleep patterns.

But Jim and Jim had some differences. One wore his hair over his forehead, the other slicked back with sideburns. One expressed himself best orally, the other was more proficient in writing. But for the most part, their profiles were remarkably similar.

Another pair, Daphne and Barbara, were called the "giggle sisters" because they were always making each other laugh. A thorough search of their adoptive families' histories revealed no gigglers. And the identical sisters handled stress by ignoring it, avoided conflict and controversy whenever possible, and showed no interest in politics.

Two other female identical twin sisters were separated at 6 weeks and reunited in their fifties. Both had nightmares, which they describe in hauntingly similar ways: Both dreamed of doorknobs and fishhooks in their mouths as they smothered to death! The nightmares began during early adolescence and had stopped in the last 10 to 12 years. Both women were bed wetters until about 12 or 13 years of age, and they reported educational and marital histories that were remarkably similar.

These sets of twins are part of the Minnesota Study of Twins Reared Apart, directed by Thomas Bouchard and his colleagues. They bring identical twins (identical genetically because they come from the same egg) and fraternal twins (dissimilar genetically because they come from two eggs) from all over the world to Minneapolis to investigate their lives. The twins are given a number of personality tests, and detailed medical histories are obtained, including information about diet, smoking, exercise habits, chest X rays, heart stress tests, and EEGs (brain-wave tests). The twins are interviewed and asked more than 15,000 questions about their family and childhood environment, personal interests, vocational orientation, values, and aesthetic judgments. They also are given ability and intelligence tests (Bouchard & others, 1981; McGue & Bouchard, in press; Tellegen & others, 1988).

The examples of Jim and Jim, the giggle sisters, and the identical twins who had the same nightmares stimulate us to think about our genetic heritage and the biological foundations of our existence. Organisms are not like billiard balls, moved by simple, external forces to predictable positions on life's pool table. Environmental experiences *and* biological foundations work together to make us who we are. Our coverage of life's biological beginnings focuses on genetics, heredity's influence on development, and the nature of heredity-environment interaction.

Genetics

Every species must have a mechanism for transmitting characteristics from one generation to the next. This mechanism is explained by the principle of genetics. Each of us carries a genetic code that we inherited from our parents. This code is located

(a)

(b)

(c)

(d)

Because of the human genetic code, a fertilized human egg cannot grow into an (a) egret, (b) eagle, or (c) elephant.

within every cell in our bodies. Our genetic codes are alike in one important way—they all contain the *human* genetic code. Because of the human genetic code, a fertilized human egg cannot grow into an eel, an egret, or an elephant.

What Are Genes?

Each of us began life as a single cell weighing about one twenty-millionth of an ounce! This tiny piece of matter housed our entire genetic code—the information about who we would become. These instructions orchestrated growth from that single cell to a person made of trillions of cells, each containing a perfect replica of the original genetic code.

The nucleus of each human cell contains 46 **chromosomes,** which are thread-like structures that come in structurally similar pairs. You inherited 23 chromosomes from your mother and another 23 chromosomes from your father. Chromosomes are composed of the remarkable substance deoxyribonucleic acid, or **DNA.** DNA is a molecule arranged in a "double helix" shape that looks like a spiral staircase (Figure 3.1). **Genes,** the units of hereditary information, are short segments of the DNA "staircase." Genes act as blueprints for cells to reproduce themselves and manufacture the proteins that maintain life. Chromosomes, DNA, and genes can be mysterious. To help you, turn mystery into understanding (Figure 3.2).

Genes are transmitted from parents to offspring by means of **gametes,** or sex cells, which are created in the testes of males and in the ovaries of females. Gametes are formed by the splitting of cells. This process is called **meiosis.** In meiosis, each pair of chromosomes in the cell separates, and one member of each pair goes into each gamete, or daughter cell. Thus, each human gamete has 23 unpaired chromosomes. **Reproduction** takes place when a female gamete (ovum) is fertilized by a male gamete (sperm) to create a single-celled **zygote** (Figure 3.3). In the zygote, two sets of unpaired chromosomes combine to form one set of paired chromosomes—one member of each pair from the mother and the other member from the father. In this manner, each parent contributes 50 percent of the offspring's heredity.

There are one hundred and ninety-three living species of monkeys and apes. One-hundred and ninety-two of them are covered with hair. The exception is the naked ape self-named, homo-sapiens.

Desmond Morris, The Naked Ape, *1967*

FIGURE 3.1   A DNA molecule. The horizontal bars are the important bases or "rungs" of the DNA ladder. The sequence of these bases plays a key role in scientists' efforts to locate the identity of a gene.

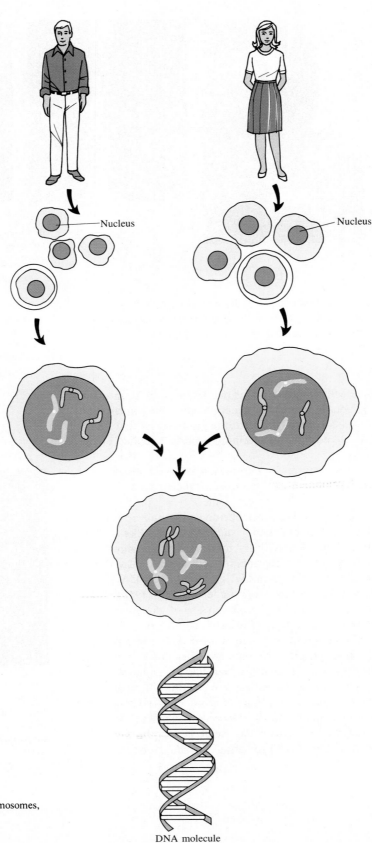

The body contains billions of cells that are organized into tissue and organs.

Nucleus

Nucleus

Each cell contains a central structure, the nucleus, which controls reproduction.

Chromosomes reside in the nucleus of each cell. The male's sperm and the female's egg are specialized reproductive cells that contain chromosomes.

At conception the offspring receives matching chromosomes from the mother's egg and the father's sperm.

The chromosomes contain DNA, a chemical substance. Genes are short segments of the DNA molecule. They are the units of hereditary information that act as a blueprint for cells to reproduce themselves and manufacture the proteins that sustain life. The rungs in the DNA ladder are an important location of genes.

FIGURE 3.2   Facts about chromosomes, genes, and DNA.

DNA molecule

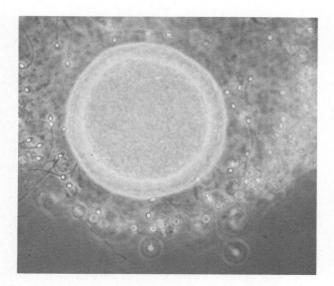

FIGURE 3.3 An ovum ready for release has been extracted and put into a nutritive solution together with a drop of specially treated seminal fluid. The sperm are eagerly striving toward the ovum. Notice the difference in size between the ovum and the sperm.

Reproduction

The ovum is about 90,000 times as large as a sperm. Thousands of sperm must combine to break down the ovum's membrane barrier to allow even a single sperm to penetrate the membrane barrier. Ordinarily, females have two X chromosomes and males have one X and one Y chromosome. Since the Y chromosome is smaller and lighter than the X chromosome, Y-bearing sperm can be separated from X-bearing sperm in a centrifuge. This raises the possibility that the offspring's sex can be controlled. Not only are the Y-bearing sperm lighter, but they are more likely to coat the ovum than the X-bearing sperm. This results in 120 to 150 males being conceived for every 100 females. But males are more likely to die (spontaneously abort) at every stage in prenatal development, so only about 106 are born for every 100 females.

Reproduction's fascinating moments have been made even more intriguing in recent years. Consider the following situation: The year is 1978. One of the most dazzling occurrences of the 1970s is about to unfold. Mrs. Brown is infertile, but her physician informs her of a new procedure that could enable her to have a baby. The procedure involves removing the mother's ovum surgically, fertilizing it in a laboratory medium with live sperm cells obtained from the father or another male donor (Figure 3.4), storing the fertilized egg in a laboratory solution that substitutes for the uterine environment, and finally implanting the egg in the mother's uterus. The procedure is called **in vitro fertilization.** For Mrs. Brown, the procedure was successful, and nine months later her daughter Louise was born.

Since the first in vitro fertilization in the 1970s, variations of the procedure have brought hope to childless couples. A woman's egg can be fertilized with the husband's sperm, or the husband and wife may contribute their sperm and egg with the resulting embryo carried by a third party, who essentially is donating her womb. A summary of nature's way of reproduction and new ways of creating babies is illustrated in Figure 3.5.

The turtle lives 'twixt plated decks
Which practically conceal its sex.
I think it clever of the turtle
In such a fix to be so fertile.

Ogden Nash, Many Long Years Ago,
1945

Drawing by Ziegler; © 1985 The New Yorker Magazine, Inc.

FIGURE 3.4   In vitro fertilization. Egg meets sperm in a laboratory dish.

The seed of the cedar will become cedar, The seed of the bramble can only become bramble.

Saint-Exupéry, Flight To Arras, *1942*

Abnormalities in Genes and Chromosomes

Geneticists and psychologists have identified a range of problems caused by some major gene or chromosome defect. In the PKU syndrome (phenylketonuria), the problem resides in a genetic code that fails to produce an enzyme necessary for metabolism. In the absence of this enzyme, the cells fail to break down an amino acid, phenylalanine, interfering with metabolic processes and generating a poisonous substance that enters the nervous system. Mental functioning rapidly deteriorates if the enzyme deficiency is not treated shortly after birth. Fortunately, the absence of this enzyme can be detected early and treated by diet to keep the phenylalanine at a very low level so that normal metabolism can proceed and the poisonous substance is not generated. The genetic code that fails to produce the enzyme involves a recessive gene. The PKU syndrome only occurs about once every 10,000 to 20,000 live births, but it accounts for about 1 percent of institutionalized mentally retarded individuals. It occurs primarily in whites.

The most common genetically transmitted form of mental retardation is Down's syndrome. The Down's syndrome child has a flattened skull, an extra fold of skin over the eyelids, and a protruding tongue. Among other characteristics are a short, thin body frame and retardation of motor abilities. The cause of Down's syndrome is an extra chromosome; Down's syndrome children have 47 chromosomes instead of the usual 46. It is not known why the extra chromosome occurs, but it may involve the health of the female ovum or the male sperm. Women in the age range of 18 to 38 are less likely to give birth to a Down's syndrome child than are younger or older women. Down's syndrome appears approximately once in every 700 live births. Black children rarely are born with Down's syndrome.

Sickle-cell anemia is another genetic disorder. It is a disease of the red blood cells and is a common disorder among blacks. About 1 in 400 black babies is affected. One in 10 black Americans is a carrier, as is 1 in 20 Latin Americans (Whaley & Wong, 1989). In sickle-cell anemia, a red blood cell is usually shaped like a disk, but a change in a recessive gene modifies its shape to a hook-shaped "sickle." These cells die quickly, causing anemia and early death because of their failure to carry oxygen to the body's cells.

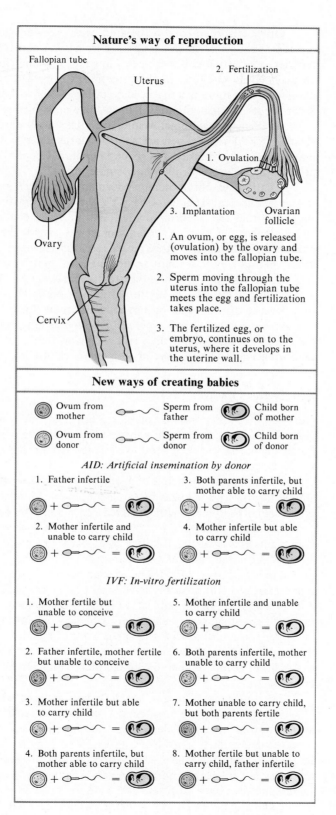

Nature's way of reproduction

Fallopian tube

Uterus

2. Fertilization

1. Ovulation

3. Implantation

Ovarian follicle

Ovary

Cervix

1. An ovum, or egg, is released (ovulation) by the ovary and moves into the fallopian tube.

2. Sperm moving through the uterus into the fallopian tube meets the egg and fertilization takes place.

3. The fertilized egg, or embryo, continues on to the uterus, where it develops in the uterine wall.

New ways of creating babies

Ovum from mother — Sperm from father — Child born of mother

Ovum from donor — Sperm from donor — Child born of donor

AID: Artificial insemination by donor

1. Father infertile

3. Both parents infertile, but mother able to carry child

2. Mother infertile and unable to carry child

4. Mother infertile but able to carry child

IVF: In-vitro fertilization

1. Mother fertile but unable to conceive

5. Mother infertile and unable to carry child

2. Father infertile, mother fertile but unable to conceive

6. Both parents infertile, mother unable to carry child

3. Mother infertile but able to carry child

7. Mother unable to carry child, but both parents fertile

4. Both parents infertile, but mother able to carry child

8. Mother fertile but unable to carry child, father infertile

FIGURE 3.5   Reproduction variations.

Other disorders are associated with sex-chromosome abnormalities. Remember that normal males have an X chromosome and a Y chromosome, and normal females have two X chromosomes. However, in **Klinefelter's syndrome,** males have an extra X chromosome (making them XXY instead of just XY): they have undeveloped testes and usually become tall and thin with enlarged breasts. This disorder occurs in approximately 1 in 800 live male births.

In **Turner's syndrome,** women are minus an X chromosome; they are XO instead of XX. These women are short in stature, with a webbing of the neck. They may be mentally retarded and sexually underdeveloped. This disorder occurs in approximately 1 in every 3,000 live female births.

Another sex-chromosome abnormality has been given considerable attention in the last several decades—the **XYY syndrome.** Early interest in this syndrome suggested that the Y chromosome found in males contributed to male aggression and violence; the extra Y chromosome was said to be responsible for excessive aggression and violence. More recent research, however, indicates that XYY males are no more likely to commit crimes than XY males (Witkin & others, 1976).

Each year in the United States, approximately 100,000 to 150,000 infants with a genetic disorder or malformation are born. These infants make up about 3 to 5 percent of the 3 million births and account for at least 20 percent of infant deaths. Prospective parents increasingly are turning to genetic counseling for assistance, wanting to know their risk of having a child born with a genetic defect or malformation. To learn more about genetic counseling, turn to Children 3.1.

Some Genetic Principles

Genetic determination is a complex affair, and much is unknown about the way genes work. But a number of genetic principles have been discovered, among them dominant-recessive genes, sex-linked genes, polygenically inherited characteristics, reaction range, and canalization.

The important principle of **dominant-recessive genes** was worked out with such simple forms of life as peas by Gregor Mendel. Mendel found that when he combined round pea plants with wrinkled pea plants, the next generation consistently came out round. The gene for round pea plants was *dominant* and the one for wrinkled plants was *recessive* (tending to go back, or "recede").

What is the color of your parents' hair? If they both have brown hair, you probably have brown hair. If one of your parents has brown hair and the other has blond hair, you still probably have brown hair because brown hair is controlled by a dominant gene; blond hair is controlled by a recessive gene. But if both of your parents have blond hair, then you probably have blond hair because there is no dominant gene to interfere with the appearance of blond hair. Examples of other dominant gene-linked characteristics are brown eyes, farsightedness, and dimples; examples of recessive gene-linked characteristics are blue eyes, normal vision, and freckles.

For thousands of years, people have wondered what determines whether an offspring will be a male or a female. Aristotle believed that the father's degree of arousal during intercourse determined the offspring's sex. The more excited the father was, the more likely the offspring would be a male, he reasoned. In the 1920s, researchers confirmed the existence of human sex chromosomes, two of the 46 chromosomes human beings normally carry. Ordinarily, females have two X chromosomes, and men have an X and a Y. (Figure 3.6 shows the chromosome makeup of a male and a female.) However, it still was not clear whether the "switch" consisted of one gene or many.

Thinking Critically
Imagine that you want to start a family. Probe your family background. What questions would you want to ask a genetic counselor?

Genetic Counseling

Bob and Mary Sims have been married for several years. They would like to start a family, but they are frightened. The newspapers and popular magazines are full of stories about infants born prematurely who don't survive, infants with debilitating physical defects, and babies found to have congenital mental retardation. The Simses feel that to have such a child would create a social, economic, and psychological strain on them and on society.

Accordingly, the Simses turn to a genetic counselor for help. Genetic counselors are usually physicians or biologists who are well versed in the field of medical genetics. They are familiar with the kinds of problems that can be inherited, the odds for encountering them, and helpful measures for offsetting some of their effects. The Simses tell their counselor that there has been a history of mental retardation in Bob's family. Bob's younger sister was born with Down syndrome, a form of mental retardation. Mary's older brother has hemophilia, a condition in which bleeding is difficult to stop. They wonder what the chances are that a child of theirs might also be retarded or have hemophilia and what measures they can take to reduce their chances of having a mentally or physically defective child.

The counselor probes more deeply, because she understands that these facts in isolation do not give her a complete picture of the possibilities. She learns that no other relatives in Bob's family are retarded and that Bob's mother was in her late forties when his younger sister was born. She concludes that the retardation was due to the age of Bob's mother and not to some general tendency for members of his family to inherit retardation. It is well known that women over 40 have a much higher probability of giving birth to retarded children than younger women have. Apparently, in women over 40, the ova (egg cells) are not as healthy in older women as in women under 40.

In Mary's case the counselor determines that there is a small but clear possibility that Mary may be a carrier of hemophilia and may transmit that condition to a son. Otherwise, the counselor can find no evidence from the family history to indicate genetic problems.

The decision then is up to the Simses. In this case, the genetic problem will probably not occur, so the choice is fairly easy. But what should parents do if they face the strong probability of having a child with a major birth defect? Ultimately, the decision depends on the couple's ethical and religious beliefs. They must decide how to balance these against the quality of their child's life.

The moral dilemma is even more acute, of course, once a pregnancy has begun. **Amniocentesis** is a test that can detect more than 100 birth defects. It is performed in the fourteenth to sixteenth weeks of pregnancy. A long, thin needle is inserted into the abdomen to extract a sample of amniotic fluid, the liquid that cushions the fetus. Fetal cells in the fluid are grown in the laboratory for two to four weeks and are then studied for the presence of defects. The later amniocentesis is performed, the better the diagnostic potential. But the earlier it is performed, the more useful it can be in deciding whether a pregnancy should be terminated.

Another type of prenatal assessment that is frequently used when a structural malformation is suspected is **ultrasound sonography.** High-frequency sound waves are directed into the pregnant woman's abdomen. The echo from the sounds is transformed into a visual representation of the fetus's inner structures. This technique has been beneficial in detecting such disorders as microencephaly, a form of mental retardation involving an abnormally small brain.

As scientists have searched for more accurate, safe assessments of high-risk prenatal circumstances, they have developed the **chorionic villus test.** Available since the mid-1980s, this test involves removing a small sample of the placenta 9 to 10 weeks into pregnancy. It takes 2 to 3 weeks to diagnose. The chorionic villus test allows a decision about abortion to be made near the end of the first trimester of pregnancy, a point when abortion is safer and less traumatic than after amniocentesis in the second trimester. These techniques provide valuable information about the presence of birth defects, but they also raise moral issues pertaining to whether an abortion should be obtained if birth defects are present. ◆

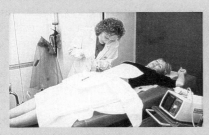

Amniocentesis being performed on a pregnant woman.

A 6-month-old infant posing with its ultrasound sonography record taken at four months into prenatal development.

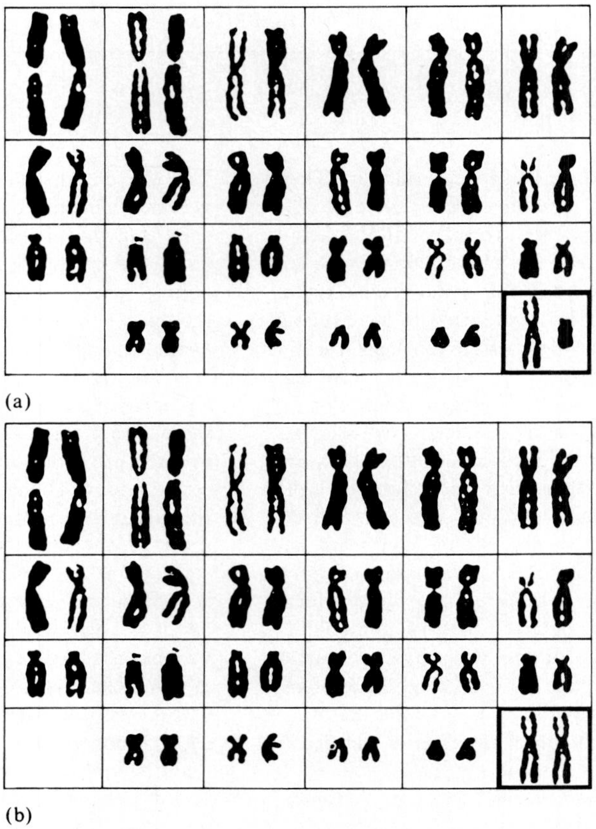

FIGURE 3.6 The genetic difference between males and females. Set (a) shows the chromosome structure of a male, and set (b) shows the chromosome structure of a female. The twenty-third pair is shown in the bottom right box of each set. Notice that the Y chromosome of the male is smaller than that of the female. To obtain this chromosomal picture, a cell is removed from the person's body, usually from the inside of the mouth. The chromosomes are magnified extensively and then photographed.

To discover how sexual differentiation takes place, David Page and his colleagues (1987) decided to study the sex chromosomes of individuals who are genetically abnormal: men with two X chromosomes and women with an X and a Y. Despite the genetic reversal, the XX men and XY women, while infertile, appeared normal. The researchers showed that one X chromosome in these men had a tiny bit of Y attached, while the women's Y chromosomes failed to have that tiny bit. They figured that a critical gene must be contained in that fragment, which sometimes breaks off from the Y.

Finding the suspect gene was a lengthy process involving several years of painstaking analysis. The researchers call the gene **testis determining factor, or TDF,** and it does appear to fix the infant's sex. To confirm their findings, Page and his coworkers plan to insert the TDF gene in a fertilized mouse egg to see whether it would transform a female embryo into a male.

Another important genetic principle is **polygenic inheritance.** Genetic transmission is usually more complex than the simple examples we just examined. Few psychological characteristics are the result of the actions of single gene pairs. Most are determined by the interaction of many different genes. There are as many as 50,000 or more genes, so you can imagine that possible combinations of these are staggering in number. Traits produced by this mixing of genes are said to be polygenically determined.

No one possesses all the characteristics that our genetic structure makes possible. The actual combination of genes produces what is known as the **genotype.** However, not all of this genetic material is apparent in our observed and measurable

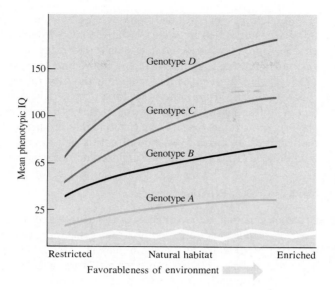

FIGURE 3.7   Hypothetical set of reaction ranges of intellectual development of several genotypes under environmental conditions that range from poor to good. Although each genotype responds favorably to improved environments, some are more responsive to environmental deprivation and enrichment than are others.

characteristics. These observed and measurable characteristics, called **phenotypes,** include physical traits, such as height, weight, eye color, and skin pigmentation, and psychological characteristics, such as intelligence, creativity, personality, and social tendencies.

For each genotype, a range of phenotypes can be expressed. Imagine that we could identify all the genes that would make a child introverted or extroverted. Would measured introversion-extroversion be predictable from knowledge of the specific genes? The answer is no, because even if our genetic model was adequate, introversion-extroversion is a characteristic shaped by experience throughout life. For example, parents may push an introverted child into social situations and encourage the child to become more gregarious.

To understand how introverted a person is, think about a series of genetic codes that predispose the child to develop in a particular way, and imagine environments that are responsive or unresponsive to this development. For example, the genotype of some persons may predispose them to be introverted in an environment that promotes a turning inward of personality, yet in an environment that encourages social interaction and outgoingness, these individuals may become more extroverted. However, it would be unlikely for the individual with this introverted genotype to become a strong extrovert. The term **reaction range** is used to describe the range of phenotypes for each genotype, suggesting the importance of an environment's restrictiveness or enrichment (Figure 3.7).

Sandra Scarr (1984) explains reaction range this way: Each of us has a range of potential. For example, an individual with "medium-tall" genes for height who grows up in a poor environment may be shorter than average. But in an excellent nutritional environment, the individual may grow up taller than average. However, no matter how well fed the person is, someone with "short" genes will never be taller than average. Scarr believes that characteristics such as intelligence and introversion work the same way. That is, there is a range within which the environment can modify intelligence, but intelligence is not completely malleable. Reaction range gives us an estimate of how modifiable intelligence is.

That which comes of a cat will catch mice.

English Proverb

Genotypes, in addition to producing many phenotypes, may show the opposite track for some characteristics—those that are somewhat immune to extensive changes in the environment. These characteristics seem to stay on a particular developmental course regardless of the environmental assaults on them (Waddington, 1957). **Canalization** is the term chosen to describe the narrow path or developmental course that certain characteristics take. Apparently, preservative forces help to protect or buffer a person from environmental extremes. For example, Jerome Kagan (1984) points to his research on Guatemalan infants who had experienced extreme malnutrition as infants yet showed normal social and cognitive development later in childhood. And some abused children do not grow up to be abusers themselves.

Methods Used by Behavior Geneticists

Behavior genetics is concerned with the degree and nature of behavior's hereditary basis. Behavior geneticists assume that behaviors are jointly determined by the interaction of heredity and environment. To study heredity's influence on development, behavior geneticists often use either the adoption study or the twin study.

In the **adoption study,** researchers compare correlations between children's characteristics and those of their biological and adoptive parents. Adopted children share half of their genes with each biological parent, but they do not share an environment with them. In contrast, they share an environment with their adopted parents but not their genes.

In the **twin study,** identical twins (called **monozygotic** twins) and fraternal twins (called **dizygotic** twins) are compared. Identical twins are born when a fertilized egg divides into two parts that then develop into two separate embryos. Since the twins come from the same fertilized egg, they share all of their genes. In contrast, fraternal twins develop when a women's ovaries release two eggs instead of one and each egg is fertilized by different sperm. Fraternal twins share the same womb, but they are no more alike genetically than any two siblings, and they may be of different sexes. By comparing groups of identical and fraternal twins, psychologists capitalize on the basic knowledge that identical twins are more similar genetically than are fraternal twins. Several problems, though, crop up when the twin-study method is used. Adults may stress the similarities of identical twins more than those of fraternal twins. And identical twins may perceive themselves as a "set" and play together more than fraternal twins. If so, observed similarities in identical twins could be environmentally influenced.

The concept of **heritability** is used in many adoption and twin studies. Heritability is a statistical estimate of the degree to which physical, cognitive, and social characteristics among individuals are a result of their genetic differences. It is measured by the use of correlational statistical procedures. The highest degree of heritability is 1.00. A heritability quotient of .80 suggests a strong genetic influence, one of .50 a moderate genetic influence, and one of .20 a much weaker, but nonetheless, perceptible genetic influence.

Although heritability values may vary considerably from one study to the next, it is possible to determine the average magnitude of a particular characteristic's quotient. For some kinds of mental retardation, the average heritability quotient approaches 1.00. That is, the environment makes almost no contribution to the characteristic's variation. This is not the same as saying the environment has no influence; the characteristic could not be expressed without the environment.

Genetics

Concept	Processes and Related Ideas	Characteristics and Description
Genes, Chromosomes, and Reproduction	Genes and chromosomes	The nucleus of each human cell contains 46 chromosomes, which are composed of DNA. Genes are short segments of DNA and act as a blueprint for cells to reproduce and manufacture proteins that maintain life.
	Reproduction	Genes are transmitted from parents to offspring by gametes, or sex cells. Gametes are formed by the splitting of cells, a process called meiosis. Reproduction takes place when a female gamete (ovum) is fertilized by a male gamete (sperm) to create a single-celled ovum. In vitro fertilization has helped to solve some infertility problems.
Abnormalities in Genes and Chromosomes	The range of problems	A range of problems are caused by some major gene or chromosome defect, among them the PKU syndrome, Down's syndrome, sickle-cell anemia, Klinefelter's syndrome, Turner's syndrome, and the XYY syndrome.
	Genetic counseling and tests	Genetic counseling has increased in popularity as couples desire information about their risk of having a defective child. Amniocentesis, ultrasonic sonography, and the chorionic villus test are used to determine the presence of defects after pregnancy has begun.
Genetic Principles	Their nature	Genetic transmission is complex, but some principles have been worked out, among them dominant-recessive genes, testis determining factor, polygenic inheritance, genotype-phenotype distinction, reaction range, and canalization.
	Methods used by behavior geneticists	Behavior genetics is the field concerned with the degree and nature of behavior's hereditary basis. Among the most important methods used by behavior geneticists are the twin study and the adoption study. The concept of heritability is used in many of the twin and adoption studies. The heritability index is not without flaws.

The heritability index is not a flawless measure of heredity's contribution to development. It is only as good as the information fed into it and the assumptions made about genetic-environment interaction. First, it is important to consider how varied the environments are that are being sampled. The narrower the range of environments, the higher the heritability index; the broader the range of environments, the lower the heritability index. Another important consideration is the reliability and validity of the measures being used in the investigation. That is, what is the quality of the measures? The weaker the measure, the less confidence we have in the heritability index. A final consideration is that the heritability index assumes that heredity and environment can be separated; information can be quantitatively added together to arrive at a discrete influence for each. In reality, heredity and environment interact; their interaction is often lost when the heritability index is computed.

So far, our coverage of the biological beginnings of the life cycle have taken us through some important aspects of heredity. A summary of these ideas is presented in Concept Table 3.1. Now let's turn our attention to some aspects of development influenced by heredity.

Heredity's Influence on Development

What aspects of development are influenced by genetic factors? They all are. However, behavior geneticists are interested in more precise estimates of the variation in a characteristic accounted for by genetic factors. Intelligence and temperament are among the most widely investigated aspects of heredity's influence on development.

Intelligence

Arthur Jensen (1969) sparked a lively and at times hostile debate when he presented his thesis that intelligence is primarily inherited. Jensen believes that environment and culture play only a minimal role in intelligence. Jensen examined several studies of intelligence, any of which involved comparisons of identical and fraternal twins. Remember that identical twins have identical genetic endowments, so their IQs should be similar. Fraternal twins and ordinary siblings are less similar genetically, so their IQs should be less similar. Jensen found support for his argument in these studies. Studies with identical twins produced an average correlation of .82; studies with ordinary siblings produced an average correlation of .50. Note the difference of .32. To show that genetic factors are more important than environmental factors, Jensen compared identical twins reared together with those reared apart; the correlation for those reared together was .89 and for those reared apart it was .78 (a difference of .11). Jensen argued that if environmental influences were more important than genetic influences, then siblings reared apart, who experienced different environments, should have IQs much farther apart.

Many scholars have criticized Jensen's work. One criticism concerns the definition of intelligence itself. Jensen believes that IQ as measured by standardized intelligence tests is a good indicator of intelligence. Critics argue that IQ tests tap only a narrow range of intelligence. Everyday problem solving, work, and social adaptability, say the critics, are important aspects of intelligence not measured by the traditional intelligence tests used in Jensen's sources. A second criticism is that most investigations of heredity and environment do not include environments that differ radically. Thus, it is not surprising that many genetic studies show environment to be a fairly weak influence on intelligence.

Jensen places the importance of heredity's influence on intelligence at about 80 percent (Jensen, 1969). Jensen is such a strong advocate of genetic influences on intelligence that he believes we can breed for intelligence. Just such an effort—the Repository for Germinal Choice—is being made today. To read more about this Nobel Prize sperm bank for breeding geniuses, turn to Children 3.2. Intelligence is influenced by heredity, but most developmentalists do not put the figure nearly as high as does Jensen. Other experts estimate heredity's influence on intelligence in the 50 percent range (Plomin, 1989; Plomin, DeFries, and McClearn, in press).

Temperament

Temperament is another widely studied aspect of human development, especially in infancy. Some infants are extremely active, moving their arms, legs, and mouths incessantly; others are tranquil. Some children explore their environment eagerly for great lengths of time; others do not. Some infants respond warmly to people; others fuss and fret. All of these behavioral styles represent a person's temperament.

Alexander Chess and Stella Thomas (Chess & Thomas, 1977; Thomas & Chess, 1987; Thomas, Chess, & Birch, 1970) define temperament broadly in terms of a person's behavioral style. They developed nine dimensions of temperament that fall into three clusters. The nine dimensions are rhythmicity of biological functions; activity level; approach to or withdrawal from new stimuli; adaptability; sensory threshold; predominant quality of mood; intensity of mood expression; distractibility; and persistence or attention span. The three temperamental clusters are easy, difficult, and slow-to-warm up. These clusters seemed to be moderately stable across the childhood years. Table 3.1 lists the nine different temperaments, their description, and the three temperamental clusters; the table also shows which of the nine dimensions were critical in spotting a cluster and what the level of responsiveness was for a critical feature. A blank space indicates that the dimension was not strongly related to cluster.

Other researchers suggest different basic dimensions of temperament. Arnold Buss and Robert Plomin (1984, 1987) believe that infants differ on three basic dimensions:

Thinking Critically
Consider your own temperament. Does it fit into one of the clusters described by Chess and Thomas? How stable has your temperament been in the course of your development? What factors contributed to this stability or lack of stability?

1. *Emotionality* is the tendency to be distressed. It reflects the arousal of the person's sympathetic nervous system. Distress develops during infancy into two separate emotional responses: fear and anger. Fearful infants try to escape something that is unpleasant; angry ones protest it. Buss and Plomin argue that children are labeled "easy" or "difficult" on the basis of their emotionality.

2. *Sociability* is the tendency to prefer the company of others to being alone. It matches up with a tendency to respond warmly to others.

3. *Activity* involves tempo and vigor of movement. Some children walk fast, are attracted to high-energy games, and jump or bounce around a lot; others are more placid.

Doran, Dr. Graham, and the Repository for Germinal Choice

Doran (a name from the Greek word meaning "gift") learned all the elements of speech by 2 years of age. An intelligence test showed that at the age of 1, his mental age was 4. Doran was the second child born through the Nobel Prize sperm bank, which came into existence in 1980. The sperm bank was founded by Robert Graham in Escondido, California, with the intent of producing geniuses. Graham collected the sperm of Nobel Prize-winning scientists and offered it free of charge to intelligent women of good stock whose husbands were infertile.

One of the contributors to the sperm bank is physicist William Shockley, who shared the Nobel Prize in 1956 for inventing the transistor. Shockley has received his share of criticism for preaching the genetic basis of intelligence. Two other Nobel Prize winners have donated their sperm to the bank, but Shockley is the only one who has been identified.

More than 20 children have been sired through the sperm bank. Are the progeny prodigies? It may be too early to tell. Except for Doran, little has been revealed about the children. Doran's genetic father was labeled "28 Red" in the sperm bank (the color apparently has no meaning). He is listed in the sperm bank's catalog as handsome, blond, and athletic, with a math SAT score of 800 and several prizes for his classical music performances. One of his few drawbacks is that he passed along to Doran an almost one-in-three chance of developing hemorrhoids. Doran's mother says that her genetic contribution goes back to the royal court of Norway and to the poet William Blake.

The odds are not high that a sperm bank will yield that special combination of factors required to produce a creative genius. George Bernard Shaw, who believed that heredity's influence on intelligence is strong, once told a story about a beautiful woman who wrote to him saying that with her body and his brain they could produce marvelous offspring. Shaw responded by saying that unfortunately the offspring might get his body and her brain.

Not surprisingly, the Nobel Prize sperm bank is heavily criticized. Some say that brighter does not mean better. They also say that IQ is not a good indicator of social competence or human contribution to the world. Other critics say that intelligence is an elusive concept to measure and that it cannot reliably be reproduced like the sperm bank is trying to do. Visions of the German gene program of the 1930s and 1940s are created. The German Nazis believed that certain traits were superior and tried to breed children with such traits and killed people without these traits.

Although Graham's Repository for Germinal Choice (as the Nobel Prize sperm bank is formally called) is strongly criticized, consider its possible contributions. The repository does provide a social service for couples who cannot conceive a child, and individuals who go to the sperm bank probably provide an enriched environment for the offspring. To once-childless parents, the offspring produced by the sperm bank, or any of the other new methods of conception available, are invariably described as miracles (Garelik, 1985). ◆

Doran, one of the offspring born through the Repository for Germinal Choice.

Robert Graham, founder of the Repository for Germinal Choice, holds a container of frozen sperm.

TABLE 3.1   *Dimensions and Clusters of Temperament in Chess and Thomas's Research*

Temperament Dimension	Description	Temperament Cluster		
		Easy Child	**Difficult Child**	**Slow-to-Warm-up Child**
Rhythmicity	Regularity of eating, sleeping, toileting	Regular	Irregular	
Activity level	Degree of energy movement		High	Low
Approach-withdrawal	Ease of approaching new people and situations	Positive	Negative	Negative
Adaptability	Ease of tolerating change in routine plans	Positive	Negative	Negative
Sensory threshold	Amount of stimulation required for responding			
Predominant quality of mood	Degree of positive or negative affect	Positive	Negative	
Intensity of mood expression	Degree of affect when pleased, displeased, happy, sad	Low to moderate	High	Low
Distractibility attention span/persistence	Ease of being distracted			

A number of scholars, including Chess and Thomas, conceive of temperament as a stable characteristic of newborns that comes to be shaped and modified by the child's later experiences (Thomas & Chess, 1987; Goldsmith, 1988; Goldsmith & others, 1987). This raises the question of heredity's role in temperament. Twin and adoption studies have been conducted to answer this question (DeFries & others, 1981; Plomin, 1989; Matheny, Dolan, & Wilson, 1976). The researchers found a heritability index in the range of .50 to .60, suggesting a moderate influence of heredity on temperament. However, the strength of the association usually declines as infants become older (Goldsmith & Gottesman, 1981). This finding supports the belief that temperament becomes more malleable with experience. Alternatively, it may be that as the child becomes older, behavioral indicators of temperament may be more difficult to spot. The biological basis of the temperament of inhibition or shyness and its developmental course is currently the interest of Jerome Kagan (1988, 1989), and Stephen Suomi (1987). To learn about how stable our tendency to be shy is and how much it can be modified, turn to Children 3.3.

The consistency of temperament depends in part on the "match" or "fit" between the child's nature and the parents' (Chess & Thomas, 1986; Plomin, DeFries, & Fulker, 1988; Plomin & Thompson, 1987; Rothbart, in press). Imagine a high-strung parent with a child who is difficult and sometimes slow to respond to the parent's affection. The parent may begin to feel angry or rejected. A father who does not need much face-to-face social interaction will find it easy to manage a similarly introverted baby, but he may not be able to provide an extroverted baby with sufficient stimulation. Parents influence infants, but infants also influence parents. Parents may withdraw from difficult children, or they may become critical and punish them; these responses may make the difficult child even more difficult. A more easygoing parent may have a calming effect on a difficult child or may continue to show affection even when the child withdraws or is hostile, eventually encouraging more competent behavior.

In sum, heredity does seem to influence temperament. But the degree of influence depends on parents' responsiveness to the child and other environmental experiences of the child.

Imperturbability in European-American, Chinese-American, and Navaho Indian Newborns

Do newborns from different cultures have different biological predispositions of temperament? In one investigation, 24 Chinese-American and 24 European-American 2-day-old babies were observed (Freedman & Freedman, 1969). The Chinese-American infants had a less rapid buildup to an excited state of arousal, showed less facial and body reddening, and showed fewer state changes. When placed in the prone position, the Chinese-Americans tended to remain inactive, face flat against the bed. By contrast, the European-Americans were more likely to lift their head or turn their face to one side. The Chinese-American babies were easier to control when crying and were able to stop by themselves without being consoled. The researchers suggested that these behaviors reflect the temperament of "imperturbability," which affects the way adults care for the infants. Further comparison of this temperament indicated that newborn Navaho Indians were more perturbable than newborn Chinese-Americans (Freedman, 1971).　　　◆

Heredity-Environment Interaction and Development

Both genes and environment are necessary for an organism—from amoeba to human being—to even exist. Heredity and environment operate—or cooperate—together to produce an individual's intelligence, temperament, height, weight, ability to pitch a baseball, career interests, and so on. Without genes, there is no organism; without environment, there is no organism (Scarr & Weinberg, 1980). If an attractive, popular, intelligent girl is elected as president of the student body, would we conclude that her success is due to environment or to heredity? Of course, it is due to both. Because the environment's influence depends on genetically endowed characteristics, we say that the two factors *interact* (Scarr, 1989; Scarr & Weinberg, 1980; Weinberg, 1989).

But as we have seen, developmental psychologists probe further to determine more precisely heredity's and environment's influence on development. What do we know about heredity-environment interaction? According to Sandra Scarr and Kenneth Kidd (1983), we know that hundreds of disorders appear because of miscodings in DNA. We know that abnormalities in chromosomal number adversely influence the development of physical, intellectual, and behavioral features. We know that genotype and phenotype do not map onto each other in a one-to-one fashion. We know that it is very difficult to distinguish between genetic and cultural transmission. There usually is a familial concentration of a particular disorder, but familial patterns are considerably different from what would be precisely predicted from simple modes of inheritance. We know that when we consider the normal range of variation, the stronger the genetic resemblance, the stronger the behavioral resemblance. This holds more strongly for intelligence than personality or interests. The influence of genes on intelligence is present early in children's development and continues through the late adulthood years. And we also know that being raised in the

Thinking Critically
Beyond the fact that heredity and environment always interact to produce development, first argue for heredity's dominance in this interaction, and, second, argue for environment's dominance.

Born to Be Shy?

Everyone has seen a shy toddler—the one who clings to a parent and only reluctantly ventures into an unfamiliar place. Faced with a stranger, the shy toddler freezes, becomes silent, and stares fearfully. The shy toddler seems visibly tense in social situations; parents of such children often report that they always seem to have been that way.

Despite parents' comments that shy children seem to have been shy from birth, psychologists have resisted the notion that such characteristics are inborn, focusing instead on the importance of early experiences. Both the research of Jerome Kagan with extremely shy children and the research of Stephen Suomi with "uptight" monkeys supports the belief that shyness is a part of a person's basic temperament.

Kagan (1987, 1989; Kagan, Reznick, & Gibbons, in press; Snidman & Kagan, 1989) collaborating with Nancy Snidman, Steven Resnick, and Jane Gibbons followed the development of extremely inhibited and uninhibited 2- to 3-year-old children for 6 years. They evaluated the children's heart rates and other physiological measures as well as observing their behavior in novel circumstances. After six years, the very inhibited children no longer behave exactly as they did when they were 2, but they still reveal the pattern of very inhibited behavior combined with intense physiological responsiveness to mild stress. Very uninhibited children typically speak within the first minute when they are observed in a social situation, but very inhibited children will sometimes wait as long as 20 minutes before they say anything.

Suomi (1987) has discovered that uptight monkeys, like Kagan's inhibited children, do not easily outgrow their intense physiological response to stress and their frozen behavioral responses to social situations. Even as late as adolescence—which is 4 to 5 years of age in monkeys—those who were uptight at birth continued to respond in intense ways to stress, but at this point they became hyperactive. As adults, they seemed to regress in the face of stress, revealing the shy, inhibited behavior seen in infancy.

Kagan says that the proper environmental context can change the tendency to be shy. But if parents let their child remain fearful for a long time, it becomes harder to modify the shyness. Kagan discovered that 40 percent of the originally inhibited children—mainly boys—became much less inhibited by 5½ years, while less than 10 percent became more timid. Based on parent interviews, parents helped their children overcome their shyness by bringing other children into the home and by encouraging the child to cope with stressful circumstances.

Modification of shyness in some cases can be extreme. Some shy individuals even become performers. Celebrities such as Johnny Carson, Carol Burnett, Barbara Walters, and Michael Jackson have strong tendencies toward shyness, but even with the biological underpinnings loaded against them, they turned the tables on heredity's influence (Asher, 1987). ◆

Extremely shy children at the age of 2 or 3 usually show similar inhibited behavior six years later, although environmental experiences can modify shyness to some degree.

"Uptight" infant monkeys show some of the same shy, inhibited behaviors as their human counterparts.

Heredity's Influence on Development and Heredity-Environment Interaction

Concept	Processes and Related Ideas	Characteristics and Description
Heredity's Influence on Development	Its scope	All aspects of development are influenced by heredity.
	Intelligence	Jensen's argument that intelligence is due primarily to heredity sparked a lively, and at times bitter, debate. Intelligence is influenced by heredity, but not as strongly as Jensen envisioned.
	Temperament	Temperament refers to behavioral style; temperament has been studied extensively. Chess and Thomas developed nine temperament dimensions and three temperament clusters. Temperament is influenced strongly by biological factors in early infancy but becomes more malleable with experience. An important consideration is the fit of the infant's temperament with the parents' temperament.
Heredity-Environment Interaction and Development	Its nature	Without genes, there is no organism; without environment, there is no organism. Because the environment's influence depends on genetically endowed characteristics, we say that the two factors interact.

same family accounts for some portion of intellectual differences among individuals, but common rearing accounts for little of the variation in personality or interests. One reason for this discrepancy may be that families place similar pressures on their children for intellectual development in the sense that the push is clearly toward the highest level, while they do not direct their children toward similar personalities or interests, in which extremes are not especially desirable. That is, most parents would like their children to have above-average intellect, but there is much less agreement about whether or not a child should be highly extroverted.

What do we need to know about the role of heredity-environment interaction in development? Scarr and Kidd (1983) commented that we need to know the pathways by which genetic abnormalities influence development. The PKU success story is but one such example. Scientists discovered the genetic linkage of the disorder and subsequently how the environment could be changed to reduce the damage to development. We need to know more about genetic-environment interaction in the normal range of development. For example, what accounts for the difference in one person's IQ of 95 and another person's IQ of 125? The answer requires a polygenic perspective and information about cultural and genetic influences.

We also need to know about heredity's influence across the entire life cycle. For instance, puberty is not an environmentally produced accident (Rowe & Rodgers, 1989); neither is menopause. While puberty and menopause can be influenced by such environmental factors as nutrition, weight, drugs, health, and the like, the basic evolutionary and genetic program is wired into the species. It cannot be eliminated, nor should it be ignored. This evolutionary and genetic perspective gives biology its appropriate role in our quest to better understand human development through the life cycle.

A summary of the main ideas in our discussion of heredity's influence on development and heredity-environment interaction is presented in Concept Table 3.2. In the next chapter we will continue our discussion of biological beginnings, turning to information about prenatal development and birth.

Summary

I. **Chromosomes, DNA, and Genes**

The nucleus of each human cell contains 46 chromosomes, which are composed of DNA. Genes are short segments of DNA and act as a blueprint for cells to reproduce and manufacture protein that maintans life.

II. **Reproduction**

Genes are transmitted from parents to offspring by gametes, or sex cells. Gametes are formed by the splitting of cells, a process called meiosis. Reproduction takes place when a female gamete (ovum) is fertilized by a male gamete (sperm) to create a single-celled zygote. In vitro fertilization has helped solve some infertility problems.

III. **Abnormalities in Genes and Chromosomes**

A range of problems are caused by some major gene or chromosome defects, among them the PKU syndrome, Down syndrome, sickle-cell anemia, Klinefelter's syndrome, and the XYY syndrome. Genetic counseling has increased in popularity, as couples desire information about their risk of having a defective child. Amniocentesis and the chorionic villus test are used to determine the presence of defects after pregnancy has begun.

IV. **Some Genetic Principles**

Genetic transmission is complex, but some principles have been worked out, among them dominant-recessive genes, testis determining factor, polygenic inheritance, genotype-phenotype distinction, reaction range, and canalization.

V. **Methods Used by Behavior Geneticists**

Behavior genetics is the field concerned with the degree and nature of behavior's heredity basis. Among the most important methods used by behavior geneticists are the twin study and the adoption study. The concept of heritability is used in many of the twin and adoption studies. The heritability index is not without flaws.

VI. **Heredity's Influence on Development**

All aspects of development are influenced by heredity. Jensen's argument that intelligence is influenced primarily by heredity sparked a lively, and at times bitter, debate. Intelligence is influenced by heredity, but not as strongly as Jensen envisioned. Temperament refers to behavioral style; termperament has been studied extensively in infancy. Chess and Thomas developed nine temperament dimensions and three temperament clusters. Temperament is strongly influenced by biological factors in early infancy but becomes more malleable with experience. An important consideration is the fit of the infant's temperament with the parents' temperament.

VII. **Heredity-Environment Interaction and Development**

Without genes, there is no organism; without environment, there is no organism. Because the environment's influence depends on genetically endowed characteristics, we say that the two factors interact.

Key Terms

chromosomes 81
DNA 81
genes 81
gametes 81
meiosis 81
reproduction 81
zygote 81
in vitro fertilization 83
PKU syndrome 84
Down's syndrome 84
sickle-cell anemia 84

Klinefelter's syndrome 86
Turner's syndrome 86
XYY syndrome 86
dominant-recessive
  genes 86
amniocentesis 87
ultrasound sonography 87
chorionic villus test 87
testis determining
  factor (TDF) 88
polygenic inheritance 88

genotype 88
phenotypes 89
reaction range 89
canalization 90
behavior genetics 90
adoption study 90
twin study 90
monozygotic 90
dizygotic 90
heritability 90

Suggested Readings

Chess, S., & Thomas, A. (1986). *Temperament in clinical practice*. New York: Guilford.
  Details of Chess and Thomas's classical longitudinal study of temperament are
  provided; applications to clinical problems are described.
Gould, S. (1983). *Hen's teeth and horse's toes: Reflections on natural history*. New York:
  Norton.
  This book is a collection of fascinating articles by a biologist interested in evolution.
  The essays originally were published in the magazine *Natural History*.
Lewontin, R. C., Rose, S., & Kamin, L. J. (1984). *Not in our genes*. New York: Pantheon.
  Argues for an environmental view of development and provides many reasons as to
  why heredity's role is overestimated.
Plomin, R., DeFries, J. C., & McClearn, G. E. (1980). *Behavioral genetics: A primer*.
  New York: W. H. Freeman.
  A good introduction to research on genes and behavior by leading behavior geneticists.
Watson, J. D. (1968). *The double helix*. New York: New American Library.
  A personalized account of the research leading up to one of the most provocative
  discoveries of the twentieth century—the DNA molecule. Reading like a mystery
  novel, it illustrates the exciting discovery process in science.

◇

The history of man for nine months preceding his birth would, probably, be far more interesting, and contain events of greater moment than all three score and ten years that follow it.

Samuel Taylor Coleridge

Prenatal Development and Birth

eresa Block's second pregnancy was difficult. Her amniotic sac ruptured, she contracted an infection that sent her temperature skyrocketing, and she had an exhausting breech delivery. Her son Robert weighed just less than 2 pounds at birth. Teresa said she had never imagined a baby looking so tiny. The first time she saw Robert, he was lying on his back attached to a respirator, and wires were connected all over his body. Robert stayed at the hospital until two weeks before his originally projected birth date, at which time he weighed 4 pounds, 8 ounces. Teresa and her husband lived in a small town 60 miles from the hospital; they commuted each day to spend time with Robert, and brought their other child along with them whenever it was practical.

A decade later, Robert is still at the bottom of the weight chart, but he is about average in height and the only physical residue of his early birth difficulties is a "lazy eye." He is 20/20 in his good eye but 20/200 in the other. He is doing special exercises for the bad eye, and his doctor thinks he is not far from the day he can go without glasses. Robert is on the soccer team and the swim team (Fincher, 1982).

Considering his circumstances, Robert had a relatively uncomplicated stay at the hospital. Not all children born so frail survive, and those who do sometimes show the consequences many years in the future.

At one time, you were an organism floating around in a sea of fluid inside your mother's womb. From the moment you were conceived until the moment you were born, some astonishing developments occurred. This chapter chronicles the truly remarkable developments from conception to birth and the nature of the birth process itself.

Prenatal Development

Imagine how you came to be. Out of thousands of eggs and millions of sperm, one egg and one sperm united to produce you. Had the union of sperm and egg come a day or even an hour earlier or later, you might have been very different—maybe even of the opposite sex.

The Course of Prenatal Development

Remember from Chapter 2 that conception occurs when a single sperm cell from the male unites with the ovum (egg) in the female's fallopian tube in a process called fertilization. The fertilized egg is called a **zygote.** By the time the zygote ends its three- to four-day journey through the fallopian tubes and reaches the uterus, it has divided into approximately 12 to 16 cells.

The period from conception until about 12 to 14 days later is called the **germinal period;** it includes the creation of the zygote, continued cell division, and attachment of the zygote to the uterine wall. Approximately one week after conception—when the zygote is composed of 100 to 150 cells—it is called the **blastula.** Differentiation of cells has already commenced in the blastula as inner and outer layers are formed. The inner layer of the blastula is called the **blastocyst,** which later develops into the embryo. The outer layer is called the **trophoblast,** which later provides nutrition and support for the embryo. About 10 days after conception, a major milestone in the germinal period is reached: **Implantation.** This is the attachment of the zygote to the uterine wall.

During the **embryonic period,** the embryo differentiates into three layers, and support systems develop. As the zygote attaches to the uterine wall, its cells form two layers; it is at this time that the mass of cells changes names from *zygote* to

What web is this
Of will be, is, and was?

Jorge Luis Borges

Beginnings

DENNIS THE MENACE

"My Mom says I come from Heaven. My Dad says he can't remember an' Mr. Wilson is positive I came from Mars!"

embryo. The embryonic period lasts from about two weeks to eight weeks after conception. The inner layer of cells is called the **endoderm;** this will develop into the digestive and respiratory systems. The outer layer of cells is divided into two parts. The outermost layer—the **ectoderm**—will become the nervous system, sensory receptors (ear, nose, and eyes, for example), and skin parts (hair and nails, for example). The middle layer—the **mesoderm**—will become the circulatory system, bones, muscle, excretory system, and reproductive system. Every body part eventually develops from these three layers. The endoderm produces primarily internal body parts, the mesoderm produces primarily parts that surround the internal areas, and the ectoderm produces primarily surface parts.

As the embryo's three layers are formed, life-support systems for the embryo mature and develop rapidly; these include the placenta, the umbilical cord, and the amnion. The **placenta** is a disk-shaped group of tissues in which small blood vessels from the mother and the offspring intertwine but do not join. The **umbilical cord** contains two arteries and one vein and connects the baby to the placenta. Very small molecules—oxygen, water, salt, food from the mother's blood, and carbon dioxide and digestive wastes from the embryo's blood—pass back and forth between the mother and infant. Large molecules cannot pass through the placental wall; these include red blood cells and harmful substances such as most bacteria, maternal wastes, and hormones. The mechanisms that govern transfer of substances across the placental barrier are complex and are still not entirely understood (Rosenblith and Sims-Knight, 1985). The **amnion,** a sort of bag or envelope that contains a clear fluid in which the developing embryo floats, is another important life-support system of the embryo. It provides an environment that is temperature and humidity controlled as well as shock proof.

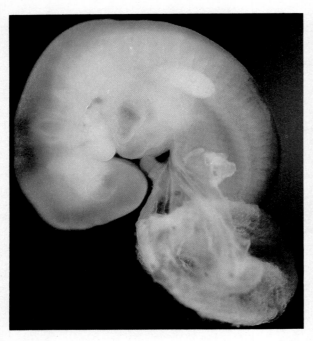

FIGURE 4.1   At 4 weeks, the embryo is about .2 inches long, and the head, eyes, and ears begin to show. The head and neck are half the body length; the shoulders will be located where the whitish arm buds are attached.

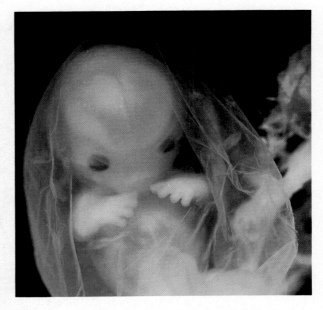

FIGURE 4.2   Fetus at 8 weeks, the beginning of the fetal period.

If I could have watched you grow
As a magical mother might.
If I could have seen through my magical
transparent belly,
There would have been such ripening
within . . .

—*Anne Sexton,* Little Girl, My String
Bean, My Lovely Woman

Before most women even know they are pregnant, some important embryonic developments take place. In the third week, the neural tube that eventually becomes the spinal cord forms. At about 21 days, eyes begin to appear, and by 24 days, the cells for the heart begin to differentiate. During the fourth week, the first appearance of the urogenital system is apparent, and arm and leg buds emerge. Four chambers of the heart take shape, and blood vessels surface. (Figure 4.1 shows a 4-week-old embryo.) From the fifth to the eighth week, arms and legs differentiate further; at this time, the face starts to form but still is not very recognizable. The intestinal tract develops and the facial structures fuse. At eight weeks, the developing organism weighs about 1/30 of an ounce and is just over 1 inch long.

The first eight weeks of development are a time when many body systems are being formed. When body systems are in the process of being formed, they are especially vulnerable to environmental changes. This process of organ formation is called **organogenesis;** it characterizes the first two months of development after conception. Later in the chapter, we will detail the environmental hazards that are especially harmful during organogenesis.

The **fetal period** begins eight weeks after conception and lasts for seven months on the average. Growth and development continue their dramatic course during this time. (Figure 4.2 shows a fetus at eight weeks after conception.) Three months after conception, the fetus is about 3 inches long and weighs about 1 ounce. It has become active, moving its arms and legs, opening and closing its mouth, and moving its head. The face, forehead, eyelids, nose, and chin are distinguishable, as are the upper arms, lower arms, hands, and lower limbs. The genitals can be identified as male or female. By the end of the fourth month, the fetus has grown to 6 inches in length and weighs 4 to 7 ounces. At this time, a growth spurt occurs in the body's lower parts. Prenatal reflexes are stronger; arm and leg movements can be felt for the first time by the mother. (Figure 4.3 shows the fetus at 4 months of age.)

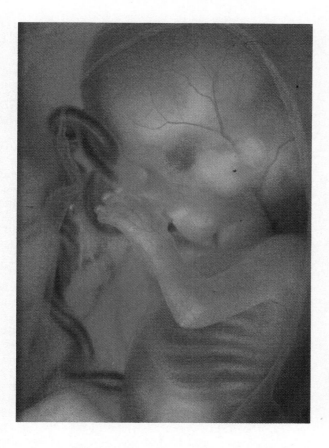

FIGURE 4.3   The fetus at 4 months. At this point the fetus has grown to approximately 6 inches in length and weighs 4–7 ounces. Arm and leg movements can be felt by the mother for the first time.

By the end of the fifth month, the fetus is about 12 inches long and weighs close to a pound. Structures of the skin have formed—toenails and fingernails, for example. The fetus is more active, showing a preference for a particular position in the womb. By the end of the sixth month, the fetus is about 14 inches long and already has gained another pound. The eyes and eyelids are completely formed. A fine layer of hair covers the head. A grasping reflex is present and irregular breathing occurs. By the end of the seventh month, the fetus is about 16 inches long and has gained another pound, now weighing about 3 pounds. During the eighth and ninth months, the fetus grows longer and gains substantial weight—about 4 pounds. At birth, the average American baby weighs 7 pounds and is 20 inches long. In these last two months, fatty tissues develop and the functioning of various organ systems—heart and kidneys, for example—is stepped up.

So the riders of the darkness pass on their circuits: the luminous island of the self trembles and waits, waits for us all my friends, where the sea's big brush recolors the dying lives, and the unborn smiles.

Lawrence Durrell

Miscarriage and Abortion

A miscarriage, or spontaneous abortion, happens when pregnancy ends before the developing organism is mature enough to survive outside the womb. This happens when the embryo separates from the uterine wall and is expelled by the uterus. Estimates indicate that about 15 to 20 percent of all pregnancies end in a spontaneous abortion, most in the first two to three months. Many spontaneous abortions occur without the mother's knowledge, and many involve an embryo or fetus that was not developing normally.

An International Perspective on Abortion Trends

An estimated 40 million abortions are legally performed each year in the world; for every two births, one pregnancy is terminated. In most countries, laws permit induced abortion, but conditions regulating the practice range from limited prohibition to an elective abortion at the request of the pregnant woman. Under limited prohibition, abortion is usually permitted on the grounds that it will save the woman's life. Most countries of Islamic faith (e.g., Indonesia, Bangladesh), half of the countries of Africa (e.g., Nigeria, the Republic of South Africa), about two-thirds of the countries of Latin America, and three countries in Western Europe (Belgium, Ireland, and Malta) fall under these prohibitive statutes. These countries make up about one-fourth of the world's population.

Thirty-nine percent of the world's population live in countries that have statutes broad enough to permit termination of pregnancy on request, usually during the first trimester. The time limit does not apply to abortions performed on medical grounds, which may be carried out even up to and beyond the twentieth week. A wide range of countries follow this policy, including the United States, Denmark, Singapore, Cuba, and Yugoslavia.

Nearly one-fourth of the world's population is governed by laws that authorize abortion on sociomedical grounds—that is, where factors such as inadequate income, poor housing, and unmarried status are considered risks to the mother's health if her pregnancy is allowed to continue. Countries such as India, Japan, most of the countries of Eastern Europe, and the United Kingdom fall into this category.

Access to legal abortion is relatively easy in most Asian countries because there are few regulations and administrative requirements. In several countries, such as China and Korea, governments have introduced a variety of incentives such as paid leave and subsidies for nourishment to encourage women to use abortion as a means of fertility regulation (Sachdev, 1988). ◆

Early in history, it was believed that a woman could be frightened into a miscarriage by loud thunder or a jolt in a carriage. Today we recognize that this occurrence is highly unlikely; the developing organism is well protected. Abnormalities of the reproductive tract and viral or bacterial infections are more likely candidates to cause spontaneous abortions. In some cases, severe traumas may be at fault.

Deliberate termination of pregnancy is a complex issue, medically, psychologically, and socially. Carrying the baby to term may affect the woman's health; the woman's pregnancy may have resulted from rape or incest; the woman may not be married; or perhaps she is poor and wants to continue her education. Abortion is again legal in the United States; in 1973, the Supreme Court ruled that any woman could obtain an abortion during the first six months of pregnancy. This decision continues to generate ethical objections from those opposed to induced abortion, especially advocates of the Right-to-Life movement. The Supreme Court also has ruled that abortion in the first trimester is solely the decision of the mother and her doctor. Cases also have added the point that the father and the parents of minor girls do not have any say during this time frame. In the second trimester, states can legislate the time and method of abortion for protection of the mother's health. In the third trimester, the fetus's right to live is the primary concern.

Ethics and the Medical Use of Fetal Tissue

The increased interest in medical uses for tissue from aborted fetuses opens up a new debate about medical technology and the beginnings of life, adding a new dimension to the long-standing controversy over abortion. Evidence is increasing that the special properties of fetal tissue make it ideal for tissue transplants to treat Parkinson's disease, Alzheimer's disease, and other disorders. Most medical researchers believe it is only a matter of time until fetal tissue is used routinely. Scientists expect fetal tissue to be especially valuable in implant treatments because it grows faster than adult tissue, is more adaptable, and causes less immunological rejection. One of the most troubling possibilities is that some women will conceive children with the intent of aborting them, either to aid a family member or to sell them for their tissue.

The laws governing organ donations require the consent of the donor, or the donor's next of kin. In the case of fetuses, tissue may be donated with the consent of the pregnant woman. Many states have laws restricting experiments on fetuses, and this may interfere with the new medical uses of fetal tissue. A recent panel on biomedical ethics at Case Western Reserve University in Cleveland made recommendations about the use of fetal tissue. First, the doctors involved in decisions regarding the abortion should conduct the procedures using fetal tissue. Second, anonymity should be maintained between the donor and the recipient, and donors and recipients should not be related. Almost everyone concerned with the use of fetal tissue agrees that it is morally wrong, although not illegal, to become pregnant for the sole purpose of aborting a fetus to obtain certain tissues. As this book went to press, the United States Department of Health and Human Services placed a moratorium on certain fetal tissue research until the ethical issues involved in fetal research become resolved (U.S. Public Health Service, 1988). Specifically, research on induced abortions, but not spontaneous abortions or stillbirths, is banned. Prior to the announcement by the Department of Health and Human Services, some ethics committees had already shut down this type of fetal research until the ethical issues could be evaluated further (Burtchaell, in press).

Biomedical ethicists say there is a big difference between taking advantage of a death to harvest tissue, and creating a life just to abort it. When an abortion is planned anyway, some ethicists say that donating the fetal tissue may help to relieve some of the sadness surrounding the decision. Donating tissue to help someone else can be helpful in the process of grieving or bereavement, say some ethicists. The National Right-to-Life Committee, however, says the idea is morally repulsive. They point out that people who kill tiny, developing babies lose any moral right to use those tissues. They also believe that the medical use of fetal tissue offers an additional rationale to some individuals who defend abortion. As can be seen, the use of fetal tissue is a debate that probably will be with us for some time to come (Lewin, 1987). ◆

An unwanted pregnancy is stressful for any woman, regardless of how she resolves the problem: ending the pregnancy, giving the child up for adoption, or keeping the child and raising it. Depression and guilt are common reactions of the woman, both before and after an induced abortion. If an abortion is performed, it should not only involve competent medical care, but the woman's psychological needs also should be considered. Yet another ethical issue related to abortion has appeared recently—medical use of tissues from aborted fetuses. To learn more about this ethical issue in abortion, turn to Children 4.1.

Thinking Critically
What are the arguments for and against abortion? Where do you stand on this sensitive ethical issue? Why?

Teratology and Hazards to Prenatal Development

Some expectant mothers carefully tiptoe about in the belief that everything they do and feel has a direct effect on their unborn child. Others behave casually, assuming that their experiences have little effect on the unborn child. The truth lies somewhere in between these two extremes. Although living in a protected, comfortable environment, the fetus is not totally immune to the larger environment surrounding the mother. The environment can affect the child in many well-documented ways. Thousands of babies born deformed or mentally retarded every year are the result of events that occurred in the mother's life as early as one or two months before conception.

Teratology

The field of study that investigates the causes of congenital (birth) defects is called **teratology.** Any agent that causes birth defects is called a *teratogen* (from the Greek word *tera,* meaning "monster"). A specific teratogen (such as a drug) usually does not cause a specific birth defect (such as malformation of the legs). So many teratogens exist, that practically every fetus is exposed to at least some teratogens. For this reason, it is difficult to determine which teratogen causes which birth defect. In addition, it may take a long time for the effects of a teratogen to show up; only about half are present at birth.

Despite the many unknowns about teratogens, scientists have discovered the identity of some of these hazards to prenatal development and the particular point of fetal development at which they do their greatest damage. As Figure 4.4 shows, sensitivity to teratogens occurs about three weeks after conception. The probability of a structural defect is greatest early in the embryonic period, because this is when organs are being formed. After organogenesis is complete, teratogens are less likely to cause anatomical defects. Exposure later during the fetal period is more likely to stunt growth or to create problems in the way organs function. The preciseness of organogenesis is evident when teratologists point out that vulnerability of the brain is greatest at 15 to 25 days after conception, the eye at 24 to 40 days, the heart at 20 to 40 days, and the legs at 24 to 36 days.

In the following sections, we explore how certain environmental agents influence prenatal development. That is, we will examine how maternal diseases and conditions as well as drugs influence the embyro or fetus.

Maternal Diseases and Conditions

Maternal diseases or infections can produce defects by crossing the placental barrier, or they can cause damage during the birth process itself.

Rubella (German measles) and syphilis (a sexually transmitted disease) are two maternal diseases that can damage prenatal development. A rubella outbreak in 1964–1965 resulted in 30,000 prenatal and neonatal (newborn) deaths, and more than 20,000 infants were born with malformations, including mental retardation, blindness, deafness, and heart problems. The greatest damage occurs when mothers contract rubella in the third and fourth weeks of pregnancy, although infection during the second month is also damaging. Elaborate efforts ensure that rubella will never again have the same disastrous effects as it did in the mid-1960s. A vaccine that prevents German measles is routinely administered to children, and mothers who plan to have children should have a blood test before they become pregnant to determine if they are immune to the disease.

Syphilis is more damaging later in prenatal development—four months or more after conception. Rather than affecting organogenesis as rubella does, syphilis damages organs after they already are formed. Damage includes eye lesions, which can cause blindness, and skin lesions. When syphilis is present at birth, other problems involving the central nervous sytem and gastrointestinal tract can develop. Most states require a pregnant woman to be given a blood test to detect the presence of syphilis.

Another infection that has received widespread attention recently is genital herpes. Increased numbers of newborns contract this virus when they are delivered through the birth canal of a mother with genital herpes. About one-third of babies delivered through an infected birth canal die; another one-fourth become brain damaged. If a pregnant woman detects an active case of genital herpes close to her delivery date, a cesarean section can be performed (in which the infant is delivered through the mother's abdomen) to keep the virus from infecting the newborn (Rice, 1989).

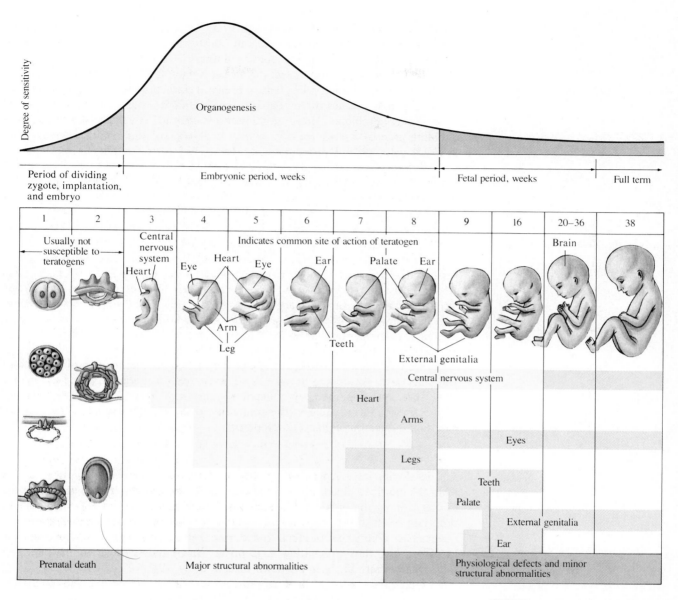

FIGURE 4.4 Teratogens and the timing of their effects on prenatal development. The danger of structural defects caused by teratogens is greatest early in embryonic development. This is the period of organogenesis, and it lasts for several months. Damage caused by teratogens during this period is represented by the dark-colored bars. Later assaults by teratogens typically occur during the fetal period and, instead of structural damage, are more likely to stunt growth or cause problems of organ function.

AIDS also may be transmitted by the mother to the offspring (Seibert & Olson, 1989). The first infant case of AIDS appeared in this country in 1979. By the end of 1991, 3,000 cumulative cases of AIDS are expected (Task Force on Pediatric AIDS, 1989). In the majority of cases, the mother's infection is linked to her own or her sexual partner's use of intravenous drugs. Most children develop symptoms in the first year of life, including bacterial infections, neurological impairment, and delayed development. Treatment of AIDS is still in the trial stages. Early recognition and treatment of the symptoms may prolong life (Novick, 1989).

The Mother's Age

When the mother's age is considered in terms of possible harmful effects on the fetus and infant, two time periods are of special interest: adolescence and the thirties and beyond. Approximately one of every five births is to an adolescent; in some

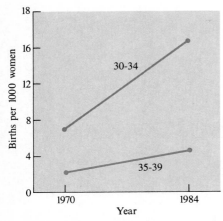

FIGURE 4.5   Birth rates for women aged
30 to 39
Source: National Center for Health Statistics.

urban areas, the figure reaches as high as one in every two births. Infants born to adolescents are often premature. The mortality rate of infants born to adolescent mothers is double that of infants born to mothers in their twenties (Graham, 1981). While such figures probably reflect the mother's immature reproductive system, they also may involve poor nutrition, lack of prenatal care, and low socioeconomic status. Prenatal care decreases the probability that a child born to an adolescent girl will have physical problems. However, adolescents are the least likely of all age groups to obtain prenatal assistance from clinics, pediatricians, and health services (Blum & Goldhagen, 1981; Timberlake and others, 1987; Worthington, 1988).

Women are increasingly seeking to establish their careers before beginning a family, delaying childbearing until their thirties (Figure 4.5). Down syndrome, a form of mental retardation, is related to the mother's age. A baby with Down syndrome rarely is born to a mother under the age of 30, but the risk increases after the mother reaches 30. By age 40, the probability is slightly over 1 in 100, and by age 50, it is almost 1 in 10. The risk also increases before age 18.

Women also have more difficulty becoming pregnant after the age of 30. In one investigation (Schwartz & Mayaux, 1982), the clients of a French fertility clinic all had husbands who were sterile. To increase their chances of having a child, they were artificially inseminated once a month for one year. Each woman had 12 chances to become pregnant. Seventy-five percent of the women in their twenties became pregnant, 62 percent of the women 31 to 35 years old became pregnant, and only 54 percent of those women over 35 years old became pregnant.

We still have much to learn about the role of the mother's age in pregnancy and childbirth. As women become more active, exercise regularly, and are careful about their nutrition, their reproductive systems may remain healthier at older ages than was thought possible in the past. Indeed, as we will see next, the mother's nutrition influences prenatal development.

Nutrition

The developing fetus depends completely on the mother for its nutrition, which comes from the mother's blood. Nutritional state is not determined by any specific aspect of diet; among the important factors are the total number of calories and the appropriate levels of protein, vitamins, and minerals. The mother's nutrition even influences her ability to reproduce. In extreme instances of malnutrition, women stop menstruating, thus precluding conception. And children born to malnourished mothers are more likely to be malformed (Hurley, 1980).

One investigation of Iowa mothers documents the important role of nutrition in prenatal development and birth (Jeans, Smith & Stearns, 1955). The diets of 400 pregnant women were studied and the status of the newborns was assessed. The mothers with the poorest diets were more likely to have offspring who weighed the least, had the least vitality, were born prematurely, or who died. In one investigation, diet supplements given to malnourished mothers during pregnancy improved the performance of offspring during the first three years of life (Werner, 1979).

Emotional State and Stress

Tales abound about the way the mother's emotional state affects the fetus. For centuries, it was thought that frightening experiences—a severe thunderstorm or a family member's death—would leave birthmarks on the child or affect the child in more serious ways. Today, we believe that the mother's stress can be transmitted to the fetus, but we have gone beyond thinking that these happenings are somehow magically produced. We now know that, when a pregnant woman experiences intense fears, anxieties, and other emotions, physiological changes occur—heart rate,

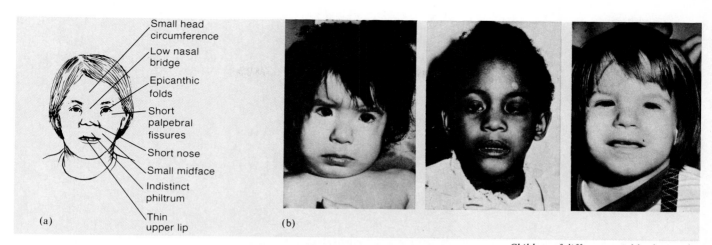

(a)

Small head circumference
Low nasal bridge
Epicanthic folds
Short palpebral fissures
Short nose
Small midface
Indistinct philtrum
Thin upper lip

(b)

Children of different racial backgrounds, diagnosed with fetal alcohol syndrome.

respiration, and glandular secretions among them. For example, the production of adrenaline in response to fear restricts blood flow to the uterine area and may deprive the fetus of adequate oxygen.

The mother's emotional state during pregnancy can influence the birth process, too. An emotionally distraught mother might have irregular contractions and a more difficult labor. This may cause irregularities in the baby's oxygen supply, or it may lead to irregularities after birth. Babies born after extended labor may adjust more slowly to their world and be more irritable. One investigation revealed a connection between the mother's anxiety during pregnancy and the newborn's condition (Ottinger & Simmons, 1964). In this study, mothers answered a questionnaire about their anxiety every three months during pregnancy. When the babies were born, the babies' weights, activity levels, and crying were assessed. The babies of the more anxious mothers cried more before feedings and were more active than the babies born to the less anxious mothers.

Drugs

How do drugs affect prenatal development? Some pregnant women take drugs, smoke tobacco, and drink alcohol without thinking about the possible effects on the fetus. Occasionally, a rash of deformed babies are born, bringing to light the damage drugs can have on the developing fetus. This happened in 1961, when many pregnant women took a popular tranquilizer called thalidomide to reduce their morning sickness. In adults, the effects of thalidomide are mild; in embryos, they are devastating. Not all infants were affected in the same way. If the mother took thalidomide on day 26 (probably before she knew she was pregnant), an arm might not grow. If she took the drug two days later, the arm might not grow past the elbow. The thalidomide tragedy shocked the medical community and parents into the stark realization that the mother does not have to be a chronic drug user for the fetus to be harmed. Taking the wrong drug at the wrong time is enough to physically handicap the offspring for life.

Heavy drinking by pregnant women also can be devastating to an offspring. A cluster of characteristics called **fetal alcohol syndrome (FAS)** identifies children born to mothers who are heavy drinkers; it includes a small head (called microencephaly) as well as defective limbs, face, and heart. Most of these children have below-average intelligence. While no serious malformations such as those found in FAS are found in infants born to mothers who are moderate drinkers, infants whose mothers drank moderately during pregnancy (for example, one to two drinks a day) were less attentive and alert, with the effects present at 4 years of age (Streissguth & others, 1984).

Fetal and neonatal deaths are higher among smoking mothers, and preterm births are higher. Respiratory problems and sudden infant death syndrome, in which the infant abruptly stops breathing, are also more common among offspring whose mothers smoke.

Thinking Critically
How can we reduce the number of offspring born to drug dependent mothers? If you had $100 million dollars to spend to help remedy this problem, what would you do?

Cigarette smoking by the pregnant woman also can adversely influence prenatal development, birth, and infant development. Fetal and neonatal deaths are higher among smoking mothers; also prevalent are higher preterm births and lower birth weights. In one investigation (Landesman-Dwyer & Sackett, 1983), 271 infant-mother pairs were studied during the infant's eight, twelfth, and sixteenth weeks of life by having each mother keep a diary of her infant's activity patterns. Mothers who smoked during pregnancy had infants who were awake on a more consistent basis, a finding one might expect, since the active chemical ingredient in cigarettes—nicotine—is a stimulant. Respiratory problems and sudden infant death syndrome (also known as crib death) are more common among the offspring of mothers who smoke. Recent evidence suggests that intervention programs designed to get pregnant women to stop smoking are successful in reducing some of the negative effects of cigarette smoking on offspring, being especially effective in raising their birth weights (Sexton & Hebel, 1984; Vorhees & Mollnow, 1987).

It is well documented that infants whose mothers are addicted to heroin show several behavioral difficulties (Hans, 1989; Hutchings & Fifer, 1986). The young infants of these mothers are addicted and show withdrawal symptoms characteristic of opiate abstinence, such as tremors, irritability, abnormal crying, disturbed sleep, and impaired motor control. Behavioral problems are still often present at the first birthday, and attention deficits may appear later in the child's development.

With the increased use of cocaine in the United States, there has been growing concern regarding the effects of cocaine on the fetuses and neonates of pregnant cocaine users. Cocaine, and its newest form crack, has been found to cause infant hypertension and damage to the offspring's heart when taken by pregnant women (Chasnoff, 1989; Lipsitt, 1989).

At this point, we have discussed a number of ideas about prenatal development. A summary of the main points in this discussion is presented in Concept Table 4.1. Next, we will turn to the study of the birth process itself.

Prenatal Development

Concept	Processes and Related Ideas	Characteristics and Description
The Course of Prenatal Development	Germinal period	The period from conception to about 10–14 days later. The fertilized egg is called a zygote. The period ends when the zygote attaches to the uterine wall.
	Embryonic period	The period that lasts from about two weeks to eight weeks after conception. The embryo differentiates into three layers; life-support systems develop; and organ systems form (organogenesis).
	Fetal period	The period that lasts from about two months after conception until nine months or when the infant is born. Growth and development continue their dramatic course and organ systems mature to the point where life can be sustained outside the womb.
Miscarriage and Abortion	Its nature and ethical issues	A miscarriage, or spontaneous abortion, happens when pregnancy ends before the developing organism is mature enough to survive outside the womb. Estimates indicate that about 15–20% of all pregnancies end this way, many without the mother's knowledge. Induced abortion is a complex issue medically, psychologically, and socially. An unwanted pregnancy is stressful for the woman regardless of how it is resolved. A recent ethical issue focuses on the use of fetal tissue in transplant operations.
Teratology and Hazards to Prenatal Development	Teratology	The field that investigates the causes of congenital (birth) defects. Any agent that causes birth defects is called a teratogen.
	Maternal diseases and conditions	Maternal diseases and infections can cause damage by crossing the placental barrier, or they can be destructive during the birth process itself. Among the maternal diseases and conditions believed to be involved in possible birth defects are rubella, syphilis, genital herpes, AIDS, the mother's age, nutrition, and emotional state and stress.
	Drugs	Thalidomide was a tranquilizer given to pregnant mothers to reduce their morning sickness. In the early 1960s, thousands of babies were malformed as a consequence of their mother taking this drug. Alcohol, cigarette smoking, heroin, and cocaine are other ways drugs can adversely affect prenatal and infant development.

The Birth Process

Delivery can be as difficult for the baby as for the mother, lasting anywhere from 4 to 24 hours, from which the newborn emerges covered with the mother's blood and a thick, greasy, white material called vernix, which eases movement through the birth canal. The newborn's head is not the most attractive in the world; it may be swollen at the top because of pressure against the pelvic outlet during the last hours of labor. The baby's face may be puffy and bluish; her ears may be pressed against her head in a bizarre position—matted forward on her cheeks, for example. Her nose may be flattened and skewed to one side by the squeeze through the pelvis. The baby may be bowlegged, and her feet may be cocked pigeon-toed from being up beside her head for so long in the mother's womb. They can be flexed and put in a normal position at birth. How stunning it must be to be thrust suddenly into a new, bright, airy world so totally different from the dark, moist warmth of the womb.

There was a star danced, and under that I was born.

William Shakespeare

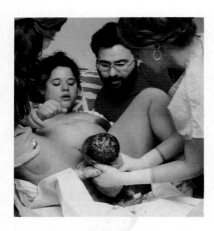

Birth is a time of dramatic transition for the fetus. The baby is on a threshold between two worlds.

We must respect this instant of birth, this fragile moment. The baby is between two worlds, on a threshold, hesitating . . .

Frederick Leboyer,
Birth Without Violence

Despite the drama of human birth, newborns who have had a comfortable stay in the womb and are born when due are well equipped by nature to withstand the birth process. There are many intriguing questions about the birth process: What kinds of childbirth strategies are available? What are the stages of birth, and what delivery complications can arise? What are preterm infants like? How can we measure the newborn's health and social responsivenes? How crucial is bonding? We will consider each of these in turn.

Childbirth Strategies

Controversy swirls over how childbirth should proceed. Some critics argue that the standard delivery practices of most hospitals and physicians need to be overhauled. Others suggest that the entire family—especially the father—should be more involved in childbirth. And others argue that procedures that ensure mother-infant bonding should be followed.

In the standard childbirth procedure that was practiced for many years—and the way you probably were delivered—the expectant mother was taken to a hospital, where a doctor was responsible for the baby's delivery. The pregnant woman was prepared for labor by having her pubic hair shaved and by having an enema. She then was placed in a labor room often filled with other pregnant women, some of whom were screaming. When she was ready to deliver, she was taken to the delivery room, which looked like an operating room. She was laid on the table with her legs in the air, and the physician, along with an anesthetist and a nurse, delivered the baby.

What could be wrong with this procedure? Critics list three things: (1) Important individuals related to the mother are excluded from the birth process. (2) The mother is separated from her infant in the first minutes and hours after birth. (3) Giving birth is treated like a disease, and a woman is thought of as a sick patient (Rosenblith & Sims-Knight, 1985). As we will see next, some alternative procedures differ radically from this standard procedure.

The **Leboyer method,** developed by French obstetrician Frederick Leboyer, intends to make the birth process less stressful for infants. Leboyer's procedure is referred to as "birth without violence." He describes standard childbirth as torture (Leboyer, 1975). He vehemently objects to holding newborns upside down and slapping or spanking them, putting silver nitrite into their eyes, separating them immediately from their mothers, and scaring them with bright lights and harsh noises in the delivery room. Leboyer also criticizes the traditional habit of cutting the umbilical cord as soon as the infant is born, a situation that forces the infant to immediately take in oxygen from the air to breathe. Leboyer believes that the umbilical cord should be left intact for several minutes to allow the newborn a chance to adjust to a world of breathing air. In the Leboyer method, the baby is placed on the mother's stomach immediately after birth so the mother can caress the infant. Then the infant is placed in a bath of warm water to relax.

While most hospitals do not use the soft lights and warm baths for the newborn suggested by Leboyer, they sometimes do place the newborn on the mother's stomach immediately after birth, believing that it will stimulate bonding between the mother and the infant.

Another well-known birth procedure that deviates markedly from the standard practice is the **Lamaze method,** a form of prepared or natural childbirth developed by Fernand Lamaze, a pioneering French obstetrician. It has become widely

Childbirth in Africa

Labor is a biological process that is virtually the same in all cultures. The *experience* of birth, though, varies extensively from one culture to another. In several cultures, giving birth is thought of as a natural process that requires no special assistance. This orientation toward birth characterizes the hunting and gathering society of the !Kung who live in Africa's Kalahari desert.

Most cultures have at least one or two attendants to help in delivering the baby. The Ngoni women of East Africa view themselves as childbirth experts. They completely exclude men from the birth sequence and keep their pregnancy a secret from the men as long as possible. When the mother-in-law discovers that her daughter-in-law's labor has started, she and other female relatives move into the woman's hut, make the husband leave, and oversee the baby's birth. The women even remove all of the husband's belongings from the hut, including his tools and clothes. Men are not permitted to return to the hut until after the baby's birth (Read, 1968). ◆

accepted in the medical profession and involves helping the pregnant mother to cope with the pain of childbirth in an active way to avoid or reduce medication. Lamaze training for parents is available on a widespread basis in the United States and usually consists of six weekly classes. In these classes, the pregnant woman learns about the birth process and is trained in breathing and relaxation exercises.

As the Lamaze method grew in popularity, it became more common for the father to participate in the exercises and to assist in the birth process. To learn more about the father's role in the Lamaze method and his participation in the birth process, turn to Children 4.2.

Medical doctors provide most maternity care in the United States. However, in many countries of the world, midwives are the primary caregiver for pregnant and laboring women. In the United States, midwives are not as well established, although all states have provisions for their practice. The emphasis of the midwife's training is that birth is a normal physiological event. Midwives support and promote the woman's physical and emotional well-being. Midwives do not care for women who have complications of pregnancy. In the United States, certified nurse-midwives are the most numerous. They generally work in close cooperation with physicians in hospitals, homes, or birthing centers.

Most births in the United States take place in a hospital. In recent years, hospitals have offered more comfortable, homelike rooms for birth. Many hospitals now have birthing rooms, where the mother can labor, give birth, and spend time with her newborn afterward. And birthing centers also have emerged as an alternative setting to hospitals if the pregnant woman is healthy and no complications are foreseen. Birthing centers provide a sense of community and learning, with social gatherings and classes often being held there.

As the Lamaze method became more popular, it became common for fathers to assist in the birth process. This photograph shows a father participating in Lamaze training.

A Father in the Delivery Room: "It Was Out of This World!"

An interesting historical accident led to one of Lamaze training's major components as it is now practiced in the United States. In France, trained women assist the woman in labor. Since such assistants are not available in the United States, fathers assumed the assistant's function. Fathers attend childbirth classes with their wives, learn the strategies required, and assist in timing contractions, massaging the mother, and giving psychological support.

The father's participation in the birth process may help to strengthen his relationship with his wife and increase the probability that he will develop a stronger attachment bond with the infant. Data supporting the belief that the father's participation in Lamaze classes and in the birth process will benefit the infant's long-term development have not been generated. However, there is something intuitively positive about the father's involvement in the birth process, if he is motivated to participate. It may increase the family's sense as a cohesive, interdependent unit that does things together. A survey indicated that the father's presence in the delivery room is a positive experience (Pawson & Morris, 1972). Only 1 of the 544 fathers sampled said that he regretted participating in the birth process. While most fathers who participate in the delivery room process provide glowing reports about the experience, many fathers feel uncomfortable and anxious about delivery room participation and have no desire to be involved.

What are some reactions of fathers who have participated in the Lamaze-type natural childbirth classes and in the birth process in the delivery room? More than 20 years ago, I was allowed in the delivery room by a progressive physician at a hospital that did not permit such practices. I still have a vivid image of those moments, moments that truly inspire a sense of awe and excitement in a father when he sees his child being born.

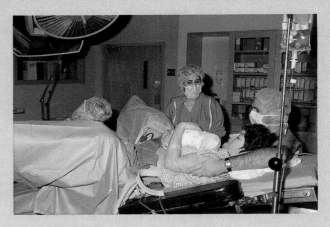

The father of a newborn is shown in the delivery room. The father's participation in the birth process strengthens his sense of involvement and commitment to the family.

One father who participated in natural childbirth classes proudly described how he felt at his accomplishments and his sense of involvement in sharing the birth of the baby with his wife:

It made me feel good to be able to help out. I know it was a painful experience, and I wanted to make it as easy as possible for her. She was willing to have the baby and go through nine months of carrying it around. The least I could do was go to the childbirth classes once a week and give her my support. There were times during her pregnancy when she did not feel well. I know she appreciated my willingness to assist her in the baby's birth. Then, in the delivery room itself—what a great, uplifting feeling. It was out of this world! I would not have missed that moment when the baby first came out for the world. ◆

Stages of Birth and Delivery Complications

The birth process occurs in three stages. For a woman having her first child, the first stage lasts an average of 12 to 24 hours: it is the longest of the three stages. In the first stage, uterine contractions are 15 to 20 minutes apart at the beginning and last up to a minute. These contractions cause the woman's cervix to stretch and open. As the first stage progresses, the contractions come closer together, appearing every 2 to 5 minutes. Their intensity increases too. By the end of the first birth stage, contractions dilate the cervix to an opening of about 4 inches so that the baby can move from the uterus to the birth canal.

The second birth stage begins when the baby's head starts to move through the cervix and the birth canal. It terminates when the baby completely emerges from the mother's body. This stage lasts for approximately 1½ hours. With each contraction, the mother bears down hard to push the baby out of her body. By the time the baby's head is out of the mother's body, the contractions come almost every minute and last for about 1 minute.

The third birth stage—known as **afterbirth**—involves the detachment and expelling of the placenta, umbilical cord, and other membranes. This final stage is the shortest of the three birth stages, lasting only minutes.

Complications can accompany the baby's delivery. When the baby moves through the birth canal too rapidly, the delivery is called **precipitate.** A precipitate delivery is one in which the baby takes less than 10 minutes to be squeezed through the birth canal. This deviation in delivery can disturb the infant's normal flow of blood, and the pressure on the infant's head can cause hemorrhaging. If the delivery takes too long, brain damage can occur because of **anoxia,** meaning that insufficient oxygen is available to the infant.

Another delivery complication involves the baby's position in the uterus. Normally, the crown of the baby's head comes through the vagina first. But in 1 of every 25 babies the head does not come through first. Some come with their buttocks first, in **breech position.** A breech baby has difficulties because his head is still in the uterus when the rest of his body is out, which can cause respiratory problems. Some breech babies cannot be passed through the cervix and must be delivered by cesarean section.

Use of Drugs During Childbirth

Drugs can be used to relieve pain and anxiety and to speed up delivery during the birth process. The widest use of drugs during delivery is to relieve the expectant mother's pain or anxiety. A wide variety of tranquilizers, sedatives, and analgesics are used for this purpose. Researchers are interested in the effects of these drugs because they can cross the placental barrier and because their use is so widespread. One survey of hospitals found that only 5 percent of deliveries involved no anesthesia (Brackbill, 1979).

One drug that has been widely used to speed up delivery is **oxytocin,** a hormone that stimulates uterine contractions. Controversy surrounds the use of this drug. Some physicians argue that it can save the mother's life or keep the infant from being damaged. They also stress that using the drug allows the mother to be well rested and prepared for the birth process. Critics argue that babies born to mothers who have taken oxytocin are more likely to have jaundice, that induced labor requires more pain-killing drugs, and that greater medical care is required after the birth, resulting in the separation of the infant and the mother.

What conclusions can be reached based on research about the influence of drugs during delivery? Four conclusions are the following (Rosenblith & Sims-Knight, 1985):

1. Research studies are few in number, and those that have been completed often have methodological problems. However, not all drugs have similar effects. Some drugs—tranquilizers, sedatives, and analgesics, for example—do not seem to have long-term effects. Other drugs—oxytocin, for example—are suspected of having long-term effects.

Thinking Critically
After reading the information on the use of drugs during childbirth, what considerations would be foremost in your mind if your offspring were about to be born? What questions about the use of drugs during delivery would you want to ask the individuals responsible for delivering the baby?

2. The degree to which a drug influences the infant is usually small. Birth weight and social class, for instance, are more powerful predictors of infant difficulties than drugs.

3. A specific drug may affect some infants but not others. In some cases, the drug may have a beneficial effect, while in others, it may have a harmful effect.

4. The overall amount of medication may be an important factor in understanding drug effects on delivery.

Preterm Infants and Age-Weight Considerations

A full-term infant is one who has grown in the womb for the full 38 to 42 weeks between conception and delivery. A **preterm infant** (also called a premature infant) is one who is born prior to 38 weeks after conception. Infants born after a regular gestation period of 38 to 42 weeks (the term *gestation* refers to the length of time between conception and birth), but who weigh less than 5½ pounds, are called **low-birth-weight infants.** Both preterm and low-birth-weight infants are considered high-risk infants (Holmes, Reich, & Gyurke, 1989; Hunt & Cooper, 1989). In one investigation (Milham & others, 1983), children were assessed at least once per year through the first four years of life. The most severe cognitive deficits appeared among those who were preterm or low-birth-weight babies and who came from an impoverished rather than a middle-class background.

THE CULTURAL WORLDS OF CHILDREN

Prenatal Development and Birth in Black Families

The 1985 Children's Defense Fund study, "Black and White Children in America: Key Facts," discovered that black children are twice as likely to

 —be born prematurely
 —have low birth weight
 —have mothers who received late or no prenatal care

are three times as likely to

 —have their mothers die in childbirth

are five times as likely to

 —be born to unmarried teenage mothers

(Edelman, 1987)   ◆

A short gestation period does not necessarily harm the infant. It is distinguished from retarded prenatal growth, in which the fetus has been damaged in some way (Kopp, 1983, 1987). The neurological development of the short-gestation infant continues after birth on approximately the same timetable as if the infant still were in the womb. For example, consider an infant born after a gestation period of 30 weeks. At 38 weeks, approximately two months after birth, this infant shows the same level of brain development as a 38-week fetus who is yet to be born. Some infants are born precariously early and have a precariously low birth weight. To learn more about these so-called kilo babies, turn to Children 4.3.

Preterm infants do have a different profile than full-term infants. For instance, Tiffany Field (1979) found that 4-month-old preterm infants vocalized less, fussed more, and avoided eye contact more than their full-term counterparts. Other researchers have found differences in the information-processing skills of preterm and full-term infants. In one investigation, Susan Rose and her colleagues (1988) found that 7-month-old high-risk preterm infants were less visually attentive to novelty and showed deficits in visual recognition memory when compared with full-term infants.

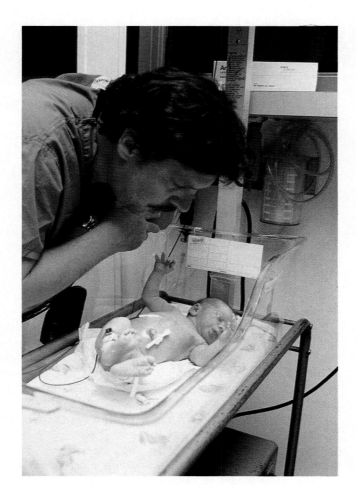

A short gestation period does not necessarily harm the infant. It is important to distinguish short gestation from retarded prenatal growth, in which the fetus has been damaged in some way.

Kilogram Kids

"Kilogram kids" weigh less than 2.3 pounds (which is 1 kilogram, or 1,000 grams) and are very premature. The task of saving such a baby is not easy. At the Stanford University Medical Center in Palo Alto, California, 98 percent of the preterm babies survive; however, 32 percent of those between 750 and 1,000 grams do not, and 76 percent of those below 750 grams do not. Approximately 250,000 preterm babies are born in the United States each year and 15 to 20,000 of these weigh less than 1,000 grams.

Neonatal intensive-care units report not only increased survival rates but decreases in the severity of the handicap of those babies that suffer handicaps. In the neonatal intensive-care units, banks of flashing lights, blinking numbers, and beeping alarms stand guard over the extreme preterm infant. She lies on a water bed that gently undulates; the water bed is in an incubator controlled for temperature and humidity by the baby's own body. So many electronic machines and computerized devices incessantly monitor, report, and sound warnings on such vital signs as brain waves, heartbeat, blood gases, and respiratory rate that a team of technicians is needed to service them around the clock. All of this care can be very expensive. Five to six months can run as high as $200,000, although it usually is within five figures.

Kilogram babies are not flawed but merely perilously ahead of schedule. After size and sex, the question parents of a preterm infant most often ask is, "What is wrong with my baby?" The baby is normal. Her form, her needs, how she is behaving—everything is precisely normal for her current stage of development. Preterm infants—even the kilogram kids— are no more sick than you are. But the kilogram kid is as close to death as you would be if you were quickly transported to the moon's surface or the ocean's bottom. Being on the moon

A "kilogram kid."

or the ocean floor is not a disease, but it certainly is life threatening. The kilogram kid has been taken from an environment to which she is beautifully adapted to one that can be deadly. Without an amniotic sac to protect her, without a placenta to feed her, breathe for her, oxygenate her blood and eliminate her waste, she needs a space suit with all those tubes and wires and needles (Fincher, 1982).   ♦

Without a doubt, preterm infants are perceived differently by the adults in their world. Consider the medical community; they know a great deal about the problems confronting preterm infants. The staff-patient ratio for preterm infants is often one of the most favorable in the hospital. And the preterm infant is immersed in an exotic environment of high-technology life-support equipment (Als, 1988). Parents undoubtedly also perceive their preterm infant differently than the parents of full-term infants. Parents know that their preterm infant is different and have reasonable fears about the infant's health and future. Preterm infants frequently remain in the hospital for a long time, making the parent's role as a competent caregiver difficult. Parents must cope with uncertainty for a lengthy period of time.

How do parents deal with their preterm infants? Before the newborn goes home from the hospital, mothers show less confidence in dealing with their preterm infant than the mothers of full-term infants. And they are less likely to hold the

Massaging and Exercising Preemies

In one recent investigation, 40 preterm infants who had just been released from the intensive-care unit and placed in a transitional nursery were studied (Field, Scafidi, & Schanberg, 1987). Twenty of the preterm babies were given special stimulation with massage and exercise techniques for three 15-minute periods at the beginning of three consecutive hours every morning for 10 weekdays. For example, the infant was placed on its stomach and gently stroked. The massage began with the head and neck and moved downward to the feet. It also moved from the shoulders down to the hands. The infant was then rolled over. Each arm and leg was flexed and extended, then both legs together were flexed and extended. Next, the massage was repeated.

The massaged and exercised preterm babies gained 47 percent more weight than their preterm counterparts who were not massaged and exercised, even though both groups had the same number of feedings per day and averaged the same intake of formula. The massaged infants were more active, more alert, and performed better on developmental tests. Also, their hospital stay was about six days shorter than the nonmassaged, nonexercised group. This saved about $3,000 per preterm infant.

The increased activity of the massaged, exercised infants would seem to work against weight gain. However, similar findings have been found with animals. The increased activity may increase gastrointestinal and metabolic efficiency.

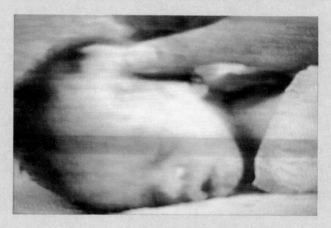

This preterm baby is being massaged as part of Tiffany Field's research investigation of the effects of massaging and exercising on infant development. The massaged and exercised infants were more active, more alert, and performed better on developmental tests than their preterm counterparts who were not massaged.

The massaged, exercised infants also were more socially interactive than the other infants. This may happen because massage stimulates intimacy between the infant and social figures in its world. ◆

baby close, cuddle, and smile at the infant than the mothers of full-term infants. Possibly such mothers feel awkward or perceive the preterm baby as more fragile than a full-term baby, which can interfere with the attachment process (Campos & others, 1983).

Because parents have to deal with infants who are physically and behaviorally different from full-term infants, the differences in the way mothers handle preterm infants may be based on their sincere motivation to competently rear their preterm infants. One recently designed program to facilitate maternal adjustment to the care of a low-birth-weight infant was successful (Rauh & others, 1988). The mothers developed more self-confidence and satisfaction with mothering, as well as more favorable perceptions of their infant's temperament. (In Children 4.4, an intervention with premature infants involving massage and exercise is described.) Other recent research indicates that as preterm infants develop, by the beginning of the preschool years many of the early differences between preterm and full-term infants have diminished, both in the child's skills and in parenting behavior (Greenberg & Crnic, 1988).

Conclusions about Preterm Infants

What conclusions can we draw from the results of research about preterm infants? Four such conclusions seem appropriate (Kopp, 1983, 1987; Kopp & Kaler, 1989):

1. As intensive-care technology has improved, there have been fewer serious consequences of preterm births. For instance, from 1961 to 1965, the manner of feeding preterm infants changed and intravenous fluid therapy came into use. From 1966 to 1968, better control of hypoxemia (oxygen deficiency) resulted. In 1971, artificial ventilation was introduced. In the mid-1970s, neonatal support systems became less intrusive and damaging to the infant.

2. Infants born with an identifiable problem are likely to have a poorer developmental future than infants born without a recognizable problem (Cohen & others, 1989). For instance, extremely sick or extremely tiny babies are less likely to survive than healthy or normal-weight babies.

3. Social class differences are associated with the preterm infant's development. The higher the socioeconomic status, the more favorable is the developmental outcome for a newborn. Social class differences are tied to many other differences. For example, quality of environment, cigarette and alcohol consumption, IQ, and knowledge of competent parenting strategies are associated with social class; less positive characteristics are associated with lower-class families.

4. We do not have solid evidence that preterm infants, as a rule, have difficulty later in school. Nor is there good evidence that these preterm children perform poorly on IQ and information-processing tests. Such claims to the contrary were made just one or two decades ago.

Measures of Neonatal Health and Responsiveness

For many years, the **Apgar scale** (Table 4.1) has been used to assess the newborn's health. One minute and five minutes after birth, the obstetrician or nurse gives the newborn a reading of 0, 1, or 2 on each of five signs: heart rate, respiratory effort, muscle tone, body color, and reflex irritability. A high total score of 7 to 10 indicates that the newborn's condition is good, a score of 5 indicates that there may be developmental difficulties, and a score of 3 or below signals an emergency and indicates that survival may be in doubt.

While the Apgar scale is used immediately after birth to identify high-risk infants who need resuscitation, another scale is used for long-term neurological assessment—the **Brazelton Neonatal Behavioral Assessment Scale** (Brazelton, 1973, 1984, 1988; Brazelton, Nugent, & Lester, 1987). This scale includes an evaluation of the newborn's reactions to people. The Brazelton scale usually is given on the third day of life and then repeated several days later. Twenty reflexes are assessed along with reactions to circumstances, such as the neonate's reaction to a rattle. The examiner rates the newborn on each of 26 different categories (Table 4.2). As an indication of how detailed the ratings are, consider item 14 in Table 4.2: "cuddliness." As shown in Table 4.3, nine categories are involved in assessing this item, with infant behavior scored on a continuum that ranges from the infant being very resistant to being held to the infant being extremely cuddly and clinging. The Brazelton scale not only is used as a sensitive index of neurological integrity in the week

TABLE 4.1 *The Apgar Scale*

	Score		
	0	**1**	**2**
Heart Rate	Absent	Slow—less than 100 beats per minute	Fast—100–140 beats per minute
Respiratory Effort	No breathing for more than 1 minute	Irregular and slow	Good breathing with normal crying
Muscle Tone	Limp and flaccid	Weak, inactive, but some flexion of extremities	Strong, active motion
Body Color	Blue and pale	Body pink, but extremities blue	Entire body pink
Reflex Irritability	No response	Grimace	Coughing, sneezing, and crying

From Virginia A. Apgar, "A Proposal for a New Method of Evaluation of a Newborn Infant" in *Anesthesia and Analgesia: Current Researches*, 32, 260–267, 1975. Copyright © 1975 International Anesthesia Research Society. Reprinted by permission.

TABLE 4.2 *The 26 Categories on the Brazelton Neonatal Behavioral Assessment Scale (NBAS)*

1. Response decrement to repeated visual stimuli
2. Response decrement to rattle
3. Response decrement to bell
4. Response decrement to pinprick
5. Orienting response to inanimate visual stimuli
6. Orienting response to inanimate auditory stimuli
7. Orienting response to animate visual stimuli—examiner's face
8. Orienting response to animate auditory stimuli—examiner's voice
9. Orienting responses to animate visual and auditory stimuli
10. Quality and duration of alert periods
11. General muscle tone—in resting and in response to being handled, passive, and active
12. Motor activity
13. Traction responses as he or she is pulled to sit
14. Cuddliness—responses to being cuddled by examiner
15. Defensive movements—reactions to a cloth over his or her face
16. Consolability with intervention by examiner
17. Peak of excitement and capacity to control self
18. Rapidity of buildup to crying state
19. Irritability during the examination
20. General assessment of kind and degree of activity
21. Tremulousness
22. Amount of startling
23. Lability of skin color—measuring autonomic lability
24. Lability of states during entire examination
25. Self-quieting activity—attempts to console self and control state
26. Hand-to-mouth activity

From B. M. Lester and T. B. Brazelton, "Cross-Cultural Assessment of Neonatal Behavior" in D. A. Wagner and H. W. Stevenson, Eds., *Cultural Perspective on Child Development*. Copyright © 1982 W. H. Freeman and Company. Reprinted by permission.

TABLE 4.3	The Assessment of Cuddliness on the Brazelton Neonatal Behavioral Assessment Scale	
Score	**Infant Behavior**
1	The infant resists being held and continually pushes away, thrashes, and stiffens.
2	The infant resists being held most of the time.
3	The infant does not resist but does not participate either, acting like a rag doll.
4	The infant eventually molds into the examiner's arms after considerable nestling and cuddling efforts by the examiner.
5	The infant usually molds and relaxes when initially held, nestling into the examiner's neck or crook of the elbow. The infant leans forward when held on the examiner's shoulder.
6	The infant always molds at the beginning, as described above.
7	The infant always molds initially with nestling and turns toward body and leans forward.
8	The infant molds and relaxes, nestles and turns head, leans forward on the shoulder, fits feet into cavity of other arm, and all of the body participates.
9	All of the above take place, and in addition, the infant grasps the examiner and clings.

From *In the Beginning: Development in the First Two Years,* by J. F. Rosenblith and J. E. Sim-Knight. Copyright © 1985 by Wadsworth, Inc. Reprinted by permission of Brooks/Cole Publishing Company, Monterey, California.

after birth, but it also is used widely as a measure in many research studies on infant development. In recent versions of scoring the Brazelton scale, Brazelton and his colleagues (1987) categorize the 26 items into four different categories—physiological, motoric, state, and interaction. They also classify the baby in global terms such as "worrisome," "normal," or "superior," based on these categories.

A very low Brazelton score can indicate brain damage. But if the infant merely seems sluggish in responding to social circumstances, parents are encouraged to give the infant attention and to undergo **Brazelton training,** which involves using the Brazelton scale to show parents how their newborn responds to people (Brazelton, 1979, 1987, 1989). As part of the training, parents are shown how the neonate can respond positively to people and how such responses can be stimulated. Brazelton training has improved the social interaction of high-risk infants and the social skills of healthy, responsive infants (Widmayer & Field, 1980; Worobey & Belsky, 1982). Considerable interest has been generated recently in increasing the caregiver's recognition and management of stress in the neonatal period (Gorski, 1988; Klaus, 1988).

Bonding

Perhaps the most controversial strategy focused on the mother's role in the newborn's life involves what is called **bonding.** Advocates of bonding argue that long-term consequences for the infant's development are set in motion during the first minutes, hours, or days of the newborn's interaction with the social world. Situations surrounding delivery may prevent or make difficult the occurrence of an emotional bond between the infant and mother. For example, preterm infants are isolated from their mothers to an even greater degree than full-term infants. In many hospitals, it is common to give the mother drugs to make the delivery less painful. The drugs may make the mother drowsy and may interfere with her ability to respond to and stimulate the newborn.

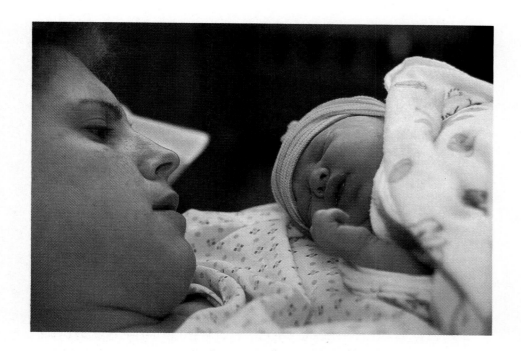

Shown here is a mother bonding with her infant moments after the baby was born. How critical is bonding for the development of social competence later in childhood?

Many pediatricians have been adamant about the importance of bonding during the initial hours and days of the newborn's life. In particular, Marshall Klaus and John Kennell (1976) influenced the introduction of bonding in many hospitals. They argue that the first few days of life are a critical period in development. During this period, close contact, especially physical contact, between the newborn and the mother is believed to create an important emotional attachment that provides a foundation for optimal development for years to come.

Is there evidence that such close contact between the mother and the newborn is absolutely critical for optimal development later in life? While some research supports the bonding hypothesis (Klaus & Kennell, 1976), a growing body of research challenges the significance of the first few days of life as a critical period (Bakeman & Brown, 1980; Rode & others, 1981). Indeed, the extreme form of the bonding hypothesis—that the newborn must have close contact with the mother in the first few days of life to develop optimally—simply is not true.

Nonetheless, the weakness of the maternal-infant bonding research should not be used as an excuse to keep motivated mothers from interacting with their infants in the postpartum period, because such contact brings pleasure to many mothers. In some mother-infant pairs—preterm infants, adolescent mothers, or mothers from disadvantaged circumstances—the practice of bonding may set in motion a climate for improved mother-infant interaction after the mother and infant leave the hospital (Maccoby & Martin, 1983).

We have discussed many dimensions of the birth process. To help you remember the main points of this discussion, turn to Concept Table 4.2. This concludes our discussion of biological beginnings. In the book's next section, we will turn our attention to the nature of infant development.

The Birth Process

Concept	Processes and Related Ideas	Characteristics and Description
Childbirth Strategies	Their nature	A controversy currently exists over how childbirth should proceed. Standard childbirth has been criticized, and the Leboyer and Lamaze methods have been developed as alternatives. Medical doctors deliver most babies in the United States, but midwives sometimes are used. Most babies in the United States are delivered in hospitals, but birthing centers also may be used.
Stages of Birth and Complications	Stages	Three stages of birth have been defined. The first lasts about 12 to 24 hours for a woman having her first child. The cervix dilates to about 4 inches. The second stage begins when the baby's head moves through the cervix and ends with the baby's complete emergence. The third stage is afterbirth.
	Complications	A baby can move through the birth canal too rapidly or too slowly. A delivery that is too fast is called precipitate; when delivery is too slow, anoxia may result.
Use of Drugs During Childbirth	Drugs used to relieve pain and anxiety and to speed up delivery	A wide variety of tranquilizers, sedatives, and analgesics are used to relieve the expectant mother's pain and anxiety, while oxytocin is used to speed up delivery. It is hard to come up with general statements about drug effects, but it is known that birth weight and social class are more powerful predictors of problems than drugs. A specific drug can have mixed effects and the overall amount of medication needs to be considered.
Preterm Infants and Age-Weight Considerations	Types	Preterm infants are those born after a briefer-than-regular time period in the womb. Infants who are born after a regular gestation period of 38 to 42 weeks but who weigh less than 5½ pounds are called low-birth-weight infants.
	Conclusions	As intensive-care technology has improved, preterm babies have benefited considerably. Infants born with an identifiable problem have a poorer developmental future than those born without a recognizable problem. Social class differences are associated with the preterm infant's development. There is no solid evidence that preterm infants perform more poorly than full-term infants when they are assessed years later in school.
Measures of Neonatal Health and Responsiveness	Types	For many years the Apgar scale has been used to assess the newborn's health. A more recently developed test—the Brazelton Neonatal Behavioral Assessment Scale—is used for long-term neurological assessment. It assesses not only the newborn's neurological integrity but also social responsiveness. If the newborn is sluggish, Brazelton training is recommended.
Bonding	Its nature	There is evidence that bonding—establishment of a close mother-infant bond in the first hours or days after birth—is not critical for optimal development, although for some mother-infant pairs it may stimulate interaction after they leave the hospital.

Summary

I. The Course of Prenatal Development

Prenatal development is divided into three periods. The germinal period lasts from conception to about 10 to 14 days. The fertilized egg is called a zygote. This period ends when the zygote attaches to the uterine wall. The embryonic period lasts from two weeks to eight weeks after conception. The embryo differentiates into three layers; life-support systems develop; and organ systems form (organogenesis). The fetal period lasts from two months after conception until nine months or when the infant is born. Growth and development continue their dramatic course, and organ systems mature to the point that life can be sustained outside the womb.

II. Miscarriage and Abortion

A miscarriage, or spontaneous abortion, happens when pregnancy ends before the developing organism is mature enough to survive outside the womb. Estimates indicate that about 15 to 20 percent of all pregnancies end this way, many without the mother's knowledge. Induced abortion is a complex issue medically, psychologically, and socially. An unwanted pregnancy is stressful for the woman regardless of how it is resolved. A recent ethical issue focuses on the use of fetal tissue in transplant operations.

III. Teratology and the Hazards to Prenatal Development

Teratology is the field that investigates the causes of congenital (birth) defects. Any agent that causes birth defects is called a teratogen. Maternal diseases and infections can cause damage by crossing the placental barrier, or they can be destructive during the birth process itself. Among the maternal diseases and conditions believed to be involved in possible birth defects are rubella, syphilis, genital herpes, the mother's age, nutrition, and emotional state and stress. Thalidomide was a tranquilizer given to pregnant mothers to reduce their morning sickness. In the early 1960s, thousands of babies were malformed as a consequence of their mother taking this drug. Alcohol, cigarette smoking, heroin, and cocaine are other ways drugs can adversely affect prenatal and infant development.

IV. Childbirth Strategies

A controversy exists over how childbirth should proceed. Standard childbirth has been criticized, and the Leboyer and Lamaze methods have been developed as alternatives. Medical doctors deliver most babies in the United States, but midwives sometimes are used. Most babies in the United States are born in hospitals, but birthing centers also may be used.

V. Stages of Birth and Complications

Three stages of birth have been defined. The first lasts about 12 to 24 hours for a woman having her first child. The cervix dilates to about 4 inches. The second stage begins when the baby's head moves through the cervix and ends with the baby's complete emergence. The third stage is afterbirth. A baby can move through the birth canal too quickly or too slowly. A delivery that is too fast is called precipitate; when delivery is too slow, anoxia may result.

VI. Use of Drugs During Childbirth

A wide variety of tranquilizers, sedatives, and analgesics are used to relieve the expectant mother's pain and anxiety, while oxytocin is used to speed up delivery. It is hard to make any general statements about drug effects, but it is known that birth weight and social class are more powerful predictors of problems than are drugs. A specific drug can have mixed effects, and the overall amount of medication needs to be considered.

VII. **Preterm Infants and Age-Weight Considerations**

Preterm infants are those born after a briefer-than-regular time period in the womb. Infants who are born after a regular gestation period of 38 to 42 weeks but who weigh less than 5½ pounds are called low-birth-weight infants. As intensive-care technology has improved, preterm babies have benefited considerably. Infants born with an identifiable problem have a poorer developmental future than those born without a recognizable problem. Social class differences are associated with the preterm infant's development. There is no solid evidence that preterm infants perform more poorly than full-term infants when they are assessed years later in school.

VIII. **Measures of Neonatal Health and Responsiveness**

For many years the Apgar Scale has been used to assess the newborn's health. A more recently developed test—the Brazelton Neonatal Behavioral Assessment Scale—is used for long-term neurological assessment. It assesses not only the newborn's neurological integrity but also social responsiveness. If the newborn is sluggish, Brazelton training is recommended.

IX. **Bonding**

There is evidence that bonding—establishment of a close mother-infant bond in the first hours or days after birth—is not critical for optimal development, although for some mother-infant pairs it may stimulate interaction after they leave the hospital.

Key Terms

zygote 104
germinal period 104
blastula 104
blastocyst 104
trophoblast 104
implantation 104
embryonic period 104
endoderm 105
ectoderm 105
mesoderm 105
placenta 105
umbilical cord 105

amnion 105
organogenesis 106
fetal period 106
teratology 110
fetal alcohol syndrome
    (FAS) 113
Leboyer method 116
Lamaze method 116
afterbirth 119
precipitate 119
anoxia 119

breech position 119
oxytocin 119
preterm infants 120
low-birth-weight
    infants 120
Apgar Scale 124
Brazelton Neonatal
    Behavioral Assessment
    Scale 124
Brazelton training 126
bonding 126

Suggested Readings

Brazelton, T. B., & Lester, B. M. (1982). *New approaches to developmental screenings of infants.* New York: Elsevier.

A group of experts on infant development relate new developments in the assessment of newborns.

Falkner, F., & Macy. C. (1980). *Pregnancy and birth.* New York: Harper & Row.

An easy-to-read description of experiences during pregnancy and the nature of childbearing.

Goldberg, S., & Devitto, B. A. (1983). *Born too soon: Preterm birth and early development.* San Francisco: W. H. Freeman.

Gives recent information about the nature of preterm infants and ways to socially interact with them.

Nilsson, L. (1966). *A child is born.* New York: Delacourt.

Contains an abundance of breathtaking photographs that take you inside the mother's womb to see the developmental unfolding of the zygote, embryo, and fetus.

III

Infancy

*A baby is the most complicated
object made by unskilled labor*

Anonymous

A s newborns, we were not empty-headed organisms. We had some basic reflexes, among them crying, kicking, and coughing. We slept a lot and occasionally we smiled, although the meaning of our first smiles was not entirely clear. We ate and we grew. We crawled and then we walked, a journey of a thousand miles beginning with a single step. Sometimes we conformed, sometimes others conformed to us. Our development was a continuous creation of more complex forms. Our helpless kind demanded the meeting eyes of love. We juggled the necessity of curbing our will with becoming what we could will freely.

Section 3 consists of three chapters. Chapter 5 focuses on physical development in infancy. Among its content is information about

—Exercise classes not being needed for babies
—What's good food for an adult is not necessarily good food for a baby
—The ability of the fetus to respond to *The Cat in the Hat*
—The young infant's ability to coordinate information from different senses

Chapter 6 focuses on cognitive development in infancy. Among its content is information about:

—Piaget's ideas on infant development
—The young infant's ability to imitate facial expressions
—Language's biological and environmental heritage
—Whether apes have language
—A modern-day wild child named Genie

Chapter 7 focuses on social development in infancy. Among its content is information about

—The role of parent-infant games such as peek-a-boo in the infant's development
—Attachment's influence
—Fathers' roles in different cultures
—What quality day care is
—The many faces of infants' emotions
—The shattered innocence of child abuse ♦

◇

*Systematic reasoning is something we could not,
as a species of individuals, do without. But neither, if we are to remain sane, can we do without
direct perception . . . of the inner and outer
world into which we have been born.*

Aldous Huxley

5

Physical Development

Thinking Critically
Other than moving a large object toward a newborn's head to see if the newborn responds to it, can you think of other techniques that could be used to determine whether a newborn can see or not?

T he creature has poor motor coordination and can move itself only with great difficulty. Its general behavior appears to be disorganized, and although it cries when uncomfortable, it uses few other vocalizations. In fact, it sleeps most of the time, about 16 to 17 hours a day. You are curious about this creature and want to know more about what it can do. You think to yourself, "I wonder if it can see? How could I find out?"

You obviously have a communication problem with the creature. You must devise a way that will allow the creature to "tell" you that it can see. While examining the creature one day, you make an interesting discovery. When you move a large object toward it, it moves its head backward, as if to avoid a collision with the object. The creature's head movement suggests that it has at least some vision.

In case you haven't already guessed, the creature you have been reading about is the human infant, and the role you played is that of a developmentalist interested in devising techniques to learn about the infant's visual perception. After years of work, scientists have developed research tools and methods sophisticated enough to examine the subtle abilities of infants and to interpret their complex actions. Videotape equipment makes it possible to investigate elusive behaviors, and high-speed computers make it possible to perform complex data analysis in minutes instead of months and years. Other sophisticated equipment is used to closely monitor respiration, heart rate, body movement, visual fixation, and sucking behavior, which provide clues to what is going on inside the infant.

Among the first things developmentalists were able to demonstrate was that infants have highly developed perceptual motor systems. Until recently, even nurses in maternity hospitals often believed that newborns were blind at birth, and they told this to mothers. Most parents were also told that their newborns could not taste, smell, or feel pain. As you will discover later in this chapter, we now know that newborns can see (albeit fuzzily), that they can taste, that they can smell, and that they can feel pain. Before we turn to the fascinating world of the infant's perception, we will discuss a number of ideas about physical development.

Physical Growth and Development in Infancy

How do infants respond to their world? What are an infant's states like? What is the nature of the infant's nutritional world? We will consider each of these questions in turn.

Reflexes

The newborn is not an empty-headed organism. Among other things, it has some basic reflexes that are genetically carried survival mechanisms. For example, the newborn has no fear of water; it will naturally hold its breath and contract its throat to keep water out.

Reflexes govern the newborn's movements, which are automatic and beyond the newborn's control. They are built-in reactions to certain stimuli. They provide young infants with adaptive responses to their environment before they have had the opportunity to learn. For instance, newborns automatically suck on an object placed in their mouth. This **sucking reflex** enables newborns to get nourishment before they have associated a nipple with food. The sucking reflex is an example of a reflex that is present at birth but later disappears. The *rooting reflex* also is present

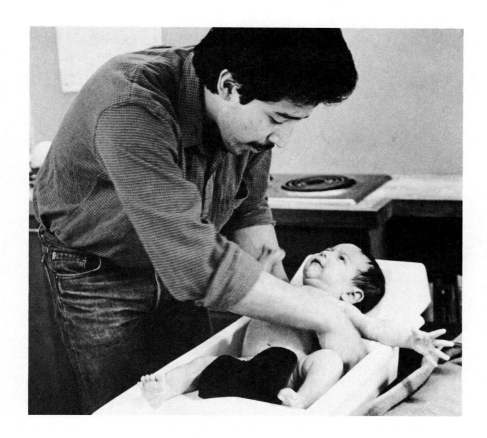

FIGURE 5.1 A Hispanic father bathing his 10-week-old son stimulates the Moro reflex. How can the father calm the infant when this reflex is stimulated?

at birth but disappears later; when the newborn's cheek is stroked or side of the mouth is touched, the newborn turns its head toward the side that was touched in an apparent effort to discover something to suck. The sucking and rooting reflexes disappear when the infant is about 3 to 4 months of age, and they are replaced by the infant's voluntary eating.

The rooting and sucking reflexes have survival value for newborn mammals, who must find the mother's breast to obtain nourishment. One of the most dramatic and frequent reflexes of the newborn—the **Moro reflex**—also has survival value (Figure 5.1). It is a vestige from our primate ancestry. If infants are handled roughly, hear loud noises, see bright lights, or feel sudden changes of position, they startle, arch their back, and throw their head back. Simultaneously, they fling out their arms and legs, then rapidly close them to the center of their body, and then flex them as if they were falling. As they cry, they startle, then cry because of the startle. This reflex—normal in all newborns—also tends to disappear at 3 to 4 months of age. Steady pressure on any part of the infant's body calms the infant. If you hold the infant's arm flexed at her shoulder, she will quiet down.

Some reflexes present in the newborn—coughing, blinking, and yawning, for example—persist throughout life. They are as important for the adult as they are for the infant. Other reflexes, though, disappear several months following birth as the infant's brain functions mature, and voluntary control over many behaviors develops. The movements of some reflexes eventually become incorporated into more complex, voluntary actions. One important example is the **grasping reflex,** which

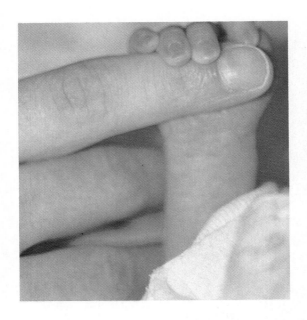

FIGURE 5.2 Shown here is the infant's powerful grasping reflex, which occurs when something touches the infant's palm.

occurs when something touches the infant's palms. The infant responds by grasping tightly (Figure 5.2). By the end of the third month, the grasping reflex diminishes and the infant shows a more voluntary grasp, which is often produced by visual stimuli. For example, when an infant sees a mobile whirling above its crib, it may reach out and try to grasp it. As its motor development becomes smoother, the infant will grasp objects, carefully manipulate them, and explore their qualities.

An overview of the main reflexes we have discussed, along with others, is given in Table 5.1. Let's look now at three important reflexes in greater detail—sucking, crying, and smiling.

Sucking

Sucking is an important means of obtaining nutrition, and it also is an enjoyable, soothing activity. An investigation by T. Berry Brazelton (1956) involved observations of infants for more than one year to determine the incidence of their sucking when they were not nursing and how their sucking changed as they grew older. More than 85 percent of the infants engaged in considerable sucking behavior unrelated to feeding. They sucked their fingers, their fists, and pacifiers. By the age of 1 year, most had stopped the sucking behavior.

Parents should not worry when infants suck their thumb, fist, or even a pacifier. Many parents, though, do begin to worry when thumb sucking persists into the preschool and elementary school years. As many as 40 percent of children continue to suck their thumbs after they have started school (Kessen, Haith, & Salapatek, 1970). Most developmentalists do not attach a great deal of significance to this behavior and are not aware of parenting strategies that might contribute to it. Individual differences in children's biological makeup may be involved to some degree in the late continuation of sucking behavior.

Infant researchers are interested in nonnutritive sucking for another reason. **Nonnutritive sucking** is used as a measure in a large number of research studies with young infants because young infants quit sucking when they attend to something, such as a picture or a vocalization. Nonnutritive sucking, then, is one of the ingenius ways developmentalists study the young infant's attention and learning.

TABLE 5.1	*Infant Reflexes*		
Reflex	**Stimulation**	**Infant's Response**	**Developmental Pattern**
Blinking	Flash of light, puff of air	Closes both eyes	Permanent
Babinski	Sole of foot stroked	Toes fan out, foot twists in	Disappears 9 mo.–1 yr.
Grasping	Palms touched	Grasps tightly	Weakens after 3 mo., disappears after 1 yr.
Moro (startle)	Sudden stimulation, such as hearing a loud noise or being dropped	Startles, arches back, throws head back, flings out arms and legs, then rapidly closes them to center of body	Disappears 3–4 mo.
Rooting	Stroke cheek or touch side of mouth	Head turns, mouth opens, sucking begins	Disappears 3–4 mo.
Stepping	Infant held above surface and feet lowered to touch surface	Feet move as if to walk	Disappears 3–4 mo.
Swimming	Put infant face down in water	Coordinated swimming movements	Disappears 6–7 mo.
Tonic neck	Place infant on back	Both hands are fisted and the head is usually turned to the right (sometimes called the "fencer's pose" because the infant looks like it is assuming a fencer's position)	Disappears 2 mo.

Nutritive sucking is the infant's route to nourishment. The sucking capabilities of neonates vary considerably; some newborns are efficient at forceful sucking and getting milk, whereas others are not so adept and get tired before they are full. Most newborns take several weeks to establish a sucking style that is coordinated with the way the mother is holding the infant, the way milk is coming out of the bottle or breast, and the infant's sucking speed and temperament.

Crying and Smiling

Crying and smiling are emotional behaviors that are important in the infant's communication with the world. Crying is the infant's first emotional or affective behavior. Newborns spend 6 to 7 percent of their day crying, although some infants cry more, and others less (Gotowiec & Ames, 1989). An infant's earliest cries are reflexive reactions to discomfort. The cries may signify information about the infant's biological state and possibly indicate distress. They are highly differentiated and have different patterns of frequency, intensity, and pause (Gustafson & Green, 1989).

Most adults can determine whether the infant's cries signify anger or pain. In one investigation, even when the crying segments were brief, adults could distinguish between aversive, arousing cries (more distressful) and those indicating hunger (less distressful). Even shortly after birth, infants' cries communicate information (Gustafson, 1989; Zeskind & Marshall, 1988).

Should a crying infant be given attention and be soothed, or does this spoil the infant? Many years ago, John Watson (1928) argued that parents spend too much time responding to the infant's crying and as a consequence reward the crying and increase its incidence. By contrast, recent arguments by ethologists such as Mary Ainsworth (1979) stress that it is difficult to respond too much to an infant's crying. Ainsworth views caregivers' responsiveness to infant crying as contributing to the

Thinking Critically
Where do you stand on the controversial issue of how much parents should respond to the cries of their infants? Should parents respond more quickly and warmly to the cries of newborns and young infants than older infants? Explain your answer.

formation of a secure attachment between the infant and the caregiver. One investigation (Bell & Ainsworth, 1972) found that mothers who responded quickly to their infant's crying at 3 months of age had infants who cried less later in the first year of life. Other research by behaviorists (Gewirtz, 1977) suggests that a quick, soothing response by a caregiver to crying increases the infant's subsequent crying. Controversy, then, still surrounds the issue of when and how caregivers should respond to infant crying.

Smiling is another important communicative behavior of the infant. Two kinds of smiling can be distinguished in infants—one reflexive, the other social. At some point in the first month after birth, an expression appears on the infant's face that adults call a smile; this is a **reflexive smile** because it does not occur in response to external stimuli. The reflexive smile occurs most often during irregular patterns of sleep and does not appear when the infant is in an alert state. A **social smile,** which typically occurs in response to a face, usually does not occur until 2 to 3 months of age (Emde, Gaensbauer, & Harmon, 1976). Some researchers believe that social smiling appears earlier than 2 months of age, arguing that an infant grins in response to voices as early as 3 weeks of age (Sroufe & Waters, 1976). The power and importance of the infant's smiles were appropriately summed up by famous attachment theorist John Bowlby (1969), "Can we doubt that the more and better an infant smiles the better is he loved and cared for? It is fortunate for their survival that babies are so designed by Nature that they beguile and enslave mothers."

Much more about Bowlby's fascinating ideas on attachment appear in Chapter 7, as well as more information about the infant's emotional worlds.

States

To chart and understand the infant's development, developmentalists have constructed different classification schemes of the infant's states (Berg & Berg, 1987; Brown, 1964 Colombo, Moss, & Horowitz, in press). One classification scheme (Brown, 1964) describes seven infant states:

1. *Deep sleep.* The infant lies motionless with eyes closed, has regular breathing, makes no vocalization, and does not respond to outside stimulation.

2. *Regular sleep.* The infant moves very little, breathing might be raspy or involve wheezing, and respirations may be normal or move from normal to irregular.

3. *Disturbed sleep.* There is a variable amount of movement, the infant's eyelids are closed but might flutter, breathing is irregular, and there may be some squawks, sobs and sighs.

4. *Drowsy.* The infant's eyes are open or partly open and appear glassy, there is little movement (although startles and free movement may occur), vocalizations are more regular than in disturbed sleep, and some transitional sounds may be made.

5. *Alert activity.* This is the state most often viewed by parents as being awake. The infant's eyes are open and bright, a variety of free movements are shown, fretting may occur, skin may redden, and there may be irregular breathing when the infant feels tension.

Infancy

6. *Alert and focused.* This kind of attention is often seen in older children but is unusual in the neonate. The child's eyes are open and bright. Some motor activity may occur, but it is integrated around a specific activity. This state may occur when focusing on some sound or visual stimulus.

7. *Inflexibly focused.* In this state, the infant is awake but does not react to external stimuli; two examples are sucking and wild crying. During wild crying the infant may thrash about, but the eyes are closed as screams pour out.

Using classification schemes such as the one just described, researchers have identified many different aspects of the infant's development. One such aspect is the sleeping-waking cycle. Each night, something lures us from our work, our play, our loved ones; the sandman's spell claims more of our time than any other pursuit. When we were infants, sleep consumed even more of our time than it does now. Newborns sleep for 16 to 17 hours a day, although some sleep more, and others less. The range is from a low of about 10 hours to a high of about 21 hours (Parmalee, Wenner, & Schulz, 1964). The longest period of sleep is not always between 11 P.M. and 7 A.M. While total sleep remains somewhat consistent for young infants, the patterns of sleep during the day do not always follow a rhythmic pattern. An infant might change from sleeping several long bouts of 7 or 8 hours to three or four shorter sessions only several hours in duration. By about 1 month of age, most infants have begun to sleep longer at night, and by about 4 months of age, they usually have moved closer to adultlike sleep patterns, spending their longest span of sleep at night and their longest span of waking during the day (Coons & Guilleminault, 1984).

However, it is common for 9-to-10-month-old infants to wake up in the middle of the night and start crying. Sometimes the crying results from some type of illness or other physically based distress (Ferber, 1989; Thorpy & Glovinsky, 1989). Most of the time, though, middle-of-the-night crying occurs because the infant is alone, usually in a dark or dimly lit room, is not very sleepy, and does not have much to do. At this point, infants use the one tool that has eliminated boredom in the past— crying. Middle-of-the-night crying is usually motivated by the infant's desire to have the company of others rather than to be alone, awake, and bored. This can become a serious inconvenience to many parents. Some couples spend long hours awake in the wee hours trying to cope with a wide-awake baby. Burton White (1988) described one such encounter. A dentist in Georgia called him long-distance. In a mildly embarrassed manner, the dentist said that he and his wife were taking a minimum of two automobile rides after midnight and before 6 A.M. each night. Like others in the same situation, they could not believe they had gotten themselves into this predicament. They finally went to a pediatrician who checked the baby's health, which was fine. He told the parents the baby was not crying at night because it was hurt or in pain. The pediatrician told them to simply let the baby cry it out at this age. This wasn't easy for the parents to do, but ignoring their 10-month old's crying in the middle of the night quickly led to much quieter nights for the parents and the infant.

Infant researchers are intrigued by different forms of infant sleep. This intrigue focuses on how much of the infant's sleep is **REM sleep** (rapid eye movement sleep) (Berg & Berg, 1987; Carskadon & Dement, 1989). Children and adults who have been awakened in sleep laboratories after being in a state of REM sleep frequently report that they have been dreaming (McCarley, 1989). Most adults spend about one-fifth of their night in REM sleep, and REM sleep usually appears about

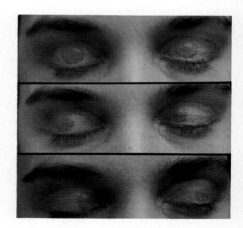

FIGURE 5.3 During REM sleep, an infant's eyes move rapidly. During REM sleep, an adult's dreams increase dramatically. About one-half of an infant's sleep is REM sleep. What might be the functions of REM sleep in the infant's development?

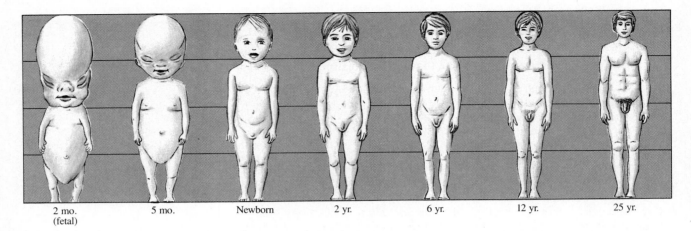

| 2 mo. (fetal) | 5 mo. | Newborn | 2 yr. | 6 yr. | 12 yr. | 25 yr. |

FIGURE 5.4   Changes in body form and proportion during prenatal and postnatal growth.

From Patten, Human Embryology. *Copyright © 1933 McGraw-Hill Book Company, New York, N.Y.*

one hour after non-REM sleep. However, about half of an infant's sleep is REM sleep; infants often begin their sleep cycle with REM rather than non-REM sleep. By the time infants reach 3 months of age, the percentage of time spent in REM sleep falls to about 40 percent and no longer does REM sleep begin the sleep cycle. The large amount of time spent in REM sleep may provide young infants with added self-stimulation, since they spend less time awake than older infants. REM sleep also may promote the brain's development.

Physical Growth and Motor Development

Physically, newborns are limited. They are tiny; from head to heels, they are only about 20 inches long and weigh 7 pounds. They are bound by where they are put, and they are at the mercy of their bodily needs. Their heart beats twice as fast as an adult's—120 beats a minute—and they breathe twice as fast as an adult does—about 33 times a minute. They urinate as many as 18 times and move their bowels from 4 to 7 times in 24 hours. On the average, they are alert and comfortable for only about 30 minutes in a 4-hour period.

The infant's pattern of physical development in the first two years of life is exciting. At birth, the neonate has a gigantic head (relative to the rest of the body) that flops around in uncontrollable fashion; she possesses reflexes that are dominated by evolutionary movements. In the span of 12 months, the infant becomes capable of sitting anywhere, standing, stooping, climbing, and usually walking. During the second year, growth decelerates,but rapid increases in such activities as running and climbing take place.

Among the important changes in growth are those involving the cephalocaudal and proximodistal sequences, gross and fine motor skills, rhythmic motor behavior, and the brain. We examine each of these in turn.

Cephalocaudal and Proximodistal Sequences

The **cephalocaudal pattern** means that the greatest growth always occurs at the top—the head—with physical growth in size, weight, and feature differentiation gradually working its way down from top to bottom (for example, neck, shoulders, middle trunk, and so on). This same pattern occurs in the head area because the top parts of the head—the eyes and brain—grow faster than the lower parts—such as the jaw. As illustrated in Figure 5.4, an extraordinary proportion of the total body is occupied by the head at birth, but by the time the individual reaches maturity, this proportion is almost cut in half.

The Precocious Motor Skills of African Infants

African infants routinely surpass American infants in their rate of learning to sit and walk, but not in learning to crawl or climb stairs. When many African parents are observed interacting with their infants, they provide the infants with experiences that seem intended to teach sitting and walking. They prop young infants in a sitting position supported by rolled blankets, exercise the newborn's walking reflex, and bounce babies on their feet. However, they discourage crawling, and stair-climbing skills may be limited because of the absence of stairs (Rogoff & Morelli, 1989).

In one investigation, observations of 24 young infants in Kenya revealed that in contrast to most American newborn babies, the Kenyan babies maintained excellent motor coordination as they were handled (Keefer & others, 1978). The researchers concluded that the ability of the young Kenyan infants to control their motor behavior was due in part to the extensive motor interaction between the infants and those around them. At birth, Kenyan newborns are jostled in outstretched arms. During the day they are played with vigorously, and during the weeks after birth they are picked up by one arm to hoist them onto their mother's hip. They are tossed into the air after a bath to shake off excess water. The motor precocity of African infants may be related to the early frequent stimulation they experience in their environment. ♦

Kenyan infants, such as the one shown here, maintain excellent motor coordination. During the day they are played with vigorously, stimulation that likely helps their motor development.

A second pattern of development—**the proximodistal pattern**— means that growth starts at the center of the body and moves toward the extremities. An example of this is the early maturation of muscular control of the trunk and arms as compared with that of the hands and fingers.

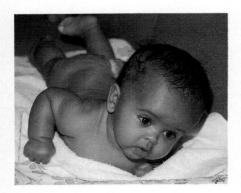

At about 4 months of age, infants develop the ability to hold their chest up in a face-down position.

Growth is the only evidence of life.

John Henry, Cardinal Newman,
Apologia pro Vita Sua, 1864

The 11-month-old is taking her first steps. Eleven months is now the average age at which American infants begin to walk, although the actual age at which such milestones take place varies as much as 4 months.

A baby is an angel whose wings decrease as his legs increase.

French Proverb

Gross and Fine Motor Skills

In addition to cephalocaudal and proximodistal growth patterns, we also can describe growth in **gross motor skills**—those involving large muscle activities such as moving one's arms and walking, and **fine motor skills**—those involving more finely tuned movements like finger dexterity.

At birth, the infant has no appreciable coordination of the chest or arms. By about 4 months of age, however, two striking accomplishments occur in turn. The first is the infant's ability to hold the chest up in a face-down position (at about 2 months). The other is the ability to reach for objects placed within the infant's direct line of vision, without making any consistent contact with the objects (because the two hands don't work together and the coordination of vision and grasping is not yet possible). A little later, at about 3 to 4 months of age, there is further progress in motor control. By 5 months, the infant can sit up with some support and grasp objects. By 6 months, the infant can roll over when lying down in a prone position.

At birth, the newborn is capable of supporting some weight with the legs. This is proven by formal tests of muscular strength. These tests use a specially constructed apparatus to measure the infant's leg resistance as the foot is pulled away by a calibrated spring device. This ability is also evidenced by the infant's partial support of its own weight when held upright by an adult. If the infant is given enough support by the adult, some forward movement is seen in a built-in stepping reflex, which disappears in a few months. Each leg is lifted, moved forward, and placed down, as if the infant were taking a series of steps. However, the sequence lasts only two to three steps, and, of course, the infant does not have sufficient balance or strength to execute the movement independently.

By about 6 months of age, infants can sit unaided. By about 7 months, they can pull to sit unaided and crawl or scoot. By about 8 months, they can pull to a stand. By about 11 months, they can walk unaided. By about 13 months, they can ride four-wheel wagons. And by about 26 months, they can ride a tricycle (White, 1988). The average age of infant motor accomplishments in the first year of life are shown in Figure 5.5. The actual month at which the milestones occur varies as much as 2 to 4 months, especially among older infants. What remains fairly uniform, however, is the sequence of accomplishments. An important implication of these infant motor accomplishments is the increasing degree of independence they bring. Infants can explore their environment more extensively and initiate social interaction with caregivers and peers.

Not content with their infants reaching the motor development milestones at an average rate, many American parents want to accelerate their infants' physical skills. Is this a wise practice? To learn more about this intriguing question, turn to Children 5.1.

Rhythmic Motor Behavior

During the first year of life, repetitive movement of the limbs, torso, and head is common. Such **rhythmic motor behavior**—kicking, rocking, waving, bouncing, banging, rubbing, scratching, and swaying—has intrigued developmentalists for many years. These infant motor behaviors stand out not only because they occur frequently, but also because of the pleasure infants seem to derive from performing the acts.

Explanations of rhythmic motor behavior are numerous. Arnold Gesell (1954) saw rocking as a specific stage of development but warned that persistent rhythmic motor behavior was a sign of developmental delay or an impoverished environment. Jean Piaget (1967) referred to kicking and waving as a stage of sensorimotor development when infants try to repeat a behavior that has an interesting effect on

FIGURE 5.5 The development of posture and locomotion in infants. The month shown is the average. The actual month at which such milestones occur varies as much as 4 months.

the environment. Psychoanalytic theorists interpret rocking as the infant's attempt to establish relations with an aloof mother. And pediatricians suggest that head banging is due to a bad temper.

More recently, Esther Thelen (1981, 1987) argued that rhythmic motor behavior serves an important adaptive function for infants in the first year of life. She believes that it is an important transition between uncoordinated activity and complex, coordinated motor behavior. She conducted extraordinarily detailed observations of 20 normal infants from the time they were 4 weeks old until they were 1 year old. More than 16,000 bouts of rhythmic behavior were observed. Infants spent about 5 percent of their time in rhythmic motor behavior, although some infants at some ages spent as much as 40 percent of the time they were observed in rhythmic motor behavior. The 47 distinct movements observed included variations of kicking, waving, bouncing, scratching, banging, rubbing, thrusting, swaying, and twisting. When stereotyped movements were grouped by body part and posture, their frequencies showed certain developmental profiles over the first year, as shown in Figure 5.6. Rhythmic leg behavior gradually increased at about 1 month, peaked at 5 to 6 months, and then declined. If all rhythmic cycles are summed, the age of peak frequency was 6 to 7 months, with a small decline in the last few months of the first year.

Babies Don't Need Exercise Classes

Six-month-old Andrew doesn't walk yet, but his mother wants him to develop his physical skills optimally. Three times a week she takes him to a recreation center where he participates with other infants in swimming and gymnastics classes. With the increased interest of today's adults in aerobic exercise and fitness, some parents have tried to give their infants a head start on becoming physically fit and physically talented. However, in 1988, the American Academy of Pediatricians issued a statement that recommends against structured exercise classes for babies. Pediatricians are seeing more bone fractures and dislocations and more muscle strains in babies now than in the past. They point out that when an adult is stretching and moving an infant's limbs, it is easy to go beyond the infant's physical limits without knowing it.

The physical fitness classes for infants range from passive fare—with adults putting infants through the paces—to programs called "aerobic" because they demand crawling, tumbling, and ball skills. However, exercise for infants is not aerobic. They cannot adequately stretch their bodies to achieve aerobic benefits. Even swimming classes before early childhood have a down side. Children cannot cognitively learn to swim until they are 3 or 4 years of age. It is not uncommon to observe 4-year-olds who have had swim classes since infancy suddenly terrified of the water because for the first time they understand that they could drown.

For optimal physical development, babies simply need touch, face-to-face contact, and brightly colored toys they can manipulate. If infants are not couch potatoes who are babysat extensively by a television set, their normal play will provide them with all the fitness training they need. ♦

Shown here are mothers and their babies in a swimming class. Pediatricians and child psychologists recommend that exercise classes, and even swimming classes, for infants are not needed, possibly having more negative than positive outcomes.

A dramatic confirmation of the developmental importance of rhythmic motor behavior was documented by Selma Fraiberg (1977) with blind infants. Motor development in blind infants was characteristically uneven. Blind infants attained postural milestones such as sitting alone, "bridging" on hands and knees, and standing at ages comparable to sighted infants. Their locomotor development was severely delayed, however, probably because of a lack of visual motivation to move foward. In normal infants, crawling follows soon after the infant assumes the hands-and-knees posture. In blind infants, there may be a delay of four or more months between these events. Nonetheless, all the infants rocked vigorously in sitting, hands-and-knees, and standing postures; but unlike in normal infants, this rocking did not disappear.

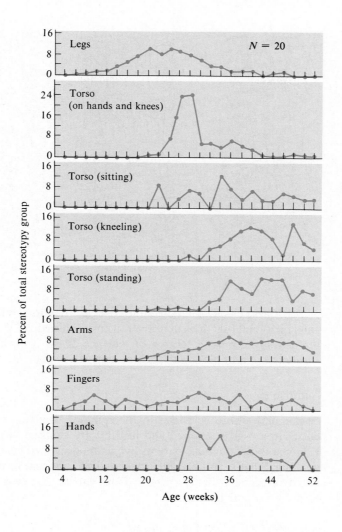

FIGURE 5.6   Frequency of rhythmic motor behavior in the first year of life. Frequencies are expressed as a percentage of the total bouts of rhythmic behavior observed at each age. The bouts are grouped by body parts.

The Brain

As the infant walks, talks, runs, shakes a rattle, smiles, and frowns, changes in the brain are occurring. Consider that the infant began life as a single cell and that in nine months was born with a brain and nervous system that contained some 10 to 100 billion nerve cells. Indeed, at birth, the infant probably had all of the nerve cells—called neurons—it was going to have in its entire life. But at birth and in early infancy, the connectedness of all of these neurons was impoverished. As shown in Figure 5.7, as the infant moves from birth to 2 years of age, the interconnections of neurons increase dramatically as the dendrites (the receiving part) of the neuron branch out.

Undoubtedly, neurotransmitters are changing through the prenatal period and during the infant years too. Neurotransmitters are the tiny chemical substances that carry information across gaps from one neuron to the next. Little is known about neurotransmitter changes in infancy, although changes in one important neurotransmitter—dopamine—has been documented in monkeys (Goldman-Rakic & others, 1983). The concentration of dopamine in the prefrontal lobe—the area of the brain involved in higher cognitive functions such as problem solving—peaks at 5 months of age, declines until about 18 to 24 months, and then increases again at 2 to 3 years

FIGURE 5.7 The development of dendritic spreading at birth, 3 months, 6 months, and 24 months in the cerebral cortex of the human infant. Note the increase in connectedness between neurons over the course of the first two years of life.

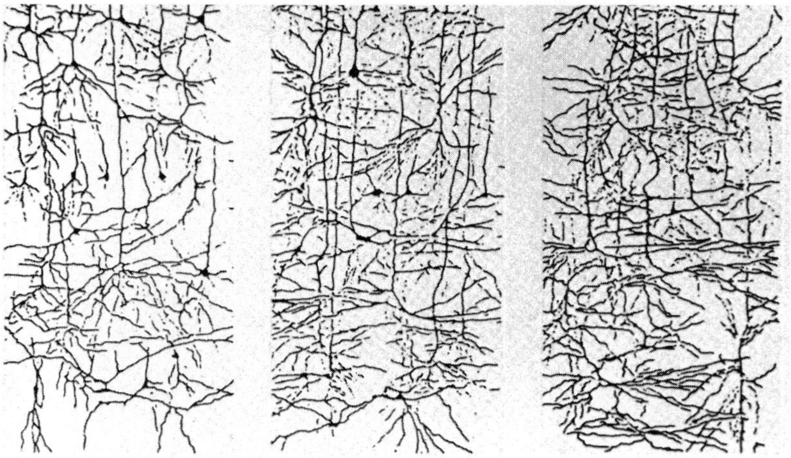

3 Months   15 Months   24 Months

of age. These changes in dopamine concentration may reflect a switch from growth and nutritional functions to neurotransmitter function for this substance. Such speculation only begins to scratch the surface of the important role neurotransmitter substances might play in the brain's early development.

Nutrition

Four-month-old Robert lives in Bloomington, Indiana, with his middle-class parents. He is well nourished and healthy. By contrast, 4-month-old Nikita lives in Ethiopia. Nikita and his parents live in impoverished conditions. Nikita is so poorly nourished that he has become emaciated and lies near death. Our coverage of infant nutrition begins with information about nutritional needs and eating behavior, then turns to malnutrition.

Nutritional Needs and Eating Behavior

The importance of adequate energy and nutrient intake consumed in a loving and supportive environment during the infant years cannot be overstated (Pipes, 1988). From birth to 1 year of age, human infants triple their weight and increase their length by 50 percent. Individual differences of infants in nutrient reserves, body composition, growth rates, and activity patterns make defining actual nutrient needs difficult. However, because parents need guidelines, nutritionists recommend that infants consume approximately 50 calories per day for each pound they weigh—more than twice an adult's requirement per pound.

Human milk, or an alternative formula if needed, is the baby's source of nutrients and energy for the first 4 to 6 months. For years, developmentalists and nutritionists have debated whether breast-feeding of an infant has substantial benefits over bottle-feeding. The growing consensus is that breast-feeding is better for the baby's health (Lozoff, 1989; Walton & Vallelunga, 1989; Worthington-Roberts, 1988). Breast-feeding provides milk that is clean and digestible and helps to immunize the newborn from disease. Breast-fed babies gain weight more rapidly than do bottle-fed babies. However, only about one-half of mothers nurse newborns, and even fewer continue to nurse their infants after several months. Mothers who work

cathy®

by Cathy Guisewite

IN ORDER TO SEND MESSAGES EFFICIENTLY, A PERSON'S NERVE CELLS MUST BE COATED WITH A SHEATH OF PROTEIN CALLED "MYELIN".

WITH SENSORY STIMULATION EXERCISES, I CAN NOT ONLY SPEED THE MYELINATION PROCESS IN MY UNBORN BABY, HAVING A DIRECT EFFECT ON COORDINATION AND INTELLECT...

...BUT I CAN ACTUALLY ENCOURAGE THE ELONGATION OF AXONS AND BRANCHING OF DENDRITES THAT ARE SO ESSENTIAL FOR THE GROWTH OF MY BABY'S BRAIN AND DEVELOPMENT OF ITS ENTIRE BODY!

ALL I EVER DID WAS KNIT YOU BOOTIES!!

Arguments continue to swirl about whether breast-feeding (left) or bottle-feeding (right) is best for an infant. Experts argue that breast-feeding is more likely to insure that the infant's nutritional requirements are met, but no long-term negative effects of bottle feeding have been documented in American children.

outside the home may find it impossible to breast-feed their young infant for many months. Even though breast-feeding provides more ideal nutrition for the infant, there is no evidence that the infant is psychologically harmed when bottle-fed.

Some years ago, controversy also surrounded the issue of whether a baby should be fed on demand or on a regular schedule. The famous behaviorist John Watson (1928) argued that scheduled feeding was superior because it increased the child's orderliness. An example of a recommended schedule for newborns was 4 ounces of formula every six hours. In recent years, demand feeding—in which the timing and amount of feeding are determined by the infant—has become more popular.

The maturation of oral and fine motor skills indicate appropriate ages for the introduction of semisolid and solid foods. Current recommendations are to introduce semisolid foods at 4 to 6 months of age and finger foods when infants reach out, grasp, and bring items to their mouth. When munching and rotary chewing begin, the use of soft-cooked foods is appropriate. Infants can begin to drink from a cup with help between 9 and 12 months of age.

What's Good Food for an Adult Can Be Bad Food for a Baby

Some yuppie parents may not know the recipe for a healthy baby: whole milk and an occasional cookie, along with fruits, vegetables, and other foods. Some affluent, well-educated parents almost starve their babies by feeding them the lowfat, low-calorie diet they eat themselves. Diets designed for adult weight loss and prevention of heart disease may actually retard growth and development in babies. Fat is very important for babies. Nature's food—the mother's breast milk—is not low in fat or calories. No child under the age of 2 should be consuming skim milk.

In a recent investigation, seven cases were documented in which babies 7 to 22 months of age were unwittingly undernourished by their health-conscious parents (Lifshitz & others, 1987). In some instances, the parents had been fat themselves and were determined that their child was not going to be. The well-meaning parents substituted vegetables, skim milk, and other lowfat foods for what they called junk food. However, for infants, broccoli is not always a good substitute for a cookie. For growing infants, high-calorie, high-energy foods are part of a balanced diet.   ♦

What hazards might the current trends in diet foods and health preoccupation on the part of parents have when it comes to choosing foods for their infants?

There has been speculation that formula feeding and the early introduction of semisolid foods might contribute to excessive intakes of energy and the development of infant obesity. It also has been speculated that obese infants often become obese adults. However, neither breast- nor bottle-feeding, nor the age of introduction of semisolid foods, are causes of obesity. Obesity in infancy also has not been a very good predictor of obesity in adulthood (Stunkard, 1989).

In the 1980s, we have become extremely nutrition conscious. Does the same type of nutrition that makes us healthy adults also make young infants healthy? For the answer to this question, turn to Children 5.2.

Malnutrition in Infancy

Severe malnutrition is still common among infants in many parts of the world. In the infant's first year of life, severe protein-calorie deficiency can cause **marasmus,** a wasting away of body tissues. The infant becomes grossly underweight, and the muscles atrophy (Figure 5.8). The main cause of marasmus is early weaning from breast milk to inadequate nutrients such as unsuitable and unsanitary cow's milk formula. Something that looks like milk but is not, also may be used, usually some form of tapioca or rice. In many of the world's developing countries, mothers used to breast-feed their infants for at least two years. To become more modern, they began to stop their breast-feeding of infants much earlier and replace it with bottle-feeding. Comparisons of breast-fed and bottle-fed infants in countries such as Afghanistan, Haiti, Ghana, and Chile document that the rate of infant deaths is much greater among bottle-fed infants than breast-fed infants, with bottle-fed infants sometimes dying at a rate five times higher than breast-fed infants (Grant, 1988).

Even if not fatal, severe and lengthy malnutrition is detrimental to physical, cognitive, and social development. And sometimes even moderate malnutrition can produce subtle difficulties in development. In one investigation of Guatemalan children, those who were chronically malnourished early in their development were shorter in stature and slower in cognitive growth in middle and late childhood (Bogin & MacVean, 1983). In another investigation, two groups of extremely malnourished black South African 1-year-old infants were studied. The children in one group were given adequate nourishment during the next six years; no intervention took place in the lives of the other group. After the seventh year, the poorly nourished group of children performed much less well on tests of intelligence than did the adequately nourished group (Bayley, 1970). In yet another investigation, the diets of rural Guatemalan infants were associated with their social development at the time they entered elementary school (Barrett, Radke-Yarrow, & Klein, 1982). Children whose mothers had been given nutritional supplements during pregnancy and who themselves had been given more nutritious, high-calorie foods in their first two years of life were more active, involved, helpful with their peers, less anxious, and happier than their counterparts who were not given nutritional supplements. The rural Guatemalan infants were only mildly undernourished in infancy, suggesting how important it is for parents to be attentive to the nutritional needs of their infants.

Up to this point, we have discussed many ideas about physical development in infancy. The main points in this discussion are summarized in Concept Table 5.1. Next, we will explore the infant's fascinating sensory and perceptual development.

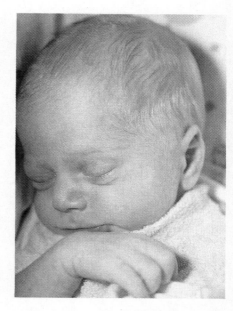

FIGURE 5.8   This malnourished infant is underweight, and its muscles have atrophied.

Thinking Critically
If and when you become a parent, what considerations would you have about the nutrition your infant gets? How important do you feel breast-feeding is for the infant's development? Explain.

Children Living Hungry in America

Harlingen, Texas, is a heavily Chicano city of approximately 40,000 near the Rio Grande. At Su Clinica ("Your Clinic"), which serves many Chicano residents, poverty and unemployment are evident in the waiting list of 800 families needing the low-cost care provided by the clinic. Many of the Chicanos working in Texas agriculture receive no health-care benefits. Few make even the minimum wage. Farm workers usually get less than $1.50 an hour for working long days in the pesticide-infected fields. The infant mortality rate for the region is listed as good, but this figure is wrong. Many of the deaths are not counted. A baby dies. It is buried. People outside the family seldom know. Many infants and young children here experience growth problems because they do not get enough to eat. This is not unique to Harlingen, Texas; many other locations in the United States have their share of impoverished families who have difficulty making ends meet and putting food on the table. Hunger and poverty are seen in children of poor Mississippi tenant farmers, of laid-off coal miners in West Virginia, of neglected parents in the ghettos of New York and Chicago. In many instances, these children are the victims of silent undernutrition, less dramatic than in Africa or Bangladesh, but no less real (Brown & Pizer, 1987). ◆

Hunger and poverty are more common in America than we often realize. Shown above are the children of a poor southern tenant farmer.

Physical Growth and Development in Infancy

Concept	Processes and Related Ideas	Characteristics and Description
Reflexes	Their nature	The newborn is no longer viewed as a passive, empty-headed organism. Newborns are limited physically, though, and reflexes—automatic movements—govern the newborn's behavior.
	Sucking	For infants, sucking is an important means of obtaining nutrition, as well as a pleasurable, soothing activity. Nonnutritive sucking is of interest to researchers because it provides a means of evaluating attention.
	Crying and smiling	Crying and smiling are affective behaviors that are important in the infant's communication with the world.
States	Classification	Researchers have put together different classification systems; one classification involved seven infant state categories, including deep sleep, drowsy, alert and focused, and inflexibly focused.
	The sleeping-waking cycle	Newborns usually sleep 16 to 17 hours a day. By 4 months, they approach adultlike sleeping patterns. REM sleep, during which children and adults are most likely to dream, occurs much more in early infancy than in childhood and adulthood. The high percentage of REM sleep—about half of neonatal sleep—may be a self-stimulatory device, or it may promote brain development.
Physical Growth and Motor Development	Cephalocaudal and proximodistal sequences	The cephalocaudal pattern is growth from the top down; the proximodistal pattern is growth from the center out.
	Gross motor and fine motor skills	Gross motor skills involve large muscle activity, as in walking. Fine motor skills involve more fine-grained activities such as manual dexterity. Both gross and fine motor skills undergo extensive change in the first two years of development.
	Rhythmic motor behavior	During the first year, rhythmic motor behavior, involving rapid repetitious movement of the limbs, torso, and head, is common; it seems to represent an important adaptive transition in development.
	The brain	There is a great deal of brain growth in infancy as well as in prenatal development. Dendritic spreading is dramatic in the first two years. Some important changes in neurotransmitters probably also take place, although these changes are just beginning to be charted.
Nutrition	Nutritional needs and eating behavior	Infants need to consume approximately 50 calories per day for each pound they weigh. Human milk, or an alternative formula, is the baby's source of nutrients for the first six months. The growing consensus is that breast-feeding is superior to bottle-feeding, but the increase in working mothers has meant fewer breast-fed babies. Parents are increasingly using a demand feeding schedule. The maturation of oral and fine motor skills indicate appropriate ages for introducing semisolid and solid foods. Obesity in infancy has not been a good predictor of obesity in adulthood. Infants should not be placed on lowfat, low-calorie diets.
	Malnutrition in infancy	Severe infant malnutrition is still prevalent in many parts of the world. Severe protein-calorie deficiency can cause marasmus, a wasting away of body tissues. It is mainly caused by early weaning from breast milk. Even if not fatal, severe and lengthy malnutrition is detrimental to physical, cognitive, and social development.

Sensory and Perceptual Development

At the beginning of this chapter, you read about how the newborn comes into the world equipped with sensory capacities. But what are sensation and perception anyway? Can a newborn see, and if so, what can it perceive? And what about the other senses—hearing, smell, taste, touch, and pain? What are they like in the newborn? These are among the intriguing questions we now explore.

What Are Sensation and Perception?

How does a newborn know that her mother's skin is soft rather than rough? How does a 5-year-old know what color her hair is? How does an 8-year-old know that summer is warmer than winter? How does a 10-year-old know that a firecracker is louder than a cat's meow? Infants and children "know" these things because of their senses. All information comes to the infant through the senses. Without vision, hearing, touch, taste, smell, and other senses, the infant's brain would be isolated from the world; the infant would live in dark silence, a tasteless, colorless, feelingless void.

Sensation occurs when information contacts sensory receptors—the eyes, ears, tongue, nostrils, and skin. The sensation of hearing occurs when waves of pulsating air are collected by the outer ear and transmitted through the bones of the inner ear to the auditory nerve. The sensation of vision occurs as rays of light contact the two eyes and become focused on the retina. **Perception** is the interpretation of what is sensed. The information about physical events that contact the ears may be interpreted as musical sounds, for example. The physical energy transmitted to the retina may be interpreted as a particular color, pattern, or shape.

Visual Perception

How do we see? Anyone who has ever taken pictures while on vacation appreciates the miracle of perception. The camera is no match for it. Consider a favorite scenic spot that you visited and photographed some time in the past. Compare your memory of this spot to your snapshot. Although your memory may be faulty, there is little doubt that the richness of your perceptual experience is not captured in the picture. The sense of depth that you felt at this spot probably is not conveyed by the snapshot. Neither is the sublety of the colors you perceived nor the intricacies of textures and shapes. Human vision is complex, and its development is complex, too.

Psychologists William James (1890) called the newborn's perceptual world a blooming, buzzing confusion. Was James right? A century later we can safely say that he was wrong. To sum up the research on infant perception with one simple statement: Infants' perception of visual information is *much* more advanced than previously thought.

Our tour of visual perception begins with the pioneering work of Robert Fantz (1958, 1961). Fantz placed infants in a "looking chamber," which has two visual displays on the ceiling of the chamber above the infant's head (Figure 5.9). An experimenter viewed the infant's eyes by looking through a peephole. If the infant was fixating on one of the displays, the experimenter could see the display's reflection in the infant's eyes (Figure 5.10). This allowed the experimenter to determine how long the infant looked at each display. The findings were simple: When presented with a pair of visual displays, an infant looked longer at one than the other.

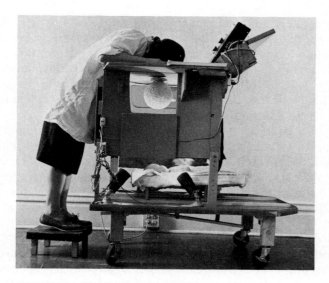

FIGURE 5.9 The "looking chamber" has been used to study visual preference in infants.

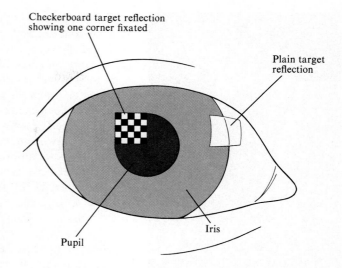

FIGURE 5.10 An infant's eye as seen by the experimenter in the test chamber when the infant is visually exposed to checked and plain squares. The more the target reflection overlays the pupil, the greater is the degree of fixation.

For instance, an infant looked longer at a display of stripes than at a solid gray patch. This demonstrates that newborns can see and also that they can tell the difference between two dissimilar objects. The newborn's visual world is not the blooming, buzzing confusion James imagined (Aslin, 1987).

Just how well can infants see? The newborn's vision is estimated to be 20/200 to 20/600 on the well-known Snellen chart that you are tested with when you have your eyes examined. This is about 10 to 30 times lower than normal adult vision (20/20). But by 6 months of age, vision is 20/100 or better (Banks & Salapatek, 1983).

The human face is perhaps the most important visual pattern for the newborn to perceive. The infant masters a sequence of steps in progressing toward full perceptual appreciation of the face (Gibson, 1969). At about 3½ weeks, the infant is fascinated with the eyes, perhaps because the infant notices simple perceptual features such as dots, angles, and circles. At 1 to 2 months of age, the infant notices and perceives contour. At 2 months and older, the infant begins to differentiate facial features: the eyes are distinguished from other parts of the face, the mouth is noticed, and movements of the mouth draw attention to it. By 5 months of age, the infant has detected other facial features—its plasticity, its solid, three-dimensional surface, the oval shape of the head, the orientation of the eyes and the mouth. Beyond 6 months of age, the infant distinguishes familiar faces from unfamiliar faces—mother from stranger, masks from real faces, and so on.

How early can infants perceive depth? To investigate this question, Eleanor Gibson and Richard Walk (1960) conducted a classic experiment. They constructed a miniature cliff with a drop-off covered by glass. The motivation for this experiment happened when Gibson was eating a picnic lunch on the edge of the Grand Canyon.

FIGURE 5.11 A child's depth perception is tested on the visual cliff. The apparatus consists of a board laid across a sheet of heavy glass, with a patterned material directly beneath the glass on one side and several feet below it on the other. Placed on the center board, the child crawls to his mother across the "shallow" side. Called from the "deep" side, he pats the glass, but despite this tactual evidence that the "cliff" is in fact a solid surface, he refuses to cross over to the mother.

She wondered whether an infant looking over the canyon's rim would perceive the dangerous drop-off and back up. In their laboratory, Gibson and Walk placed infants on the edge of a visual cliff (Figure 5.11) and had their mothers coax them to crawl out onto the glass. Most infants would not crawl out on the glass, choosing instead to remain on the shallow side, indicating that they could perceive depth. Because the 6-to 14-month-old infants had extensive visual experience, this research did not answer the question of whether depth perception is innate.

Exactly how early in life does depth perception develop? Since younger infants do not crawl, this question is difficult to answer. Research with 2-to 4-month-old infants shows differences in heart rate when the infants are placed directly on the deep side of the visual cliff instead of the shallow side of the cliff (Campos, Langer, & Krowitz, 1970). However, an alternative interpretation is that young infants respond to differences in some visual characteristic of the deep and shallow cliffs, with no actual knowledge of depth.

We have discussed a good deal of research on visual perception in infancy. Many fundamental aspects of vision are in working order by birth, and many others are present by several months of age (Granrud, 1989). Yet, perception is not complete by 1 or 2 years of age. Many aspects of perception continue to grow more efficient and accurate during the childhood years (Bornstein, 1988).

Hearing

Immediately after birth, infants can hear, although their sensory thresholds are somewhat higher than those of adults. That is, a stimulus must be louder to be heard by a newborn than by an adult. Not only can a newborn hear, but the possibility has been raised that the fetus can hear as it nestles within its mother's womb. To learn more about this possibility, turn to Children 5.3.

Smell

Infants can smell soon after birth. In one investigation (Lipsitt, Engen, & Kaye, 1963), infants less than 24 hours old made body and leg movements and showed changes in breathing when they were exposed to asafetida, a bitter and offensive odor. The infant sense of smell is not just for unpleasant odors. They apparently can recognize the smell of their mother's breasts, which presumably is pleasant. In one study (MacFarlane, 1975), infants from 2 to 7 days old were exposed to two breast pads, one to their right and one to their left. One of these breast pads had been used by the infant's mother, and the other was clean. The infants were more likely to turn toward their mother's breast pad than toward the clean breast pad. Infants this young, though, may not respond only to their mother's breast pad, but to any mother's breast pad. To test this, MacFarlane (1975) replaced the clean breast pad with another mother's breast pad. Two-day-old infants showed no preference; it may not be until several weeks of age that infants recognize their own mother's smell.

Taste

Sensitivity to taste may be present before birth. When saccharin was added to the amniotic fluid of a near-term fetus, increased swallowing was observed (Windle, 1940). Sensitivity to sweetness is clearly present in the newborn. When sucks on a nipple are rewarded with a sweetened solution, the amount of sucking increases

The Fetus and The Cat in the Hat

The fetus can hear sounds in the last few months of pregnancy: the mother's voice, music, loud sounds from television, the roar of an airplane, and so on. Given that the fetus can hear sounds, two psychologists wanted to find out if listening to Dr. Seuss's classic story *The Cat in the Hat,* while still in the mother's womb, would produce a preference for hearing the story after birth (Spence & DeCasper, 1982). Sixteen pregnant women read *The Cat in the Hat* to their fetuses twice a day over the last six weeks of their pregnancies. When the babies were born, they were given a choice of sucking on either of two nipples. Sucking on one nipple produced a recording of their mothers reading *The King, the Mice and the Cheese,* a story with a different rhyme and pace to it. Sucking on the other nipple produced a recording of their mothers reading *The Cat in the Hat.* The newborns preferred listening to *The Cat in the Hat,* which they had heard frequently as a fetus.

Two important conclusions can be drawn from this investigation. First, it reveals how ingenious scientists have become at assessing the development not only of infants but fetuses as well, in this case discovering a way to "interview" newborn babies who cannot yet talk. Second, it reveals the remarkable ability of the brain to learn even before the infant is born. ◆

What ingenious method did researchers develop to discover whether the fetus could hear its mother reading The Cat in the Hat?

(Lipsitt & others, 1976). In another investigation (Steiner, 1979), newborns showed a smilelike expression after being stimulated with a sweetened solution but pursed their lips after being stimulated with a sour solution.

Touch

Just as newborns respond to taste, they also respond to touch. A touch to the cheek produces a turning of the head, while a touch to the lips produces sucking movements. An important ability that develops in infancy is to connect information about vision with information about touch. One-year-olds clearly can do this and it appears that 6-month-olds can too. (Acredolo & Hake, 1982). Whether still younger infants can coordinate vision and touch is yet to be determined.

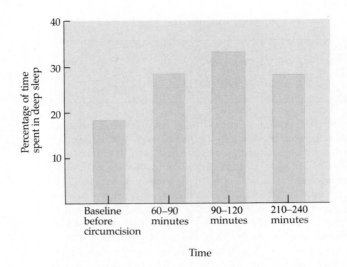

FIGURE 5.12   Percentage of time spent in deep sleep by male newborns before and after circumcision.

Pain

If and when you have a son and need to consider whether he should be circumcised, the issue of an infant's pain perception probably will become important to you. Circumcision is usually performed on young boys about the third day after birth. Will your young son experience pain if he is circumcised when he is 3 days old? Increased crying and fussing occur during the circumcision procedure, suggesting that 3-day-old infants experience pain (Gunnar, Malone, & Fisch, 1987; Porter, Porges, & Marshall, 1988).

In the recent investigation by Megan Gunnar and her colleagues (1987), the healthy newborn's ability to cope with stress was evaluated. The newborn infant males cried intensely during the circumcision, indicating that it was stressful. The researchers pointed out that it is rather remarkable that the newborn infant does not suffer serious consequences from the surgery. Rather, the circumcised infant displays amazing resiliency and ability to cope. Within several minutes after the surgery, the infant can nurse and interact in a normal manner with his mother. And, if allowed, the newly circumcised newborn drifts into a deep sleep that seems to serve as a coping mechanism. As shown in Figure 5.12, the percentage of time spent in deep sleep was greater in the 60 to 240 minutes after the circumcision than before it.

For many years, doctors have performed operations on newborns without anesthesia. The accepted standard medical practice was followed because of the dangers of anesthesia and the supposition that newborns do not feel pain. Recently, as researchers have convincingly demonstrated that newborns feel pain, the longstanding medical practice of operating on newborns without using anesthesia is being challenged.

Bimodal Perception

Are young infants so competent they can relate and integrate information in several sensory modalities? The ability to relate and integrate information about two sensory modalities—such as vision and hearing—is called **bimodal perception.** An increasing number of developmentalists believe that the young infant experiences

Yellow Kangaroos, Gray Donkeys, Thumps, Gongs, and 4-Month-Old Infants

Imagine yourself playing basketball or tennis. There are obviously many visual inputs: the ball coming and going, other players moving around, and so on. But there also are many auditory inputs: the sound of the ball bouncing or being hit and the grunts, groans, and curses emitted by yourself and others. There is also good correspondence between much of the visual and auditory information: When you see the ball bounce, you hear a bouncing sound; when a player leaps, you hear a groan.

We live in a world of objects and events that can be seen, heard, and felt. When mature observers look at and listen to an event simultaneously, they experience a unitary episode. All of this is so commonplace that it scarcely seems worth mentioning. But consider the task of the very young infant with little practice at perceiving. Can she put vision and sound together as precisely as adults?

To test bimodal perception, Elizabeth Spelke (1979) performed three experiments with the following structure: Two simple films were shown side by side in front of a 4-month-old infant. One film showed a yellow kangaroo bouncing up and down, and the other showed a gray donkey bouncing up and down. There also was an auditory sound track—a repeating thump or gong sound. A number of measures assessed the infant's tendency to look at one film instead of the other.

In Experiment 1, the animal in one of the films bounced at a slower rate than the animal in the other. And the sound track was synchronized either with the film of the slow-bouncing animal or with the film of the fast-bouncing animal. Infants' first looks were toward the film that was specified by the sound track. Experiments 2 and 3 explored two components of the relation between the sound track and the matching film: common tempo and simultaneity of sounds and bounces. The findings indicated that the infants were sensitive to both of these components.

Spelke's clever demonstration suggests that infants only 4 months old do not experience a world of unrelated visual and auditory dimensions; they can perceive them as united. ◆

related visual and auditory worlds (Bahrick, 1988; Gibson & Spelke, 1983; Kagan, 1987; Rose & Ruff, 1987). To learn more about bimodal perception, turn to Children 5.4. Keep in mind, though, that bimodal perception in young infants remains a controversial concept. For example, in one recent investigation of 6-month-old infants, the auditory sense dominated the visual sense, restricting bimodal perception (Lewkowicz, 1988).

The claim that the young infant can relate information from one sensory dimension to another has important conceptual ties. Piaget argued that the main perceptual abilities—visual, auditory, and tactile, for example—are completely uncoordinated at birth, and that young infants do not have bimodal perception. According to Piaget, it is only through months of sensorimotor interactions with the world that bimodal perception is possible. For Piaget, infant perception is much like a representation of the world that builds up as the infant constructs an image of experiences. Piaget's theory is aptly called a **constructivist view** of perception. By contrast, a number of experts on infant perception argue that infants are born with bimodal perception abilities that enable them to display bimodal perception early in infancy (Gibson, 1979, 1986, in press). This perspective is called the **direct perception view.** In this view, infants only have to attend to the appropriate information, they do not have to build up an internal representation to see them.

While the bimodal perception and constructivist-direct perception arguments have not completely been settled, what we do know today is that young infants know a lot more than we used to think they did. They see more and hear more than we used to think was possible. In our tour of the infant's perceptual world, we have

Thinking Critically
Increasingly, developmentalists are becoming surprised by the early competencies of newborns and young infants. Are we going too far, though, in believing that newborns and young infants are competent in dealing with their world, or are they really as sophisticated as the new wave of research would seem to suggest?

Perceptual Development in Infancy

Concept	Processes and Related Ideas	Characteristics and Description
What Are Sensation and Perception?	Sensation	When information contacts sensory receptors—eyes, ears, tongue, nostrils, and skin.
	Perception	The interpretation of what is sensed.
Developmental Theories of Perception	Ecological or direct perception view	The view developed by the Gibsons that the infant perceives the world by picking up perceptual invariants in the environment.
	Constructivist view	The view developed by Piaget that what the infant perceives is a construction based on a combination of sensory input and information retrieved from memory.
Visual Perception	The newborn's visual world	William James said it is a blooming, buzzing confusion; he was wrong. The newborn's perception is more advanced than we previously thought.
	Visual preferences	Fantz's research—by showing how infants prefer striped to solid patches—demonstrated that newborns can see.
	Quality of vision	The newborn is about 20/600 on the Snellen chart; by 6 months vision has improved to at least 20/100.
	The human face	Is an important visual pattern for the newborn. The infant gradually masters a sequence of steps in perceiving the human face.
	Depth perception	A classic study by Gibson and Walk (1960) demonstrated through the use of the visual cliff that 6-month-old infants can perceive depth.
Other Senses	Hearing	The fetus can hear several weeks before birth; immediately after birth newborns can hear, although their sensory threshold is higher than adults'.
	Smell, taste, touch, and pain	Each of these senses is present in the newborn. Research on circumcision shows that 3-day-old males experience pain and have the ability to adapt to stress.
Bimodal Perception	Its nature	Considerable interest focuses on the infant's ability to relate information across perceptual modalities; the coordination and integration of perceptual information across two modalities—such as the visual and the auditory senses—is called bimodal perception. Research indicates that infants as young as 4 months of age have bimodal perception.

discussed a number of senses—vision, hearing, smell, taste, touch, and pain. Main ideas related to these aspects of infants' perceptual development are summarized in Concept Table 5.2. In the next chapter, we will continue our discussion of infant development, turning to the nature of infants' cognitive development.

Summary

I. Reflexes
The newborn is no longer viewed as a passive, empty-headed organism. Physically, newborns are limited, however, and reflexes (automatic movements) govern the newborn's behavior. Sucking is an important means of obtaining nutrition, as well as

a pleasurable, soothing activity, for infants. Nonnutritive sucking is of interest to researchers because it provides a means of evaluating attention. Crying and smiling are affective behaviors that are important in the infant's communication with the world.

II. **States**

Researchers have put together different classification systems; one classification involved seven infant state categories, including deep sleep, drowsy, alert and focused, and inflexibly focused. Newborns usually sleep 16 to 17 hours a day. By 4 months, they approach adultlike sleeping patterns. REM sleep, during which children and adults are most likely to dream, occurs much more often in early infancy than in childhood or adulthood. The high percentage of REM sleep—about half of neonatal sleep—may be a self-stimulatory device, or it may promote brain development.

III. **Physical Growth and Development in Infancy**

The cephalocaudal pattern is growth from the top down; the proximodistal pattern is growth from the center out. Gross motor skills involve large muscle activity as in walking; fine motor skills involve more fine-grained activities, such as manual dexterity. Both gross and fine motor skills undergo extensive change in the first two years of a child's development. During the first year, rhythmic motor behavior— involving rapid, repetitive movement of the limbs, torso, and head—is common; this type of movement seems to represent an important adaptive transition in development. A great deal of brain growth occurs in infancy as well as in prenatal development. Dendritic spreading is dramatic in the first two years of life. Some important changes in neurotransmitters probably also occur, although these changes are just beginning to be charted.

IV. **Nutritional Needs and Eating Behavior**

Infants need to consume about 50 calories per day for each pound they weigh. Human milk, or alternative formula, is the baby's source of nutrients for the first six months. The growing consensus is that breast-feeding is superior to bottle-feeding, but the increase in working mothers has meant fewer breast-fed babies. Parents are increasingly using a demand feeding schedule. The maturation of oral and fine motor skills indicate appropriate ages for introducing semisolid and solid foods. Obesity in infancy has not been a good predictor of obesity in adulthood. Infants should not be placed on lowfat, low-calorie diets.

V. **Malnutrition in Infancy**

Severe infant malnutrition is still prevalent in many parts of the world. Severe protein-calorie deficiency can cause marasmus, a wasting away of body tissues. It is caused mainly by early weaning from breast milk. Even if not fatal, severe and lengthy malnutrition is detrimental to physical, cognitive, and social development.

VI. **Sensation and Perception**

Sensation is when information contacts sensory receptors—eyes, ears, tongue, nostrils, and skin. Perception is the interpretation of what is sensed.

VII. **Visual Perception**

William James said that the newborn's world is like a blooming, buzzing confusion. He was wrong. The newborn's perception is more advanced than previously thought. Fantz's research—by showing that infants prefer stripes to solids—demonstrated that newborns can see. The human face is an important visual pattern for the newborn. The infant gradually masters a sequence of steps in perceiving the human face. A classic study by Gibson and Walk demonstrated through the use of the visual cliff that 6-month-old infants can perceive depth.

VIII. **Other Senses**

The fetus can hear several weeks before birth; immediately after birth newborns can hear, although their sensory threshold is higher than adults'. Smell, taste, touch, and pain are present in the newborn. Research on circumcision shows that 3-day-old males experience pain and have the ability to cope with stress.

IX. **Bimodal Perception**

Considerable interest focuses on the infant's ability to relate information across perceptual modalities; the coordination and integration of perceptual information across two modalities—such as the visual and auditory senses—is called bimodal perception. Research suggests that infants as young as 4 months of age have bimodal perception.

Key Terms

sucking reflex 138
Moro reflex 139
grasping reflex 139
nonnutritive sucking 140
reflexive smile 142
social smile 142
REM sleep 143

cephalocaudal pattern 144
proximodistal pattern 145
gross motor skills 146
fine motor skills 146
rhythmic motor
   behavior 146

marasmus 153
sensation 156
perception 156
bimodal perception 160
constructivist view 161
direct perception view 161

Suggested Readings

Banks, M. S. & Salapatek, P. (1983). Infant visual perception. In P. E. Mussen (Ed.), *Handbook of child psychology* (4th ed., Vol. 2). New York: Wiley.
This authoritative version of research on infant perception covers in great detail the topics discussed in this chapter.

Caplan, F. (1981). *The first twelve months of life.* New York: Bantam.
An easy-to-read, well-written account of each of the first 12 months of life. Includes extensive information about motor milestones.

Lamb, M. E. & Bornstein, M. C. (1987). *Development in infancy.* New York: Random House.
This portrayal of the infant by two leading researchers includes individual chapters on perceptual development as well as the ecology of the infant's development.

Osofsky, J. D. (1987). *Handbook of infant development* (2nd ed.). New York: Wiley.
Leading experts in the field of infant development have contributed chapters on a far ranging set of topics about infants.

Williams, S. R., & Worthington-Roberts, B. S. (1988). *Nutrition through the life-style.* St. Louis: Times Mirror/Mosby.
An up-to-date, authoritative examination of nutrition in development with separate chapters on breast-feeding and nutrition in infancy.

There was a child who went forth every day
And the first object he looked upon,
that object he became.
And that object became part of him for
the day, or a certain
part of the day, or for many years,
or stretching cycles of years.

Walt Whitman

6

Cognitive Development

Matthew is 1 year old. He has already seen over 1,000 flash cards with pictures of shells, flowers, insects, flags, countries, and words on them. His mother, Billie, has made almost 10,000 of the 11-inch-square cards for Matthew and his 4-year-old brother, Mark. Billie has religiously followed the regimen recommended by Glenn Doman, the director of the Philadelphia Institute for the Achievement of Human Potential and the author of *How to Teach Your Baby to Read.* Using his methods, learned in a course called "How to Multiply Your Baby's Intelligence," Billie is teaching Matthew Japanese and even a little math. Mark is learning geography, natural science, engineering, and fine arts as well.

Parents using the card approach print one word on each card using a bright red felt-tipped pen. The parent repeatedly shows the card to the infant while saying the word aloud. The first word usually is *mommy,* then comes *daddy,* the baby's name, parts of the body, and all the things the infant can touch. The infant is lavishly praised when he recognizes the word. The idea is to imprint the large red words in the infant's memory, so that in time, he accumulates an impressive vocabulary and begins to read. The parent continues to feed the infant with all manner of information in small, assimilable bits, just as Billie Rash has done with her two boys.

With this method, the child should be reading by 2 years of age, and by 4 or 5 should have begun mastering some math and be able to play the violin, not to mention the vast knowledge of the world he should be able to display because of a monumental vocabulary. Maybe the SAT or ACT test you labored through on your way to college might have been conquered at the age of 6 if your parents had only been enrolled in "How to Multiply Your Baby's Intelligence" course and made 10,000 flash cards for you.

Is this the best way for an infant to learn? A number of developmentalists believe Doman's "better baby institute" is a money-making scheme and is not based on sound scientific evidence. They believe that we should not be trying to accelerate the infant's learning so dramatically. Rather than have information poured into infants' minds, infants should be permitted more time to spontaneously explore the environment and construct their knowledge. Jean Piaget called "What should we do to foster cognitive development?" the American question, because it was asked of him so often when he lectured to American audiences. Developmentalists worry that children exposed to Doman's methods will burn out on learning. What probably is more important is providing a rich and emotionally supportive atmosphere for learning.

The excitement and enthusiasm surrounding the infant's cognition has been fueled by an interest in what an infant knows at birth and soon after, by continued fascination about innate and learned factors in the infant's cognitive development, and by controversies over whether infants construct their knowledge (as Piaget believed) or whether they know their world more directly through the environment's influence on behavior. Primary topics include Piaget's theory of infant development, the nature of attention, memory, and imitation, measurement of infants' intelligence, and where the infant's language comes from and how it develops. We will examine each of these topics in turn.

Piaget's Theory of Infant Development

The poet Noah Perry once asked, "Who knows the thoughts of a child?" Piaget knew as much as anyone. Through careful, inquisitive interviews and observations of his own three children—Laurent, Lucienne, and Jacqueline—Piaget changed the way we think about children's conception of the world. Remember that we studied an overview of Piaget's theory in Chapter 2. It may be helpful for you to review the basic features of his theory at this time.

Piaget believed that the child passes through a series of stages of thought from infancy to adolescence. Passage through the stages results from biological pressures to _adapt_ to the environment (assimilation and accommodation) and to organize structures of thinking. The stages of thought are *qualitatively* different from one another; the way a child reasons at one stage is very different from the way she reasons at another stage. This contrasts with the quantitative assessments of intelligence made through the use of standardized intelligence tests, where the focus is on what the child knows, or how many questions the child can answer correctly (Ginsburg & Opper, 1988). According to Piaget, the mind's development is divided into four such qualitatively different stages: sensorimotor, preoperational, concrete operational, and formal operational. Here our concern is with the stage that characterizes infant thought—the sensorimotor stage.

The Stage of Sensorimotor Development

Piaget's sensorimotor stage lasts from birth to about 2 years of age, corresponding to the period of infancy. During this time, mental development is characterized by considerable progression in the infant's ability to organize and coordinate sensations with physical movements and actions—hence, the name *sensorimotor* (Piaget, 1952).

At the beginning of the sensorimotor stage, the infant has little more than reflexive patterns with which to work. By the end of the stage, the 2-year-old has complex sensorimotor patterns and is beginning to operate with a primitive system of symbols. Unlike other stages, the sensorimotor stage is subdivided into six substages, which describe qualitative changes in sensorimotor organization. The term **scheme** (or schema) refers to the basic unit for an organized pattern of sensorimotor functioning.

Piaget was a masterful observer of his three children. The following observation of his son, Laurent, provides an excellent example of the infant's emerging coordination of visual and motor schemes and eloquently portrays how infants learn about their hands.

At 2 months, Laurent by chance discovers his right index finger and looks at it briefly. Several days later, he briefly inspects his open right hand, perceived by chance. About a week later, he follows its spontaneous movement for a moment, then he holds his two fists in the air and looks at the left one. Then he slowly brings it toward his face and rubs his nose with it, then his eye. A moment later the left hand again approaches his face. He looks at it and touches his nose. He does that again and laughs five or six times while moving the left hand to his face. He seems

We are born capable of learning.

Jean Jacque Rousseau

to laugh before the hand moves, but looking has no influence on its movement. He laughs beforehand but begins to smile again on seeing the hand. Then he rubs his nose. At a given moment, he turns his head to the left, but looking has no effect on the direction. The next day, the same reaction occurs. And, then another day later, he looks at his right hand, then at his clasped hands. Finally, on the day after that, Piaget says that Laurent's looking acts on the orientation of his hands, which tend to remain in the visual field (Piaget, 1936).

With a given substage, there may be different schemes—sucking, rooting, and blinking in Substage 1, for example. In Substage 1, they are basically reflexive in nature. From substage to substage, the schemes change in organization. This change is at the heart of Piaget's description of the stages. The six substages of sensorimotor development are (1) simple reflexes; (2) first habits and primary circular reactions; (3) secondary circular reactions; (4) coordination of secondary circular reactions; (5) tertiary circular reactions, novelty, and curiosity; and (6) internalization of schemes.

In Substage 1, **simple reflexes,** which corresponds to the first month after birth, the basic means of coordinating sensation and action is through reflexive behaviors, such as rooting and sucking, which the infant has at birth. In Substage 1, the infant exercises these reflexes. More importantly, the infant develops an ability to produce behaviors that resemble reflexes in the absence of obvious reflexive stimuli. The newborn may suck when a bottle or nipple is only nearby, for example. When the baby was just born, the bottle or nipple would have produced the sucking pattern only when placed directly in the newborn's mouth or touched to the lips. Reflexlike actions in the absence of a triggering stimulus is evidence that the infant is initiating action and is actively structuring experiences in the first month of life.

In Substage 2, **first habits and primary circular reactions,** which develops between 1 and 4 months of age, the infant learns to coordinate sensation and types of schemes or structures—that is, habits and primary circular reactions. A *habit* is a scheme based upon a simple reflex, such as sucking, that has become completely divorced from its eliciting stimulus. For example, an infant in Substage 1 might suck when orally stimulated by a bottle or when visually shown the bottle, but an infant in Substage 2 might exercise the sucking scheme even when no bottle is present.

A **primary circular reaction** is a scheme based upon the infant's attempt to reproduce an interesting or pleasurable event that initially occurred by chance. In a popular Piagetian example, a child accidentally sucks his fingers when they are placed near his mouth; later, he searches for his fingers to suck them again, but the fingers do not cooperate in the search because the infant cannot coordinate visual and manual actions. Habits and circular reactions are stereotyped in that the infant repeats them the same way each time. The infant's own body remains the center of attention; there is no outward pull by environmental events.

In Substage 3, **secondary circular reactions,** which develops between 4 and 8 months of age, the infant becomes more object oriented or focused on the world, moving beyond preoccupation with the self in sensorimotor interactions. The chance shaking of a rattle, for example, may fascinate the infant, and the infant will repeat this action for the sake of experiencing fascination. The infant imitates some simple actions of others, such as the baby talk or burbling of adults, and some physical gestures. However, these imitations are limited to actions the infant is already able to produce. Although directed toward objects in the world, the infant's schemes lack an intentional, goal-directed quality.

In Substage 4, **coordination of secondary reactions,** which develops between 8 and 12 months of age, several significant changes take place. The infant readily combines and recombines previously learned schemes in a *coordinated* way. She may look at an object and grasp it simultaneously, or visually inspect a toy, such as a rattle, and finger it simultaneously in obvious tactile exploration. Actions are even more outwardly directed than before. Related to this coordination is the second achievement—the presence of *intentionality,* the separation of means and goals in accomplishing simple feats. For example, the infant might manipulate a stick (the means) to bring a desired toy within reach (the goal). She may knock over one block to reach and play with another one.

In Substage 5, **tertiary circular reactions, novelty, and curiosity,** which develops between 12 and 18 months of age, the infant becomes intrigued by the variety of properties that objects possess and by the multiplicity of things she can make happen to objects. A block can be made to fall, spin, hit another object, slide across the ground, and so on. **Tertiary circular reactions** are schemes in which the infant purposely explores new possibilities with objects, continually changing what is done to them and exploring the results. Piaget says that this stage marks the developmental starting point for human curiosity and interest in novelty. Previous circular

Piaget's six Substages of sensorimotor development. In Substage 1 (a), the infant practices the reflexive behavior of sucking. In Substage 2 (b), the infant will practice the sucking reflex when no bottle is present. In Substage 3 (c), the infant becomes more object oriented. In Substage 4 (d), the infant begins to coordinate action. In Substage 5 (e), the infant becomes intrigued by an object's variety of properties. In Substage 6 (f), the infant's functioning shifts to a symbolic plane.

Encouraging Babies' Curiosity: From "Feely Boxes" to Peek-a-boo

Curiosity is a special interest of infants. Around the first birthday, an infant's curiosity rapidly expands. Some infant behaviors that indicate the emergence of curiosity include

—interest in the effects of their actions (e.g., dropping, banging) on objects

—interest in small particles

—interest in voices

—interest in sounds

—interest in faces

—interest in exploring living areas

What are some ways to encourage an infant's curiosity? Among the possibilities are "feely boxes," hiding an object in a matchbox, playing with small objects and containers, finding a wrapped toy, playing in the kitchen cabinet, and playing peek-a-boo (White, 1988).

Making a "Feely Box." Put the following materials into a cardboard box: tissue paper, foam rubber sponge, and an elastic strip. While you and the baby are sitting on the floor, take one object out of the box at a time. Show the baby how to handle the piece (stroke, stretch, crumble, and so on) and talk to the baby about how the object feels. Allow the baby to handle the object and see what the baby does with it. Encourage the baby to play freely with these materials from time to time. Occasionally, add new materials to the baby's collection.

Hiding Objects in a Matchbox. Place an object inside a matchbox, and help the infant learn how to slide the box open to get at the object. Show and tell the baby what you are doing. Then let the baby try it.

Playing with Small Objects and Containers. Make available several containers such as

—wicker basket

—large coffee can

—cardboard box about 10 inches deep

Fill the container with objects such as the following:

—drawers that fit the container

—beads too large to put into the mouth

—blocks

—spools

—small plastic animals

An important task for parents is to encourage their infants' curiosity. Letting infants explore and play with safe, unbreakable objects, such as the plastic glasses shown here, is one way to encourage curiosity.

Finding a Wrapped Toy. Wrap the baby's favorite toy in a bag or a piece of paper so she has to do a little work to get to the toy. She may just rip open the packaging. Don't discourage this but tell her to try again and show her how to use her fingers to open the package without destroying the paper.

Playing in a Kitchen Cabinet. Select a lower kitchen cabinet and stock it with safe, unbreakable objects. When you are working in the kitchen, let the baby crawl on the kitchen floor. Partially open the cabinet door. If left alone, the baby will probably start examining the objects. The baby will have an opportunity to touch them, bang them together, and listen to the sounds they make. Let the baby play freely, but talk to the baby during the play and make sure the play is safe.

Peek-a-boo. Sit across from the baby on the floor and say, "I have a new way to play peek-a-boo. Watch." Place your hands on the baby's wrists and cover the baby's eyes with the palms of the baby's hands. Wait for a second, then remove the baby's hands and say, "Peek-a-boo!" Repeat the sequence several times and then show the baby how to play the game with your hands and eyes. After playing the game for several days, encourage the baby to cover and uncover her eyes without your help. ◆

(a)

(b)

Object permanence is one of the infant's significant accomplishments. How do developmentalists study the infant's sense of object permanence?

reactions have been devoted exclusively to reproducing former events, with the exception of imitation of novel acts, which occurs as early as Substage 4. The tertiary circular act is the first to be concerned with novelty. More about the infant's curiosity and ways to encourage it appears in Children 6.1.

In Substage 6, **internalization of schemes,** which develops between 18 and 24 months, the infant's mental functioning shifts from a purely sensorimotor plane to a symbolic plane, and the infant develops the ability to use primitive symbols. For Piaget, a *symbol* is an internalized sensory image or word that represents an event. Primitive symbols permit the infant to think about concrete events without directly acting them out or perceiving them. Moreover, symbols allow the infant to manipulate and transform the represented events in simple ways. In a favorite Piagetian example, Piaget's young daughter saw a matchbox being opened and closed; sometime later, she mimicked the event by opening and closing her mouth. This was an obvious expression of her image of the event. In another example, a child opened a door slowly to avoid disturbing a piece of paper lying on the floor on the other side. Clearly, the child had an image of the unseen paper and what would happen to it if the door opened quickly. Recently, however, developmentalists have debated whether 2-year-olds really have such representations of action sequences at their command (Corrigan, 1981; Escalona, 1988).

Object Permanence

One of the infant's most significant accomplishments is the development of object permanence (Flavell, 1985). **Object permanence** is the development of the ability to understand that objects and events continue to exist even when the infant is not in direct contact with them. Imagine what thought would be like if you could not distinguish between yourself and your world. Your thought would be chaotic, disorderly, and unpredictable. This is what the mental life of the newborn is like; there is no self-world differentiation and no sense of object permanence (Piaget, 1952).

TABLE 6.1 *The Six Substages of Object Permanence*

Stage	Behavior
Sensorimotor Substage 1	There is no apparent object permanence. When a spot of light moves across the visual field, the infant follows it but quickly ignores its disappearance.
Sensorimotor Substage 2	A primitive form of object permanence develops. Given the same experience, the infant looks briefly at the spot where the light disappeared, with an expression of passive expectancy.
Sensorimotor Substage 3	The infant's sense of object permanence undergoes further development. With the newfound ability to coordinate simple schemes, the infant shows clear patterns of searching for a missing object, with sustained visual and manual examination of the spot where the object apparently disappeared.
Sensorimotor Substage 4	The infant actively searches for a missing object in the spot where it disappeared, with new actions to achieve the goal of searching effectively. For example, if an attractive toy has been hidden behind a screen, the child may look at the screen and try to push it away with a hand. If the screen is too heavy to move or is permanently fixed, the child readily substitutes a secondary scheme—for example, crawling around it or kicking it. These new actions signal that the infant's belief in the continued existence of the missing object is strengthening.
Sensorimotor Substage 5	The infant now is able to track an object that disappears and reappears in several locations in rapid succession. For example, a toy may be hidden under different boxes in succession in front of the infant, who succeeds in finding it. The infant is apparently able to hold an image of the missing object in mind longer than before.
Sensorimotor Substage 6	The infant can search for a missing object that disappeared and reappeared in several locations in succession, as before. In addition, the infant searches in the appropriate place even when the object has been hidden from view as it is being moved. This activity indicates that the infant is able to "imagine" the missing object and to follow the image from one location to the next.

By the end of the sensorimotor period, however, both are clearly present. The transition between these states is not abrupt; it is marked by qualitative changes that reflect movement through each substage of sensorimotor thought.

The principal way that object permanence is studied is by watching the infant's reaction when an attractive object or event disappears. If the infant shows no reaction, it is assumed that he believes it no longer exists. By contrast, if the infant is surprised at the disappearance and searches for the object, it is assumed that he believes it continues to exist. According to Piaget, six distinct substages characterize the development of object permanence. Table 6.1 shows how these six substages reflect Piaget's substages of sensorimotor development.

(a)   (b)

Although Piaget's stage sequence is the best summary of what might happen as the infant fathoms the permanence of things in the world, some contradictory findings have emerged. Piaget's stages broadly describe the interesting changes reasonably well, but the infant's life is not so neatly packaged into distinct organizations as Piaget believed. Some of Piaget's explanations for the causes of change are debated.

Habituation is a common occurrence in the infant's perceptual world. In (a) the infant is attending to the blocks hanging overhead. In (b), the infant has become bored with the blocks and looks away from them. Habituation is like getting bored with a stimulus.

Habituation, Memory, and Imitation

Other processes that developmentalists believe are involved in the infant's cognitive development are habituation, memory, and attention, each of which we will consider in turn.

Habituation

If a stimulus—a sight or sound—is presented to an infant several times in a row, the infant usually pays less attention to it each time, suggesting that he is bored with it. This is the process of **habituation**—repeated presentation of the same stimulus that causes reduced attention to the stimulus (Kaplan, Rudy, & Werner, 1989; Tamis-LeMonda & Bornstein, 1989). If a different stimulus is then presented, the infant perks up and pays attention to it, suggesting that he can discriminate between the two. This is the process of **dishabituation.** Among the measures infant researchers have used to study whether habituation or dishabituation is occuring are heart and respiration rates, sucking behavior (sucking stops when the young infant attends to an object), and the length of time the infant looks at an object. Newborn infants can habituate to repetitive stimulation in virtually every sensory modality—vision, audition, touch, and so on (Rovee-Collier, 1987). However, habituation becomes more acute during the first three months of life. The extensive assessment of habituation in recent years has resulted in its use as a measure of an infant's maturity and well-being. Infants who have brain damage or have suffered birth traumas such as lack of oxygen do not habituate well and may later have developmental and learning problems.

Man is the only animal that can be bored.

Erich Fromm, The Sane Society, *1955*

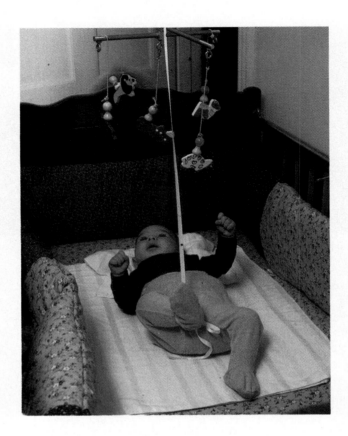

FIGURE 6.1   The technique used in Rovee-Collier's investigation of infant memory. The mobile is connected to the infant's ankle by the ribbon and moves in direct proportion to the frequency and vigor of the infant's kicks.

A knowledge of habituation and dishabituation can benefit parent-infant interaction. Infants respond to changes in stimulation. If stimulation is repeated often, the infant's response will decrease to the point that the infant no longer responds to the parent. In parent-infant interaction, it is important for parents to do novel things and to repeat them often until the infant stops responding. The wise parent senses when the infant shows an interest and that many repetitions of the stimulus may be necessary for the infant to process the information. The parent stops or changes behaviors when the infant redirects her attention (Rosenblith & Sims-Knight, 1985).

Memory

Researchers also have found that infants have surprisingly good memories. **Memory** is a central feature of cognitive development, pertaining to all situations in which an individual retains information over time. Sometimes, information is retained for only a few seconds, and at other times for a lifetime. Memory is involved when we look up a telephone number and dial it, when we remember the name of our best friend from elementary school, and when an infant remembers who her mother is.

Carolyn Rovee-Collier and her colleagues (Rovee-Collier, 1987; Borovsky, Hill, & Rovee-Collier, 1987) hung a mobile over an infant's crib and attached a ribbon to one of the baby's limbs (Figure 6.1). Six-week-old infants quickly discovered which arm or leg would move the mobile. Two weeks later, the infants were placed in the same situation. They *remembered* which arm or leg to move, even though they were not attached to the mobile. These early signs of memory are the basis of the kinds of learning from experience that continue throughout our lifetime. Ongoing investigation of such abilities underscores just how surprisingly competent young infants are.

Is the infant's memory of the mobile conscious? As children and adults, our memory often involves conscious feelings, such as "I have seen that before," as well as additional retrieval abilities, such as "Where have I seen that before—was it at the zoo?" These conscious feelings probably are not present in the memory of young infants, who do not have the ability to consciously recall or reflect about objects when they are not present (Flavell, 1985).

Just when do infants acquire the ability to consciously remember the past? In one investigation, parents kept diaries of their 5- to 11-month-olds' memories (Ashmead & Perlmutter, 1979). An entry in one of the diaries describes the behavior of a 9-month-old girl who was looking for ribbons that had been removed from the drawer where they had been kept. She first looked in the "old" drawer. Failing to find the ribbons, she searched other drawers until she found them. The next day, the young girl went directly to the "new" drawer to find the ribbons. More formal experiments support the existence of such memory in infants over 6 months of age (Fox, Kagan, & Weiskopf, 1979). For example, when an object is shown to an infant and then subsequently removed, the 7-month-old infant will search for it, but a younger infant will not. The memory of infants in the first six months of life is not like what we, as adults, commonly think of as memory; it is not conscious memory for specific past episodes but rather learning of adaptive skills.

Why does conscious memory develop later than other learning and memory skills? Possibly conscious memory must await the maturation of certain brain structures, such as the hippocampus (Diamond, 1989). Possibly conscious memory depends on the development of cognitive structures, as Piaget's theory suggests.

Despite evidence of conscious memory in the first year of life, such recall is believed to be minimal until the child is about 3 years of age. Try to recall a specific episode in the first 3 years of your life, such as the birth of a sibling. Can you remember anything at all about the first three years of your life? As children and adults, we have little or no memory of events we experienced before 3 years of age. This phenomenon is called **infantile amnesia.** In one investigation (Sheingold & Tenney, 1982), college students who had at least one younger sibling were interviewed and asked such questions as, "Who told you that your mother was leaving to go to the hospital to have a baby?" "What time of day did she go to the hospital?" "Did you visit your mother in the hospital?" Recall for the college students is shown in Figure 6.2. Recall was virtually zero unless their siblings were 3 years younger or more, supporting the concept of infantile amnesia.

Imitation

In the last chapter, we described how infants display a variety of their own emotions. But can they also imitate someone else's emotional expressions? If an adult smiles, will the baby follow with a smile? If an adult protrudes her lower lip, wrinkles her forehead, and frowns, will the baby show a saddened look? If an adult opens her mouth, widens her eyes, and raises her eyebrows, will the baby follow suit? Could infants only 1 day old do these things?

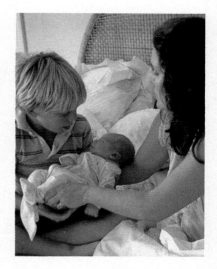

What is meant by infantile amnesia?

Thinking Critically
Can you think of ways to measure infantile amnesia other than asking if you remember a sibling being born?

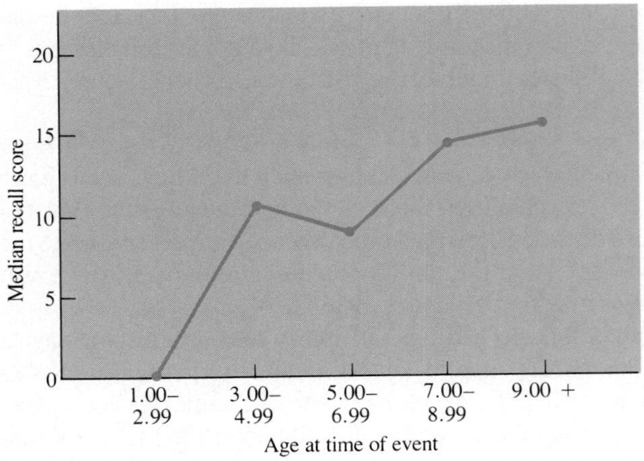

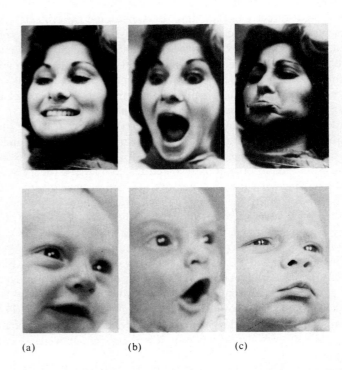

FIGURE 6.2 Median recall scores as a function of age for sibling births reported by college students.

FIGURE 6.3 Sample photographs of a model's (*a*) happy, (*b*) surprised, and (*c*) sad expressions, and an infant's corresponding expressions.

(a)   (b)   (c)

We are, in truth, more than half what we are by imitation.

Lord Chesterfield,
Letters to His Son, 1750

Tiffany Field and her colleagues (1982) explored these questions with newborns only 36 hours after their birth. The model held the newborn's head upright with the model's and the newborn's faces separated by 10 inches. The newborn's facial expressions were recorded by an observer who stood behind the model. The observer could not see which facial expressions the model was showing. The model expressed one of three emotions: happiness, sadness, or surprise (Figure 6.3). As shown in Figure 6.4, infants were most likely to imitate the model's display of surprise by widely opening their mouths. When the infants observed a happy mood, they frequently widened their lips. When the model expressed sadness, the infants followed with lips that reflected pouting. Other research supports the belief that

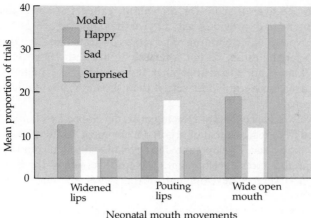

FIGURE 6.4　Imitations of adult emotions by 36-hour-old newborns. The graph shows the mean proportion of trials during which newborn mouth movements followed a model's facial expression. Mouth movements included widened lips (happy), pouting lips (sad), and wide open mouth (surprised).

young infants can imitate an adult's emotional expressions, but it is open to interpretation whether the imitation is learned or an innate ability (Meltzoff, 1988; Meltzoff & Kuhl, 1989).

Individual Differences in Intelligence

So far we have stressed general statements about how the cognitive development of infants progresses, emphasizing what is typical of the largest number of infants or the average infant. But the results obtained for most infants do not apply to all infants. Individual differences in infant cognitive development have been studied primarily through the use of developmental scales or infant intelligence tests.

It is advantageous to know whether an infant is advancing at a slow, normal, or advanced pace of development. In Chapter 4, we discussed the Brazelton Neonatal Behavioral Assessment Scale, which is widely used to evaluate newborns. Developmentalists also want to know how development proceeds during the course of infancy as well. If an infant advances at an especially slow rate, then some form of enrichment may be necessary. If an infant develops at an advanced pace, parents may be advised to provide toys that stimulate cognitive growth in slightly older infants.

The infant testing movement grew out of the tradition of IQ testing with older children. However, the measures that assess infants are necessarily less verbal than IQ tests that assess the intelligence of older children. The infant developmental scales contain far more items related to perceptual motor development. They also include measures of social interaction.

The most important early contributor to the developmental testing of infants was Arnold Gesell (1934). He developed a measure that was used as a clinical tool to help sort out potentially normal babies from abnormal ones. This was especially useful to adoption agencies who had large numbers of babies awaiting placement. Gesell's examination was used widely for many years and still is frequently used by pediatricians in their assessment of normal and abnormal infants. The version of the Gesell test now used has four categories of behavior: motor, language, adaptive, and personal-social. If the examiner wishes, the scores in these four domains can be combined into one overall score for the infant, called the **developmental quotient (DQ).** Gesell intended to provide a way to give the infant an overall score, much like the IQ score given to older children. The scores on tests like the Gesell that obtain an overall DQ for the infant do not correlate highly with IQ scores obtained later in childhood. This is not surprising, since the nature of the items on the developmental scales are considerably less verbal than the items on intelligence tests given to older children.

The **Bayley Scales of Infant Development,** developed by Nancy Bayley (1969), are widely used in the assessment of infant development. Unlike Gesell, whose scales were clinically motivated, Bayley wanted to develop scales that could document infant behavior and predict later development. The early version of the Bayley scales covered only the first year of development; in the 1950s, the scales were extended to assess older infants.

The version of the scales used today has three components—a Mental scale, a Motor scale, and an Infant Behavior Profile (which is based on the examiner's observations of the infant during testing). Our major interest here is the infant's cognitive development; the Mental scale includes assessment of the following:

—auditory and visual attention to stimuli
—manipulation, such as combining objects or shaking a rattle
—examiner interaction, such as babbling and imitation
—relation with toys, such as banging spoons together
—memory involved in object permanence, such as when the infant finds a hidden toy
—goal-directed behavior that involves persistence, such as putting pegs in a board
—ability to follow directions and knowledge of objects' names, such as understanding the concept of "one"

How well should a 6-month-old perform on the Bayley Mental scale? The 6-month-old infant should be able to vocalize pleasure and displeasure, persistently search for objects that are just out of immediate reach, and approach a mirror when the examiner places it in front of the infant. How well should a 12-month-old perform? By 12 months of age, the infant should be able to inhibit behavior when commanded to do so, imitate words the examiner says (such as "Mama"), and respond to simple requests (such as "Take a drink"). Figure 6.5 shows an infant being given the Bayley scales.

Infant tests of intelligence have been valuable in assessing the effects of malnutrition, drugs, maternal deprivation, and environmental stimulation on infants' development. They have met with mixed results in predicting later intelligence. Global developmental quotient or IQ scores for infants have not been good predictors of childhood intelligence. However, specific aspects of infant intelligence are related to specific aspects of childhood intelligence. For example, in one recent investigation, infant language abilities as assessed by the Bayley test predicted language, reading, and spelling ability at 6–8 years of age (Siegel, 1989). Infant perceptual motor skills predicted visual-spatial, arithmetic, and fine-motor skills at 6 to 8 years of age. These results indicate that an item analysis of infant scales like the Bayley can provide information about the development of specific intellectual functions and the domain specific nature of cognitive growth.

Thinking Critically
Is an older infant's intelligence just quantitatively more than a younger infant's intelligence, or is it qualitatively different? How would Piaget have answered this question?

FIGURE 6.5   The Mental Scale of the Bayley test includes assessment of the infant's auditory and visual attention to objects.

The explosion of interest in infant development has produced many new measures especially tasks that evaluate the way the infant processes information (Ensher & Meller, 1989; Fagan & Khevel, 1989; Gottfried & Bathurst, 1989; Rose, 1989). Evidence is accumulating that measures of habituation and dishabituation predict intelligence in childhood (Bornstein, 1989; Bornstein & Sigman, 1986; Sigman & others, 1989). Quicker decays or less cumulative looking in the habituation situation and greater amounts of looking in the dishabituation situation reflect more efficient information processing. Both types of attention—decrement and recovery—when measured in the first six months of infancy, are related to higher IQ scores on standardized intelligence tests given at various times between infancy and adolescence. In sum, more precise assessment of the infant's cognition with information-processing tasks involving attention have led to the conclusion that continuity between infant and childhood intelligence is greater than was previously believed (Bornstein & Krasnegor, 1989).

Thus far, we have described several important ideas about the infant's cognitive development. To help you remember the main points of this discussion, turn to Concept Table 6.1. Next, we will study another key dimension of the infant's development—language.

Infant Cognitive Development

Concept	Processes and Related Ideas	Characteristics and Description
Piaget's Theory of Infant Development	Sensorimotor stage	Lasts from birth to about 2 years of age; involves progression in the infant's ability to organize and coordinate sensations with physical movements. The sensorimotor stage has six substages: simple reflexes, first habits and primary circular reactions; secondary circular reactions; coordination of secondary circular reactions; tertiary circular reactions, novelty, and curiosity; and internalization of schemes.
	Object permanence	Refers to the development of the ability to understand that objects and events continue to exist even though the infant no longer is in contact with them. Piaget believed that this ability developed over the course of the six substages.
Habituation, Memory, and Imitation	Habituation	The repeated presentation of the same stimulus causes reduced attention to the stimulus. If a different stimulus is presented and the infant pays attention to it, dishabituation is occurring. Newborn infants can habitate, but habituation becomes more acute over the first three months of infancy.
	Memory	Memory is the retention of information over time. In the first six months, infants learn adaptive skills, but conscious memory does not develop until later in the first year. Infantile amnesia is our inability to remember anything that happened in the first three years of our life.
	Imitation	Infants only 1 day old imitate facial expressions of emotion by adults; whether the imitation is learned or innate is open to interpretation.
Individual Differences in Intelligence	History	Developmental scales for infants grew out of the tradition of IQ testing with older children. These scales are less verbal than IQ tests. Gesell was an early developer of an infant test. His scale is still widely used by pediatricians; it provides a DQ (developmental quotient).
	Bayley Scales	The developmental scales most widely used today, developed by Nancy Bayley. Consist of a Motor scale, a Mental scale, and an Infant Behavior Profile.
	Conclusions about infant tests and continuity in mental development	Global infant intelligence measures are not good predictors of childhood intelligence. However, specific aspects of infant intelligence, such as information-processing tasks involving attention, have been better predictors of childhood intelligence, especially in a specific area.

Language Development

In the thirteenth century, the Holy Roman Emperor Frederick II had a cruel idea. He wanted to know what language children would speak if no one talked to them. He selected several newborns and threatened the adults who cared for them with their lives if they ever talked to the infants. Frederick never found out what language the children spoke because they all died.

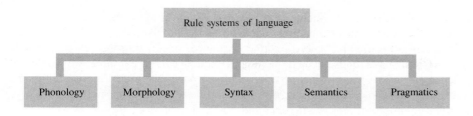

FIGURE 6.6   Language rule systems.

These cruel circumstances bring up an important issue in language—namely, what are the biological and environmental contributions to language? The contributions of biology and environment figure prominently throughout our discussion of language.

What Is Language?

Every human society has language. Human languages number in the thousands, differing so much on the surface that many of us despair at learning more than even one. Yet all human languages have some things in common.

Language has been defined by one expert as a sequence of words (Miller, 1981). This definition describes language as having two different characteristics—the presence of words and sequencing. But language has other characteristics as well. The use of language is a highly creative process. For example, you can understand this sentence even though you have never seen or heard it. And you can create a unique sentence that you have not seen or heard before. This creative aspect of language is called **infinite generativity,** the individual's ability to generate an infinite number of meaningful sentences using a finite set of words and rules. Yet another characteristic of language is **displacement.** This means that we can use language to communicate information about another place and time, although we also use language to describe what is going on in our immediate environment. A final important characteristic of language is its different rule systems. These include phonology, morphology, syntax, semantics, and pragmatics, which we now discuss in turn (Figure 6.6).

Language's Rule Systems

Language is comprised of basic sounds, or *phonemes*. In the English language there are approximately 36 phonemes. The study of language's sound system is called **phonology;** phonological rules ensure that certain sound sequences occur (e.g., *sp, ar, ba*) and others do not (e.g., *zx, qp*). A good example of a phoneme in the English language is /k/, the sound represented by the letter *k* in the word *ski* and by the letter *c* in the word *cat*. While the /k/ sound is slightly different in these two words, the variation is not distinguished and the /k/ sound is viewed as a single phoneme.

Language also is characterized by a string of sounds that give meaning to what we say and hear. The string of sounds is a *morpheme;* **morphology** refers to the rules for combining morphemes. Every word in the English language is made up of one or more morphemes. Not all morphemes are words, however (e.g., *pre-, -tion,* and *-ing*). Some words consist of a single morpheme (e.g., *help*). Other words are made

up of more than one morpheme (e.g., *helper,* which has two morphemes, *help +
er,* with the morpheme *er* meaning "one who"—in this case, "one who helps"). Just
as phonemes ensure that certain sound sequences occur, morphemes ensure that
certain strings of sounds occur in particular sequences. For example, we would not
reorder *helper* to *erhelp.* Morphemes have fixed positions in the English language,
and these morphological rules ensure that some sequences appear in words (e.g.,
combining, popular, and *intelligent*) and others do not (e.g., *forpot, skiest*).

Syntax is the way words are combined to form acceptable phrases and sentences. Because you and I share the same syntactic understanding of sentence structure, if I say to you, "Bob slugged Tom" and "Bob was slugged by Tom," you know
who did the slugging and who was slugged in each case. You also understand that
the sentence "You didn't stay, did you?" is a grammatical sentence, but that "You
didn't stay, didn't you?" is unacceptable and ambiguous.

A concept closely related to syntax is **grammar,** the formal description of syntactical rules. In elementary school and high school, most of us learned rules about
sentence structure. Linguists devise rules of grammar that are similar to those you
learned in school but are much more complex and powerful. Many contemporary
linguists distinguish between the "surface" and "deep" structure of a sentence. **Surface structure** is the actual order of words in a sentence; **deep structure** is the syntactic relation of the words in a sentence. By applying syntactic rules in different
ways, one sentence (the surface structure) can have two very different deep structures. For example, consider this sentence: "Mrs. Smith found drunk on her lawn."
Was Mrs. Smith drunk or did she find a drunk on the lawn? Either interpretation
fits the sentence, depending on the deep structure applied.

Semantics refers to the meaning of words and sentences. Every word has a set
of semantic features. *Girl* and *woman,* for example, share the same semantic features as the words *female* and *human* but differ in regard to age. Words have semantic restrictions on how they can be used in sentences. The sentence "The bicycle
talked the boy into buying a candy bar" is syntactically correct but semantically
incorrect. The sentence violates our semantic knowledge—bicycles do not talk.

A final set of language rules involves **pragmatics**—the ability to engage in
appropriate conversation. Certain pragmatic rules ensure that a particular sentence
will be uttered in one context and not in another. For example, you know that it is
appropriate to say "Your new haircut certainly looks good" to someone who just
had his or her hair styled, but that it is inappropriate for you to say "That new
hairstyle makes you look awful." Through pragmatics we learn to convey intended
meaning with words, phrases, and sentences. Pragmatics helps us to communicate
more smoothly with others (Anderson, 1989).

Is this ability to generate rule systems for language and then use them to create
an almost infinite number of words, learned, or is it the product of biology and evolution?

Language's Biological Basis

In 1882, 2-year-old Helen Keller was left deaf, blind, and mute by a severe illness.
By the time she was 7 years old, she feared the world she could neither see nor hear.
Alexander Graham Bell suggested to her parents that they hire a tutor named Anne
Sullivan to help Helen overcome her fears (Figure 6.7). By using sign language,

*The adjective is the banana peel of the
parts of speech.*

Clifton Fadiman, Reader's Digest, *1956*

FIGURE 6.7   Helen Keller learning
language from Anne Sullivan
Source: UPI, Bettman Archive, Luis Lord.

Infancy

Newborn birds come into the world ready to sing the song of their species. They are biologically equipped to learn their species' song early in their development. Contemporary language researchers believe biology's contributions to language are very strong.

Anne was able to teach Helen a great deal about language. Helen Keller became an honors graduate of Radcliffe College and had this to say: "Whatever the process, the result is wonderful. Gradually from naming an object, we advance step by step until we have traversed the vast distance between our first stammered syllable and the sweep of thought in a line of Shakespeare."

What is the process of learning language like? Helen Keller had the benefit of a marvelous teacher, which suggests that experience is important in learning language. But might there have been biological foundations responsible for Helen's ability to communicate? Did Helen, despite her condition, have some biological predisposition to learn language?

The Biological Story

Newborn birds come into the world ready to sing the song of their species. They listen to their parents sing the song a few times and then they have learned it for the rest of their lives. Noam Chomsky (1957) believes that the language of human beings works in much the same way. Chomsky says that we are biologically predisposed to learn language at a certain time and in a certain way. Chomsky's ideas prompted David McNeil (1970) to propose that the child comes into the world with a **language acquisition device (LAD)** that is wired to detect certain language categories—phonology, syntax, and semantics, for example. McNeil also believes that we are able to detect deep and surface structures in language.

The contemporary view of language continues to stress that biology has a very strong role in language (Bates, O'Connell, & Shore, 1987; Miller, 1981; Wilks, in press). For example, George Miller (1981) argues that biology is far more important than environment in determining language's nature. In his view, the fact that evolution shaped humans into linguistic creatures is inevitable.

Ape Talk—From Gua to Nim Chimpsky

It is the early 1930s. A 7-month-old chimpanzee named Gua has been adopted by humans (Kellogg & Kellogg, 1933). Gua's adopters want to rear her alongside their 10-month-old son, Donald. Gua was treated much the way we rear human infants today—her adopters dressed her, talked with her, and played with her. Nine months after she was adopted, the project was discontinued because the parents feared that Gua was slowing down Donald's progress.

About 20 years later, another chimpanzee was adopted by human beings (Hayes & Hayes, 1951). Viki, as the chimp was called, was only a few days old at the time. The goal was straightforward: teach Viki to speak. Eventually she was taught to say "Mama," but only with painstaking effort. Day after day, week after week, the parents sat with Viki and shaped her mouth to make the desired sounds. She ultimately learned three other words—Papa, cup, and up—but she never learned the meanings of these words and her speech was not clear.

Approximately 20 years later, another chimpanzee named Washoe was adopted when she was about 10 months old (Gardner & Gardner, 1971). Recognizing that the earlier experiments with chimps had not demonstrated that apes have language, the trainers tried to teach Washoe the American sign language, which is the sign language of the deaf. Daily routine events, such as meals and washing, household chores, play with toys, and car rides to interesting places provided many opportunities for the use of sign language. In two years Washoe learned 38 different signs and by the age of 5 she had a vocabulary of 160 signs. Washoe learned how to put signs together in novel ways, such as "you drink" and "you me tickle" (Figure 6.A).

Yet another way to teach language to chimpanzees exists. The Premacks (Premack & Premack, 1972) constructed a

FIGURE 6.A   Washoe is learning to ask for objects by means of sign language.

set of plastic shapes that symbolized different objects and were able to teach the meanings of the shapes to a 6-year-old chimpanzee, Sarah. Sarah was able to respond correctly using such abstract symbols as "same as" or "different from." For example, she could tell you that "banana is yellow" is the same as "yellow color of banana." Sarah eventually was able to "name" objects, respond "yes," "no," "same as," and "different from" and tell you about certain events by using symbols (such as putting a banana on a tray). Did Sarah learn a generative language capable of productivity? Did the signs Washoe learned have an underlying system of language rules?

Herbert Terrace (1979) doubts that these apes have been taught language. Terrace was part of a research project designed to teach language to an ape by the name of Nim

Both physical and cultural evolution help to explain the development of language skills. The brain, nervous sytem, and vocal system changed over hundreds of thousands of years. Before *Homo sapiens,* the physical equipment to produce language was not present. Then social evolution occurred as human beings, with their newly evolved language capacity, had to generate a way of communicating. *Homo sapiens* went beyond the groans and shrieks of its predecessors with the development of abstract speech. Estimates of how long ago human beings acquired language vary

FIGURE 6.B   Nim Chimpsky learning sign language.

Chimpsky (named after famous linguist Noam Chomsky) (Figure 6.B). Initially, Terrace was optimistic about Nim's ability to use language as human beings use it, but after further evaluation he concluded that Nim really did not have language in the sense that human beings do. Terrace says that apes do not spontaneously expand on a trainer's statements as people do; instead, the apes just imitate their trainer. Terrace also believes that apes do not understand what they are saying when they speak; rather they are responding to cues from the trainer that they are not aware of.

The Gardners take exception to Terrace's conclusions (Gardner & Gardner, 1986). They point out that chimpanzees use inflections in sign language to refer to various ac-

tions, people, and places. They also cite recent evidence that the infant chimp Loulis learned over 50 signs from his adopted mother Washoe and other chimpanzees who used sign language.

The ape language controversy goes on. It does seem that chimpanzees can learn to use signs to communicate meanings, which has been the boundary for language. Whether the language of chimpanzees possesses all of the characteristics of human language such as phonology, morphology, syntax, semantics, and pragmatics is still being argued (Maratsos, 1983; Rumbaugh, 1988).   ◆

from about 20,000 to 70,000 years. This means that language is a very recent acquisition in evolutionary time. The role of language in human evolution has stimulated psychologists to think about the possibility that animals have language. Do chimpanzees and apes have language, for example? Is their language similar to human language? To discover the answer to this intriguing question and to learn about the way scientists teach apes and chimpanzees language, read Children 6.2.

Is There a Critical Period for Language Learning?

In addition to considering continuities in language between people and animals and the role of evolution, another biological aspect of language involves the issue of whether there is a critical period for learning language. If you have listened to former Secretary of State Henry Kissinger speak, you have some evidence for the belief that there exists a critical period for learning language. If a person over 12 years of age emigrates to a new country and then starts to learn its language, the individual probably will speak the language with a foreign accent for the rest of his life. Such was the case with Kissinger. But if an individual emigrates as a young child, the accent goes away as the new language is learned (Asher & Garcia, 1969; Oyama, 1973). Similarly, speaking like a native New Yorker is less related to how long you have lived in the city than to the age at which you moved there. Speaking with a New York "dialect" is more likely if you moved there before the age of 12. Apparently, puberty marks the close of a critical period for acquiring the phonological rules of different languages and dialects.

Eric Lenneberg (1962) speculated that lateralization of language in the brain also is subject to a similar critical period. He says that up until about 12 years of age, a child who has suffered damage to the brain's left hemisphere can shift language to the brain's right hemisphere; after this period, the shift is impossible. The idea of a critical period for shifting lateralization is controversial, and research on the issue is inconclusive (de Villiers & de Villiers, 1978).

The experiences of a modern-day wild child named Genie raises further interest in the idea of whether a critical time period for acquiring language exists. To learn more about Genie, turn to Children 6.3.

Such findings confirm the belief that language must be triggered to be learned and that the optimal time for that triggering is during the early years of childhood. Clearly, biology's role in language is powerful, but even the most heavily inherited aspects of human development require an environment for their expression.

The Behavioral View and Environmental Influences

Behaviorists view language as just another behavior, like sitting, walking, or running. They argue that language represents chains of responses (Skinner, 1957) or imitation (Bandura, 1977). But many of the sentences we produce are novel; we have not heard them or spoken them before. For example, a child hears the sentence, "The plate fell on the floor," and then says, "My mirror fell on the blanket," after she drops the mirror on the blanket. The behavioral mechanisms of reinforcement and imitation cannot completely explain this.

While spending long hours observing parents and their young children, Roger Brown (1973) searched for evidence that parents reinforce their children for speaking in grammatical ways. He found that parents did sometimes smile and praise their children for sentences they liked, but that they also reinforced sentences that were ungrammatical. Brown concluded that no evidence exists to document that reinforcement is responsible for language's rule systems.

Another criticism of the behavioral view is that it fails to explain the extensive orderliness of language. The behavioral view predicts that vast individual differences should appear in children's speech development because of each child's unique

Genie, Modern-Day Wild Child

Genie was found in 1970 in California. At the time, she was 13 years old and had been reared by a partially blind mother and a violent father. She was discovered because her mother applied for assistance at a public welfare office. At the time, Genie could not speak and could not stand erect. She had lived in almost total isolation during her childhood years. Naked and restrained by a harness that her father had fashioned, she was left to sit on her potty seat day after day. She could move only her hands and feet and she had virtually nothing to do every day of her life. At night, she was placed in a kind of straight jacket and caged in a crib with wire mesh sides and an overhead cover. She was fed, although sparingly. When she made a noise, her father beat her. He never spoke to her with words but growled and made barking sounds toward her.

Genie underwent extensive rehabilitation and training over a number of years (Curtiss, 1977). During her therapy, Genie learned to walk with a jerky motion and was toilet trained. She learned to recognize many words and to speak. At first she spoke in one-word utterances and eventually began to string together two-word utterances. She began to create some two-word sequences on her own, such as "big teeth," "little marble," and "two hand." Later she was able to put together three words—"small two cup," for example.

But unlike normal children, Genie never learned how to ask questions and she never understood grammar. Even four years later, after she began to put words together, her speech

Artist's drawing of the modern-day wild child, Genie, after she was found.
Illustration by Roger Burkhart.

sounded like a garbled telegram. Genie never understood the differences between pronouns and between passive and active verbs. She continues as an adult to speak in short, mangled sentences, such as "father hit leg," "big wood," and "Genie hurt." ◆

learning history. But as we have seen, a compelling fact about language is its structure and ever-present rule systems. All infants coo before they babble. All toddlers produce one-word utterances before two-word utterances, and all state sentences in the active form before they state them in the passive form.

However, we do not learn language in a social vacuum. Most children are bathed in language from a very early age. We need this early exposure to language to acquire competent language skills (Schegloff, 1989; Snow, 1989a). The Wild Boy of Aveyron did not learn to communicate effectively after being reared in social isolation for years. Genie's language was rudimentary even after a number of years of extensive training.

What are some of the ways the environment contributes to language development? Imitation is one important candidate. A child who is slow in developing her language ability can be helped if parents use carefully selected lists of words and grammatical constructions in their speech to the child (Snow, 1989b; Stine & Bohannon, 1984; Whitehurst & Valdez-Menchaca, 1988). Recent evidence also suggests that parents provide more corrective feedback for children's ungrammatical utterances than Brown originally thought (Bohannon & Stanowicz, 1988; Penner, 1987). Nonetheless, a number of language experts believe that imitation and reinforcement facilitate language but are not absolutely necessary for its acquisition (de Villiers & de Villiers, 1978).

One intriguing role of the environment in the young child's acquisition of language involves *motherese,* or the **baby-talk register,** a characteristic way of talking to young language learners. A *register* is a way of speaking to people (or pets) in a particular category, such as babies or foreigners. *Motherese* is somewhat of a misnomer because mothers, fathers, and people in general talk to babies this way. If you pay attention to your behavior when you talk to a baby, you will notice some interesting things. Your sentences will be short, you will use exaggerated intonation contours (speaking with great ups and downs in pitch), you will pause for long periods between sentences, and you will place great stress on important words. The baby-talk register is virtually universal. It was documented as early as the first century B.C. and is present in diverse languages (Brown, 1986; Grieser & Kuhl, 1988). When parents are asked why they use baby talk, they point out that it is designed to teach their baby to talk. Older peers also talk baby talk to infants, but observations of siblings indicate that the affectional features are dropped when sibling rivalry is sensed (Dunn & Kendrick, 1982).

Other than the baby-talk register, are there other strategies adults use to enhance the child's acquisition of language? Four candidates are recasting, echoing, expanding, and labeling. **Recasting** is phrasing the same or a similar meaning of a sentence in a different way, perhaps turning it into a question. For example, if the child says, "The dog was barking," the adult can respond by asking, "When was the dog barking?" The effects of recasting fit with suggestions that "following in order to lead" helps a child to learn language (Schaffer, 1977). That is, letting a child initially indicate an interest and then proceeding to elaborate that interest—commenting, demonstrating, and explaining—may enhance communication and help language acquisition. In contrast, an overly active, directive approach to communicating with the child may be harmful (Rice, 1989).

Echoing is repeating what the child says to you, especially if it is an incomplete phrase or sentence. **Expanding** is restating what the child has said in a linguistically sophisticated form. **Labeling** is identifying the names of objects. Young children are forever being asked to identify the names of objects. Roger Brown (1986) identified this as the great word game and claimed that much of the early vocabulary acquired by children is motivated by this adult pressure to identify the words associated with objects.

How Language Develops

In describing language, we have touched on language development many times. You just read about the baby-talk register parents use with their infants. Earlier we discussed Frederick II's effort to learn which language children would speak, the Wild Boy of Aveyron, Genie, and Donald and Gua.

Thinking Critically
In our discussion of language, we have emphasized the role of biological and environmental factors. How might cognitive factors be involved in language development?

Young children acquire language very quickly.

When does an infant utter her first word? The event usually occurs at about 10 to 13 months of age, although some infants take longer. Many parents view the onset of language development as coincident with this first word, but some significant accomplishments are attained earlier. Before babies say words, they babble, emitting such vocalizations as "goo-goo" and "ga-ga." Babbling starts at about 3 to 6 months of age; the start is determined by biological maturation, not reinforcement or the ability to hear. Even deaf babies babble for a time (Lenneberg, Rebelsky, & Nichols, 1965). Babbling exercises the baby's vocal apparatus and facilitates the development of articulation skills that are useful in later speech (Clark & Clark, 1977). But the purpose of a baby's earliest communication is to attract attention from parents and others in the environment. Infants engage the attention of others by making or breaking eye contact, by vocalizing sounds, or by performing manual actions such as pointing. All of those behaviors involve pragmatics.

A child's first words include those that name important people (dada), familiar animals (kittie), vehicles (car), toys (ball), food (milk), body parts (eye), clothes (hat), household items (clock), or greeting terms (bye). These were the first words of babies 50 years ago; they are the first words of babies today (Clark, 1983). At times it is hard to tell what these one-word utterances mean. One possibility is that they stand for an entire sentence in the infant's mind. Because of limited cognitive or linguistic skills, possibly only one word comes out instead of the whole sentence. This is called the **holophrase hypothesis**—that is, a single word is used to imply a complete sentence.

Children pick up words as pigeons peas.
John Ray, English Proverbs, 1670

First Words of Japanese Babies

Among the first words babies hear in Japan is the baby's own name. Other early words often are concerned with body functions and help the baby become aware of its physical self-identity. Some words are related to feeding, others with elimination, and yet others with activities and accomplishments such as crawling, dressing, washing, and bathing. In each case, the training involves words that encourage the gradual development of self-control. Japanese parents carefully guide the child in the "proper" way to do things, often through clearly defined physical assistance (Hendry, 1986). ◆

For words that a child uses as nouns, the meanings can be overextended or underextended. Eve Clark (1983) has studied early words and described a number of **overextensions.** For instance, when a child learns to say the word *dada* for *father,* she often applies the term beyond the class of individuals it was intended to represent, using it for other men, strangers, or boys, for example. With time, such overextension decreases and eventually disappears. **Underextension** occurs when a child fails to use a noun to name a relevant event or object. For instance, the child may learn to use the word *boy* to describe a 5-year-old neighbor but will not apply the word to a male infant or a 9-year-old male.

By the time children are 18 to 24 months of age, they usually utter two-word statements. During this two-word stage, they quickly grasp the importance of expressing concepts and the role that language plays in communicating with others. To convey meaning with two-word utterances, the child relies heavily on gesture, tone, and context. The wealth of meaning children can communicate with a two-word utterance includes the following (Slobin, 1972):

Identification: See doggie.
Location: Book there.
Repetition: More milk.
Nonexistence: Allgone thing.
Negation: Not wolf.
Possession: My candy.
Attribution: Big car.
Agent-action: Mama walk.
Action-direct-object: Give papa.
Action-instrument: Cut knife.
Question: Where ball?

One of the striking aspects of this list is that it is used by children all over the world. The examples are taken from utterances in English, German, Russian, Turkish, and Samoan, but the entire list could be derived from a 2-year-old's speech in any language.

A child's two-word utterance differs substantially from adult word combinations. Language usage at this time is called **telegraphic speech.** When we send telegrams to individuals, we try to be short and precise, excluding any unnecessary words. As indicated in the examples of telegraphic speech from children around the world, articles, auxiliary verbs, and other connectives usually are omitted. Of course, telegraphic speech is not limited to two-word utterances. "Mommy give ice cream," or "Mommy give Tommy ice cream," also are examples of telegraphic speech.

One- and two-word utterances classify children's language development in terms of the number of utterances. Roger Brown (1973) expanded this concept by proposing that **mean length of utterance (MLU)** is a good index of a child's language

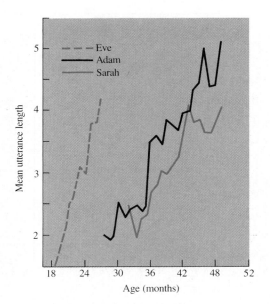

maturity. Brown identified five stages based on an estimation of the number of words per sentence that a child produces in a sample of about 50 to 100 sentences. The mean length of utterance for each stage is as follows:

Stage	*MLU*
1	1+ to 2.0
2	2.5
3	3.0
4	3.5
5	4.0

The first stage begins when the child generates sentences consisting of more than one word, such as examples of two-word utterances we gave. The 1+ designation suggests that the average number of words in each utterance is greater than one but not yet two, because some of the child's utterances are still holophrases. This stage continues until the child averages two words per utterance. Subsequent stages are marked by increments of 0.5 in mean length of utterance.

Brown's stages are important for several reasons. First, children who vary in chronological age as much as one-half to three-fourths of a year still have similar speech patterns. Second, children with similar mean lengths of utterance seem to have similar rule systems that characterize their language. In some ways, then, MLU is a better indicator of language development than chronological age. Figure 6.8 shows the individual variation in chronological age that characterizes children's MLU.

As we have just seen, language unfolds in a sequence. At every point in development, the child's linguistic interaction with parents and others obeys certain principles. Not only is this development strongly influenced by the child's biological wiring, but the language environment the child is bathed in from an early age is far more intricate than was imagined in the past (von Tetzchner & Siegel, 1989). The main ideas we have discussed about language development are summarized in Concept Table 6.2. In the next chapter, we will continue our discussion of infant development, turning to information about the infant's social worlds.

Infancy

Language Development

Concept	Processes and Related Ideas	Characteristics and Description
What Is Language?	Its nature	A sequence of words that involves infinite generativity, displacement, and rules systems. Rule systems include phonology, morphology, syntax, semantics, and pragmatics.
The Biological Basis of Language	The biological story	Chomsky believes that we are biologically prewired to learn language. McNeil says that we have a language acquisition device that includes wiring for surface and deep structures. The fact that evolution shaped human beings into linguistic creatures is undeniable.
	Critical period	The experiences of Genie and other children suggest that the early childhood years are an optimal time for learning language. If exposure to language does not come before puberty, lifelong deficits in grammar result.
The Behavioral View and Environmental Influences	The behavioral view	Language is just another behavior. Behaviorists believe that language is learned primarily through reinforcement and imitation, although they probably play a facilitative rather than a necessary role.
	Environmental influences	Most children are bathed in language early in their development. Among the ways adults teach language to infants are the baby-talk register, recasting, echoing, expanding, and labeling.
How Language Develops	Its nature	Vocalization begins with babbling at about 3 to 6 months of age. A baby's earliest communication skills are pragmatic. One-word utterances occur at about 10 to 13 months; the holophrase hypothesis has been applied to this. By 18 to 24 months, most infants use two-word utterances. Language at this point is referred to as telegraphic. Brown developed the idea of mean length of utterance (MLU). Five stages of MLU have been identified, providing a valuable indicator of language maturity.

Summary

I. **Piaget's Theory of Infant Development**
The stage of sensorimotor development lasts from birth to about 2 years of age. It involves progression in the infant's ability to organize and coordinate sensations with physical movements. The sensorimotor stage has six substages: simple reflexes, first habits and primary circular reactions; secondary circular reactions; tertiary circular reactions, novelty, and curiosity; and internalization of schemes. Object permanence is an important accomplishment in infant cognitive development; it refers to the development of the ability to understand that objects and events continue to exist even though the infant is no longer in contact with them. Piaget believed that this ability developed over the course of the six substages.

II. **Habituation**
Habituation is the repeated presentation of a stimulus, causing reduced attention to the stimulus. If a different stimulus is presented and the infant pays attention to it, dishabituation is occurring. Newborn infants can habituate, although habituation becomes more acute over the first three months of infancy.

III. **Memory**

Memory is the retention of information over time. In the first six months, infants learn adaptive skills, but conscious memory does not develop until later in the first year. Infantile amnesia is our inability to remember anything that happened in the first three years of our life.

IV. **Imitation**

Infants only 1 day old imitate facial expressions of emotion by adults. Whether the imitation is learned or innate is open to interpretation.

V. **Individual Differences in Intelligence**

Developmental scales for infants grew out of the tradition of IQ testing with older children. These scales are less verbal than IQ tests. Gesell was an early pioneer in the development of infant scales. His scale is still widely used by pediatricians; it provides a DQ (developmental quotient). The Bayley Scales are the most widely used today. They consist of a Motor scale, a Mental scale, and an Infant Behavior Profile. Global infant intelligence measures do not predict childhood intelligence. However, specific aspects of infant intelligence, such as information processing tasks involving attention, are better predictors of childhood intelligence, especially in a specific area.

VI. **What Is Language?**

Language is a sequence of words that involves infinite generativity, displacement, and rule systems. Rule systems include phonology, morphology, syntax, semantics, and pragmatics.

VII. **The Biological Basis of Language**

Chomsky believes that we are biologically prewired to learn language. McNeil says that we have a language acquisition device that includes wiring for surface and deep structures. The fact that evolution shaped human beings into linguistic creatures is undeniable. The experiences of Genie and other children suggest that the early childhood years are an optimal time for learning language. If exposure to language does not come before puberty, lifelong deficits in grammar result.

VIII. **The Behavioral View and Environmental Influences**

Language is just another behavior in the behavioral view. Behaviorists believe that language is learned primarily through reinforcement and imitation, although they probably play a facilitative rather than a necessary role. Most children are bathed in language early in their development. Among the ways adults teach language to infants are the baby-talk register, recasting, echoing, expanding, and labeling.

IX. **How Language Develops**

Vocalization begins with babbling at about 3 to 6 months of age. A baby's earliest communication skills are pragmatic. One-word utterances occur at about 10 to 13 months; the holophrase hypothesis has been applied to this. By 18 to 24 months, most infants use two-word utterances. Language at this point is referred to as telegraphic. Brown developed the idea of mean length of utterance (MLU). Five stages of MLU have been identified, providing a valuable indicator of language maturity.

Key Terms

scheme 169
simple reflexes 170
first habits and primary
   circular reactions 170
primary circular
   reactions 170
secondary circular
   reactions 170
coordination of secondary
   reactions 171
tertiary circular reactions,
   novelty, and
   curiosity 171
tertiary circular
   reactions 171
internalization of
   schemes 173

object permanence 173
habituation 175
dishabituation 175
memory 176
infantile amnesia 177
developmental quotient
   (DQ) 180
Bayley Scales of Infant
   Development 180
language 183
infinite generativity 183
displacement 183
phonology 183
morphology 183
syntax 184
grammar 184
surface structure 184

deep structure 184
semantics 184
pragmatics 184
language acquisition device
   (LAD) 185
baby-talk register 190
recasting 190
echoing 190
expanding 190
labeling 190
holophrase hypothesis 191
overextensions 192
underextension 192
telegraphic speech 193
mean length of utterance
   (MLU) 193

Suggested Readings

Bruner, J. (1983). *Child talk*. New York: Norton.
   A fascinating view of the child's language development by one of the leading cognitive
   theorists.
Curtiss, S. (1977). *Genie*. New York: Academic Press.
   Susan Curtiss tells the remarkable story of Genie, a modern-day wild child and her
   ordeal of trying to acquire language.
Ginsburg, H., & Opper, S. (1979). *Piaget's theory of intellectual development* (2nd ed.).
   Englewood Cliffs, NJ: Prentice-Hall.
   One of the best explanations and descriptions of Piaget's theory of infant
   development.
Maratsos, M. (1983). Some current issues in the study of the acquisition of grammar. In
   P. H. Mussen (Ed.), *Handbook of child psychology* (4th ed., Vol. 2). New York:
   Wiley.
   A thorough, informative review of what we know about language development.
Rovee-Collier, C. (1987). Learning and memory in infancy. In J. D. Osofsky (Ed.),
   Handbook of infant development. New York: Wiley.
   One of the leading researchers on infant memory describes how infants learn and
   remember; special attention is given to habituation.

7

Social Development

he newborns of some species function independently in the world; other species are not so independent. At birth, the opossum is still considered fetal and is capable of finding its way around only in its mother's pouch, where it attaches itself to her nipple and continues to develop. This protective environment is similar to the uterus. By contrast, the wildebeest must run with the herd moments after birth. The newborn wildebeest's behavior is far more adult than the opossum's, although the wildebeest does have to obtain food through suckling. The maturation of the human infant lies somewhere between these two extremes; much learning and development must take place before the infant can sustain itself (Maccoby, 1980) (Figure 7.1).

Because it cannot sustain itself, the human infant requires extensive care. What kind of care is needed and how does the infant begin the road to social maturity? Much of the interest in infant care focuses on attachment, although the infant's development of emotions, trust, sense of self, and independence are important as well. Before we tackle these important dimensions of the infant's social development, some basic ideas about sociocultural and family processes need to be considered.

FIGURE 7.1 Variations in the dependency of newborns in different species. (a) The newborn opossum is fetal, capable of finding its way around only in its mother's pouch, where it attaches itself to her nipple and continues to develop. (b) By contrast, the wildebeest runs with the herd moments after birth. (c) The human newborn's maturation lies somewhere in between that of the opossum and that of the wildebeest.

(a)

(b)

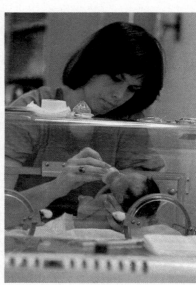

(c)

Infancy

Sociocultural and Family Processes

In Brazil, almost every middle-class family can afford a nanny, and there is no such thing as a babysitting problem. However, because many of the nannies believe in black magic, it is not beyond the realm of possibility for Brazilian parents to return home from a movie and find their infant screaming, presumably, according to the nanny, from a voodoo curse. Contrast the world of the middle-class Brazilian family with the world of the typical family in Thailand, where farm families are large and can afford to educate only their most promising child—determined by which child is most capable of learning English. Such sociocultural and family experiences play important roles in the infant's development.

Sociocultural Influences

Sociocultural influences range from the broad-based, global inputs of culture to a mother or father's affectionate touch. A view that captures the complexity of this sociocultural world as developed by Urie Bronfenbrenner (1979, 1989). Figure 7.2 portrays Bronfenbrenner's ecological model for understanding sociocultural influences. Notice that the child is placed in the center of the model and that the child's most direct interactions are with the **microsystem**—the setting in which the child lives. These contexts include the child's family, school, peers, and neighborhood. The child is not viewed as a passive recipient of experiences in these settings, but as someone who helps to construct the environment. Most research on sociocultural

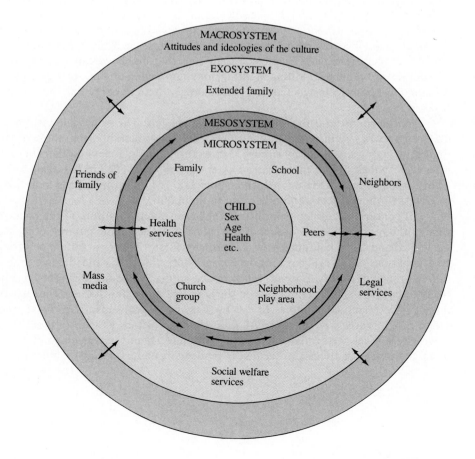

FIGURE 7.2   Bronfenbrenner's ecological model. Bronfenbrenner's model provides one of the most systematic analyses of the environment's role in the child's development. The model ranges from the micro, fine-grained analyses of face-to-face interactions between children and social agents to their molar influences of culture.

(a)

(b)

FIGURE 7.3 (a) The peaceful !Kung of Southern Africa discourage any kind of aggression; the !Kung are called the "harmless people." (b) Hardly harmless, the violent Yanomamo Indians of South America are told that manhood cannot be achieved unless they are capable of killing, fighting, and pummeling others.

influences focuses on the microsystem, emphasizing the infant's attachment to parents, parenting strategies, sibling relationships, peer relations and friendships, and school experiences.

The **mesosystem** involves relations between microsystems or connections between contexts. Examples include the relation of family experiences to school experiences, school experiences to church experiences, or family experiences to peer experiences. For example, a child whose parents have rejected him may have difficulty developing a positive relationship with his teachers. Developmentalists increasingly believe that it is important to observe the child's behavior in multiple settings—such as family, peer, and school contexts—to provide a more complete picture of the child's social development.

Children also experience their environment in a more indirect way. The **exosystem** is involved when experiences in another social setting—in which the child does not have an active role—influences what the child experiences in an immediate context. For example, work experiences may affect a woman's relationship with her husband and children. She may receive a promotion that requires more travel. This might increase marital conflict and change caregiving, perhaps increasing father care or day care. Another example of an exosystem is the city government, which is responsible for the quality of parks and recreation facilities available to children.

The most abstract level in Bronfenbrenner's analysis of sociocultural influences is the **macrosystem**—the attitudes and ideologies of the culture. People in a particular culture share some broad-based beliefs. The people of Russia have certain beliefs; the people of China have certain beliefs; so do the people of a South Sea island culture. Consider the !Kung of southern Africa and the Yanomamo Indians of South America (Figure 7.3). The !Kung are peaceful people. They discourage any kind of aggression on the part of their children and resolve disputes calmly. The !Kung are described as "harmless people." By contrast, the Yanamamo Indians are called the "fierce people." They teach their sons that manhood cannot be attained unless they are capable of killing, fighting, and pummeling others. As they grow up, Yanamamo boys are instructed at great length in how to carry out these violent tasks.

Within countries, subcultures have shared beliefs. The values and attitudes of children growing up in an urban ghetto may differ considerably from those of children growing up in a wealthy suburb. For example, middle-class mothers verbally interact with their infants more than do lower-class mothers (Tulkin & Kagan, 1971). They respond more to the infant's frets, entertain the infant more, are more likely to give the infant objects, and talk more to the infant.

Of concern to developmentalists is the lower-class subculture of the poor. Although the most noticeable aspect of the poor is their economic poverty, other psychological and social characteristics are present. First, the poor are often powerless. In occupations, they rarely are the decision makers; rules are handed down to them in an authoritarian way. Second, the poor are vulnerable to disaster. They are not likely to be given advance notice when they are laid off from work, and they usually do not have financial resources to fall back on when problems arise. Third, their range of alternatives is restricted. A limited range of jobs is open to them. Even when alternatives are available, they may not know about them or may not be prepared to make a wise decision, because of inadequate education and inability to read

Mother-Child Interaction in an Inner-City Housing Project

Some young children are brought up in the blighted urban areas of high-rise housing projects. Many of them are the children of single mothers. The small apartments and public housing rules discourage extended families. High-rise buildings frequently eliminate the possibility of free play outside by young children.

Young mothers isolated in these small apartments with their young children are often separated from family members by the expense and trouble of cross-town public transportation. The mothers watch television, talk on the phone, or perform household and caregiving chores. Playmates for their children are scarce. So are toys. The mother's girlfriends, the older children of neighbors, visits to the grocery store, the welfare office, and the laundromat may represent the only breaks in daily apartment routines. So may the usually traumatic visits to the health clinic.

One mother agreed to let researcher Shirley Heath (in press) tape-record her interactions with her children over a two-year period and to write notes about her activities with them. Within 500 hours of tape and more than 1,000 lines of notes, the mother living in a high-rise urban housing project initiated talk with one of her three preschool children on only 18 occasions (other than giving them a brief directive or asking a quick question). Few of the mother's conversations involved either planning or executing actions with or for her children.

Heath (1989) points out that the lack of family and community supports is widespread in urban housing projects, especially among black Americans. The deteriorating, impoverished conditions of these inner-city areas severely impede the ability of young children to develop the cognitive and social skills they need to function competently.   ◆

well. Fourth, there is little prestige in being poor. This lack of prestige is transmitted to the child early in life; the poor child observes other children who wear nicer clothes and live in more attractive houses. Whether a child grows up in poverty or in a comfortable middle-class setting, experiences in the family constitute the most important sociocultural setting in the child's life.

Family Processes

Most of us began our lives in families and spent thousands of hours during our childhood interacting with our parents. Some of you already are parents; others of you may become parents. What is the transition to parenthood like? What is the nature of family processes?

Transition to Parenthood

When people become parents through pregnancy, adoption, or stepparenting, they face disequilibrium and must adapt. Parents want to develop a strong attachment with their infant, but they still want to maintain a strong attachment to their spouse and friends and possibly continue their careers. Parents ask themselves how this new being will change their lives. A baby places new restrictions on partners; no longer will they be able to rush out to a movie on a moment's notice, money will not be readily available for vacations and other luxuries. Dual-career parents ask, "Will it harm the baby to place her in day care? Will we be able to find responsible babysitters?"

The excitement and joy that accompany the birth of a healthy baby are often followed by "postpartum blues" in mothers—a depressed state that lasts as long as nine months into the infant's first year (Fleming & others, 1988; Osofsky, 1989). The early months of the baby's physical demands may bring not only the joy of intimacy but also the sorrow of exhaustion. Pregnancy and childbirth are demanding physical events that require recovery time for the mother. As one mother told it:

> When I was pregnant, I felt more tired than ever before in my life. Since my baby was born, I am 100 percent more tired. It's not just physical exhaustion from the stress of childbirth and subsequent days of interrupted sleep, but I'm slowed down emotionally and intellectually as well. I'm too tired to make calls to find a babysitter. I see a scrap of paper on the floor, and I'm too tired to pick it up. I want to be taken care of and have no demands made of me other than the baby's. *Ourselves and our Children*, 1978, pp. 42–43.

Many fathers are not sensitive to these extreme demands placed on the mother. Busy trying to make enough money to pay the bills, fathers may not be at home much of the time. A father's ability to sense and adapt to the stress placed on his wife during the first year of the infant's life has important implications for the success of the marriage and the family.

Becoming a father is both wonderful *and* stressful. In a longitudinal investigation of couples from late pregnancy until three-and-one-half years after the baby was born, Carolyn and Phillip Cowan (Cowan, 1988; Cowan & Cowan, 1989, in press) found that the couples enjoyed more positive marital relations before the baby was born than after. Still, almost one-third showed an increase in marital satisfaction. Some couples said that the baby had both brought them closer together *and* moved them farther apart. They commented that being parents enhanced their sense of themselves and gave them a new, more stable identity as a couple. Babies opened men up to a concern with intimate relationships, and the demands of juggling work and family roles stimulated women to manage family tasks more efficiently and pay attention to their personal growth.

At some point during the early years of the child's life, parents do face the difficult task of juggling their roles as parents and self-actualizing adults. Until recently in our culture, nurturing our children and having a career were thought to be incompatible. Fortunately, we have come to recognize that the balance between caring and achieving, nurturing and working—although difficult to manage—can be accomplished.

We may never know the love of our parents, until we become parents.

Henry Ward Beecher, 1887

The interaction of mothers and their infants is symbolized as a dance or a dialogue in which the successive actions of the partners are closely coordinated. This coordinated dance or dialogue can assume the form of synchrony, as shown here in the interaction of a synchronous mother-infant pair.

Reciprocal Socialization

For many years, socialization between parents and children was viewed as a one-way process: Children were considered to be the products of their parents' socialization techniques. By contrast, socialization between parents and their children is now viewed as reciprocal: Children socialize their parents just as parents socialize children. This process is called **reciprocal socialization.** For example, the interaction of mothers and their infants is symbolized as a dance or a dialogue in which successive actions of the partners are closely coordinated. This coordinated dance or dialogue can assume the form of mutual synchrony (each person's behavior depends on the partner's previous behavior), or it can be reciprocal in a more precise sense; the actions of the partners can be matched, as when one partner imitates the other or when there is mutual smiling (Cohn & Tronick, 1988).

When reciprocal socialization has been investigated in infancy, mutual gaze or eye contact has been found to play an important role in early social interaction (Fogel, 1988; Fogel, Toda, & Kawai, 1988). In one investigation, the mother and infant engaged in a variety of behaviors while they looked at each other; by contrast, when they looked away from each other, the rate of such behaviors dropped considerably (Stern & others, 1977). In sum, the behaviors of mothers and infants involve substantial interconnection and synchronization.

Scaffolding describes the manner in which some competent parents interact with their infants (Bruner, 1989). In scaffolding, mothers provide a framework around which they and their infants interact. For example, in the game of peek-a-boo, mothers initially cover their babies, then remove the covering, and finally register "surprise" at the reappearance. As infants become more skilled at peek-a-boo, the infants do the covering and uncovering. Recently, researchers have documented the importance of scaffolding in infant development. In the investigation by Deborah Vandell and Kathy Wilson (1988), infants who had more extensive scaffolding experiences with their parents, especially in the form of turn-taking, were more likely to engage in turn-taking as they interacted with their peers. More about the role of peek-a-boo and other parent-infant social games appears in Children 7.1.

Pat-a-Cake and Peek-a-Boo

Pat-a-cake and peek-a-boo are among infants' most enjoyable games. But they are more than just fun and games. These games and others function to introduce infants to social behavior's rules. Games like pat-a-cake and peek-a-boo are highly repetitive with simple roles for both parents and the infant. They help infants learn the rules of give-and-take during conversations. And, even when infants are too young to play an active role in the games, the repetitive structure of the games may help them to sense the turn-taking aspects of social interaction.

Infant researcher Tiffany Field (1987) observed that, in addition to *pat-a-cake* and *peek-a-boo*, other infant games function to introduce social behavior's rules and turn-taking sequences. These included:

Tell me a story. Parents ask babies to tell a story and the baby coos or utters some other sound. The parent then provides the words for both the story

and the reactions to the story. This game teaches infants that their responses will produce a response from parents.

I'm gonna get you. Wide-eyed parents time after time loom toward the infant, saying "Ah, boom!" or "I'm gonna get you." The repetitious behavior usually brings forth a smile or laugh from the infant. Parents usually continue the game until the infant no longer smiles or laughs.

Walking fingers or **creepie crawlies.** Parents use their fingers to crawl, spiderlike, up the infant's body, usually making the infant laugh.

So big. Parents extend the infant's arms upwards and say, "So big. My goodness, you are so big." This activity provides the infant with a combination of visual, auditory, and tactile stimulation. ◆

(a)

(a) Pat-a-cake; (b) peek-a-boo, and (c) so-big are excellent games for parents to play with their infants. Through such games, children learn social rules, especially turn-taking.

(b)

(c)

The Family as a System

As a social system, the family can be thought of as a constellation of subsystems defined in terms of generation, gender, and role. Divisions of labor among family members define particular subunits, and attachments define others. Each family member is a participant in several subsystems—some dyadic (involving two people), some polyadic (involving more than two people). The father and child represent one dyadic subsystem, the mother and father another; the mother-father-child represent one polyadic subsystem, the mother and two siblings another (Belsky, Rovine, & Fish, 1989).

An organizational scheme that highlights the reciprocal influences of family members and family subsystems is shown in Figure 7.4 (Belsky, 1981). As the arrows in the figure show, marital relations, parenting, and infant behavior can have both direct and indirect effects on each other. An example of a direct effect is the influence of the parent's behavior on the child; an example of an indirect effect is how the relationship between the spouses mediates the way a parent acts toward the child. For example, marital conflict might reduce the efficiency of parenting, in which case marital conflict would be an indirect effect on the child's behavior. In the family system, the infant's most important experiences involve the process of attachment.

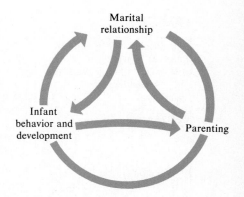

FIGURE 7.4   Direct and indirect effects of family interaction. Jay Belsky developed this model to describe the way that family interaction patterns can have both direct and indirect effects. For example, the parent's behavior can have a direct effect on the infant's development, or the marital relationship can have indirect effects on the infant's development by influencing parenting behavior.

Attachment

A small curly-haired girl named Danielle, age 11 months, begins to whimper. After a few seconds, she begins to wail. The psychologist observing Danielle is conducting a research study on the nature of attachment between infants and their mothers. The psychologist is watching Danielle's cry. Subsequently, the mother reenters the room, and Danielle's crying ceases. Quickly, Danielle crawls over to where her mother is seated and reaches out to be held. This scenario is one of the main ways that psychologists study the nature of attachment during infancy.

What Is Attachment?

In everyday language, attachment refers to a relationship between two individuals in which each individual feels strongly about the other and does a number of things to continue the relationship. Many pairs of people are attached: relatives, lovers, a teacher and a student. In the language of developmental psychology, though, **attachment** is often restricted to a relationship between particular social figures and to a particular phenomenon thought to reflect unique characteristics of the relationship. The developmental period is infancy, the social figures are the infant and one or more adult caregivers, and the phenomenon in question is a bond (Hartup, 1989; Vaughn & others, in press).

When researchers investigate attachment, what dimensions do they study? The most frequently used indicators of attachment are maintaining contact and proximity, protest at separation, and stranger anxiety. Infants often try to maintain physical contact with their caregiver in every way possible. If the caregiver moves across the room, the infant follows. If the caregiver puts the infant down, the infant may cling tenaciously. If the caregiver looks away, the infant may try to regain the caregiver's attention by calling, pulling on the caregiver, or shifting locations. Consider 2-year-old David, whose father turned away to read the newspaper. Young David grabbed his father's face and forcibly turned it to reestablish visual contact.

Sometimes, when the caregiver leaves, the infant cannot maintain physical contact or may not actively try to do so. Instead, the infant may protest the departure by whining, crying, thrashing about, or otherwise indicating displeasure. This type of behavior has been referred to as **separation anxiety.** Closely associated with separation anxiety is a set of behaviors that occur when the caregiver returns after

< cathy>

cathy ®   **by Cathy Guisewite**

Panel 1: YOU SHOULDN'T RUSH TO COMFORT HIM EVERY TIME HE OPENS HIS MOUTH. / THANK YOU, DR. SPOCK. / WAAH!

Panel 2: FOR THE REST OF HIS LIFE, HE'LL EXPECT YOU TO COME RUNNING EVERY TIME HE LETS OUT A LITTLE PEEP! IT'S UNFAIR TO HIM AND DEMEANING TO YOU!!

Panel 3: CATHY, UH... / COMING, MAX! JUST A SECOND! I'M ON MY WAY!

Panel 4: LOOK WHO'S TALKING.

FIGURE 7.5   Shown here is one of the monkeys in Harlow's classic "contact comfort" study. Regardless of whether they were fed by the wire mother or by the cloth mother, the infant monkeys overwhelming preferred to be in contact with the cloth mother, demonstrating the importance of contact comfort in attachment.

such a separation episode. The infant may smile, giggle, quickly approach, and cling to the caregiver. The corollary is not always simple, though. Consider young David again. He and his 7-year-old sister spent a week with a babysitter while their parents vacationed. When his parents returned, David's reaction was more one of shock than glee. He held his distance, resisted efforts to be held or kissed, and made a nasty face.

Infants also may behave in ways that reflect distress and fear—when an unfamiliar individual approaches, for example. Crying, clinging to the caregiver, and moving away from or averting the gaze of the stranger are all examples of these behaviors. **Stranger anxiety,** or fear of strangers, is the term developmentalists use to describe this type of behavior. In many infants, but not all, stranger anxiety appears later than attachment to a specific caregiver. For example, in one investigation, specific attachment to the mother occurred at about 6 months, followed by stranger anxiety at about 8 months (Schaffer & Emerson, 1964). However, stranger anxiety is influenced by the nature of the situation. Infants are less afraid of a nice stranger than a nasty stranger, and they are less afraid of a stranger when they are sitting on their mother's lap than when they are not (Clarke-Stewart, 1978).

There is no shortage of theories about infant attachment. Freud believed that the infant becomes attached to the person or object that provides oral satisfaction; for most infants, this is the mother, since she is most likely to feed the infant.

But is feeding as important as Freud thought? A classic study by Harry Harlow and Robert Zimmerman (1959) suggests that the answer is no. These researchers evaluated whether feeding or contact comfort was more important to infant attachment. Infant monkeys were removed from their mothers at birth and reared for six months by surrogate (substitute) "mothers." As shown in Figure 7.5, one of the mothers was made of wire, the other of cloth. Half of the infant monkeys were fed by the wire mother, half by the cloth mother. Periodically the amount of time the infant monkeys spent with either the wire or the cloth monkey was computed. Figure 7.6, indicates that regardless of whether they were fed by the wire or the cloth mother, the infant monkeys spent far more time with the cloth mother. This study clearly demonstrates that feeding is not the crucial element in the attachment process and that contact comfort is important.

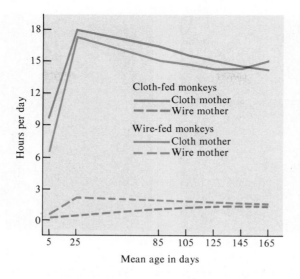

FIGURE 7.6 Harlow and Zimmerman's wire and cloth monkey study. The average amount of time infant monkeys spent in contact with their cloth and wire mothers is shown. The infant monkeys spent most of their time with the cloth monkey, regardless of which mother fed them (Harlow & Zimmerman, 1959).

Most toddlers develop a strong attachment to a favorite soft toy or a particular blanket. Toddlers may carry the toy or blanket with them everywhere they go, just as Linus does in the "Peanuts" cartoon strip, or they may run for the toy or blanket only in moments of crisis, such as after an argument or a fall. By the time they have outgrown the security object, all that may be left is a small fragment of the blanket, or an animal that is hardly recognizable, having had a couple of new faces and all its seams resewn half a dozen times. If parents try to replace the security object with something newer, the toddler will resist. There is nothing abnormal about a toddler carrying around a security blanket. Children know that the blanket or teddy bear is not the mother, and yet they react affectively to these objects and derive comfort from them as if they were the mother. Eventually they abandon the security object as they grow up and become more sure of themselves.

Might familiarity breed attachment? The famous study by Konrad Lorenz (1965) suggests that the answer is yes. Remember from our description of this study in Chapter 2 that newborn goslings became attached to "father" Lorenz rather than to their mother because he was the first moving object they saw. The time period during which familiarity is important for goslings is the first 36 hours after birth; for human beings, it is more on the order of the first year of life.

Erik Erikson (1968) believes that the first year of life is the key time frame for the development of attachment. Recall his proposal—also discussed in Chapter 11—that the first year of life represents the stage of trust versus mistrust. A sense of trust requires a feeling of physical comfort and a minimal amount of fear and apprehension about the future. Trust in infancy sets the stage for a lifelong expectation that the world will be a good and pleasant place to be. Erikson also believes that responsive, sensitive parenting contributes to the infant's sense of trust.

The ethological perspective of British psychiatrist John Bowlby (1969, 1980, 1989) also stresses the importance of attachment in the first year of life and the responsiveness of the caregiver. Bowlby believes that the infant and the mother instinctively form an attachment. He argues that the newborn is biologically equipped to elicit the mother's attachment behavior. The baby cries, clings, coos, and smiles.

Soft toys or a particular blanket are common attachment objects of toddlers. Most toddlers eventually abandon the security object as they grow up and become more sure of themselves.

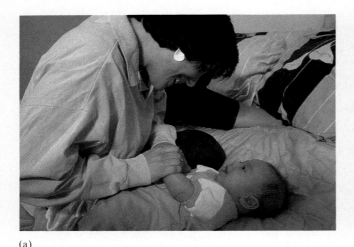

(a)

(b)

The attachment theorists argue that early experience plays an important role in the child's social behavior later in development. (a) Secure attachment to the mother in infancy was related to (b) the preschool child's social competence as reflected in more happy feelings and less frustration in one investigation (Matas, Arend, & Sroufe, 1978).

Later the infant crawls, walks, and follows the mother. The goal for the infant is to keep the mother nearby. Research on attachment supports Bowlby's view that at about 6 to 7 months of age, attachment of the infant to the caregiver intensifies (Sroufe, 1985).

Individual Differences

Although attachment to the caregiver intensifies midway through the first year, isn't it likely that some babies have a more positive attachment experience than others? Mary Ainsworth (1979) thinks so and says that this variation can be categorized as secure or insecure attachment. In **secure attachment,** the infant uses the caregiver, usually the mother, as a secure base from which to explore the environment. The securely attached infant moves freely away from the mother but processes her location through periodic glances. The securely attached infant also responds positively to being picked up by others, and when put back down, moves freely to play. An insecurely attached infant, by contrast, avoids the mother or is ambivalent toward her. The insecurely attached infant fears strangers and is upset by minor, everyday separations.

Ainsworth believes that the insecurely attached infant can be classified as either anxious-avoidant or anxious-resistant, making three main attachment categories: secure (type B), anxious-avoidant (type A), and anxious-resistant (type C). **Type B babies** use the caregiver as a secure base from which to explore the environment. **Type A babies** exhibit insecurity by avoiding the mother (for example, ignoring her, averting her gaze, and failing to seek proximity). **Type C babies** exhibit insecurity by resisting the mother (for example, clinging to her but at the same time fighting against the closeness, perhaps by kicking and pushing away).

Why are some infants securely attached and others insecurely attached? Following Bowlby's lead, Ainsworth believes that attachment security depends on how sensitive and responsive the caregiver is to the infant's signals. For example, infants who are securely attached are more likely to have mothers who are more sensitive, accepting, and expressive of affection toward them than those who are insecurely attached (Pederson & others, 1989).

If early attachment to the caregiver is important, it should relate to the child's social behavior later in development. Research by Alan Sroufe (1985, 1987) documents this connection. In one investigation, infants who were securely attached to

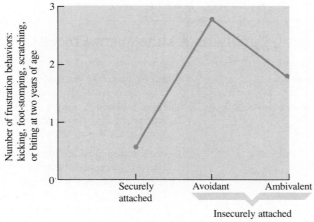

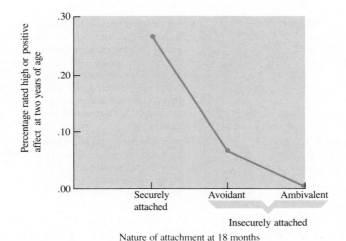

FIGURE 7.7   Research by Alan Sroufe and his colleagues demonstrates that secure attachment in infancy is related to the child's social competence. In this study (Matas, Arend, & Sroufe, 1978), infants who were securely attached to their mothers at 18 months of age showed less frustration behavior (*top figure*) and more positive affect (*bottom figure*) at 2 years of age.

their mothers early in infancy were less frustrated and happier at 2 years of age than their insecurely attached counterparts (Figure 7.7) (Matas, Arend, & Sroufe, 1978). And, in another longitudinal investigation, securely attached infants were more socially competent and had better grades in the third grade (Egeland, 1989).

Attachment, Temperament, and the Wider Social World

Not all developmentalists believe that a secure attachment in infancy is the only path to competence in life. Indeed, some developmentalists believe that too much emphasis is placed on the importance of the attachment bond in infancy. Jerome Kagan (1987, 1989), for example, believes that the infant is highly resilient and adaptive; he argues that the infant is evolutionarily equipped to stay on a positive developmental course even in the face of wide variations in parenting. Kagan and others stress that genetic and temperament characteristics play more important roles in the child's social competence than the attachment theorists like Bowlby, Ainsworth, and Sroufe are willing to acknowledge (Fish, 1989; Fox & others, 1989). For example, an infant may have inherited a low tolerance for stress; this, rather than an insecure attachment bond, may be responsible for his inability to get along with peers.

Sociocultural, Family, and Attachment Processes

Concept	Processes and Related Ideas	Characteristics and Description
Sociocultural Influences	Bronfenbrenner's ecological model	The child is placed at the center of this model. The four environmental systems in the model are microsystem, mesosystem, exosystem, and macrosystem.
Family Processes	Transition to parenthood	Produces a disequilibrium, requiring considerable adaptation. Becoming a parent is both wonderful *and* stressful.
	Reciprocal socialization	Children socialize their parents just as parents socialize their children. Scaffolding, synchronization, and mutual regulation are important dimensions of reciprocal socialization.
	The family as a system	The family is a system of interacting individuals with different subsystems, some dyadic, others polyadic. Belsky's model describes direct and indirect effects.
Attachment	What is attachment?	Attachment is a relationship between two people in which each person feels strongly about the other and does a number of things to ensure the relationship's continuation. In infancy, attachment refers to the bond between the caregiver and the infant. Feeding is not the critical element in attachment, although contact comfort, familiarity, and trust are important. Bowlby's ethological theory stresses that the mother and infant instinctively trigger attachment. Attachment to the caregiver intensifies at about 6–7 months.
	Individual differences	Ainsworth believes that individual differences in attachment can be classified into secure, avoidant, and resistant categories. Ainsworth believes that securely attached babies have sensitive and responsive caregivers. In some investigations, secure attachment is related to social competence later in childhood. Attachment is related to intergenerational relations.
	Attachment, temperament, and the wider social world	Some developmentalists believe that too much emphasis is placed on the role of attachment; they believe that genetics and temperament, on the one hand, and the diversity of social agents and contexts on the other, deserve more credit.

Another criticism of the attachment theory is that it ignores the diversity of social agents and social contexts that exist in the infant's world. Experiences with both the mother and the father, changing gender roles, day care, the mother's employment, peer experiences, socioeconomic status, and cultural values are not considered adequately in the attachment concept (Lamb & others, 1984). In all of these perspectives, the importance of social relationships with parents is recognized; their differences lie in the criticalness of the attachment bond. Keep in mind that there is currently a great deal of controversy surrounding the concept of secure attachment. Some experts argue for its primacy in influencing the child's competent development, and others argue that it is given too much weight.

Thus far we have discussed a number of important ideas about sociocultural, family, and attachment processes. These ideas are summarized in Concept Table 7.1. Now we turn our attention to other caregivers and settings in the infant's development, evaluating, first, the father's role, and second, day care.

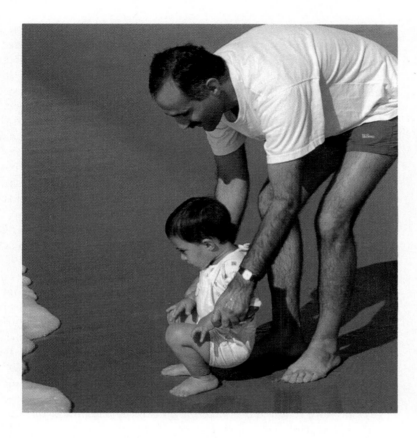

In the 1970s, the current image of the father as an active, nurturant, caregiving parent emerged.

The Father's Role

A father gently cuddles his infant son, softly stroking his forehead. Another father dresses his infant daughter as he readies her for her daily trip to a day-care center. How common are these circumstances in the life of fathers and their infants? Has the father's role changed dramatically?

The father's role has undergone major changes (Bronstein, 1988; Lamb, 1986, 1987; Pleck, 1984). During the colonial period in American history, fathers were mainly responsible for moral teaching. Fathers provided moral guidance and values, especially through religion. With the Industrial Revolution, the father's role changed; now he had the responsibility as the breadwinner, a role that continued through the Great Depression. By the end of World War II, another role for fathers emerged, that of a gender role model. While being a breadwinner and moral guardian continued to be important father roles, attention shifted to his role as a male, especially for sons. Then, in the 1970s, the current interest in the father as an active, nurturant, caregiving parent emerged. Rather than only being responsible for the discipline and control of older children and with providing the family's economic base, the father now is being evaluated in terms of his active, nurturant involvement with his children, even infants.

Are fathers more actively involved with their children than they were 10 to 20 years ago? Few data document changes in the father's involvement from one point in history to another. One study (Juster, in press), however, compared the

All men know their children mean more than life.

Euripides, 426 B.C.

father's involvement in 1975 and 1981. In 1981, fathers spent about one-fourth more time in direct interaction with the child than in 1975. Mothers increased their direct interaction about 7 percent over this time period, but fathers—while increasing their direct interaction—still were far below mothers in this regard. In this study, the father's involvement was about one-third that of the mother, both in 1975 and in 1981. If the mother is employed, does the father increase his involvement with his children? Only slightly. In sum, the father's active involvement with the child has increased somewhat, although this involvement does not approach the mother's, even when she is employed. Although fathers are spending more time with their infants and children, the evidence so far indicates that increased time does not necessarily mean quality time. In one recent investigation, there was no relationship between the amount of time fathers spent with their 5-year-old children and the quality of fathering (Grossman, Pollack, & Golding, 1988).

Can fathers take care of infants as competently as mothers can? Observations of fathers and their infants suggest that fathers have the ability to act sensitively and responsively with their infants (Parke, in press; Parke & Sawin, 1980). Probably the strongest evidence of the placticity of male caregiving abilities is derived from information about male primates who are notoriously low in their interest in offspring but are forced to live with infants whose female caregivers are absent. Under these circumstances, the adult male competently rears the infants (Parke & Suomi, 1981). But remember, while fathers can be active, nurturant, involved caregivers with their infants, most of the time they choose not to follow this pattern.

Do fathers behave differently toward infants than mothers do? While maternal interactions usually center around child-care activities—feeding, changing diapers, bathing—paternal interactions are more likely to include play. Fathers engage in more rough-and-tumble-play, bouncing the infant, throwing him up in the air, tickling him, and so on (Lamb, 1986). Mothers do play with infants, but their play is less physical and arousing than that of fathers.

In stressful circumstances, do infants prefer their mother or father? In one investigation (Lamb, 1977), 20 12-month-olds were observed interacting with their parents. With both parents present, infants preferred neither their mother nor their father. The same was true when the infant was alone with the mother or the father. But the entrance of a stranger, combined with boredom and fatigue, produced a shift in the infant's social behavior toward the mother. In stressful circumstances, then, infants show a stronger attachment to the mother.

Might the nature of parent-infant interaction be different in families that adopt nontraditional gender roles? This question was investigated by Michael Lamb and his colleagues (1982). They studied Swedish families in which the fathers were the primary caregivers of their firstborn, 8-month-old infants. The mothers were working full time. In all observations, the mothers were more likely to discipline, hold, soothe, kiss, and talk to the infants than the fathers. These mothers and fathers dealt with their infants differently, along the lines of American fathers and mothers following traditional gender roles. Having fathers assume the primary caregiving role did not seem to substantially alter the way they interacted with the infant. This may be because of biological reasons or because of deeply ingrained socialization patterns in cultures. To learn more about the father's role in different cultures, turn to Children 7.2, where you will read about Swedish fathers, Chinese fathers, and Pgymy fathers.

Thinking Critically
The father's role has changed considerably in the twentieth century. What do you think the father's role in the child's development will be like in the twenty-first century?

Infancy

Swedish Fathers, Chinese Fathers, and Pygmy Fathers

Sweden has been a forerunner in promoting the father's involvement with infants. The Swedish government prominently displays posters of a large, muscular man holding a tiny baby, an effort to communicate that "real men" can be actively involved in infant care. This message is important, because many men still feel that active, nurturant parenting and masculinity are incompatible (Lamb, 1987). In Sweden, fathers, like mothers, can take parental leave during the first 12 months of the infant's life, the first nine being fully paid leave. He can stay home and take care of the child and has the right to reduce his working time up to two hours per day until the child is 8 years old (Hwang, 1987).

The father's role in China has been slower to change than in Sweden, but it is changing. Traditionally, in China, the father has been expected to be strict, the mother kind. The father is characterized as a stern disciplinarian, concerned very little with the child's feelings; the child is expected to fear the father. The notion of the strict father has ancient roots. The Chinese character for father (*fu*) evolved from a primitive character representing the hand holding a cane, which symbolizes authority. However, the twentieth century has witnessed a decline in the father's absolute authority.

Younger fathers are becoming more inclined to emphasize the child's expression of opinions and independence, and they also are becoming more involved in child care, influenced to some degree by the increased employment of mothers. Intergenerational tension has resulted between fathers and sons, as younger generations behave in less traditional ways (Ho, 1987).

A culture markedly different from Sweden and China is the Aka pygmy culture of the south central region of Africa. Over the course of a year, the Aka spend about 56 percent of their time hunting, 27 percent of their time gathering food, and 17 percent of their time doing village work. What is the Aka pygmy father's role in the infant's development? Aka fathers are intimate and affectionate with their infants. They are not the infant's vigorous playmate like the American father is, but Aka fathers hold their infants extensively, possibly because the infant mortality rate is very high (Hewlitt, 1987).

North America harbors some rather unique cultures. We can better understand the father's role in our own culture when we compare it with the father's role in other cultures, such as Swedish, Chinese, and Aka pygmy. ◆

This Chinese father enjoys an outing with his toddler.

Aka pygmy fathers hold their infants extensively. This Aka father soothes his infant during the middle of the night. The father sings quietly as he dances and plays with the rattle.

The young children shown here are at a day-care center while their parents are at work. Day care has become a basic need of the American family. What are some variations in the type of day care children can experience?

Day Care

Each weekday at 8:00 A.M., Ellen Smith takes her 1-year-old daughter to the day-care center at Brookhaven College in Dallas. Then Mrs. Smith goes off to work and returns in the afternoon to take Tanya home. Now, after three years at the center, Mrs. Smith reports that her daughter is adventuresome and interacts confidently with peers and adults. Mrs. Smith believes that day care has been a wonderful way to raise Tanya.

In Los Angeles, however, day care has been a series of horror stories for Barbara Jones. After two years of unpleasant experiences with sitters, day-care centers, and day-care homes, Mrs. Jones quit her job as a successful real estate agent to stay home and take care of her 2½-year-old daughter, Gretchen. "I didn't want to sacrifice my baby for my job," said Mrs. Jones, who was unable to find good substitute care in day-care homes. When she put Gretchen into a day-care center, she said that she felt her daughter was being treated like a piece of merchandise—dropped off and picked up.

Many parents worry whether day care will adversely affect their children. They fear that day care will reduce the infant's emotional attachment to them, retard the infant's cognitive development, fail to teach the child how to control anger, and allow the child to be unduly influenced by their peers. How extensive is day care? Are the worries of these mothers justified?

In the 1980s, far more young children are in day care than at any other time in history; about 2 million children currently receive formal, licensed day care, and more than 5 million children attend kindergarten. Also, uncounted millions of children are cared for by unlicensed babysitters. Day care clearly has become a basic need of the American family (Phillips, in press).

The type of day care that young children receive varies extensively. Many day-care centers house large groups of children and have elaborate facilities. Some are commercial operations, others nonprofit centers run by churches, civic groups, and employers. Home care frequently is provided in private homes, at times by child-care professionals, at others by mothers who want to earn extra money.

The quality of care children experience in day care varies extensively. Some caregivers have no training, others extensive training; some day-care centers have a low caregiver-child ratio, others have a high caregiver-child ratio. Some experts recently have argued that the quality of day care most children receive in the United States is poor. Jay Belsky (Belsky & Rovine, 1988) not only believes that the quality of day care children experience is generally poor, he also believes this translates into negative developmental outcomes for children. Belsky concludes that extensive day-care experience during the first 12 months of life—as typically experienced in the United States—is associated with insecure attachment, as well as increased aggression, noncompliance, and possibly social withdrawal during the preschool and early elementary school years.

A recent study by Deborah Vandell and Mary Anne Corasaniti (1988) supports Belsky's beliefs. They found that extensive day care in the first year of the infant's life was associated with long-term negative outcomes. In contrast to children who began full-time day care later, children who began full-time day care (defined as more than 30 hours per week) as infants were rated by parents and teachers as being less compliant and as having poorer peer relations. In the first grade, they received lower grades and had poor work habits by comparison.

Mobile Crèches In India

In most developing countries, the availability of day-care facilities has grown, but most facilities often are in a form that denies access to the poorest children. One out of every six children in the world is Indian, and day care for Indian families is badly needed. Commitment of women to formal employment and shortage of services often pulls an older daughter out of school to take care of an infant or forces working mothers to take small children with them to work sites where they face added hazards. One strategy has been to develop mobile crèches (traveling day nurseries), a program of intensive, integrated child care. When a crèche is established, employers are contacted so that the basic amenities of shelter, water, and other resources can be shared. Basic care facilities are then established on the work site and locally recruited child-care workers are trained. The daily crèche routine emphasizes cleanliness, nutrition, play, and affectionate interaction with adults. Clinics are held regularly at the crèches, with doctors visiting about once a week. While the mobile crèches are still being used only on a small scale, in some cases they have been very effective. In some slum settlements of large cities and rural villages, they represent the first time families have had day care available. Critics of the mobile crèches say that in some instances they are too preoccupied with custodial care of young children and not concerned enough with young children's developmental needs (de Souza, 1979; MacPherson, 1987).   ◆

Provision of day care in most developing countries has improved, but this often has been in a form that denies access to the poorest children. In some locations in India, mobile day-care centers have provided intensive integrated child services to young children in slum settlements within large cities and rural villages.

Belsky's conclusions about day care are controversial. Other respected researchers have arrived at a different conclusion; their review of the day-care research suggests no ill effects of day care (Clarke-Stewart, 1989; Scarr, 1984; Scarr, Lande & McCartney, in press).

What can we conclude? Does day care have adverse effects on children's development? Trying to combine the results into an overall conclusion about day-care effects is a problem because of the different types of day care children experience and the different measures used to assess the outcome. Belsky's analysis does suggest that parents should be very careful about the quality of day care they select for their infants, especially those 1 year of age or less. Even Belsky agrees, though, that day care itself is not the culprit; rather it is the quality of day care that is problematic in this country. Belsky acknowledges that no evidence exists to show that children in high-quality day care are at risk in any way (Belsky, 1988; Doll, 1988).

What constitutes a high-quality day-care program for infants? The demonstration program developed by Jerome Kagan and his colleagues (1978) at Harvard University is exemplary. The day-care center included a pediatrician, a nonteaching director, and an infant-teacher ratio of 3 to 1. Teachers' aides assisted at the center. The teachers and aids were trained to smile frequently, to talk with the infants, and to provide them with a safe environment that included many stimulating toys. No adverse effects of day care were observed in this project. More information about what to look for in a quality day-care center is presented in Children 7.3. Using such criteria, Carolee Howes (1988) discovered that children who entered low-quality child care as infants were least likely to be socially competent in early childhood (less compliant, less self-controlled, less task-oriented, more hostile, and having more problems in peer interaction).

Edward Zigler (1987) recently proposed a solution to the day-care needs of families. Zigler says that we should not think of school as an institution, but rather as a building, one that is owned by tax-paying parents who need day care for their children. Part of the school building would be for teaching and part would be for child care and supervision. This system could provide parents with competent developmental child-care services. Zigler believes it should be available to every child over the age of 3. He does not think children should start formal schooling at age 3; they would be in the schools only for day care. At the age of 5, children would start kindergarten, but only for half days. If the child has a parent at home, the child would spend the remainder of the day at home. If the parents are working, the child would spend the second half of the day in the day-care part of the school. For children aged 6 to 12, after-school and vacation care would be available to those who need it.

Zigler does not believe that teachers should provide day care; they are trained as educators and are too expensive. What we need, he says, is a child development associate, someone who is trained to work with children, someone we can afford to pay. This is a large vision, one that involves a structural change in society and a new face for our school system. Zigler believes that a bill legislating such experimental schools will soon be introduced in Congress. As Zigler remembers, between the fall of 1964 and the summer of 1965, we managed to put 560,000 children into Head Start programs, an educational program for impoverished children. He believes we can do the same thing with day care (Trotter, 1987).

Thinking Critically
Of the criteria listed in Children 7.3, which do you believe are the most important if your own children were going to day care? Are there criteria not listed in the box that you believe should be considered?

Infancy

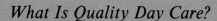

What Is Quality Day Care?

A major concern about quality day care is that the facilities should provide more than custodial care. While adequate food, warmth, and shelter are important, by themselves they do not constitute good day care. Experts recommend that parents seeking day care for their children concern themselves with the following:

1. **Nutrition, Health, and Safety.** A balanced, nutritionally sound diet should be provided; the child's health should be carefully monitored, and provisions for a sick child should be available; the physical environment should be free of hazards and the child's safety should be of utmost concern.
2. **Child–Caregiver Ratio.** The number of children for each caregiver is an important consideration. For children under the age of 2, no more than five children should be cared for by a single caregiver; an even lower ratio is better.
3. **Caregiver Training and Behavior.** A competent caregiver does not need a Ph.D. in child development, but the caregiver should have some training and extensive experience in working with children. The caregiver should smile at the child, talk with the child, ask the child questions, and provide many stimulating toys.
4. **Peers, Play, and Exploration.** Infants and children spend considerable time with peers in day care. Caregivers need to supervise peer relations carefully, providing a good balance of structured and unstructured play, handling aggression and a lack of self-control judiciously. Exploration should be encouraged; adequate, safe space in which to curiously and creatively investigate the world should be available.
5. **Language and Cognitive Development.** Language and cognitive development, as well as social development, should be emphasized. Conversation between the caregivers and children should be plentiful, and attention should be given to stimulating the child's cognitive abilities; books for children should be readily available. Long hours should not be spent watching television.
6. **Coordination of Home and Day Care.** What goes on in the child's home should be coordinated with what goes on in day care. Caregivers in quality day care maintain open communication with parents, being receptive to parent questions. ◆

Emotional and Personality Development

The sociocultural world, family processes, attachment, the father's role, and day care—all are important ingredients of the infant's social being. But there is more to understanding the nature of the infant; emotions, trust, independence, and development of a sense of self also play key roles in understanding the infant's social development.

Emotional Development

If you cannot name an emotion, you cannot experience it. That was the dominant view of infant emotion for much of this century. But now a different picture has emerged, one that recognizes the infant's repertoire of emotions. Just as we found in Chapters 5 and 6, that vision, hearing, and the ability to remember and learn are more highly developed in infancy than was originally believed, we now know that interest, distress, and disgust are present early in infancy and can be communicated to parents. Much earlier than the arrival of language, infants add other emotions like joy, anger, surprise, shyness, and fear to their capabilities.

What are the functions of emotions in infancy? Emotions are adaptive and promote survival, serve as a form of communication, and provide regulation (Barrett & Campos, 1987; Bretherton & others, 1986; Izard and Malatesta, 1987; Lewis, 1989). For example, various fears—such as fear of the dark and fear of sudden changes in the environment—are adaptive because there are clear links between such events and possible danger. Infants also use emotions to inform others about their feelings and needs. The infant who smiles probably is telling others that she is feeling pleasant; the infant who cries probably is communicating that something is unpleasant. Infants also use emotions to increase or decrease the distance between themselves and others. The infant who smiles may be encouraging someone to come closer; the infant who displays anger may be suggesting that an intruder should go away. And emotions influence the information the infant selects from the perceptual world and the behaviors the infant displays.

Joy
Mouth forms smile, cheeks lifted, twinkle in eyes

Anger
Brows drawn together and downward, eyes fixed, mouth squarish

Interest
Brows raised or knit, mouth softly rounded, lips pursed

Disgust
Nose wrinkled, upper lip raised, tongue pushed outward

Surprise
Brows raised, eyes widened, mouth rounded in oval shape

Distress
Eyes tightly closed, mouth, as in anger, squared and angular

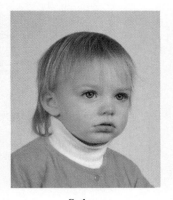

Sadness
Brows' inner corners raised, drawn out and down

Fear
Brows level, drawn in and up, eyelids lifted, mouth retracted

FIGURE 7.8   Facial expressions of emotion and their characteristics.

How can we find out if the infant is displaying emotion? Carroll Izard (1982) developed a system for decoding the emotional expressions on infants' faces. Izard wanted to discover which emotions were inborn, which emerged later, and under which conditions they were displayed. The conditions included being given an ice cube, having tape put on the backs of their hands, being handed a favorite toy and then having it taken away, being separated from and reunited with their mothers, being approached by a stranger, having their heads gently restrained, having a ticking clock held next to their ears, having a balloon pop in front of their faces, and being given camphor to sniff and lemon rind and orange juice to taste.

Izard's system for coding emotions has the imposing name Maximally Discriminative Facial Movement Coding System, or **MAX** for short. the coder, using MAX, watches slow-motion and stop-action videotapes of the infant's facial reactions to the circumstances described earlier. Anger, for example, is indicated when the brows are sharply lowered and drawn together, the eyes are narrowed or squinted, and the mouth is open in an angular, square shape. The key elements of emotional facial codes in infants are shown in Figure 7.8 and the developmental timetable of their emergence in infancy is shown in Table 7.1.

TABLE 7.1	*The Developmental Course of Infant Emotions*	
Emotional Expression	**Approximate Time of Emergence**
Interest ªNeonatal smile (a sort of half smile that appears spontaneously for no apparent reason) ªStartled response ªDistress Disgust	Present at birth
Social smile	4–6 weeks
Anger Surprise Sadness	3–4 months
Fear Shame/Shyness	5–7 months 6–8 months
Contempt Guilt	Second year of life

ªThe neonatal smile, the startled response, and distress in response to pain are precursors of the social smile and the emotions of surprise and sadness, which appear later. No evidence exists to suggest that they are related to inner feelings when they are observed in the first few weeks of life.

Personality Development

The individual characteristics of the infant that are often thought of as central to personality development are trust, the self, and independence.

Trust

According to Erik Erikson (1968), the first year of life is characterized by the stage of development, trust versus mistrust. Following a life of regularity, warmth, and protection in the mother's womb, the infant faces a world that is less secure. Erikson believes that infants learn trust when they are cared for in a consistent, warm manner. If the infant is not well fed and kept warm on a consistent basis, a sense of mistrust is likely to develop.

We briefly described Erikson's ideas about the role of trust in attachment earlier. His thoughts have much in common with Mary Ainsworth's concept of secure attachment. The infant who has a sense of trust is likely to be securely attached and have confidence to explore new circumstances; the infant who has a sense of mistrust is likely to be insecurely attached and to not have such confidence and positive expectations.

Trust versus mistrust is not resolved once and for all in the first year of life; it arises again at each successive stage of development. There is both hope and danger in this. The child who enters school with a sense of mistrust may trust a particular teacher who has taken the time to make herself trustworthy. With this second chance he overcomes his early mistrust. By contrast, a child who leaves infancy with a sense of trust can still have his sense of mistrust activated at a later stage, perhaps if his parents are separated or divorced under conflicting circumstances. An example is

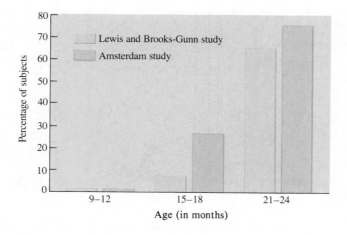

instructive (Elkind, 1970). A 4-year-old boy was being seen by a clinical psychologist at a court clinic because his adoptive parents, who had had him for six months, now wanted to give him back to the agency. They said he was cold and unloving, stole things, and could not be trusted. He was indeed a cold and apathetic boy, but with good reason. About a year after his illegitimate birth, he was taken away from his mother, who had a drinking problem and was shuttled back and forth among several foster homes. At first he tried to relate to people in the foster homes, but the relationships never had an opportunity to develop because he was moved so frequently. In the end, he gave up trying to reach out to others because the inevitable separations hurt too much. Like the burned child who dreads the flame, this emotionally burned child shunned the pain of close relationships. He had trusted his mother, but now he trusted no one. Only years of devoted care and patience could now undo the damage to this child's sense of trust.

The Developing Sense of Self and Independence

Individuals carry with them a sense of who they are and what makes them different from everyone else. They cling to this identity and begin to feel secure in the knowledge that this identity is becoming more stable. Real or imagined, this sense of self is a strong motivating force in life. When does the individual person begin to sense a separate existence from others?

Children begin to develop a sense of self by learning to distinguish themselves from others. To determine whether infants can recognize themselves, psychologists have used mirrors. In the animal kindom, only the great apes learn to recognize their reflection in the mirror, but human infants accomplish this feat by about 18 months of age. How does the mirror technique work? The mother puts a dot of rouge on her infant's nose. The observer watches to see how often the infant touches his nose. Next, the infant is placed in front of a mirror and observers detect whether nose touching increases. Figure 7.9 reveals that in two separate investigations in the second half of the second year of life, infants recognized their own image and coordinated the image they saw with the actions of touching their own body (Amsterdam, 1968; Lewis, 1987; Lewis & others, 1989).

This 18-month-old shows a sense of self.

Thinking Critically
In addition to the description of the 4-year-old boy from an adopted family, can you think of other examples in which trust during infancy is an important aspect of development? Try to come up with at least two other specific cases.

The infant's development of a sense of self, then, is based both on the infant's relationship with caregivers and on the infant's developing cognitive skills, especially the ability to represent an image. Language may also be wrapped up in the representation of the self early in life. In one investigation (Pipp, Fischer, & Jennings, 1987), at 18 to 23 months of age, girls detected more features of themselves than did boys. This is the age at which one type of representational ability, use of sophisticated language, is first emerging, and girls seem to be more advanced in this ability than boys.

Not only does the infant develop a sense of self in the second year of life, but independence becomes a more central theme in the infant's life as well. The theories of Margaret Mahler and Erik Erikson have important implications for both self-development and independence. Mahler (1979) believes that the child goes through a separation and then an individuation process. Separation involves the infant's movement away from the mother and individuation involves the development of self.

Mother-child interaction can interfere with the development of individuation. For example, Anna's mother was often emotionally unavailable. Never certain of her mother's availability, Anna was preoccupied with it; she found it difficult to explore her surroundings. After a brief spurt of practicing, she would return to her mother and try to interact with her in an intense way. Sometimes she would spill cookies on the floor, always with an eye to gaining her mother's attention. Anna's mother was absorbed with her own interests. During the preschool years, Anna threw temper tantrums and clinged to her teacher. Then the clinging would turn to hitting and yelling. In Mahler's view, Anna wanted only one thing to happen: She wanted her mother to return through the door. As can be seen in Anna's case, an unsatisfactory mother-infant relationship led to problems in her development of independence.

Erikson (1968), like Mahler, believes that independence is an important issue in the second year of life. Erikson describes the second stage of development as autonomy versus shame and doubt. Autonomy builds on the infant's developing mental and motor abilities. At this point in development, the infant not only can walk but also can climb, open and close, drop, push and pull, hold and let go. The infant feels pride in these new accomplishments and wants to do everything himself, whether it is flushing the toilet, pulling the wrapping off of a package, or deciding what to eat. It is important for parents to recognize the toddler's need to do what he is capable of doing at his own pace and in his own time. Then, he can learn to control his muscles, his impulses, himself, and his environment. But when caregivers

One great splitting of the whole universe into two halves is made by each of us . . . We call the two halves "me" and "not me."

William James, Principles of Psychology, *1890*

I am what I can will freely.

Erik Erikson, 1968

Erikson, like many other theorists, believes independence is an important theme of life's second year. The 2-year-old boy shown here has developed the autonomy to climb to the sink and get his own drink of water.

are impatient and do for him what he is capable of doing himself, shame and doubt are developed. Every parent has rushed a child from time to time. It is only when parents are consistently overprotective and critical of accidents (wetting, soiling, spilling, or breaking, for example) that the child develops an excessive sense of shame with respect to others and an excessive sense of doubt about his ability to control himself and his world.

Erikson also believes that the autonomy versus shame and doubt stage has important implications for the development of independence and identity during adolescence. The development of autonomy during the toddler years gives the adolescent the courage to be an independent individual who can choose and guide her own future.

Too much autonomy, though, can be as harmful as too little. A 7-year-old boy who had a heart condition learned quickly how afraid his parents were of any signs of his having cardiac problems. It was not long before he ruled the household. The family could not go shopping or for a drive if the boy did not approve. On the rare occasions his parents defied him, he would get angry, and his purple face and gagging would frighten them into submission. This boy actually was scared of his power and eager to relinquish it. When the parents and the boy realized this, and recognized that a little shame and doubt were a healthy opponent of an inflated sense of autonomy, the family began to function much more smoothly (Elkind, 1970).

Consider also Robert, age 22 months, who has just come home from watching his 5-year-old brother, William, take a swimming lesson. Their mother has gone in the kitchen to get dinner ready when she hears a scream. She hurries into the living room and sees Robert's teeth sunk into William's leg. The next day, Robert is playing with a new game and he can't get it right. He hurls it across the room and just misses his mother. That night his mother tells him it is time for bed. Robert's response: "No." Sometimes the world of the 2-year-old becomes very frustrating. Much of their frustration stems from their inability to control the adult world. Things are

Caregiving and Child Competencies in Japan and America

Reports about Japanese and American cultures have long included commentaries about both striking similarities and conspicuous differences in the psychological makeups of the two cultures' adults and children (Bornstein, 1989). Americans are described as ethnically heterogeneous, self-assertive, individualistic, and future-oriented. Japanese are described as ethnically homogeneous, inner-oriented, devoted to group identity, and traditional-oriented. Yet, in today's world, America and Japan are remarkably similar in terms of educational levels, economic and living standards, and social aspirations.

How do Japanese and American cultures view the development of children? Both Japanese and American cultures are child-centered. Despite recent rapid modernization, Japan remains a culturally insulated society in terms of family life, and a value system dating from ancient China still underpins conceptions of child rearing. Thus, while both cultures are child-centered, Japanese and American parents perceive and treat children somewhat differently. Most Japanese mothers see their infants as extensions of themselves and organize their interactions to strengthen mutual dependence between themselves and their infants. By contrast, American mothers are more likely to encourage the autonomy of their infants and to organize their interactions to foster independence in their offspring.

Japanese and American parents also differ in their beliefs about the developmental paths their children should follow to reach culture-specific goals. Patience, persistence, and conformity are virtues promoted in Japanese children. Originality, exploration, and self-assertion are encouraged in American children. In one investigation, Japanese mothers expected their children to show early mastery of emotional maturity, self-control, and social courtesy, whereas American mothers expected their children to show early mastery of verbal comprehension and individualistic behavior (Hess & others, 1980). Thus, even with somewhat similar ultimate goals, the Japanese and American cultures differ fundamentally in the way they rear children and in the competencies they want their children to display. ◆

too big to manage, to push around, or to make happen what the toddler wants. The toddler wants to be in the driver's seat of every car, to push every cart by herself, and to throw herself into every doll bed. Two-year-olds want to play the dominant role in almost every situation. When things don't go their way, toddlers can become openly defiant even though they were placid as babies earlier in life. Called the "terrible twos" by Arnold Gesell, this developmental time frame can try the patience of the most even-tempered parents. Nonetheless, calm, steady affection and firm patience can help to disperse most of toddlerhood's tensions. Fortunately, the defiance is only temporary in most children's development.

Problems and Disturbances

Problems and disturbances in infancy can arise for a number of reasons. All development—normal and abnormal—is influenced by the interaction of heredity and environment. In a comprehensive study of children at risk, a variety of biological, social, and developmental characteristics were identified as predictors of problems and disturbances at age 18. They included moderate to severe perinatal (at or near birth) stress and birth defects, low socioeconomic status at 2 and 10 years of age, level of maternal education below 8 years, low family stability between 2 and 8 years, very low or very high infant responsiveness at 1 year, a Cattell score below 80 at age 2 (the Cattell is one of the early measures of infant intelligence), and the need for long-term mental health services or placement in a learning-disability class at age 10. When four or more of these factors were present, the stage was set for serious coping problems in the second decade of life (Werner & Smith, 1982). Among the problems in infancy that deserve special consideration are child abuse and autism.

Child Abuse

Unfortunately, parental hostility toward children in some families escalates to the point where one or both parents abuse the child. Child abuse is an increasing problem in the United States. Estimates of its incidence vary, but some authorities say that as many as 500,000 children are physically abused every year. Laws in many states now require doctors and teachers to report suspected cases of child abuse. Yet, many cases go unreported, especially those of battered infants (Fontana, 1988; Hutchings, 1988).

Child maltreatment is such a disturbing circumstance that many people have difficulty understanding or sympathizing with parents who abuse or neglect their children (Crittenden, 1988a, b). Our response is often outrage and anger directed at the parent. This outrage focuses our attention on parents as bad, sick, monstrous, sadistic individuals who cause their children to suffer. Experts on child abuse believe that this view is too simple and deflects attention away from the social context of the abuse and parents' coping skills. It is especially important to recognize that child abuse is a diverse condition, that it is usually mild to moderate in severity, and that it is only partially caused by individual personality characteristics of parents (Emery, 1989; Haugard & Emery, in press).

The Multifaceted Nature of Child Maltreatment
While the public and many professionals use the term *child abuse* to refer to both abuse and neglect, developmentalists increasingly are using the term *child maltreatment*. This term reduces the emotional impact of the term *abuse* and acknowledges that maltreatment includes several different conditions. Among the different types of maltreatment are physical and sexual abuse, fostering delinquency, lack of supervison, medical, educational, and nutritional neglect, and drug or alcohol abuse (Garbarino, 1989). Approximately 20 percent of the reported cases involve abuse alone, 46 percent neglect alone, 23 percent both abuse and neglect, and 11 percent sexual abuse (American Association for Protecting Children, 1986). Abused children are more likely to be angry or wary than neglected children, who tend to be passive (Lynch & Roberts, 1982).

Severity of Abuse

The concern about child abuse began with the identification of the "battered child syndrome" and has retained the characteristic of severe, brutal injury for several reasons. First, the media tend to underscore the most bizarre and vicious incidents. Second, much of the funding for child-abuse prevention, identification, and treatment depends on the public's perception of the horror of child abuse and the medical professions' lobby for funds to investigate and treat abused children and their parents. The emphasis is often on the worst cases. These horrific cases do exist, and are indeed terrible, but they make up only a small minority of abused children. Less than 1 percent of abused children die, and another 11 percent suffer life-threatening, disabling injuries (American Association for Protecting Children, 1986). By contrast, almost 90 percent suffer temporary physical injuries. These milder injuries, though, are likely to be repeatedly experienced in the context of daily hostile family exchanges. Similarly, neglected children, who suffer no physical injuries, often experience extensive, long-term psychological harm.

The Cultural Context of Maltreatment

The extensive violence of the American culture is reflected in the occurrence of violence in the family. A regular diet of violence appears on television screens, and parents often resort to power assertion as a disciplinary technique. In China, where physical punishment is rarely used to discipline children, the incidence of child abuse is reported to be very low. In the United States, many abusing parents report that they do not have sufficient resources or help from others. This may be a realistic evaluation of the situation experienced by many low-income families, who do not have adequate preventive and supportive services (Rodrigquez-Haynes & Crittenden, 1988).

Community support systems are especially important in alleviating stressful family situations and thereby preventing child abuse. An investigation of the support systems in 58 counties in New York State revealed a relation between the incidence of child abuse and the absence of support systems available to the family. Both family resources—relatives and friends, for example—and such formal community support systems as crisis centers and child abuse counseling were associated with a reduction in child abuse (Garbarino, 1976).

Family Influences

To understand abuse in the family, the interaction of all family members needs to be considered, regardless of who actually performs the violent acts against the child (Daro, 1988). For example, even though the father may be the one who physically abuses the child, contributions by the mother, the child, and siblings also should be evaluated. Many parents who abuse their children come from families in which physical punishment was used. These parents view physical punishment as a legitimate way of controlling the child's behavior, and physical punishment may be a part of this sanctioning. Children themselves may unwittingly contribute to child abuse: An unattractive child receives more physical punishment than an attractive child, and a child from an unwanted pregnancy may be especially vulnerable to abuse (Harter, Alexander, & Neimeyer, 1988). Husband-wife violence and financial problems may result in displaced aggression toward a defenseless child. Displaced aggression is commonly involved in child abuse. One form of child maltreatment can be devastating to the child—sexual abuse, which is described in Children 7.4.

Shattered Innocence

Headlines about day-care center scandals and feminist protests against sexist exploitation have increased public awareness of what we now know is a widespread problem: children's sexual abuse. It has been estimated that as many as 40 million American children are sexually abused—about one in six. A 1984 Gallup poll of 2,000 men and women in 210 Canadian communities found that 22 percent of the respondents were sexually abused as children. Clearly, children's sexual abuse is more widespread than was thought in the past. One reason the problem of children's sexual abuse was a dark secret for so long is that people understandably kept this painful experience to themselves.

The sexual abuse of children occurs most often between the ages of 9 and 12, although the abuse of 2- and 3-year-olds is not unusual. The abuser is almost always a man, and he typically is known to the child, often being a relative. In many instances, the abuse is not limited to a single episode. No race, ethnic group, or economic class is immune.

While children do not react uniformly to sexual abuse, certain behaviors and feelings occur with some regularity. The immediate effects include sleeping and eating disturbances, anger, withdrawal, and guilt. The children often appear to be afraid or anxious. Two additional signs occur so often that professionals rely on them as indicators of abuse when they are present together. The first is sexual preoccupation—excessive or public masturbation and an unusually strong interest in sexual organs, play, and nudity. The second sign consists of a host of physical complaints or problems, such as rashes, headaches, and vomiting, all without medical explanation. When it is discovered that these children have been sexually abused, a check of their medical records usually produces years of such mysterious ailments. While there are patterns in the immediate effects of sexual abuse of children, it is far more difficult to connect such abuse with later psychological problems. It is impossible to say that every child who has been abused will develop this or that problem, and we still have not developed a profile of the child abuse victim that everyone can agree upon.

One of the most disturbing findings about childhood sexual abuse is its strong intergenerational pattern. Boys who are sexually abused are far more likely to turn into offenders, molesting the next generation of children; girls who are sexually abused are more likely to produce children who are abused. And victimization can lead to revictimization. Individuals who have been sexually abused as children may become later victims of rape or attempted rape. Women, of course, are not to blame for being victims.

How can the intergenerational transmission of abuse be broken? In one recent investigation, the group of adults most likely to break the abuse cycle were more likely to receive emotional support from a nonabusive adult, participate in therapy, and have a less abusive and more stable, emotionally supportive and satisfying relationship with a mate (Egeland, Jacobvitz, & Papatola, in press; Egeland, Jacobvitz, & Sroufe, 1987). The prognosis also is better if a person has not been abused by more than one person, when force is not used during the abuse, and when the abuser is not a close relative (Kohn, 1987). ◆

Infantile Autism

As its name suggests, **infantile autism** has its onset in infancy. It is a severe developmental disturbance that includes deficiencies in social relationships, abnormalities in communication, and restricted, repetitive, and stereotyped patterns of behavior (Dawson, 1989; Hertzig & Shapiro, in press; Rutter & Schopler, 1987; Tager-Flusberg, in press). Social deficiencies include a failure to use an eye-to-eye gaze to regulate social interaction, rarely seeking others for comfort or affection, rarely initiating play with others, and having no peer relations involving mutual sharing of interests and emotions. As babies, these children require very little from their parents. They do not demand much attention and they do not reach out (literally or figuratively) for their parents. They rarely smile. When someone tries to hold them, they usually withdraw by arching their back and pushing away. In their cribs or playpens, they appear oblivious to what is going on around them, often sitting and staring into space for long periods of time.

In addition to these social deficiencies, these children also show communication abnormalities that focus on the problems of using language for social communication: poor synchrony and lack of reciprocity in conversation, and stereotyped,

The Father's Role, Day Care, Emotional Development, and Personality Development

Concept	Processes and Related Ideas	Characteristics and Description
The Father's Role	Its nature	Over time, the father's role in the child's development has evolved from moral teacher to breadwinner to gender role model to active, nurturant caregiver.
	Father-child interaction and attachment	Fathers have increased their interaction with their children, but they still lag far behind mothers, even when the mother is employed. Fathers can act sensitively to the infant's signals, but most of the time they do not. The mother's role in the infant's development is primarily caregiving. That of the father involves playful interaction. Infants generally prefer their mother under stressful circumstances even in nontraditional families, as when the father is the main caregiver, the behaviors of mothers and fathers follow traditional gender lines.
Day Care	Its nature	Day care has become a basic need of the American family; more children are in day care today than at any other time in history.
	Quality of care and effects on development	The quality of day care is uneven. Belsky concluded most day care is inadequate and that extensive day care in the first 12 months of the infant's life has negative developmental outcomes. Other experts disagree with Belsky. Day care remains a controversial topic. Quality day care can be achieved and it seems to have few adverse effects on children.

repetitive use of language. As many as one of every two autistic children never learns to speak. Those who do learn to speak sometimes display **echolalia,** a condition in which children echo what they hear. If you ask, "How are you, Chuck?" Chuck responds, "How are you, Chuck?" Autistic children also confuse pronouns, inappropriately substituting *you* for *I,* for example (Durand & Crimmins, 1987.)

Stereotyped patterns of behavior by autistic children include compulsive rituals, repetitive motor mannerisms, and distress over changes in small details of the environment. Rearrangement of a sequence of events or even furniture in the course of a day may cause autistic children to become extremely upset, suggesting that they are not flexible in adapting to new routines and changes in their daily lives.

What causes autism? Autism seems to involve some form of organic brain dysfunction and may also have a hereditary basis. There has been no satisfactory evidence developed to document that family socialization causes autism (Rutter & Schopler, 1987).

At this point we have discussed several ideas about the father's role, day care, emotional development, and personality development in infancy. A summary of these ideas is presented in Concept Table 7.2. This chapter concludes our discussion of infant development. In the next section, we will continue our journey through development, moving into the early childhood years.

Concept	Processes and Related Ideas	Characteristics and Description
Emotional and Personality Development	Emotional development	Emotions in infancy are adaptive and promote survival, serve as a form of communication, and provide regulation. Izard developed the MAX system for coding infant facial expressions of emotion. Using this system, it was found that interest and disgust are present in the newborn, and that a social smile, anger, surprise, sadness, fear, and shame/shyness develop in the first year, while contempt and guilt develop in the second year.
	Trust	Erikson argues that the first year is characterized by the crisis of trust versus mistrust; his ideas about trust have much in common with Ainsworth's secure attachment concept.
	Developing a sense of self and independence	At some point in the second half of the second year of life, the infant develops a sense of self. Independence becomes a central theme in the second year of life. Mahler argues that the infant separates herself from the mother and then develops individuation. Erikson stresses that the second year of life is characterized by the stage of autonomy versus shame and doubt.
Problems and Disturbances	Child abuse	An understanding of child abuse requires information about cultural, familial, and community influences. Sexual abuse of children is now recognized as a more widespread problem than was believed in the past.
	Infantile autism	Is a severe disorder that first appears in infancy. It involves an inability to relate to people, speech problems, and upset over change in routine or environment. Autism seems to involve some form of organic brain and genetic dysfunction.

Summary

I. **Sociocultural Influences**
Bronfenbrenner developed a comprehensive ecological model that places the child at the center of the model; the four environmental systems in the model are microsystem, mesosystem, exosystem, and macrosystem.

II. **Family Processes**
The transition to parenthood produces a disequilibrium that requires considerable adaptation. It is not unusual for postpartum blues to characterize mothers in the several months after the infant's birth. Infants socialize parents just as parents socialize infants—the process of reciprocal socialization. Parent-infant relationships are mutually regulated by the parent and the infant. In infancy, much of the relationship is driven by the parent, but as the infant gains self-control, the relationship is initiated more on an equal basis. The family is a system of interacting individuals with different subsystems, some dyadic, others polyadic. Belsky's model describes direct and indirect effects.

III. **What Is Attachment?**
Attachment is a relationship between two people in which each person feels strongly about the other and does a number of things to ensure the relationship's continuation. In infancy, attachment refers to the bond between the caregiver and

the infant. Feeding is not the critical element in attachment, although contact comfort, familiarity, and trust are important. Bowlby's ethological theory stresses that the mother and infant instinctively trigger attachment. Attachment to the caregiver intensifies at about 6 to 7 months.

IV. **Individual Differences in Attachment, Temperament, and the Wider Social World**
Ainsworth believes that individual differences in attachment can be classified into secure, avoidant, and resistant categories. Ainsworth believes that securely attached babies have sensitive and responsive caregivers. In some investigations, secure attachment is related to social competence later in childhood. Attachment is related to intergenerational relations. Some developmentalists believe that the role of attachment is emphasized too much; they believe that genetics and temperament on the one hand, and the diversity of social agents and contexts on the other, deserve more credit.

V. **The Father's Role**
Over time, the father's role has evolved from moral teacher to breadwinner to gender role model to active, nurturant caregiver. Fathers have increased their interaction with their children, but fathers still lag far behind mothers, even when the mother is employed. Fathers can act sensitively to the infant's signals, but most of the time they do not. The mother's role in the infant's development is primarily caregiving, and that of the father involves playful interaction. Infants generally prefer their mother under stressful circumstances. Even in nontraditional families, as when the father is the primary caregiver, the behaviors of mothers and fathers follow traditional gender lines.

VI. **Day Care**
Day care has become a basic need of the American family. More children are in day care today than at any other time in history. The quality of day care is uneven. Belsky contends that most day care is inadequate and that extensive day care in the first 12 months of the infant's life has negative developmental outcomes. Other experts disagree with Belsky. Day care remains a controversial topic. Quality day care can be achieved and it seems to have little adverse effects on children.

VII. **Emotional Development**
Emotions in infancy are adaptive and promote survival, serve as a form of communication, and provide regulation. Izard developed the MAX system for coding infant facial expressions of emotion. Using this system, it was found that interest and disgust are present in the newborn, and that a social smile, anger, surprise, sadness, fear, and shame and shyness develop in the first year while contempt and guilt develop in the second year.

VIII. **Personality Development**
Erikson argues that the first year of life is characterized by the crisis of trust versus mistrust; his ideas about trust have much in common with Ainsworth's concept of secure attachment. At some point in the second half of the second year of life, the infant develops a sense of self, and independence becomes a central theme. Mahler argues that the infant separates herself from the mother and then develops individuation. Erikson stresses that the second year of life is characterized by the stage of autonomy versus shame and doubt.

IX. **Problems and Disturbances**
Abnormal development, like normal development, is caused by the interaction of heredity and environment. An understanding of child abuse requires an analysis of cultural, familial, and community influences. Sexual abuse of children is now recognized as a more widespread problem than was believed in the past. Infantile autism is a severe disorder that first appears in infancy. It involves an inability to relate to people, speech problems, and upset over change in routine or environment. Autism seems to involve some form of organic brain and genetic dysfunction.

Key Terms

microsystem 201
mesosystem 202
exosystem 202
macrosystem 202
reciprocal
  socialization 205
scaffolding 205

attachment 207
separation anxiety 207
stranger anxiety 208
secure attachment 210
type A babies 210
type B babies 210

type C babies 210
MAX 221
infantile autism 229
echolalia 230

Suggested Readings

Birns, B., & Daye, D. (Eds.) (1988). *Motherhood and child care.* Boston: Auburn House.
  A number of articles that describe the mother's role in the infant's development are
  provided; included is an excellent chapter on day care.
Crittenden, P. (1988). Family and dyadic patterns of functioning in maltreating families.
  In K. Browne, C. Davies, & P. Stratton (Eds.). *Early prediction and prevention of
  child abuse.* New York: John Wiley.
  An excellent overview of family patterns of child maltreatment.
Izard, C. E. (1982). *Measuring emotion in infants and children.* New York: Cambridge
  University Press.
  Izard, one of the leading figures in the study of infant emotions, describes in
  fascinating detail how to assess the emotions of infants and young children.
Kohn, A. (1987). *No contest: The case against competition.* Boston: Houghton Mifflin.
  The dark secrets of children's sexual abuse is told with extensive examples of case
  studies to illustrate its psychological damage.
Lamb, M. E. (1987). *The father's role: Cross-cultural perspectives.* Hillsdale, NJ:
  Erlbaum.
  Intriguing descriptions of the father's role in different cultures are provided. Includes
  information about English, American, Israeli, Italian, Chinese, Swedish, and Aka
  pygmy fathers.
Sroufe, L. A., & Fleeson, J. (1986). Attachment and the construction of relationships. In
  W. Hartup and Z. Rubin (Eds.), *Relationships and development.* Hillsdale, NJ:
  Erlbaum.
  Gives insight into the importance of attachment in our development of relationships.

IV

Early Childhood

You are troubled at seeing him spend his early years doing nothing. What! Is it nothing to be happy? Is it nothing to skip, to play, to run about all day long? Never in his life will he be so busy as now.

Jean-Jacques Rousseau

I n early childhood, our greatest untold poem was being only 4 years old. We skipped and ran and played all the sun long, never in our lives so busy, busy being something we had not quite grasped yet. Who knew our thoughts, which we worked up into small mythologies all our own? Our thoughts and images and drawings took wings. The blossoms of our heart, no wind could touch. Our small world widened as we discovered new refuges and new people. When we said "I," we meant something totally unique, not to be confused with any other.

Section 4 consists of three chapters. Chapter 8's contents include ideas about

—Young children's physical development
—Body growth and change
—Rough-and-tumble play and laughing faces
—Nutrition
—Sugar and children's behavior
—The state of illness and health in the world's children
—Young children "buckling up" for safety

Among Chapter 9's contents are ideas about

—Young children's cognitive development
—Preoperational development
—Where pelicans kiss seals, cars float on clouds, and humans are tadpoles
—*Winnie-the-Pooh* and Piaget
—Language development
—Early childhood education
—Whether preschool is crucial

Among Chapter 10's contents are ideas about

—Young children's social development
—Making the grade as parents
—Peer relations
—Pervasiveness of play in children's lives
—Superheros
—Television's role and *Sesame Street* in different countries around the world

◇

All the sun long I was running . . .

Dylan Thomas

8

Physical Development

A t 2 years of age, Tony is no saint. Tony's growing demand for autonomy keeps his mother busy hour after hour. Only a year earlier, he had learned to walk. Now he is running away from her into neighbors' yards and down the aisles of grocery stores. Trying out his new skills, he is constantly testing his parents and finding out the limits of his behavior.

By about his third birthday, Tony's behavior takes a slightly different turn. His temper tantrums have not entirely disappeared—the "terrible twos" can last into the fourth year—but much of his negative behavior has gone away. Every week produces a palate of new words and new tricks of climbing, skipping, and jumping. Tony is beginning to be able to make his body do what he wants it to do. As he moves through the preschool years, he learns how to draw and how to play different ball games. He is boastful, too, about his newly developed competencies. Tony says, "I'm bigger now, aren't I?" "I'm not a little baby anymore am I?" Tony is right. He is not a baby anymore. His babyhood is gone.

By 4 years of age, Tony has become even more adventuresome, exploring his world with fascination and abandon. By age 5, Tony is a self-assured child. He has good coordination and he delights at alarming his parents with his hair-raising stunts on any suitable climbing object. Our coverage of early childhood's physical development focuses on body growth and change, motor development, nutrition, and health and illness. We will consider each of these topics in turn.

Body Growth and Change

Remember from Chapter 5 that the infant's growth in the first year is extremely rapid and follows cephalocaudal and proximodistal patterns. At some point around the first birthday, most infants have begun to walk. During the infant's second year, the growth rate begins to slow down, but both gross and fine motor skills progress rapidly. The infant develops a sense of mastery through increased proficiency in walking and running. Improvement in fine motor skills—such as being able to turn the pages of a book one at a time—also contribute to the infant's sense of mastery in the second year. The growth rate continues to slow down in early childhood. Otherwise, we would be a species of giants.

Height and Weight

The average child grows 2½ inches in height and gains between 5 and 7 pounds a year during early childhood. As the preschool child grows older, the percentage of increase in height and weight decreases with each additional year. Figure 8.1 shows the average height and weight of children as they age from 3 to 6 years. Girls are only slightly smaller and lighter than boys during these years, a difference that continues until puberty. During the preschool years, both boys and girls slim down as the trunk of their bodies lengthens. Although their heads are still somewhat large for their bodies, by the end of the preschool years, most children have lost their top-heavy look. Body fat also shows a slow, steady decline during the preschool years, so that the chubby baby often looks much leaner by the end of early childhood. Girls have more fatty tissue than boys, and boys have more muscle tissue.

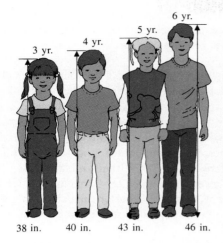

Physical Growth, Ages 3 to 6 (50th Percentile)				
	Height (Inches)		Weight (Pounds)	
Age	Boys	Girls	Boys	Girls
3	38	37¾	32¼	31¾
3½	39¼	39¼	34¼	34
4	40¼	40½	36½	36¼
4½	42	42	38½	38½
5	43¼	43	41½	41
5½	45	44½	45½	44
6	46	46	48	47

FIGURE 8.1 Average height and weight of children as they age from 3 to 6.

If the growth rate did not slow down in early childhood, we would become a species of giants.

Most preschool children are fascinated by bodies, especially their own, but also the bodies of family members and friends. Children have lots of questions about how they work. Jonathan, age 4, says, "You know, I sometimes wonder about what is inside me. I bet it is all wet with blood and other stuff moving around. Outside of me it is all dry. You wouldn't know my inside by looking at the outside part." Jason, age 5, asks, "How does my brain work?" Jennifer, age 5, asks, "Why do we eat food? What happens to the food after we eat it?" Budding 4-year-old biologists like Jonathan, Jason, and Jennifer are telling us they want to know more about their body's machinery. Two recommended books to help answer some of children's curious questions about their bodies are *The Body Book* by Claire Raynor and *Blood and Guts* by Linda Allison.

Growth patterns vary individually. Think back to your preschool years. This was probably the first time you noticed that some children were taller than you, some shorter; that some were fatter, some thinner; that some were stronger, some weaker. Much of the variation is due to heredity, but environmental experiences are involved to some extent. A review of the heights and weights of children around the world concluded that the two most important contributors to height differences are ethnic origin and nutrition (Meredith, 1978). Urban, middle-class, and firstborn children were taller than rural, lower-class, and later-born children. Children whose mothers smoked during pregnancy were 1/2″ shorter than children whose mothers did not smoke during pregnancy. In the United States, black children are taller than white children.

Why are some children unusually short? The culprits are congenital factors (genetic or prenatal problems), a physical problem that develops in childhood, or an emotional difficulty. In many cases, children with congenital growth problems can be treated with hormones. Usually, this treatment is directed at the pituitary, the body's master gland, located at the base of the brain. This gland secretes growth-related hormones. With regard to physical problems that develop during childhood, malnutrition and chronic infections can stunt growth, although if the problems are properly treated, normal growth usually is attained. And some developmentalists believe that emotional problems can produce shorter stature. For example, Lita Gardner (1972) argued that depriving children of affection causes stress and alters the release of hormones by the pituitary gland. This type of growth retardation due to emotional deprivation is called **deprivation dwarfism.** Some children who are small and weak but who are not dwarfs also may show the effects of an impoverished emotional environment, although most parents of these children say they are small and weak because they have a poor body structure or constitution.

The Brain

One of the most important physical developments during early childhood is the continuing development of the brain and nervous system. While the brain continues to grow in early childhood, it does not grow as rapidly as in infancy. By the time children have reached 3 years of age, the brain is three-quarters of its adult size. By age 5, the brain has reached about nine-tenths its adult size.

The brain and the head grow more rapidly than any other parts of the body. The top parts of the head, the eyes, and the brain grow faster than the lower portions, such as the jaw. Figure 8.2 reveals how the growth curve for the head and brain advances more rapidly than the growth curve for height and weight. At 5 years of age, when the brain has attained approximately 90 percent of its adult weight, the 5-year-old's total body weight is only about one-third of what it will be when the child reaches adulthood.

Some of the brain's increase in size is due to the increase in the number and size of nerve endings within and between areas of the brain. These nerve endings continue to grow at least until adolescence. Some of the brain's increase in size also

Swiftly the brain becomes an enchanted loom, where millions of flashing shuttles weave a dissolving pattern—always a meaningful pattern—though never an abiding one.

Sir Charles Sherrington, 1906

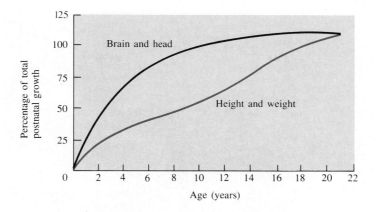

FIGURE 8.2 Growth curves for the head and brain and for height and weight. The more rapid growth of the brain and head can be easily seen. Height and weight advance more gradually over the first two decades of life (After Damon, 1977).

is due to the increase in **myelination,** a process in which nerve cells are covered and insulated with a layer of fat cells. This process has the effect of increasing the speed of information traveling through the nervous system. Some developmentalists believe myelination is important in the maturation of a number of children's abilities. For example, myelination in the areas of the brain related to hand-eye coordination is not complete until about 4 years of age. Myelination in the areas of the brain related to focusing attention is not complete until the end of middle and late childhood (Tanner, 1978).

The increasing maturation of the brain, combined with opportunities to experience a widening world, contributes enormously to children's emerging cognitive abilities. Consider a child who is learning to read and is asked by the teacher to read aloud to the class. Input from the child's eyes is transmitted to the child's brain, then passed through many brain systems, which translate (process) the patterns of black and white into codes for letters, words, and associations. The output occurs in the form of messages to the child's lips and tongue. The child's own gift of speech is possible because brain systems are organized in ways that permit language processing.

Visual Perception

Visual maturity increases during the early childhood years. Only toward the end of early childhood are most children's eye muscles adequately developed to allow them to move their eyes efficiently across a series of letters (Vurpillot, 1968). And preschool children are often farsighted, not being able to see up close as well as they can far away. By the time they enter the first grade, though, most children can focus their eyes and sustain their attention quite well.

Depth perception continues to mature during the preschool years. However, because of young children's lack of motor coordination, they may trip and spill drinks, fall from a jungle gym, or produce poor artwork.

Some young children develop a "lazy eye." The technical term for this is **functional amblyopia,** which usually results from not using one eye enough to avoid the discomfort of double vision produced by imbalanced eye muscles. Children with a lazy eye have no way of knowing that they are not seeing adequately, even though

Preschool children lead very active lives. Their movement through their environment now becomes more automatic and purposeful than in infancy.

their vision is decreased because one eye is doing most of the work. Treatment may include patching the stronger eye for several months to encourage the use of the affected eye, wearing glasses, doing eye exercises. Occasionally, surgery may be required on the muscles of the eye.

What signs suggest that a child might be having vision problems? These include rubbing of the eyes, excessive blinking, squinting, appearing irritable when playing games that require good distance vision, shutting or covering one eye, and tilting the head or thrusting it forward when looking at something. A child who shows any of these behaviors should be examined by an ophthalmologist (Ashburn, 1986).

Motor Development

Running as fast as you can, falling down, getting right back up and running just as fast as you can . . . building towers with blocks . . . scribbling, scribbling, and more scribbling . . . cutting paper with scissors. During your preschool years you probably developed the ability to perform all of these activities.

Gross Motor Skills

The preschool child no longer has to make an effort simply to stay upright and to move around. As children move their legs with more confidence and carry themselves more purposefully, the process of moving around in the environment becomes more automatic.

At 3 years of age, children are still enjoying simple movements such as hopping, jumping, and running back and forth, just for the sheer delight of performing these activities. They take considerable pride in showing how they can run across a room and jump all of six inches. The run-and-jump will win no Olympic gold medals, but for the 3-year-old the activity is a source of considerable pride and accomplishment.

By 4 years of age, children are still enjoying the same kind of activities, but they have become more adventurous. They scramble over low jungle gyms as they display their athletic prowess. Although they have been able to climb stairs with one foot on each step for some time now, they are just beginning to be able to come down the same way. They still often revert to marking time on each step.

By 5 years of age, children are even more adventuresome than when they were 4. As our description of Tony at the beginning of the chapter indicated, it is not unusual for self-assured 5-year-olds to perform hair-raising stunts on practically any climbing object. Five-year-olds run hard and enjoy races with each other and their parents.

You probably have arrived at one important conclusion about preschool children: They are very, very active. Indeed, researchers have found that 3-year-old children have the highest activity level of any age in the entire human life span. They fidget when they watch television. They fidget when they sit at the dinner table. Even when they sleep, they move around quite a bit. Because of their activity level and the development of large muscles, especially in the arms and legs, preschool children need daily exercise. As part of their increased activity level in early childhood, young children often engage in rough-and-tumble play. To learn more about the nature of young children's rough-and-tumble play, turn to Children 8.1.

Fine Motor Skills

At 3 years of age, children are still emerging from the infant ability to place and handle things. Although they have had the ability to pick up the tiniest objects between their thumb and forefinger for some time now, they are still somewhat clumsy at it. Three-year-olds can build surprisingly high block towers, each block being placed with intense concentration but often not in a completely straight line. When 3-year-olds play with a form board or a simple jigsaw puzzle, they are rather rough in placing the pieces. Even when they recognize the hole a piece fits into, they are not very precise in positioning the piece. They often try to force the piece in the hole or pat it vigorously.

At 4 years of age, children's fine motor coordination has improved substantially and become much more precise. Sometimes 4-year-old children have trouble building high towers with blocks because in their desire to place each of the blocks perfectly they may upset those already stacked. By age 5, children's fine motor coordination has improved further. Hand, arm, and body all move together under better command of the eye. Mere towers no longer interest the 5-year-old, who now wants to build a house or a church complete with steeple, though adults may still need to be told what each finished project is meant to be.

Fine motor skills develop during the preschool years. As shown here, 3-year-old children can build surprisingly tall towers of blocks.

That energy which makes a child hard to manage is the energy which afterward makes him a manager of life.

Henry Ward Beecher,
Proverbs from Plymouth Pulpit, *1887*

Rough-and-Tumble Play and Laughing Faces

Four-year-old Harry is standing on the playground outside his nursery school. He watches as two other boys mix some water with the sand where they are playing. Harry takes off and runs full speed into the sand area where they are playing, diving into the water and sand and the other two boys. The three of them wrestle for a few moments. Harry then takes off running and one of the sand players calls out, "Harry, you bum," and the two chase after Harry. They catch Harry and all three tumble to the ground in a heap. However, there is a look on their faces that you might not expect. Rather than hatred and anger, all three boys are observed to be occasionally smiling and laughing. This is *rough-and-tumble play,* play that involves running, jumping, chasing, fleeing, open-hand hitting or hitting at, and a laughing face (Eibl-Eibesfeldt, 1989; Smith, 1989). Rough-and-tumble play is distinguished from *aggression,* which involves hitting with clenched fists, frowning, and hostile intentions.

Rough-and-tumble play and aggression also tend to occur in different settings. Rough-and-tumble play usually occurs on playgrounds with soft surfaces. Aggression is more likely to occur in the context of property disputes (Humphreys & Smith, 1987). During rough-and-tumble play, children usually alternate roles between aggressor and victim, but this alternation does not characterize aggression. At the end of rough-and-tumble play, children do not separate as they do at the end of aggressive acts; rough-and-tumble play and aggression are not the same thing.

Rough-and-tumble play can serve positive educational and developmental functions (Humphreys and Smith, 1987; Pellegrini, 1987). In rough-and-tumble play, children learn to use and practice skills that are important for social competence. For example, in rough-and-tumble play, children alternate between being the victim and the victimizer. This reciprocal role taking may be involved in children's ability to understand the perspective of others.

In one recent investigation, the benefits of rough-and-tumble play were evident (Pelegrini, 1987; Pelegrini & Perlmutter, 1988). Children from kindergarten and the second and fourth grades were observed on the playground during their recess. The results confirmed that children's rough-and-tumble play was positively related to social competence but that aggression was not. And rough-and-tumble play did not usually lead to aggression. Instead, rough-and-tumble play tended to lead to games with rules and desirable forms of prosocial play. Children who engaged in aggression did not engage in rough-and-tumble play. Also children who engaged in rough-and-tumble play were more popular with their peers than were those who engaged in aggression. Other researchers have found that boys are more likely to engage in rough-and-tumble play than girls are (DiPietro, 1980).

Young children need to spend considerable time playing outdoors or in spacious indoor settings. This physical play time should be part of any educational program. Researchers have found that children who are confined to classrooms for longer periods of time engage in more intense rough-and-tumble play than do children who are confined for shorter periods (Smith & Hagen, 1980). It is important for teachers to be able to distinguish between rough-and-tumble play and aggression, and to support rough-and-tumble play and to discourage aggression. ◆

What are some of the main ways we can tell the difference between children's rough-and-tumble play and aggression?

(a)

(b)

(c)

(d)

The young child's developing ability to hold a pencil reveals growth in fine motor coordination. As shown in Figure 8.3, toddlers tend to grab the pencil in the palm of their hand and make rough, crude movements with it. During early childhood, children become more proficient at using a pencil, learning to use their fingers and wrist to manipulate the tip rather than the whole pencil (Goodman, 1979).

As we have seen, both the gross motor and fine motor skills of children improve dramatically during early childhood. A summary of some of the major motor and perceptual milestones from 2 or 3 to 6 or 6½ years of age is presented in Table 8.1.

How do developmentalists measure motor development? One widely used measure is the **Denver Developmental Screening Test.** It was devised to be a simple, inexpensive, fast method to diagnose developmental delay in children from birth

FIGURE 8.3 The young child's development of fine motor coordination reflected in the ability to hold a pencil. (*a*) The toddler grabs the whole pencil and is able to make only crude markings with it. (*b, c*) During early childhood, children use fewer arm and shoulder movements and more finger movements. (*d*) By the end of early childhood, children have learned to use their fingers and wrist to manipulate the tip rather than the whole pencil (Goodman, 1979, p. 96).

TABLE 8.1 Motor and Perceptual Development in Early Childhood

The following tasks are reasonable to expect in 75 to 80 percent of the children of the indicated ages. Children should be tested individually. The data upon which this is based have been collected from children in white middle-class neighborhoods.

A child failing to master four to six of the tasks for his or her age probably needs (a) a more thorough evaluation and (b) some kind of remedial help. Various sex differences are indicated.

2 to 3 Years	Yes	No
1. Displays a variety of scribbling behavior	___	___
2. Can walk rhythmically at an even pace	___	___
3. Can step off low object, one foot ahead of the other	___	___
4. Can name hands, feet, head, and some face parts	___	___
5. Opposes thumb to fingers when grasping objects and releases objects smoothly from finger-thumb grasp	___	___
6. Can walk a 2-inch wide line placed on ground, for 10 feet	___	___

4 to 4½ Years	Yes	No
1. Forward broad jump, both feet together and clear of ground at the same time	___	___
2. Can hop two or three times on one foot without precision or rhythm	___	___
3. Walks and runs with arm action coordinated with leg action	___	___
4. Can walk a circular line a short distance	___	___
5. Can draw a crude circle	___	___
6. Can imitate a simple line cross using a vertical and horizontal line	___	___

5 to 5½ Years	Yes	No
1. Runs 30 yards in just over 8 seconds	___	___
2. Balances on one foot (girls 6 to 8 seconds) (boys 4 to 6 seconds)	___	___
3. Child catches large playground ball bounced to him or her chest-high from 15 feet away, four to five times out of five	___	___
4. Rectangle and square drawn differently (one side at a time)	___	___
5. Can high-jump 8 inches or higher over bar with simultaneous two-foot takeoff	___	___
6. Bounces playground ball, using one or two hands, a distance of 3 to 4 feet	___	___

6 to 6½ Years	Yes	No
1. Can block-print first name in letters 1½ to 2 inches high	___	___
2. Can gallop, if it is demonstrated	___	___
3. Can exert 6 pounds or more of pressure in grip strength measure	___	___
4. Can walk balance beam 2 inches wide, 6 inches high, and 10 to 12 inches long	___	___
5. Can run 60 feet in about 5 seconds	___	___
6. Can arise from ground from back lying position, when asked to do so as fast as he or she can, in 2 seconds, or under	___	___

From B. Cratty, *Psychomotor Behavior in Education and Sport.* © 1974 Charles C Thomas, Publisher, Springfield, Illinois.

through 6 years of age. The test is individually administered and includes an evaluation of language and personal-social ability in addition to separate assessments of gross and fine motor skills. Among the gross motor skills that are measured are the child's ability to sit, walk, broad jump (now called the long jump), pedal a tricycle, throw a ball overhand, catch a bounced ball, hop on one foot, and balance on one foot. Fine motor skills that are measured include the child's ability to stack cubes, reach for objects, and draw a person.

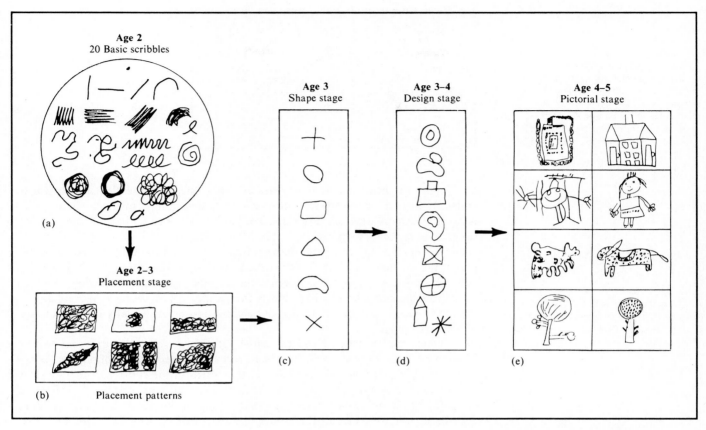

Age 2
20 Basic scribbles

(a)

Age 2–3
Placement stage

(b)   Placement patterns

Age 3
Shape stage

(c)

Age 3–4
Design stage

(d)

Age 4–5
Pictorial stage

(e)

FIGURE 8.4   The stages of young children's artistic drawings (Kellogg, 1970, pp. 34–35).

Young Children's Artistic Drawings

The development of fine motor skills in the preschool years allows children to become budding artists. There are dramatic changes in how children depict what they see. Art provides unique insights into children's perceptual worlds—what they are attending to, how space and distance are viewed, how they experience patterns and forms. Rhoda Kellogg is a creative teacher of preschool children who has been observing and guiding young children's artistic efforts for many decades. She has assembled an impressive array of tens of thousands of drawings produced by more than 2,000 preschool children. Adults who are unfamiliar with young children's art often view the productions of this age group as meaningless scribbles. Kellogg (1970) has tried to change this perception by showing that young children's artistic productions are orderly, meaningful, and structured.

By their second birthday, children can scribble. Scribbles represent the earliest form of drawing. Every form of graphic art, no matter how complex, contains the lines found in children's artwork, which Kellogg calls the 20 basic scribbles. These include vertical, horizontal, diagonal, circular, curving, waving or zigzag lines, and dots. As young children progress from scribbling to picture making, they go through four distinguishable stages: placement, shape, design, and pictorial (Figure 8.4).

Even the earliest drawings of children are not placed at random on the page. Instead they are drawn on the page in placement patterns. The spaced border pattern is shown in Figure 8.3b. Sixteen other placement patterns are developed, with

The youth of an art is, like the youth of anything else its most interesting period.

Samuel Butler, Note-Books, *1912*

FIGURE 8.5 The first two cats are typical of a young child's early efforts at drawing animals: They are humanlike, standing upright. As children become more aware of the nature of cats, they draw them more catlike, standing on all four feet, as shown in the cat at the right.

Thinking Critically
Should parents and preschool teachers let the young child's artistic and drawing skills develop naturally, or should they try to train them? Explain.

all 17 patterns present at 2 to 3 years of age. This stage is called the **placement stage.** By their third birthday, children can draw diagrams in different shapes. This is called the **shape stage** (Figure 8.3c). Young children draw six basic shapes: circles, squares or rectangles, triangles, crosses, X's, and forms. In the next stage, which occurs rather quickly after the shape stage, young children mix two basic shapes into a more complex design. This is called the **design stage** (Figure 8.3d). Finally, between the ages of 4 and 5, children enter the **pictorial stage** of drawing, in which their drawings begin to look like objects that adults can recognize (Figure 8.3e). In the next chapter, we further study young children's art, especially the role of cognitive development.

Young children often use the same formula for drawing different things. Though modified in small ways, one basic form can cover a range of objects. When children begin to draw animals, they portray them in the same way they portray humans: standing upright with a smiling face, legs, and arms (Figure 8.5). Pointed ears may be the only clue adults have as to nature of the particular beast. As children become more aware of the nature of a cat, their drawings acquire more catlike features and the cat is shown on all four feet, tail in the air (Goodman, 1979).

Handedness

For centuries left-handers have suffered unfair discrimination in a world designed for the right-hander. Even the devil himself was portrayed as a left-hander. For many years, teachers forced all children to write with their right hand even if they had a left-hand tendency. Fortunately, today most teachers let children write with the hand they favor.

Some children are still discouraged from using their left hand, even though many left-handed individuals have become very successful. Their ranks include Leonardo da Vinci, Benjamin Franklin, and Pablo Picasso. Each of these famous men was known for his imagination of spatial layouts, which may be stronger in left-handed individuals. Left-handed athletes also are often successful; since there are fewer left-handed athletes, the opposition is not as accustomed to the style and approach of "lefties." Their serve in tennis spins in the opposite direction, their curve ball in baseball swerves the opposite way, and their left foot in soccer is not the one children are used to defending against. Left-handed individuals also do well intellectually. In a recent analysis of the Scholastic Aptitude Test (SAT) scores of more than 100,000 students, 20 percent of the top scoring group was left-handed, which is twice the rate of left-handedness found in the general population (Bower, 1985). Quite clearly, many left-handed people are competent in a wide variety of human activities ranging from athletic skills to intellectual accomplishments.

Early Childhood

Being left-handed has not always had its advantages in our world. Despite society's penalties for being left-handed, most lefties are successful in coping with life in a right-handed world. Children should not be forced to write with their right hand if they have left-handed tendencies.

When does hand preference develop? Adults usually notice a child's hand preference during early childhood, but researchers have found handedness tendencies in the infant years. Even newborns have some preference for one side of their body over the other. In one research investigation, 65 percent of infants turned their head to the right when they were lying on their stomachs in the crib. Fifteen percent preferred to face toward the left. These preferences for the right or left were related to later handedness (Michel, 1981). By about 7 months of age, infants prefer grabbing with one hand or the other, and this is also related to later handedness (Ramsay, 1980). By 2 years of age, about 10 percent of children favor their left hand (Hardyck & Petrinovich, 1977). Many preschool children, though, use both hands, with a clear hand preference not completely distinguished until later in development. Some children use one hand for writing and drawing, and the other hand for throwing a ball. My oldest daughter, Tracy, confuses the issue even further. She writes left-handed and plays tennis left-handed, but she plays golf right-handed. During her early childhood, her handedness was still somewhat in doubt. My youngest daughter, Jennifer, was left-handed from early in infancy. Their left-handed orientation has not handicapped them in their athletic and academic pursuits, although Tracy once asked me if I would buy her a pair of left-handed scissors.

What is the origin of hand preference? Genetic inheritance and environmental experiences have been proposed as causes. In one investigation, a genetic interpretation was favored. The handedness of adopted children was not related to the handedness of their adopted parents but was related to the handedness of their biological parents (Carter-Saltzman, 1980).

At this point we have discussed a number of ideas about the nature of physical and motor development in early childhood. A summary of these ideas is presented in Concept Table 8.1. We now turn to another important concern in early childhood nutrition.

Body Growth and Change, and Motor Development

Concept	Processes and Related Ideas	Characteristics and Description
Physical Development	Height and weight	The average child grows 2½ inches in height and gains between 5 and 7 pounds a year during early childhood. Growth patterns vary individually, though. Some children are unusually short because of congenital problems, a physical problem that develops in childhood, or emotional problems.
	The brain	A key aspect of growth. By age 5, the brain has reached 9/10 of its size. Some of its increased size is due to increases in the number and size of nerve endings, some to myelination. Increasing brain maturation contributes to improved cognitive abilities.
	Visual perception	Visual maturity increases in early childhood. Some children develop functional amblyopia, or a "lazy eye."
Motor Development	Gross motor skills	Improve dramatically during early childhood. Children become increasingly adventuresome as their gross motor skills improve. Young children's lives are extremely active, more active than at any other point in the life cycle. Rough-and-tumble play often occurs, especially in boys, and it can serve positive educational and developmental functions.
	Fine motor skills	Also improve substantially during early childhood. The Denver Developmental Screening Test is one widely used measure of gross and fine motor skills.
	Young children's artistic drawings	The development of fine motor skills in the preschool years allows young children to become budding artists. Scribbling begins by 2 years of age and is followed by four stages of drawing, culminating in the pictorial stage at 4 to 5 years of age.
	Handedness	At one point, all children were taught to be right-handed. In today's world, the strategy is to allow children to use the hand they favor. Left-handed children are as competent in motor skills and intellect as right-handed children. Both genetic and environmental explanations of handedness have been given.

Nutrition

Four-year-old Bobby is on a steady diet of double cheeseburgers, french fries, and chocolate milkshakes. Between meals he gobbles up candy bars and marshmallows. He hates green vegetables. Only a preschooler, Bobby already has developed poor nutrition habits. What are a preschool child's energy needs? What is a preschooler's eating behavior like?

Energy Needs

Feeding and eating habits are important aspects of development during early childhood. What children eat affects their skeletal growth, body shape, and susceptibility to disease. Recognizing that nutrition is important for the child's growth and development, the federal government provides money for school lunch programs. An

TABLE 8.2	Recommended Energy Intakes for Children Ages 1 through 10			
Age	Weight (kg)	Height (cm)	Energy Needs (calories)	Calorie Ranges
1–3	13	90	1,300	900–1,800
4–6	20	112	1,700	1,300–2,300
7–10	28	132	2,400	1,650–3,300

Source: Food and Nutrition Board, 1980.

average preschool child requires 1,700 calories per day. Table 8.2 shows the increasing energy needs of children as they move from infancy through the childhood years. Energy requirements for individual children are determined by the **basal metabolism rate (BMR),** which is the minimum amount of energy a person uses in a resting state, rate of growth, and activity. Energy needs of individual children of the same age, sex, and size vary. Reasons for these differences remain unexplained. Differences in physical activity, basal metabolism, and the efficiency with which children use energy are among the candidates for explanation (Pipes, 1988).

Eating Behavior

A special concern in our culture is the amount of fat in our diets. While some health-conscious mothers may be providing too little fat in their infant's and children's diets, other parents are raising their children on diets in which the percentage of fat is far too high. Our changing life-styles, in which we often eat on the run and pick up fast-food meals, probably contribute to the increased fat levels in children's diets. Most fast-food meals are high in protein, especially meat and dairy products. But the average American child does not need to be concerned about getting enough protein. What must be of concern is the vast number of young children who are being weaned on fast foods that are not only high in protein but also high in fat. Eating habits become ingrained very early in life, and unfortunately, it is during the preschool years that many people get their first taste of fast foods. The American Heart Association recommends that the daily limit for calories from fat should be approximately 35 percent. Compare this figure with the figures in Table 8.3. Clearly, many fast-food meals contribute to excess fat intake by children.

Thinking Critically
Why have we become, simultaneously, a health-conscious nation and a nation with poor health habits?

Being overweight can be a serious problem in early childhood. Consider Ramon, a kindergartner who always begged to stay inside to help during recess. His teacher noticed that Ramon never joined the running games the small superheroes played as they propelled themselves around the playground. Ramon is an overweight 4-year-old boy. Except for extreme cases of obesity, overweight preschool children are usually not encouraged to lose a great deal of weight, but to slow their rate of weight gain so that they will grow into a more normal weight for their height by thinning out as they grow taller. Prevention of obesity in children includes helping children and parents see food as a way to satisfy hunger and nutritional needs, not as proof of love or as a reward for good behavior. Snack foods should be low in fat, simple sugars, and salt, and high in fiber. Routine physical activity should be a daily occurrence. The child's life should be centered around activities, not meals (Javernik, 1988).

TABLE 8.3	Fat and Calorie Intake of Selected Fast-Food Meals		
Selected Meal		**Calories**	**Percentage of Calories from Fat**
Burger King Whopper, fries, vanilla shake		1,250	43
Big Mac, fries, chocolate shake		1,100	41
McDonald's Quarter-Pounder with cheese		418	52
Pizza Hut 10-inch pizza with sausage, mushrooms, pepperoni, and green pepper		1,035	35
Arby's roast beef plate (roast beef sandwich, two potato patties, and coleslaw), chocolate shake		1,200	30
Kentucky Fried Chicken dinner (three pieces of chicken, mashed potatoes and gravy, coleslaw, roll)		830	50
Arthur Treacher's fish and chips (two pieces breaded, fried fish, french fries, cola drink)		900	42
Typical restaurant "diet plate" (hamburger patty, cottage cheese, etc.)		638	63

From Virginia DeMoss, "Good, the Bad and the Edible" in *Runner's World,* June 1980. Copyright Virginia DeMoss. Reprinted with permission.

There is concern not only about excessive fat in children's diets, but about excessive sugar. To learn more about the effects of sugar on young children's behavior, turn to Children 8.2.

In sum, while there is individual variation in appropriate nutrition for children, their diets should be well balanced and should include fats, carbohydrates, protein, vitamins, and minerals. An occasional candy bar does not hurt and can even benefit a growing body, but a steady diet of hamburgers, french fries, milkshakes, and candy bars should be avoided.

Health and Illness

What is the status of children's illness and health around the world? What is the nature of illness, health, and development during the early childhood years? We will consider each of these questions in turn.

The State of Illness and Health in the World's Children

A simple child,
That lightly draws its breath,
What should it know of death?

William Wordsworth, "We Are Seven,"
1798

Of every three deaths in the world, one death is of a child under the age of 5. Every week, more than a quarter of a million young children still die in developing countries in a quiet carnage of infection and undernutrition (Grant, 1988).

What are the main causes of death and child malnutrition in the world?

—*Diarrhea* is the leading cause of childhood death. However, approximately 70 percent of the more than 4 million children killed by diarrhea in 1989 could have been saved if all parents had available a low-cost breakthrough known as **oral rehydration therapy (ORT)**. This

Sugar and Children's Inappropriate Behavior

Robert, age 3, loves chocolate. His mother lets him have three chocolate candy bars each day. Robert also drinks an average of four cans of caffeine cola a day, and he eats sugar-coated cereal each morning at breakfast. It is estimated that the average American child consumes almost 2 pounds of sugar per week (Riddle & Prinz, 1984). How does sugar consumption influence the health and behavior of young children?

The association of sugar consumption and children's health problems—dental cavities and obesity, for example—has been widely documented (Rogers & Morris, 1986). In recent years, a growing interest in the influence of sugar on children's behavior has surfaced. In one investigation, eight preschool children on separate mornings each received 6 ounces of juice, sweetened one morning with sucrose and on the other with an artificial sweetener (Goldman & others, 1986). The children were observed for 90 minutes following the drinks. After the sucrose drink, the young children exhibited more inappropriate behavior: They were less attentive and overly active, for example. Other findings support the belief that sugar consumption by young children increases their aggression, especially in unstructured circumstances and when the child is bored (Goldman & others, 1987).

Is sugar consumption related to preschool children's aggression?

The jury is still out on how extensively sugar affects children's behavior. Some reviews conclude that we do not have good evidence for sugar's role in promoting aggressive or hyperactive behavior (e.g., Pipes, 1988). However, investigatons such as the one described here argue for a closer look at the contribution of sugar to children's behavior. ◆

treatment encompasses a range of techniques designed to prevent dehydration during episodes of diarrhea by giving the child fluids by mouth. When a child has diarrhea, dehydration can often be prevented by giving the child a large volume of water and other liquids.

—More than 3 million children were killed in 1987 by *measles, tetanus,* and *whooping cough.* Another 200,000 have been permanently disabled by polio. The efforts in the 1980s have made immunization widely available, and the lives of many children have been saved by vaccination costing only about $5 a child. What is needed is improved communication to inform parents in developing countries and around the world of the importance of a course of vaccinations for their children.

—*Acute respiratory infections,* mainly *pneumonias,* killed 2 to 3 million children under the age of 5 in 1987. Most of these children could have been saved by 50¢ worth of antibiotics administered by a community health worker with a few months of training. Most of the children's parents could have sought out the low-cost help if they had known how to distinguish between a bad cough and a life-threatening lung infection.

Oral Rehydration Therapy in Bangladesh

Bangladesh is where much of the pioneering work on oral rehydration therapy has been carried out. Still, 10 percent of all children born in Bangladesh die before the age of 5 from dehydration and malnutrition brought about by diarrhea. The majority of Bangladesh women are illiterate, so health workers must go to considerable lengths to contact families and instruct them in how to give oral rehydration therapy. A homemade solution was needed that every household could afford. The solution that was decided upon was a three-finger pinch of salt and a four-finger scoop of molasses dissolved in water, a solution that has been very effective. Close to 1,000 oral rehydration workers have been trained to go from door to door in villages. More than 5 million mothers have had half an hour instruction with an oral rehydration worker. Mothers are taught that it is a mistake to stop giving food and drink to the child, because this only increases the danger of dehydration. The worker shows the mother how to prepare the solution and then watches the mother make it. Although average usage rates have yet to rise above 60 percent, further promotion of the technique is occurring through the use of posters, leaflets, television, and radio (MacPherson, 1987). ◆

Malnourished children from Bangladesh. While oral rehydration therapy is being used in Bangladesh, 10 percent of all children born in Bangladesh die before reaching the age of 5 from dehydration and malnutrition brought about by diarrhea.

—*Undernutrition* was a contributing cause in about one-third of the 14 million child deaths in the world in 1987. While not having enough to eat is still a fundamental problem in some of the world's poorest countries, the major cause of undernutrition in the world is not a shortage of food in the home. Rather, it is a lack of basic services and a shortage of information about preventing infection and using food to promote growth. Making sure that parents know that they can protect their children's nutritional health by such means as birth spacing, care during pregnancy, breast-feeding, immunization, preventing illness, special feeding before and after illness, and regularly checking the child's weight gain can overcome many cases of malnutrition and poor growth in today's world.

—A contributing factor in at least one-fourth of today's child deaths is the *timing of births*. Births that are too numerous or too close, or mothers who are too young or too old carry a much higher risk for both the mother and the child. Using this knowledge and today's low-cost ways of timing births is one of the most powerful and least expensive means for raising the child survival rate and improving children's health around the world.

—Also, more than half of all illnesses and deaths among children is associated with inadequate *hygiene*. In communities without a safe water supply and sanitation, it is very difficult to prevent the contamination of food and water. Some low-cost methods can prevent the spread of germs, and all families should be informed of these sanitation measures.

In summary, most child malnutrition, as well as most child deaths, could now be prevented by parental actions that are almost universally affordable and are based on knowledge that is already available. An overview of the leading causes of children's death and the ways these problems could be prevented is presented in Table 8.4.

Among the nations with the highest mortality rate under age 5 are Asian nations such as Afghanistan and African nations such as Ethiopia (Grant, 1988). In Afghanistan, in 1986, for every 1,000 children born alive, 325 died before the age of 5; in Ethiopia, the figure was 255 per 1,000. Among the countries with the lowest mortality rate under age 5 are Scandinavian countries such as Sweden and Finland, where only 7 of every 1,000 children born died before the age of 5 in 1986. The United States mortality rate under age 5 is better than that of most countries, but of 131 countries for which figures were available in 1986, 20 countries had better rates than the United States. In 1986, for every 1,000 children born alive in the United States, 13 died before the age of 5.

Fortunately, in the United States the dangers of many diseases such as measles, rubella (German measles), mumps, whooping cough, diphtheria, and polio are no longer present. The vast majority of children in the United States have been immunized against such major childhood diseases. It is important, though, for parents to recognize that these diseases, while no longer afflicting our nation's children, do require a sequence of vaccinations. Without the vaccinations, children can still get the diseases.

The disorders most likely to be fatal during the preschool years are birth defects, cancer, and heart disease. Death rates from these problems have been reduced in recent years because of improved treatments and health care (Garrison and McQuiston, 1989).

Thinking Critically
What responsibility do the wealthier nations of the world have for fostering and financially supporting health and nutrition services for children in developing countries? Explain.

TABLE 8.4   *Annual Deaths of Children Under the Age of 5 in Developing Countries in 1987*

Deaths in Millions (Cumulative)	Causes	Prevention
14	Diarrheal diseases 5 million	Of which approximately 3.5 million were caused by dehydration that could have been prevented or treated by low-cost action using ORT
13	(also a major cause of malnutrition)	
12		
11		
10		
9	Malaria 1 million	Can be drastically reduced by low-cost drugs if parents know signs and can get help
8	Measles 1–9 million	Can be prevented by one vaccination, but is is essential to take the child at the right time— as soon as possible after the age of 9 months
7	(also a major cause of malnutrition)	
6	Acute respiratory infections 2–9 million	0–6 million whooping cough deaths can be prevented by a full course of DPT vaccine—most of the rest can be prevented by low-cost antibiotics if parents know danger signs and can get help
5		
4		
3	Tetanus 0–8 million	Neonatal tetanus kills 0–8 million. Can be prevented by immunizatin of mother-to-be
2	Other 2–4 million	Many of which can be avoided by prenatal care, breast-feeding, and nutrition education

From J. P. Grant, *State of the World's Children,* Copyright © 1988 Oxford University Press, Oxford, England.
Of the 14 million child deaths each year approximately 10 million are from only four major causes and all are now susceptible to effective low-cost actions by well-informed and well-supportd parents.
For the purpose of this chart, one cause of death has been allocated for each child death when, in fact, children die of multiple causes and malnutrition is a contributory cause in approximately one-third of all child deaths.

Health, Illness, and Development

While there has been great national interest in the psychological aspects of adult health, only recently has a developmental perspective on psychological aspects of children's health been proposed. The uniqueness of young children's health-care needs is evident when we consider their motor, cognitive, and social development (Maddux & others, 1986). For example, think about the infant's and preschool child's motor development—inadequate to ensure personal safety while riding in an automobile. Adults must take preventive measures to restrain infants and young children in car seats. More about ways children can be encouraged to use seat belts

Playgrounds for young children should be designed with the child's safety in mind, and the outdoor play environment should promote young children's motor, cognitive, and social development.

when riding in a car is presented in Children 8.3. Young children may lack the intellectual skills—including reading ability—to discriminate between safe and unsafe household substances. And they may lack the impulse control to keep them from running out into a busy street while chasing after a ball or a toy.

Playgrounds for young children need to be designed with the child's safety in mind (Frost & Wortham, 1988). The initial steps in ensuring children's safety is to walk with children through the existing playground or the site where the playground is to be developed, talking with them about possible safety hazards, letting them assist in identifying hazards, and indicating how they can use the playground safely. The outdoor play environment should enhance the child's motor, cognitive, and social development. The inadequate attention to the safety of children on playgrounds is evident in the following statistic: More than 305,000 preschool children were treated in emergency rooms with playground-related injuries from 1983 through 1987. One of the major problems is that playground equipment—superstructures incorporating climbers, swings, slides, clatter bridges and sliding poles—is not constructed

Buckle Up for Safety

Each year more American children are injured or die as a result of automobile accidents than as a result of any other type of accident or disease. According to recent statistics from the National Safety Council, about 1,500 deaths and 125,000 injuries occur each year in children 14 years of age and under. There seems to be a strong consensus that safety belts and child safety seats, if used properly, could eliminate about half of these deaths and injuries (Scott, 1985).

In the face of such evidence, one natural question is, How can we get children to use safety belts consistently? For those children old enough to understand and take responsibility for themselves, how can we make "buckling up" a high-frequency behavior when children get into a car?

A recent study by Karen Sowers-Hoag, Bruce Thyer, and Jon Bailey (1987) offers a simple, but powerful, answer. The authors reviewed what other experts had tried. Many of these efforts, not unexpectedly, were directed toward adults. Typical intervention programs included reminder flyers placed on automobile windshields, safety-belt lotteries, dashboard reminder stickers, and "flash-for-life" cards used as prompts for unbuckled drivers. Only modest gains were observed in the number of individuals buckling up in these programs.

The researchers thought that it was important to direct efforts at children themselves—to try to invent a program that would get large numbers of children to buckle up and to demonstrate the lasting effects of behavior change. They identified 16 children ranging from 4 to 7 years of age, all of whom attended an after-school program and none of whom buckled

up when they drove home with their parents at the end of the school day.

Following a baseline period of observing the children, the behavior modification consisted of four parts. First, one of the authors presented educational facts about the use of safety belts and discussed famous role models known to use safety belts, such as airline and jet fighter pilots, race car drivers, and well-known movie stars. Second, the same author taught children how to be assertive about the use of seat belts by role playing a number of situations children might encounter. Third, the children engaged in behavioral rehearsal during which they went to the school parking lot and practiced getting into and out of the front and back seats of several cars, buckling the seat belts in the cars and practicing how to accomplish this quickly. Finally, a lottery was set up and any child observed buckling up on the after-school trip home was eligible to win a prize in the next day's lottery. Half of the children won prizes in the lottery, including stickers, toy cars, and coloring books. The results of the study were impressive. On many of the days, all of the children buckled up. And in follow-up observations through approximately 100 days, a high percentage of the children were still buckling up. Even when the children were not being observed, interviews with the parents indicated that the children were consistently buckling up in other situations as well. These findings are important because they report a relatively simple educational technique that takes only a few hours to implement and because the results may save a child's life one day.   ♦

Safety belts and child safety seats, if used properly, can eliminate about half of the 1,500 deaths and 125,000 injuries that occur each year in children under 14 years of age. How can we get children to "buckle up" consistently?

over impact-absorbing surfaces, such as wood chips and sand. A 1-foot fall head first into concrete, or a 4-foot fall head first onto packed earth can be fatal. The wood chips and sand under equipment should be kept at a minimum of 8 inches deep.

Health-education programs for preschool children need to be cognitively simple. There are three simple but important goals for health-education programs for preschool children (Parcel & others, 1979): (1) Be able to identify feelings of wellness and illness and be able to express them to adults; (2) be able to identify appropriate sources of assistance for health-related problems; and (3) be able to independently initiate the use of sources of assistance for health problems.

Caregivers have an important health role for young children (Farmer, Peterson, & Kashani, 1989). For example, by controlling the speed of the vehicles they drive, by decreasing their drinking—especially before driving—and by not smoking around children, caregivers enhance children's health. In one recent investigation, it was found that, if the mother smokes, her children are twice as likely to have respiratory ailments (Etzel, 1988). The young children of single, unemployed, smoking mothers are also three times more likely to be injured. Smoking may serve as a marker to identify mothers less able to supervise young children. In sum, caregivers can actively affect young children's health and safety by training and monitoring recreational safety, self-protection skills, proper nutrition, and dental hygiene.

Illnesses, especially those that are not life threatening, provide an excellent opportunity for the young child to expand his or her development. The preschool period is a peak time for illnesses such as respiratory infections (colds, flu) and gastrointestinal upsets (nausea, diarrhea). The illnesses usually are of short duration and are often handled outside the medical community, through the family, day care, or school. Such minor illnesses can increase the young child's knowledge of health and illness and sense of empathy (Parmalee, 1986).

Young children may confuse terms such as "feel bad" with bad behavior and "feel good" with good behavior. Examples include

"I feel bad. I want aspirin."
"I feel bad. My tummy hurts."
"Bobby hurt me."
"I bad girl. I wet my pants."
"Me can do it. Me good girl."
"I'm hurting your feeling, 'cause I was mean to you."
"Stop, it doesn't feel good."

Young children often attribute their illness to what they view as a transgression, such as having eaten the wrong food or playing outdoors in the cold when told not to. In illness and wellness situations, adults have the potential to help children sort out distressed feelings resulting from emotional upsets and from physical illness. For example, a mother might say to her young daughter, "I know you feel bad because you are sick like your sister was last week, but you will be well soon just as she is now." Or a mother might comment, "I know you feel bad because I am going on a trip and I can't take you with me, but I will be back in a few days" (Parmalee, 1986).

Thus far, we have discussed a number of ideas about nutrition, health, and illness in early childhood. These ideas are summarized in Concept Table 8.2. In the next chapter, we will turn our attention to the cognitive development of young children.

Nutrition, Health, and Illness

Concept	Processes and Related Ideas	Characteristics and Description
Nutrition	Energy needs	Increase as children go through the childhood years. Energy requirements vary according to basal metabolism, rate of growth, and activity.
	Eating behavior	Many parents are raising children on diets that are too high in fat and sugar. Children's diets should include well-balanced proportions of fats, carbohydrates, protein, vitamins, and minerals.
Health and Illness	The state of illness and health in the world's children	One death of every three in the world is the death of a child under age 5. Every week, more than a quarter of a million children die in developing countries. The main causes of death and child malnutrition in the world are diarrhea, measles, tetanus, whooping cough, acute respiratory infections, (mainly pneumonias), and undernutrition. Contributing factors include the timing of births and hygiene. Most child malnutrition and child deaths could be prevented by parental actions that are affordable and based on knowledge that is available today. The United States has a relatively low rate of child deaths compared to other countries, although the Scandinavian countries have the best rates. The disorders most likely to be fatal during the preschool years are birth defects, cancer, and heart disease.
	Illness, health, and development	Children's health care needs involve their motor, cognitive, and social development.

Summary

I. **Body Growth and Change**

The average child grows 2½ inches in height and gains between 5 and 7 pounds a year during early childhood. Growth patterns vary individually, though. Some children are unusually short because of congenital problems, a physical problem that develops in childhood, or emotional problems. A key aspect of growth is brain development. By age 5, the brain has reached nine-tenths of its size. Some of its increased size is due to increases in the number and size of nerve endings, some to myelination. Increasing brain maturation contributes to improved cognitive abilities. Visual maturity increases in early childhood. Some children develop functional amblyopia, or "lazy eye."

II. **Gross Motor Development**

Gross motor development improves dramatically in early childhood. Children become increasingly adventuresome as their gross motor skills improve. Young children are extremely active, more active than at any other point in the life cycle. Rough-and-tumble play often occurs, especially in boys, and it can serve positive educational and developmental outcomes.

III. **Fine Motor Skills and Young Children's Artistic Drawings**

Fine motor skills also improve substantially during early childhood. The Denver Developmental Screening Test is one widely used measure of gross and fine motor skills. The development of fine motor skills in early childhood allows young children to become budding artists. Scribbling begins by 2 years of age and is followed by four stages of drawing, culminating in the pictorial stage at 4 to 5 years of age.

IV. Handedness

At one point, all children were taught to be right-handed. In today's world, the strategy is to allow children to use the hand they favor. Left-handed children are as competent in motor skills and intellectual pursuits as right-handed children. Both genetic and environmental explanations of handedness have been given.

V. Nutrition

Energy needs increase through the childhood years. Energy requirements vary according to basal metabolism, rate of growth, and activity. Many parents are raising children on diets that are too high in fat and sugar. Children's diets should include well-balanced proportions of fats, carbohydrates, protein, vitamins, and minerals.

VI. The State of Illness and Health in the World's Children

Of every three deaths in the world, one death is of a child under the age of 5. Every week, more than a quarter of a million children die in developing nations. The main causes of death and malnutrition in the world are diarrhea, measles, tetanus, whooping cough, acute respiratory infections (mainly pneumonias), and undernutrition. Contributing factors include hygiene and the timing of births. Most child malnutrition and child deaths could be prevented by parental actions that are affordable and based on knowledge that is available today. The United States has a relatively low rate of child deaths compared to other countries, although the Scandinavian countries have the best rates. The disorders most likely to be fatal during the preschool years are birth defects, cancer, and heart disease.

VII. Health, Illness, and Development

Children's health care needs involve their motor, cognitive, and social development.

Key Terms

deprivation dwarfism 242
myelination 243
functional amblyopia 243
Denver Developmental
  Screening Test 247

placement stage 250
shape stage 250
design stage 250

pictorial stage 250
basal metabolism rate
  (BMR) 253
oral rehydration therapy
  (ORT) 254

Suggested Readings

Clark, J. E. & Humphrey, J. H. (Eds.) (1985). *Motor development: Current selected research*. Princeton, NJ: Princeton Book Company.
    A collection of articles by leading experts on children's motor development. Includes detailed information about the growth of various motor and athletic skills in the preschool years.

Grant, J. P. (1988). *The state of the world's children*. New York: UNICEF and Oxford University Press.
    Provides an analysis of children's illness, health, and death in 131 countries around the world. Detailed charts about death rates and nutrition. Recommends ways to reduce the child death rate and malnutrition.

Pipes, P. (1988). Nutrition in childhood. In S. R. Williams & B. S. Worthington (Eds.), *Nutrition throughout the life cycle*. St. Louis: Times Mirror/Mosby.
    An excellent overview of nutrition requirements in childhood. Discusses nutrition concerns related to growth and positive health.

Young Children, published by the National Association for the Education of Young Children, Washington, DC.
    This journal includes a variety of articles about young children's physical, cognitive, and social development. Special attention is given to how various aspects of development can be fostered in our nation's preschool programs. Look through the issues of the last five years to get a feel for the important concerns in this area.

The greatest poem ever known
Is one all poets have outgrown:
The poetry, innate, untold,
Of being only four years old.

Christopher Morley

Cognitive Development

A my began attending a Montessori school when she was 3 years old and has been attending the school for more than a year now. Her mother was interested in a preschool program for Amy that involved academic instruction rather than play. Amy's mother talked to a number of mothers in her neighborhood, read extensively about different approaches to early childhood education, and visited eight different preschool programs to observe a typical day and talk with teachers before making her decision about which school would be best for Amy.

Montessori schools are patterned after the educational philosophy of Maria Montessori, an Italian physician-turned-educator, who crafted a revolutionary approach to young children's education at the beginning of the twentieth century. Her work began with a group of mentally retarded children in Rome. She was successful in teaching them to read, write, and pass examinations designed for normal children. Some time later, she turned her attention to poor children from the slums of Rome and had similar success in teaching them. Her approach has since been adopted extensively in private nursery schools in the United States.

The **Montessori approach** is at once a philosophy of education, a psychology of the child, and a group of practical educational exercises that can be used to teach children. Children are given considerable freedom and spontaneity in choosing activities, and they can move from one activity to another when they desire. Each child is encouraged to work independently, to complete tasks in a prescribed manner once they have been undertaken, and to put materials away in assigned places. The teacher is a facilitator rather than a director or controller of learning. She shows the child how to perform intellectual activities, demonstrates interesting ways to explore curriculum materials, and offers help when the child requests it.

Some developmentalists, favor the Montessori approach, but others believe that it neglects children's social development. For example, while Montessori fosters independence and the development of cognitive skills, verbal interaction between the teacher and child and peer interaction are deemphasized. Montessori's critics also argue that imaginative play is restricted. Later in this chapter, other preschool education programs will be described. Keep the Montessori approach in mind so that you can compare its focus with that of these other approaches.

The cognitive world of the preschool child is creative, free, and fanciful. In their art, suns sometimes show up as green, and skies yellow. Cars float on clouds, pelicans kiss seals, and people look like tadpoles. The preschool child's imagination works overtime and their mental grasp of the world improves. Our coverage of cognitive development in early childhood focuses on Piaget's stage of preoperational thought, information processing, language development, Vygotsky's theory of development, and early childhood education.

Piaget's Stage of Preoperational Thought

Remember from Chapter 6 that, during Piaget's sensorimotor stage of development, the infant progresses in the ability to organize and coordinate sensations and perceptions with physical movements and actions. What kinds of changes take place in the preoperational stage?

The Nature of Preoperational Thought

Since this stage of thought is called preoperational, it would seem that not much of importance occurs until full-fledged operational thought appears. Not so. The preoperational stage stretches from approximately the age of 2 to the age of 7. It is a time when stable concepts are formed, mental reasoning emerges, egocentrism begins strongly and then weakens, and magical beliefs are constructed. Preoperational thought is anything but a convenient waiting period for concrete operational thought, although the label *preoperational* emphasizes that the child at this stage does not yet think in an operational way. What are **operations?** They are internalized sets of actions that allow the child to do mentally what before was done physically. Operations are highly organized and conform to certain rules and principles of logic. The operations appear in one form in concrete operational thought and in another form in formal operational thought. Thought in the preoperational stage is still flawed and not well organized. Preoperational thought is the beginning of the ability to reconstruct at the level of thought what has been established in behavior. Preoperational thought also involves a transition from primitive to more sophisticated use of symbols. Preoperational thought can be subdivided into two substages: the symbolic function substage and the intuitive thought substage.

Symbolic Function Substage

The symbolic function substage of preoperational thought occurs roughly between the ages of 2 to 4. By 2 years of age, the child has the ability to mentally picture objects that are not present. The ability to engage in such symbolic thought is referred to as symbolic function, and it vastly expands the child's mental world during this time. Young children use scribbled shapes to represent people, houses, cars, clouds, and so on. More on young children's scribbles and art appears in Children 9.1. Other examples of symbolism in early childhood are the prevalence of pretend play (see Chapter 10) and language. In sum, the ability to think symbolically and represent the world mentally predominates during this early substage of preoperational thought. However, while the young child makes distinct progress during the symbolic function substage, her thought still has several important limitations, two of which are egocentrism and animism.

    Egocentrism is a salient feature of preoperational thought. It is the inability to distinguish between one's own perspective and someone else's perspective. The following telephone conversation between 4-year-old Mary, who is at home, and her father, who is at work, typifies Mary's egocentric thought:

> *Father:* Mary, is Mommy there?
> *Mary:* (Silently nods.)
>
> *Father:* Mary, may I speak to Mommy?
> *Mary:* (Nods again silently.)

Mary's response is egocentric in that she fails to consider her father's perspective before replying. A nonegocentric thinker would have responded verbally.

    Piaget and Barbara Inhelder (1969) initially studied young children's egocentrism by devising the three mountains task (Figure 9.1). The child walks around the model of the mountains and becomes familiar with what the mountains look like from different perspectives. The child can see that there are different objects on the mountains as well. The child is then seated on one side of the table on which the

There are no days in life so memorable as those which vibrated to some stroke of imagination.

Ralph Waldo Emerson,
The Conduct of Life, *1860*

Where Pelicans Kiss Seals, Cars Float on Clouds, and Humans Are Tadpoles

At about 3 years of age and sometimes even 2, children's spontaneous scribbles begin to resemble pictures. One 3½-year-old child looked at the scribble he had just drawn and said it was a pelican kissing a seal (Figure 9.A). At about 3 to 4 years of age, children begin to create symbols of humans. Invariably the first symbols look curiously like tadpoles; see the circle and two lines in Figure 9.B—the circle represents a head and the two lines are legs.

These observations of children's drawings were made by Denise Wolf, Carol Fucigna, and Howard Gardner at Harvard University. They point out that many people think young children draw a person in this rather odd way because it is the best they can do. Piaget said children intend their drawings to be realistic; they draw what they know rather than what they see. So the tadpole with its strange exemptions of trunk and arms might reflect a child's lack of knowledge of the human body and how its parts fit together. However, children know more about the human body than they are capable of drawing. One 3-year-old child drew a tadpole but described it in complete detail, pointing out where the feet, chin, and neck were. When 3- and 4-year-old children are asked to draw someone playing ball, they produce symbols of humans that include arms, since the task implicitly requires arms (Figure 9.C).

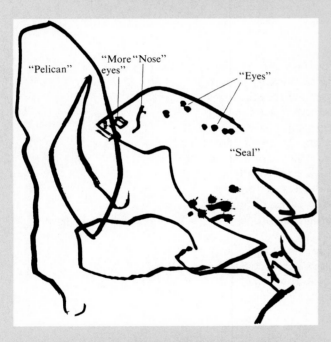

FIGURE 9.A   Halfway into this drawing, the 3½-year-old artist said it was "a pelican kissing a seal." D. Wolf/J. Nove.

FIGURE 9.B   The 3-year-old's first drawing of a person: a "tadpole" consisting of a circle with two lines for legs.

Possibly because preschool children are not very concerned about reality, their drawings are fanciful and inventive (Figure 9.D). Suns are blue, skies are yellow, and cars float on clouds in the preschool child's symbolic world. The symbolism is simple but strong, not unlike the abstractions found in some contemporary art. In the elementary school years, the child's symbols become more realistic, neat, and precise. Suns are yellow, skies are blue, and cars are placed on roads (Figure 9.E).

A child's ability to symbolically represent the world on paper is related to the development of perceptual motor skills. But once such skills are developed, some artists revert to the style of young children's drawings. As Picasso once commented, "I used to draw like Raphael but it has taken me a whole lifetime to learn to draw like children" (Winner, 1986). ♦

FIGURE 9.C   A young child, asked to draw people playing ball, includes only a single arm on the figures playing ball; the fourth figure, an observer, is armless.

FIGURE 9.D   This 6-year-old's drawing is free, fanciful, and inventive.

FIGURE 9.E   An 11-year-old's drawing is neater and more realistic than the 6-year-old's drawing, but it is also less inventive.

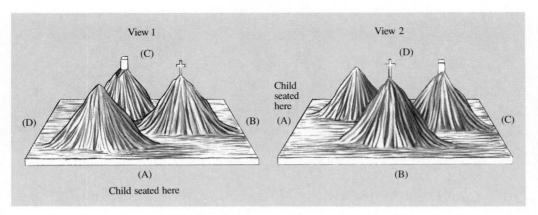

FIGURE 9.1 The three mountains task devised by Piaget and Inhelder (1967). View 1 shows the child's perspective from where he is sitting. View 2 is an example of the photograph the child would be shown mixed in with others from different perspectives. For the child to correctly identify this view, he has to take the perspective of a person sitting at spot (B). Invariably, the preschool child who thinks in a preoperational way cannot perform this task. When asked what the perspective or view of the mountains will look like from position (B), the child selects a photograph taken from location (A), the view he has at the time.

mountains are placed. The experimenter takes a doll and moves it to different locations around the table, at each location asking the child to select from a series of photos, the one photo that most accurately reflects the view the doll is seeing. Children in the preoperational stage often pick the view they have from where they are sitting rather than the view that the doll has. Perspective-taking does not seem to develop uniformly in the preschool child, who frequently shows perspective skills on some tasks but not others (Rubin, 1978; Shantz, 1983).

Animism, another facet of preoperational thought, is the belief that inanimate objects have "lifelike" qualities and are capable of action. The young child might show animism by saying, "That tree pushed the leaf off, and it fell down," or "The sidewalk made me mad; it made me fall down." The young child who uses animism fails to distinguish the appropriate occasions for using human and nonhuman perspectives. Some developmentalists, though, believe that animism represents incomplete knowledge and understanding, not a general conception of the world (Dolgin & Behrend, 1984; Bullock, 1985).

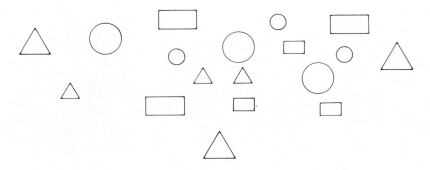

FIGURE 9.2　A random array of objects.

Intuitive Thought Substage

Tommy is 4 years old. Although he is starting to develop his own ideas about the world he lives in, his ideas are still simple and he is not very good at thinking things out. He has difficulty understanding events he knows are taking place but cannot see. He has little control over reality, to which his fantasized thoughts bear little resemblance. He cannot yet answer the question, What if? in any reliable way. For example, he has only a vague idea of what would happen if a car hit him. He also has difficulty negotiating traffic because he cannot do the mental calculations necessary to estimate whether an approaching car will hit him when he crosses the road (Goodman, 1979).

As preschool children become older, they move from the symbolic thought substage to an inner world of thinking that is more intuitive—that is, knowing without the use of rational thinking. The preoperational stage of thought continues until about 7 years of age for most children. The **intuitive thought substage** stretches from approximately 4 to 7 years of age. During this time, children begin to reason primitively and want to know the answers to all sorts of questions.

Children's thinking in this substage is prelogical. While they reason and search for many answers, their reasoning is highly imperfect when measured against adult standards. Piaget referred to this period as *intuitive* because, on one hand, young children seem so sure about their knowledge and understanding, yet on the other hand, they are so unaware of how they know what they know.

An example of the young child's reasoning ability is the difficulty she has putting things into their correct classes. Faced with a random collection of objects that can be grouped together on the basis of two or more properties, the preoperational child is seldom capable of using these properties consistently to sort the objects into appropriate categories. Look at the collection of objects in Figure 9.2. You would respond to the direction "Put the things together that you believe belong together" by sorting the characteristics of size and shape together. Your sorting might look something like that shown in Figure 9.3. In the social realm, the 4-year-old girl might be given the task of dividing her peers into groups according to whether they are friends and whether they are boys or girls. She would be unlikely to arrive at the following classification: friendly boys, friendly girls, unfriendly boys, unfriendly girls. Another example of classification shortcomings involves the preoperational child's understanding of religious concepts (Elkind, 1976). When asked, "Can you be a Protestant and an American at the same time?" 6- and 7-year-olds usually say no; 9-year-olds are likely to say yes, understanding that objects can be cross-classified simultaneously.

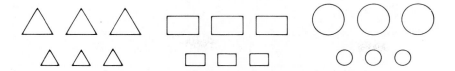

FIGURE 9.3   An ordered array of objects.

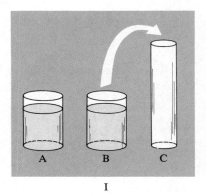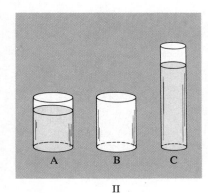

I   II

FIGURE 9.4   Piaget's beaker task. Piaget used the beaker task to determine whether children had conservation of liquid. In I, two identical beakers (A and B) are presented to the child; then (in II), the experimenter pours the liquid from B into beaker C, which is taller and thinner than A or B. The child is now asked if beakers A and C have the same amount of liquid. The preoperational child says no, responding that the taller, thinner beaker (C) has more.

Many of these examples show a characteristic of preoperational thought called **centration**—the focusing, or *centering,* of attention on one characteristic to the exclusion of all others. Centration is most clearly evidenced in the young child's lack of **conservation**—the idea that an amount stays the same regardless of how its container changes. To adults, it is obvious that a certain amount of liquid stays the same regardless of a container's shape. But this is not obvious at all to young children; instead, they are struck by the height of the liquid in the container. In the conservation task—Piaget's most famous—the child is presented with two identical beakers, each filled to the same level with liquid (Figure 9.4). The child is asked if these beakers have the same amount of liquid, and she usually says yes. Then, the liquid from one beaker is poured into a third beaker, which is taller and thinner than the first two (Figure 9.4). The child is then asked if the amount of liquid in the tall, thin beaker is equal to that which remains in one of the original beakers. If the child is less than 7 or 8 years old, she usually says no and justifies her answer in terms of the differing height or width of the beakers. Older children usually answer yes and justify their answers appropriately ("If you poured the milk back, the amount would still be the same").

In Piaget's theory, failing the conservation of liquid task is a sign that children are at the preoperational stage of cognitive development, while passing this test is a sign that they are at the concrete operational stage. In Piaget's view, the preoperational child not only fails to show conservation of liquid, but also of number, matter, length, volume, and area (Figure 9.5).

Thus far, we have discussed a number of Piaget's ideas about preoperational thought, among them egocentrism, animism, and conservation. To learn more about these fascinating aspects of preschool children's thoughts, turn to Children 9.2, where you will discover how these concepts were included in the story *Winnie-the-Pooh.*

False would be a picture which insisted on the brutal egocentrism of the child, and ignored the physical beauty which softens it.

A. A. Milne

Type of conservation	Initial presentation	Manipulation	Preoperational child's answer

Number

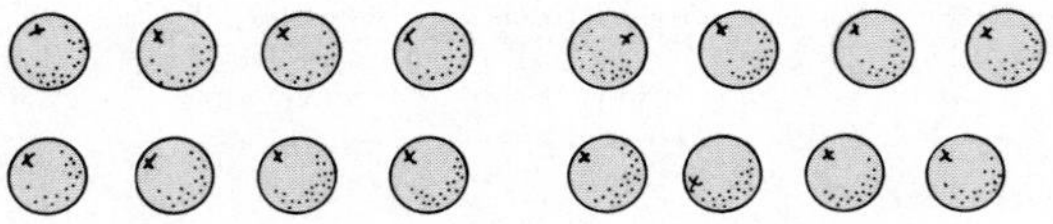

Two identical rows of objects are shown to the child, who agrees they have the same number.

One row is lengthened and the child is asked whether one row now has more objects.

Yes, the longer row.

Matter

Two identical balls of clay are shown to the child. The child agrees they are equal.

The experimenter changes the shape of one of the balls and asks the child whether they still contain equal amounts of clay.

No, the longer one has more.

Length

Two sticks are aligned in front of the child. The child agrees that they are the same length.

The experimenter moves one stick to the right, then asks the child if they still are equal in length.

No, the one on the top is longer.

Volume

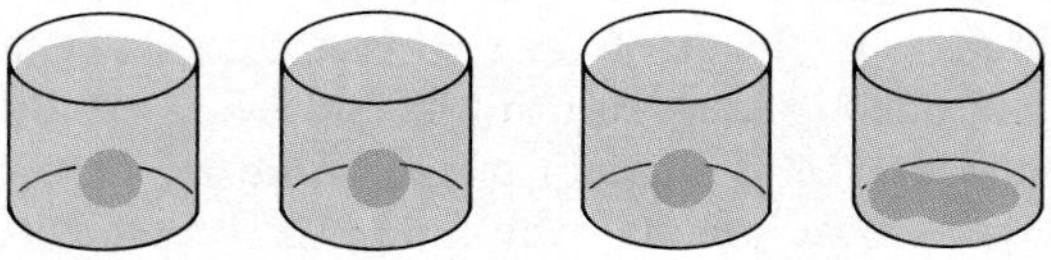

Two balls are placed in two identical glasses with an equal amount of water. The child sees the balls displace equal amounts of water.

The experimenter changes the shape of one of the balls and asks the child if it still will displace the same amount of water.

No, the longer one on the right displaces more.

Area

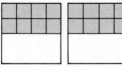

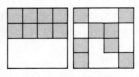

Two identical sheets of cardboard have wooden blocks placed on them in identical positions. The child agrees that the same amount of space is left on each piece of cardboard.

The experimenter scatters the blocks on one piece of cardboard and then asks the child if one of the cardboard pieces has more space covered up.

Yes, the one on the right has more space covered up.

FIGURE 9.5   The domains of conservation.

274   Early Childhood

Piglet, Pooh, and Piaget

According to psychologist Dorothy Singer (1972), if Piaget had opened the pages of *Winnie-the-Pooh,* he would have discovered how A.A. Milne used some of the same concepts Piaget believed were so prominent in the preschool child's thought. Milne's psychological insight gives life and meaning to a little story about an imaginary forest peopled with animals from the nursery.

We first meet Edward Bear as he is being dragged down the stairs on the back of his head. "It is, as far as he knows, the only way of coming down the stairs." This example of egocentrism sets the tone for the rest of the book. The narrator tells us that Edward's name is Winnie-the-Pooh. When asked if Winnie is not a girl's name, Christopher replies with a second example of egocentrism. "He's Winnie-ther-Pooh. Don't you know what *ther* means?" Again, an example of egocentrism. Christopher knows, so no further explanation is necessary, or forthcoming. Piglet, an egocentric friend of Pooh, is a weak and timid pig, and he is certain that everyone knows when he is in distress. But Pooh is just as egocentric when he interprets a note. Pooh recognizes only the letter *P* and each *P* convinces him further that *P* means "Pooh" so "it's a very important Missage to me." In a later chapter, Pooh eats a jar of honey that he had intended to give to everyone else on his birthday. In egocentric form, though, Pooh rationalizes his gluttony and decides to give everyone the empty jar: "It's a very nice pot. Everyone could keep things in it."

Milne recognized the pervasiveness of animism in young children's thought. Each of the imaginary characters displays a talent for animism. In the first chapter, Pooh develops an elaborate plan to steal some honey from a bee's hive. He disguises himself as a cloud in a blue sky. He rolls over and over in the mud until he is as dark as a thundercloud. He borrows a sky-blue balloon from Christopher and floats off into the sky, singing as he goes. The singing cloud is an example of animism.

Milne's story of the birthday of Eeyore (the cynical and pessimistic donkey) illustrates the principle of conservation. Piglet plans to give Eeyore a big red balloon. On the way,

How were Piaget's ideas about cognitive development exemplified in A. A. Milne's classic book, Winnie the Pooh?

Piglet catches his foot in a rabbit's hole and falls down. When he recovers, he finds out to his dismay that the balloon has burst. All that he has left is a small piece of a damp rag. Nevertheless, Piglet is determined to give a present to Eeyore. When he finally reaches Eeyore, the conversation goes like this:

"Eeyore, I brought you a balloon."

"Balloon," said Eeyore, . . .

"one of those big colored things you blow up? Gaiety, song-and-dance, here we are and there we are?"

"Yes . . . but I fell down . . . and I burst the balloon."

"My birthday balloon?"

"Yes, Eeyore," said Piglet, sniffing a little. "Here it is. With—many happy returns of the day."

"My present?"

Piglet nodded again.

"The balloon?"

"Yes."

"Thank you, Piglet," said Eeyore,

"you don't mind my asking," he went on, "but what color was this balloon when it—when it *was* a balloon?"

Poor Eeyore cannot understand that red remains red even when the balloon is small and no longer round or full. ♦

Some developmentalists do not believe Piaget was entirely correct in his estimate of when children's conservation skills emerge. For example, Rochel Gelman (1969, 1979; Gelman & Baillargeon, 1983) has shown that by improving the child's attention to relevant aspects of the conservation task, the child is more likely to conserve. Gelman has also demonstrated that attentional training on one type of task, such as numbers, improves the preschool child's performance on another type of task, such as mass. Thus, Gelman believes that conservation appears earlier than Piaget thought and that the process of attention is especially important in explaining conservation.

Yet another characteristic of the preoperational child is that they ask a barrage of questions. The child's earliest questions appear around the age of 3, and by the age of 5, the child has just about exhausted the adults around him with "Why" questions. The child's questions yield clues about mental development and reflect intellectual curiosity. These questions signal the emergence of the child's interest in reasoning and figuring out why things are the way they are. Samples of the questions children ask during the questioning period of 4 to 6 years of age are (Elkind, 1976)

"What makes you grow up?"
"What makes you stop growing?"
"Why does a lady have to be married to have a baby?"
"Who was the mother when everybody was a baby?"
"Why do leaves fall?"
"Why does the sun shine?"

Thinking Critically
Is preoperational thought something that develops through maturation, or is it something that can be taught? Explain your answer.

Earlier we mentioned that Gelman's research demonstrated that children may fail a Piagetian task because of their failure to attend to relevant dimensions of the task—length, shape, density, and so on. Gelman and other developmentalists also believe that many of the tasks used to assess cognitive development may not be sensitive to the child's cognitive abilities. Thus, rather than limitations on cognitive development, the limitations may be due to the tasks used to assess cognitive development. Gelman's research reflects the thinking of information-processing psychologists who place considerable importance on the tasks and procedures involved in assessing children's cognition.

Information Processing

Not only can we study the stages of cognitive development that young children go through, as Piaget did, but we also can study the different cognitive processes of young children's mental worlds. Two limitations on preschool children's thoughts are attention and memory, important domains involved in the way young children process information. Yet advances in these two domains also are made during early childhood. What are the limitations and advances in attention and memory during the preschool years?

Attention

Remember from Chapter 6 that attention was discussed in the context of habituation, which is something like being bored, in that the infant becomes disinterested in a stimulus and no longer attends to it. Habituation actually can be described as a decrement in attention, while dishabituation is the recovery of attention. The importance of these aspects of attention in infancy for the preschool years was underscored by research showing that both decrement and recovery of attention, when measured in the first six months of infancy, were associated with higher intelligence in preschool years (Bornstein & Sigman, 1986).

While the infant's attention has important implications for cognitive development in the preschool years, significant changes in the child's ability to pay attention take place in the preschool years. The toddler wanders around, shifting

This young boy's attention is riveted on the dandelion he has just picked; so is the dog's attention. Preschool children are able to attend for longer periods of time than infants are.

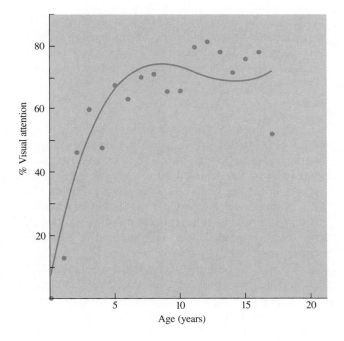

FIGURE 9.6   Increase in visual attention to television during the preschool years. In this elaborate study, two video cameras and a time-lapse recorder were used to observe young children's attention to television in their homes. Visual attention to television dramatically increased during the preschool years.

attention from one activity to another, generally seeming to spend little time focused on any one object or event. By comparison, the preschool child might be observed watching television for a half-hour. In one investigation (Anderson & others, 1985), young children's attention to television in the natural setting of the home was videotaped. Ninety-nine families that included 460 individuals were observed for 4,672 hours. Visual attention to television dramatically increased during the preschool years (Figure 9.6).

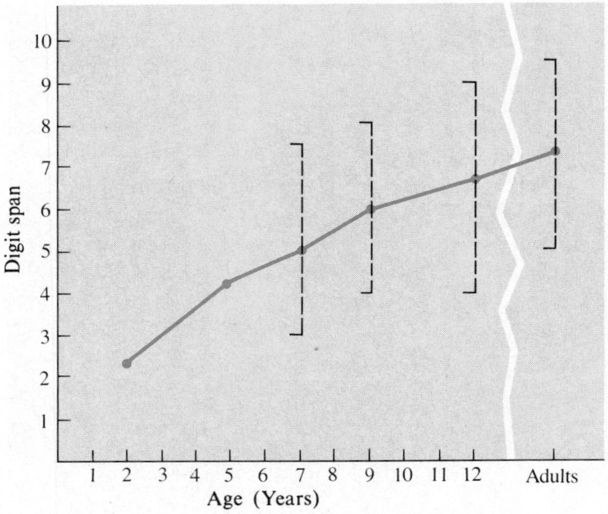

FIGURE 9.7 Memory span and age.
Memory span increased from about two
digits in 2- to 3-year-old children to about
five digits in 7-year-old children. Between
7 and 13 years of age, memory span only
increased by 1½ digits. The dotted lines
represent how widely the memory span
scores varied at different ages.

One deficit in attention during the preschool years concerns those dimensions that stand out or are *salient* compared to those that are relevant to solving a problem or performing well on a task. For example, a problem might have a flashy, attractive clown that presents the directions for solving a problem. Preschool children are influenced strongly by the features of the task that stand out, such as the flashy, attractive clown. After the age of 6 or 7, children attend more efficiently to the dimensions of the task that are relevant, such as the directions for solving a problem. Developmentalists believe this change reflects a shift to cognitive control of attention so that children act less precipitously and reflect more (Paris & Lindauer, 1982).

Memory

Memory is a central process in children's cognitive development; it involves the retention of information over time. Conscious memory comes into play as early as 7 months of age, although as children and adults, we have little or no memory of events we experienced before the age of 3. Among the interesting questions about memory in the preschool years are those involving short-term memory.

In **short-term memory,** we can retain information for up to 15 to 30 seconds, assuming there is no rehearsal. Using rehearsal, we can keep information in short-term memory much longer. One method of assessing short-term memory is the memory-span task. If you have taken an IQ test, you probably were exposed to one of these tasks. You simply hear a short list of stimuli—usually digits—presented at a rapid pace (one per second, for example). Then you are asked to recite the digits back. Research with the memory-span task suggests that short-term memory increases during early childhood. For example, in one investigation, memory span increased from about two digits in 2- to 3-year-old children to about five digits in 7-year-old children; yet between 7 and 13 years of age, memory span increased only by 1½ digits (Dempster, 1981) (Figure 9.7). Keep in mind, though, memory span's individual differences, which is why IQ and various aptitude tests are used.

Why are there age differences in memory span? Rehearsal of information is important; older children rehearse the digits more than younger children. Speed and efficiency of processing information are important too, especially the speed with which memory items can be identified. For example, in one investigation, children were

*I come into the fields and spacious
palaces of my memory, where are
treasures of countless images of things in
every manner.*

St. Augustine

Piaget's Stage of Preoperational Thought and Information Processing

Concept	Processes and Related Ideas	Characteristics and Description
Preoperational Thought	Its nature	The beginning of the ability to reconstruct at the level of thought what has been established in behavior, and a transition from primitive to more sophisticated use of symbols. The child does not yet think in an operational way; operations are internalized sets of actions that allow the child to do mentally what was done physically before.
	Symbolic function substage	Occurs roughly between 2 to 4 years of age. The ability to think symbolically and represent the world mentally develops. Thought still has several important limitations, two of which are egocentrism and animism.
	Intuitive thought substage	Stretches from approximately 4 to 7 years of age. The substage is called intuitive because, on one hand, children seem so sure about their knowledge, yet on the other hand, they are so unaware of how they know what they know. The preoperational child lacks conservation, the idea that amount stays the same or is conserved regardless of how the shape that contains it changes. One of the main reasons young children cannot conserve is the process of centration, or focusing of attention on one characteristic to the exclusion of all others. Gelman believes that conservation occurs earlier than Piaget thought and the process of attention is important in its appearance. The preoperational child also asks a barrage of questions, showing an interest in reasoning and finding out why things are the way they are.
Information Processing	Attention	The child's attention dramatically improves during early childhood. One deficit in attention in early childhood is that the child attends to the salient rather than the relevant features of a task.
	Memory	Significant changes in short-term memory occur during early childhood. For example, memory span increases substantially. Improvement in short-term memory is influenced by increased rehearsal and speed of processing.

tested on their speed at repeating words presented orally (Case, Kurland, & Goldberg, 1982). Speed of repetition was a powerful predictor of memory span. Indeed, when the speed of repetition was controlled, the 6-year-olds' memory spans were equal to those of young adults!

Thus far, we have discussed a number of ideas about preoperational thought and information processing. These ideas are summarized in Concept Table 9.1. Next, we will evaluate the nature of young children's language development.

Language Development

Young children's understanding sometimes gets way ahead of their speech. One 3-year-old, laughing with delight as an abrupt summer breeze stirred his hair and tickled his skin, commented, "It did winding me!" Adults would be understandably perplexed if a young child ventured, "Anything is not to break, only plates and glasses," when she meant, "Nothing is breaking except plates and glasses." Many of the oddities of young children's language sound like mistakes to adult listeners. But from the children's point of view, they are not mistakes; they represent the way young children perceive and understand their world at that point in their development. Our coverage of language in early childhood focuses on elaboration of Roger Brown's stages of language development, rule systems, and literacy.

Elaboration of Brown's Stages

In Chapter 6, we briefly described Roger Brown's five stages of language development. Remember that Brown (1973, 1986) believes that mean length of utterance (MLU) is a good index of a child's language maturity. He identified five stages of a child's language development based on MLU. Other aspects of the stages include an age range, characteristics, and typical sentences.

In *Stage I,* occurring from 12 to 26 months of age, the MLU is 1.00 to 2.00. Vocabulary consists mainly of nouns and verbs, with several adjectives and adverbs. Word order is preserved. Typical sentences are "Mommy bye-bye," and "Big doggie."

In *Stage 2,* occurring from 27 to 30 months, MLU is 2.00 to 2.50. Plurals are correctly formed, past tense is used, *be* is used, definite (the) and indefinite (a, an) articles are used, and so are some prepositions. Typical sentences are "Dolly in bed," "Them pretty," and "Milk's all gone."

In *Stage 3,* occurring from 31 to 34 months of age, MLU is 2.50 to 3.00. Yes-no questions appear, *wh-* questions (who, what, where) proliferate, negatives (no, not, non) are used, and so are imperatives (command or request). Typical sentences are "Daddy come home?" and "Susie no want milk."

In *Stage 4,* occurring from 35 to 40 months, MLU is 3.00 to 3.75. One sentence is sometimes embedded in another. Typical sentences include, "I think it's red," and "Know what I saw."

In *Stage 5,* occurring from 41 to 46 months, MLU is 3.75 to 4.50. Simple sentences and propositional relations are coordinated. Typical sentences are "I went to Bob's and had ice cream," and "I like bunnies 'cause they're cute." A summary of Brown's five stages is given in Table 9.1.

Rule Systems

Language consists of rule systems. The five main rule systems are phonological, morphological, syntactic, semantic, and pragmatic. What kinds of changes take place in these rule systems during early childhood?

As children move beyond two-word utterances, there is clear evidence that they know morphological rules. Children begin using the plurals and possessive forms of nouns (e.g., *dogs* and *dog's*), putting appropriate endings on verbs (e.g., *s* when the subject is third-person singular, *-ed* for the past tense, and *-ing* for the present progressive tense), using prepositions (*in* and *on*), articles (e.g., *a* and *the*), and various forms of the verb *to be* (e.g., "I was going to the store"). Some of the best evidence for morphological rules appears in the form of **overgeneralizations** of these rules. Have you ever heard a preschool child say "foots" instead of "feet," or "goed" instead of "went?" If you do not remember having heard such things, talk to some parents who have young children. You will hear some interesting errors in the use of morphological rule endings.

But whatever the process, the result is wonderful, gradually from naming an object we advanced step-by-step until we have traversed the vast distance between our first stammered syllable and the sweep of thought in a line of Shakespeare.

Helen Keller

"No, Timmy, not 'I sawed the chair'. It's 'I saw the chair' or 'I have seen the chair'."

© Glenn Bernhardt.

TABLE 9.1   *Brown's Stages of Language Development*

Stage	Age Range (months)	Mean Length of Utterance (average number of words per sentence)	Characteristics	Typical Sentences
1	12–26	1.00–2.00	Vocabulary consists mainly of nouns and verbs with a few adjectives and adverbs; word order is preserved	Baby bath.
2	27–30	2.00–2.50	Correct use of plurals; use of past tense, use of *be,* definite and nondefinite articles, some prepositions	Cars go fast.
3	31–34	2.50–3.00	Use of yes-no questions, *wh-* questions (who, what, where); use of negatives and imperatives	Put the baby down.
4	35–40	3.00–3.75	Embedding one sentence within another	That's the truck mommy buyed me.
5	41–46	3.75–4.50	Coordination of simple sentences and propositional relations	Jenny and Cindy are sisters.

From J. U. Dumtschin, "Recognize Language Development and Delay in Early Childhood" in *Young Children*, pp. 16–24, March 1988. Copyright © 1988 by the National Association for the Education of Young Children. Reprinted by permission.

In a classic experiment, Jean Berko (1958) presented preschool and first-grade children with cards such as the one shown in Figure 9.8. Children were asked to look at the card while the experimenter read the words on the card aloud. Then the children were asked to supply the missing word. This might sound easy, but Berko was interested not just in the children's ability to recall the right word but their ability to say it "correctly" (with the ending that was dictated by morphological rules). "Wugs" would be the correct response for the card in Figure 9.8. Although the children's answers were not perfectly accurate, they were much better than chance. Moreover, the children demonstrated their knowledge of morphological rules not only with the plural forms of nouns ("There are two wugs"), but also with possessive forms of nouns and with the third-person singular and past-tense forms of verbs. What makes the study by Berko impressive is that most of the words were fictional; they were created especially for the experiment. Thus, the children could not base their responses on remembering past instances of hearing the words. It seems, instead, that they were forced to rely on *rules*. Their performance suggested that they did so successfully.

Similar evidence that children learn and actively apply rules can be found at the level of syntax. After advancing beyond two-word utterances, the child speaks word sequences that show a growing mastery of complex rules for how words should be ordered. Consider the case of *wh-* questions: "Where is Daddy going?" and "What is that boy doing?" for example. To ask these questions properly, the child has to know two important differences between *wh-* questions and simple affirmative statements (e.g., "Daddy is going to work" and "That boy is waiting on the school bus").

FIGURE 9.8   In Jean Berko's (1958) study, young children were presented cards such as this one with a "wug" on it. Then the children were asked to supply the missing word; in supplying the missing word, they had to say it correctly, too. "Wugs" is the correct response here.

First, a *wh-* word must be added at the beginning of the sentence. Second, the auxiliary verb must be "inverted"—that is, exchanged with the subject of the sentence. Young children learn quite early where to put the *wh-* word, but they take much longer to learn the auxiliary-inversion rule. Thus, it is common to hear preschool children asking such questions as "Where daddy is going?" and "What that boy is doing?"

As children move into the elementary school years, they become skilled at using syntactical rules to construct lengthy and complex sentences. Sentences such as "The man who fixed the house went home" and "I don't want you to use my bike" are impressive demonstrations of how the child can use syntax to combine ideas into a single sentence. Just how a young child achieves the mastery of such complex rules, while at the same time she may be struggling with relatively simple arithmetic rules, is a mystery we have yet to solve.

Regarding semantics, as children move beyond the two-word stage, their knowledge of meanings also rapidly advances. The speaking vocabulary of a 6-year-old child ranges from 8,000 to 14,000 words (Carey, 1977). Assuming that word learning began when the child was 12 months old, this translates into a rate for new word meanings of five to eight words a day between the ages of 1 and 6. After five years of word learning, the 6-year-old child does not slow down. According to some estimates, the average child of this age is moving along at the awe-inspiring rate of 22 words a day (Miller, 1981)! How would you fare if you were given the task of learning 22 new words every day? It is truly miraculous how quickly children learn language (Winner & Gardner, 1988).

Although there are many differences between a 2-year old's language and a 6-year-old's language, none are more important than those pertaining to pragmatics—that is, rules of conversation. A 6-year-old is simply a much better conversationalist than a 2-year-old is. What are some of the improvements in pragmatics that are made in the preschool years? At about 3 years of age, children improve in their ability to talk about things that are not physically present; that is, they improve their command of the characteristic of language known as displacement. One way displacement is revealed is in games of pretend. Although a 2-year-old might know the word *table,* he is unlikely to use this word to refer to an imaginary table that he pretends is standing in front of him. But a child over 3 probably has this ability, even if he does not always use it. There are large individual differences in preschoolers' talk about imaginary people and things.

Somewhat later in the preschool years—at about 4 years of age—children develop a remarkable sensitivity to the needs of others in conversation (Gleason, 1988). One way in which they show such sensitivity is their use of the articles *the* and *an* (or *a*). When adults tell a story or describe an event, they generally use *an* (or *a*) when they first refer to an animal or an object, and then use *the* when referring to it later (e.g., "Two boys were walking through the jungle when *a* fierce lion appeared. *The* lion lunged at one boy while the other ran for cover"). Even 3-year-olds follow part of this rule (they consistently use the word *the* when referring to previously mentioned things). However, using the word *a* when something is initially mentioned develops more slowly. Although 5-year-old children follow this rule on some occasions, they fail to follow it on others.

Thinking Critically
If you were an early childhood education instructor, what would you want to be aware of to detect language delay in young children?

Another pragmatic ability that appears around 4 to 5 years of age involves speech style. As adults, we have the ability to change our speech style according to the social situations and persons with whom we are speaking. An obvious example is that adults speak in a simpler way to a 2-year-old child than to an older child or to an adult. Interestingly, even 4-year-old children speak differently to a 2-year-old than to a same-aged peer (they "talk down" to the 2-year-old by using shorter utterance lengths). They also speak differently to an adult than to a same-aged peer, using more polite and formal language with the adult (Shatz & Gelman, 1973).

Literacy and Early Childhood Education

The concern about our nation's literacy—the ability to read and write—has led to a careful examination of preschool and kindergarten children's experiences with the hope that a positive orientation toward reading and writing can be developed early in life (Early Childhood and Literacy Development Committee, 1986; Fox, 1987; Jalongo & Zeigler, 1987). Literacy begins in infancy. Reading and writing skills in young children should build on their existing understanding of oral and written language. Learning should occur in a supportive environment, one in which children can generate a positive perception of themselves and develop a positive attitude toward reading and writing (Bloome, in press; Garton & Pratt, 1989).

All young children should experience feelings of success and pride in their early reading and their writing. Like this young girl, children should be encouraged to be active participants in the reading process.

Unfortunately, in the push to develop a nation of literate people by emphasizing the early development of reading and writing skills, some dangers have emerged (Early Childhood and Literacy Development Committee, 1986). Too many preschool children are being subjected to rigid, formal prereading programs with expectations and experiences that are too advanced for children of their levels of development. Too little attention is being given to the individual development of young children's learning styles and skills. Too little attention is being placed on reading for pleasure and this may keep children from associating reading with enjoyment. The pressure to achieve high scores on standardized tests that often are inappropriate for preschool children has resulted in a curriculum that is too advanced and too intense. Such programs frequently restrict curiosity, critical thinking, and creative expression.

What should a literacy program for preschool children be like? Instruction should be built on what children already know about oral language, reading, and writing. All young children should experience feelings of success and pride in their early reading and writing exercises. Teachers need to help them perceive themselves as people who can enjoy exploring oral and written language. Reading should be integrated into the broad communication process, which includes speaking, listening, and writing, as well as other communication systems such as art, math, and music. Children's early writing attempts should be encouraged without concern for the proper formation of letters or correct conventional spelling (Figure 9.9). Children should be encouraged to take risks in reading and writing, and errors should be viewed as a natural part of the child's growth. Teachers and parents should take time to regularly read to children from a wide variety of poetry, fiction, and nonfiction. Teachers and parents should present models for young children to emulate by using language appropriately, listening and responding to children's talk, and engaging in their own reading and writing. And children should be encouraged to be active participants in the learning process rather than passive recipients of knowledge. This can be accomplished by using activities that stimulate experimentation with talking, listening, writing, and reading.

Jason, age 2 years, 2 months

Michelle, age 4 years, 6 months

Katie is going to run and skip and jump around

Katie, age 6 years, 6 months

FIGURE 9.9 These early efforts at writing by young children are full of errors. Many children's errors are a natural part of their growth and development. Children should be encouraged to take risks in writing without worrying about mistakes.

Vygotsky's Theory of Development

Children's cognitive and language development do not develop in a social vacuum. Lev Vygotsky (1896–1934), a Russian psychologist, recognized this important point about children's minds more than half a century ago. Vygotsky's theory is receiving increased attention as we move toward the close of the twentieth century, especially his belief that the child's developing mind is embedded in culture and society (Belmont, 1989; Rogoff, in press; Rogoff & Morelli, 1989). Before we turn to Vygotsky's ideas on language and thought, and culture and society, let's examine his concept called the zone of proximal development.

Zone of Proximal Development

A key idea in Vygotsky's view is the **zone of proximal development (ZPD).** This zone has a lower limit and an upper limit. The lower limit is the level of problem solving reached by a child working independently. The upper limit is the level of additional responsibility the child can currently accept with the assistance of an able instructor. Vygotsky's emphasis on the ZPD underscored his belief in the importance of social influences on cognitive development and the role of instruction in children's development. Tasks in the ZPD are too difficult to perform alone. They require assistance from an adult or a skilled child. As children experience the verbal instruction or demonstration, they organize the information into their existing mental structures so they can eventually perform the skill or task without assistance.

The zone of proximal development is conceptualized as a measure of learning potential. IQ also is a measure of learning potential. However, IQ emphasizes that intelligence is a property of the child, while ZPD emphasizes that learning is interpersonal, a dynamic social event that depends on a minimum of two minds, one better informed or more drilled than the other. It is inappropriate to say that the child *has* a ZPD; rather, a child *shares* a ZPD with an instructor.

The practical teaching involved in ZPD begins toward the zone's upper limit, where the child is able to reach the goal only through close collaboration with the instructor. With adequate continuing instruction and practice, the child organizes and masters the behavioral sequences necessary to perform the target skill. As the instruction continues, the performance transfers from the instructor to the child as the teacher gradually reduces the explanations, hints, and demonstrations until the child is able to adequately perform alone. Once the goal is achieved, it may become the foundation for the development of a new ZPD.

Learning by toddlers provides an example of how the zone of proximal development works. The toddler has to be motivated and must be involved in activities that involve the skill at a reasonably high level of difficulty—that is, toward the zone's upper end. The teacher must have the know-how to exercise the target skill at any level required by the activity. And the teacher must be able to locate and stay in the zone. The teacher and the child have to adapt to each other's requirements. The reciprocal relationship between the toddler and the teacher adjusts dynamically as the division of labor is negotiated and aimed at increasing the weaker partner's share of the goal attainment.

In one research investigation of toddler-mother dyads, the pair was put to work on a number of problems with arrays of various numbers (few versus many objects) and varying complexity (simple counting versus number reproduction) (Saxe, Guberman, & Gearhart, 1987). The mothers were told to treat this as an opportunity to encourage learning and understanding of their child. Based on videotaped interactions of the mothers and their toddlers, the mothers adjusted their task goals to meet their children's abilities. Importantly, the mothers also adjusted the quality of their assistance during the problem-solution period in direct response to the children's successes and failures.

Language and Thought

In Vygotsky's view, the child's mental or cognitive structures are made of relations between mental functions. The relation between language and thought is believed to be especially important in this regard (Langer, 1969; Vygotsky, 1962). Vygotsky said that language and thought initially develop independently of each other but eventually merge.

Two principles govern the merging of thought and language. First, all mental functions have external or social origins. Children must use language and communicate with others before they focus inward to their own mental processes. Second, children must communicate externally and use language for a long period of time before the transition from external to internal speech takes place. This transition period occurs between 3 and 7 years of age and involves talking to oneself. After a while, the self-talk becomes second nature to children and they can act without verbalizing. When this occurs, children have internalized their egocentric speech in the form of inner speech, which becomes the thoughts of the child. Vygotsky believed that children who engage in a large amount of private speech are more socially competent than those who do not use it extensively. He argued that private speech represents an early transition in becoming more socially communicative.

Vygotsky's theory challenges Piaget's ideas on language and thought. Vygotsky argued that language, even in its earliest forms, is socially based, whereas Piaget emphasized young children's egocentric and nonsocially oriented speech. Young children talk to themselves to govern their behavior and to guide themselves. By contrast, Piaget stressed that young children's egocentric speech reflects social and cognitive immaturity.

Culture and Society

Many developmentalists who work in the field of culture and development find themselves comfortable with Vygotsky's theory, which focuses on the sociocultural context of development (Rogoff & Morelli, 1989). Vygotsky's theory offers a portrayal of human development that is inseparable from social and cultural activities. Vygotsky emphasized how the development of higher mental processes such as memory, attention, and reasoning involve learning to use the inventions of society, such as language, mathematical systems, and memory devices. He also emphasized how children are aided in development by the guidance of individuals who are already skilled in these tools.

Vygotsky stressed both the institutional and the interpersonal levels of social contexts. At the institutional level, cultural history provides organizations and tools useful to cognitive activity through institutions such as school and inventions such as the computer and literacy. Institutional interaction gives the child broad behavioral and societal norms to guide their lives. The interpersonal level has a more direct influence on the child's mental functioning. According to Vygotsky (1962),

The Development of Social Understanding in a Culture

Cognitive psychologist Jerome Bruner (1989) shares Vygotsky's belief that one of developmental psychology's most important agendas is to focus more extensively on the inseparability of human growth from the culture in which it occurs. According to Bruner, cultural location identifies us and makes understandable our cognitive interpretations of the world and ourselves. Bruner argues that an important focus of this cultural emphasis is to carefully examine the everyday, ordinary happenings that take place in a child's life and the meanings children attach to them.

One effort in this direction was recently accomplished by Judy Dunn (1988), who observed children's development of social understanding in the context of their everyday lives. Dunn pointed out that children's self-interests often conflict with the self-interests of others. Sometimes these conflicts lead to confrontations in which the child does not win. In the process of managing these interpersonal matters, children learn to verbally support what they are doing by producing justifications for their behavior. Learning how to tell about and represent themselves in transactions with others enhances children's sense of self and helps them to develop practical social understanding in how to get along in the culture in which they live. ◆

skills in mental functioning develop through immediate social interaction. Information about cognitive tools, skills, and interpersonal relations are transmitted through direct interaction with people. Through the organization of these social interactional experiences embedded in a cultural backdrop, children's mental development matures.

In Chapter 10, Vygotsky's ideas about the nature of children's play are discussed. For now, though, we turn to a topic in which Vygotsky's views are increasingly being put to use—early childhood education.

Early Childhood Education

With increased understanding of how young children develop and learn has come greater emphasis on young children's education. We explore the following questions about early childhood education: What is child-centered kindergarten? What are the main effects of early childhood education? What should be the nature of early childhood education for disadvantaged children? Does it really matter if children attend preschool before kindergarten?

Child-Centered Kindergarten

Kindergarten programs vary a great deal. The Montessori approach described at the beginning of the chapter is one variation. Some approaches place more emphasis on young children's social development, others on their cognitive development. Some experts on early childhood education believe that the curriculum of too many of

In the child-centered kindergarten, education involves the whole child and includes firsthand experiences with people and materials, such as the art experience of this preschool child at Hackensack Christian School in New Jersey.

today's kindergarten and preschool programs place too much emphasis on achievement and success, putting pressure on young children too early in their development (Bredekamp & Shepard, 1989; Charlesworth, 1989; Elkind, 1987, 1988; Moyer, Egertson, & Isenberg, 1987). Placing such heavy emphasis on success is not what kindergartens were originally intended to do. In the 1840s, Friedrich Froebel's concern for quality education for young children led to the founding of the kindergarten, literally "a garden for children." The founder of the kindergarten understood that, like growing plants, children require careful nurturing. *Unfortunately, too many of today's kindergartens have forgotten the importance of careful nurturing for our nation's young children.*

In the **child-centered kindergarten,** education should involve the whole child and include physical, social and cognitive development. Instruction should be organized around each child's developmental needs, interests, and learning styles. The process of learning, rather than the finished product, should be emphasized. Each child follows a unique developmental pattern, and young children learn best through firsthand experiences with people and materials. Play is extremely important in the child's total development. *Experimenting, exploring, discovering, trying out, restructuring, speaking,* and *listening* are all words that describe excellent kindergarten programs. Such programs are closely attuned to the developmental status of 4- and 5-year-old children. They are based on a state of being, not on a state of becoming (Ballenger, 1983).

How Does Early Childhood Education Influence Children's Development?

Because kindergarten and preschool programs are so diverse, it is difficult to make overall conclusions about their effects on children's development. Nonetheless, in one review of early childhood education's influence (Clarke-Stewart & Fein, 1983), it was concluded that children who attend preschool or kindergarten

—interact more with peers, both positively and negatively
—are less cooperative with and responsive to adults than home-reared children
—are more socially competent and mature in that they are more confident, extroverted, assertive, self-sufficient, independent, verbally expressive, knowledgeable about the social world, comfortable in social and stressful circumstances, and better adjusted when they go to school (exhibiting more task persistence, leadership, and goal direction, for example)
—are less socially competent in that they are less polite, less compliant to teacher demands, louder, and more aggressive and bossy, expecially if the school or family supports such behavior.

In sum, early childhood education generally has a positive effect on children's development, since the behaviors just mentioned—while at times negative—seem to be in the direction of developmental maturity in that they increase as the child ages through the preschool years.

Education for Disadvantaged Young Children

For many years, children from low-income families did not receive any education before they entered the first grade. In the 1960s, an effort was made to try to break the cycle of poverty and poor education for young children in the United States through compensatory education. As part of this effort, **Project Head Start** began in the summer of 1965, funded by the Economic Opportunity Act. The program was designed to provide children from low-income families with an opportunity to experience an enriched environment. It was hoped that early intervention might counteract the disadvantages these children had experienced and place them on an equal level with other children when they entered the first grade.

Project Head Start consisted of many different types of preschool programs in different parts of the country. Initially, little effort was made to find out whether some programs worked better than others, but it became apparent that some programs did work better than others. Consequently, **Project Follow Through** was established in 1967. A significant aspect of this program was planned variation, in which different kinds of educational programs were devised to see whether specific programs were effective. In the Follow Through programs, the enriched planned variation was carried through the first few years of elementary school.

Were some Follow Through programs more effective than others? Many of the different variations were able to produce the desired effects on children. For example, children in academically oriented, direct-instruction approaches did better on achievement tests and were more persistent on tasks than were children in the other approaches. Children in affective education approaches were absent from school less often and showed more independence than children in other approaches. Thus, Project Follow Through was important in demonstrating that variation in early childhood education does have significant effects in a wide range of social and cognitive areas (Stallings, 1975).

The effects of early childhood compensatory education continue to be studied, and recent evaluations support the positive influence on both the cognitive and social worlds of disadvantaged young children (Haskins, 1989; Kagan, 1988; Lee, Brooks-Gunn, & Schnur, 1988). Of special interest are the long-term effects such intervention might produce. Model preschool programs lead to lower rates of placement in special education, dropping out of school, grade retention, delinquency, and use of welfare programs. Such programs might also lead to higher rates of high school graduation and employment. For every dollar invested in high-quality, model preschool programs, taxpayers receive about $1.50 in return by the time the participants reach the age of 20 (Haskins, 1989). The benefits include savings on public school education (such as special-education services), tax payments on additional earnings, reduced welfare payments, and savings in juvenile justice system costs. Predicted benefits over a lifetime are much greater to the taxpayer, a return of $5.73 on every dollar invested.

One long-term investigation of early childhood education was conducted by Irving Lazar, Richard Darlington, and their colleagues (1982). They pooled their resources into what they called a consortium for longitudinal studies, developed to share information about the long-term effects of preschool programs so that better designs and methods could be created. At the time the data from the 11 different early education studies were analyzed together, the children ranged in age from 9 to 19 years. The early education models varied substantially, but all were carefully planned and executed by experts in early childhood education. Outcome measures

Cognitive Development

Kindergarten in Japan

Two Japanese preschool girls are the last to arrive at their kindergarten. In Japanese kindergartens, leaving one's shoes outside the door is common practice.

In Japan, the majority of children attend kindergarten. Some Japanese kindergartens have specific aims such as early musical training or the practice of Montessori aims. In large cities some kindergartens are attached to universities where there also are primary and secondary schools. Many parents believe that this enhances their children's chances of eventually being admitted to the university and therefore of securing a good job as an adult. Some of these kindergartens interview 3-year-olds for prospective admission; others prefer to assess the child's mother. The possibility of upward mobility by gaining admission to top-rated schools and universities had led to an early emphasis on intellectual activities. Private kindergartens all over Japan respond to this demand, and many have special small classes to train specific skills. The overintellectualization of Japanese kindergartens is viewed as a problem by many Japanese. In recent years, an emphasis on free play as a specialty is appearing in some of the more progressive kindergartens. In many Japanese kindergartens, children wear the same uniforms, including caps, which are of different colors to indicate the classroom to which they belong. They have identical sets of equipment kept in identical drawers and shelves. This is not intended to turn the young children into robots, as some Americans have observed, but to impress upon them that other people just like themselves have needs and desires that are equally important (Hendry, 1986).

A custom in Japan is for people to leave their shoes outside the door before entering. Most of the Japanese kindergarten children have learned to follow this tradition, although several young girls hesitate to join the large group of children inside. Notice the identical uniforms worn by the Japanese kindergarten girls. ◆

included indicators of school competence (such as special education and grade retention), abilities (as measured by standardized intelligence and achievement tests), attitudes and values, and impact on the family. The results indicated substantial benefits of competent preschool education with low-income children on all four dimensions investigated. In sum, there is ample evidence that well-designed and well-implemented early childhood education programs with low-income children are successful (Haskins, 1989; Kagan, 1988).

Does It Really Matter if Children Attend Preschool Before Kindergarten?

According to education expert David Elkind (1987, 1988), parents who are exceptionally competent and dedicated and who have both the time and the energy can provide the basic ingredients of early childhood education in their home. If parents have the competence and resources to provide young children with a variety of learning experiences, with exposure to other children and adults (possibly through neighborhood play groups), along with opportunities for extensive play, then home schooling may sufficiently educate young children. However, if parents do not have the commitment, the time, the energy, and the resources to provide young children with an environment that approximates a good early childhood program, then it

Is Preschool Crucial?

David Elkind (1988) raises a key question about the role of preschools. With more and more two-career and single-parent families, fewer parents are available to provide the type of home schooling that young children need to help them fully realize their abilities. Public school programs, along with privately funded preschool programs, can provide an educational setting for children whose parents cannot provide it at home. Twenty-three states already have legislation pending to provide schooling for 4-year-old children, underscoring the growing belief that early childhood education should be a legitimate component of public education.

There are dangers, though. Because of the dangers, some experts on early childhood education have been reluctant to support the institutionalization of education for 4-year-old children. According to Elkind (1988), early childhood education is not well understood by officials at higher levels of education. Thus, the danger is that public preschool education for 4-year-old children will become little more than a downward extension of education for elementary schoolchildren. This is already occurring in preschool programs in which testing, workbooks, and group drill are imposed on 4- and 5-year-old children.

Elkind believes that early childhood education should become a part of public education but on its own terms. Early childhood has its own curriculum, its own methods of evaluation and classroom management, and its own teaching-training programs. There is some overlap with curriculum, evaluation, classroom management, and teacher training at the upper levels of schooling, but they are certainly not identical.

does matter whether a child attends preschool. In this case, the issue is not whether preschool is important, but whether home schooling can closely duplicate what a competent preschool program can offer.

We should always keep in mind the unfortunate idea of early childhood education as an early start to ensure the participants will finish early or on top in an educational race. David Elkind (1988) points out that perhaps the choice of the phrase "head start" for the education of disadvantaged children was a mistake. "Head Start" does not imply a race. Not surprisingly, when middle-class parents heard that low-income children were getting a "head start," they wanted a "head start" for their own young children. In some instances, starting children in formal academic training too early can produce more harm than good. In Denmark, where reading instruction follows a language experience approach and formal instruction is delayed until the age of 7, illiteracy is virtually nonexistent. By contrast, in France, where state-mandated formal instruction in reading begins at age 5, 30 percent of the children have reading problems. Education should not be stressful for young children. Education for young children should not be solely a preschool prep school. More about the role of preschool programs in young children's development appears in Children 9.3, where we discuss the increasing number of public preschools.

Thus far, we have discussed a number of ideas about young children's language development and early childhood education. These ideas are summarized in Concept Table 9.2. In the next chapter, we will turn our attention to the social worlds of young children.

Thinking Critically
Are parents too concerned and pushy about their young children's preschool education? Are we putting too much pressure on young children in our nation's preschools?

Language Development and Early Childhood Education

Concept	Processes and Related Ideas	Characteristics and Description
Language Development	Elaboration of Brown's stages	Roger Brown's five stages represent a helpful model for describing young children's language development. They involve mean length of utterance, age ranges, characteristics of language, and sentence variations.
	Rule systems	Involve changes in phonology, morphology, syntax, semantics, and pragmatics during the early childhood years.
	Literacy and early childhood	There has been increased interest in teaching young children reading and writing skills. Unfortunately, this had led to some dangers, with too many preschool children subjected to rigid, intense programs too advanced for their development. Young children need to develop positive feelings about their reading and writing skills through a supportive environment. Children should be active participants and be immersed in a wide range of interesting and enjoyable listening, talking, writing, and reading experiences.
Vygotsky's Theory of Development	Zone of proximal development	Has a lower and an upper limit. Lower limit is level of problem solving reached by child working independently; upper limit is level of additional responsibility child can accept with assistance of an able instructor.
	Language and thought	Language and thought develop independently and then merge. The merging of language and thought takes place between 3 and 7 years of age and involves talking to oneself.
	Culture and society	Vygotsky's theory stresses how the child's mind develops in the context of the sociocultural world. Cognitive skills develop through social interaction embedded in a cultural backdrop.
Early Childhood Education	Child-centered kindergarten	Involves education of the whole child, with emphasis on individual variation, the process of learning, and the importance of play in development.
	How does early childhood education influence children's development?	Difficult to evaluate, but the effects overall seem to be positive. However, outcome measures reveal areas in which social competence is more positive, others in which it is less competent.
	Education for disadvantaged young children	Compensatory education has tried to break through the poverty cycle with programs like Head Start and Follow Through. Long-term studies reveal that model preschool programs have positive effects on development.
	Does it really matter if children attend preschool before kindergarten?	Parents can effectively educate their young children just as schools can. However, many parents do not have the commitment, time, energy, and resources needed to provide young children with an environment that approaches a competent early childhood education program. Too often, parents see education as a race, and preschool as a chance to get ahead in the race. However, education is not a race and it should not be stressful for young children. Public preschools are appearing in many states. A concern is that they should not become merely simple versions of elementary school. Early childhood education has some issues that overlap with upper levels of schooling, but in many ways the agenda of early childhood education is different.

Summary

I. **The Nature of Preoperational Thought**
Preoperational thought is the beginning of the ability to reconstruct at the level of thought what has been established in behavior, and a transition from primitive to more sophisticated use of symbols. The child does not yet think in an operational way. Operations are internalized sets of actions that allow a child to do mentally what was done before physically.

II. **Symbolic Function Substage**
The symbolic function substage occurs roughly between 2 and 4 years of age. The ability to think symbolically and represent the world mentally develops. Thought still has several important limitations, two of which are egocentrism and animism.

III. **Intuitive Thought Substage**
The intuitive thought substage stretches from approximately 4 to 7 years of age. The substage is called intuitive because, on one hand, children seem very sure of their knowledge, yet on the other hand, they are unaware of how they know what they know. The preoperational child lacks conservation, the idea that amount stays the same or is conserved regardless of how the shape of the container changes. One of the main reasons young children cannot conserve is the process of centration, or focusing of attention on one characteristic to the exclusion of all others. Gelman believes that conservation occurs earlier than Piaget thought it did and that the process of attention is important in its appearance. The preoperational child also asks a barrage of questions, showing an interest in reasoning and finding out why things are the way they are.

IV. **Information Processing**
Two important dimensions of information processing that change during early childhood are attention and memory. The child's attention dramatically improves during early childhood. One deficit in attention during early childhood is that the child attends to the salient rather than to the relevant features of a task. Significant changes in short-term memory take place during early childhood. For example, memory span increases substantially. Improvement in short-term memory is influenced by increased rehearsal and speed of processing.

V. **Language Development**
Roger Brown's five stages represent a helpful model for describing young children's language development. They involve mean length of utterance, age ranges, characteristics of language, and sentence variations. The rule systems of language—phonology, morphology, syntax, semantics, and pragmatics—change during early childhood. Interest in teaching young children reading and writing skills has increased. Unfortunately, this increase has led to some dangers, with too many preschool children subjected to rigid, intense programs too advanced for their development. Young children need to develop positive feelings about reading and writing skills through a supportive environment. Children should be active participants and be immersed in a wide range of interesting, enjoyable listening, talking, writing, and reading experiences.

VI. **Vygotsky's Theory**
Vygotsky's theory has received increased attention in recent years. Vygotsky emphasized the importance of the zone of proximal development, which has a lower limit and an upper limit. The lower limit is the level of problem solving the child reaches when working independently, the upper level is the additional responsibility the child can accept with the assistance of an able instructor. Vygotsky said that

language and thought develop independently, then merge between 3 and 7 years of age, with a key factor being internal speech, or talking to oneself. Vygotsky's theory stresses how the child's mind develops in the sociocultural world. Cognitive skills develop through social interaction embedded in a cultural backdrop.

VII. **Child-Centered Kindergarten and Early Childhood Education's Influence on Development**

Child-centered kindergarten involves education of the whole child, emphasizing individual variation, the process of learning, and the importance of play in development. It is difficult to evaluate the influence of early childhood education on development. Overall, though, the effects do appear to be positive. However, outcomes reveal some areas in which social competence is positive, and other areas in which it is less positive.

VIII. **Education for the Disadvantaged**

Compensatory education has tried to break through the poverty cycle with programs like Head Start and Follow Through. Long-term studies reveal that model preschool programs have positive developmental outcomes.

IX. **Does It Really Matter if Children Attend Preschool Before Kindergarten?**

Parents can effectively educate their young children, just as schools can. However, many parents do not have the commitment, time, energy, and resources needed to provide young children with an environment that approaches a competent early childhood education program. Too often, parents see education as a race, and preschool as a chance for their children to get ahead in the race. However, education is not a race and it should not be stressful for young children. Public preschools are appearing in many states. A concern is that they should not become merely simple versions of elementary school. Early childhood education has some issues that overlap with upper levels of schooling, but in many ways the agenda of early childhood education is different.

Key Terms

Montessori approach 266
operations 267
symbolic function
   substage 267
egocentrism 267
animism 271

intuitive thought
   substage 272
centration 273
conservation 273
short-term memory 278
overgeneralizations 280

zone of proximal
   development (ZPD) 286
child-centered
   kindergarten 289
Project Head Start 290
Project Follow
   Through 290

Suggested Readings

Clarke-Stewart, K. A., & Fein, G. G. (1983). Early childhood programs. In P. H. Mussen (Ed.), *Handbook of child psychology* (4th ed, Vol. 2). New York: Wiley.
A comprehensive review of what we know about early childhood education.

Daehler, M. W., & Bukatko, D. (1985). *Cognitive development.* New York: Random House.
A thorough review of children's cognitive development is provided. Topics include the development of attention, memory, and reasoning.

Dumtschin, J. U. (1988, March). Recognize language development and delay in early childhood. *Young Children,* pp. 16–24.
Presents an up-to-date overview of what language delay is, how parents and preschool teachers can recognize it, and what can be done about it.

Elkind, D. (1988, January). Educating the very young: A call for clear thinking. *NEA Today,* pp. 22–27.
Elkind, a leading expert on early childhood education, discussed what early childhood programs should teach and what the possible benefits of preschool and kindergarten education are.

Kessel, F. (Ed.) (1988). *The development of language and language researchers.* Hillsdale, NJ: Erlbaum.
A number of chapters by experts on language development are presented; includes a chapter by Berko-Gleason on language and socialization and a chapter by Winner and Gardner on creating a world with words.

Piaget, J. (1987) (Translated from French by Helga Feider). *Possibility and necessity.* Minneapolis, MN: University of Minnesota Press.
Children's understanding of possibility and how they learn to choose among alternatives was a major interest of Piaget late in his life. This book includes a description of a number of problems Piaget devised to assess these possibilities and choices.

◇

Saturday morning was come, and all the summer world was bright and fresh, and brimming with life. There was a song in every heart; and if the heart was young the music issued at the lips.

Tom Sawyer, The Adventures of Huckleberry Finn

10

Social Development

D avid, Ruth, Shaun, and Ilene are black kindergarten children playing at their school (Griffing, 1980). Their kindergarten has three centers for dramatic play: a house, a grocery store, and a doctor's office. Props include realistic toys, large boxes, ropes, and other unstructured materials. The girls put on hats and carry purses. They go the grocery store with pretend money to buy some food to take on a picnic. David crawls under the table in the home area with some tools in his hand. "I'm fixing the car," he says proudly. "We got to fix the car before we can go anywhere." Shaun joins him. Shaun begins to play the cashier of the store. The two boys lie on their backs beneath the imaginary car, using hammer, pliers, screwdriver, and pretend screws to fix it.

Returning home with bags of food from the store, Ruth tells Shaun and David, "Boys, let's get ready for the picnic." David slides out from under the car. He takes the grocery bags and hands them to Shaun. David then turns to Ilene, "I told you not to wear your new hat!" Ilene complies, "Okay." She removes the hat, then directs David to "pick up all the stuff and put it in the car." David picks up the doll and says, "Okay, I'll take the baby."

All four children load things on the table (car). Ilene explains to some invisible person still at home, "We'll be back tomorrow." David adds, "We're going to Hollywood." Ilene says, "Here is a nice spot right here." David chirps in, "This is Hollywood." They start to unload the car. Ruth comments, "Watch the eggs, they might break." She tells David, "Don't put the baby on the table." (The table is now the picnic table.)

This series of play episodes illustrates some of the positive benefits of dramatic play for young children. The play is rich in symbols—the transformations in self, objects, and situations into characters, objects, and events that existed only in the children's imaginations. There was extensive social interaction and verbal communication, with children playing roles and carrying them out in a cooperative fashion. In several instances, the children were flexible in adapting to the views of others, and occasionally they expressed the thoughts and feelings of the characters. This type of play provides young children with valuable opportunities to practice social and cognitive skills (Griffing, 1983).

Young children participating in a play at the Children's Center in Woodstock, New York. Young children's play is imaginative and symbolic.

Early Childhood

We will spend considerable time describing the fascinating world of children's play in this chapter. We will also focus on young children's peer relations, television, and personality development. But to begin, we continue our emphasis on the importance of families in children's socialization. Carl Jung once captured the importance of parenting by commenting that we reach backward to our parents and forward to our children, and through their children to a future we will never see, but about which we need to care.

Families

In Chapter 7, we learned that attachment is an important aspect of family relationships during infancy. Remember that some experts believe attachment to a caregiver during the first several years of life is the key ingredient in the child's social development, increasing the probability the child will be socially competent and well adjusted in the preschool years and beyond. We also learned that other experts believe secure attachment has been overemphasized and that the child's temperament, other social agents and contexts, and the complexity of the child's social world are also important in determining the child's social competence and well-being. Some developmentalists also emphasize that the infant years have been overdramatized as determinants of life-span development, arguing that social experiences in the early childhood years and later deserve more attention than they sometimes have been given.

In this chapter, we will go beyond the attachment process as we explore the different types of parenting styles to which children are exposed, sibling relationships, and how more children are now experiencing socialization in a greater variety of family structures than at any other point in history. Keep in mind as we discuss these aspects of families the importance of viewing the family as a system of interacting individuals who reciprocally socialize and mutually regulate each other.

Parenting Styles

Parents want their children to grow into socially mature individuals, and they may feel frustrated in trying to discover the best way to accomplish this. Developmentalists have long searched for the ingredients of parenting that promote competent social development in children. For example, in the 1930s, John Watson argued that parents were too affectionate with their children. In the 1950s, a distinction was made between physical and psychological discipline, with psychological discipline, especially reasoning, emphasized as the best way to rear a child. In the 1970s and beyond, the dimensions of competent parenting have become more precise.

Especially widespread is the view of Diana Baumrind (1971), who believes parents should be neither punitive nor aloof, but should instead develop rules for their children and be affectionate with them. She emphasizes three types of parenting that are associated with different aspects of the child's social behavior: authoritarian, authoritative, and laissez-faire (permissive). More recently, developmentalists have argued that permissive parenting comes in two different forms: permissive indulgent and permissive indifferent. What are these forms of parenting like?

Authoritarian parents are restrictive, punitive, exhort the child to follow their directions, respect work and effort, place limits and controls on the child, and offer little verbal-give-and-take between the child and parent. **Authoritarian parenting** is associated with these child behaviors: anxiety about social comparison, failure to initiate activity, and ineffective social interaction.

What characteristics would this father need to show in his interaction with his son to be labeled an authoritative parent?

TABLE 10.1	Classification of parenting styles. The four types of parenting—authoritarian, authoritative, permissive indulgent, and permissive indifferent—involve the dimensions of acceptance, responsiveness, demand, and control.	
	Accepting, Responsive	Rejecting, Unresponsive
Demanding, Controlling	Authoritative	Authoritarian
Undemanding, Uncontrolling	Permissive Indulgent	Permissive Indifferent

Source: After Maccoby and Martin, 1983.

Authoritative parenting encourages that child to be independent but still places limits, demands, and controls on the child's actions. Verbal give-and-take is extensive, and parents are warm and nurturant toward the child. Authoritative parenting is associated with the child's social competence, especially self-reliance and social responsibility.

Permissive indulgent parenting is undemanding but accepting and responsive. These parents are involved in their child's life but allow them extensive freedom and do not control their negative behavior. Their children grow up learning that they can get by with just about anything; they disregard and flaunt rules. In one family with permissive indulgent parents, the 14-year-old son moved his parents out of their master bedroom suite and claimed it—along with their expensive stereo system and color television—for himself. The boy is an excellent tennis player, but he behaves in the fashion of John McEnroe, throwing fits on the tennis court. He has few friends, is self-indulgent, and has never learned to abide by rules and regulations. Why should he? His parents never made him follow any.

Permissive indifferent parenting is a style in which parents are highly uninvolved in their children's lives; these parents are neglecting and unresponsive. This type of parenting consistently is associated with a lack of self-control on the part of children. In our discussion of parenting styles, we have talked about parents who vary on the dimensions of acceptance, responsiveness, demand, and control. As shown in Table 10.1, four parenting styles—authoritarian, authoritative, permissive indulgent, and permissive indifferent—can be described in terms of these dimensions. Further advice for parents that dovetails with the concept of authoritative parenting is presented in Children 10.1.

Parents also need to adapt their behavior toward the child based on the child's developmental maturity. Parents should not treat the 5-year-old the same as the 2-year-old. The 5-year-old and the 2-year-old have different needs and abilities. In the first year, parent-child interaction moves from a heavy focus on routine caretaking—feeding, changing diapers, bathing, and soothing—to later include more noncaretaking activities like play and visual-vocal exchanges. During the child's second and third years, parents often handle disciplinary matters by physical manipulation: They carry the child away from a mischievous activity to the place they want the child to go; they put fragile and dangerous objects out of reach; they sometimes spank. But as the child grows older, parents turn increasingly to reasoning, moral exhortation, and giving or withholding special privileges. As children move toward the elementary school years, parents show them less physical affection,

There's no vocabulary for love within a family, love that's lived in but not looked at, love within the light of which all else is seen, the love within which all other love finds speech. This love is silent.

T. S. Eliot, The Elder Statesman

Making the Grade as Parents

In the 1980s, the Missouri Department of Education hired Michael Meyerhoff and Burton White to design a model parent-education program and help set it up in four school districts across the state: one urban, one suburban, one small town, and one rural town. The families cover a wide range of social and economic backgrounds. The services include get-togethers—at which 10 to 20 parents meet with a parent educator at the resource center—and individual home visits by a parent educator. Services begin during the final three months of pregnancy and continue until the child's third birthday, with increasing emphasis on private visits after the child is 6 months old. The average amount of contact with the families is once a month for an hour and a half.

During group and private sessions, parents are given basic information about what kinds of parenting practices are likely to help or hinder their children's progress. Table 10.A shows the dos and don'ts told to parents, advice that makes sense and is likely to promote the child's competence (Meyerhoff & White, 1986; White, 1988).

TABLE 10.A   *A Primer in Competent Parenting*

The following recommendations are based on the lessons Michael Meyerhoff and Burton White learned from the parents of competent preschool children.

Things to Do:	**Things Not to Do:**
Provide children with the maximum opportunity for exploration and investigation.	Don't confine your children regularly for long periods of time.
Be available to act as your children's personal consultant as much as possible. You don't have to hover, but be around to provide attention and support as needed.	Don't allow them to concentrate their energies on you so much that independent exploration and investigation are excluded.
Respond to your children promptly and favorably as often as you can, providing appropriate enthusiasm and encouragement.	Don't ignore attention getting to the point where children have to throw a tantrum to gain your interest.
Set limits—do not give in to unreasonable requests or permit unacceptable behavior to continue.	Don't worry that your children won't love you if you say "no" on occasion.
Talk to your children often. Make an effort to understand what they are trying to do and concentrate on what they see as important.	Don't try to win all the arguments, especially during the second half of the second year when most children are passing through a normal period of negativism.
Use words they understand but also add new words and related ideas.	Don't be overprotective.
Provide new learning opportunities. Having children accompany you to the supermarket or allowing them to bake cookies with you is more enriching than sitting them down and conducting a flash card session.	Don't bore your child if you can avoid it.
Give your children a chance to direct some of your shared activities from time to time.	Don't worry about when children learn to count or say the alphabet.
Try to help your children be as spontaneous emotionally as your own behavior patterns will allow.	Don't worry if they are slow to talk, as long as they seem to understand more and more language as time goes by.
Encourage your child's pretend activities, especially those in which they act out adult roles.	Don't try to force toilet training; it will be easier when they are 2.
	Don't spoil your children, giving them the notion that the world was made just for them.

The Strong Family Ties of Mexican Children

A basic value in Mexico is represented by the saying "As long as our family stays together, we are strong." Mexican children are brought up to stay close to their family, often playing with their siblings rather than with schoolmates or neighborhood children, as American children usually do. Unlike the father in many American families, the Mexican father is the undisputed authority on all family matters and is usually obeyed without question. The mother is revered as the primary source of affection and care. This emphasis on family attachment leads the Mexican to say, "I will achieve mainly because of my family, and for my family, rather than myself." By contrast, the self-reliant American would say, "I will achieve mainly because of my ability and initiative and for myself rather than for my family." Unlike most Americans, families in Mexico tend to stretch out in a network of relatives that often runs to scores of individuals. Both societies have undergone considerable change in recent decades. Whether Mexican children will gradually take on characteristics of American children, or whether American children will shift closer to Mexican children, is difficult to predict. The cultures of both countries will probably move to a new order more in keeping with future demands, retaining some common features of the old while establishing new priorities and values (Holtzmann, 1982). ♦

The Hispanic family reunion of the Limon family in Austin, Texas. Hispanic American children often grow up in families with a network of relatives that runs into scores of individuals.

Early Childhood

become less protective, and spend less time with them (Maccoby & Martin, 1983). Throughout childhood, socialization is reciprocal: Children socialize their parents, just as parents socialize their children. As we will see next, in most families, there also are siblings to be socialized and socialized by.

Sibling Relationships and Birth Order

Sandra describes to her mother what happened in a conflict with her sister:

> We had just come home from the ball game. I sat down on the sofa next to the light so I could read. Sally (the sister) said, "Get up. I was sitting there first. I just got up for a second to get a drink." I told her I was not going to get up and that I didn't see her name on the chair. I got mad and started pushing her. Her drink spilled all over her. Then she got really mad; she shoved me against the wall, hitting and clawing at me. I managed to grab a handful of hair.

At this point, Sally comes into the room and begins to tell her side of the story. Sandra interrupts, "Mother, you always take her side." Sound familiar? Any of you who have grown up with siblings probably have a rich memory of aggressive, hostile interchanges; but sibling relationships have many pleasant, caring moments as well. Children's sibling relationships include helping, sharing, teaching, fighting, and playing. Children can act as emotional supports, rivals, and communication partners (Zukow, 1989; Vandell, 1987). More than 80 percent of American children have one or more siblings (brothers or sisters). Because there are so many possible sibling combinations, it is difficult to generalize about sibling influences. Among the factors to be considered are the number of siblings, age of siblings, birth order, age spacing, sex of siblings, and whether sibling relationships are different from parent-child relationships.

Is sibling interaction different than parent-child interaction? There is some evidence that it is. Observations indicate that children interact more positively and in more varied ways with their parents than with their siblings (Baskett & Johnson, 1982). Children also follow their parents' dictates more than those of their siblings, and they behave more negatively and punitively with their siblings than with their parents.

In some instances, siblings may be stronger socializing influences on the child than parents are (Cicirelli, 1977). Someone close in age to the child—such as a sibling—may be able to understand the child's problems and be able to communicate more effectively than parents can. In dealing with peers, coping with difficult teachers, and discussing taboo subjects such as sex, siblings may be more influential in the socialization process than parents.

Birth order is a special interest of sibling researchers. When differences in birth order are found, they usually are explained by variations in interactions with parents and siblings associated with the unique experiences of being in a particular position in the family. This is especially true in the case of the firstborn child. The oldest child is the only one who does not have to share his parents' love and affection with other siblings—until another sibling comes along. An infant requires more attention than an older child; this means that the firstborn sibling now gets less attention than before the newborn arrived. Does this result in conflict between parents and the firstborn? In one research study, mothers became more negative, coercive,

Thinking Critically
Sibling rivalry is a common occurrence in families. What aspects of family life are likely to increase sibling rivalry? What techniques could be used to reduce sibling conflict?

Sibling relationships include (a) fighting, but they also include (b) sharing and teaching.

restraining, and played less with the firstborn following the birth of a second child (Dunn & Kendrick, 1982). Even though a new infant requires more attention from parents than does an older child, an especially intense relationship seems to be maintained between parents and firstborns throughout the life cycle. Parents have higher expectations for, put more pressure for achievement and responsibility on, and interfere more with the activities of firstborn than later-born children (Rothbart, 1971).

Birth order also is associated with variations in sibling relationships. The oldest sibling is expected to exercise self-control and show responsibility in interacting with younger siblings. When the oldest sibling is jealous or hostile, parents restrain her and protect the younger sibling. The oldest sibling is more dominant, competent, and powerful than the younger siblings; the oldest sibling also is expected to assist and teach younger siblings. Indeed, researchers have shown that older siblings are both more antagonistic—hitting, kicking, and biting—and more nurturant toward their younger siblings than vice versa (Abramovitch, & others, 1986). There also is something unique about same-sex sibling relationships. Aggression, dominance, and cheating occur more in same-sex relationships than in opposite-sex sibling relationships (Minnett, Vandell, & Santrock, 1983).

Given the differences in family dynamics involved in birth order, it is not surprising that firstborns and later-borns have different characteristics. Firstborn children are more adult oriented, helpful, conforming, anxious, self-controlled, and less

Early Childhood

The Only-Child Policy in China

What would it be like to grow up in a world where almost everyone is an only child, where few people really know what it is like to have brothers and sisters, where couples who dare to have two—or worse, three—children are criticized for being selfish? This world can now be glimpsed in Shanghai and several other Chinese cities where the one-child family has become much more prevalent because of the strong motivation to limit population growth in the People's Republic of China. While the policy is still new and its effects not fully examined, China's kindergartens and early elementary school classrooms are being increasingly populated by only children. The changes could stimulate people to look to society for social bonds and services they once depended on families to give them. China's culture is providing a giant laboratory for revealing what a world minus siblings is like. It will be intriguing to follow the outcomes (Huang, 1982; Pines, 1981).   ◆

To harness their population explosion, China has instituted a one-child policy. What might a world without siblings mean for Chinese families?

aggressive than their siblings. Parental demands and high standards established for firstborns result in these children excelling in academic and professional endeavors. Firstborns are overrepresented in *Who's Who* and Rhodes scholars, for example. However, some of the same pressures placed on firstborns for high achievement may be the reason they also have more guilt, anxiety, difficulty in coping with stressful situations, and higher admission to child guidance clinics.

What is the only child like? The popular conception of the only child is a "spoiled brat" with such undesirable characteristics as dependency, lack of self-control, and self-centered behavior. But researchers present a more positive portrayal of the only child, who often is achievement oriented and displays a desirable personality, especially in comparison to later-borns and children from large families (Falbo & Polit, 1986).

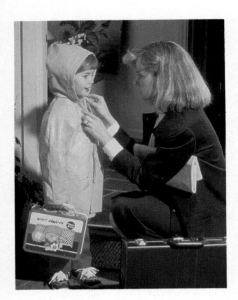

What issues do women face as they combine career and family?

The Changing Family in a Changing Society

Children are growing up in a greater variety of family structures than ever before in history. Many mothers spend the greatest part of their day away from their children, even their infants. More than one of every two mothers with a child under the age of 5 is in the labor force; more than two of every three with a child from 6 to 17 years of age is. And the increasing number of children growing up in single-parent families is staggering. One estimate suggests that 25 percent of the children born between 1910 and 1960 lived in a single-parent family at some time during their childhood. However, 40 to 50 percent of the individuals born in the 1970s have spent part of their childhood in a single-parent family (Bane, 1978). Furthermore, about 11 percent of all American households now are made up of so-called blended families—that is, families with stepparents or cohabiting adults. And, as we saw in Chapter 7, fathers perform more child-rearing duties than in the past.

Working Mothers

Because household operations have become more efficient and family size has decreased in America, it is not certain that children with mothers working outside the home actually receive less attention than children in the past whose mothers were not employed. Outside employment—at least for mothers with school-aged children—may simply be filling time previously taken up by added household burdens and more children. It also cannot be assumed that, if the mother did not go to work, the child would benefit from the time freed by streamlined household operations and smaller families. Mothering does not always have a positive effect on the child. The educated, nonworking mother may overinvest her energies in her children, fostering an excess of worry and discouraging the child's independence. In such situations, the mother may inject more parenting than the child can profitably handle.

As Lois Hoffman (1979, 1989) comments, maternal employment is a part of modern life. It is not an aberrant aspect of it, but a response to other social changes that meets the needs the previous family ideal of a full-time mother and homemaker cannot. Not only does it meet the parent's needs, but in many ways, it may be a pattern better suited to socializing children for the adult roles they will occupy. This is especially true for daughters, but it is also true for sons. The broader range of emotions and skills that each parent presents is more consistent with this adult role. Just as his father shares the breadwinning role and the child-rearing role with his mother, so the son, too, will be more likely to share these roles. The rigid gender role stereotyping perpetuated by the divisions of labor in the traditional family is not appropriate for the demands children of either sex will have made on them as adults. The needs of the growing child require the mother to loosen her hold on the child, and this task may be easier for the working woman whose job is an additional source of identity and self-esteem.

Effects of Divorce on Children

Early studies of the effects of divorce on children followed a **father absence tradition**; children from father-absent and father-present families were compared, and differences in their development were attributed to the absence of the father. But family structure (such as father present, divorced, and widowed) is only one of many factors that influence the child's adjustment. The contemporary approach advocates evaluating the strengths and weaknesses of the child prior to divorce, the nature of events surrounding the divorce itself, and postdivorce family functioning. Support systems (babysitters, relatives, day care), an ongoing, positive relationship between the custodial parent and the ex-spouse, authoritative parenting, financial stability, and the child's competencies at the time of the divorce are related to the child's adjustment (Block, Block, & Gjerde, 1986; Chase-Landsdale & Hetherington, in press; Hetherington, Cox, & Cox, 1982; Kelly, 1987; Santrock & Warshak, 1986; Wallerstein & Kelly, 1980).

Many separations and divorces are highly emotional affairs that immerse the child in conflict (Parish, 1988; Parish & Osterberg, 1985). Conflict is a critical aspect of family functioning that seems to outweigh the influence of family structure on the child's development. Children in divorced families low in conflict function better than children in intact, never-divorced families high in conflict, for example (Rutter, 1983; Wallerstein, Corbin, & Lewis, 1988). Although escape from conflict may be a positive benefit for children, in the year immediately following the divorce, the conflict does not decline, but instead increases. At this time, children—especially boys—in divorced families show more adjustment problems than children in homes with both parents present. During the first year after the divorce, the child often experiences a poor quality of parenting; parents seem preoccupied with their own needs and adjustment—experiencing anger, depression, confusion, and emotional instability—which inhibits their ability to respond sensitively to the child's needs. During the second year after the divorce, parents are more effective in their child-rearing duties, especially with daughters (Hetherington, Cox, & Cox, 1982).

Recent evaluations by Mavis Hetherington and her colleagues (Hetherington, 1989; Hetherington, Hagan, & Anderson, 1989) of children six years after the divorce of their parents found that living in nonremarried mother-custody homes had long-term negative effects on boys, with negative outcomes appearing consistently from preschool to adolescence. In contrast, most girls from these families recovered from divorce early in their lives. However, although preadolescent girls in divorced families adapted reasonably well, at the onset of adolescence, these girls engaged in frequent conflict with their mothers, behaved in noncompliant ways, had lower self-esteem, and experienced more problems in heterosexual relations.

The sex of the child and the sex of the custodial parent are important considerations in evaluating the effects of divorce on children. One research study directly compared children living in father-custody and mother-custody families (Santrock & Warshak, 1979, 1986). On a number of measures, including videotaped observations of parent-child interaction, children living with the same-sex parent were more socially competent—happier, more independent, and more mature—and had higher self-esteem than children living with the opposite-sex parent. Other research recently has supported these findings (Camara & Resnick, 1987; Furstenberg, 1988; Maccoby & Mnookin, 1989).

Support systems are especially important for low-income divorced families (Coletta, 1978; Hetherington, Hagan, & Anderson, 1989). The extended family and community services may play a critical role in the functioning of low-income divorced families. These support systems may be crucial for low-income divorced families with infants and young children, because the majority of these parents must work full-time but still may not be able to make ends meet (Wilson, 1989).

Thinking Critically
Imagine you are a judge in a custodial dispute. What are some of the key factors you will consider in awarding custody?

Child Custody in the People's Republic of the Congo

Legal provisions for child custody in the People's Republic of the Congo are typical of many developing countries. As a general rule, since men are in much better economic circumstances than women, with the exception of the very youngest, children are left to the responsibility of the husband in cases of breakdowns in marriage. Only a small portion of the population in poor countries have access to formal law. In most countries, the majority of poor people settle child-custody matters outside the formal legal system (Tchibinda & Mayetela, 1983). ◆

The age of the child at the time of the divorce also needs to be considered. Young children's responses to divorce are mediated by their limited cognitive and social competencies, their dependency on their parents, and their restriction to the home or inferior day care (Hetherington, Hagan, & Anderson, 1989). During the interval immediately following divorce, young children less accurately appraise the divorce situation. These young children may blame themselves for the divorce, may fear abandonment by both parents, and may misperceive and be confused by what is happening (Wallerstein, Corbin, & Lewis, 1988).

The cognitive immaturity that creates extensive anxiety for children who are young at the time of their parents' divorce may benefit the children over time. Ten years after the divorce of their parents, adolescents have few memories of their own earlier fears and suffering or of their parents' conflict (Wallerstein, Corbin, & Lewis, 1988). Nonetheless, approximately one-third of these children continue to express anger about not being able to grow up in an intact, never-divorced family. Those who were adolescents at the time of their parents' divorce were more likely to remember the conflict and stress surrounding the divorce some 10 years later in their early adult years. They too expressed disappointment at not being able to grow up in an intact family and wondered if their life wouldn't have been better if they had been able to do so.

In sum, large numbers of children are growing up in divorced families. Most children initially experience considerable stress when their parents divorce, and they are at risk for developing problem behaviors. However, divorce also can remove children from marriages in which there is a great deal of conflict. Many children emerge from divorce as competent individuals. In recent years, researchers have moved away from the view that single-parent families are atypical or pathological, focusing more on the diversity of children's responses to divorce and the factors that facilitate or disrupt the development and adjustment of children in these family circumstances (Hetherington, Hagan, & Anderson, 1989).

Thus far, we have discussed a number of ideas about family relationships in early childhood. A summary of these ideas is presented in Concept Table 10.1. We now turn to the intriguing world of children's peer relations and play.

Parenting Styles, Sibling Relationships, and the Changing Family

Concept	Processes and Related Ideas	Characteristics and Description
Parenting Styles	The four major categories	Authoritarian, authoritative, permissive indulgent, and permissive indifferent are four main categories of parenting. Authoritative parenting is associated with children's social competence more than the other styles.
	Maturation of the child	Parents need to adapt their interaction strategies as the child grows older, using less physical manipulation and more reasoning in the process.
Sibling Relationships	Their nature	More than 80 percent of American children have one or more siblings. Siblings interact with each other in more negative, less positive, and less varied ways than parent and children interact. In some cases, siblings are stronger socializing influences than parents.
	Birth order	The relationship of the firstborn child and parents seems to be especially close and demanding, which may account for the greater achievement orientation and anxiety in firstborn children.
The Changing Family	Working mothers	A mother's working full-time outside the home can have both positive and negative effects on the child; there is no indication that long-term effects are negative overall.
	Divorce	The early father-absent tradition has been supplanted by an emphasis on the complexity of the divorced family, pre- and postdivorce family functioning, and varied responses to divorce. Among the factors that influence the child's adjustment in divorced families are conflict, time since divorce, sex of the child and sex of the custodial parent, support systems, and age of the child.

Peers and Play

Peer relations take up an increasing amount of time during early childhood. Many of children's greatest frustrations and happiest moments come when they are with their peers. And early childhood is a time when play becomes a central theme of the child's life.

Peer Relations

Peers are children who are of about the same age or maturity level. Same-age peer interaction serves a unique role in our culture (Hartup, 1983). Age grading would occur even if schools were not age graded and children were left to choose the composition of their own societies. After all, one can only learn to be a good fighter among age mates: The bigger guys will kill you, the little ones are no challenge. One of the most important functions of the peer group is to provide a source of information and comparison about the world outside the family. From the peer group, children receive feedback about their abilities. Children evaluate what they do in terms of whether it is better than, as good as, or worse than what other children do. It is hard to do this at home, because siblings are usually older or younger.

Peer relations play powerful roles in children's lives. Through commerce with peers, children learn about the world outside their family and learn how other children about their age behave, think, and feel.

Are peers necessary for development? When peer monkeys who have been reared together are separated from one another, they become depressed and less advanced socially (Suomi, Harlow, & Domek, 1970). The literature on human development contains a classic example of the importance of peers in social development. Anna Freud (Freud & Dann, 1951) studied six children from different families who banded together after their parents were killed in World War II. Intensive peer attachment was observed; the children were a tightly knit group, dependent on one another and aloof with outsiders. Even though deprived of parental care, they became neither delinquent nor psychotic.

The frequency of peer interaction, both positive and negative, continues to increase throughout early childhood (Hartup, 1983). Although aggressive interaction and rough-and-tumble play increase, the *proportion* of aggressive exchanges to friendly interchanges decreases, especially among middle-class boys. With age, children tend to abandon this immature and inefficient social interaction and acquire more mature methods of relating to peers.

What are some similarities and differences in peer and parent-child relationships? Children touch, smile, frown, and vocalize when they interact with both parents and other children. However, rough-and-tumble play occurs mainly with other children, not with adults. In times of stress, children usually move toward their parents rather than their peers.

Early Childhood

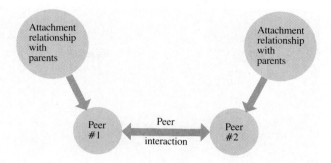

FIGURE 10.1   Peer interaction: the influence of the relationship histories of each peer. In the investigation by Olweus (1980), bullies had parents who were rejecting, had discord, used power assertive discipline, and were permissive toward aggression; by contrast, the mothers of "whipping boys" were anxious and overinvolved with their sons and eschewed aggression.

The worlds of parent-child and peer relations are distinct, but they are coordinated, too. Some developmentalists believe that secure attachment to parents promotes healthy peer relations (e.g., Ainsworth, 1979; Sroufe, in press). However, as we discussed in Chapter 7, others believe the route to competency, including positive peer relations, is not always through secure attachment (e.g., Kagan, 1987). Nonetheless, the data are consistent with the theory that children's relationships with their parents serve as emotional bases for exploring and enjoying peer relations (Hartup, 1983; Pettit, Dodge, & Brown, 1988).

One investigation (Olweus, 1980) reveals how the relationship history of each peer helps to predict the nature of peer interaction (Figure 10.1). Some boys were typically aggressive and other boys were the recipients of aggression throughout the preschool years. The "bullies" as well as the "whipping boys" had distinctive relationship histories. The bullies' parents treated them with rejection and discord, power assertion, and permissiveness for aggression. By contrast, the whipping boys' mothers were anxious and overinvolved with their children and eschewed aggression. The well-adjusted boys were not as involved in aggressive interchanges. Their parents did not sanction aggression; their responsive involvement with their children promoted the development of self-assertion as an adaptive pattern (Olweus, 1989).

Play

An extensive amount of peer interaction during early childhood involves play. American children's freewheeling play once took place in rural fields and city streets, using equipment largely of their own making. Today, play is increasingly confined to backyards, basements, playrooms, and bedrooms, and derives much of its content from video games, television dramas, and Saturday morning cartoons (Sutton-Smith, 1985). Modern children spend an increasingly large part of their lives alone with their toys, which was inconceivable several centuries earlier. Childhood was once a part of collective village life. Children did not play separately, but joined youth and adults in seasonal festivals that intruded upon the work world with regularity and boisterousness (Figure 10.2).

Play's Functions

Play is essential to the young child's health. As today's children move into the twenty-first century and continue to experience pressure in their lives, play becomes even more crucial (Block & Pellegrini, 1989; Isenberg & Quisenberry, 1988). Play increases affiliation with peers, releases tension, advances cognitive development, increases exploration, and provides a safe haven in which to engage in potentially

And that park grew up with me; that small world widened as I learned its secret boundaries, as I discovered new refuges in the woods and jungles; hidden homes and lairs for the multitudes of imagination, for cowboys and Indians, and the tall-terrible half-people who rode on nightmares through my bedroom. But it was not the only world—that world of rockery, gravel path, playbank, bowling green, bandstands, reservoir, dahlia garden, where an ancient keeper named smoky, was the whiskered snake in the grass one must keep off. There was another world where with my friends I used to dawdle on half holidays along the bent and devon-facing seashore, hoping for gold watches or the skull of a sheep or a message in a bottle to be washed up by the tide.

Dylan Thomas

FIGURE 10.2 *Children's Games* by
Pieter Breughel, 1560. Is the play of
today's children different than the play of
children in collective village life?
The Kunthistorisches Museum, Vienna.

dangerous behavior. Play increases the probability that children will converse and interact with each other. During this interaction, children practice the roles they will assume later in life.

For Freud and Erikson, play was an especially useful form of human adjustment, helping the child master anxieties and conflicts. Because tensions are relieved in play, the child can cope with life's problems. Play permits the child to work off excess physical energy and to release pent-up tensions. **Play therapy** allows the child to work off frustrations and is a medium through which the therapist can analyze the child's conflicts and ways of coping with them. The child may feel less threatened and be more likely to express his true feelings in the context of play.

Piaget (1962) saw play as a medium that advances children's cognitive development. At the same time, he said that the child's cognitive development *constrains* the way she plays. Play permits children to practice their competencies and acquired skills in a relaxed, pleasurable way. Piaget believed that cognitive structures need to be exercised, and play provides the perfect setting for this exercise. For example, a child who has just learned to add or multiply begins to play with numbers in different ways as she perfects these operations, laughing as she does so.

Vygotsky (1962), whose developmental theory was discussed in Chapter 9, also believed that play is an excellent setting for cognitive development. He was especially interested in the symbolic and make-believe aspects of play, as when a child substitutes a stick for a horse and rides the stick as if it is a horse (Smolucha, 1989). For young children, the imaginary situation is real. Parents should encourage such imaginary play because it advances the child's cognitive development, especially creative thought (Arman-Nolley, 1989).

Daniel Berlyne (1960) described play as exciting and pleasurable in itself because it satisfies the exploratory drive each of us possesses. This drive involves curiosity and a desire for information about something new or unusual. Play is a means

whereby children can safely explore and seek out new information—something they might not otherwise do. Play encourages this exploratory behavior by offering children the possibilities of novelty, complexity, uncertainty, surprise, and incongruity (Görlitz & Wohlwill, 1986).

Play is an elusive concept. It ranges from an infant's simple exercise of a newfound sensorimotor talent to a preschool child's riding a tricycle to an older child's participation in organized games. One expert on play and games observed that there is no universally accepted definition of play because it encompasses so many different kinds of activities (Sutton-Smith, 1973).

Types of Play

Many years ago, Mildred Parten (1932) developed one of the most elaborate attempts to categorize children's play. Based on observations of children in free play at nursery school, Parten arrived at these play categories:

1. *Unoccupied.* The child is not engaging in play as it is commonly understood. He may stand in one spot, look around the room, or perform random movements that do not seem to have a goal. In most nursery schools, **unoccupied play** is less frequent than other forms.

2. *Solitary.* The child plays alone and independently of those around him. The child seems engrossed in what he is doing and does not care much about anything else that is happening. Two- and three-year-olds engage more frequently in **solitary play** than older preschoolers do.

3. *Onlooker.* The child watches other children playing. He may talk with them and ask them questions but does not enter into their play behavior. The child's active interest in other children's play distinguishes **onlooker play** from unoccupied play.

4. *Parallel.* The child plays alone, but with toys like those that other children are using or in a manner that mimics the behavior of other children who are playing. The older the child, the less frequently he engages in this type of play; even older preschool children, though, engage in **parallel play** quite often.

5. *Associative.* Social interaction with little or no organization involved is called **associative play.** In this type of play, children seem to be more interested in associating with each other than in the tasks they are performing. Borrowing or lending toys and following or leading one another in line are examples of associative play.

6. *Cooperative.* Social interaction in a group with a sense of group identity and organized activity characterizes **cooperative play.** Children's formal games, competition aimed at winning something, and groups formed by the teacher for doing things together are examples of cooperative play. Cooperative play is the prototype for the games of middle childhood; little of it is seen in the preschool years.

Parten's research on play was conducted more than half a century ago. To determine whether her findings were out of date, Keith Barnes (1971) used Parten's categories of play to observe a group of preschoolers. He found that children in the 1970s did not engage in as much associative and cooperative play as they did in the 1930s. These changes in play probably occurred because children have become more passive as a consequence of heavy television viewing and because toys are more abundant and attractive than they were 40 years ago. Today, solitary play may be more natural, and parents may encourage children to play by themselves more than parents did years ago. The developmental changes that were observed by Parten also were observed by Barnes. That is, 3-year-old children engaged in solitary play and parallel play more than 5-year-old children did, and 5-year-old children engaged in cooperative and associative play more than other types of play (Figure 10.3).

Another form of play that is pervasive in early childhood is **pretend play.** When children engage in pretend play, they transform the physical environment into a symbol (Fein, 1986; Howes, Unger, & Seidner, 1989). Make-believe play appears rather abruptly in the toddler's development, at about 18 months of age, continues

Early Childhood

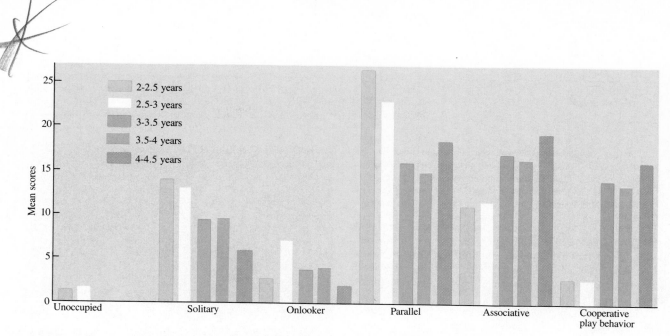

FIGURE 10.3 Mean scores in five categories of social play for 2-, 3-, and 4-year-olds

to develop between 3 to 4 years of age, peaks between 5 to 6 years of age, and then declines. In the early elementary school years, children's interests shift to games.

It is not unusual for young children to create imaginary companions—children, animals, or fanciful versions of friendly monsters. Some imaginary friends are created for companionship. One 3-year-old had two such companions, "Agoo" and "Day-Day," who would come to play with her when no one else was available. Imaginary friends usually have sterling qualities. They behave exactly as the child wants, they never argue, and they do not insist on having their turn. Sometimes an imaginary friend is a scapegoat. "Court" always seemed to be around when 4-year-old Matt did anything wrong. Another 4-year-old *never* forgets to flush the toilet—it is always his imaginary friend, "George". The imaginary friends are taken seriously by young children. It does not help to tell preschool children that they do not exist. There is nothing abnormal about young children having imaginary friends. It is quite normal (Rubin & Fisher, 1982).

Catherine Garvey (1977) has spent many years observing young children's play. She indicates that three elements are found in almost all of the pretend play she has observed: props, plot, and roles. Children use objects as *props* in their pretend play. Children can pretend to drink from a real cup or from a seashell. They even can create a make-believe cup from thin air, if nothing else is available. Most pretend play also has a story line, though the *plot* may be quite simple. Pretend play themes often reflect what children see going on in their lives, as when they play family, school, or doctor. Fantasy play also can take its theme from a story children have heard, or a show they have seen. In pretend play, children try out many different *roles*. Some roles, like mother or teacher, are derived from reality. Other roles, like cowgirls or Superman, come from fantasy. More about the nature of young children's superhero play appears in Children 10.2.

Superhero Play

Jonathan runs into the classroom, charges over to the block cabinet, and selects a long, thin board. He shoves it under his sweater, takes a fighting stance, and announces, "I have the power." He laughingly advances toward his playmates, who run from him, leaping, shouting, and giggling.

Another day of superhero play has begun. Superhero play is a common occurrence in young children's lives and there is little doubt that they find it exhilarating. Marilyn Kostelnik, Alice Whiren, and Laura Stein (1988) recently described why children find superhero play so attractive and how it relates to their development.

Superhero characters have been endowed with powers and qualities that embody the best of human nature. Consider Superman, Wonder Woman, Princess Leia, and He-Man. These superheroes and superheroines

—are unquestionably good, being wise, fearless, clever, and strong.
—possess powers children wished they had themselves. The superheroes have amazing speed, strength, or endurance. They can fly, swim under water for miles, or change the shape of their bodies.
—solve every problem and overcome all obstacles. Their solutions are always accepted.
—are in control. No one tells them what to do.
—know what is right. They rarely, if ever, make a mistake.
—Receive praise and recognition from powerful adults. Everyone wants to be their friend.

Children have little power in their world because it is dominated by adults. Yet, through their play, children can take on powerful roles that allow them to dominate villains or experience circumstances that entail no real risk. Feelings of fear and vulnerability can be overcome and transformed through playful shows of courage, strength, and wisdom. Superhero play also provides children the opportunity to pretend to be someone they admire and would like to resemble. And because superheroes are all good and antiheroes are all bad, children have clear, precise models for imitation. Finally, as with all other forms of dramatic play, through superhero play, children improve their language skills, problem solving abilities, and cooperation.

How can teachers and parents help children make superhero play a constructive experience? They can

—help children recognize the humane characteristics of superheroes they admire. For example, a teacher might say, "Barbara, you must have felt as helpful

A preschool "He-Man" engaged in superhero play.

as Wonder Woman when you carried the chairs over to the table."
—discuss real heroes and heroines with children. Introduce children to people such as Martin Luther King, Jr. and Helen Keller.
—help children understand what happened when play goes awry. Children often are surprised when one of them is injured or frightened during play. The teacher might say, "Jane did not know you were playing," or "That was a real hit, not a pretend hit."
—make clear that aggression is unacceptable. Children's aggressive acts need to be stopped, and adults need to make it clear that aggression will not be tolerated.

In summary, superhero play is a specialized form of dramatic or pretend play that is considerably appealing to young children. While superhero play should not be actively promoted, when carefully monitored and directed, superhero play can have positive benefits. ♦

Television

Few developments in society over the past 25 years have had a greater impact on children than television has. Many children spend more time in front of the television set than they do with their parents. In Chapter 9, we saw that children's attention to television increases dramatically during the preschool years. Although it is only one mass medium that affects children's behavior, television is the most influential. The persuasion capabilities of television are staggering; the 20,000 hours of television watched by the time the average American adolescent graduates from high school are greater than the number of hours spent in the classroom. Television's influence on children has been studied extensively, including its role in aggression, prosocial behavior, and eating behavior.

Television has been called many things, not all of them good. Depending on one's point of view, it may be a "window on the world," the "one-eyed monster," or the "boob tube." Television has been attacked as one of the reasons that scores on national achievement tests in reading and mathematics are lower now than in the past. Television, it is claimed, attracts children away from books and schoolwork. In one recent study (Huston, Seigle, & Bremer, 1983), children who read printed materials, such as books, watched television less than those who did not read. Furthermore, critics argue that television trains children to become passive learners; rarely, if ever, does television require active responses from the observer.

Television also is said to deceive; that is, it teaches children that problems are resolved easily and that everything always comes out right in the end. For example, TV detectives usually take only 30 to 60 minutes to sort through a complex array of clues to reveal the killer—and they *always* find the killer! Violence is a way of life on many shows. It is all right for police to use violence and to break moral codes in their fight against evildoers. The lasting results of violence are rarely brought home to the viewer. A person who is injured suffers for only a few seconds; in real life, the person might need months or years to recover, or might not recover at all. Yet, one out of every two first-grade children says that the adults on television are like adults in real life (Lyle & Hoffman, 1972).

A special concern is how ethnic minorities are portrayed on television. Ethnic minorities have historically been underrepresented and misrepresented on television. Ethnic-minority characters—whether black, Asian, Hispanic, or Native American—have traditionally been presented as less dignified and less positive than white characters (Condry, 1989). In one recent investigation, character portrayals of ethnic minorities were examined during heavy children's viewing hours (weekdays 4–6 P.M. and 7–11 P.M.) (Williams & Condry, 1989). The percentage of white characters far exceeded the actual percentage of whites in the United States; the percentage of black, Asian, and Hispanic characters fell short of the population statistics. Hispanic characters were especially underrepresented—only 0.6 percent of the characters were Hispanic, while the Hispanic population in the United States is 6.4 percent of the total U.S. population. Minorities tended to hold lower status jobs and were more likely than whites to be cast as criminals or victims.

There are some positive aspects to television's influence on children. For one, television presents children with a world that is different than the one in which they live. It exposes children to a wider variety of viewpoints and information than they might get from only their parents, teachers, and peers. And some television programs have educational and developmental benefits. One of television's major programming attempts to educate children is *Sesame Street,* which is designed to teach children both cognitive and social skills. The program began in 1969 and is still going strong.

"Mrs. Horton, could you stop by school today?"

Copyright © 1981 Martha F. Campbell.

Television has been called a lot of things, not all of them good. Special concerns are shown for the high degree of violence, such as that displayed on the Saturday morning cartoon shows these young children are watching.

Sesame Street demonstrates that education and entertainment can work well together. Through *Sesame Street,* children experience a world of learning that is both exciting and entertaining. *Sesame Street* also follows the principle that teaching can be accomplished in both direct and indirect ways. Using the direct way, a teacher might tell children exactly what they are going to be taught and then teach them. However, in real life, social skills are often communicated in indirect ways. Rather than merely telling children, "You should cooperate with others," TV can show children so that children can figure out what it means to be cooperative and what the advantages are.

Just how much television do young children watch? They watch a lot, and they seem to be watching more all the time. In the 1950s, 3-year-old children watched television for less than one hour a day; 5-year-olds watched just over two hours a day. But in the 1970s, preschool children watched television for an average of four hours a day; elementary schoolchildren watched for as long as six hours a day (Friedrich & Stein, 1973). In the 1980s, children averaged 11 to 28 hours of television per week (Huston, Watkins, & Kunkel, 1989), which is more than for any other activity except sleep. Of special concern is the extent to which children are exposed to violence and aggression on television. Up to 80 percent of the prime time shows include violent acts, including beatings, shootings, and stabbings. The frequency of violence increases on the Saturday morning cartoon shows, which average more than 25 violent acts per hour.

Some psychologists believe that television violence has a profound influence on shaping children's aggressive thoughts and behaviors; others believe that the effects are exaggerated (Liebert & Sprafkin, 1988). Does television violence merely stimulate a child to go out and buy a Darth Vadar ray gun? Or does it trigger an attack on a playmate and even increase the number of violent attacks and murders?

Early Childhood

Sesame Street around the World

When *Sesame Street* first appeared in 1969, the creators of the show had no idea that this "street" would lead to locations as distant as Kuwait, Israel, Latin America, and the Philippines. In the 20 years since *Sesame Street* first aired in the United States, the show has been televised in 84 countries. Thirteen foreign language versions of the show have been produced. Following is a sampling of *Sesame Street* productions in various countries:

Plaza Sesamo, Latin America The show is seen in 17 South and Central American countries, as well as in Puerto Rico. The diversity of cultures and life-styles in Latin America is given special emphasis.

Rechov Sumsum, Israel The set represents a typical Israeli neighborhood, with old houses next to modern apartment buildings. Its puppet characters include Kippy, a full-size pink porcupine who is naive, friendly, and opinionated. Moishe Oofnick is a shaggy grouch. Reflecting the diversity of Israel's population, the cast includes people from different ethnic and religious backgrounds who live in harmony.

Sesamstraat, The Netherlands Children are familiarized with the concept of school and any anxieties they might have about school are dispelled. Some segments encourage children to discuss their fears openly. Other segments show interactions between disabled and nondisabled children. One of the puppets is Pino, a 7-foot-tall blue bird who is eager to learn.

Barrio Sesamo, Spain The bakery is *Barrio Sesamo's* central meeting place. The residents include two full-size puppets. Espinete, a special friend of the children, is a hedgehog who tries to get the cast members to play games whenever possible. Don Pimpon is a shaggy old codger, at times a bit absent-minded, who has traveled extensively and entertains with stories of his adventures (Corwin, 1989). ◆

Don Pimpón of Spain's "Barrio Sesamo."

Violence on television is associated with aggression in individuals who watch it. For example, in one investigation, the amount of television violence watched by children when they were in elementary school was associated with how aggressive they were at age 19 and at age 30 (Eron, 1987; Lefkowitz & others, 1972). In another investigation, long-term exposure to television violence increased the likelihood of aggression in 1,565 boys aged 12 to 17 (Belson, 1978). Boys who watched the most aggression on television were the most likely to commit some violent action, swear, be aggressive in sports, threaten violence toward another boy, write slogans on walls, or break windows. The types of television violence most often associated with aggression were realistic, took place between individuals in close relationships rather than between strangers, and were committed by the "good guys" rather than the "bad guys."

But it is another step to conclude that television violence in itself causes aggressive behavior. Children who watch the most violence may be more aggressive in the first place; other factors such as poverty and unpleasant life experiences may be culprits, too. So far we have not been able to establish a causal link between television violence and aggression (Freedman, 1984; Heath, Bresolin, & Rinaldi, 1989). Like other behaviors, aggression is multiply determined.

Television can also teach children that it is better to behave in positive, prosocial ways than in negative, antisocial ways. Aimee Leifer (1973) demonstrated that television is associated with prosocial behavior in young children; she selected a number of episodes from the television show *Sesame Street* that reflected positive social interchanges. She was especially interested in situations that taught children how to use their social skills. For example, in one interchange, two men were fighting over the amount of space available to them; they gradually began to cooperate and to share the space. Children who watched these episodes copied these behaviors and, in later social situations, they applied the prosocial lessons they had learned.

When we watch television, we are exposed to commercials as well as regular programming. For example, the average television-viewing child sees 30,000 commercials per year (Condry, Bence, & Schiebe, 1988)! A significant portion of the commercials that are shown during children's television shows involve food products that are high in sugar (Barcus, 1978). In one investigation, children 3 to 6 years old were exposed to television cartoons over a four-week period; the advertising content of the shows consisted of either commercials for food products with added sugar, food products with no added sugar, or pronutritional public service announcements, with or without adult comments about the product portrayed (Galst, 1980). As shown in Table 10.2, the most effective treatment in reducing the child's selection of sugar snacks was exposure to commercial food products without added sugar combined with pronutritional public service announcements with accompanying positive comments by an adult.

How actively do parents discuss television with their children? For the most part, parents do not discuss the content of television shows with their children. Parents need to be especially sensitive to young children's viewing habits because the age period of 2½ to 6 is when long-term television-viewing habits begin to be established. Children from families of lower socioeconomic status watch television more

TABLE 10.2 *Average Proportion of Snacks with Added Sugar Selected During Four Weeks of Experimental Intervention*

Intervention Week	Condition				
	S–NC	NS–NC	S–C	NS–C	CT
3	.86	.88	.80	.71	.90
4	.74	.80	.73	.58	.84
5	.77	.86	.76	.68	.87
6	.83	.81	.83	.71	.88

Note: S–NC Commercials for food products with added sugar viewed without adult commentary.

NS–NC No sugar added and public service announcement without adult commentary.

S–C Sugar added and adult commentary.

NS–C No sugar added and pronutritional public service announcement with adult commentary.

CT The control condition, in which children had no television exposure.

Notice that the most effective treatment in reducing the child's selection of sugar snacks was exposure to commercial food products without added sugar and pronutritional public service announcements with accompanying positive comments by an adult (the NS–C condition with the lower proportions, .71 in week three, .58 in week four, .68 in week five, and .71 in week six).

than children from families of higher socioeconomic status (Huston, Seigle, & Bremer, 1983). And children who live in families involved in high conflict watch more television than children who live in families low in conflict (Price & Feshbach, 1982). In one recent investigation (Tangney, 1988), parents who showed more empathy and were more sensitive to their children had children who preferred less fantasy fare on television. In dysfunctional families, children may use the lower developmental level of fantasy-oriented children's programs to escape from the taxing, stressful circumstances of the home.

Thus far, we have discussed a number of ideas about peers, play, and television. These ideas are summarized in Concept Table 10.2. Next, we will turn to some further developments in early childhood, those pertaining to the self, gender roles, and moral development.

Personality Development

During early childhood, children's sense of self develops, their sense of gender roles and being male or female emerges, and their sense of morality intensifies.

The Self

We saw in Chapter 7, that toward the end of the second year of life, children develop a sense of self. Erikson believed that early childhood is a time when the self develops further and comes to grips with the crisis of initiative versus guilt, when it is important to consider distinctions between the self as "I" and "me," and when the child begins to understand that the self has both inner and outer dimensions.

Peers, Play, and Television

Concept	Processes and Related Ideas	Characteristics and Description
Peers	The nature of peer relations	Peers are powerful social agents. The term *peers* refers to children who are of about the same age or maturity level. Peers provide a source of information and comparison about the world outside the family.
	The development of peer relations	The frequency of peer interaction, both positive and negative, increases during the preschool years.
	The distinct but coordinated worlds of parent-child and peer relations	Peer relations are both like and unlike family relations. Children touch, smile, and vocalize when they interact with parents and peers. However, rough-and-tumble play occurs mainly with peers. In times of stress, children generally seek out their parents. Healthy family relations usually promote healthy peer relations.
Play	Functions	Includes affiliation with peers, tension release, advances in cognitive development, exploration, and provision of a safe haven in which to engage in potentially dangerous activities.
	Types	Unoccupied, solitary, onlooker, parallel, associative, and cooperative play are among the most characteristic play styles. One of the most enjoyable forms of play in early childhood is pretend play, in which the child transforms the physical environment into a symbol.
Television	Functions	Includes provision of information and entertainment. Television provides a portrayal of the world beyond the family, teachers, and peers. However, television may train children to become passive learners, is deceiving, and often takes children away from reading and studying.
	Children's exposure	Children watch huge amounts of television, with preschool children watching an average of four hours a day. Up to 80 percent of prime-time shows have violent episodes.
	Aggressive behavior, prosocial behavior, eating behavior, and social context	Television violence is associated with children's aggression, but no causal link has been established. Prosocial behavior on television also is associated with increased positive in young children. The average television-viewing child sees more than 20,000 commercials per year! Commercials influence children's food preferences. Parents rarely discuss television's content with their children. Television-viewing habits often are formed in the early childhood years.

Initiative Versus Guilt

According to Erikson (1968), the psychosocial stage that characterizes early childhood is *initiative versus guilt.* By now, the child has become convinced that she is a person of her own; during early childhood, she must discover what kind of person she will become. She is deeply identified with her parents, who most of the time appear to her to be powerful and beautiful, although often unreasonable, disagreeable, and sometimes even dangerous. During early childhood, children use their perceptual, motor, cognitive, and language skills to make things happen. They have a surplus of energy that permits them to forget failures quickly and to approach new areas that seem desirable—even if they seem dangerous—with undiminished zest and some increased sense of direction. On their own *initiative,* then, children at this stage exhuberantly move out into a wider social world.

The great governor of initiative is *conscience*. Children now not only feel afraid of being found out, but they also begin to hear the inner voice of self-observation, self-guidance, and self-punishment. Their initiative and enthusiasm may bring them not only rewards, but also punishments. Widespread disappointment at this stage leads to an unleashing of guilt that drastically lowers the child's self-concept.

Whether children leave this stage with a sense of initiative that outweighs their sense of guilt depends considerably on how parents respond to their self-initiated activities. Children who are given freedom and opportunity to initiate motor play such as running, bike riding, sledding, skating, tussling, and wrestling have their sense of initiative supported. Initiative also is supported when parents answer their children's questions and do not deride or inhibit fantasy or play activity. In contrast, if children are made to feel that their motor activity is bad, that their questions are a nuisance, and that their play is silly and stupid, then they may develop a sense of guilt over self-initiated activities that will persist through life's later stages (Elkind, 1970).

The Self's "I" and "Me"

Early in psychology's history, William James (1890) distinguished between the "I" as knower and the "me" as the aggregate of things known about the self. Today, we continue to distinguish between the self's "I" and "me" (Ruble, 1987; Wylie, 1979). The information-processing perspective is at the forefront of recapturing the interest in the "I" part of the self (Lapsley & Quintana, 1985). For example, there is a clear indication that people remember information more efficiently when it is encoded about the self than when it is not self-referenced. For example, if a young child is trying to learn the definition of the word *win,* she will do so more effectively if she associates the word with herself, such as thinking of the time last week when she won a game (Rogers, Kuiper, & Kirker, 1977).

The greatest interest in the self, however, has focused on "me," represented by children's self-concept and self-esteem. Remember from Chapter 2 that Carl Rogers' humanistic perspective emphasized the importance of self-concept in understanding the child's personality; indeed, Rogers believed that self-concept is the core, organizing force of personality. Children develop their picture of "me" through interactions with significant others, especially parents. Rogers believed that children are especially sensitive to praise and blame from adults. For example, the child's thoughts may add up to this conclusion: You are bad, your behavior is bad, and you are not loved or lovable when you behave in this way.

How can the child develop a healthy, positive self-concept? Rogers said that parents should love the child unconditionally; through positive regard from parents, the child experiences the feeling of being accepted, loved, and special. Even when a child's behavior is obnoxious, below acceptable standards, or inappropriate, the child needs to be respected, comforted, and loved. Parents need to distinguish between the child as a person of worth and dignity and the child's behavior, which may not deserve positive regard (Rogers, 1974).

One investigation of parenting and children's self-esteem revealed the importance of consistent parenting and sensitivity of parents to the young child's signals (Burkett, 1985). In particular, parents' respect for their children as individual people separate from them and as having their own needs were the best predictors of the preschool child's self-esteem.

An increasing number of clinicians and developmentalists believe that the core of the self—its basic inner organization—is derived from regularities in experience (Kohut, 1977; Sroufe, in press). The child carries forward into early childhood a

When I say "I," I mean a thing absolutely unique, not to be confused with any other.

Ugo Betti, The Inquiry, *1944*

Children as young as 3 years of age have a basic idea that they have a private interior self to which others do not have access.

history of experiences with caregivers that provide the child with expectations about whether the world is pleasant or unpleasant. In early childhood, the child continues to experience the positive or negative affect of caregivers. Despite developmental changes and context changes (such as increased peer contact or a wider social world), an important feature of the self's healthy development is continuity in caregiving and support, especially in the face of environmental challenges and stresses. As the child moves through the early childhood years, this continuity and support in caregiving gives the child confidence to show initiative and to increasingly be the author of her own experiences, something that enhances self-pride and self-esteem. Many clinicians stress that difficulties in interpersonal relationships derive from low self-esteem, which in turn derives from a lack of nurturance and support (Erikson, 1968; Kohut, 1977; Rogers, 1974; Sullivan, 1953).

The Self's Emerging Inner and Outer Dimensions

Children as young as 3 years of age have a basic idea that they have a private self to which others do not have access (Flavell, Shipstead, & Croft, 1978). For example, consider this exchange between an experimenter and a 3-year-old:

> (Can I see you thinking?) "No." (Even if I look in your eyes, do I see you thinking?) "No." (Why not?) "Cause I don't have any big holes." (You mean there would have to be a hole there for me to see you thinking?) Child nods. (p. 16)

Another child said that the experimenter could not see his thinking processes because he had a skin over his head.

Once they have developed an awareness of an inner self, between the ages of 3 to 4 children distinguish between this inner self and their outer or bodily self. Indeed, when asked to describe themselves, preschool children present a self portrait of external characteristics. They describe themselves in terms of how they look ("I'm big"), where they live ("I live in Chicago"), and the activities in which they participate ("I play with dolls"). It is not until about 6 to 7 years of age that children begin to describe themselves more in terms of psychological traits—how they feel, their personality characteristics, and their relationships with others, for example.

Gender Roles

As the child develops during the preschool years, gender roles become increasingly important in personality development. **Gender roles** are social expectations of how we should act and think as males and females. Developmentalists have described the biological, cognitive, and environmental contributions to gender roles, and they have charted the course of gender role development in early childhood.

Biological Influences

One of Freud's basic assumptions is that human behavior and history are directly related to reproductive processes. From this assumption arises the belief that sexuality is essentially unlearned and instinctual. Erikson (1968) extended this argument, claiming that the psychological differences between males and females stem from anatomical differences. Erikson argued that, because of genital structure, males are more intrusive and aggressive, females more inclusive and passive. Erikson's belief has become known as "anatomy is destiny." Critics of the anatomy is destiny view believe that Erikson has not given experience an adequate audience. They argue that males and females are more free to choose their gender role than Erikson allows. In response to the critics, Erikson has modified his view, saying that females in today's world are transcending their biological heritage and correcting society's overemphasis on male intrusiveness.

Biology's influence on gender roles also involves sex hormones, among the most powerful and subtle chemicals in nature. These hormones are controlled by the master gland in the brain, the pituitary. In females, hormones from the pituitary carry messages to the ovaries to produce the hormone **estrogen.** In males, the pituitary messages travel to the testes, where the sex hormone **androgen** is manufactured.

The secretion of androgen from the testes of the young male fetus (or the absence of androgen in the female) completely controls sexual development in the womb. If enough androgen is produced, as happens with a normal developing boy, male organs and genitals develop. When the hormone level is imbalanced (as in a developing male with insufficient androgen, or a female exposed to excess androgen), the genitals are intermediate between male and female (Money, 1987; Money & Ehrhardt, 1972). Such individuals are referred to as **hermaphrodites.**

Although estrogen is the dominant sex hormone in females and androgen fills this role in males, each person's body contains both hormones. The amount of each hormone varies from one person to the next; for example, a boy's bass voice is based on the presence of more androgen than a tenor's voice (Durden-Smith & Desimone, 1983). As we move from animals to humans, hormonal control over sexual behavior is less dominant. For example, when the testes of the male rat are removed through castration, sexual behavior declines and eventually ceases. But in human beings, castration produces much greater variation in sexual behavior.

No one argues about the presence of genetic, biochemical, and anatomical differences between the sexes. Even psychologists with a strong environmental orientation acknowledge that boys and girls will be treated differently because of their

What are little boys made of?
Frogs and snails,
And puppy dogs' tails.

What are little girls made of?
Sugar and spice
And all that's nice.

J. O. Halliwell, Nursery Rhymes of
England, *1844*

physical differences and their different roles in reproduction. The importance of biological factors is not at issue. What is at issue is the directness or indirectness of their effects on social behavior (Huston, 1983). For example, if a high androgen level directly influences the central nervous system, which in turn produces a higher activity level, then the effect is more direct. By contrast, if a high level of androgen produces strong muscle development, which in turn causes other people to expect the child to be a good athlete and in turn leads her to participate in sports, then the biological effect is more direct.

While nearly everyone is an interactionist in thinking that children's behavior as males and females is due to an interaction of biological and environmental factors, an interactionist position means different things to different people (Hinde, 1989; Maccoby, 1987, 1989; Money, 1987). For some it suggests that certain environmental conditions are required to make preprogrammed dispositions appear. For others it suggests that the same environment will have different effects depending on the predisposition of the child. For yet others it means that children shape their environments, including their interpersonal environments, and vice versa. Circular processes of influence and counterinfluence develop over time. Throughout childhood, boys and girls are involved in active construction of their own version of acceptable masculine and feminine behavior patterns. As we see next, cognitive factors play an important role in this active construction.

Cognitive Influences

Cognitive factors influence gender roles during early childhood through self-categorization and language. Lawrence Kohlberg (1966) argued that to have an idea of what is masculine or feminine, a child must be able to categorize objects into the two groups—masculine and feminine. According to Kohlberg, the categories become relatively stable by the age of 6. That is, by the age of 6, children have a fairly definite idea of which category is theirs. They also understand what is entailed in belonging to one category or the other and seldom fluctuate in their category judgments. From Kohlberg's perspective, this self-categorization is the impetus for gender role development. Kohlberg reasons that gender role development proceeds in the following sequence: I am a boy, and I want to do boy things; therefore, the opportunity to do boy things is rewarding. Having acquired the ability to categorize, children strive toward consistency in the use of the categories and their actual behavior. The striving for consistency forms the basis for gender role development (Carter, 1989; Martin, 1989; Ruble, 1987).

An important theme in the cognitive approach to children's gender role development is that the child's mind is set up to perceive and organize information according to a network of associations called a schema. A **gender schema** organizes the world in terms of female and male (Bem, 1985; Leinbach & Hort, 1989). Gender is a powerful organizing category to which children connect many experiences and attitudes. The gender schema approach emphasizes children's active construction of their gender role but also accepts that societies determine which schemata are important and the associations involved.

Gender roles also are present in the language children use and are exposed to (Graddol & Swann, 1989). The nature of the language children hear most of the time is sexist. That is, the English language contains sex bias, especially in the use of "he" and "man" to refer to everyone. For example, in one recent investigation, mothers and their 1- to 3-year-old children looked at popular children's books, such as *The Three Bears* (DeLoache, Cassidy, & Carpenter, 1987). The three bears almost always were boys, and 95 percent of all characters of indeterminate gender role were referred to by the mothers as males.

Environmental Influences

In our culture, adults discriminate between the sexes shortly after the infant's birth. The "pink and blue" treatment may be applied to girls and boys even before they leave the hospital. Soon afterward, differences in hairstyles, clothes, and toys become obvious. Adults and other children reward these differences throughout childhood, but girls and boys also learn appropriate gender role behavior by watching what other people say and do. For example, a 7-year-old boy who knows he is a boy and readily labels objects appropriately as male or female may have parents who support equality between the sexes; his behavior probably will be less stereotyped along masculine lines than that of boys reared in more traditional homes.

In recent years, the idea that parents are the critical socialization agents in gender role development has come under fire. Parents are only one of many sources through which the child learns about gender roles. Schools, peers, the media, and other family members are other sources. Yet it is important to guard against swinging too far in this direction, because parents do play important roles in children's gender roles, especially in the early years of development.

Parents, by action and by example, influence their children's gender role development. In the psychoanalytic view, this influence stems principally from the child's identification with the parent of the same sex. The child develops a sense of likeness to the parent of the same sex and strives to emulate that parent. But in reality, fathers and mothers are both psychologically important for children. Fathers seem to play an especially important part in gender role development. They are more likely to act differently toward sons and daughters than mothers are (Huston, 1983; Lamb, 1986). Parents provide the earliest discrimination of gender roles in the child's development, but before long, peers and teachers join the societal process of providing feedback about masculine and feminine roles.

Many parents encourage boys and girls to engage in different types of play and activities even during infancy. Girls are more likely to be given dolls to play with and, when old enough, are more likely to be assigned babysitting duties. Girls are encouraged to be more nurturant and emotional than boys, and fathers are more likely to engage in rough-and-tumble play with sons than with daughters. With increasing age, boys are permitted more freedom by parents who allow them to be away from home without supervision than are girls.

Without much doubt, parents do treat boys and girls differently in many instances. However, when parents treat boys and girls differently, it is not always easy to sort through the direction of the effects (Maccoby, 1987). Do young boys like rough-and-tumble play because their fathers trained them to enjoy it, or because they, as well as their fathers, have a low threshold for initiation of this male-male pattern? The same types of questions crop up with regard to higher rates of punishment and other coercive treatment directed to boys by their parents. Is this a form of differential pressure initiated by parents that produces distinctively male behavior in boys, or is it a consequence of something boys are doing in interacting with their parents that elicits this kind of parent behavior? Probably reciprocal and circular processes are at work as parents differentially socialize their sons and daughters and their sons and daughters socialize them.

As reflected in this tug-of-war battle between boys and girls, the playground in elementary school is like going to "gender school." Elementary school children show a clear preference for being with and liking same-sex peers.

Parents provide the earliest discrimination of gender roles in children's development, but peers and teachers soon join the societal process of responding to and providing feedback about masculine and feminine behavior (Sheldon, 1989). Most children have already acquired a preference for masculine or feminine toys and activities before they are exposed to school. During the preschool and elementary school years, teachers and peers maintain these preferences through feedback. Children who play in sex-appropriate activities tend to be rewarded for doing so by their peers. Those who play in cross-sexed activities tend to be criticized by their peers or left to play alone. Children show a clear preference for being with and liking same-sexed peers (Maccoby & Jacklin, in press), and this tendency often becomes stronger as children move from the preschool years through the middle elementary school years (Hayden-Thomson, Rubin, & Hymel, 1987). This increase probably reflects children's growing awareness of culturally prescribed expectancies for males and females.

Even when a deliberately engineered program of reinforcing children for cross-sex play reduces segregation temporarily, playmate choices return quickly toward a segregated pattern once the behavior modification program is discontinued (Serbin, Tonick, & Sternglanz, 1977).

After extensive observations of school playgrounds, two researchers characterized the play settings as "gender school," pointing out that boys teach each other the required masculine behavior and enforce it strictly (Luria & Herzog, 1985).

Girls also pass on the female culture (distinctively female games such as jump rope or jacks) and congregate mostly with each other. Individual "tomboy" girls can join boys' activities without losing their status in the girls' groups, but the reverse is not true for boys, reflecting our society's greater sex-typing pressure for boys.

Gender segregation is important because it provides the conditions under which two different childhood cultures are formed and maintained (Maccoby, 1987). Children's bias toward same-sex play suggests that any society, or any set of parents, would have to exert extensive pressure to get children to select playmates without regard to gender. Yet adults clearly do affect the extent that play is segregated by establishing the conditions under which play normally occurs.

In school, teachers react more negatively to boys than to girls in early schooling and are more likely to reward feminine behavior in boys and girls—being quiet, conforming, and unassertive, for example (Fagot, 1975). However, in one investigation in which the teachers were males, feminine and masculine behavior were rewarded equally (McCandless, 1973). This raises the intriguing but untested question of whether there would be more support for masculine behavior in children's early schooling if more of the teachers were males.

The Development of Gender Roles

During the age period from 18 months to 3 years, children start expressing considerable interest in gender-typed activities and classify themselves according to gender. From 3 to 7 years of age, children begin to acquire an understanding of gender constancy and increasingly enjoy being with same-sex peers. During early childhood, young children also tend to make grand generalizations about gender roles. For example, 3-year-old William accompanied his mother to the doctor's office. A man in a white coat walked by and William said, "Hi, Doc." Then a woman in a white coat walked by and William greeted her, "Hi, nurse." William's mother asked him how he knew which individual was a doctor and which was a nurse. William replied, "Because doctors are daddies and nurses are mommies." As Piaget warned, young children are very sure of their thoughts, yet they often inaccurately understand the world. William's "nurse" turned out to be his doctor, and vice versa (Carper, 1978).

Moral Development

In one sense, moral development has a longer history than any other topic we discuss in this book. In prescientific periods, philosophers and theologians heatedly debated the child's moral status at birth, which they felt had important implications for how the child should be reared. Recall from Chapter 1 the original sin, *tabula rasa,* and innate goodness views of the child. Today, people are hardly neutral about moral development. Most have strong opinions about what is acceptable and unacceptable behavior, ethical and unethical conduct, and the ways that acceptable and ethical conduct should be fostered in children (Kurtines & Gewirtz, 1989).

Moral development concerns rules and conventions about what people *should* do in their interactions with other people. In studying these rules, developmentalists examine three different domains. First, how do children *reason* or *think* about rules for ethical conduct? For example, consider cheating. The child can be presented with a story in which someone has a conflict about whether or not to cheat in a particular situation, such as taking a test in school. The child is asked to decide what is appropriate for the character to do and why. The focus is placed on children's *reasoning* that is used to justify their moral decisions.

Second, how do children actually *behave* in moral circumstances? In our example of cheating, the emphasis is on observing the child's cheating and the environmental circumstances that produced and maintain the cheating. Children might be shown some toys and then be asked to select the one they believe is the most attractive. The experimenter then tells the young child that that particular toy belongs to someone else and is not to be played with. Observations of different conditions under which the child deviates from the prohibition or resists temptation are then conducted.

Third, how does the child *feel* about moral matters? In the example of cheating, does the child feel enough guilt to resist temptation? If children do cheat, do feelings of guilt after the transgression keep them from cheating the next time they face temptation? In the remainder of this section, we will focus on these three facets of moral development: thought, action, and feeling. Then, we will evaluate the positive side of children's moral development: altruism.

Piaget's View of Moral Reasoning

Interest in how the child thinks about moral issues was stimulated by Piaget (1932), who extensively observed and interviewed children from the ages of 4 to 12. He watched them play marbles, seeking to learn how they used and thought about the game's rules. He also asked children questions about ethical rules—theft, lies, punishment, and justice, for example. Piaget concluded that children think in two distinctly different ways about morality depending on their developmental maturity. The more primitive way of thinking—**heteronomous morality**—is displayed by younger children (from 4 to 7 years of age). The more advanced way of thinking—**autonomous morality**—is displayed by older children (10 years of age and older). Children 7 to 10 years of age are in a transition between the two stages, evidencing some features of both.

What are some characteristics of heteronomous morality? The heteronomous thinker judges the rightness or goodness of behavior by considering the consequences of the behavior, not the intentions of the actor. For example, the heteronomous thinker says that breaking 12 cups accidently is worse than breaking 1 cup intentionally while trying to steal a cookie. For the moral autonomist, the reverse is true. The actor's intentions assume paramount importance. The heteronomous thinker also believes that rules are unchangeable and are handed down by all-powerful authorities. When Piaget suggested that new rules be introduced into the game of marbles, the young children resisted. They insisted that the rules had always been the same and could not be altered. By contrast, older children—who were moral autonomists—accept change and recognize that rules are merely convenient, socially agreed-upon conventions, subject to change by consensus.

The heteronomous thinker also believes in **immanent justice**: If a rule is broken, punishment will be meted out immediately. He believes that the violation is connected in some automatic way to the punishment. Thus, young children often look around worriedly after committing a transgression, expecting inevitable punishment. Older children, who are moral autonomists, recognize that punishment is socially mediated and occurs only if a relevant person witnesses the wrongdoing and that, even then, punishment is not inevitable.

Piaget argued that, as children develop, they become more sophisticated in thinking about social matters, especially about the possibilities and conditions of cooperation. Piaget believed that this social understanding comes about through the mutual give-and-take of peer relations. In the peer group, where others have power and status similar to the individual, plans are negotiated and coordinated, and disagreements are reasoned about and eventually settled. Parent-child relations, in which parents have the power and the child does not, are less likely to advance moral reasoning because rules are often handed down in an authoritarian way. Later, in Chapter 13, we will discuss another highly influential cognitive view of moral development, that of Lawrence Kohlberg.

Thinking Critically
In the cognitive developmental view, parents are not thought to be especially important in the child's moral development. Have the cognitive developmentalists underestimated the importance of parents in children's moral development? Explain your answer.

Moral Behavior

The study of moral behavior has been influenced by social learning theory. The processes of reinforcement, punishment, and imitation are used to explain children's moral behavior. When children are rewarded for behavior that is consistent with laws and social conventions, they are likely to repeat that behavior. When models who behave morally are provided, children are likely to adopt their actions. And when children are punished for immoral behavior, those behaviors are likely to be reduced or eliminated. However, because punishment may have adverse side effects, it needs to be used judiciously and cautiously.

Another important point needs to be made about the social learning view of moral development: Moral behavior is influenced extensively by the situation. What children do in one situation is often only weakly related to what they do in other situations. A child may cheat in math class, but not in English class; a child may steal a piece of candy when others are not present, and not steal it when they are present; and so on. More than half a century ago, morality's situational nature was observed in a comprehensive study of thousands of children in many different situations—at home, at school, and at church, for example. The totally honest child was virtually nonexistent; so was the child who cheated in all situations (Hartshorne & May, 1928–30).

Social learning theorists also believe that the ability to resist temptation is closely tied to the development of self-control. Children must overcome their impulses for something they want that is prohibited. To accomplish this self-control, they must learn to be patient and to delay gratification. Today, social learning theorists believe that cognitive factors are important in the child's development of self-control. For example, in one investigation (Mischel & Patterson, 1976), children's cognitive transformations of desired objects helped children to become more patient. Preschool children were asked to do a boring task. Close by was an enticing mechanical clown who tried to persuade the children to come play with him. The children who had been trained to say to themselves, "I'm not going to look at Mr. Clown when Mr. Clown says to look at him," controlled their behavior and continued working on the dull task much longer than those who did not instruct themselves.

Moral Feelings and Guilt

In the psychoanalytic account of guilt, children avoid transgressing to avoid anxiety. By contrast, a child with little guilt has little reason to resist temptation. Guilt is responsible for harnessing the id's evil drives and for maintaining the world as a safe place to be. Early childhood is a special time for the development of guilt. It

The young girl on the left is engaging in altruistic behavior by unselfishly helping the young girl on the right.

is during this time period, thought Freud, that through identification with parents and parents' use of love withdrawal for discipline, children turn their hostility inward and experience guilt. The guilt is primarily unconscious and reflects the structure of the personality known as the superego. Remember also that Erikson believes early childhood has special importance in the development of guilt; he even called the major conflict to be resolved in early childhood *initiative versus guilt*.

Moral feelings or affect have traditionally been thought of in terms of guilt, but recently there has been considerable interest in empathy's role in the child's moral development. **Empathy** is the ability to understand the feelings of another individual, and as we will see next, it is believed to be an important aspect of the child's altruism.

Altruism

In studying guilt, cheating, lying, stealing, and resistance to temptation, we are investigating the antisocial, negative side of moral development. Today, we recognize that it is important not to dwell too much on the dark side of morality; perhaps we should spend more time evaluating and promoting the positive side of morality—prosocial behavior, altruism, and empathy, for example.

Altruism is an unselfish interest in helping someone. Human acts of altruism are plentiful: the hard-working laborer who places a $5 dollar bill in a Salvation Army kettle, rock concerts organized by Bob Geldof and Willie Nelson to feed the hungry and help farmers, and a child who takes in a wounded cat and cares for it. How do psychologists account for such frequent accounts of altruism?

Reciprocity and exchange are important aspects of altruism (Brown, 1986). Reciprocity is found throughout the human world. It is not only the highest moral principle in Christianity, but it is also present in every widely practiced religion in the world—Judaism, Hinduism, Buddism, and Islam. Reciprocity encourages us to do unto others as we would have them do unto us. Certain human sentiments are wrapped up in this reciprocity. Trust probably is the most important principle over the long run; guilt emerges if we do not reciprocate; and anger results if someone else does not reciprocate. Not all human altruism is motivated by reciprocity and social exchange, but this view alerts us to the importance of considering self-other interactions and relationships in understanding altruism. The circumstances most likely to involve altruism are empathetic or sympathetic emotion for an individual in need or a close relationship between the benefactor and the recipient (Batson, 1989; Eisenberg, 1989).

Although altruism increases as children get older, examples of caring for others and comforting someone in distress are abundant during the preschool years (Eisenberg, 1987; Iannotti, 1985). In the following episode, even 2-year-old John shows altruistic concerns:

Today, Jerry was kind of cranky; he just started completely bawling and he wouldn't stop. John kept coming over and handing Jerry toys, trying to cheer him up, so to speak. He'd say things like, "Here, Jerry," and I said to John: "Jerry's sad; he doesn't feel good; he had a shot today." John would look at me with his eyebrows kind of wrinkled together like he really understood that Jerry was crying because he was unhappy, not that he was just being a crybaby. He went over and rubbed Jerry's arm and said, "Nice Jerry" and continued to give him toys (Zahn-Waxler, Radke-Yarrow, & King, 1979, pp. 321–322).

One way to explain altruism's presence in young children is their motivation to understand the feelings of others and to experience those feelings themselves (Denham, 1986; Fogel & Melson, 1987; Melson & Fogel, 1988). If we see people cry or become sad and we share their distress, we may become motivated to help them relieve the distress. The empathy we feel and share with others, then, may be altruism's engine. The early preschool years may have a special importance in understanding empathy and altruism because it is at this point in development that children begin to recognize that other people have their own feelings and needs. Are there ways parents can develop these positive feelings in their young children? The following are some suggestions:

—Expose children to a wide range of feelings; it is hard for children to empathize with someone who is experiencing an emotion the children have never felt.
—Direct the child's attention to others' feelings saying to the child something like, "How do you think Sam felt when you socked him?"
—Ensure that children have models around them in their daily lives who not only show altruistic behavior but who verbalize the empathic feelings that underlie it.

Emerson once said, "The meaning of good and bad, better and worse, is simply helping or hurting." By developing the capacity for empathy and altruism young children possess, we can become a nation of *good* people who *help* rather than *hurt*.

Thus far, we have discussed a number of ideas about the self, gender roles, and moral development in young children. These ideas are summarized in Concept Table 10.3. This chapter concludes our discussion of early childhood. In the next section, we will turn our attention to middle and late childhood.

Personality Development

Concept	Processes and Related Ideas	Characteristics and Description
The Self	Initiative versus guilt	Erikson believes early childhood is a period when the self involves resolving the conflict between initiative versus guilt.
	"I" versus "Me"	"I" is the self as knower, "me" is the object of what is known, which usually is studied by investigating the child's self-concept. Rogers believes the child's self-concept can be improved by unconditionally loving the child.
	Inner and outer dimensions	Children as young as 3 years old have a basic idea that they have a private self. Between the ages of 3 and 4, children distinguish between the inner self and their outer, bodily self.
Gender Roles	Their nature	Gender roles are social expectations of how we should act and think as males and females. Gender roles are influenced by biological, cognitive, and social factors.
	Biological influences	Freud's and Erikson's theories promoted the idea that anatomy is destiny. Hormones influence sexual development. Today's developmentalists are all interactionists in terms of biological and environmental influences on gender roles, but interaction means different things to different people.
	Cognitive influences	Cognitive factors that influence gender roles include self-categorization and language development. An important theme in the cognitive approach is that children develop a gender schema.
	Environmental influences	Environmental factors that influence gender roles include parent-child relations, peer relations, and teacher-child relations.
	Gender role development	Considerable development in gender roles occurs during early childhood. At this time, young children often make grand generalizations about gender roles.
Moral Development	Its nature	Concerns rules and regulations about what people should do in their interactions with others. Developmentalists study how children think, behave, and feel about such rules and regulations.
	Piaget's view	Distinguished between the heteronomous morality of younger children and the autonomous morality of older children.
	Moral behavior	Has been influenced by social learning theory. Emphasis is placed on situational influences and the child's development of self-control.
	Moral feelings and guilt	Psychoanalytic theory emphasizes moral feelings and guilt. Erikson even calls early childhood the initiative vs. guilt stage. Recently, there has been interest in empathy's role.
	Altruism	An unselfish interest in helping someone. Reciprocity and exchange are important aspects of altruism. Empathy plays a key role in the development of altruism in young children.

Summary

I. **Parenting Styles**

Four major categories of parenting styles are authoritarian, authoritative, permissive indulgent, and permissive indifferent. Authoritative parenting is associated with children's social competence more than the other styles. Parents need to adapt their interaction strategies as the child grows older, using less physical manipulation and more reasoning in the process.

II. Sibling Relationships

More than 80 percent of American children have one or more siblings. Siblings interact with each other in more negative, less positive, and less varied ways than parents and children interact. In some cases, siblings are stronger socializing influences than parents. The relationship of the firstborn child to parents seems to be especially close and demanding, which may account for the greater achievement and anxiety found in firstborn children.

III. The Changing Family

A mother's working full-time outside the home can have positive or negative effects on the child; there is no indication of long-term negative effects overall. Family conflict seems to outweigh family structure in its impact on the child; conflict is greatest in the first year after the divorce. A continuing, ongoing positive relationship with the ex-spouse is important for the child's adjustment. Support systems are significant in the child's adaptation to divorce. Boys fare better in father-custody families, girls in mother-custody families.

IV. Peers

Peers are powerful social agents. The term *peers* refers to children who are of about the same age or maturity level. Peers provide a source of information and comparison about the world outside the family. The frequency of peer interaction, both positive and negative, increases during the preschool years. Peer relations are both similar to and different from family relations.

V. Play

Play's functions include affiliation with peers, tension release, advances in cognitive development, exploration, and provision of a safe haven in which to engage in potentially dangerous activities. The types of play include unoccupied, solitary, onlooker, parallel, associative, and cooperative play, as well as pretend play.

VI. Television

Television's functions include entertainment and information. Television presents a more diverse view of the world than can be experienced in one's family, school, or peer group. However, television may train children to become passive learners, is deceiving, and often takes children away from studying and reading. Children watch huge amounts of television, and this watching is associated with their aggression, altruism, eating behavior, and social contexts of viewing.

VII. The Self

Erikson believes early childhood is a period when the self involves resolving the conflict between initiative versus guilt, when it is important to consider the distinction between "I" and "me," and when the child begins to understand that the self has both inner and outer dimensions. "I" is the self as knower, "me" is the object of what is known, which usually is studied by investigating the child's self-concept. Rogers believes the child's self-concept can be improved by unconditionally loving the child.

VIII. Gender Roles

Gender roles are social expectations of how we should act and think as males and females. Gender roles are influenced by biological, cognitive, and environmental factors. Freud's and Erikson's theories promoted the idea that anatomy is destiny; hormones influence sexual development, although not as pervasively in human beings as in animals. Today's developmentalists are all interactionists in terms of biological and environmental influences on gender roles, but interaction means different things to different people. Cognitive factors that influence gender roles are self-categorization and language development. An important theme in the cognitive approach is that children develop a gender schema. Environmental factors are parent-child relations, peer relations, and teacher-child relations. Considerable development in gender roles occurs during early childhood. At this time, young children often make grand generalizations about gender roles.

IX. Moral Development

Moral development concerns rules and regulations about what people should do in their interactions with others. Developmentalists study how children think, behave, and feel about such rules and regulations. Piaget distinguished between the heteronomous morality of younger children and the autonomous morality of older children. The study of moral behavior has been influenced by social learning theory. Emphasis is placed on the importance of situational influences and the development of self-control. Psychoanalytic theory emphasizes the importance of moral feelings and guilt. Erikson even called early childhood the initiative vs. guilt stage. Altruism is an unselfish interest in helping someone. Reciprocity and exchange are important aspects of altruism. Empathy plays a key role in the development of altruism in young children.

Key Terms

authoritarian parenting 301
authoritative parenting 302
permissive indulgent
    parenting 302
permissive indifferent
    parenting 302
father absence
    tradition 308
peers 311
play theory 314

unoccupied play 315
solitary play 316
onlooker play 316
parallel play 316
associative play 316
cooperative play 316
pretend play 316
gender roles 327
estrogen 327

androgen 327
hermaphrodites 327
gender schema 328
moral development 331
heteronomous morality 332
autonomous morality 332
immanent justice 332
empathy 334
altruism 334

Suggested Readings

Hartup, W. W. (1983). The peer system. In P. H. Mussen (Ed.), *Handbook of child psychology* (4th ed., Vol. 4). New York: Wiley.

A detailed look at the development of peer relations from one of the leading experts in the field, Willard Hartup.

Hetherington, E. M., Hagan, M. S., & Anderson, E. R. (1989). Family transitions: A child's perspective. *American Psychologist, 44,* 303–312.

Hetherington is a leading researcher in the investigation of the effects of divorce on children's development. In this article, she and her colleagues review the recent literature on divorce, giving special attention to transitions in divorced and stepparent families.

Liebert, R. M., & Sprakin, J. N. (1988). *The early window: Effects of television on children and youth* (3rd ed.). Elmsford, NY: Pergamon.

An updated account of theory and research that addresses the effects of television on children's development.

Reinisch, J. M., Rosenblum, L. A., & Sanders, S. A. (Eds.). (1987). *Masculinity/ femininity.* New York: Oxford University Press.

An outstanding collection of articles by leading experts such as Eleanor Maccoby, John Money, and Jacqueline Eccles. Includes a special section of papers on the development of gender roles.

Rubin, K. H., Fein, G. G., & Vandenberg, B. (1983). Play: In P. H. Mussen (Ed.), *Handbook of child psychology* (4th ed., Vol. 4). New York: Wiley.

A thorough, detailed analysis of what we know about children's play; describes directions in which developmentalists' interests in play are moving.

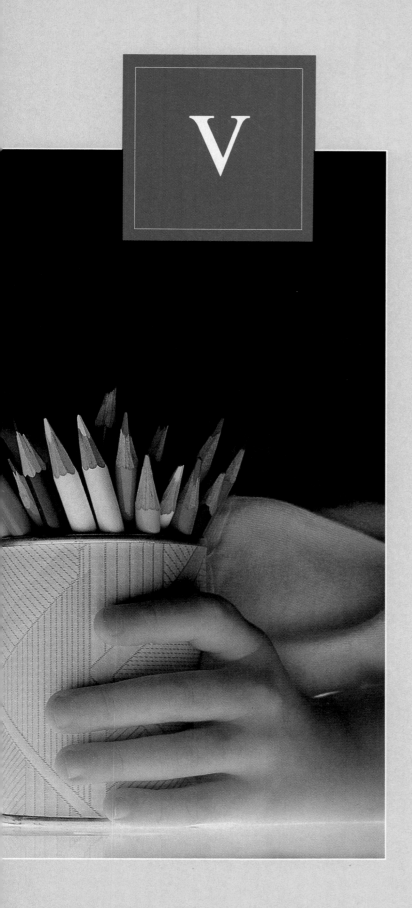

Middle and Late Childhood

◆

Blessed be childhood, which brings something of heaven into the midst of our rough earthliness.

Henri Frédéric Amiel,
Journal, *1868*

I n middle and late childhood, children are on a different plane, belonging to a generation and feeling all their own. It is the wisdom of the human life cycle that at no time are children more ready to learn than at the end of early childhood's expansive imagination. Children develop a sense of wanting to make things, and not just to make them, but to make them well and even perfectly. Their thirst is to know and to understand. They are remarkable for their intelligence and for their curiosity. Their parents continue to be important influences in their lives, but their growth also is shaped by successive choirs of friends. They don't think much about the future or about the past, but they enjoy the present moment.

Section 5 consists of three chapters. Chapter 11 describes children's physical development in middle and late childhood. Among its contents is information about

—Body changes
—Children's writing skills
—Handicapped children
—Health
—Daily hassles and daily uplifts in children's lives
—A program called Heart Smart for improving children's cardiovascular fitness
—Coping with stress

Chapter 12 describes children's cognitive development in middle and late childhood. Among its contents is information about

—Piaget's theory and concrete operational thought
—Information processing
—The information age and children's education
—Whether intelligence has one face or many faces
—Language development
—Reading and literacy
—Achievement in minority group children

Chapter 13 describes children's social competence in middle and late childhood. Among its contents is information about

—Parent-child issues
—Stepfamilies
—Latchkey children
—Peer relations
—Schools
—The jigsaw classroom
—The self and social competence
—Androgyny
—Moral development
—Problems and disturbances

11

Physical Development

Standing on the balance beam at a sports school in Beijing, China, 6-year-old Zhang Liyin stretches her arms outward as she gets ready to perform a backflip on the beam. She wears an elite bright-red gymnastic suit given to only the best 10 girls in her class of 6-to 8-year-olds (Figure 11.1). But her face wears a dreadful expression; she can't drum up enough confidence to do the flip. Maybe it is because she has had a rough week; a purple bruise decorates one leg, and a nasty gash disfigures the other. Her coach, a woman in her twenties, makes Zhang jump from the beam and escorts her to the high bar, where she is instructed to hang for three minutes. If Zhang falls, she must pick herself up and try again. But she does not fall, and she is escorted back to the beam, where her coach puts her through another tedious routine.

Zhang attends the sports school in the afternoon. The sports school is a privilege given to only 260,000 of China's 200 million students of elementary to college age. The Communist party has decided that sports is one avenue China can pursue to prove that China has arrived in the modern world. The sports schools designed to produce Olympic champions were the reason for China's success in the 1984 and 1988 Olympics. These schools are the only road to Olympic stardom in China. There are precious few neighborhood playgrounds. And for every 3.5 million people, there is only one gymnasium.

Many of the students who attend the sports schools in the afternoon live and study at the schools as well. Only a few attend a normal school and then come to a sports school in the afternoon. Because of her young age, Zhang stays at home during the mornings and goes to the sports school from noon until 6 P.M. A part-timer like Zhang can stay enrolled until she no longer shows potential to move up to the next step. Any child who seems to lack potential is asked to leave.

Zhang was playing in a nursery school class when a coach from a sports school spotted her. She was selected because she had broad shoulders, narrow hips, straight legs, symmetrical limbs, an open-minded attitude, vivaciousness, and an outgoing personality. If Zhang continues to show progress, she could be asked to move to full time next year. At age 7, she would then go to school there and live in a dorm six days a week. If she becomes extremely competent at gymnastics, Zhang could be moved over to Shishahai, where the elite gymnasts train and compete.

At Shishahai, the day begins at 6 A.M. with breakfast, followed by four hours of academic classes and study until 11:30 A.M. Then follows lunch and a nap until 2:30, four grueling hours of athletic training, dinner at 7, more studies from 7 to 9, and lights out at 9:30. No TVs are allowed in the school, no in-room phones are permitted, and dating is prohibited. Coca-Cola, VCRs, and Colonel Sanders may have arrived in Beijing, but they won't be found at the Shishahai sports school.

Possibly someday Zhang will be one of the special ones, achieving a good education, a good salary, and perhaps an Olympic medal. But for now, she is just one of many aspirants. Every day she is tested to see if she is on schedule for stardom (Reilly, 1988).

By American standards, Zhang's life sounds rigid and punitive. Although achievement in sports has a lofty status in American society, children are not trained with the intensity now being witnessed in China, Eastern European nations such as East Germany, and the Soviet Union.

Thinking Critically
Is the policy of China and other countries that use massive efforts to discover and train potential Olympic athletes at very young ages a wise one? What needs and concerns of children are involved?

346   Middle and Late Childhood

FIGURE 11.1 The training of future Olympians in the sports schools of China. Six-year-old Zhang Liyin is the third from the left. She hopes someday to become an Olympic gymnastics champion. Attending the sports school is considered an outstanding privilege; it is given to only 260,000 of China's 200 million children.

Later in this chapter, we cover further information about the nature of children's sports and physical fitness. We also will study handicapped children, as well as children's health, stress, and coping. But to begin, we turn to the nature of children's body changes in middle and late childhood.

Body Changes

The period of middle and late childhood involves slow, consistent growth. This is a period of calm before the rapid growth spurt of adolescence. Among the important aspects of body change in this developmental period are those involving the skeletal system, the muscular system, and motor skills.

The Skeletal and Muscular Systems

During the elementary school years, children grow an average of 2 to 3 inches a year until, at the age of 11, the average girl is 4 feet 10 inches tall and the average boy is 4 feet, 9½ inches tall. Children's legs become longer and their trunks slimmer. During the middle and late childhood years, children gain about 5 to 7 pounds a year. The weight increase is due mainly to increases in the size of the skeleton and muscular systems, as well as the size of some body organs. Muscle mass and strength gradually increase as "baby fat" decreases. The loose movements and knock knees of early childhood give way to improved muscle tone. The increase in muscular strength is due to heredity and to exercise. Children double their strength capabilities during these years. Because of their greater number of muscle cells, boys are usually stronger than girls (Whaley & Wong, 1989).

Elementary schoolchildren should be involved in active, rather than passive, activities. Physical action, such as that involved in games like soccer, is essential for children to develop their physical skills.

Motor Skills

During middle and late childhood, children's motor development becomes much smoother and more coordinated than it was in early childhood. For example, only one child in a thousand can hit a tennis ball over the net at the age of 3, yet by the age of 10 or 11, most children can learn to play the sport. Running, climbing, skipping rope, swimming, bicycle riding, and skating are just a few of the many physical skills elementary schoolchildren can master. And when mastered, these physical skills are a source of great pleasure and accomplishment for children. In gross motor skills involving large muscle activity, boys usually outperform girls rather handily.

As children move through the elementary school years, they gain greater control over their bodies and can sit and attend for longer periods of time. However, elementary schoolchildren are far from having physical maturity, and they need to be active. Elementary schoolchildren become more fatigued by long periods of sitting than by running, jumping, or bicycling. Physical action is essential for these children to refine their developing skills, such as batting a ball, skipping rope, or

FIGURE 11.2 Improvement of fine motor control is evidenced by changes in handwriting. These children were asked to write their names on a blank piece of paper. As the children increase in age, their writing becomes smaller, and the evenness and the uniformity of letter configurations improve. Females generally exhibit more highly developed fine-motor skills during these years because of advanced neurological development. Note the immaturity in discrimination as well as coordination of the 4-year-olds; the reversal of letters of a 6-year-old (Bridget); the mixture of upper- and lowercase letters of the 6-year-olds; and the letter dropping of the 8-year-old. All are common for the ages of the children (Schuster, 1986, p. 449).

balancing on a beam. An important principle of practice for elementary school-children, therefore, is that they should be engaged in *active*, rather than passive, activities (Katz & Chard, in press).

Increased myelinization of the central nervous system is reflected in the improvement of fine motor skills during middle and late childhood. Children's hands are used more adroitly as tools. Six-year-olds can hammer, paste, tie shoes, and fasten clothes. By 7 years of age, children's hands become steadier. At this age, children prefer a pencil to a crayon for printing, and reversal of letters is less common. Printing becomes smaller. Between 8 to 10 years of age, the hands can be used independently with more ease and precision. Fine motor coordination develops to the point where children can write rather than print words. Letter size becomes smaller and more even. By 10 to 12 years of age, children begin to show manipulative skills similar to the abilities of adults. The complex, intricate, and rapid movements needed to produce fine-quality crafts or playing a difficult piece on a muscial instrument can be mastered. Figure 11.2 reflects the improvement in children's fine motor skills as they move through the elementary school years (Schuster, 1986). One final point: Girls usually outperform boys in fine motor skills. More about children's writing appears in Children 11.1.

"Keep Him away from the Cords because He Can Get Aledrcouted"

Many language arts texts, workbooks, and worksheets commonly seen in today's elementary schools encourage children to conform and write in much the same way. In classrooms that emphasize the *process* of writing as well as the product, children are treated much more individually when working on their writing. In the process orientation to writing, children are expected to choose their own topics and to make decisions about length, organization, style, spelling, and revision strategies. Allowing children to "invent" their own spelling as they write removes some of the obstacles in communicating meaning for young writers (Graves, 1983; Sowers, 1987).

Ruth Hubbard (1988) described a second-and-third-grade classroom in which the process orientation to writing was being used. The teacher wanted her students to explore different groups of animals: birds, mammals, amphibians, reptiles, and fish. She converted her classroom into a giant zoo, with a rabbit, a guinea pig, a shark, various other fish, a chameleon, an African frog, and a snake. A bird feeder also was set up outside the window. On the first day, children were given notebooks. Each day they were expected to write their observations of the animals in these journals.

After a week of observing the animals groups, the children chose the one group they wanted to learn to take care of, to observe, to read about, and to write about daily. Following is an excerpt by Ilana's journal:

> I nonist that a rabbit stays away from someone he is not used to. If he is not used to you, he will stay away or bit you. Jil was treing to pet the rabbit but he hede and woulden't come out. But Rachael could take it out and it would not be afaered. I found out that Cuddle can't eat news paper

because the ink can get in to him and he can die! If you let him out you must keep him away from cords because he can get aledrcouted.

Another child chose to study the guinea pig. This child's account of the guinea pig appears in Figure 11.A.

There is much to commend about the process orientation to writing. The approach allows children's individuality to emerge in their writing rather than turning them into robots who produce an endless recitation of facts and a rigid writing style, and develop anxieties about penmanship and spelling. While penmanship and spelling cannot be allowed to go completely unguided, many elementary schoolteachers have been overly concerned about these competencies. The fine motor skills and cognitive development of many children simply are not adequate to allow the children to produce perfect letters and spelling. I vividly remember my youngest daughter's experience with a first-grade teacher who made the children spend 45 minutes each school day perfecting their penmanship. Jennifer started bringing home papers with "sad faces," exclamation points, and negative remarks because she had not tilted her *y*'s just right. A conference with the teacher and the principal led to an elimination of the negative feedback. By the end of the first grade, Jennifer was motorically mature enough to tilt her *y*'s correctly, but many other children were not. Imagine how much more productive, creative, and enjoyable those 45 minutes each school day would have been for the children if the teacher had emphasized the process of writing and the individual abilities of the children rather than forcing them to conform to a rigid penmanship routine. ◆

Handicapped Children

The elementary school years are a time when handicapped children become more sensitive about their differentness and how it is perceived by others. One 6-year-old girl came home from school and asked, "Am I disabled or handicapped?" Another articulate 6-year-old girl described in detail how her premature birth was the cause of her cerebral palsy: "I was a teensy-weensy baby. They put me in an incubator and I almost died." Later, when asked about being teased by her classmates because she could not walk, she replied, "I hate their guts, but if I said anything the teacher would get mad at me." A 7-year-old handicapped boy commented about how he had successfully completed a rocket-making course during the summer; he was the youngest and the most knowledgeable child in the class: "For the first time, some kids really liked me" (Howard, 1982). Life is not always fair, especially for handicapped children. As evidenced by the comments of the handicapped children just

April 9, 1986
Guinea pigs do
get there hair
cuts. The guinea
pigs hair grows
one inch a
month. Shonna's
guinea pig. is six
inches long. Also
today two Fish
died. The Fish
group thinks that
when the Fish go
under the fillter they
die, I do not no how,

FIGURE 11.A   A child's written description of a guinea pig entered into a daily journal in a second- to third-grade classroom (Hubbard, 1988, p. 37).

mentioned, adjusting to the world of peers and school often is painful and difficult. Our coverage of handicapped children focuses on the scope and education of handicapped children, learning disabilities, and attention-deficit disorder.

Scope and Education of Handicapped Children

An estimated 10 to 15 percent of the United States population of children between the ages of 5 and 18 are handicapped in some way (Table 11.1). The estimates range from 0.1 percent who are visually impaired to the 3 to 4 percent who have speech handicaps. Estimates vary because of problems in classification and testing. Experts sometimes differ in how they define the various categories of handicapped children. And different tests may be used by different school systems or psychologists to assess whether a child is handicapped.

TABLE 11.1 *Estimates of the Percentage and Number of Handicapped Children in the United States*

Handicap	Percentage of Population	Number of Children Ages 5 to 18*
Visual impairment (includes blindness)	0.1	55,000
Hearing impairment (includes deafness)	0.5–0.7	275,000–385,000
Speech handicap	3.0–4.0	1,650,000–2,200,000
Orthopedic and health impairments	0.5	275,000
Emotional disturbance	2.0–3.0	1,100,000–1,650,000
Mental retardation (both educable and trainable)	2.0–3.0	1,100,000–1,650,000
Learning disabilities	2.0–3.0	1,100,000–1,650,000
Multiple handicaps	0.5–0.7	275,000–385,000
Total	10.6–15.0	5,830,000–8,250,00

From *The Exceptional Student in the Regular Classroom,* Third Edition by Bill R. Gearheart and Mel W. Weishahn, © 1984. Reprinted by permission of Merrill Publishing Company, Columbus, Ohio.
*Number of children based on 1985 population estimates

All states have now been ordered by the federal government to ensure a free, appropriate education for all handicapped children. The initial impetus for this order was **Public Law 94–142,** the Education for All Handicapped Children Act, passed by Congress in 1975. One key provision of the act is the development of an individualized education program for each identified handicapped child.

Another provision of the Public Law 94–142 is to provide the **least restrictive environment** for the education of handicapped children. Each state must ensure that all handicapped students are educated with students who are not handicapped. Special-education classes, separate schooling, or other removal of handicapped children from the regular education environment should occur only when the nature or severity of the handicap is such that an education in regular classes with the use of supplementary aids and services cannot be satisfactorily achieved (Gaylord-Ross, 1989; Lipsky & Gartner, 1989).

The least restrictive environment provision establishes a policy that is usually referred to as **mainstreaming.** This means that as many handicapped children as possible should enter the mainstream of education by attending school in classes with nonhandicapped children. Even under PL 94–142 and its emphasis on mainstreaming, certain types of handicapped children, such as those with hearing impairments, usually spend part of each day in separate classes taught by specially trained teachers. The results of mainstreaming have met with mixed results. In some schools, teachers assign children to environments that are not the best contexts for learning (Brady & others, 1988). Some people believe that mainstreaming means there will be a number of profoundly retarded, drugged children sitting in classrooms in dazed, unresponsive states. Others believe that including handicapped children in regular classrooms will detract from the quality of education given to nonhandicapped children. The picture is not as bleak as some of these criticisms suggest. Virtually all profoundly retarded children are institutionalized and will never be schooled in public classrooms. Only the mildly retarded are mainstreamed. Mainstreaming makes children and teachers become more aware of the special needs of handicapped people.

In practice, mainstreaming has not been the simple solution its architects hoped for. Many handicapped children require extensive and expensive services to help them become effective learners in the regular classroom. As school systems have

Thinking Critically
Is mainstreaming the best way for handicapped children to be educated? What needs and concerns of handicapped and nonhandicapped children should be considered?

Middle and Late Childhood

The Status of Special Education in Vietnam

Lack of funds and lack of special-education personnel make the training of hand-icapped and exceptional children a precarious situation in Vietnam. As a result of the Vietnam War, many children are handicapped both physically and emotionally. Services for these children are limited. Vietnam needs assistance to train special-education personnel, develop methods of instruction appropriate for local needs, and funds to build and operate schools for many handicapped children. The need is being recognized, but economic factors and lack of facilities for training special-education personnel restrict growth in this area to a very slow pace (Csapo, 1986). ◆

What are some of the most important issues in the special education of the handicapped?

become increasingly strapped financially, many services for handicapped children have been cut back. Some teachers, already burdened with heavy course loads and time demands, have felt overwhelmed by the added requirement of developing spe-cial teaching arrangements for handicapped children. And the social interaction of handicapped and nonhandicapped children has not always gone smoothly in main-streamed classrooms (Gallagher, Trohanis, & Clifford, 1989).

The hope that mainstreaming would be a positive solution for all handicapped children needs to be balanced with the reality of each individual handicapped child's life and that particular child's special needs. The specially tailored education pro-gram should meet with the acceptance of the child's parents, counselors, educational authorities and, when feasible, the children themselves (Hallahan & others, 1988).

Is there a disadvantage to referring to these children as handicapped or dis-abled? Children who are labeled as handicapped or disabled may feel permanently stigmatized and rejected, and they may be denied opportunities for full develop-ment. Children labeled as handicapped or disabled may be assigned to inferior educational programs or placed in institutions without the legal protection given to "normal" individuals. Paradoxically, however, if handicapped or disabled children are not labeled, they may not be able to take advantage of the special programs designed to help them (Hobbs, 1975; Horne, 1988).

There are no quick fixes for the education of handicapped children. While progress has been made in recent years to provide supportive instruction for handicapped children, increasing effort needs to be devoted to developing the skills of handicapped children (Hynd & Obrzut, 1986). Handicapped children have a strong will to survive, to grow, and to learn. They deserve our very best educational efforts (Wood, 1988).

Learning Disabilities

Paula doesn't like kindergarten and can't seem to remember the names of her teacher or classmates. Bobby's third-grade teacher complains that his spelling is awful and that he is always reversing letters. Ten-year-old Tim hates to read. He says it is too hard for him and the words just don't make any sense to him. Each of these children is learning disabled. Children with **learning disabilities** (1) are of normal intelligence or above, (2) have difficulties in several academic areas but usually do not show deficits in others, and (3) are not suffering from some other conditions or disorders that could explain their learning problems (Reid, 1988). The breadth of definitions of learning disabilities has generated controversy about just what learning disabilities are (Chalfant, 1989; Siegel, 1988; Siegel & Ryan 1989; Silver, 1989).

Within the global concept of learning disabilities fall problems in listening, thinking, memory, reading, writing, spelling, and math. Attention deficits involving an inability to sit still, pay attention, and concentrate also are classified under learning disabilities. Table 11.2 reveals the heterogeneity of characteristics that lead teachers to classify children as learning disabled. Estimates of the number of learning-disabled children in the United States are as broad as the definition, ranging from 1 to 30 percent (Lerner, 1988). The United States Department of Education puts the number of identified learning-disabled children between the ages of 3 and 21 at approximately 2 million.

Improving the lives of learning-disabled children will come from (1) recognizing the complex, multifaceted nature of learning disabilities—(biological, cognitive, and social aspects of learning disabilities need to be considered) and (2) becoming more precise in our analysis of the learning environments in which learning-disabled children participate (Lerner, 1989). The following discussion of one subtype of learning disability, attention-deficit disorder, exemplifies consideration of this complexity and preciseness.

Attention-Deficit Disorder

Matthew failed the first grade. His handwriting was messy. He did not know the alphabet and never attended very well to the lessons the teacher taught. Matthew is almost always in motion. He can't sit still for more than a few minutes at a time. His mother describes him as always being fidgety. Matthew has an **attention-deficit disorder,** sometimes commonly referred to as hyperactivity. Children are described as having an attention-deficit disorder if they are extremely active, impulsive, distractible, and excitable (Barkeley, in press; Silver, 1987). In short, they do not pay attention and have difficulty concentrating on what they are doing. Estimates of the number of children with attention-deficit disorder vary from less than 1 percent to 5 percent. While young children or even infants show characteristics of this disorder,

TABLE 11.2 *Descriptions of Behavior Most Frequently Checked by Teachers for Second-Grade Children Meeting Diagnostic Guidelines for Learning Disabilities*

Description of Behavior	Percentage of Children for Whom Description was Checked	Description of Behavior	Percentage of Children for Whom Description Was Checked
1. Substitutes words that distort meaning ("when" for "where")	70	19. Reverses and/or rotates letters and numbers (reads *b* for *d, u* for *n*, and *6* for *9*) far more than most peers	47
2. Reads silently or aloud far more slowly than peers (word by word while reading aloud)	68	20. Difficulty with arithmetic (e.g., can't determine what number follows 8 or 16, may begin to add in the middle of a subtraction problem)	46
3. Unusually short attention span for daily work	67	21. Poor drawing of crossing, wavy lines compared with peers' drawing	46
4. Easily distracted from schoolwork (can't concentrate with even the slightest disturbances from other students' moving around or talking quietly)	66	22. Omits words while reading grade-level material aloud (omits more than one of every 10)	44
5. Can't follow written directions that most peers can follow, when read orally or silently	65	23. Poor drawing of a person compared with peers' drawings	43
6. Does very poorly in written spelling tests compared with peers	64	24. Can read orally but does not comprehend the meaning of written grade-level words (word caller)	43
7. Can't sound out or "unlock" words	64	25. Excessive inconsistency in quality of performance from day to day and even hour to hour	43
8. Reading ability at least three-fourths of a year below most peers	63	26. Seems quite immature (doesn't act his or her age)	43
9. Has trouble telling time	62	27. Unable to learn the sounds of letters (can't associate appropriate phoneme with its grapheme)	41
10. Doesn't seem to listen to daily classroom instructions or directions (often asks to have them repeated whereas rest of class goes ahead)	61	28. Avoids work calling for concentrated visual attention	39
11. Is slow to finish work (doesn't apply self, daydreams a lot, falls asleep in school)	56	29. Mistakes own left from right (confuses left-hand side of paper)	39
12. Repeats the same behavior over and over	56	30. Demands unusual amount of attention during regular classroom activities	39
13. Has trouble organizing written work (seems scatterbrained, confused)	56	31. Loses place more than once while reading aloud for more than one minute	38
14. Can't correctly recall oral directions (e.g., item 10 above) when asked to repeat them	54	32. Cannot apply the classroom or school regulations to own behavior whereas peers can	37
15. Poor handwriting compared with peers' writing	52	33. Tense or disturbed (bites lip, needs to go to the bathroom often, twists hair, high-strung)	36
16. Reverses and/or rotates letters, numbers, or words (writes *p* for *q, saw* for *was, 2* for *7*) far more frequently than peers	52	34. Poor drawing of diamond compared with peers' drawings	36
17. Seems very bright in many ways but does poorly in school	50	35. Overactive (can't sit still in class—shakes or swings legs, fidgety)	34
18. Points at words while reading silently or aloud	49		

Children with attention-deficit disorder do not pay attention and have difficulty concentrating on what they are doing. The social and physical environments in which children live, as well as children's biological makeup, are involved in attention-deficit disorder.

the vast majority of hyperactive children is identified in the first three grades of elementary school when teachers recognize that they have great difficulty paying attention, sitting still, and concentrating on their schoolwork.

What makes Jimmy so impulsive, Sandy so distractible, and Harvey so excitable? Possible causes include heredity, prenatal damage, diet, family dynamics, and the physical environment. As we saw in Chapter 3, the influence of heredity on temperament is increasingly considered, with activity level being one aspect of temperament that differentiates one child from another very early in development. Approximately 4 times as many boys as girls are hyperactive. This sex difference may be due to differences in the brains of boys and girls determined by genes on the Y chromosome. The prenatal hazards we discussed in Chapter 4 also may produce hyperactive behavior. Excessive drinking by women during pregnancy is associated with poor attention and concentration by their offspring at 4 years of age, for example (Streissguth & others, 1984). With regard to diet, severe vitamin deficiencies can lead to attentional problems. Vitamin B deficiencies are of special concern. Caffeine and sugar also may contribute to attentional problems.

The social and physical environments in which children live also contribute to attentional problems (Henker & Whalen, 1989). Children with attention-deficit disorder are more likely to come from families who frequently move and who are more concerned with controlling the child's behavior than with the child's academic work (Lambert & Hartsough, 1984). Hyperactive children are more likely to misbehave when they are in exciting but unstructured circumstances (such as a typical birthday party) or in circumstances with many behavioral demands (such as a typical school classroom). Lead poisoning also can produce attention problems and hyperactive behavior.

Children with attention-deficit disorder may continue to have problems in adolescence, although by that time the attentional problem is usually less severe. By adulthood, approximately one-third to one-half continue to be troubled by their attentional difficulties (Weiss & Hechtman, 1986).

Body Changes and Handicapped Children

Concept	Processes and Related Ideas	Characteristics and Description
Body Changes	The skeletal and muscular systems	During the elementary school years, children grow an average of 2 to 3 inches a year. Muscle mass and strength gradually increase. Legs lengthen and trunks slim down as "baby fat" decreases. Growth is slow and consistent.
	Motor skills	During the middle and late childhood years, children's motor development becomes much smoother and more coordinated. Children gain greater control over their bodies and can sit and attend for longer frames of time. However, their lives should be activity oriented and very active. Increased myelinization of the central nervous system is reflected in improved fine motor skills. Improved fine motor development is reflected in children's handwriting skills over the course of middle and late childhood. Boys are usually better at gross motor skills, girls at fine motor skills.
Handicapped Children	Scope and education of handicapped children	Approximately 10 to 15 percent of children in the United States are estimated to be handicapped in some way. Public Law 94–142 ordered a free, appropriate education for every handicapped child. The law emphasizes an individually tailored education program for every child and provision of a least restrictive environment, which has led to extensive mainstreaming of handicapped children into the regular classroom. Mainstreaming has been a controversial topic. Another issue is the labeling of handicapped children and its benefits and drawbacks.
	Learning disabilities	Such children have normal or above-normal intelligence, have difficulties in some areas but not others, and do not suffer from some other disorder that could explain their learning problems. Learning disabilities are complex and multifaceted and require precise analysis.
	Attention-deficit disorder	A disorder that is classified under learning disabilities. Sometimes called hyperactivity, it describes children who are extremely active, impulsive, distractible, and excitable. Possible causes include heredity, prenatal damage, diet, family dynamics, and physical environment. Amphetamines have been used with some success in treatment, but they do not work for all hyperactive children.

A wide range of psychotherapies and drug therapy has been used to improve the lives of hyperactive children. For unknown reasons, some drugs that stimulate the brains and behaviors of adults have a quieting effect on the brains and behaviors of children. The drugs most widely prescribed for hyperactive children are amphetamines, especially Ritalin. Amphetamines work effectively for some hyperactive children, but not all (Batshaw & Perret, 1986). As many as 20 percent of hyperactive children treated with Ritalin do not respond to it. Even when Ritalin works, it is also important to consider the social worlds of the hyperactive child. The teacher is especially important in this social world, helping to monitor the child's academic and social behavior to determine whether the drug works and whether the prescribed dosage is correct.

Thus far, we have discussed several ideas about body changes and handicapped children. These ideas are summarized in Concept Table 11.1. Next, we will focus on the increased interest in children's health.

Health

Although we have become a health-conscious nation, many children as well as adults do not practice good health habits. Too much junk food and too much couch-potato behavior describes all too many children. Our exploration of the health of elementary schoolchildren focuses on the holistic health orientation, the health status of elementary schoolchildren, and the role of exercise in children's lives.

The Holistic Health Orientation

Oriental physicians, around 2600 B.C. and Greek physicians around 500 B.C. recognized that good habits are essential to good health. Instead of blaming magical thinking or the gods for illness, they realized that human beings have the capability of exercising some control over their health. The physician was viewed as a guide, assisting the patient in restoring a natural physical and emotional balance. In more recent times, medical doctors have tended to specialize. Although this tendency continues, as we move toward the twenty-first century an interest in integrated health care has once again emerged. Family medicine is now viewed as an important approach in caring for children's health problems. A child's illness and health are multidimensional and complex, often requiring knowledge about different medical and psychological disciplines.

The new approach to preventing illness and promoting health is called **holistic health.** Instead of linking a child's illness to a specific cause such as genes or germs, this approach recognizes the complex, multidimensional nature of illness and health. Genes and germs might be involved, say the holistic health advocates, but a better understanding of the child's problem will occur if we know something about psychological factors, the family's life-style, and the nature of the health-care delivery system. Interest in the psychological factors involved in illness and the promotion of health led to the development of a new division in 1978 in the American Psychological Association called health psychology (Matarazzo, 1979). Every indication points toward health psychology playing an increasingly important role in understanding children's illnesses and promoting children's health.

Children's Health Status and Their Understanding of Health

Among the most common ailments of children in the elementary school years are respiratory infections. Children in this age range may get as many as six to seven respiratory infections a year (Behrman & Vaughan, 1983), although the average is 3.5 per year. Colds, gastrointestinal infections, and pneumonia account for more than 70 percent of school absenteeism.

Dental problems also are common in middle and late childhood. Permanent teeth are developing so rapidly in this time frame that children should have their teeth checked every 6 months. Primary teeth begin to fall out around the age of 6. These are replaced by permanent teeth at the rate of about four per year. Children's dental problems continue at a high rate in the United States. By age 12, the majority of children have more than four decayed or filled surfaces in their permanent teeth, and by age 17 more than 11 such dental problems (U.S. Department of Health and Human Services, 1981). But there is some positive news: More than one-third of children have no tooth decay. Fluoride supplements either in the local water supply or in tablet form, seem to be responsible for the reduction in children's cavities we are now witnessing.

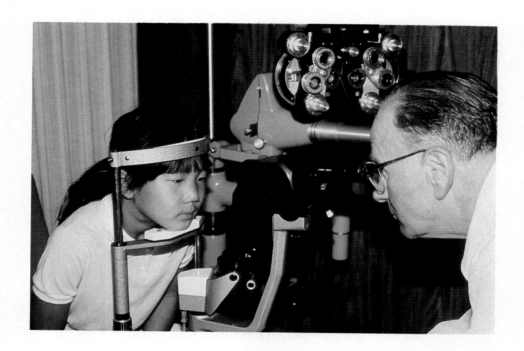

All children should have a visual examination when they enter school, especially since only one-third of all children who need visual correction are identified during the preschool years.

Vision problems also are common for children. Visual maturity is usually reached between the ages of 6 to 7. Although visual screening tests are recommended during the preschool years, all children should have a visual examination when they enter school. Only one-third of the children who need visual correction are identified during the preschool years (Ismail & Lall, 1981). Children with vision problems usually do not complain of poor vision because they do not know how accurately they are supposed to see their world. By age 11, 17 percent of children have poor distance vision and 10 percent have poor near vision, but many of these children have not yet been fitted with eyeglasses.

Hearing problems in children are frequently overlooked. Parents often believe that the hearing-impaired child is just not paying attention, doesn't understand, or easily forgets. Recurrent or chronic ear infections, fluid in the middle ear, frequent exposure to loud noises, and illnesses such as measles or mumps can produce hearing problems. Five percent of children tested do not pass auditory screening tests (Schuster, 1986).

When elementary schoolchildren are asked about their health, they seem to understand that good health is something they have to work at on a regular basis. Early positive attitudes toward health and exercise are thought to be an important factor in the child's ability to maintain a healthy life-style (Ferguson & others, 1989). But while elementary schoolchildren and adolescents may recognize the contributions of nutrition and exercise to health, their behavior does not always follow suit. Adolescents seem to have an especially difficult time applying health information and knowledge to their own personal lives. For example, in one investigation, adolescents reported that they probably would never have a heart attack or a drinking problem but that other adolescents would. The adolescents also said that no relation existed between their risk of heart attack and how much they exercised, smoked, or ate red meat or high-cholesterol foods such as eggs, even though they correctly recognized that factors such as family history influence risk (Weinstein, 1984). Many adolescents appear to have unrealistic, overly optimistic beliefs about their immunity from health risks.

Exercise is an important component of children's lives. Everything we know about children's development suggests that children's lives should be active and involve a number of physical activities.

We are underexercised as a nation. We look instead of play. We ride instead of walk. Our existence deprives us of the minimum of physical activity essential for healthy living.

John F. Kennedy, 1961

Exercise

Many of our patterns of health and illness are longstanding. Our experiences as children contribute to our health practices as adults. Did your parents seek medical help at your first sniffle, or did they wait until your temperature reached 104 degrees? Did they feed you heavy doses of red meat and sugar or a more rounded diet with vegetables and fruit? Did they get you involved in sports or exercise programs, or did you lie around watching television all the time?

Are children getting enough exercise? The 1985 School Fitness Survey tested 18,857 children aged 6 to 17 on nine fitness tasks. Compared to a similar survey in 1975, there was virtually no improvement on the tasks. For example, 40 percent of the boys 6 to 12 years of age could do no more than one pull-up, and a full 25 percent could not do any! Fifty percent of the girls aged 6 to 17 and 30 percent of the boys aged 6 to 12 could not run a mile in less than 10 minutes. In the 50-yard dash, the adolescent girls in 1975 were faster than the adolescent girls in 1985.

Some experts suggest that television is at least partially to blame for the poor physical condition of our nation's children. In one investigation, children who watched little television were significantly more physically fit than their heavy-television-viewing counterparts (Tucker, 1987). The more children watch television, the more they are likely to be overweight. No one is quite sure whether this is because children spend their leisure time in front of the television set instead of chasing each other around the neighborhood or whether they tend to eat a lot of junk food they see advertised on television.

Some of the blame also falls on the nation's schools, many of which fail to provide physical education classes on a daily basis. In the recently completed 1985 School Fitness Survey, 37 percent of the children in the first through the fourth grades take gym classes only once or twice a week. The investigation also revealed that parents are poor role models when it comes to physical fitness. Less than 30 percent of the parents of children in grades 1 through 4 exercised three days a week.

The family plays an important role in children's exercise. A wise strategy is for families to participate in activities that parents and children can enjoy together, such as hiking.

Roughly half said they never get any vigorous exercise. In another study, observations of children's behavior in physical education classes at four different elementary schools revealed how little vigorous exercise is done in these classes (Parcel & others, 1987). Children moved through space only 50 percent of the time they were in the class, and they moved continuously an average of only 2.2 minutes. In summary, not only do children's school weeks not include adequate physical education classes, but the majority of children do not exercise vigorously even when they are in physical education classes. Furthermore, most children's parents are poor role models for vigorous physical exercise.

Does it make a difference if we push children to exercise more vigorously in elementary school? One recent investigation says yes (Tuckman & Hinkle, 1988). One hundred fifty-four elementary schoolchildren were randomly assigned to either three 30-minute running programs per week or to regular attendance in physical education classes. Although the results sometimes varied according to sex, for the most part the cardiovascular health as well as the creativity of children in the running program were enhanced. For example, the boys in this program had less body fat and the girls had more creative involvement in their classrooms.

The family, in addition to the school, plays an important role in the child's exercise program. A wise strategy is for the family to take up activities involving vigorous physical exercise that parents and children can enjoy together. Running, swimming, cycling, and hiking are especially recommended. In encouraging children to exercise more, parents should not push them beyond their physical limits or expose them to competitive pressures that take the fun out of sports and exercise. For example, long-distance running may be too strenuous for young children and could result in bone injuries. Recently, there has been an increase in the number of children competing in strenuous athletic events such as marathons and triathalons. Doctors are beginning to see some injuries in children that they previously saw only in adults. Some injuries, such as stress fractures and tendonitis, stem from the overuse of young, still-growing bodies (Risser, 1989). If left to their own devices, how many 8-year-old children would want to prepare for a marathon? It is recommended that parents downplay cutthroat striving and encourage healthy sports that children can enjoy (Puffer, 1987).

Thinking Critically
Imagine that you are the physical education coordinator for the elementary schools in a large city. Describe the ideal program you would want to implement to improve children's physical fitness.

Stress and Coping

An exciting prospect of health psychology is that psychological principles can be used to prevent illness and promote health in children or to reduce illness and restore health even when children have learned bad health habits (Hurrelmann, 1989). So far in this book, we have discussed many different aspects of nutrition, illness, and exercise that affect children's health. Understanding children's health from a holistic perspective also requires information about the nature of stress and coping.

No one knows whether today's children experience more stress than their predecessors did, but it does seem that their stressors have increased. Among the stress-related questions we evaluate are: What is the body's response to stress? How are life events and daily hassles related to children's stress? How is Type A behavior related to children's stress? How can children cope with stress? How do children cope with death?

The Body's Response to Stress

According to the Austrian-born founding father of stress research, the late Hans Selye (1974, 1983), stress is simply the wear and tear the body suffers as a result of the demands placed on it. To describe the common effects on the body when demands are placed on it, Selye developed the concept of the **general adaptation syndrome,** which moves through three stages. In the first stage, the alarm stage, the child's body detects the presence of stress and tries to eliminate it. Muscle tone is lost, temperature decreases, and blood pressure drops. Then, a rebound called countershock occurs. The adrenal cortex enlarges and hormone release increases. The alarm stage is short. Before long, the child moves into a more prolonged defense against stress, the resistance stage. The child tries an all-out effort to combat stress. If the effort fails and the stress persists, the child goes into the exhaustion stage, during which time defenses degenerate rapidly. As the exhaustion deepens, the strain on the child's body increases. The strain usually is felt the most in the child's weakest parts. For one child, the strain might produce high blood pressure; for another, depression; and for yet another, migraine headaches.

Most research on stress has focused on negative experiences. As yet, we know little about the nature of stress that occurs when a child is chosen to be captain of the team or wins first place in a science fair. Adults rank these kinds of positive experiences as having low levels of stress for children. Selye (1983) recognized that not all stress is bad for children. He called the positive features of stress, **eustress.**

Life Events and Daily Hassles

Children can experience a spectrum of stresses that range from ordinary to severe (Brenner, 1984; Dubow & Tisak, inpress). At the ordinary end are experiences that occur in most children's lives and for which there are reasonably well defined coping patterns. For example, most parents are aware that siblings are jealous of each other and that when one sibling does well at something, the other sibling or siblings will be jealous. They know how jealousy works and ways they can help children cope with it. More severe stress occurs when children are separated from their parents. Healthy coping patterns for this stressful experience are not spelled out well. Some children are well cared for, but others are ignored when divorce, death, illness, or

(a)

(b)

(a) The tense life of this child living in poverty does not show up on scales of life events, yet the everyday pounding such children experience can add up to a highly stressful life. (b) Children's daily uplifts, such as the rewarding feeling this boy is having because of his mother's positive comments about his computer skills, are also important to examine in our effort to understand children's stress and coping.

foster placement causes a separation (Honig, 1986). Even more severe are the experiences of children who have lived for years with neglect or abuse. Victims of incest also experience severe stress and have difficulty coping with their unwanted experiences.

In many instances, more than one stress occurs at a time in a child's life. When several stresses are combined, the effects may be compounded. For example, in one investigation, Michael Rutter (1979) found that boys and girls who were under two chronic life stresses were four times as likely to eventually need psychological services as those who had to cope with only one chronic stress. A similar multiplier effect was found in children who experienced more than one short-term strain at a time.

Recently, psychologists have emphasized that life's daily experiences as well as life's major events may be the culprits in stress. Enduring a tense family life and living in poverty do not show up on scales of major life events in children's development, yet the everyday pounding children take from these living conditions can add up to a highly stressful life and eventually psychological disturbance or illness (Compas, 1989; Folkman & others, 1986; Lazarus & Folkman, 1984; Wertlieb, 1989). More about the daily hassles and uplifts in the lives of children appears in Children 11.2.

It's not the large things that send a man to the madhouse . . . No, it's the continuing series of small tragedies that send a man to the madhouse . . . Not the death of his love but a shoelace that snaps with no time left.

Charles Bukowski

Daily Hassles and Uplifts in Children's Lives

Robbie is a sixth-grade boy. He gets punished a lot for doing things wrong, and he also feels that he gets punished a lot even when he doesn't do things wrong. He hasn't been doing well in school, and his father yelled at him last night for not working on his homework. The night before, his mother and father got into a big argument, and his mother threw a lamp across the room and broke it. Last week at school, Robbie got into a fight with another kid and was sent to the principal's office for discipline. His best friend moved away two months ago, and since that time Robbie hasn't found anyone he likes nearly as well. Robbie's life is filled with daily hassles.

Stephanie is a sixth-grade girl. She gets good marks at school, enjoys playing with her friends, and feels that her teacher is pleased with her. Her parents spend a lot of time with her, and last week she enjoyed going out to dinner with them. Yesterday her mother took her shopping and bought her a new dress. Stephanie also enjoys talking on the phone with her friends. She plays goalie on her girl's soccer team, and two days ago her team won, a victory that moved them into first place in their league.

In a recent research investigation, Allen Kanner and his colleagues (1987) studied the daily hassles and daily uplifts of 232 sixth-grade boys and girls. As shown in Tables 11.A and 11.B, the daily experiences of Robbie and Stephanie represent the types of hassles and uplifts young adolescents encounter as they go through their everyday lives. In general, boys and girls reported the same number of hassles and uplifts.

The researchers also examined the relationship of the hassles and uplifts to the presence of anxiety, depression, distress, self-restraint, perceived support from friends, perceived competence, and general self-worth. The results were in the expected direction: Daily hassles were associated with negative outcomes, and daily uplifts were associated with positive outcomes. Uplifts were especially important in contributing to adaptive outcomes. ◆

TABLE 11.A   *Percentage of Sample Endorsing Items on the Children's Hassles Scale*

Item Content	Percentage of Occurrence*
You had to clean up your room.	83
You felt bored and wished there was something interesting to do.	81
Another kid could do something better than you could.	75
You lost something.	73
Your brothers and sisters bugged you.	73
You got punished when you did something wrong.	66
You didn't like the way you looked and wished you could be different (taller, stronger, better-looking).	66
You had to go to bed when you didn't feel like it.	64
Your mother or father forgot to do something they said they would do.	62
Kids at school teased you.	61
Your mother or father got sick.	59
Your schoolwork was too hard.	59
You didn't know the answer when the teacher called on you.	58

From A. D. Kanner, et al., "Uplifts, Hassles, and Adaptational Outcomes in Early Adolescents" in *Journal of Early Adolescence*, 7:371–394, 1987. Copyright © 1987 Sage Publications, Inc., Newbury Park, California. Reprinted by permission.
*Refers to the percentage of children who said the item made them feel bad.

Stress, Illness, and Type A Behavior

What do migraine headaches, indigestion, high blood pressure, and hives have in common? They are all stress-related ailments. It has long been known that life's hassles can produce ulcers, asthma, high blood pressure, skin eruptions, migraine headaches, and allergy attacks. In recent years, though, considerable attention also has been given to the **Type A behavioral pattern**—a cluster of characteristics that include being excessively competitive, having an accelerated pace of ordinary activities, being impatient, doing several things at the same time, and being unable to

Item Content	Percentage of Occurrence*
Your mother or father didn't have enough time to do something with you.	57
Your mother or father wasn't home when you expected them.	55
You didn't have enough privacy (a time and place to be alone) when you wanted it.	54
You were punished for something you didn't do.	50
You didn't do well at sports.	45
Your teacher was mad at you because of your behavior.	44
Your mother and father were fighting.	43
When the kids were picking teams, you were one of the last ones to be picked.	39
Your pet died.	36
Your mother or father was mad at you for getting a bad school report.	35
You got into a fight with another kid.	35
Your best friend didn't want to be your best friend anymore.	30

TABLE 11.B *Percentage of Sample Endorsing Items on the Children's Uplifts Scale*

Item Content	Percentage of Occurrence
You got a good mark at school.	95
You had a good time playing with your friends.	93
Your teacher was pleased with you.	89
You went out to eat.	88
There was a school holiday.	88
Your mother or father spent time with you.	87
You got a phone call or a letter.	87
You had fun joking with the kids at school.	83
You learned something new.	83
You got some new clothes.	82
Your friends wanted you to be on their team.	81
Your parents were pleased with a good grade that you got.	80
You did something special with your mother or father.	79
You made or fixed something by yourself.	78
You won a game.	77
You got a present you really wanted.	76
You did well at sports.	75
You found something you thought you had lost.	73
You helped your brother or sister.	71
You made a new friend.	68
You played with your pet.	64
Your mother or father agreed with you that something wasn't your fault.	64
You were helped by your brother or sister.	63
You had a good time at a party.	60
You gave a talk at school that went well.	41

From A. D. Kanner, et al., "Uplifts, Hassles, and Adaptational Outcomes in Early Adolescents" in *Journal of Early Adolescence*, 7:381, 1987. Copyright © 1987 Sage Publications, Inc., Newbury Park, California. Reprinted by permission.

Note: The numbers reflect the percentage of children who indicated that the item made them feel good.

hide the fact that time is a struggle in life (Friedman & Rosenman, 1974). Most of the research on Type A behavior has been conducted with adults. Currently, the Type A behavior cluster is controversial. Some researchers argue that only specific components of the cluster, especially hostility, are linked with coronary disease (Dembrowski & Czajkowski, 1989; Siegman, 1989; Williams, 1989). Others still believe that the Type A behavioral cluster as a whole is related to cardiovascular disease (Fischman, 1987).

Danger in the Texture of Bianca's Life

Two low-lying, dilapidated brick housing projects border the neighborhood where 9-year-old Bianca lives. Just around the corner from Bianca's house is a middle school where teenagers and some school dropouts hang out, selling drugs and causing trouble. They spill into Bianca's neighborhood, producing ripples of fear, especially in young children. One sunny afternoon, Bianca rides her bicycle up and down the street. She does not stray far from home. A few blocks away, another child, about Bianca's age, is hit on the head and knocked off his new bike by an older boy, who rides away on the bicycle.

"I could see two men jump out of a car and grab me," says Bianca. "I yelled at the bus driver to let me off. When he turned toward me, he was wearing a hood, and his eyes were big flames of fire like he was the devil. He was laughing and wouldn't open the door. I couldn't get out of the bus. I started yelling and screaming. I have never been so scared in my life." At that instant, Bianca's mother runs into her room to see what is wrong as she responds to her screams. She wakes Bianca up and tells her, "Don't worry, honey, it's only a dream. You will be fine." Her mother hugs her and continues to reassure her (Ludtke, 1988). ◆

"You're a Type A just like your father."

Reprinted from Psychology Today *Magazine. Copyright © 1986 American Psychological Association.*

Recent research with children does reveal that those with a Type A behavioral pattern have more illnesses, cardiovascular symptoms, muscle tension, and sleep disturbances (Eagleston & others, in press; Thoresen & others, 1985). Some researchers have found that Type A children are more likely to have Type A parents. This association seems to be stronger for fathers and sons than for parents and daughters (Eagleston & others, in press; Weidner, Sexton, Matarazzo, & Friend, 1988). In one investigation, when Type A parents were observed interacting with their sons and daughters, the parents often criticized their failures and compared them to others when evaluating their performance (Eagleston & others, in press). Such stressful family experiences may set the tone for ineffective ways of coping with stress and a tendency to develop cardiovascular symptoms. In other research, the Type A behavioral pattern was more stable among adolescents than among children (Steinberg, 1986).

One large-scale investigation, the Bogalusa Heart Study, involves an ongoing evaluation of 8,000 boys and girls in Bogalusa, Louisiana (Berensen, 1989, Downey & others, 1987). Observations show that the precursors of heart disease begin at a young age with many children already possessing one or more clinical risk factors—hypertension, obesity, or adverse lipoprotein changes. Based on the Bogalusa Heart Study, a cardiovascular health intervention model for children and young adolescents has been developed. The model is called Heart Smart. An overview of Heart Smart is given in Children 11.3.

Coping with Stress

How can children cope with stress? In some cases, certain coping techniques may be used more at one developmental level than another (Altshuler & Ruble, in press; Brenner, 1984). For example, 3-year-old children are more likely to cope with loneliness by inventing imaginary companions than are 10-year-olds. Yet most coping

Heart Smart

The school is the focus of the Heart Smart intervention. Since 95 percent of children and adolescents aged 5 to 18 are in school, schools are an efficient context in which to educate individuals about health. Special attention is given to teachers, who serve as role models. Teachers who value the role of health in life and who engage in health-enhancing behavior present children and adolescents with positive models for health. Teacher in-service education is conducted by an interdisciplinary team of specialists including physicians, psychologists, nutritionists, physical educators, and exercise physiologists. The school's staff is introduced to heart health education, the nature of cardiovascular disease, and risk factors for heart disease. Coping behavior, exercise behavior, and eating behavior are discussed with the staff. And a Heart Smart curricula is explained. For example, the Heart Smart curricula for grade 5 includes the content areas of cardiovascular health (such as risk factors associated with heart disease), behavior skills (for example, self-assessment and monitoring), eating behavior (for example, the effects of food on health), and exercise behavior (for example, the effects of food on health), and exercise behavior (for example, the effects of exercise on the heart).

The physical education component of Heart Smart involves two to four class periods each week to incorporate a "Superkids-Superfit" exercise program. The physical education instructor teaches skills required by the school system plus aerobic activities aimed at cardiovascular conditioning including jogging, race walking, interval workouts, rope skipping, circuit training, aerobic dance, and games. Classes begin and end with five minutes of walking and stretching.

The school lunch program serves as an intervention site where sodium, fat, and sugar levels are decreased. Children and adolescents are given reasons why they should eat healthy foods such as a tuna sandwich and why they should not eat unhealthy foods such as a hot dog with chili. The school lunch program includes a salad bar where children and adolescents can serve themselves. The amount and type of snack foods sold on the school premises is monitored.

High-risk children—those with elevated blood pressure, cholesterol, and weight—are identified as part of Heart Smart. A multidisciplinary team of physicians, nutritionists, nurses, and behavioral counselors work with the high-risk boys and girls and their parents through group-oriented activities and individual-based family counseling. High-risk boys and girls and their parents receive diet, exercise, and relaxation prescriptions in an intensive 12-session program, followed by long-term monthly evaluations.

Extensive assessment is a part of this ongoing program. Short-term and long-term changes in children's knowledge about cardiovascular disease and changes in their behavior are being assessed. ◆

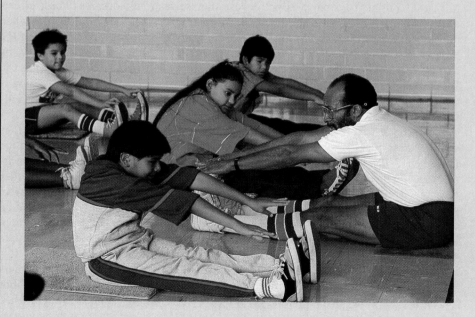

A gymnastics class for third and fourth grades at the Govalle School in Austin, Texas. One of the most important components of heart disease prevention programs is a regular, vigorous exercise workout.

mechanisms can be used effectively throughout the childhood years. As part of coping with stress, children usually call on more than one strategy at a time. For example, on the day when Brian's kitten died, he constructed a shoe box coffin for it, which he ceremonially buried in the backyard. A favorite television show helped him to keep his mind off the loss for a while, he spoke sadly of the kitten at supper, was distracted by a game of cards with his older brother, then returned to his grieving at bedtime, crying himself to sleep. Most of the time, children are not conscious of their coping strategies. They simply act without thinking when they are under stress. For example, when his brother went away to college, Kevin responded by spending hours perfecting minute details on his model airplanes. The concentration made him feel better, but he was not aware that this was a way of coping with sadness and loss.

It is important to determine whether children's coping modes are a way of avoiding or facing stress. Strategies that allow children to go on with their lives without confronting the causes of the tension are usually believed to be more useful over the short term. Adaptations that acknowledge and accept the stress are usually believed to be more useful over the long term (Brenner, 1984).

What are some of the ways children avoid stress? Denial, regression, withdrawal, and impulsive acting out are the most common responses. When children use *denial,* they act as if the stress does not exist. For example, a 7-year-old girl goes on playing with her toys while being told that her father has died. Denial can relieve pain and can help to preserve a child's equilibrium. Children also may deny by using fantasy to mask reality. For example, 3-year-old Bob constructs an imaginary friend to keep him company. When children act younger than their years and engage in earlier behaviors, they are using *regression.* For example, children may become dependent and demanding. This may lead to more physical comforting and affection than usual, thus reducing stress. *Withdrawal* is when children remove themselves either physically or mentally from the stress. They might run away from the stressful environment or become very quiet or almost invisible. To escape mentally, they might focus on their pet or lose themselves in daydreams. These efforts afford them temporary refuge from the stress. *Impulsive acting out* occurs when children act impulsively and sometimes flamboyantly to avoid thinking either of the past or of the consequences of their current actions. They conceal their pain by making others angry at them, seeking easy and quick solutions to reduce their misery. By doing so, they draw attention to themselves, and momentarily their tension is eased. However, in the long run, this coping strategy is almost guaranteed to be self-destructive.

In contrast to these evasive strategies, there are ways children accept and face stress. These include altruism, humor, suppression, anticipation, and sublimation (Brenner, 1984; Vaillant, 1977). As with the evasive strategies, each of these strategies has both positive and negative aspects. When children use *altruism,* they forget their own troubles by helping others, especially their parents and siblings. They feel good about their helper role. However, sometimes children who use altruism as a coping strategy do not let themselves be carefree. Their seriousness may push them into adultlike behavior too early in their development. Children also sometimes joke about their difficulties, using humor to express anger and tension. However, if this is taken to its extreme, children may lose the ability to cry and to reach out to others for help. *Suppression* allows children to set aside their tensions temporarily. For hours they may forget their cares, yet they are not afraid to go back to them when their free time is over. When a family death occurs, preschool children may unconsciously suppress the knowledge. They may cry for a while, then go and play as if nothing happened. The negative side is that children may suppress feelings to the point of denial. Children who use *anticipation* are able to foresee and plan for their

Participation in various activities can give children under stress a great deal of satisfaction and helps them to cope with the stress.

next stressful episode. When the stress appears, they are better prepared to protect themselves and to accept what they cannot avoid. Anticipation can be a strong coping mechanism. It becomes negative when children become too fearful and develop compulsive needs to know and plan in rigid, overly compulsive ways. With *sublimation,* children discover ways to vent their anger, overcome their fears, or express their sadness by becoming absorbed in games, sports, or hobbies. These activities are enjoyable and compensate for their stress. Sublimation becomes negative when children become so engrossed in these activities that they ignore other pleasures or family needs.

How can parents, teachers, and helping professionals most effectively work with children in stressful circumstances? Avis Brenner (1984) proposes three intelligent strategies: removing at least one stressor; teaching new coping strategies; and showing children ways they can transfer existing coping strategies to other, more appropriate life circumstances.

Based on Michael Rutter's (1979) research indicating the multiple effects of stress, it makes sense that removing one stress or hassle can help children feel stronger and more competent. For example, consider Lisa, who had been coming to school hungry each morning. Her teacher arranged for Lisa to have a hot breakfast at school each morning, which improved her concentration in school. This in turn helped Lisa to suppress for a time her anxieties about her parents' impending divorce.

Children who have a number of coping techniques seem to have the best chance of adapting and functioning competently in the face of stress. By learning new coping techniques, children may no longer feel as incompetent, and their self-confidence may improve. For example, Kim was relieved when a clinical psychologist helped her to anticipate what it would be like to visit her seriously ill sister. She had been frightened by the hospital and used withdrawal as part of her coping, saying she did not want to see her sister, even though she missed her a great deal. Children tend to apply their coping strategies only in the situations in which stress develops. Adults can show children how to use these coping skills to their best advantage in many other situations as well. For example, Jennifer used altruism to cope when her mother was hospitalized for cancer. She coped with the separation by mothering her father, her little brother, and her classmates. Her classmates quickly became annoyed with her and began to tease her. Jennifer's teacher at school recognized the problem and helped Jennifer express her altruism by taking care of the class's pet animals and by being responsible for some daily cleanup chores. Her mothering of the children stopped, and so did the teasing. By following such guidelines, both professionals and laypeople can help children cope more effectively with stress.

Coping with Death

Children who have healthy and positive relationships with their parents before a parent dies cope with the death more effectively than children with unhappy prior relationships with the parent. The years of warmth and caring have probably taught the child effective ways of coping with such a traumatic event. Also, children who are given high-quality care by surviving family members during the mourning period, or who are effectively helped by caregivers in other contexts, experience less separation distress (Brenner, 1984; Garmezy, 1983).

Sometimes the death of a sibling is even more difficult for children to understand and accept than the loss of a parent. Many children believe that only old people die, so the death of a child may stimulate children to think about their own immortality. The majority of children, though, seem to be able to cope with a sibling's death effectively if they are helped through a mourning period.

Knowing what children think about death can help adults to understand their behavior in the period following the loss of a parent or sibling (Brenner, 1984). When a 3-year-old boy creeps from his bed every night and runs down the street searching for his mother who has just died, is he mourning for her? When a 6-year-old girl spends an entire afternoon drawing pictures of graveyards and coffins, is she grieving? When a 9-year-old boy can't wait to go back to school after the funeral so he can tell his classmates about how his sister died, is he denying grief? All of these are ways in which children cope with death. And all follow children's logic.

Children 3 to 5 years old think that dead people continue to live, but under changed circumstances (Lonetto, 1980). The missing person is simply missing, and young children expect the person to return at some point. When the person does not come back, they may feel hurt or angry at being abandoned. They may declare that they want to go to heaven to bring the dead person home. They may ask their caregivers where the dead person's house is, where the dead person eats, and why the dead person won't be cold if the person is buried without a coat and hat in winter.

Though children vary somewhat in the age at which they begin to understand death, the limitations of preoperational thought make it difficult for a child to comprehend death before the age of 7 or 8. Young children blame themselves for the death of someone they knew well, believing that the event may have happened because they disobeyed the person who died. Children under 6 rarely understand that death is universal, inevitable, and final. Instead, young children usually think that only people who want to die, or who are bad or careless, actually do die. At some

Health, Stress, and Coping

Concept	Processes and Related Ideas	Characteristics and Description
Health	The holistic health orientation	Instead of linking illness only to a specific cause such as genes or germs, this approach recognizes the complex, multidimensional nature of illness and health. Includes focus on psychological factors and life-style.
	Children's health status and their understanding of health	Among the common ailments of the elementary school years are respiratory, dental, vision, and hearing problems. Elementary schoolchildren seem to understand that health is something that has to be worked at on a regular basis, but many of them do not adopt good health habits.
	Exercise	Every indication suggests that our nation's children are not getting enough exercise. Television viewing, parents being poor role models for children's exercise, and the lack of adequate physical education classes in schools may be to blame.
Stress and Coping	The body's response to stress	Selye described stress as the wear and tear on the body due to the demands placed on it. He developed the concept of the general adaptation syndrome, which moves through three stages. Most research on stress focuses on negative experiences (distress), but in some instances stress may be positive (eustress).
	Life events and daily hassles	Children can experience a spectrum of stresses that range from ordinary to severe. Two or more stresses can have multiplier effects. Recently, it has been argued that life's daily hassles and uplifts are important to consider in evaluating children's stress.
	Stress, illness, and Type A behavior	Stress can be involved in illnesses such as migraine headaches, ulcers, asthma, skin problems, allergy attacks, and high blood pressure. Children with a Type A behavioral pattern do have more illnesses, cardiovascular symptoms, muscle tension, and sleep disturbances. Debate focuses on the precise nature of the Type A components and the role of parents.
	Coping with stress	Avoiding stress is wiser as a short-term strategy than as a long-term strategy. Avoiding stress can be accomplished by denial, regression, withdrawal, and impulsive acting out. Accepting and facing stress include altruism, humor, suppression, anticipation, and sublimation. Adults can help children deal with stress by removing at least one stressor, teaching new coping strategies, and showing the children how to transfer stress to other circumstances.
	Coping with death	A positive close relationship with a parent before the death of the parent and high-quality care by surviving individuals help a child to cope. Young children do not understand the nature of death, believing that it is not final. By the middle of the elementary school years, they comprehend its final, irreversible nature.

point around the middle of the elementary school years, children begin to grasp the concept that death is the end of life and is not reversible. They come to realize that they too will die someday.

Thus far, we have discussed several ideas about children's health, stress, and coping. These ideas are summarized in Concept Table 11.2. This concludes our discussion of physical development in middle and late childhood. In the next chapter, we will turn our attention to children's cognitive development in middle and late childhood.

Summary

I. **The Skeletal and Muscular Systems**
During the elementary school years, children grow an average of 2 to 3 inches a year. Muscle mass and strength gradually increase. Legs become longer and trunks slimmer as "baby fat" decreases. Growth is slow and consistent.

II. **Motor Skills**
During the middle and late childhood years, children's motor development becomes much smoother and more coordinated. Children gain greater control over their bodies and can sit and attend for longer periods of time. However, their lives should be activity focused and very active. Increased myelinization of the central nervous system is reflected in improved fine motor skills. Improved fine motor development is reflected in children's writing skills over the course of middle and late childhood. Boys are usually better at gross motor skills, girls at fine motor skills.

III. **Scope and Education of Handicapped Children**
As estimated 10 to 15 percent of children in the United States are handicapped in some way. Public Law 94–142 ordered a free, appropriate education for every handicapped child. The law emphasizes an individually tailored program for every child and provision of a least restrictive environment, which has led to extensive mainstreaming of handicapped children into the regular classroom. Mainstreaming has been a controversial topic. Another issue is the labeling of handicapped children and its benefits and drawbacks.

IV. **Learning Disabilities**
Children with learning disabilities have normal or above-normal intelligence, have difficulties in some areas but not in others, and do not suffer from some other disorder that could explain their learning problems. Learning disabilities are complex and multifaceted and require precise analysis.

V. **Attention-Deficit Disorder**
This is a disorder that is classified under learning disabilities. Sometimes called hyperactivity, it describes children who are extremely active, impulsive, distractible, and excitable. Possible causes include heredity, prenatal damage, diet, family dynamics, and the physical environment. Amphetamines have been used with some success in the treatment of the disorder but they do not work with all hyperactive children.

VI. **The Holistic Health Orientation**
A holistic health orientation has become increasingly popular. Instead of linking illness only to a specific cause, such as genes or germs, the approach recognizes the complex, multidimensional nature of illness and health. It emphasizes psychological factors and life-style.

VII. **Children's Health Status and Their Understanding of Health**
Among the common ailments of the elementary school years are respiratory, dental, vision, and hearing problems. Elementary schoolchildren seem to understand that health is something that has to be worked at on a regular basis, but many children do not adopt good health habits.

VIII. **Exercise**
Every indication suggests that our nation's children are not getting enough exercise. Television viewing, parents being poor role models for exercise, and the lack of adequate physical education classes in schools may be the culprits.

IX. **The Body's Response to Stress, Life Events, and Daily Hassles**
Hans Selye described stress as the wear and tear on the body because of the demands placed on it. He developed the concept of the general adaptation syndrome, which moves through three stages. Most research on stress focuses on negative experiences (distress) but in some instances stress may be positive (eustress).

Children can experience a spectrum of stresses that range from ordinary to severe. Two or more stresses can have multiplier effects. Recently, it has been argued that life's daily hassles and uplifts are important to consider in evaluating children's stress.

X. **Stress, Illness, and Type A Behavior**

Stress can be involved in illnesses such as migraine headaches, ulcers, asthma, skin problems, allergy attacks, and high blood pressure. Children with a Type A behavioral pattern do have more illnesses, cardiovascular symptoms, muscle tension, and sleep disturbances. Debate focuses on the precise nature of the Type A components and the role of parents.

XI. **Coping with Stress**

Avoiding stress is wiser as a short-term strategy than as a long-term strategy. Avoiding stress can be accomplished by denial, regression, withdrawal, and impulsive acting out. Ways of accepting and facing stress include altruism, humor, suppression, anticipation, and sublimation. Adults can help children deal with stress by removing at least one stressor, teaching new coping strategies, and showing children how to transfer feelings of stress to other circumstances.

XII. **Coping with Death**

A positive close relationship with a parent before the death of the parent and high-quality care by surviving individuals help the child to cope. Young children do not understand death, believing that it is not final. By the middle of the elementary school years, children comprehend its final, irreversible nature.

Key Terms

Public Law 94–142 352
least restrictive
environment 352
mainstreaming 352

learning disabilities 354
attention-deficit
disorder 354
holistic health 358

general adaptation
syndrome 362
eustress 362
Type A behavioral
pattern 364

Suggested Readings

Batshaw, M. L., & Perret, Y. M. (1986). *Children with handicaps*. Baltimore: Brookes.
A comprehensive treatment of handicapped children. Includes chapters on dental care, vision, hearing, attention-deficit disorder, and cerebal palsy.

Brenner, A. (1984). *Helping children cope with stress*. Lexington, MA: D. C. Heath.
An excellent, insightful portrayal of children's stress and effective ways to cope with the stress.

Journal of School Health
This journal includes a number of articles about children's nutrition, health, illness, and exercise. Leaf through the issues of the last several years to get a feel for the type of interventions being used in school settings to improve children's health.

Melamed, B. G., Matthews, K., Routh, D. K., Stabler, B., & Schniederman, N. (Eds.). (1988). *Child health psychology*. Hillsdale, NJ: Erlbaum.
Includes chapters by experts on child health psychology. Ideas about prevention and life-style, personality and emotional behavior, developmental aspects of illness, and chronic health problems in children are covered.

Reid, D. K. (1988). *Teaching the learning disabled*. Boston, MA: Allyn & Bacon.
A recent, up-to-date, authoritative treatment of learning disabilities, including many valuable suggestions for working with learning-disabled students.

Children are remarkable for their intelligence
and ardor, for their curiosity, their intolerance
of shams, the clarity . . . of their vision.

Aldous Huxley

Cognitive Development

ntelligence and intelligence tests frequently make the news. The following story appeared in the *Los Angeles Times:*

> IQ testing that leads to the placement of an unusually large number of black children in so-called mentally retarded classes has been ruled unconstitutional by a federal judge. On behalf of five black children, Chief District Court Judge Robert Peckham said the use of standardized IQ tests to place children in educable mentally retarded (EMR) classes violated recently enacted federal laws and the state and federal constitutions. . . . Peckham said the history of IQ testing and special education in California "revealed an unlawful discriminatory intent . . . not necessarily to hurt black children, but it was an intent to assign a grossly disproportionate number of black children to the special, inferior and dead-end EMR classes." (October 18, 1979)

As you might expect, this story sparked impassioned debate (Kail & Pellegrino, 1985). The use of IQ tests to selectively place children in special classes continues to be debated.

Robert Sternberg recalls being terrified of taking IQ tests as a child. He says that he froze when the time came to take such tests. When he was in the sixth grade, he was sent to take an IQ test with the fifth graders; he still talks about how embarrassing and humiliating the experience was. Sternberg recalls that maybe he was dumb, but knows that he wasn't *that* dumb. He finally overcame his anxieties about IQ tests and performed much better on them. Sternberg became so fascinated with IQ tests that he devised his own at the age of 13 and began assessing the intellectual abilities of his classmates until the school psychologist scolded him. Later in the chapter, you will see that Sternberg recently has developed a provocative theory of intelligence.

Intellectual performance and achievement are prized by our society and promoted by parents who enthusiastically encourage their charges to become brighter and more strongly motivated to achieve success. During middle and late childhood, the push for intellectual performance and achievement becomes more apparent to childen than earlier in their development. Now, they are usually spending far more of their time in the achievement setting of school and are placed in circumstances that call on them to exhibit their intellectual skills in more pressurized ways than when they were in early childhood. Our coverage of children's cognitive development in middle and late childhood focuses on Piaget's theory and concrete operational thought, information processing, intelligence, language, and achievement.

Piaget's Theory and Concrete Operational Thought

According to Piaget (1967), the preschool child's thought is preoperational. Preoperational thought involves the formation of stable concepts, the emergence of mental reasoning, the prominence of egocentrism, and the construction of magical belief systems. Thought during the preschool years is still flawed and not well organized. Piaget believed that concrete operational thought does not appear until about the age of 7, but as we saw in Chapter 9, Piaget may have underestimated some of the cognitive skills of preschool children. For example, by carefully and cleverly designing experiments on understanding the concept of number, Rochel Gelman (1972) demonstrated that some preschool childen show conservation, a concrete operational skill. In Chapter 9, we explored concrete operational thought by

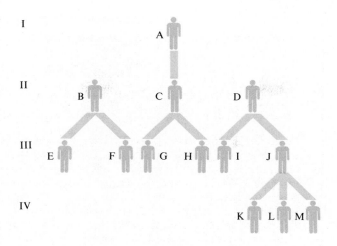

FIGURE 12.1 A family tree of four generations (I–IV). The preoperational child has trouble classifying the members of the four generations; the concrete operational child can classify the members vertically, horizontally, and obliquely (up and down and across).

describing the preschool child's flaws in thinking about such concrete operational skills as conservation and classification; here we will cover the characteristics of concrete operational thought again, this time emphasizing the competencies of elementary schoolchildren. Applications of Piaget's ideas to children's education and an evaluation of Piaget's theory are also considered.

Concrete Operational Thought

Remember that, according to Piaget, concrete operational thought is made up of operations—mental actions or representations that are reversible. In the well-known test of reversibility of thought involving conservation of matter, the child is presented with two identical balls of clay. The experimenter rolls one ball into a long, thin shape; the other remains in its original ball shape. The child is then asked if there is more clay in the ball or in the long, thin piece of clay. By the time children reach the age of 7 or 8, most answer that the amount of clay is the same. To answer this problem correctly, children have to imagine that the clay ball is rolled out into a long, thin strip and then returned to its original round shape. This type of imagination involves a reversible mental action. Thus, a concrete operation is a reversible mental action on real, concrete objects. Concrete operations allow the child to coordinate several characteristics rather than focus on a single property of an object. In the clay example, the preoperational child is likely to focus on height *or* width. The concrete operational child coordinates information about both dimensions.

Many of the concrete operations identified by Piaget focus on the way children reason about the properties of objects. One important skill that characterizes the concrete operational child is the ability to classify or divide things into different sets or subsets and to consider their interrelationships. An example of the concrete operational child's classification skills involves a family tree of four generations (Figure 12.1) (Furth & Wachs, 1975). This family tree suggests that the grandfather (A) has three children (B, C, & D), each of whom has two children (E through J), and that one of these children (J) has three children (K, L, & M). A child who comprehends the classification system can move up and down a level (vertically), across a level (horizontally), and up and down and across (obliquely) within the system. The concrete operational child understands that person J can at the same time be father, brother, and grandson, for example.

Classification Skills of the African Kpelle

Remembering or classifying lists of unrelated objects can be unusual activities outside literate or school-related activities. The most appropriate categories in literate circumstances may not be valued in other circumstances. For example, in one investigation of a classification problem given to members of the Kpelle culture in Liberia (located on the eastern coast of Africa), the individuals sorted 20 objects into functional groups—such as knife with an apple, and a potato with a hoe—rather than into categories the researcher considered correct (Glick, 1975). Upon further questioning, the Kpelle said that this was the way a wise person would do things. The researcher asked how a fool would classify the objects. He was told what he initially expected to be the correct answers, such as four neat piles of food in one category, four tools in another category, and so on.

   The subjects in the Kpelle study were illiterate and had no schooling. Individuals who have had more schooling—such as older children and individuals in Western cultures—may excel on many cognitive tasks because the skills and social situations involved in testing resemble the activities practiced in schools. In everyday life, people classify and remember things to achieve functional goals. In schools and on tests, they perform to satisfy an adult's request. Persons with little schooling have more experience in doing cognitive activities at the request of an adult without having a clear practical goal (Rogoff & Mistry, in press; Rogoff & Morelli, 1989).   ◆

While concrete operational thought is more advanced than preoperational thought, it has its limitations. Concrete operational thought is limited in that the child needs to have clearly available perceptual physical supports. That is, the child needs to have objects and events present to reason about them. The concrete operational thinker is not capable of imagining the necessary steps to complete an algebraic equation, for example. More information about thought that is more advanced than concrete operational thought appears in Chapter 15, where we discuss formal operational thought.

Piaget and Education

Americans interested in improving children's intellect moved swiftly to embrace Piaget and apply his ideas to children's education (Murray, 1978). Two social crises, the proliferation of behaviorism and the psychometric IQ approach to intelligence, made the adoption of Piaget's theory inevitable. The first social crisis was the post-Sputnik concern of a country preoccupied with its deteriorating position as the world's leader in engineering and science, and the second was the need for compensatory education for minority groups and the poor. Curriculum projects that soon came into being after these social crises included the "new math," Science Curriculum Improvement Study, Project Physics, and Man: A Course of Study. All of these projects were based on Piaget's notion of cognitive developmental changes. Piaget's theory contains information about the child's reasoning in math, science, and logic—information not found anywhere else in developmental psychology.

Piaget was not an educator and never pretended to be. But he did provide a sound conceptual framework from which to view educational problems. What are some of the principles in Piaget's theory of cognitive development that can be applied to children's education? David Elkind (1976) described three. First, the foremost issue in education is *communication*. In Piaget's theory, the child's mind is not a blank slate; to the contrary, the child has a host of ideas about the physical and natural world, but these ideas differ from those of adults. We must learn to comprehend what children are saying and to respond in the same mode of discourse that children use. Second, the child is always unlearning and relearning in addition to acquiring knowledge. Children come to school with their own ideas about space, time, causality, quantity, and number. Third, the child is by nature a knowing creature, motivated to acquire knowledge. The best way to nurture this motivation for knowledge is to allow the child to spontaneously interact with the environment; education needs to ensure that it does not dull the child's eagerness to know by providing an overly rigid curricula that disrupts the child's own rhythm and pace of learning.

Piagetian Contributions and Criticisms

Piaget was a genius at observing children, and his insights are often surprisingly easy to verify. Piaget showed us some important things to look for in development, including the shift from preoperational to concrete operational thought. He also showed us how we must make experiences fit our cognitive framework, yet simultaneously adapt our cognitive orientation to experience. Piaget also revealed how cognitive change is likely to occur if the situation is structured to allow gradual movement to the next higher level.

The thirst to know and understand . . .
these are the goods in life's rich hand.

Sir William Watson, 1905

But Piaget's view has not gone unquestioned. Four sorts of findings question the Piagetian approach to cognitive development (Beilin, 1989; Bjorklund, 1989; Mandler, 1983; Small, 1990; Sugarman, 1989). First, Piaget conceived of stages as unitary structures of thought, so his theory assumes that there is a synchrony in development. That is, various aspects of a stage should emerge at about the same time. However, several concrete operational concepts do not appear in synchrony. For example, children do not learn to conserve at the same time they learn to cross-classify. Second, small changes in the procedures involved in a Piagetian task sometimes have significant effects on a child's cognition. Third, in some cases, children who are at one cognitive stage—such as preoperational thought—can be trained to reason at a higher cognitive stage—such as concrete operational thought. This poses a problem for Piaget, who argued that such training works only on a superficial level and is ineffective unless the child is at a transitional point from one stage to the next. Fourth, some cognitive abilities emerge earlier than Piaget believed and their subsequent development may be more prolonged than he thought. Conservation of number has been demonstrated in children as young as 3 years of age, although Piaget did not believe that it came about until 7 years of age; some aspects of formal operational thought that involve abstract reasoning do not consistently appear as early in adolescence as Piaget believed.

FIGURE 12.2 Use of the keyword method to improve children's memory. To help children remember the state capitals, the keyword method was used. A special component of the keyword method is the use of mental imagery, which was stimulated by the presentation to the children of a vivid visual image, such as the one shown here of two apples being married. The strategy is to help the children to associate *apple* with Annapolis and *marry* with Maryland (Levin, 1980).

Information Processing

Among the highlights of changes in information processing during middle and late childhood are improvements in memory, schemata, and scripts. Remember also, from Chapter 9, that the attention of most children improves dramatically during middle and late childhood, and that at this time children attend more to the task-relevant features of a problem than to the salient features.

Memory

In Chapter 8, we concluded that tasks involving short-term memory—the memory span task, for example—reveal a considerable increase in short-term memory during early childhood, but after the age of 7 do not show as much increase. Is the same pattern found for **long-term memory,** information we retain indefinitely that can be used over and over again? Long-term memory shows a different pattern of development than short-term memory during childhood: Long-term memory increases with age during middle and late childhood. Two aspects of memory related to improvement in long-term memory are control processes and learner characteristics.

If we know anything at all about long-term memory, it is that long-term memory depends on the learning activities that people engage in when learning and remembering information. Most such activities fit into the category of effortful **control processes.** That is, they are not automatic, they require work and effort. These activities are under the learner's conscious control. They are also appropriately referred to as *strategies* (McGilly & Siegler, 1989; Siegler, 1987, 1989). Three important control processes involved in children's memory are rehearsal, organization, and imagery.

One control process or strategy for improving children's memory is **rehearsal,** which involves the repetition of information after it has been presented—as when a child is trying to remember a phone number, for example. Researchers have found that children's spontaneous use of rehearsal increases between the ages of 5 and 10 (Flavell, Beach, & Chinsky, 1966). The use of organization also improves memory. As with rehearsal, children in middle and late childhood are more likely to spontaneously organize information to be remembered than are children in early childhood (Moely & others, 1969).

Another control process that develops as children move through middle and late childhood is imagery. A powerful imagery strategy is the *keyword method,* which has been used to practical advantage by teaching elementary schoolchildren how to quickly master new information such as foreign vocabulary words, the states and capitals of the United States, and the names of United States presidents. For example, in remembering that Annapolis is the capital of Maryland, children were taught the keywords for the states, such that when a state was given (*Maryland*), they could supply the keyword (*marry*) (Levin, 1980). Then, children were given the reverse type of keyword practice with the capitals. That is, they had to respond with the capital (*Annapolis*) when given a keyword (*apple*). Finally, an illustration was provided (Figure 12.2). The keyword strategy's use of vivid mental imagery, such as the image in Figure 12.2, was effective in increasing children's memory of state capitals. Developmentalists today encourage the use of imagery in our nation's schools, believing that it helps to increase the child's memory (McDaniel & Pressley, 1987).

What are the effects of knowledge on memory?

In addition to these control processes, the characteristics of the child influence memory. Apart from the obvious variable of age, many characteristics of the child determine the effectiveness of memory. These characteristics include attitude, motivation, and health. However, the characteristic that has been examined the most thoroughly is the child's previously acquired knowledge. What the child knows has a tremendous effect on what the child remembers. In one investigation, 10-year-old children who were chess experts remembered chessboard positions much better than adults who did not play much chess (Chi, 1978). However, the children did not do as well as the adults when both groups were asked to remember a group of random numbers; the children's expertise in chess gave them superior memories, but only in chess.

The two factors of knowledge and control factors are tightly intertwined. Indeed, one important type of memory knowledge actually concerns control processes; this knowledge is **metamemory**—knowledge about one's memory (Brown & others, 1983; Flavell, 1985; Flavell & Wellman, 1977). Researchers have found that children's metamemory improves from the preschool years through adolescence; for example, preschool children are less efficient at monitoring their own memory than are children in the fourth grade (Flavell, Friedrichs, & Hoyt, 1970).

Schemata and Scripts

Many developmentalists believe that it is necessary to consider the concepts of schemata and scripts when we try to explain children's knowledge. When we reconstruct information, we often fit it into information already existing in our mind. The existing information we have about various concepts, events, and knowledge is called **schemata** (singular, *schema*). Schemata come from prior encounters with the environment and influence the way children encode, make references about, and retrieve information. Children have schemata for stories, scenes, spatial layouts (a bathroom or a park), and common events (going to a restaurant, playing with toys, practicing soccer). Schemata for events are called **scripts** (Schank & Abelson, 1977). Children's first scripts appear very early in development, perhaps as early as the

Children have schemata—existing information in their minds—about many different aspects of our world. The children shown here have a schema for the woods and lake where they are that helps them to keep from getting lost.

Thinking Critically
Imagine that you have been asked to develop an information-processing curriculum for first-grade students. What would be the curriculum's main themes?

first year of life. Children clearly have scripts by the time they enter school (Firush & Cobb, 1989; Flannagan & Tate, 1989; Furman & Walden, 1989); as they develop, their scripts become less crude and more sophisticated. For example, a 4-year-old's script for a restaurant might include information only about sitting down and eating food. By middle and late childhood, the child adds information about the types of people who serve food, paying the cashier, and so on to the restaurant script.

So far, we have learned a great deal about the way children process information about their world. Through a number of chapters, we have studied how children attend to information, perceive it, retain it over time, and draw inferences about it. Recently, ways the information-process approach can be applied to children's education have been considered (Gagne, 1985; White, in press). To learn more about this application, turn to Children 12.1.

Thus far, we have discussed a number of ideas about Piaget's theory and concrete operational thought, and about information processing. These ideas are summarized in Concept Table 12.1. We now turn our attention to the nature of children's intelligence.

Information Processing, the Information Age, and Children's Education

When you were in elementary school, did any teacher at any time work with you on improving your memory strategies? Did any of your teachers work with you on your reading skills after the first and second grades? Did any of your teachers discuss with you ways in which imagery could enhance your processing of information? If you are like most people, you spent little or no time in elementary school on improving these important processes involved in our everyday encounters with the world.

Why is it so important to improve the information-processing skills of children? Think for a moment about yourself and the skills necessary for you to be successful in adapting to your environment and for improving your chances of getting a good job and having a successful career. To some extent, knowledge itself is important; more precisely, content knowledge in certain areas is important. For example, if you plan to become a chemical engineer, you will need knowledge of chemistry. Our schools have done a much better job of imparting knowledge than of instructing students how to process information.

Another important situation in your life when instruction in information processing would have helped you tremendously was when you took the SAT or ACT test. SAT cram courses are popping up all over the United States, in part because schools have not done a good job of developing information-processing skills. For example, is speed of processing information important on the SAT? Most of you probably felt that you did not have as much time as you would have liked to handle difficult questions. Are memory strategies important on the SAT? You had to read paragraphs and hold a considerable amount of information in your mind to answer some of the questions. And you certainly had to remember how to solve a number of math problems. Didn't you also have to remember the definitions of a large number of vocabulary words? And what about problem solving, inferencing, and understanding? Remember the difficult verbal problems you had to answer and the inferences you had to make when reasoning was required?

The story of information processing is one of attention, perception, memory (especially the control processes in memory), thinking, and the like. These information-processing skills become even more crucial in education when we consider that we are now in the midst of a transition from an industrial to a postindustrial information society, with approximately 65 to 70 percent of all workers involved in ser-

vices. The information revolution has required workers to process huge amounts of information in a rapid fashion, to have efficient memories, to attend to relevant details, to reason logically about difficult issues, and to make inferences about information that may be fuzzy or unclear. Students graduate from high school, college, or graduate school and move into jobs requiring information-processing skills, yet they have had little or no instruction in improving these skills.

At this time, we do not have a specified curriculum of information processing that can be taught in a stepwise, developmental fashion to our nation's children. We also do not have the trained personnel for this instruction. Furthermore, some information-processing experts believe that processes such as attention and memory cannot be trained in a general way. They argue that information processing is domain or content specific. That is, we should work on improving information-processing skills that are specific to math or specific to history. They do believe, though, that an infusion of the information-processing approach into all parts of the curriculum would greatly benefit children (Glazer & Bassok, 1989).

Researchers are beginning to study the importance of information-processing skills for school learning (Jones & Idol, 1989; Kinsch, 1989; Resnick, 1989). What information-processing skills need to be considered when instructing children in specific content areas—reading, writing, math, and science, for example? Successful students—those who get better grades and higher achievement test scores—are better at information-processing skills such as focusing attention, elaborating and organizing information, and monitoring their study strategies. As yet, though, we do not know to what extent these information-processing skills can be taught. Nonetheless, in one investigation, children who were taught effective ways to elaborate information remembered it more efficiently (Gagne & others, in press). Elaboration refers to more extensive processing. Getting children to think of examples of a concept is a good way to improve their memory of the concept; so is getting children to think about how the concept relates to themselves. Other experts in cognitive psychology also believe that information-processing skills can be taught. For example, Joan Baron and R. J. Sternberg (1987) believe that we need to teach children to think in less irrational ways. Children need to be more critical of the first ideas that pop into their minds. They should be taught to think longer about problems and to search in more organized ways for evidence to support their views. ◆

Piaget's Theory and Concrete Operational Thought, and Information Processing

Concept	Processes and Related Ideas	Characteristics and Description
Piaget's Theory and Concrete Operational Thought	Concrete operational thought	Concrete operational thought is made up of operations, mental actions, or representations that are reversible. The concrete operational child shows conservation and classification skills. The concrete operational child needs clearly available perceptual supports to reason; later in development, thought becomes more abstract.
	Piaget and education	Piaget's ideas have been applied extensively to children's education. Emphasis is on communication and the belief that the child has many ideas about the world, that the child is always learning and unlearning, and that the child is by nature a knowing creature.
	Contributions and criticisms	Piaget was a genius at observing children and he developed fascinating insights about children's cognition; he showed us some important things to look for in development and mapped out some general cognitive changes in development. Criticisms of Piaget focus on the belief that the stages are not as unitary as he thought, that small changes in procedures affect the child's cognition, that children can sometimes be trained to think at higher stages, and that some cognitive skills appear earlier than Piaget thought, while others are more protracted than he thought.
Information Processing	Memory	Children's long-term memory improves during middle and late childhood. Control processes or strategies such as rehearsal, organization, and imagery are among the important influences that are responsible for improved long-term memory. Children's knowledge also influences their memory. A special type of knowledge—metamemory—concerns control processes.
	Schemata and scripts	Schemata refer to the existing information we have about concepts, events, and knowledge; scripts are schemata for events. Children's schemata and scripts become more complex and sophisticated in middle and late childhood.

Intelligence

Intelligence is an abstract concept that is difficult to define. While many psychologists and laypeople equate intelligence with verbal ability and problem-solving skills, others prefer to define it as the individual's ability to learn from and adapt to the experiences of everyday life. If we were to settle on a definition of intelligence based on these criteria, it would be that **intelligence** is verbal ability, problem-solving skills, and the ability to learn from and adapt to the experiences of everyday life.

The components of intelligence are very close to the information-processing and language skills we have discussed at various points in children's development. The difference between how we discussed information-processing skills and language and how we will discuss intelligence lies in the concepts of individual differences and assessment. Individual differences simply are the consistent, stable ways we differ from each other. The history of the study of intelligence has focused extensively on individual differences and their assessment. For example, an intelligence test will inform us whether a child can reason more logically than most other children who have taken the test. Our coverage of intelligence focuses on the components of intelligence, cultural bias, knowledge versus process, the use and misuse of intelligence tests, and the extremes of intelligence. As you think about intelligence, keep in mind our discussion of intelligence in Chapter 3, in which we concluded that intelligence is influenced by the interaction of heredity and environment, rather than either factor alone.

One Face or Many?

Is it more appropriate to think of intelligence as an individual's general ability or as a number of specific abilities? As we explore different approaches to what intelligence is and how it should be measured, you will discover that intelligence probably is *both*.

Alfred Binet (1857–1911) constructed the first intelligence test.

Alfred Binet and the Binet Tests

In 1904, the French Ministry of Education asked psychologist Alfred Binet to devise a method that would determine which students did not profit from typical school instruction. School officials wanted to reduce overcrowding by placing those who did not benefit from regular classroom teaching in special schools. To meet this request, Binet and his student Theophile Simon developed an intelligence test. The test, referred to as the 1905 Scale, consisted of 30 different items ranging from the ability to touch one's nose or ear when asked to the ability to draw designs from memory and define abstract concepts.

Binet developed the concept of **mental age** (**MA**)—an individual's level of mental development relative to others. Binet reasoned that mentally retarded children would perform like normal children of a younger age. He developed norms for intelligence by testing 50 nonretarded children from 3 to 11 years of age. Children suspected of mental retardation were tested, and their performance was compared with children of the same chronological age in the normal sample. Average mental-age scores (MA) correspond to chronological age (CA), which is age since birth. A bright child has an MA above CA, a dull child has an MA below CA.

The term **intelligence quotient** (**IQ**) was devised by William Stern. IQ is the child's mental age divided by chronological age multiplied by 100:

$$IQ = \frac{MA}{CA} \times 100$$

If mental age is the same as chronological age, then the child's IQ is 100; if mental age is above chronological age, the IQ is more than 100; if mental age is below chronological age, the IQ is less than 100.

Over the years, psychologists have made great efforts to standardize the Binet test, which has been given to thousands of children and adults of different ages, selected at random from different parts of the United States. By administering the test to large numbers of people and recording the results, intelligence has been found to approximate a **normal distribution** (Figure 12.3). This type of distribution is symmetrical, with a majority of cases falling in the middle of a possible range of scores and few scores appearing toward the ends of the range.

The current Stanford-Binet (named after Stanford University, where revisions of the test were constructed) is given to persons from the age of 2 through adulthood. It includes a wide variety of items, some requiring verbal responses, others nonverbal

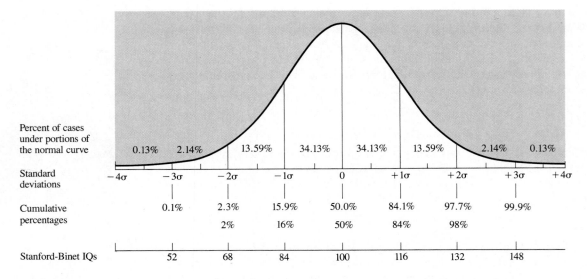

Percent of cases under portions of the normal curve

0.13% 2.14% 13.59% 34.13% 34.13% 13.59% 2.14% 0.13%

Standard deviations

−4σ   −3σ   −2σ   −1σ   0   +1σ   +2σ   +3σ   +4σ

Cumulative percentages

0.1%   2.3%   15.9%   50.0%   84.1%   97.7%   99.9%

2%   16%   50%   84%   98%

Stanford-Binet IQs

52   68   84   100   116   132   148

FIGURE 12.3   The normal curve and Stanford-Binet IQ scores (Sattler, 1982). The distribution of IQ scores approximates a normal curve. Most of the population falls in the middle range of scores. Notice that extremely high and extremely low scores are very rare. Slightly more than two-thirds of the scores fall between 84 and 116. Only about 1 in 50 individuals has an IQ of more than 132 and only about 1 in 50 individuals has an IQ of less than 68.

responses. For example, items that characterize a 6-year-old's performance on the test include the verbal ability to define at least six words such as *orange* and *envelope,* and the nonverbal ability to trace a path through a maze. Items that reflect the average adult's intelligence include defining words such as *disproportionate* and *regard,* explaining a proverb, and comparing idleness and laziness.

The fourth edition of the Stanford-Binet was published in 1985 (Thorndike, Hagan, & Sattler, 1985). One important addition to this version is the analysis of responses in four content areas: verbal reasoning, quantitative reasoning, abstract/visual reasoning, and short-term memory (Keith & others, 1988). A general composite score is also obtained to reflect overall intelligence. The Stanford-Binet continues to be one of the most widely used individual tests of children's intelligence.

The Wechsler Scales

Besides the Stanford-Binet, the other most widely used individual intelligence tests are the **Wechsler scales,** developed by David Wechsler. They include the Wechsler Adult Intelligence Scale-Revised (WAIS-R); the Wechsler Intelligence Scale for Children-Revised (WISC-R), for use with children between the ages of 6 and 16; and the Wechsler Preschool and Primary Scale of Intelligence (WPPSI), for use with children from the ages of 4 to 6½ (Wechsler, 1949, 1955, 1967, 1974, 1981).

The Wechsler scales not only provide an overall IQ, but the items are grouped according to 12 subscales, six of which are verbal and six of which are nonverbal. This allows the examiner to obtain separate verbal and nonverbal IQ scores and to see quickly in which areas of mental performance the child is below average, average, or above average. The inclusion of a number of nonverbal subscales makes the Wechsler test more representative of verbal *and* nonverbal intelligence; the Binet test includes some nonverbal items but not as many as the Wechsler scales. Eleven of the 12 subscales on the Wechsler Intelligence Scale for Children-Revised are shown in Figure 12.4, along with examples of each subscale.

Verbal subtests

General information
The individual is asked a number of general information questions about experiences that are considered normal for individuals in our society.
   For example, "How many wings does a bird have?"

Similarities
The individual must think logically and abstractly to answer a number of questions about how things are similar.
   For example, "In what way are boats and trains the same?"

Arithmetic reasoning
Problems measure the individual's ability to do arithmetic mentally and include addition, subtraction, multiplication, and division.
   For example, "If two buttons cost 14¢, what will be the cost of a dozen buttons?"

Vocabulary
To evaluate word knowledge, the individual is asked to define a number of words. This subtest measures a number of cognitive functions, including concept formation, memory, and language.
   For example, "What does the word *biography* mean?"

Comprehension
This subtest is designed to measure the individual's judgment and common sense.
   For example, "What is the advantage of keeping money in the bank?"

Digit span
This subtest primarily measures attention and short-term memory. The individual is required to repeat numbers forward and backward.
   For example, "I am going to say some numbers and I want you to repeat them backward: 4   7   5   2   8."

Picture completion
A number of drawings are shown, each with a significant part missing. Within a period of several seconds, the individual must differentiate essential from nonessential parts of the picture and identify which part is missing. This subtest evaluates visual alertness and the ability to organize information visually.
   For example, "I am going to show you a picture with an important part missing. Tell me what is missing."

Picture arrangement
A series of pictures out of sequence are shown to the individual, who is asked to place them in their proper order to tell an appropriate story. This subtest evaluates how individuals integrate information to make it logical and meaningful.
   For example, "The pictures below need to be placed in an appropriate order to tell a meaningful story."

FIGURE 12.4   The subtests of the WISC-R and examples of each subtest.

[*continued on next page*]

Object assembly
The individual is asked to assemble pieces into something. This subtest measures visual-motor coordination and perceptual organization.

For example, "When these pieces are put together correctly, they make something. Put them together as quickly as you can."

Block design
The individual must assemble a set of multi-colored blocks to match designs that the examiner shows. Visual-motor coordination, perceptual organization, and the ability to visualize spatially are measured.

For example, "Use the four blocks on the left to make the pattern on the right."

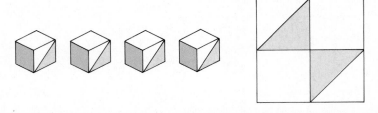

Coding
This subtest evaluates, how quickly and accurately an individual can link code symbols and digits. The subtest assesses visual-motor coordination and speed of thought.

For example, "As quickly as you can, transfer the appropriate code symbols to the blank spaces."

Note: A sixth nonverbal scale, Mazes, is not shown because it is rarely used by examiners. Digit Span also is considered to be an optional subtest, but examiners are more likely to administer it than the optional performance subtest, Mazes.

FIGURE 12.4 Continued

Japanese Question the Value of IQ Tests

In Japan, intelligence is a private matter. You don't hear people talking about someone being very bright, the way we often do in the United States. In Japan, a very high IQ is usually thought of as unrealistic. Some psychologists have claimed that Japanese children have the highest mean IQ in the world and that the gap between them and the rest of the world is growing. Such comments catch the attention of Americans and Europeans, but they attract little interest in Japan. Faith in hard work and a belief in group achievement help to explain the relative lack of interest in individual differences in intelligence in Japan (Hathaway, 1984). ◆

Multiple Faces of Intelligence

Long before David Wechsler analyzed intelligence in terms of general and specific abilities (giving the child an overall IQ but also providing information about specific subcomponents of intelligence), Charles Spearman (1927) proposed that intelligence has two factors. Spearman's **two-factor theory** argued that we have both a general intelligence, which he called g, and a number of specific intelligences, which he called s. Spearman believed that these two factors could account for a person's performance on an intelligence test. One recent classification developed by Howard Gardner (1983, 1989) also describes intelligence as having many faces. By turning to Children 12.2, you can read about Gardner's seven frames of mind. Clearly, there is disagreement about whether intelligence is a general ability or a number of specific abilities, and if there are specific abilities, disagreement about just what those are (Carroll, 1989).

Are Intelligence Tests Culturally Biased?

Many of the early intelligence tests were culturally biased, favoring urban children over rural children, middle-class children over lower-class children, and white children over minority children. The norms for the early tests were based almost entirely on white, middle-class children. And some of the items themselves were culturally biased. For example, one item on an early test asked what you should do if you find a 3-year-old child in the street; the correct answer was "Call the police." Children from impoverished inner-city families might not choose this answer if they have had bad experiences with the police; rural children might not choose it, because they may not have police nearby. Such items do not measure the knowledge necessary to adapt to one's environment or to be "intelligent" in an inner-city minority neighborhood or in rural America (Scarr, 1984). The contemporary versions of intelligence tests attempt to reduce cultural bias (Angoff, 1989).

Bird to Beethoven—Seven Frames of Mind

Larry Bird, the 6'9" superstar of the Boston Celtics, springs into motion. Grabbing a rebound off the defensive board, he quickly moves across two-thirds the length of the 94-foot basketball court, all the while processing the whereabouts of his five opponents and four teammates. As the crowd screams, Bird calmly looks one way, finesses his way past a defender, and whirls a behind-the-back pass to a fast-breaking teammate, who dunks the ball for two points. Is there specific intelligence to Bird's movement and perception of the spatial layout of the basketball court?

Now we turn the clock back 200 years. A tiny boy just 4 years old is standing on a footstool in front of a piano keyboard practicing. At the age of 6, the young boy is given the honor of playing concertos and trios at a concert. The young boy is Ludwig van Beethoven, whose musical genius was evident at a young age. Did Beethoven have a specific type of intelligence, one we might call musical intelligence?

Bird and Beethoven are different types of people with different types of abilities. Howard Gardner (1983), in his book, *Frames of Mind,* argues that Bird's and Beethoven's talents represent two of seven intelligences that we possess. The seven types of intelligence Gardner believes human beings possess are verbal, mathematical, ability to spatially analyze the world, movement skills, insightful skills for analyzing ourselves, insightful skills for analyzing others, and musical skills.

Gardner believes that each of the seven intelligences can be destroyed by brain damage, that each involves unique cognitive skills, and that each shows up in exaggerated fashion in both the gifted and idiots savants (individuals who are mentally retarded but who have unbelievable skill in a particular domain, such as drawing, music, or computing). I remember vividly an individual from my childhood who was mentally retarded but could instantaneously respond with the correct day of the week (say Tuesday or Saturday) when given any date in history (say June 4, 1926, or December 15, 1746).

Gardner is especially interested in musical intelligence, particularly when it is exhibited at an early age. He points out that musically inclined preschool children not only have the remarkable ability to learn musical patterns easily, but that they rarely forget them. He recounts a story about Stravinsky, who as an adult could still remember the musical patterns of the tuba, drums, and piccolos of the fife-and-drum band that marched outside his home when he was a young child.

To measure musical intelligence in young children, Gardner might ask a child to listen to a melody and then ask the child to recreate the tune on some bells he provides. He believes such evaluations can be used to develop a profile of a child's intelligence. He also believes that it is during this early time in life that parents can make an important difference in how a child's intelligence develops.

Critics of Gardner's approach point out that we have geniuses in many domains other than music. There are outstanding chess players, prize fighters, writers, politicians, physicians, lawyers, preachers, and poets, for example; yet we do not refer to chess intelligence, prize-fighter intelligence, and so on. ◆

Even if the content of test items is appropriate, another problem may exist with intelligence tests. Since many questions are verbal in nature, minority groups may encounter problems in understanding the language of the questions (Gibbs & Huang, 1989). Minority groups often speak a language that is very different from standard English. Consequently, they may be at a disadvantage when they take intelligence tests oriented toward middle-class whites. Such cultural bias is dramatically underscored by tests like the one in Figure 12.5. The items in this test were developed to reduce the cultural disadvantage black children might experience on traditional intelligence tests.

Culture-fair tests were devised to reduce cultural bias. Two types of culture fair tests have been developed. The first includes items that are familiar to individuals from all socioeconomic and ethnic backgrounds, or items that are at least familiar to the people taking the test. A child might be asked how a bird and a dog

Larry Bird, NBA superstar of the Boston Celtics. Howard Gardner believes Bird's movement skills and spatial perception are forms of intelligence.

Ludwig van Beethoven. Gardner also argues that musical skills, such as those shown by Beethoven, are a form of intelligence.

are different, on the assumption that all children have been exposed to birds and dogs. The second type of culture-fair test has all the verbal items removed. Figure 12.6 shows a sample item from the Raven Progressive Matrices Test, which exemplifies this approach. Even though tests like the Raven Test are designed to be culture fair, people with more education score higher on them than those with less education (Anastasi, 1988).

Culture-fair tests remind us that traditional intelligence tests are probably culturally biased, yet culture-fair tests do not provide a satisfactory alternative. Constructing a test that is truly culture fair—one that rules out the role of experience emanating from socioeconomic and ethnic background—has been difficult and may be impossible. Consider, for example, that the intelligence of the Iatmul people of Papua, New Guinnea, involves the ability to remember the names of some 10,000 to 20,000 clans; by contrast, the intelligence of islanders in the widely dispersed Caroline Islands involves the talent of navigating by the stars.

1. A "gas head" is a person who has a:
   (a) fast-moving car
   (b) stable of "lace"
   (c) "process"
   (d) habit of stealing cars
   (e) long jail record for arson
2. "Bo Diddley" is a:
   (a) game for children
   (b) down-home cheap wine
   (c) down-home singer
   (d) new dance
   (e) Moejoe call
3. If a pimp is uptight with a woman who gets state aid, what does he mean when he talks about "Mother's day"?
   (a) second Sunday in May
   (b) third Sunday in June
   (c) first of every month
   (d) none of these
   (e) first and fifteenth of every month
4. A "handkerchief head" is:
   (a) a cool cat
   (b) a porter
   (c) an Uncle Tom
   (d) a hoddi
   (e) a preacher
5. If a man is called a "blood," then he is a:
   (a) fighter
   (b) Mexican-American
   (c) Negro
   (d) hungry hemophile
   (e) red man, or Indian
6. Cheap chitlings (not the kind you purchase at a frozen-food counter) will taste rubbery unless they are cooked long enough. How soon can you quit cooking them to eat and enjoy them?
   (a) forty-five minutes
   (b) two hours
   (c) twenty-four hours
   (d) one week (on a low flame)
   (e) one hour

Answers: 1. c 2. c 3. e 4. c 5. c 6. c

FIGURE 12.5   Sample items from the Chitling Intelligence Test.
Source: Adrian Dove, 1968.

Knowledge Versus Process in Intelligence

The information-processing approach we have discussed raises two interesting questions about intelligence: What are the fundamental information-processing abilities? And how do these abilities develop?

Few of us would deny that changes in both processing and knowledge occur as we develop. However, a consensus does not exist on something more fundamental. We accumulate knowledge as we grow from an infant to an adult, but the thing that may be growing is simply a reserve of processing capacity. That is, your greater processing capacity as an adult might be what allows you to learn more than you could as a child. By contrast, your greater processing capacity as an adult may be a consequence of your greater knowledge, which allows you to process information more effectively. It is not easy to choose between these two possibilities, and the issue has been called the great **structure-process dilemma** of intelligence (Keil, 1984). That is, what are the mechanisms of intelligence and how do they develop? Does information-processing ability change, or do knowledge and expertise change? Or do both change?

To make the structure-process dilemma more concrete, consider a simple computer metaphor. Suppose we have two computers, each capable of solving multiplication problems (e.g., 13×24, 45×21), but one computer works faster than the other. How can the difference be explained? One possibility is that the faster computer has a greater capacity—that is, core memory—in which to do mental work. This greater core memory, which psychologists refer to as *working memory,* might allow the computer to work on two or more components of a problem at once. Another explanation is that the faster computer might have a greater store of relevant knowledge. Perhaps in its data bank (long-term memory) is a complete multiplication table to compute amounts up to 99×99. The slower computer might have a table up to 12×12 (as do most humans). The faster computer need not be fundamentally faster. Its subroutines may be relatively slow, but it is able to perform the multiplication task because of knowledge, not because of processing capacity.

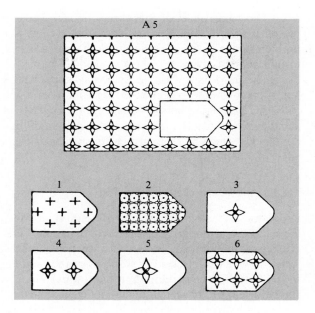

FIGURE 12.6 Sample item from the Raven Progressive Matrices Test. The individual is presented with a matrix arrangement of symbols, such as the one at the top of this figure, and must then complete the matrix by selecting the appropriate missing symbol from a group of symbols.

Explaining intelligence is similar to explaining the difference between the fast and slow computers: Is processing or knowledge responsible for how intelligence changes with age? Based on research on memory, the answer is probably both (Zembar & Naus, 1985). If so, the essential task becomes one of determining the ways that processing and knowledge interact in the course of intellectual development.

The modern information-processing approach does not argue that knowledge is unimportant. Many information-processing psychologists believe that attention should be given to the knowledge base generated by intellectual processes. One information-processing approach to intelligence that recognizes the importance of both process and knowledge is the model of R. J. Sternberg (1988, 1989). Sternberg believes that every person has three types of intelligence; for this reason, he calls his approach the **triarchic theory of intelligence.** Consider Ann, who scores high on traditional intelligence tests such as the Stanford-Binet and is a star analytical thinker. Consider Todd, who does not have the best test results but has an insightful and creative mind. And consider Art, a street-smart boy who has learned how to deal with his world in practical ways, although his scores on traditional intelligence tests are low.

Sternberg calls Ann's analytical thinking and abstract reasoning *componential intelligence;* it is the closest to what we call intelligence in this chapter and is what is commonly measured by intelligence tests. Todd's insightful and creative thinking is called *experiential intelligence* by Sternberg. And Art's street smarts and practical know-how is called *contextual intelligence* by Sternberg (Figure 12.7).

In Sternberg's view of componential intelligence, the basic unit of intelligence is a *component,* defined simply as a basic unit of information processing. Sternberg believes that components include those used to acquire or store information, to retain or retrieve information, to transfer information, to plan, make decisions, and solve problems, and to carry out problem-solving strategies or translate thoughts into performance.

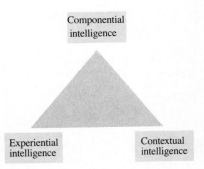

FIGURE 12.7 Sternberg's triarchic theory of intelligence

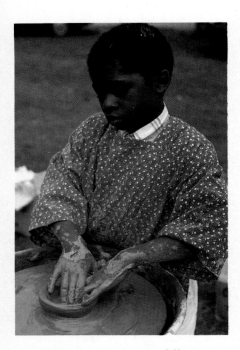

Intelligence comes in many different forms. Developmentalists debate the nature of the forms and how many there are. For example, Sternberg argues that children's intelligence comes in three forms: componential, experiential, and contextual. Which of these forms would this young boy's behavior fit?

Thinking Critically
How close are Piaget's view of intelligence and the intelligence test approach to intelligence? Explain your answer.

The second part of Sternberg's model focuses on experience. An intelligent person is able to solve new problems quickly but also learns how to solve familiar problems in an automatic way so that her mind is free to handle problems requiring insight and creativity.

The third part of the model involves practical knowledge, such as how to get out of trouble, how to replace a fuse, and how to get along with people. Sternberg calls this practical knowledge *tacit knowledge.* It includes all of the information about getting along in the world that is not taught in school. Sternberg believes that tacit knowledge is more important for success in life than explicit, or "book," knowledge.

The Use and Misuse of Intelligence Tests

Psychological tests are tools. Like all tools, their effectiveness depends on the knowledge, skill, and integrity of the user. A hammer can be used to build a beautiful kitchen cabinet or it can be used as a weapon of assault. Like a hammer, intelligence tests can be used for positive purposes or they can be badly abused. It is important for both the test constructor and the test examiner to be familiar with the current state of scientific knowledge about intelligence and intelligence tests (Anastasi, 1988).

Even though they have limitations, intelligence tests are among psychology's most widely used tools. To be effective, though, intelligence tests must be viewed realistically. They should not be thought of as a fixed, unchanging indicator of a person's intelligence. They also should be used in conjunction with other information about a person and should not be relied upon as the sole indicator of intelligence. For example, an intelligence test should not be used as the sole indicator of whether a child should be placed in a special-education or gifted class. The child's developmental history, medical background, performance in school, social competencies, and family experiences should be taken into account, too.

The single number provided by many IQ tests can easily lead to stereotypes and expectations about a person. Many people do not know how to interpret the results of an intelligence test, and sweeping generalizations about a person are too often made on the basis of an IQ score. Imagine, for example, that you are a teacher sitting in the teacher's lounge the day after school has started in the fall. You mention a student—Johnny Jones—and a fellow teacher remarks that she had Johnny in class last year; she remarks that he was a real dunce and points out that his IQ is 78. You cannot help but remember this information, and it may lead you to think that Johnny Jones is not very bright so it is useless to spend much time teaching him. In this way, IQ scores are misused and stereotypes are formed (Rosenthal, 1987; Rosenthal & Jacobsen, 1968).

We have a tendency in our culture to consider intelligence or a high IQ as the ultimate human value. It is important to keep in mind that our value as people includes other matters: consideration of others, positive close relationships, and competence in social situations, for example. The verbal and problem-solving skills measured on traditional intelligence tests are only one part of human competence.

Despite their limitations, when used judiciously by a competent examiner, intelligence tests provide valuable information about people. There are not many alternatives to intelligence tests. Subjective judgments about individuals simply reintroduce the biases the tests were designed to eliminate.

The Extremes of Intelligence

The atypical person has always been of interest to developmentalists. Intellectual atypicality has intrigued many psychologists and drawn them to study both the mentally retarded and the mentally gifted.

Mental Retardation

The most distinctive feature of mental retardation is inadequate intellectual functioning. Long before formal tests were introduced to assess intelligence, the mentally retarded were identified by a lack of age-appropriate skills in learning and caring for oneself. With the development of intelligence tests, more emphasis was placed on IQ as an indicator of mental retardation. But it is not unusual to find two retarded persons with the same low IQ, one of whom is married, employed, and involved in the community and the other requiring constant supervision in an institution. These differences in social competence led developmentalists to include deficits in adaptive behavior in their definition of mental retardation. The currently accepted definition of **mental retardation** refers to the condition of a person who has a low IQ, usually below 70 on a traditional intelligence test, and who has difficulty adapting to everyday life. About 5 million Americans fit this definition of mental retardation (Baumeiser, 1987; Robinson, 1987; Zigler, 1987).

There are different classifications of mental retardation. About 80 percent of the mentally retarded fall into the mild category, with IQs of 50 to 70. About 12 percent are classified as moderately retarded, with IQs of 35 to 49; these individuals can attain a second-grade level of skills and may be able to support themselves as adults through some type of labor. About 7 percent of the mentally retarded fall into the severe category, with IQs of 20 to 34; these individuals learn to talk and engage in very simple tasks, but they require extensive supervision. Only 1 percent of the mentally retarded are classified as profoundly retarded with IQs below 20; they are in constant need of supervision.

What causes retardation? The causes are divided into two categories: organic and cultural-familial. Individuals with **organic retardation** are retarded because of a genetic disorder or brain damage. *Organic* refers to the tissues or organs of the body, so in organic retardation, some physical damage has taken place. Down's syndrome, a form of organic retardation (Figure 12.8), occurs when an extra chromosome is present. The condition may be influenced by the health of the female ovum or the male sperm. Although those who suffer organic retardation are found across the spectrum of mental retardation IQ distribution, most have IQs between 0 and 50.

Persons with **cultural-familial retardation** make up the majority of the mentally retarded population; they have no evidence of organic damage or brain dysfunction. Their IQs range from 50 to 70. Developmentalists seek to discover the cause of this type of retardation in the impoverished environments these individuals probably have experienced. Even with organic retardation, though, it is wise to think about the contributions of genetic-environment interaction. Parents with low IQs not only may be more likely to transmit genes for low intelligence to their offspring, but they also tend to provide them with a less enriched environment (Garber, 1988; Landesman & Ramey, 1989).

FIGURE 12.8   A child with Down's syndrome.

Never to be cast away are the gifts of the gods, magnificent.

Homer, The Iliad, *9th century,* B.C.

"I'm a gifted child."

Drawing by Drucker; © 1981 The New Yorker Magazine, Inc.

Giftedness

Conventional wisdom has identified some individuals in all cultures and historical periods as gifted because they have talents not evident in the majority of people. Despite this widespread recognition of the gifted, developmentalists have difficulty reaching a consensus on the precise definition and measurement of giftedness (Hoge, 1987). Some experts view the gifted as the top end of a continuum of intelligence (Zigler & Farber, 1985). Some of these advocates view this ability as a general characteristic that is perhaps hereditary. Others see the gifted as people who express specific talents that have been nurtured environmentally (Wallach, 1985). A comprehensive definition of a **gifted** person is an individual with intelligence well above average (an IQ of 120 or more), having a superior talent for something, or both. Most school systems emphasize intellectual superiority and academic aptitude when selecting children for special instruction; however, they rarely consider competence in the visual and performing arts (art, drama, dance), psychomotor abilities (tennis, golf, basketball), or other special aptitudes.

Lewis Terman (1925) began a classic study of the gifted more than 60 years ago. Terman studied approximately 1,500 children whose Stanford-Binet IQs averaged 150. His goal was to follow these children through their adult lives. The study will not be complete until the year 2010.

The accomplishments of the 1,500 children in Terman's study are remarkable. Of the 800 males, 78 have obtained Ph.D.s (they include two past presidents of the American Psychological Association), 48 have earned M.D.s, and 85 have been granted law degrees. Nearly all of these figures are 10 to 30 times greater than the amount found among 800 men of the same age chosen randomly from the overall population. These findings challenge the commonly held belief that the intellectually gifted are somehow emotionally or socially maladjusted. This belief is based on striking instances of mental disturbances among the gifted. Sir Isaac Newton,

Vincent Van Gogh, Leonardo da Vinci, Socrates, and Edgar Allan Poe all had emotional problems, but these are exceptions rather than the rule; no relationship between giftedness and mental disturbance in general has been found. Recent studies support Terman's conclusion that, if anything, the gifted tend to be more mature and have fewer emotional problems than others (Janos & Robinson, 1985).

In one investigation, people with exceptional talents as adults were interviewed about what they believe contributed to their giftedness (Bloom, 1983). The 120 people had excelled in one of six fields: concert pianists and sculptors (arts), Olympic swimmers and tennis champions (psychomotor), and research mathematicians and research neurologists (cognitive). They said that the development of their exceptional accomplishments required special environmental support, excellent teaching, and encouragement. Each experienced years of special attention under the tutelage and supervision of a remarkable set of teachers and coaches. They also were given extensive support and encouragement from parents. All of these stars devoted exceptional time to practice and training, easily outdistancing the amount of time spent in all other activities combined. Of course, not every parent wants to raise a star, but too many parents develop unrealistic expectations for their offspring, putting unbearable pressure on them and wanting them to achieve things that far exceed their talents. For every Chris Evert, there are thousands of girls with only mediocre tennis talent whose parents have wanted them to become "another" Chris Evert. Such unreal expectations always meet with failure and place children under considerable stress. And all too often parents try to push children and adolescents into activities that bore rather than excite them (Feldman, 1989; Hennessey & Amabile, 1988).

Each of us would like to be talented. And if each of us has children we would like to be able to develop the talents of our children. Some children become extraordinarily gifted, reaching the status of "star." Becoming a "star" takes years of special tutelage with remarkable coaches, extensive support by parents, and day after day, week after week, month after month, and year after year of practice.

Creativity

Most of us would like to be gifted *and* creative. Why was Thomas Edison able to invent so many things? Was he simply more intelligent than most other people? Did he spend long hours toiling away in private? Surprisingly, when Edison was a young boy, his teacher told him that he was too dumb to learn anything! Other examples of famous people whose creative genius went unnoticed when they were young include American film producer Walt Disney, who was fired from a newspaper job because he did not have any good ideas; Italian singer Enrico Caruso, whose music teacher told him that his voice was terrible; and British statesman and author Winston Churchill, who failed one year of secondary school. One reason such individuals are underestimated is the difficulty of defining and measuring creativity.

Experts who study intelligence and creativity believe that the two are not the same (Monroe, 1988; Wallach, 1985; Winner, 1989). One distinction is between **convergent thinking,** which produces one correct answer, and **divergent thinking,** which produces many different answers to the same question (Guilford, 1967). For example, the following problem-solving task has one correct answer and requires convergent thinking: "How many quarters should you get for 60 dimes?" But the next question has many possible answers and requires divergent thinking: "What are some unique things that can be done with a paper clip?" A degree of creativity is needed to answer this question. Other examples of divergent thinking are generated by the following: Name words that belong to a particular class. For example, name as many objects as you can that weigh less than 1 pound. Even when you are not asked to, do you give divergent answers? For example, if you are asked what things can be done with a paper clip, do you spontaneously generate different categories of use for the paper clip? For more examples of items on tests of creativity, turn to Figure 12.9.

Thinking Critically
What should be the criteria for placing a child in a gifted program?

1. *Sketches:* Add just enough detail to the circle below to make a recognizable object (two examples of acceptable responses are shown).

2. *Word fluency:* Write as many words as you can think of with the first and last letters R_____M ("rim" would be one).

3. *Name grouping:* Classify the following six names in as many different ways as you can (a person might group 1, 3, and 4 together because each has two syllables).

    1. GERTRUDE 2. BILL
    3. ALEX   4. CARRIE
    5. BELLE   6. DON

4. *Making objects:* Using two or more of the forms shown below, make a face. Now make a lamp (examples of good responses are shown).

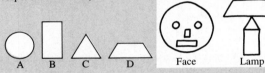

FIGURE 12.9 Creativity examples. Sample items from Guilford's (1967) Divergent Productions Tests.

Creativity is the ability to think about something in a novel way and to come up with unique solutions to problems. When people in the arts and sciences who fit this description are asked what enables them to produce their creative works, they say that they generate large amounts of associative content when solving problems and that they have the freedom to entertain a wide range of possible solutions in a playful way (Wallach & Kogan, 1965).

How strongly is creativity related to intelligence? A certain level of intelligence seems to be required to be creative in most fields, but many highly intelligent people (as measured by IQ tests) are not very creative.

Some experts remain skeptical that we will ever fully understand the creative process. Other experts believe that a psychology of creativity is in reach. Most experts do agree that the concept of creativity as spontaneously bubbling up from a magical well is a myth. Momentary flashes of insight, accompanied by images, make up only a small part of the creative process. At the heart of the creative process are ability and experience that shape an individual's intentional and sustained effort, often over the course of a lifetime. As we learn more about creativity, we come to understand how important it is as a human resource (Gardner & Perkins, 1989; Wolf, 1989).

Language Development

As children develop during middle and late childhood, changes in their vocabulary and grammar take place. Reading assumes a prominent role in their language world. An increasingly important consideration is bilingualism. We will consider each of these aspects of children's language development in turn.

Vocabulary and Grammar

During middle and late childhood, a change occurs in the way children think about words. They become less tied to the actions and perceptual dimensions associated with words, and they become more analytical in their approach to words. For example, when asked to say the first thing that comes to mind when they hear a word such as *dog,* preschool children often respond with a word related to the immediate context of a dog. A child might associate *dog* with a word that indicates its appearance (*black, big*) or to an action associated with it (*bark, sit*). Older children more frequently respond to *dog* by associating it with an appropriate category (*animal*) or to information that intelligently expands the context (*cat, veternarian*) (Holzman, 1983). The increasing ability elementary children have to analyze words helps them to understand words that have no direct relationship to their own personal experiences. This allows children to add more abstract words to their vocabulary. For example, *precious stones* may be understood by understanding the common characteristics of *diamonds* and *emeralds.* Also, children's increasing analytic abilities allow them to distinguish between similar words such as *cousin* and *nephew,* or *city, village,* and *suburb.*

Children make similar advances in grammar. The elmentary schoolchild's improvement in logical reasoning and analytical skills helps in the understanding of such constructions as the appropriate use of comparatives (*shorter, deeper*) and subjectives ("If you were president, . . ."). By the end of the elementary school years, children can usually apply many of the appropriate rules of grammar when asked to (de Villiers & de Villiers, 1978).

Reading, Information Processing, and Literacy

Reading becomes a special skill during the elementary school years. Not being a competent reader places a child at a substantial disadvantage in relation to his or her peers. Our coverage of reading focuses on learning-to-read techniques, information processing, and literacy.

Learning-to-Read Techniques

In the history of learning-to-read techniques, three approaches have dominated: (1) the **ABC method,** which emphasizes memorizing the names and letters of the alphabet; (2) the **whole-word method,** which focuses on learning direct associations between whole words and their meanings; and (3) the **phonics method,** which stresses the sounds that letters make when in words (such sounds can differ from the names of these letters, such as when the sound of the name of the letter *C* is not found in *cat*). The ABC method is in ill repute today. Because of the imperfect relationship

Reading becomes a special skill during the elementary school years. A special concern of our nation is the improvement of children's reading skills from low-income, ethnic minority backgrounds.

between the names of letters and their sounds in words, the technique is regarded as ineffective, if not harmful, in teaching children to read. Despite its poor reputation, the ABC method was that by which many children in past generations learned to read successfully.

Disputes in recent years have centered on the merits of the whole-word and phonics methods. Although some research has been done comparing these two techniques, the findings have not been conclusive (Carbo, 1987; Crowder, 1982). However, there is evidence that drill practice with the sounds made by letters in words (part of some phonics methods) improves reading ability (Williams, 1979). Many current techniques of reading instruction incorporate components of both whole-word and phonics (Durkin, 1987; Karlin & Karlin, 1987).

Information Processing

Reading is more than the sum of whole-word and phonics methods. Information-processing skills are also involved in successful reading (Hall, 1989). To understand how information processing is basic to becoming a good reader, consider the circumstances of Sam Winter, a fifth-grade student (Santrock & Yussen, 1989). Sam left his book on the dining room table one morning and went off to school. It is a popular novel, written for 9-to-12-year-olds. The book, called *Bridge to Terabithia,* describes how two children in a rural elementary school in contemporary Maryland start a friendship.

Sam's 4-year-old sister, Nancy, spied the inviting cover of the book shortly after Sam left, scooped it up, and headed for her room to "read" it. For a while, Nancy stared at the book's cover drawing of the two children, then she turned the book upside down to contemplate the drawing from that perspective. A few moments later, Nancy was poring over the story. A quick "reader," Nancy finished the entire 128-page book in about six minutes. In that six minutes she studied each of the 12 drawings in the book and thought about what each drawing represented. Nancy also picked out several capital letters she knew (*B, A, D, Z, M, N, C, Y*) and spotted some familiar numbers on different pages (0, 1, 3, 6). She returned the book to the dining room table when she finished.

Sam came home from school to have lunch. After eating a hamburger, he decided to spend a little time reading and picked up *Bridge to Terabithia*. He sat quietly for 15 minutes and read the eight pages of Chapter 2, which introduce Leslie, a bright 11-year-old girl. A few of the words in the chapter were unfamiliar, but Sam got the idea that Leslie is an unusual girl. She looks like a boy, says whatever she pleases, and knows a lot about everything. The other character in the story, Jess, kind of liked Leslie, and Sam figured that the rest of the book would be about the two of them.

Nancy, still eating lunch, hollered at Sam, "Did you finish the book?"

Sam smiled, "You can't read this book, Nancy. You're just a little kid."

Their mother intervened to prevent a predictable fight. "Well, tell us what you read, Nancy."

"A boy . . . um . . . a girl . . . a little dog house . . . a *B*, a *6*."

Sam laughed and Mrs. Winters complimented Nancy for reading so well. After Sam was comfortably off to school and Nancy was occupied with her crayons and coloring book, Mrs. Winters sat down with *Bridge to Terabithia* to see what she could learn from the novel. She skimmed the book in 20 minutes, forming a general idea of the plot outline. As she read, she made some mental notes about words and concepts she would later discuss with Sam, because she was fairly certain he had not understood them. She also considered whether the book was a good selection for Sam. Was the book's difficulty level about right for Sam, and would he assimilate the moral lessons the author was trying to communicate?

When children read, they process information and interpret it. So reading serves as a practical example to illustrate the approach of information processing we have talked about at various other times in this book. Remember that information processing is concerned with how children analyze the many different sources of information available to them in the environment and how they make sense of those experiences. When children read, for example, they have available to their senses a rich and complex set of visual symbols. The symbols are associated with sounds, the sounds are combined to form words, and the words and large units that contain them (phrases, sentences, paragraphs) have conventional meanings.

To read effectively, children have to perceive and attend to these symbols. Notice that while Sam and Mrs. Winters attended to words and sentences, Nancy attended primarily to pictures, letters of the alphabet, and numbers. Another process in reading is holding the information in memory while new information is taken in. Notice that Mrs. Winters, because she can read so much faster than Sam, was able to retain meanings skimmed from the entire novel during a 20-minute reading session, while Sam held in memory only the meanings from one chapter. A number of information-processing skills then, are involved in the ability of children to read effectively. And, as shown in Figure 12.10, they also are involved in the increased intricacies of children's art.

FIGURE 12.10 The intricacies of this 10-year old boy's art reflect the development of information processing skills during the middle- and late-childhood years.

Thinking Critically
Should a national literacy test be developed and given to all school children? Explain your answer.

Literacy

The United States is in the midst of educational reform. State after state is making legislated changes at all levels of schooling to try to improve public education. One concern has been popularized by E. D. Hirsch (1987) in his book *Cultural Literacy*. Hirsch's ideas are related to children's reading ability and have been receiving a great deal of attention in the educational community.

The following is a list of terms drawn from Hirsch's book. Read each term and see if you can silently identify its basic meaning in some way. For example, define it, give an example of it, or explain its significance, however crudely.

> 1066   Zurich   mainspring   golden   fleece
> burgher   golden   rule   nicotine   probate   court

These words were selected at random from a glossary of several thousand words in Hirsch's book. Hirsch believes that, to function in society, every literate adult should have learned every term in the glossary. The list includes terms drawn from history, literature, government, science, mathematics, art, geography, and other areas of knowledge.

Few educators could or would want to argue against the notion that accumulating a broad base of knowledge is important. But, should we be content with "shallow" knowledge of the sort that would be encouraged by a test, which Hirsch recommends should be given to every student to see whether children's knowledge is improving? Should everyone be a broad, Renaissance collector of information? And shouldn't we also be concerned about improving children's information-processing skills? (Santrock & Yussen, 1989).

Bilingualism

Octavio's Mexican parents moved to the United States one year before Octavio was born. They do not speak English fluently and have always spoken to Octavio in Spanish. At 6 years of age, Octavio has just entered the first grade at an elementary school in San Antonio, Texas, and he speaks no English. What is the best way to teach Octavio? How much easier would elementary school be for Octavio if his parents had been able to speak to him in Spanish and English when he was an infant?

A difficult task faced by the more than 6 million children who come from homes in which the primary language is not English is to master both their native tongue, spoken at home, and English, to make their way in the larger society.

Well over 6 million children in the United States come from homes in which the primary language is not English. Often, like Octavio, they live in a community in which this same non-English language is the main means of communication. These children face a more difficult task than most of us: They must master the native tongue of their family to communicate effectively at home and they must also master English to make their way in the larger society. The number of bilingual children is expanding at such a rapid rate in our country (some experts predict a tripling of their number early in the twenty-first century) that they constitute an important subgroup of language learners to be dealt with by society. Although the education of such children in the public schools has a long history, only recently has a national policy evolved to guarantee a quality language experience for them.

Great debates have raged over how best to conduct this bilingual education (Baker, 1987; Odlin, 1989; Romaine, 1989; Hakuta & Garcia, 1989). Does a person teach English as a foreign language, adopting the child's native tongue as the language of the classroom, or does one treat English as a second, equal language and strive for balance in usage of English and the native tongue? The answer to this question has important consequences for the way in which school curricula and texts are written in cities with large concentrations of Spanish-speaking children (such as New York City, Miami, San Antonio, and Los Angeles).

Annie and Tony's Disagreement about Spanish

Annie picked up Spanish when she was a child by spending time with her Mexican grandmother. She says she probably knows more Spanish than all her cousins put together. She often used her second language during her summer job as a long-distance operator. She is currently majoring in journalism at college. Annie says, "I'm really embarrassed that my younger brothers don't speak Spanish. I think they should know it. That's our background, our ancestry." Tony, age 10, seems to take as much pride in not speaking Spanish as Annie does in her fluency. Says Tony, "This is America. I don't talk Spanish. I talk to my grandparents in English. They answer me in Spanish. I don't know what they are saying." Annie shakes her head sadly, "He is embarrassed to use Spanish. I tell him that people pay to learn Spanish. It is important nowadays." ♦

Achievement

Yet another important dimension of cognitive development in middle and late childhood is children's achievement. We are a species motivated to do well at what we attempt, to gain mastery over the world in which we live, to explore with enthusiasm and curiosity unknown environments, and to achieve the heights of success. We live in an achievement-oriented world with standards that tell children that success is important. The standards suggest that success requires a competitive spirit, a desire to win, a motivation to do well, and the wherewithal to cope with adversity and persist until an objective is reached. Some developmentalists, though, believe that we are becoming a nation of hurried, "wired" people who are raising our children to become the same way—uptight about success and failure and far too worried about what we accomplish in comparison to others (Elkind, 1981). It was in the 1950s that an interest in achievement began to flourish. The interest initially focused on the need for achievement.

Need for Achievement

Think about yourself and your friends for a moment. Are you more achievement oriented than they are, or are you less so? If we asked you and your friends to tell stories about achievement-related themes, could we accurately determine which of you is the most achievement oriented?

David McClelland (1955) stressed that individuals vary in their motivation for achievement and that we can measure these differences. McClelland referred to achievement motivation as *n* **achievement** (need for achievement), the individual's motivation to overcome obstacles, to seek success, and to expend effort in completing tasks. To measure achievement, children were shown ambiguous pictures that were likely to stimulate achievement-related responses. Then they were asked to tell a story about the picture; their comments were scored according to how strongly they reflected achievement (McClelland & others, 1953).

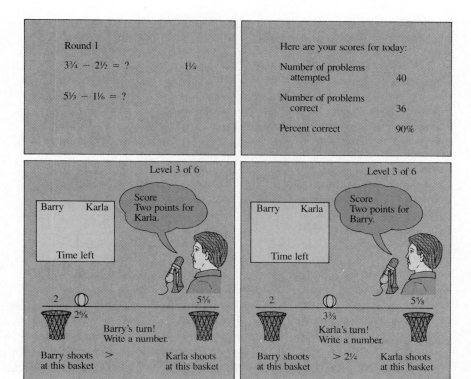

FIGURE 12.11 Examples of educational computer programs involving drill (top panel) versus game (lower panels) formats. The top panel shows a typical panel of a drill and practice program in which the child is praised after getting the problem right. The bottom panel is an example from the Fractions Basketball program developed by Sharon Dugdale and David Kibbey, 1973.

A host of studies have correlated achievement-related responses with different aspects of the individual's experiences and behavior. The findings are diverse, but they do suggest that achievement-oriented individuals have a stronger hope for success than a fear of failure, are moderate rather than high or low risk-takers, and persist for appropriate lengths of time in solving difficult problems (Atkinson & Raynor, 1974). Early research indicated that independence training by parents promoted children's achievement, but more recent research reveals that parents, to increase achievement, need to set high standards for achievement, model achievement-oriented behavior, and reward their children for their achievements (Huston-Stein & Higgens-Trenk, 1978).

Intrinsic and Extrinsic Motivation

As part of their interest in achievement motivation, psychologists have focused on the internal and external factors that contribute to such motivation. Considerable enthusiasm has greeted the issue of whether we should emphasize intrinsic or extrinsic motivation. Imagine that you must teach children about the addition and subtraction of fractions and help them practice these problems. One possibility would be to develop a simple "drill-and-practice" exercise that provides each child with a sequence of problems and, after each correct answer, praise. Such programs are indeed widespread. An alternative approach might be to present the same sequence of problems in the form of an instructional computer game tailored to enhance the child's motivation. These programs are becoming available, but they are less common than the drill-and-practice type. "Fractions Basketball" is one example developed by the PLATO PROJECT at the University of Illinois (Dugdale & Kibbey, 1980). Figure 12.11 shows how the drill-and-practice program and the computer game strategy vary (Lepper, 1985; Lepper & Gurtner, 1989).

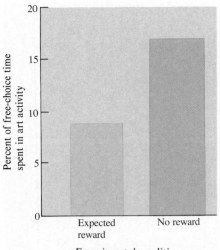

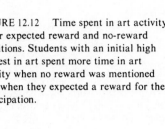

FIGURE 12.12   Time spent in art activity under expected reward and no-reward conditions. Students with an initial high interest in art spent more time in art activity when no reward was mentioned than when they expected a reward for the participation.

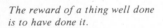
The interest in intrinsic motivation comes from ideas about motivation for challenge, competence, effectiveness, and mastery (Harter, 1981; White, 1959); curiosity, incongruity, complexity, and discrepancy (Berlyne, 1960); and perceived control and self-determination (Deci, 1975). **Intrinsic motivation** invovles an underlying need for competence and self-determination. By contrast, **extrinsic motivation** involves external factors in the environment, especially rewards. If you work hard in school because a personal standard of excellence is important to you, intrinsic motivation is involved. But if you work hard in school because you know it will bring you a higher-paying job when you graduate, extrinsic motivation is at work.

An important consideration when motivating a child to do something is whether or not to offer an incentive (Ames & Ames, 1989; Rotter, 1989). If a child is not doing competent work, is bored, or has a negative attitude, it may be worthwhile to consider incentives to improve motivation. However, there are times when external rewards can get in the way of motivation. In one investigation, children with a strong interest in art spent more time in a drawing activity when they expected no reward than their counterparts who knew that they would be rewarded (Figure 12.12) (Lepper, Greene, & Nisbett, 1973).

Intrinsic motivation implies that internal motivation should be promoted and external factors deemphasized. In this way, children learn to attribute to themselves the cause of their success and failure, and especially how much effort they expend. But in reality, achievement is motivated by both internal and external factors; children are never divorced from their external environment. Some of the most achievement-oriented children are those who have both a high personal standard for achievement and are also highly competitive. In one investigation, low-achieving boys and girls who engaged in individual goal setting and were given comparative information about peers worked more math problems and got more of them correct than their counterparts who experienced either condition alone (Schunk, 1983). Other research suggests that social comparison by itself is not a wise strategy (Nicholls, 1984). The argument is that social comparison puts the child in an ego-involved, threatening, self-focused state rather than in a task-involved, effortful, strategy-focused state.

Middle and Late Childhood

Middle-class black children, like their middle-class white counterparts, have high expectations and understand that success is due to effort and not to luck.

Achievement in Minority-Group Children

One of the main limitations of existing research on minority-group achievement is that there has been so little of it. The research literature on achievement has focused heavily on white males. Too often, research on minority groups has been interpreted as "deficits" by middle-class, white standards. Rather than characterizing individuals as *culturally different,* many conclusions unfortunately characterize the cultural distinctiveness of blacks, Hispanics, and other minority groups as deficient in some way.

Much of the research on minority group children is plagued by a failure to consider socioeconomic status (determined by some combination of education, occupation, and income). In many instances, when race *and* socioeconomic status (also called social class) are investigated in the same study, social class is a far better predictor of achievement orientation than race (Graham, 1986). Middle-class individuals fare better than their lower-class counterparts in a variety of achievement-oriented circumstances—expectations for success, achievement aspirations, and recognition of the importance of effort, for example (McAdoo & McAdoo, 1985).

Sandra Graham has conducted a number of investigations that reveal not only stronger social class than racial differences, but also the importance of studying minority-group motivation in the context of general motivational theory (Graham, 1984, 1986, 1987). Her inquiries focus on the causes blacks give for their achievement orientation—why they succeed or fail, for example. She is struck by how consistently middle-class black children do not fit our stereotypes of either deviant or special populations. They, like their middle-class white counterparts, have high expectations and understand that failure is often due to lack of effort rather than to luck.

The Achievement and Adjustment of Asian-American Children

Suzanna Kang is a 17-year-old Korean-American student at T. C. Williams High School in Alexandria, Virginia. She fits the stereotype of Asian-American students. She is bright, hard working, and carries a 4.0 grade point average. Suzanna likes science and math, is headed for a college scholarship, and is very close to her family. Says Suzanna, "I guess I do fit the Asian-American superachiever image, but I know there are many Asian-American children who are not doing so well, especially those who have recently immigrated to this country. Many of them are struggling to learn English." The whiz kid image fits many of the children of Asian immigrant families who arrived in the United States in the late 1960s and early 1970s. Many of these immigrants came from Hong Kong, South Korea, India, and the Philippines. The image also fits many of the more than 100,000 Indochinese (primarily Vietnamese) immigrants who arrived in the United States after the end of the Vietnam War in 1975. Both groups included mostly middle- to upper-income professional people who were reasonably well educated and who passed along to their children a strong interest in education and a solid work ethic. For thousands of other Asian-Americans, including a high percentage of the 600,000 Indochinese refugees who fled Vietnam, Laos, and Cambodia in the late 1970s, the problems are legion. Many in this wave of refugees lived in poor surroundings in their homelands. They came to the United States with few skills and little education. They speak little English and have a difficult time finding a decent job. They often share housing with relatives. Adjusting to school is difficult for their children. Some drop out. Some are attracted to gangs and drugs. Better school systems use a variety of techniques to help these Asian-Americans, including English as a Second Language class, as well as a range of social services. ◆

Many Asian-American children are very successful in academic settings and have strong achievement orientations. However, large numbers of Asian-American refugee children, especially those from Indochina, live in low-income surroundings and share the problems of other children of poverty. It is important to keep in mind that every ethnic group is diverse.

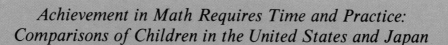

Achievement in Math Requires Time and Practice: Comparisons of Children in the United States and Japan

Harold Stevenson and his colleagues (1986) recently conducted a detailed investigation of math achievement in first- and fifth-grade children from the United States and Japan. The final sample included 240 first graders and 240 fifth graders from each country. Extensive time was spent developing the math test that was given to the children, the children were observed in their classrooms, and additional information was obtained from mothers, teachers, and the children themselves. As shown in Table 12.A, the Japanese children clearly outscored the American children on the math test in both the first and fifth grades. And, by the fifth grade, the highest average score of any of the American classrooms fell *below* the worst performing score of the Japanese classrooms.

What are some reasons for these dramatic differences between American and Japanese children's math achievement? Curriculum did not seem to be a factor. Neither did the educational background of the children's parents. And

neither did intelligence; the American children sampled actually scored slightly higher than the Japanese children on such components of intelligence as vocabulary, general information, verbal ability, and perceptual speed. Possibly the Japanese teachers had more experience? Apparently, this was not the case, since in terms of educational degrees and years of teaching experiences, no differences were found.

The amount of time spent in school and math classes probably was an important factor. The Japanese school year consists of 240 days of instruction and each school week is 5½ days long. The American school year consists of 178 days of instruction and each school week is 5 days long. In the fifth grade, Japanese children were in school an average of 37.3 hours per week, American children only 30.4 hours. Observations in the children's classrooms revealed that Japanese teachers spent far more time teaching math than did American teachers; approximately one-fourth of total classroom time in the first grade was spent in math instruction in Japan, only approximately one-tenth in the United States. Observations also indicated that the Japanese children attended more efficiently to what the teacher was saying than American children did. And Japanese children spent far more time doing homework than American children—on weekends, 66 minutes versus 18 minutes, respectively.

And in another recent investigation, Chinese children were assigned more homework and spent more time on homework than Japanese children, who, in turn, were assigned more homework and spent more time on homework than American children (Chen & Stevenson, 1989). Chinese children had more positive attitudes about homework than Japanese children, who in turn had more positive attitudes about homework than American children.

The conclusion: Learning requires time and practice. When either is reduced, learning is impaired. ◆

TABLE 12.A	*Average Mathematics Achievement by Japanese and American Children*	
Country	**Boys**	**Girls**
Grade 1		
Japan	20.7	19.5
United States	16.6	17.6
Grade 5		
Japan	53.0	53.5
United States	45.0	43.8

From H. W. Stevenson, et al., "Achievement in Mathematics" in H. W. Stevenson, et al. (eds.), *Child Development and Education in Japan.* Copyright © 1986 W. H. Freeman and Company. Used by permission.

We can compare not only the achievement orientation of children from different ethnic groups and social classes, but also the achievement orientation of children in different countries. Quite clearly, American children are more achievement oriented than children in many other countries. However, there has recently been concern about the achievement American children display in comparison to children in other countries that have developed strong educational orientations—Russia and Japan, for example. To learn more about the achievement orientation of American children compared to Japanese children, turn to Children 12.3.

Intelligence, Language, and Achievement

Concept	Processes and Related Ideas	Characteristics and Description
Intelligence	What is intelligence?	An abstract concept that is measured indirectly. Psychologists rely on intelligence tests to estimate intelligence. Verbal ability, problem-solving skills, and the ability to learn from and adapt to everyday life are involved in intelligence.
	One face or many?	The Binet and Wechsler scales are the most widely used individual tests of intelligence. Both evaluate intelligence as a general ability, while the Wechsler also evaluates a number of components of intelligence. Psychologists debate whether intelligence is a general ability or a number of specific abilities.
	Issues in intelligence	Three prominent issues in intelligence are the cultural bias of intelligence tests, knowledge versus process, and the use and misuse of intelligence tests
	The extremes of intelligence	These involve mental retardation, giftedness, and creativity. A mentally retarded person has a low IQ and has difficulty adapting to everyday life. A gifted person is one who has well-above-average intelligence, a superior talent, or both. Creativity is the ability to think in a novel or unusual way and to come up with unique solutions to problems.
Language	Vocabulary and grammar	In middle and late childhood, children become more analytical and logical in their approach to words and grammar.
	Reading, information processing, and literacy	In the history of learning to read, three techniques dominate: ABC, whole-word, and phonics. Current strategies often focus on some combination of the whole-word and phonics methods. But reading is much more than the sum of these approaches. Understanding how reading works requires consideration of information processing. Of current interest is literacy, with debate focusing on how it should be achieved.
	Bilingualism	This has become a major issue in our nation's schools, with debate raging over the best way to conduct bilingual education
Achievement	Its nature	Early interest, stimulated by McClelland's ideas, focused on the need for achievement. Contemporary ideas include the distinction between intrinsic and extrinsic motivation, as well as a concern for achievement motivation in minority-group children.

Thus far, we have discussed many ideas about the nature of children's intelligence, language, and achievement. These ideas are summarized in Concept Table 12.2. In the next chapter we will turn to children's social development in middle and late childhood.

Summary

I. Piaget's Theory and Concrete Operational Thought

Concrete operational thought is made up of operations, mental actions that are reversible. The concrete operational child shows conservation and classification skills. The concrete operational child needs clearly available perceptual supports to reason; later in development, thought becomes more abstract. Piaget's ideas have been applied extensively to education. Piaget was a genius at observing children; he showed us some important things to look for and mapped out some general cognitive changes. Criticisms of his theory focus on such matters as stages, which are not as unitary as he believed and do not always follow the timetable he envisioned.

II. Information Processing

Children's long-term memory improves during middle and late childhood. Control processes or strategies such as rehearsal, organization, and imagery are among the important influences responsible for memory improvement. Children's knowledge also influences their memory; a special kind of knowledge—metamemory—concerns control processes. Schemata and scripts become more prominent in the cognitive world of the elementary schoolchild.

III. Intelligence

Intelligence is an abstract ability that is measured indirectly. Psychologists use intelligence tests to estimate intelligence. Verbal ability, problem-solving skills, and the ability to learn from and adapt to everyday life are involved in intelligence. The Binet and Wechsler scales are the most widely used individual tests of intelligence. Both evaluate intelligence as a general ability, while the Wechsler evaluates a number of other components of intelligence. Psychologists debate whether intelligence is a general ability or a number of specific abilities. Three prominent issues in intelligence are the cultural bias of intelligence tests, knowledge versus process, and the use and misuse of intelligence tests.

IV. The Extremes of Intelligence

These involve mental retardation, giftedness, and creativity. A mentally retarded person has a low IQ and has difficulty adapting to everyday life. A gifted person is one who has well-above-average intelligence, a superior talent, or both. Creativity is the ability to think in a novel or unusual way and to come up with unique solutions to problems.

V. Language

In the middle and late childhood years, children become more analytical and logical in their approach to words and grammar. In the history of learning to read, ABC, whole-word, and phonics methods have dominated. Current strategies often focus on some combination of the whole-word and phonics methods. But reading is much more than the sum of these approaches. Understanding how reading works requires consideration of information processing. Of current interest is literacy, with debate focusing on how it should be achieved. Bilingualism has become a major issue in our nation's schools, with debate raging over the best way to conduct bilingual education.

VI. **Achievement**

Early interest, stimulated by McClelland's ideas, focused on the need for achievement. Contemporary ideas include the distinction between intrinsic and extrinsic motivation, as well as a concern for achievement motivation in minority-group children.

Key Terms

long-term memory 380
control processes 380
rehearsal 380
metamemory 381
schemata 381
scripts 381
intelligence 384
mental age (MA) 385
intelligence quotient
  (IQ) 385
normal distribution 385

Wechsler scales 386
two-factor theory 389
culture-fair tests 390
structure-process
  dilemma 392
triarchic theory of
  intelligence 393
mental retardation 395
organic retardation 395
cultural-familial
  retardation 395

gifted 396
convergent thinking 397
divergent thinking 397
creativity 398
ABC method 399
whole-word method 399
phonics method 399
n achievement 404
intrinsic motivation 406
extrinsic motivation 406

Suggested Readings

Anastasi, A. (1988). *Psychological testing* (6th ed.). New York: Macmillan.
This widely used text on psychological testing provides extensive information about intelligence tests for children.

Hirsch, E. D. (1987). *Cultural literacy*. Boston: Houghton Mifflin.
An engaging critique of school practices. Hirsch pushes for the adoption of a national test for literacy.

Horowitz, F. D., & O'Brien, M. (Eds.). (1985).
The gifted and the talented. Washington, DC: The American Psychological Association. This volume pulls together what we currently know about the gifted and the talented. Experts contributed chapters on the diverse nature of the gifted and the talented.

Kail, R. (1984). *The development of memory in children*. San Francisco: W. H. Freeman.
A readable review of developmental changes in children's memory. Includes information about many aspects of memory such as metamemory, control processes, and long-term memory.

McAdoo, H. P., & McAdoo, J. L. (1985). *Black children: Social, educational, and parental environments*. Beverly Hills, CA: Sage.
This book provides a contemporary look at the nature of achievement orientation in black children.

McDaniel, M. A., & Pressley, M. (1987). *Imagery and related mnemonic processes*. New York: Springer-Verlag.
This book provides a number of excellent strategies, especially those involving imagery, for improving children's memory.

◇
_____

*Children know nothing about childhood and
have little to say about it. They are too busy
becoming something they have not quite grasped
yet, something which keeps changing . . . Nor
will they realize what is happening to them until
they are too far beyond it to remember how it
felt.*
_____

Alistair Reed

Social Development

C an children in middle and late childhood understand concepts like discrimination, economic inequality, affirmative action, and comparable worth? Probably not, if we used these terms. But might we be able to construct circumstances illustrating these concepts that they might be able to understand? Phyllis Katz (1987) asked a group of children to pretend that they had taken a long ride on a spaceship to a make-believe planet called Pax and to give opinions about different situations in which they found themselves. The situations involved conflict, socioeconomic inequality, and civil-political rights. Conflict items included asking what a teacher should do when two students were tied for a prize or when they had been fighting. The economic equality dilemmas included a proposed field trip that not all students could afford, a comparable worth situation in which janitors were paid more than teachers, and an employment situation that discriminated against those with dots on their noses instead of stripes. The rights items dealt with minority rights and freedom of the press.

The elementary schoolchildren did indeed recognize injustice and often came up with interesting solutions to problems. For example, all but two children believed that teachers should earn as much as janitors. The holdouts said that teachers should make less because they stay in one room or because cleaning toilets is disgusting and therefore deserves higher wages. Children were especially responsive to the economic inequality items. All but one thought that not giving a job to a qualified applicant who had different physical characteristics (a striped nose rather than a dotted nose) was unfair. The majority recommended an affirmative action solution—giving the job to the one from the discriminated minority. None of the children verbalized the concept of freedom of the press or seemed to understand that a newspaper could have the right to criticize a mayor in print without being punished. Some of the courses of action suggested by the students were intriguing. Several argued that the reporters should be jailed. One child said that if she were mayor, she would worry, make speeches, and say, "I didn't do anything wrong," not unlike what American presidents have done in recent years. Another child said that the mayor should not put newspaper people out of work because that might make them print more bad things. "Make them write comics instead," he suggested.

Children believed that poverty exists on earth, but mainly in Africa, big cities, or Vietnam. War was mentioned as the biggest problem on earth, although children were not certain where that is currently occurring. Other problems mentioned were crime, hatred, school, smog, and meanness. Overall, the types of rules the children believed a society should abide by were quite sensible; almost all included the need for equitable sharing of resources and work, and prohibition against aggression.

Later in this chapter, we will further discuss children's thoughts about rules and regulations, as we continue our description of moral development. Additional aspects of the self and gender roles also are presented. To begin the chapter, we examine the social worlds of children's families, peers, and schools in middle and late childhood.

Families

As children move into the middle and late childhood years, parents spend considerably less time with them. In one investigation, parents spent less than half as much time with their children aged 5 to 12 in caregiving, instruction, reading, talking, and playing as when the children were younger (Hill & Stafford, 1980). This drop

in parent-child interaction may be even more extensive in families with little parental education. While parents spend less time with their children in middle and late childhood than in early childhood, parents continue to be extremely important socializing agents in their children's lives. What are some of the most important parent-child issues in middle and late childhood?

While parents spend less time with children in middle and late childhood, parents continue to be very important socializing agents in their children's lives.

Parent-Child Issues

Parent-child interactions during early childhood focus on such matters as modesty, bedtime regularities, control of temper, fighting with siblings and peers, eating behavior and manners, autonomy in dressing, and attention seeking. While some of these issues—fighting and reaction to discipline, for example—are carried forward into the elementary school years, many new issues appear by the age of 7 (Maccoby, 1984). These include whether children should be made to perform chores, and, if so, whether they should be paid for them; how to help children learn to entertain themselves rather than relying on parents for everything; and how to monitor children's lives outside the family in school and peer settings.

School-related matters are especially important for families during middle and late childhood. Later in this chapter, we will see that school-related difficulties are the number one reason that children in this age group are referred for clinical help.

Children must learn to relate to adults outside the family on a regular basis—adults who interact with the child much differently than parents. During middle and late childhood, interactions with adults outside the family involve more formal control and achievement orientation.

Discipline during middle and late childhood is often easier for parents than it was during early childhood; it may also be easier than during adolescence. In middle and late childhood, children's cognitive development has matured to the point where it is possible for parents to reason with them about resisting deviation and controlling their behavior. By adolescence, children's reasoning has become more sophisticated and they may be less likely to accept parental discipline. Adolescents also push more strongly for independence, which contributes to parenting difficulties. Parents of elementary schoolchildren use less physical discipline than do parents of preschool children. By contrast, parents of elementary schoolchildren are more likely to use deprivation of privileges, appeals directed at the child's self-esteem, comments designed to increase the child's sense of guilt, and statements indicating to the child that she is responsible for her actions.

During middle and late childhood, some control is transferred from parent to child, although the process is gradual and involves **coregulation** rather than control by either the child or the parent alone (Maccoby, 1984). The major shift to autonomy does not occur until about the age of 12 or later. During middle and late childhood, parents continue to exercise general supervision and exert control while children are allowed to engage in moment-to-moment self-regulation. This coregulation process is a transition period between the strong parental control of early childhood and the increased relinquishment of general supervision of adolescence.

During this coregulation, parents should

—monitor, guide, and support children at a distance;
—effectively use the times when they have direct contact with the child;
—strengthen in their children the ability to monitor their own behavior, to adopt appropriate standards of conduct, to avoid hazardous risks, and to sense when parental support and contact are appropriate.

In middle and late childhood, parents and children increasingly label each other and make attributions about each others' motives. Parents and children do not react to each other only on the basis of each others' past behavior; rather, their reactions to each other are based on how they interpret behavior and their expectations for behavior. Parents and children label each other broadly. Parents label their children smart or dumb, introverted or extraverted, mannerly or unruly, and lazy or hard-working. Children label their parents as cold or warm, understanding or not understanding, and so on. Even though there probably are specific circumstances when children and parents do not conform to these labels, the labels represent a distillation of many hours, days, months, and years of learning what each other is like as a person.

Life changes in parents also influence the nature of parent-child interaction in middle and late childhood; parents become more experienced in child rearing. As child-rearing demands are reduced in middle and late childhood, mothers are more likely to consider returning to a career or beginning a new career. Marital relationships change as less time is spent in child rearing and more time is spent in career development, especially for mothers.

Societal Changes in Families

As we discussed in Chapter 10, increasing numbers of children are growing up in divorced and working-mother families. But there are several other major shifts in the composition of family life that especially affect children in middle and late childhood. Parents are divorcing in greater numbers than ever before, but many of them remarry. It takes time for parents to marry, have children, get divorced, and then remarry. Consequently, there are far more elementary and secondary schoolchildren than infant or preschool children living in stepfamilies. In addition, an increasing number of elementary and secondary schoolchildren are latchkey children.

Stepfamilies

The number of remarriages involving children has steadily grown in recent years, although both the rate of increase in divorce and stepfamilies slowed in the 1980s. Stepfather families, in which a woman has custody of children from a previous marriage, make up 70 percent of stepfamilies. Stepmother families make up almost 20 percent of stepfamilies, and a small minority are blended with both partners bringing children from a previous marriage. A substantial percentage of stepfamilies produce children of their own.

Research on stepfamilies has lagged behind research on divorced families, but recently a number of investigators have turned their attention to this increasingly common family structure (Bray, 1988; Furstenburg, 1988; Hetherington, Hagan, & Anderson, 1989; Pasley & Ihinger-Tallman, 1987; Santrock & Sitterle, 1987; Santrock, Sitterle, & Warshak, 1988). Following remarriage of their parents, children of all ages show a resurgence of behavior problems. Younger children seem to eventually form an attachment to a stepparent and accept the stepparenting role. However, the developmental tasks facing adolescents make them especially vulnerable to the entrance of a stepparent. At the time they are searching for an identity and exploring sexual and other close relationships outside the family, a nonbiological parent may increase the stress associated with these important tasks.

Following the remarriage of the custodial parent, an emotional upheaval usually occurs in girls, and problems in boys often intensify. Over time, preadolescent boys seem to improve more than girls in stepfather families. Sons who frequently are involved in conflicted or coercive relations with their custodial mothers probably have much to gain from living with a warm, supportive stepfather. In contrast, daughters who have a close relationship with their custodial mothers and considerable independence frequently find a stepfather both disruptive and constraining.

Children's relationships with their biological parents are more positive than with their stepparents, regardless of whether a stepmother or a stepfather family is involved. However, stepfathers are often distant and disengaged from their stepchildren. As a rule, the more complex the stepfamily, the more difficult the child's adjustment. Families in which both parents bring children from a previous marriage have the highest level of behavioral problems.

In sum, as with divorce, entrance into a stepfamily involves a disequilibrium in children's lives. Most children initially find their parents' remarriage as stressful. Remarriage, though, can remove children from stressful single-parent circumstances and provide additional resources for children, such as increased involvement with parents and improved economic circumstances. Many children emerge from their remarried family as competent individuals. As with divorced families, it is

Thinking Critically
What might parents do to improve the adjustment of children in stepfamilies?

important to consider the complexity of stepfamilies, the diversity of possible outcomes for the child, and the factors that facilitate children's adjustment in stepfamilies (Hetherington, Hagan, & Anderson, 1989; Santrock, Sitterle, & Warshak, 1988).

Latchkey Children

We concluded in Chapter 10 that the mother's working outside the home does not necessarily have negative outcomes for her child. However, a certain set of children from working-mother families deserve further scrutiny: latchkey children. These children typically do not see their parents from the time they leave for school in the morning until about 6:00 or 7:00 P.M. They are called latchkey children because they are given the key to their home, take the key to school, and then use it to let themselves into the home while their parents are still at work. Latchkey children are largely unsupervised for two to four hours a day during each school week. During the summer months, they may be unsupervised for entire days, five days a week.

Thomas and Lynette Long (1983) interviewed more than 1,500 latchkey children. They concluded that a slight majority of these children had had negative latchkey experiences. Some latchkey children may grow up too fast, hurried by the responsibilities placed on them (Elkind, 1981). How do latchkey children handle the lack of limits and structure during the latchkey hours? Without limits and parental supervision, latchkey children find their way into trouble more easily, possibly stealing, vandalizing, or abusing a sibling. The Longs point out that 90 percent of the juvenile delinquents in Montgomery County, Maryland, are latchkey children. Joan Lipsitz (1983), in testifying before the Select Committee on Children, Youth, and Families, called the lack of adult supervision of children in the after-school hours one of today's major problems. Lipsitz calls it the "three-to-six o'clock problem" because it is during this time that the Center for Early Adolescence in North Carolina, of which Lipsitz is director, experiences a peak of referrals for clinical help. And in a 1987 national poll, teachers related the latchkey children phenomenon the number one reason that children have problems in school (Harris, 1987).

But while latchkey children may be vulnerable to problems, the experiences of latchkey children vary enormously, just as do the experiences of all children with working mothers. Parents need to give special attention to the ways in which their latchkey children's lives can be effectively monitored. Variations in latchkey experiences suggest that parental monitoring and authoritative parenting help the child cope more effectively with latchkey experiences, especially resisting peer pressure (Galambos & Maggs, 1989; Steinberg, 1986). The degree of developmental risk to latchkey children remains undetermined. One positive sign is that researchers are beginning to conduct more fine-grained analysis of children's latchkey experiences to determine which aspects of latchkey circumstances are the most detrimental (Rodman & others, 1988; Steinberg, 1988).

Peer Relations

During middle and late childhood, children spend an increasing amount of time in peer interaction. In one investigation, children interacted with peers 10 percent of their day at the age of 2, 20 percent at age 4, and more than 40 percent between the ages of 7 and 11. Episodes with peers totaled 299 times per typical school day (Barker & Wright, 1955).

What do children do when they are with their peers? For one, they play a lot, as reflected in the game playing of these two 10-year-old boys.

What do children do when they are with their peers? In one study, sixth graders were asked what they do when they are with their friends (Medrich & others, 1982). Team sports accounted for 45 percent of boys' nominations but only 26 percent of girls'. General play, going places, and socializing were common listings for both sexes. Most peer interactions occur outside the home (although close to home), occur more often in private than in public places, and occur more between children of the same sex than between children of different sexes.

Peer Popularity, Rejection, and Neglect

Children often think, "What can I do to get all of the kids at school to like me?" or "What's wrong with me? Something must be wrong with me or I would be more popular." What makes a child popular with peers? Children who give out the most reinforcements are often popular. So is a child who listens carefully to other children and maintains open lines of communication with peers. Being themselves, being happy, showing enthusiasm and concern for others, and being self-confident but not conceited are characteristics that serve children well in their quest for popularity among peers (Hartup, 1983).

Recently, developmentalists have distinguished between two types of children who are not popular with their peers: those who are neglected and those who are rejected (Asher & Parker, in press; Parker & Asher, 1987). **Neglected children,** while they may not have friends, are not especially disliked by their peers. However, **rejected children** are overtly disliked by their peers. Rejected children are more likely to be disruptive and aggressive than neglected children. And rejected children are more likely to continue to be unaccepted by peers even when they move into a new setting; neglected children seem to get a new social life in new groups. Rejected children say they are lonelier and less happy as well. And rejected children have more serious adjustment problems later in life. In sum, children who are rejected by their peers are at greater risk for adjustment problems; the risk status of children who are neglected by their peers is less certain (Dodge & others, 1986; Price & Dodge, in press).

Social Cognition

Earlier we found that the mutual cognitions of children and parents become increasingly important in family relationships during middle and late childhood. Children's social cognitions about their peers also become increasingly important for understanding peer relationships in middle and late childhood. Of special interest are how children process information about peer relations and their social knowledge.

A boy accidentally trips and knocks a peer's soft drink out of his hand. The peer misinterprets the encounter as hostile, which leads him to retaliate aggressively against the boy. Through repeated encounters of this kind, other peers come to perceive the aggressive boy as habitually acting in inappropriate ways. Kenneth Dodge (1983) argues that children go through five steps in processing information about their social world: decoding social cues, interpreting, searching for a response, selecting an optimal response, and enacting. Dodge has found that aggressive boys are more likely to perceive another child's actions as hostile when the child's intention is ambiguous. And when aggressive boys search for cues to determine a peer's intention, they respond more rapidly, less efficiently, and less reflectively than nonaggressive children. These are among the social cognitive factors believed to be involved in the nature of children's conflicts (Shantz, 1988).

Social knowledge also is involved in children's ability to get along with peers. An important part of children's social life involves what goals to pursue in poorly defined or ambiguous situations. Social relationship goals are also important, such as how to initiate and maintain a social bond. Children need to know what scripts to follow to get children to be their friends. For example, as part of the script for getting friends, it helps to know that saying nice things, regardless of what the peer does or says, will make the peer like the child more.

From a social cognitive perspective, children who are maladjusted do not have adequate social cognitive skills to skillfully interact with others (Berndt & Ladd, 1989; Kelly & deArmas, 1989; Weisberg, Caplan, & Sivo, 1989). One investigation explored the possibility that children who are maladjusted do not have the social cognitive skills necessary for positive social interaction (Asarnow & Callan, 1985). Boys with and without peer adjustment difficulties were identified, and their social cognitive skills were assessed. Boys without peer adjustment problems generated more alternative solutions to problems, proposed more assertive and mature solutions, gave less intense aggressive solutions, showed more adaptive planning, and evaluated physically aggressive responses less positively than boys with peer adjustment problems.

The world of peers is one of varying acquaintances; children interact with some children they barely know and with others for hours every day. It is to the latter type—friends—that we now turn.

Friends

"My best friend is nice. She is honest and I can trust her. I can tell her my innermost secrets and know that nobody else will find out about them. I have other friends, but she is my best friend. We consider each other's feelings and don't want to hurt each other. We help each other out when we have problems. We make up funny names for people and laugh ourselves silly. We make lists of which boys we think are the ugliest, which are the biggest jerks, and so on. Some of these things we share with other friends, some we don't." This is a description of a friendship by a 10-year-old girl. It reflects the belief that children are interested in specific peers—in Barbara and Tommy—not just any peers. They want to share concerns, interests, information, and secrets with them.

Why are children's friendships important? They serve six functions: companionship, stimulation, physical support, ego support, social comparison, and intimacy/affection (Gottman & Parker, 1987; Parker & Gottman, 1989). Concerning companionship, friendship provides children with a familiar partner and playmate, someone who is willing to spend time with them and join in collaborative activities.

Children's friendships serve a number of important functions, including companionship, stimulation, physical support, ego support, social comparison, and intimacy/affection.

A man's growth is seen in the successive choirs of his friends.

Ralph Waldo Emerson, 1841

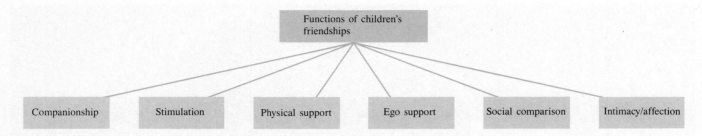

FIGURE 13.1   The functions of children's
friendships.

Concerning stimulation, friendship provides children with interesting information, excitement, and amusement. Concerning physical support, friendship provides time, resources, and assistance. Concerning ego support, friendship provides the expectation of support, encouragement, and feedback that helps the child maintain an impression of herself as a competent, attractive, and worthwhile individual. Concerning social comparison, friendship provides information about where the child stands vis-à-vis others and whether the child is doing OK. Concerning intimacy and affection, friendship provides children with a warm, close, trusting relationship with another individual in which self-disclosure takes place (Figure 13.1).

While friendships exist in early childhood, they become more predominant during middle and late childhood. Robert Selman (1980) proposed a developmental model that highlights the changing faces of friendship. Friendship begins at 3 to 7 years of age with momentary friendships; friends are valued because they are nearby and have nice toys. At 4 to 9 years, friendship involves one-way assistance; a friend is a friend because he does what you want him to do. At 6 to 12 years of age, friendship consists of two-way fair-weather cooperation, followed at 9 to 15 years of age by intimate, mutually shared relationships. Finally, at 12 years of age and older, children gain enough perspective for autonomous, interdependent friendships to become possible.

Two of friendship's most common characteristics are intimacy and similarity. **Intimacy** in friendships is defined as self-disclosure and the sharing of private thoughts. Research reveals that intimate friendships may not appear until early adolescence (Berndt, 1982; Berndt & Perry, 1990; Buhrmester, 1989). Also, throughout childhood, friends are more similar than dissimilar in terms of age, sex, race, and many other factors. Friends often have similar attitudes toward school, similar educational aspirations, and closely aligned achievement orientations. Friends like the same music, the same kind of clothes, and the same kind of leisure activities.

Schools

The world rests on the breath of the children in the schoolhouse.

The Talmud

It is justifiable to be concerned about the impact of schools on children: By the time students graduate from high school, they have spent 10,000 hours in the classroom. Children spend many years in schools as members of a small society in which there are tasks to be accomplished, people to be socialized and socialized by, and rules that define and limit behavior, feelings, and attitudes.

As children enter the first grade, what changes do they experience?

The Transition to School

For most children, entering the first grade signals a change from being a "home-child" to being a "schoolchild" in which new roles and obligations are experienced. Children take up a new role (being a student), interact and develop relationships with new significant others, adopt new reference groups, and develop new standards by which to judge themselves. School provides children with a rich source of new ideas to shape their sense of self.

A special concern about children's early school experiences is emerging. Evidence is mounting that early schooling proceeds mainly on the basis of negative feedback. For example, children's self-esteem in the latter part of elementary school is lower than it is in the earlier part, and older children rate themselves as less smart, less good, and less hard-working than do younger ones (Blumenfeld & others, 1981). In one recent investigation, the first year of school was identified as a period of considerable importance in shaping achievement, especially for ethnic-minority children (Alexander & Entwisle, 1988). Black and white children began school with similar achievement test scores, but by the end of the first year, black children's performance lagged noticeably behind that of white children, and the gap widened over the second year of schooling. The grades teachers gave to black children in the first two grades of school also were lower than those they gave to white children.

Thinking Critically
Why does early elementary school involve so much negative feedback? What aspects of our culture and the nature of education are responsible?

Schools in the Soviet Union

Soviet schools have 10 grades, called forms, which correspond roughly to the 12 grades in American schools. Children begin school at age 7 and attend classes 5½ days a week. In the higher forms, students report that they average doing two to three hours of homework each night. Beginning in the third form, Russian students study both Russian and English. Since most of the Soviet Union's 15 republics have native languages other than Russian, many students study their native language as well. Because of the emphasis on teaching English in their schools, most Soviet citizens under the age of 35 speak at least some English (Cameron, 1988).   ♦

Students in the USSR—their red ties show their identification with the Communist government as members of the young pioneers. How much more likely are these students able to read English than are American students able to read Russian?

In school, as well as out of school, children's learning, like children's development, is *integrated* (NAEYC, 1988). One of the main pressures on elementary teachers has been the need to "cover the curriculum." Frequently, teachers have tried to do so by tightly scheduling discrete time segments for each subject. This approach ignores the fact that children often do not need to distinguish learning by subject area. For example, they advance their knowledge of reading and writing when they work on social studies projects; they learn mathematical concepts through music and physical education (Katz & Chard, in press; Van Deusen-Henkel & Argondizza, 1987). A curriculum can be facilitated by providing learning areas in which children plan and select their activities. For example, the classroom may include a fully equipped publishing center, complete with materials for writing, illustrating, typing, and binding student-made books; a science area with animals and plants for observation and books to study; and other similar areas (Van Deusen-Henkel & Argondizza, 1987). In this type of classroom, children learn reading as they discover information about science; they learn writing as they work together on interesting projects. Such classrooms also provide opportunities for spontaneous play, recognizing that elementary schoolchildren continue to learn in all areas through unstructured play, either alone or with other children.

The following poem by Kathy Davis, age 8, reveals the special place school can be in the lives of children:

> Montlake School is the neatest around
> And if they tried to close it down,
> Tell it like this, Tell it like that,
> Montlake's the best and that's a fact.
> We're all good friends. We like each other.
> Just like we're sister and brother.
> If you're looking for a place that's great
> Why don't you try Room Eight.
> (Ludtke, 1988, p. 36)

Teachers and Peers

Teachers and peers have a prominent influence in middle and late childhood. Teachers symbolize authority and establish the classroom's climate, conditions of interaction among students, and the nature of group functioning. The peer group is an important source of status, friendship, and belonging in the school setting; the peer group also is a learning community in which social roles and standards related to work and achievement are formed.

Almost everyone's life is affected in one way or another by teachers. You were probably influenced by teachers as you grew up; you may become a teacher yourself or work with teachers through counseling or psychological services; and you may one day have children whose education will be guided by many different teachers through the years. You can probably remember several of your teachers vividly: Perhaps one never smiled, another required you to memorize everything in sight, and yet another always appeared happy and vibrant and encouraged verbal interaction. Psychologists and educators have tried to create a profile of a good teacher's personality traits, but the complexity of personality, education, learning, and individual differences make the task difficult. Nonetheless, some teacher traits are associated with positive student outcomes more than others; enthusiasm, ability to plan, poise, adaptability, warmth, flexibility, and awareness of individual differences are a few (Gage, 1965).

Erik Erikson (1968) believes that good teachers should be able to produce a sense of industry, rather than inferiority, in their students. Good teachers are trusted and respected by the community and know how to alternate work and play, study and games, says Erikson. They know how to recognize special efforts and to encourage special abilities. They also know how to create a setting in which children feel good about themselves and how to handle those children to whom school is not important. In Erikson's (1968) own words, children should be "mildly but firmly coerced into the adventure of finding out that one can learn to accomplish things which one would never have thought of by oneself" (p. 127).

Teacher characteristics and styles are important, but they need to be considered in concert with what children bring to the school situation (Linney & Seidman, 1989). Some children may benefit more from structure than others, and some teachers may be able to handle a flexible curriculum better than others. The importance of both children's characteristics and the treatments or experiences they are given in classrooms is known as **aptitude-treatment interaction (ATI).** Aptitude refers to academic potential and personality dimensions on which students differ; treatment refers to educational techniques—structured versus flexible classrooms, for example (Cronbach & Snow, 1977). Research has shown that children's achievement level (aptitude) interacts with classroom structure (treatment) to produce the best learning and most enjoyable learning environment (Peterson, 1977). That is, students who are highly achievement oriented usually do well in a flexible classroom and enjoy it; low-achievement-oriented students usually fare worse and dislike the flexibility. The reverse often appears in structured classrooms.

Social Class and Ethnicity

Sometimes it seems as though the main function of schools is to train children to contribute to a middle-class society. Politicians who vote on school funding are usually middle-class, school board members are usually middle-class, and principals and teachers are usually middle-class. Critics argue that schools have not done a good job of educating lower-class children to overcome the barriers blocking the enhancement of their position (Alexander & Entwisle, 1988; McAdov, 1988).

Teachers have lower expectations for children from low-income families than for children from middle-income families. A teacher who knows that a child comes from a lower-class background may spend less time trying to help the child solve a problem and may anticipate that the child will get into trouble. The teacher may believe that the parents in low-income families are not interested in helping the child, so she may make fewer efforts to communicate with them. There is evidence that teachers with lower-class origins may have different attitudes toward lower-class students than teachers from middle-class origins (Gottlieb, 1966). Perhaps because they have experienced many inequities themselves, teachers with lower-class origins may be more empathetic to problems that lower-class children encounter. When asked to rate the most outstanding characteristics of their lower-class students, middle-class teachers checked lazy, rebellious, and fun-loving; lower-class teachers checked happy, cooperative, energetic, and ambitious. The teachers with lower-class backgrounds perceived the lower-class children's behaviors as adaptive; the middle-class teachers viewed the same behaviors as falling short of middle-class standards.

In his famous speech "I Have a Dream," Martin Luther King said, "I have a dream that my four little children will one day live in a nation where they will not be judged by the color of their skin but by the content of their character." Children from lower-class backgrounds are not the only students who had difficulties in school; so have children from different ethnic backgrounds (Tharp, 1989). In most American schools, blacks, Mexican-Americans, Puerto Ricans, Native Americans, Japanese, and Asian-Indians are minorities. Many teachers have been ignorant of the different cultural meanings non-Anglo children have learned in their community (Huang & Gibbs, 1989). The social and academic development of children from minority groups depends on teacher expectations, the teacher's experience in working with children from different backgrounds, the curriculum, the presence of role models in the schools for minority students, the quality of relations between school personnel and parents from different ethnic, economic, and educational backgrounds, and the relations between the school and the community (Minuchin & Shapiro, 1983).

THE CULTURAL WORLDS OF CHILDREN

Some critics argue that one of the main functions for schools has been to train children to contribute to a middle-class, white society. These critics argue that schools have not done a competent job of educating low-income, ethnic minority children.

A Black Student's View of Public Schools

"Black and Hispanic students have less chance of building strong relationships with teachers because their appearance and behavior may be considered offensive to middle-class white teachers. These students show signs of what white teachers, and some teachers of color, consider disrespect, and they do not get the nurturing relationships that develop respect and dedication. They are considered less intelligent, as can be seen in the proportion of blacks and Hispanics in lower-level as opposed to upper-level classes. There is less teacher-student contact with "underachievers," because they are guided into peer tutoring programs. . . . The sad part is that many students believe that this type of teaching is what academic learning is all about. They have not had the opportunity to experience alternative ways of teaching and learning. From my experience in public school, it appears that many minority students will never be recognized as capable of analytical and critical thinking."

Imani Perry, 15-year-old black student

Source: Perry, 1988 ♦

The Jigsaw Classroom

Aronson stressed that the reward structure of the elementary school classrooms needed to be changed from a setting of unequal competition to one of cooperation among equals, without making any curriculum changes. To accomplish this, he put together the **jigsaw classroom.** How might this work? Consider a class of 30 students, some white, some black, some Hispanic. The lesson to be learned in the class focuses on the life of Joseph Pulitzer. The class might be broken up into five groups of six students each, with the groups being as equal as possible in terms of ethnic composition and academic achievement level. The lesson about Pulitzer's life could be divided into six parts, with one part given to each member of the six-person group. The parts might be paragraphs from Pulitzer's biography, such as how the Pulitzer family came to the United States, Pulitzer's childhood, his early work, and so on. The components are like parts of a jigsaw puzzle. They have to be put together to form the complete puzzle.

Each student in the group is given an allotted time to study his part. Then the group meets and each member tries to teach a part to the group. After an hour or so, each member is tested on the entire life of Pulitzer, with each member receiving an individual rather than a group score. Each student, therefore, must learn the entire lesson; learning depends on the cooperation and effort of the other members. Aronson (1986) believes that this type of learning increases the stu-

dents' independence through cooperatively reaching the same goal.

The strategy of emphasizing cooperation rather than competition and the jigsaw classroom have been widely used in classrooms in the United States. A number of research studies reveal that this type of cooperative learning is associated with increased self-esteem, better academic performance, friendships among classmates, and improved interethnic perceptions (Aronson, 1986; Slavin, 1987, 1989).

While the cooperative classroom strategy has many merits, it may have a built-in difficulty that restricts its effectiveness. Academic achievement is as much an individual as a team "sport" (Brown, 1986). It is individuals, not groups, who enter college, take jobs, and follow careers. A parent with an advantaged child in the jigsaw classroom might react with increased ethnic hostility when the child brings home a lower grade than he had been used to getting before the jigsaw classroom was introduced. The child tells the father, "The teacher is getting us to teach each other. In my group, we have a kid named Carlos who can barely speak English." While the jigsaw classroom can be an important strategy for reducing interracial hostility, caution needs to be exercised in its use because of the unequal status of the participants and the individual nature of achievement. ◆

Our most basic common link is that we all inhabit the planet. We all breathe the same air. We all cherish our children's future.

John F. Kennedy, address,
The American University, 1963

When the schools of Austin, Texas, were desegregated through extensive busing, the outcome was increased racial tension among blacks, Mexican-Americans, and whites, producing violence in the schools. The superintendent consulted with Eliot Aronson, a prominent social psychologist, who was at the University of Texas at Austin at the time. Aronson thought it was more important to prevent racial hostility than to control it. This led him to observe a number of elementary school classrooms in Austin. What he saw was fierce competition between persons of unequal status. To learn how Aronson proposed to reduce the tension and fierce competition, turn to Children 13.1.

Thus far, we have discussed many ideas about families, peers, and schools in middle and late childhood. These ideas are summarized in Concept Table 13.1. We turn next to children's personality development in middle and late childhood, exploring the self, gender roles, and moral development.

Personality Development

Children's expanding social worlds and increased cognitive sophistication in middle and late childhood contribute to their perceptions of themselves, to their social competence, to their gender roles, and to their thoughts about right and wrong.

Families, Peers, and Schools

Concept	Processes and Related Ideas	Characteristics and Description
Families	Parent-child interaction and issues	Parents spend less time with children during middle and late childhood, including less time in caregiving, instruction, reading, talking, and playing. Nonetheless, parents still are powerful and important socializing agents in this period. New parent-child issues emerge, and discipline changes. Control is more coregulatory, children and parents label each other more, and parents mature just as children do.
	Societal changes in families	During middle and late childhood, two major changes in many children's lives are movement into a stepfamily and becoming a latchkey child. Just as divorce produces disequilibrium and stress for children, so does the entrance of a stepparent. Over time, preadolescent boys seem to improve more than girls in stepfather families. Adolescence appears to be an especially difficult time for adjustment to the entrance of a stepparent. Latchkey children may become vulnerable when they are not monitored by adults in the after-school hours.
Peer Relations	Peer interaction	Children spend considerably more time with peers in middle and late childhood.
	Popularity, rejection, and neglect	Listening skills and effective communication, being yourself, being happy, showing enthusiasm and concern for others, and indicating self-confidence but not conceit are predictors of peer popularity. Rejected children are at risk for adjustment problems; the risk status of neglected children is less clear.
	Social cognition	Social information-processing skills and social knowledge are two important dimensions of social cognition in peer relations.
	Friends	Children's friendships serve six functions: companionship, stimulation, physical support, ego support, social comparison, and intimacy/affection. Intimacy and similarity are two common characteristics of friendships.
Schools	Transition to school	Children spend more than 10,000 hours in the classroom as members of a small society in which there are tasks to be accomplished, people to be socialized and socialized by, and rules that define and limit behavior. A special concern is that early schooling proceeds mainly on the basis of negative feedback to children. The curriculum in elementary schools should be integrated.
	Teachers and peers	Teachers and peers have prominent influences in middle and late childhood. Aptitude-treatment interaction is an important consideration.
	Social class and ethnicity	Schools have a stronger middle-class than lower-class orientation. Many lower-class children have problems in schools, as do children from ethnic minorities. Efforts are being made to reduce this bias, among them the jigsaw classroom.

The Self and Social Competence

What are some important changes in the self and the self-concept in middle and late childhood? What makes a child socially competent in this period of development? What did Erikson believe was the most important consideration in middle and late childhood? We will consider each of these questions in turn.

(a)

(b)

(c)

(d)

On Susan Harter's Perceived Competence Scale for Children, children answer questions about their (a) general self-worth, such as how happy they are; (b) cognitive skills, such as how good they are at schoolwork; (c) social skills, such as whether they have a lot of friends; and (d) physical skills, such as how good they are in sports.

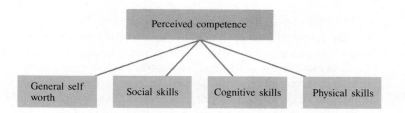

FIGURE 13.2   The Harter Perceived Competence Scale for Children.

Self-Concept

An important dimension of children's self-concept is their increasing ability to understand how others view them. Young children have difficulty understanding another person's perception of them, and often they are unaware of the impressions their behavior makes on others. But gradually, children come to understand that their behavior triggers reactions from others, and they begin to monitor their actions, acting differently depending on whom they are with and which aspect of their social self they wish to be seen. This is a time when children are more cautious about revealing themselves to others (Maccoby, 1980).

Closely related to self-concept is *self-esteem*—the value people place on themselves and their behavior. Children with high self-esteem feel good about themselves and evaluate their abilities highly (Isberg & others, 1989). In one investigation, a measure of self-esteem was administered to elementary schoolboys, and the boys and their mothers were interviewed about their family relationships (Coopersmith, 1967). Based on these assessments, the following parenting attributes were associated with the boys' high self-esteem:

—expression of affection
—concern about the child's problems
—harmony in the home
—participation in joint family activities
—availability to give competent, organized help to the boys when
  they need it
—setting clear and fair rules
—abiding by these rules
—allowing the children freedom within well-prescribed limits

Efforts to measure self-concept and self-esteem have been numerous, but one measure deserves special attention. Susan Harter (1982) developed the **Perceived Competence Scale for Children.** This measure consists of four components. One set of questions measures general self-worth ("I am sure of myself"; "I am happy the way I am"). Self-perceptions of skills in three different areas represent other sets of questions: cognitive ("I am good at schoolwork"; "I remember things easily"); social ("I have a lot of friends"; "Most kids like me"); and physical ("I do well at sports"; "I'm usually chosen first for games"). Harter's scale does an excellent job of separating the child's self-perceptions about abilities in different skill areas; and when general self-worth is measured, questions that focus on overall perceptions of the self are used rather than questions that are directed at specific skill domains. Notice that Harter calls her scale an assessment of perceived competence. Notice also that one of the important domains of perceived competence is social competence. Indeed, in recent years, developmentalists have shown an increased interest in mapping out what social competence is (Figure 13.2).

When I was one,
I had just begun.
When I was two,
I was nearly new.
When I was three,
I was hardly me.
When I was four,
I was not much more.
When I was five,
I was just alive.
But now I am six, I'm as clever as ever.
So I think I'll be six now for ever and
ever.

A. A. Milne, Now We Are Six

Social Competence

Socially competent children are able to use resources within themselves and in the environment to achieve positive developmental outcomes (Waters & Sroufe, 1983). Resources within the self include self-esteem, self-control, delay of gratification, resilience to stress, and a healthy orientation toward achievement and work. For example, socially competent children feel good about themselves and have confidence in their abilities; they can control their behavior in the face of temptation and threat; they are able to delay gratification when appropriate rather than seeking immediate satisfaction; they cope effectively with stress (often viewing stress as a challenge rather than as a threat); and they persist in achieving goals. Parents are important resources in children's environment throughout childhood; in early childhood and beyond, peers assume more importance.

The dimensions of social competence may be different at various points in development. Dependency is a positive feature of social competence in the first year but later takes on more negative tones. We have seen that Erikson believes that development of trust is the most salient component of social competence in the first year, that autonomy has this distinction in the second year, and that initiative is the key aspect of social competence to develop during early childhood. What does Erikson believe is the most important dimension of social competence during middle and late childhood?

Industry Versus Inferiority

Erikson's fourth stage of the human life cycle, industry versus inferiority, appears during middle and late childhood. The term *industry* expresses a dominant theme of this period: Children become interested in how things are made and how they work. It is the Robinson Crusoe age in that the enthusiasm and minute detail Crusoe uses to describe his activities appeal to the child's budding sense of industry. When children are encouraged in their efforts to make and build and work—whether building a model airplane, constructing a treehouse, fixing a bicycle, solving an addition problem, or cooking—their sense of industry increases. However, parents who see their children's efforts at making things as "mischief" or "making a mess" encourage children's development of a sense of inferiority.

Children's social worlds beyond their families also contribute to a sense of industry. School becomes especially important in this regard. Consider a child who is slightly below average in intelligence. He is too bright to be in special classes but not bright enough to be in gifted classes. He fails frequently in his academic efforts, developing a sense of inferiority. By contrast, consider a child whose sense of industry is derogated at home. A series of sensitive and committed teachers may revitalize his sense of industry (Elkind, 1970).

Gender Roles

Children's social competence and personality also involve gender roles. Nowhere in the social and personality development of children have more sweeping changes occurred in recent years than in the area of gender roles. Not too long ago, it was widely believed that boys should grow up to be "masculine" and girls should grow up to be "feminine." The feedback children received from parents, peers, teachers, and television was consistent with this thinking. Today, diversity characterizes the gender roles of children and the feedback they receive from their environment. A

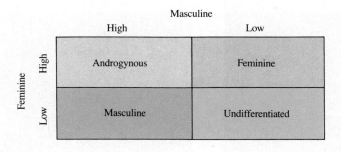

FIGURE 13.3 Categories used in androgyny scales.

	Masculine	
	High	Low
High (Feminine)	Androgynous	Feminine
Low (Feminine)	Masculine	Undifferentiated

young girl's mother may promote femininity, but the girl may be close friends with a "tomboy" in the neighborhood, and she may have teachers who encourage her assertiveness.

Masculinity, Femininity, and Androgyny

In the past, the well-adjusted male was expected to be independent, aggressive, and power-oriented; the well-adjusted female was expected to be dependent, nurturant, and uninterested in power and dominance. By the mid-1970s, though, gender roles were changing. Many females were unhappy with the label "feminine" and felt stigmatized by its association with characteristics such as passiveness and unassertiveness. Many males were uncomfortable with being called "masculine" because of its association with such characteristics as insensitivity and aggression.

Many laypeople as well as developmentalists believed that something more than "masculinity" and "femininity" was needed to describe the changing gender roles. The byword became **androgyny,** meaning the combination of masculine and feminine characteristics in the same individual (Bem, 1977; Spence & Helmreich, 1978). The androgynous child might be a male who is assertive (masculine) and nurturant (feminine) or a female who is dominant (masculine) and sensitive to others' feelings (feminine).

The primary characteristics used to assess androgyny are self-assertiveness and integration (Ford, 1986). The self-assertive characteristics include leadership, dominance, independence, competitiveness, and individualism. Integrative characteristics include sympathy, affection, and understanding. The androgynous child is simply a female or male who has a high degree of both feminine and masculine characteristics. No new characteristics are used to describe the androgynous individual. An individual can be classified as masculine, feminine, or androgynous. A fourth category, **undifferentiated,** is used to assess gender roles; this category describes a person who has neither masculine nor feminine characteristics. The four classifications of gender roles are presented in Figure 13.3.

Debate still flourishes on what components ought to go into making up the masculine and feminine categories. Because the components are combined to make up the androgyny category, the composition of masculinity and femininity is crucial to what it means to be androgynous. The nature of androgyny raises an important issue in psychology. When a concept or construct is developed and evaluated, the dimensions of the concept must be pinned down. Specifying the dimensions of a concept in a logical, organized, and empirical way is one of psychology's great lessons. Unfortunately, in the case of androgyny, this lesson has sometimes been lost.

(a)

(b)

Androgyny consists of (a) self-assertive characteristics, such as those shown by this young girl's independence, competitiveness, and individualism; and (b) integrative characteristics, such as those shown by these young boys' sympathy, affection, and understanding.

The concept of androgyny has often been based on a hodgepodge of stereotypical ideas, especially those of college students, about personality differences between males and females (Downs & Langlois, 1988; Gill & others, 1987; Ford, 1986).

Adding to the complexity of determining whether a child is masculine, feminine, or androgynous is the child's developmental level (Maccoby, 1987a). A 4-year-old boy would be labeled masculine if he enjoyed and frequently engaged in rough-and-tumble play, if he preferred to play with blocks and trucks, and if he tended to play outdoors in the company of other boys during periods of free play at his preschool. A 4-year-old girl would be labeled feminine if she liked to wear dresses, played with dolls and art materials, and did not get into fights. At age 10, a masculine boy would be one who engaged in active sports, avoided girls, and was not especially diligent about his schoolwork. At age 10, a feminine girl would be one who had one or two close girlfriends, did not try to join boys' sports play groups, paid attention to the teacher in class, liked to babysit, and preferred romantic television fare. At age 15, a masculine boy would be one who excelled in spatial-visual tasks, liked and did well in math, was interested in cars and machinery, and knew how to repair mechanical gadgets. At age 15, a feminine girl would be more interested in English and history than in math or science and would wear lipstick and makeup. These examples are not exhaustive, but they give the flavor of how the characteristics of masculinity and femininity depend to some degree on the child's developmental status.

In a recent longitudinal investigation, both the developmental and the multifaceted nature of gender roles were evident (Maccoby & Jacklin, in press). When the children were almost 4 years old, parents were asked whether their daughters were flirtatious, liked frilly clothes, cared how their hair looked, and liked to wear jewelry. These items formed a feminine scale. A second scale inquired about how rough and noisy their daughter was in playing with her age mates, whether she preferred to play with boys, girls, or both equally, whether she ever got into fights, and what her favorite pretend roles were. On the basis of these items, a "tomboy" scale was constructed, indicating the girl's motivation to play with boys, engage in rough and noisy play, fight occasionally, and engage in masculine fantasy roles. Somewhat surprising, the girls who were the most feminine on the first scale also were somewhat more likely to be tomboys. This finding raises several important points. Clearly, persons may show some dimensions but not others among the set of stereotyped masculine or feminine attributes. Also, different aspects of the clusters may take on more or less importance at different ages. For example, two attributes—sexual attractiveness and gentle-kind-considerate-nurturant qualities—are probably involved in the concept of femininity at all ages, but the sexual aspect probably is dominant in adolescence, while the second component may emerge most strongly in adulthood when many women are involved in the care of their children.

According to Martin Ford (1986), gender roles can be better understood by describing masculinity in terms of self-assertion and femininity in terms of integration. *Self-assertion* includes such components as leadership, dominance, independence, competitiveness, and individualism. *Integration* includes such components as sympathy, affection, and understanding. An androgynous individual would be high on both self-assertion and integration. Sandra Gill and her colleagues (1987) believe gender roles can be better understood by describing masculinity in terms of an instrumental orientation and femininity in terms of an expressive orientation. An **instrumental orientation** is concerned with the attainment of goals and an emphasis on a person's accomplishments. An **expressive orientation** is concerned with facilitating social interaction, interdependence, and relationships. In both the descriptions by Ford and Gill and her colleagues, we find the same dual emphasis on the individual and social relations that also is proposed as the best way to describe social competence.

Which children are the most competent? Children who are undifferentiated in terms of gender roles are the least competent. They are the least socially responsible, they have the least self-control, and they receive the poorest grades in school (Ford, 1986). Psychologists do not understand this category well, and consequently they classify few children in this way. But what about the majority of children, those who are masculine, feminine, or androgynous? Which of these groups is the most competent?

This is not an easy question to answer because the dimensions of androgyny and the dimensions of competence are not clearly spelled out in research. In many instances, androgynous children are the most competent; however, the criteria for competence are varied. If the criteria for competence involve self-assertion and integration or an instrumental and an expression orientation, then androgynous children usually are more competent. However, if the criteria for competence involve primarily self-assertion or an instrumental orientation, then a masculine gender role is favored. If the criteria involve primarily self-assertion, then a masculine gender role is favored; if they involve primarily integration or an expressive orientation,

Thinking Critically
How extensively are parents rearing their children to become androgynous? Are parents rearing girls to be more androgynous than they are their sons? Are middle-class parents more likely to rear their children to be androgynous than parents from low-income backgrounds? Explain.

Gender-Role Socialization in Egypt

In recent decades, roles assumed by males and females in the United States are believed to have become increasingly similar—that is, androgynous. In some countries, gender roles have remained more gender specific than in the United States. Egypt is one example of such a country. The division of labor between Egyptian males and females is pronounced: Egyptian males are socialized to work in the public sphere, females in the private world of home and child rearing. The Islamic religion dictates that the man's duty is to provide for his family, the woman's duty to care for her family and household (Dickerscheid & others, 1988).

Any deviations from this traditional gender role orientation are severely disapproved of. Many cultures around the world socialize children and adolescents to behave, think, and feel in gender-specific ways. Kenya and Nepal are two other cultures where children and adolescents are brought up following very strict gender-specific guidelines (Munroe & others, 1984). While in the United States and other western cultures, many parents are rearing their children and adolescents to be more androgynous, this gender role orientation has not touched the lives of people in many of the world's nations. ◆

In Egypt near the Aswan Dam, women are returning from the Nile River where they have filled their water jugs. How might gender role socialization for girls in Egypt compare to that in the United States?

Middle and Late Childhood

TABLE 13.1	Adjectives That Describe Possible Gender Differences	
What are the differences in the behavior and thoughts of boys and girls? Indicate whether you think each noun below *best* describes boys or girls—or neither—in our society. Follow your first impulse and be honest.		
Noun	**Girls**	**Boys**
Verbal skills	☐	☐
Sensitivity	☐	☐
Activity	☐	☐
Competitiveness	☐	☐
Compliance	☐	☐
Dominance	☐	☐
Math skills	☐	☐
Suggestibility	☐	☐
Sociability	☐	☐
Aggression	☐	☐
Visual-spatial skills	☐	☐

then a feminine gender role is preferred. For example, masculine persons might be more competent in school achievement and work, and feminine individuals more competent in relationships and helping.

The self-assertive and instrumental dimensions of gender roles have been valued in our culture more than the integrative or expressive dimensions. When psychologists have assessed the relation of gender roles to competence, their criteria for competence have included twice as many self-assertive and instrumental as integrative and expressive items. A disturbing outcome of such cultural standards and research bias is that masculine dimensions are perceived to mean competence. We need to place a higher value on the integrative and expressive dimensions of our own lives and our children's lives and to give these dimensions adequate weight in our assessment of competence.

Gender Differences

In addition to studying cultural expectations and attitudes about gender, we can also examine whether boys and girls differ in certain ways. To sample some of the possible differences in gender, turn to Table 13.1. According to a classic review of gender differences, Eleanor Maccoby and Carol Jacklin (1974) concluded that boys have better math skills, have superior visual-spatial ability (the kind of skills an architect would need to design a building's angles and dimensions), and are more aggressive, while girls are better at verbal skills. Recently, Eleanor Maccoby (1987b) revised her conclusion about several gender-role dimensions. She commented that research evidence suggests that boys now are more active than girls, and she is less certain that girls have greater verbal ability than boys, mainly because boys score as high as girls on the verbal part of the Scholastic Aptitude Tests (SAT).

Evidence is accumulating that some gender differences are vanishing, especially in verbal ability (Feingold, 1988; Hyde & Linn, 1986; Jacklin, 1989). In a recent analysis, Alan Feingold (1988) evaluated gender differences in cognitive abilities on two widely used tests—the Differential Aptitude Test and the SAT—from

1947 to 1983. Girls scored higher than boys in grammar, spelling, and perceptual speed; boys scored higher in spatial visualization, high school mathematics, and mechanical aptitude. No gender differences were found on verbal reasoning, arithmetic, and reasoning about figures. Gender differences declined precipitously over the years. One important exception to the rule of vanishing gender differences is the well-documented gender gap at the upper levels of performance on high school mathematics that has remained constant over three decades.

Few data about gender differences seem to be cast in stone. As our culture has changed, so have some of our findings about gender differences and similarities. As our expectations and attitudes about gender roles have become more similar for boys and girls, gender differences in many areas are vanishing.

But there are skill areas in which gender differences remain strong, one of them being math (Ducey, 1989). A special concern about gender roles in today's society focuses on computer ability. In two recent novels, *Turing's Man* (Bolter, 1984) and *The Second Self* (Turkle, 1984), technology overwhelms humanity. In both stories, females have no important roles in the technological, computer culture. One character notes: "There are few women hackers. This is a male world" (Turkle, 1984). Unfortunately, both boys and girls are socialized to associate computer programming with math skills, and programming is typically taught in math departments by males. Male-female ratios in computer classes range from 2:1 to 5:1, although computers in offices tend to be used equally by females and males. Males also have more positive attitudes toward computers. One hopes that Turkle's male computer hacker will not serve as the model for future computer users (Lockheed, 1985).

Moral Development

Remember from Chapter 10 our description of Piaget's view of moral development. Piaget believed that younger children are characterized by heteronomous morality, but that by 10 years of age they have moved into a higher stage called autonomous morality. According to Piaget, older children consider the intentions of the individual, believe that rules are subject to change, and are aware that punishment does not always follow a wrongdoing. A second major cognitive perspective on moral development was proposed by Lawrence Kohlberg.

Kohlberg stressed that moral development is based primarily on moral reasoning and unfolds in stages (Colby & Kohlberg, 1987; Kohlberg, 1958, 1976, 1986; Kohlberg & Higgins, 1987). Kohlberg arrived at his view after some 20 years of using a unique interview with children. In the interview, children are presented with a series of stories in which characters face moral dilemmas. The following is the most popular Kohlberg dilemma:

> In Europe a woman was near death from a special kind of cancer. There was one drug that the doctors thought might save her. It was a form of radium that a druggist in the same town had recently discovered. The drug was expensive to make, but the druggist was charging 10 times what the drug cost him to make. He paid $200 for the radium and charged $2,000 for a small dose of the drug. The sick woman's husband, Heinz, went to everyone he knew to borrow the money, but he could only get together $1,000 which is half of what it cost. He told the druggist that his wife was dying and asked him to sell it cheaper or let him pay later. But the druggist said, "No, I discovered the drug, and I am going to make money from it." So Heinz got desperate and broke into the man's store to steal the drug for his wife. (Kohlberg, 1969, p. 379)

This story is one of 11 devised by Kohlberg to investigate the nature of moral thought. After reading the story, the interviewee answers a series of questions about the moral dilemma. Should Heinz have stolen the drug? Was stealing it right or wrong? Why? Is it a husband's duty to steal the drug for his wife if he can get it no other way? Would a good husband steal? Did the druggist have the right to charge that much when there was no law setting a limit on the price? Why or why not?

Based on the reasons interviewees gave for this and other moral dilemmas, Kohlberg believed three levels of moral development exist, each of which is characterized by two stages:

Level One: Preconventional Reasoning

At the low level of **preconventional reasoning,** children show no internalization of moral values. Moral reasoning is controlled by external punishments and rewards.

> **Stage 1: Punishment and obedience orientation.** Moral thinking is based on punishments. Children obey because adults tell them to obey.

> **Stage 2: Individualism and purpose.** Moral thinking is based on rewards and self-interest. Children obey when they want to obey and when it is in their best interest to obey. What is right is what feels good and what is rewarding.

Level Two: Conventional Reasoning

At the level of **conventional reasoning,** internalization is intermediate. The child abides by certain standards (internal), but they are the standards of others (external).

> **Stage 3: Interpersonal Norms.** The person values trust, caring, and loyalty to others as the basis of moral judgments. At this stage, children often adopt their parents' moral standards, seeking to be thought of by their parents as a "good girl" or a "good boy."

> **Stage 4: Social System Morality.** Moral judgments are based on understanding the social order, law, justice, and duty.

Level Three: Postconventional Moral Reasoning

At the highest level, **postconventional reasoning,** morality is completely internalized and not based on others' standards. The person recognizes alternative moral courses, explores the options, and then decides on a personal moral code.

> **Stage 5: Community Rights Versus Individual Rights.** The person understands that values and laws are relative and that standards may vary from one person to another. The person recognizes that laws are important for society but also knows that laws can be changed. The person believes that some values, such as liberty, are more important than the law.

> **Stage 6: Universal Ethical Principles.** In rare instances, persons have developed a moral standard based on universal human rights. When faced with a conflict between law and conscience, the person will follow conscience, even though the decision might involve personal risk.

Stage description	Examples of moral reasoning that support Heinz's theft of the drug	Examples of moral reasoning that indicate Heinz should not steal the drug
Preconventional morality		
Stage 1: Avoid punishment	Heinz should not let his wife die; if he does, he will be in big trouble.	Heinz might get caught and sent to jail.
Stage 2: Seek rewards	If Heinz gets caught, he could give the drug back and maybe they would not give him a long jail sentence.	The druggist is a businessman and needs to make money.
Conventional morality		
Stage 3: Gain approval/ avoid disapproval especially with family	Heinz was only doing something that a good husband would do; it shows how much he loves his wife.	If his wife dies, he can't be blamed for it; it is the druggist's fault. He is the selfish one.
Stage 4: Conformity to society's rules	If you did nothing, you would be letting your wife die; it is your responsibility if she dies. You have to steal it with the idea of paying the druggist later.	It is always wrong to steal; Heinz will always feel guilty if he steals the drug.
Postconventional morality		
Stage 5: Principles accepted by the community	The law was not set up for these circumstances; taking the drug is not really right, but Heinz is justified in doing it.	You can't really blame someone for stealing, but extreme circumstances don't really justify taking the law into your own hands. You might lose respect for yourself if you let your emotions take over; you have to think about the long term.
Stage 6: Individualized conscience	By stealing the drug, you would have lived up to society's rules, but you would have let down your conscience.	Heinz is faced with the decision of whether to consider other people who need the drug as badly as his wife. He needs to act by considering the value of all the lives involved.

FIGURE 13.4   Examples of moral reasoning at Kohlberg's six stages in response to the Heinz and the druggist story.

Some specific responses to the dilemma of Heinz and the druggist are given in Figure 13.4, which should provide you with a better sense of reasoning at the six stages in Kohlberg's theory. Notice that whether Heinz steals the drug is not the important issue in Kohlberg's cognitive developmental theory. What is crucial is how the person reasons about the moral dilemma.

Kohlberg believed that these levels and stages occur in a sequence and are age related: Before age 9, most children reason about moral dilemmas in a preconventional way; by early adolescence, they reason in more conventional ways; and by early adulthood, a small number of people reason in postconventional ways. In a 20-year longitudinal investigation, the uses of stages 1 and 2 decreased. Stage 4, which did not appear at all in the moral reasoning of the 10-year-olds, was reflected in 62 percent of the moral thinking of the 36-year-olds. Stage 5 did not appear until the age of 20 to 22 and never characterized more than 10 percent of the individuals. Thus, the moral stages appeared somewhat later than Kohlberg initially envisioned, and the higher stages, especially stage 6, was extremely elusive (Colby & others, 1983). Recently, stage 6 was removed from the Kohlberg scoring manual, but it is still considered to be theoretically important in the Kohlberg scheme of moral development. A recent review of data from 43 studies in 27 diverse world cultures provided striking support for the universality of Kohlberg's first four stages, although there was more cultural diversity at stages 5 and 6 (Snarey, 1987).

Children's Moral Development: East Versus West

In contrast to Kohlberg's view on the cultural universality of moral judgment, a number of experts believe that, except for the incest taboo, the substance of moral prohibition varies across cultures and is deeply embedded in the values of each culture. An example of the varied moral orientation of children in different cultures appears in the research of James Garbarino and Urie Bronfenbrenner (1976). They argue that increased exposure to multiple social agents and multiple political views advances the child's moral development. Their research reveals that children who grow up in a culture that is more sociopolitically plural (such as the United States and West Germany) are less likely to be authority oriented and to have more plural ideas about moral dilemmas than their counterparts who grow up in less sociopolitical cultures (such as Poland and Hungary). Families also probably are involved. In the East, the family is expected to support the governmental regime, so family styles there are likely to be more monolithic. In Western cultures, where more individual freedom is allowed, more diverse family styles are common and children are exposed to more varied cultural experiences. ◆

Kohlberg's provocative view has generated considerable research on moral development, and his theory has not gone unchallenged (Kurtines & Gewirtz, in press; Puka, in press). One criticism of Kohlberg's view is that moral reasons can often be a shelter for immoral behavior, bank embezzlers and politicians, for example, address the loftiest of moral virtues when analyzing moral dilemmas, but their own behavior may be immoral. No one wants a nation of cheaters and thieves who reason at the postconventional level; the cheaters and thieves may know what is right and what is wrong but still do what is wrong.

A second major criticism of Kohlberg's view is that it does not adequately reflect connectedness with and concern for others. Carol Gilligan (1982, 1985) argues that Kohlberg's theory emphasizes a **justice perspective,**—that is, a focus on the rights of the individual. People are differentiated and seen as standing alone in making moral decisions. By contrast, the **care perspective** sees people in terms of their connectedness with others, and the focus is on interpersonal communication. According to Gilligan, Kohlberg vastly underplayed the care perspective in moral development. She believes this may be because most of his research was with males rather than with females. More insight into Gilligan's belief in the importance of the care perspective in understanding children's moral development appears in Children 13.2.

Gilligan also thinks that moral development has three basic levels. She calls Level 1 preconventional morality, which reflects a concern for self and survival. Level 2, conventional morality, shows a concern for being responsible and caring for others. Level 3, postconventional morality, shows a concern for self and others as interdependent. Gilligan believes that Kohlberg underemphasized the care perspective in the moral development of *both* males and females and that morality's highest level for both sexes involves a search for moral equality between one's self and others.

Amy Says They Should Just Talk It Out and Find Some Other Way to Make Money

The main character in Kohlberg's most widely used dilemma is a male, Heinz. Females may have a difficult time identifying with him. Some of Kohlberg's dilemmas are gender neutral, but one concerns the captain of a company of marines, which is highly masculine. The subjects in Kohlberg's original research were all males. Going beyond her critique of Kohlberg's failure to consider females, Gilligan (1982) argues that an important voice is not present in his view. Following are two excerpts from children's responses to the story of Heinz and the druggist, one from 11-year-old Jake, the other from 11-year-old Amy. Jake's comments:

> For one thing, human life is worth more than money, and if the druggist only makes $1,000, he is still going to live, but if Heinz doesn't steal the drug, his wife is going to die. (*Why is life worth more than money?*) Because the druggist can get $1,000 later from rich people with cancer, but Heinz can't get his wife again. (Gilligan, 1982, p. 26)

Amy's comments:

> I think there might be other ways besides stealing it, like if he could borrow the money or make a loan or something, but he really shouldn't steal the drug—but his wife shouldn't die either. (*Why shouldn't he steal the drug?*) If he stole the drug, he might save his wife then, but if he did, he might have to go to jail, and then his wife might get sicker again, and he couldn't get more of the drug, and it might not be good. So, they should really just talk it out and find some other way to make the money. (Gilligan, 1982, p. 28)

Jake's comments are a mixture of Kohlberg's stages 3 and 4, but they also include some of the components of a mature level 3 moral thinker. Amy, by contrast, does not fit into Kohlberg's scoring system so well. Jake sees the problem as one of rules and balancing the rights of people. However, Amy views the problem as involving relationships: The druggist's failure to live up to his relationship to the needy woman, the need to maintain the relationship between Heinz and his wife, and the hope that a bad relationship between Heinz and the druggist can be avoided. Amy concludes that the characters should talk it out and try to repair their relationships. ♦

Problems and Disturbances

In a large-scale investigation, researchers found that children from a lower-class background have more problems and disturbances than children from a middle-class background (Achenbach & Edelbrock, 1981). Most of the problems reported for children from a lower-class background were undercontrolled, externalizing behaviors—destroying others' things and fighting, for example; these behaviors also were more characteristic of boys than of girls. The problems and disturbances of middle-class children and girls—anxiety or depression, for example—were more likely to be overcontrolled and internalizing.

The behavioral problems that most likely caused children to be referred to a clinic for mental health treatment were those in which the children felt unhappy, sad, or depressed, and were not doing well in school (Figure 13.5). Difficulties in

Sadness and depression are often reflected in the faces of children referred to psychological clinics.

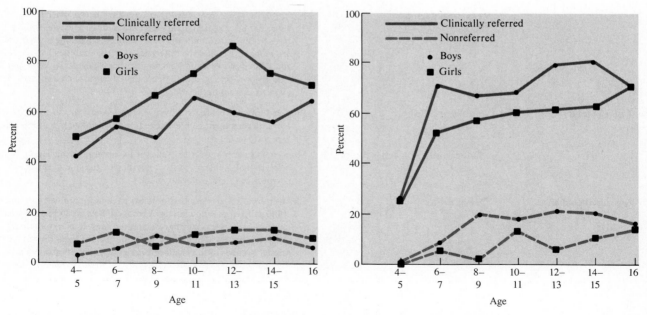

FIGURE 13.5   The two items most likely to differentiate between clinically referred children and nonreferred children (Achenbach & Edelbrock, 1981).

school achievement, whether secondary to other kinds of disturbances or primary problems in themselves, seem to account for the greatest number of clinical referrals for children (Weiner, 1980). Investigations of underachieving children often reveal that they are more likely than their achieving counterparts to feel hostility that they cannot express directly. Parental demands for extraordinarily high achievement are likely to trigger poor school performance, which can be an indirect retaliation toward the achievement-demanding parents.

The Self and Social Competence, Gender Roles, and Moral Development

Concept	Processes and Related Ideas	Characteristics and Description
The Self and Social Competence	Self-concept	An important dimension of children's self-concept is their increasing ability to understand how they are viewed by others. Closely related to self-concept is self-esteem; healthy relations with parents improve a child's self-esteem. Harter's Perceived Competence Scale for Children investigates four domains: general self-worth, social skills, cognitive skills, and physical skills.
	Social competence	Socially competent children can draw on effective resources from within themselves and from the environment. The criteria for social competence may vary with the child's developmental status.
	Industry versus inferiority	Erikson's fourth psychosocial stage; he believes that social competence in middle and late childhood rests on the child's ability to resolve this conflict positively.
Gender Roles	Masculinity, femininity, and androgyny	Gender roles focus on society's expectations for males and for females. Recent interest emphasizes the concept of androgyny, the belief that competent persons have both masculine and feminine characteristics. The four gender-role classifications are masculine, feminine, androgynous, and undifferentiated. Debate surrounds the criteria for masculine, feminine, and androgynous categories. The most widely used criteria for masculinity are self-assertion and instrumental orientation; for femininity they are integration and expressive orientation.
	Gender differences	In the 1970s, it was concluded that boys have better math skills, have superior visual-spatial ability, and are more aggressive, while girls have better verbal abilities. Today's conclusions suggest that boys are more active, and the difference in verbal abilities has virtually vanished. The other differences—math, visual-spatial ability, and aggression—persist, although continued cultural change may chip away at these differences.
Moral Development	Kohlberg's theory	Proposed three levels (each with two stages) that vary in the degree moral development is internalized: preconventional, conventional, and postconventional.
	Criticisms of Kohlberg's theory	Moral reasons can always be a shelter for immoral behavior. Gilligan believes that Kohlberg vastly underplayed the role of the care perspective in moral development.
Problems and Disturbances	Their nature	Children from lower-class backgrounds have more problems than children from middle-class backgrounds. Boys and children from lower-class backgrounds have a greater number of externalized problems; girls and children from middle-class backgrounds have a greater number of internalized problems. Difficulties in school are the most common reason children are referred for clinical help.

Thus far, we have discussed many ideas about the self, gender roles, moral development, and problems and disturbances in middle and late childhood. These ideas are summarized in Concept Table 13.2. This chapter concludes our description of development in middle and late childhood. In the next section, we will turn to the study of adolescent development, first evaluating physical development.

Summary

I. Families

Parents spend less time with children during middle and late childhood, including less time in caregiving, instruction, reading, talking, and playing. Nonetheless, parents are still powerful and important socializing agents in this period. New parent-child issues emerge and discipline changes. Control is more coregulatory, children and parents label each other more, and parents mature just as children do. During middle and late childhood, two major changes in many children's lives are movement into a stepfamily and becoming a latchkey child. Just as divorce produces disequilibrium and stress for children, so does the entrance of a stepparent. Over time, preadolescent boys seem to improve more than girls in stepfather families. Adolescence appears to be an especially difficult time for adjustment to the entrance of a stepparent. Latchkey children may become vulnerable when they are not monitored in the after-school hours.

II. Peer Relations

Children spend considerably more time with peers in middle and late childhood. Listening skills and effective communication, being oneself, being happy, showing enthusiasm and concern for others, and indicating self-confidence but not conceit are predictors of peer popularity. Rejected children are at risk for adjustment problems; the risk status of neglected children is less clear. Social information-processing skills and social knowledge are two important dimensions of social cognition in peer relations. Children's friendships serve six functions: companionship, stimulation, physical support, ego support, social comparison, and intimacy/affection. Intimacy and similarity are two common characteristics of friendships.

III. Schools

Children spend more than 10,000 hours in the classroom as members of a small society in which there are tasks to be accomplished, people to be socialized and socialized by, and rules that define and limit behavior, feelings, and attitudes. A special concern is that early schooling proceeds mainly on the basis of negative feedback to children. The curriculum in elementary schools should be integrated. Teachers and peers play prominent roles in the school's influence on children. A profile of a good teacher's personality traits has been difficult to establish, although some traits are clearly superior to others. Aptitude-treatment interaction is an important consideration. Schools have a stronger middle-class than lower-class orientation. Not only do many lower-class children have problems in schools, so do children from ethnic minorities. Efforts are being made to reduce this bias, among them the jigsaw classroom.

IV. Self-Concept

An important dimension of a child's self-concept is the increasing ability to understand how he or she is perceived by others. Closely related to self-concept is self-esteem; healthy relationships with parents improve children's self-esteem. Harter's Perceived Competence Scale for Children investigates four domains: general self-worth, social skills, cognitive skills, and physical skills.

V. Social Competence

Socially competent children can draw on effective resources from within themselves and from the environment. The criteria for social competence may vary with the child's developmental status.

VI. Masculinity, Femininity, and Androgyny

Gender roles focus on society's expectations for males and for females. Recent interest emphasizes the concept of androgyny, the belief that competent individuals have both masculine and feminine characteristics. The four gender-role classifications are masculine, feminine, androgynous, and undifferentiated. Debate surrounds the criteria for masculine, feminine, and androgynous categories. The most widely used criteria for masculinity are self-assertion and instrumental orientation, and for femininity integration and expressive orientation.

VII. **Gender Differences**

In the 1970s, it was concluded that boys have better math skills, have superior visual-spatial ability, and are more aggressive, while girls have better verbal abilities. Today's conclusions suggest that boys are more active, and the difference in verbal abilities has virtually vanished. The other differences—math, visual-spatial ability, and aggression—persist, although continued cultural change may chip away at these differences.

VIII. **Moral Development**

Kohlberg proposed three levels (each with two stages) that vary in the degree moral development is internalized: preconventional, conventional, and postconventional. Kohlberg's theory has not gone uncriticized. Moral reasons can always be a shelter for immoral behavior. Also, Gilligan believes that Kohlberg vastly underplayed the role of the care perspective in moral development.

IX. **Problems and Disturbances**

Children from lower-class backgrounds have more problems and disturbances than children from middle-class backgrounds. Boys and children from lower-class backgrounds have more externalized problems; girls and children from middle-class backgrounds have more internalized problems. Difficulties in school are the most common reason children are referred for clinical help.

Key Terms

coregulation 418
neglected children 422
rejected children 422
intimacy 424
aptitude-treatment
    interaction (ATI) 428
jigsaw classroom 430
Perceived Competence
    Scale for Children 433
androgyny 435
undifferentiated 435

instrumental
    orientation 437
expressive orientation 437
preconventional
    reasoning 441
punishment and obedience
    orientation 441
individualism and
    purpose 441
conventional reasoning 441

interpersonal norms 441
social system morality 441
postconventional
    reasoning 441
community rights versus
    individual rights 441
universal ethical
    principles 441
justice perspective 443
care perspective 443

Suggested Readings

Development during middle childhood (1984). Washington, DC: National Academy Press.
  An excellent collection of essays about what is currently known about the elementary
  school years. Includes chapters on families, peers, self, and problems and disturbances.

Gilligan, C. (1982). *In a different voice.* Cambridge, MA: Harvard University Press.
  Advances Gilligan's provocative view that a care perspective is a missing voice in
  Kohlberg's theory.

Gottman, J. M., & Parker, J. G. (Eds.). (1987). *Conversations of friends.* New York:
  Cambridge University Press.
  An excellent volume on how children become friends; explores the rich conversations
  of children.

Hyde, J. S. (1985). *Half the human experience* (3rd ed.). Lexington, MA: D. C. Heath.
  An excellent overview of gender roles, with special attention given to the female role.

Minuchin, P. P., & Shapiro, E. K. (1983). The school as a context for social development.
  In P. H. Mussen (Ed.), *Handbook of child psychology* (4th ed., Vol. 4). New York:
  Wiley.
  An authoritative review of the school's role in children's development.

VI

Adolescence

In no order of things is adolescence the simple time of life.

Jean Erskine Stewart

◆

I n no order of things is adolescence the time of simple life. Adolescents feel like they will live forever. At times, they are sure that they know everything. They clothe themselves with rainbows and go brave as the zodiac, flashing from one end of the world to the other both in mind and body. In many ways, today's adolescents are privileged, wielding unprecedented economic power. At the same time, they move through a seemingly endless preparation for life. They try on one face after another, seeking to find a face of their own. In their most pimply and awkward moments, they become acquainted with sex. They play furiously at "adult games" but are confined to a society of their own peers. They want their parents to understand them. Their generation of young people is the fragile cable by which the best and the worst of their parents' generation is transmitted to the present. In the end, there are only two lasting bequests parents can leave youth, one being roots, the other wings.

Section 6 consists of three chapters. Chapter 14 describes the nature of physical development in adolescence. In it is information about

—Stereotyping adolescents
—Puberty's fascinating moments
—The difficult journey to sexual maturity
—Three adolescent mothers: Angela, Michelle, and Stephanie
—Problems and disturbances
—Frog and Dolores, whose lives are wrapped in an escalating world of drugs and gang violence

Chapter 15 describes the nature of cognitive development in adolescence. It contains information about

- —Personal fables and pregnancies
- —Values, religion, and cults
- —Schools
- —Helping Hispanic students stay in school and go to college
- —Careers and work

Chapter 16 describes the nature of social development in adolescence. Among its contents is information about

- —Families
- —Developmental trajectories and delayed childbearing
- —Peer pressure
- —Cliques
- —Dating
- —Adolescents' motivation to find out who they are
- —Culture
- —The dreams and struggles of John David Gutierrez
- —Rites of passage

14

Physical Development

I'm pretty confused. I wonder whether I'm weird or normal. My body is starting to change but I sure don't look like a lot of my friends. I still look like a kid for the most part. My best friend is only 13, but he looks like he is 16 or 17. I get nervous in the locker room during PE class because when I go to take a shower I'm afraid somebody is going to make fun of me since I'm not as physically developed as some of the others.

—Robert, age 12

I don't like my breasts. They are too small and they look funny. I'm afraid guys won't like me if they don't get bigger.

—Angie, age 13

I can't stand the way I look. I have zits all over my face. My hair is dull and stringy. It never stays in place. My nose is too big. My lips are too small. My legs are too short. I have four warts on my left hand and people get grossed out by them. So do I. My body is a disaster!

—Ann, age 14

I'm short and I can't stand it. My father is six feet tall and here I am only five foot four. I'm 14 already. I look like a kid and I get teased a lot, especially by other guys. I'm always the last one picked for sides in basketball because I'm so short. Girls don't seem to be interested in me either because most of them are taller than I am.

—Jim, age 14

The comments of these four adolescents in the midst of pubertal change underscore the dramatic upheaval in our bodies following the calm, consistent growth of middle and late childhood. Young adolescents develop an acute concern about their bodies. Columnist Bob Greene (1988) recently dialed a party line called Connections in Chicago to discover what young adolescents were saying to each other. The first thing the boys and girls asked—after first names—was physical descriptions. The idealism of the callers was apparent. Most of the girls described themselves as having long blond hair, standing five feet five inches tall, and weighing about 110 pounds. Most of the boys said that they had brown hair, lifted weights, stood six feet tall, and weighed 170 pounds.

Puberty's changes are perplexing to adolescents as they go through them. Although the changes are perplexing and call forth self-doubts, questions, fears, and anxieties, most of us survive the adolescent years quite well. Later in the chapter we will study puberty's fascinating moments and adolescents' problems and disturbances, but first we will focus on the nature of adolescent development.

The Nature of Adolescent Development

As in the development of children, genetic, biological, environmental, and social factors interact in adolescent development. Also, continuity and discontinuity characterize adolescent development. The genes inherited from parents still influence an adolescent's thought and behavior, but inheritance now interacts with the social conditions of the adolescent's world, such as family, peers, friendships, dating, and school experiences. An adolescent has experienced thousands of hours of interaction

BLOOM COUNTY   by Berke Breathed

© 1986, Washington Post Writers Group.
Reprinted with permission.

with parents, peers, and teachers in the past 10 to 13 years of development. Yet new experiences and developmental tasks appear during adolescence. Relationships with parents take a different form, moments with peers become more intimate, dating occurs for the first time, as do sexual exploration and possibly intercourse. The adolescent's thoughts are more abstract and idealistic. Biological changes trigger a heightened interest in body image. Adolescence, then, is both continuous and discontinuous with childhood.

As in the concept of child development, the concept of adolescence was speculative before the nineteenth and twentieth centuries. In 1904, G. Stanley Hall, known as the father of the scientific study of adolescence, published his ideas in a two-volume set, *Adolescence*. According to Hall, adolescence is a time of storm and stress, full of contradictions and wide swings in mood. Thoughts, feelings, and actions oscillate between conceit and humility, self-control and temptation, happiness and sadness. The adolescent may be nasty one moment, kind the next. The adolescent wants to be alone, then, seconds later, wants close companionship. Because he viewed adolescence as a turbulent time charged with conflict, Hall's perspective became known as the **storm and stress view.**

Today, we do not view adolescence as the jaundiced time Hall envisioned. The vast majority of adolescents make the transition from childhood to adulthood competently. As with any period of development, adolescent life has its peaks and valleys, issues to be negotiated, mistakes and adjustments, highs and lows, ebbs and flows. Today we view adolescence in a much more balanced, positive way than earlier in this century.

Current interest in the history of adolescence raises the possibility that adolescence is a historical invention. While adolescence has a biological base, sociohistorical conditions also contributed to the emergence of the concept of adolescence. American society may have "inflicted" the status of adolescence on its youth through child-saving legislation (Elder & Caspi, in press; Lapsley, Enright, & Serlin, 1985). By developing laws for youth only, adults placed young people in a submissive position, one that restricted their options, encouraged dependency, and made their move into the adult world more manageable. From 1890 to 1920, every state developed

A few years ago it occurred to me that when I was a teenager, in the early depression years, there were no teenagers! The teenager has sneaked up on us in our own lifetime, and yet it seems he has always been with us. . . . The teenager had not yet been invented, though, and there did not yet exist a special class of beings, bounded in a certain way—not quite children and certainly not adults.

A. K. Cohen, Foreward, in P. Musgrove, Youth and the Social Order

The vast majority of adolescents make the transition from childhood to adulthood competently. As with any period of development, there are hills and valleys, issues to be negotiated, mistakes and adjustments, highs and lows, ebbs and flows in life. Today we view adolescence in a much more balanced, positive way than we did earlier in this century.

laws that excluded youth from work and required them to attend school. During this time, the number of students who graduated from high school increased 600 percent (Tyack, 1976). By 1950, the developmental period we refer to as adolescence had come of age. Not only did it possess physical and social identity, but it received legal attention, too. By this time, every state had developed special laws for youths between the ages of 16 to 18 or 20.

It is easy to develop stereotypes about adolescents. A sampling: "They say they want to work, but they are all lazy." "They're all sex fiends." "They're all into drugs, every last one of them." "Kids today don't have the moral fiber of my generation." "The problem with today's adolescents is that they have it too easy." "They're a bunch of smart-alecks." Researchers have found that the layperson does have a number of stereotypes about adolescents (Hill, 1983; Youniss & Smollar, 1985). Some of the stereotypes about adolescents have stemmed from the visible, rebellious adolescents of the 1960s and 1970s. One expert on adolescence labeled the stereotyping of adolescents as stressed, rebellious, and incompetent the **adolescent generalization gap** rather than the "generation" gap, meaning that widespread generalizations have been made about adolescents based on information about a limited group of adolescents (Adelson, 1979).

An investigation by Daniel Offer and his colleagues (1988) further documents that the vast majority of adolescents are competent human beings without deep emotional turmoil. The self-images of adolescents from around the world were sampled—from the United States, Australia, Bangladesh, Hungary, Israel, Italy, Japan, Taiwan, Turkey, and West Germany. A healthy self-image characterized at least 73 percent of the adolescents studied. They appeared to be moving toward adulthood with a healthy integration of previous experiences, self-confidence, and optimism about the future. Although the adolescents differed somewhat, they were happy most of the time, they enjoyed life, they perceived themselves as able to exercise self-control, they valued work and school, they expressed confidence about their sexual selves, they indicated positive feelings toward their family, and they felt they had the capability to cope with life's stresses . . . not exactly a storm and stress portrayal of adolescents.

Some of the readiness to assume the worst about adolescents may involve the short memories of adults. With little effort, most adults can remember behavior of their own that stretched the patience of their elders, or even shocked them. In matters of taste and manners, young people of every generation have seemed radical, unnerving, and different from adults—different in how they look, how they behave, the music they enjoy, their hairstyles, and the clothing they choose. But it is an enormous error to confuse the adolescent's enthusiasm for trying on new identities and enjoying moderate amounts of outrageous behavior with hostility toward parental and societal standards. Acting out and boundary testing are time-honored ways in which adolescents move toward accepting, rather than rejecting, parental values.

It does little good, and can do considerable disservice, to think of adolescence as a time of rebellion, crisis, pathology, and deviation. Far better, and far more accurate, is a vision of adolescence as a time of evaluation, a time of decision making, a time of commitment as youth carve out their place in the world. How competent they will become often depends on their access to a range of legitimate opportunities and to the long-term support of adults who deeply care about them (William T. Grant Foundation Committee, 1988).

Puberty

In *Diary of a Young Girl,* Anne Frank (1952) wrote, "I think that what is happening to me is so wonderful and not only what can be seen on my body, but all that is taking place inside. I never discuss myself with anybody; that is why I have to talk to myself about them." Anne Frank was describing the changes of puberty. Our discussion of puberty focuses on defining its boundaries and determinants, hormonal changes, physical changes, individual variation, and the psychological dimensions of puberty.

The Boundaries and Determinants of Puberty

Puberty can be distinguished from adolescence. For most of us, puberty has ended long before adolescence is finished, although puberty is the most important marker of the beginning of adolescence. What is puberty? Puberty is a rapid change to physical maturation involving hormonal and bodily changes that occur primarily during early adolescence.

Imagine a toddler displaying all the features of puberty—a 3-year-old girl with fully developed breasts or a boy just slightly older with a deep male voice. That is what we would see by the year 2250 if the age at which puberty arrives kept getting younger at its present pace. In Norway, **menarche**—the girl's first menstruation—occurs at just over 13 years of age, compared to 17 years of age in the 1840s. In the United States, where children mature up to a year earlier than children in European countries, the age of menarche has been declining an average of about four months per decade for the past century (Figure 14.1). Fortunately, however, we are unlikely to see pubescent toddlers, because what has happened in the past

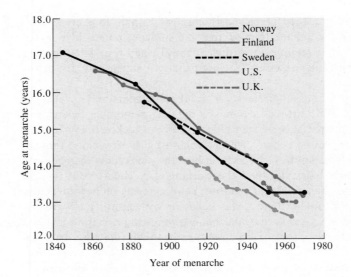

FIGURE 14.1   Median age of menarche in selected northern European countries and the United States from 1845 to 1969 (Roche, 1977).

century is special. Our best guess is that the "something special" is a higher level of nutrition and health. The available information suggests that menarche began to occur earlier at about the time of the Industrial Revolution, a time associated with increased standards of living and advances in medical science (Petersen, 1979).

Puberty is not simply an environmental accident; genetic factors are also involved. As we indicated earlier, while nutrition, health, and other factors affect puberty's timing and variations in its makeup, the basic genetic program is wired into the nature of the species (Scarr & Kidd, 1983).

Another key factor in puberty's occurrence is body mass. For example, menarche occurs at a relatively consistent weight in girls. A body weight of approximately 106 ± 3 pounds signals menarche and the end of the adolescent growth spurt. And for menarche to begin and continue, fat must make up 17 percent of the girl's total body weight.

Hormonal Changes

Behind the first whisker in boys and behind the widening of hips in girls is a flood of **hormones,** powerful chemical substances secreted by the endocrine glands and carried through the body by the bloodstream. The key to understanding the endocrine system's role in pubertal change involves the **hypothalamic-pituitary-gonadal axis** (Nottelman & others, 1987). The *hypothalamus* is a structure in the higher portion of the brain, and the *pituitary* is the body's master gland. It is located at the base of the brain. Its reference as the master gland comes from the ability to regulate a number of other glands. The term *gonadal* refers to the sex glands—the testes in males and the ovaries in females. How does this hormonal system work? While the pituitary gland monitors endocrine levels, it is regulated by the hypothalamus. The pituitary gland sends a signal via a *gonadotropin* (a hormone that stimulates the testes or ovaries) to the appropriate gland to manufacture the hormone. Then, the pituitary gland, through interaction with the hypothalamus, detects when the optimal level is reached and responds by maintaining gonadotropin secretion (Petersen & Taylor, 1980).

The concentrations of certain hormones increase dramatically during adolescence. In boys, **testosterone** is associated with the development of external genitals, an increase in height, and a change in voice. In girls, **estradiol** is associated with breast, uterine, and skeletal development (Dillon, 1980). In one investigation, testosterone levels increased eighteen-fold in boys but only two-fold in girls during puberty; estradiol increased eight-fold in girls but only two-fold in boys (Nottelmann & others, 1987). This same influx of hormones may be associated with psychological adjustment in adolescence. In the same investigation, a higher concentration of testosterone was present in boys who rated themselves more socially competent (Nottelmann & others, 1987). In another investigation of 60 normal boys and girls in the same age range, girls with higher estradiol levels expressed more anger and aggression (Inhoff-German & others, 1988).

Physical Changes

As indicated in Figure 14.2, the growth spurt for girls occurs approximately two years earlier than for boys. The growth spurt for girls begins at approximately 10½ years of age and lasts for about two years. During this time, girls increase in height by about 3½ inches per year. The growth spurt for boys begins at about 12½ years of age and also lasts for about two years. Boys usually grow about 4 inches per year during this time frame (Tanner, 1970).

Think back to the onset of your puberty. Of the striking changes that were taking place in your body, what was the first change that occurred? Researchers have found that male pubertal characteristics develop in this order: increase in penis and testicle size, appearance of straight pubic hair, minor voice change, first ejaculation (which usually occurs through masturbation or a wet dream), appearance of kinky pubic hair, onset of maximum growth, growth of hair in armpits, more detectable voice changes, and growth of facial hair. Three of the most noticeable areas of sexual maturation in boys are penis elongation, testes development, and growth of facial hair. The normal range and average age of development for these sexual characteristics, along with height spurt, is shown in Figure 14.3.

Puberty: the time of life when the two sexes begin to first become acquainted.

Samuel Johnson

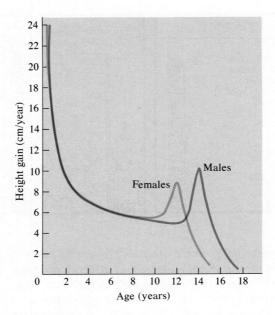

FIGURE 14.2 Growth curves for height in boys and girls. These curves represent the rate of growth of a typical boy and girl at a given age (Tanner & others, 1966).

As reflected in the adolescents who are dancing here, females experience pubertal change much earlier than boys, approximately two years on the average.

What is the order of appearance of physical changes in females? First, either the breasts enlarge or pubic hair appears. Hair will later appear in the armpits. As these changes occur, the female grows in height and her hips become wider than her shoulders. Her first menstruation comes rather late in the pubertal cycle. Initially her menstrual cycles may be highly irregular. For the first several years, she may not ovulate every menstrual cycle. In some instances it is only after two years after her period begins that she becomes fertile. No voice changes comparable to those in pubertal males take place in pubertal females. By the end of puberty, the female's breasts have become more fully rounded. Two of the most noticeable aspects of the female's pubertal change are pubic hair and breast development. Figure 14.4 shows the normal range and average of development of these sexual characteristics as well as information about menarche and height gain.

Considerable individual variation characterizes pubertal change (Brooks-Gunn & Warren, 1989; Lerner, Lerner & Tubman, 1989). For most boys, the pubertal sequence may begin as early as 10 years of age or as late as 13½; it may end as early as 13 years or as late as 17 years. The normal range is wide enough, that in two boys of the same chronological age, one may complete the pubertal sequence before the other one has begun it. For girls, the age range of the first menstrual period is even wider. Menarche is considered to be within a normal range if it appears between the ages of 9 and 15 (Hill, 1980; Brooks-Gunn, 1988).

Psychological Dimensions of Puberty

A host of psychological changes accompany an adolescent's pubertal development. Imagine yourself as you were at the beginning of puberty. Not only did you probably begin to think of yourself differently, but your parents and peers probably began acting differently toward you. Maybe you were proud of your changing body, even

Adolescence

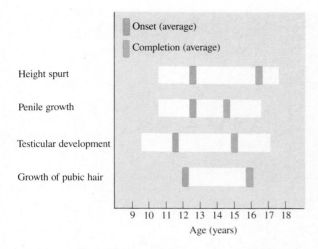

FIGURE 14.3   Normal range and average age of development of sexual characteristics in males.
From J. M. Tanner, "Growing Up" in Scientific American, *1973. Copyright © 1973 by Scientific American, Inc. All rights reserved.*

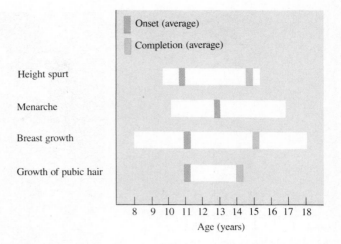

FIGURE 14.4   Normal range and average age of development of sexual characteristics in females.
From J. M. Tanner, "Growing Up" in Scientific American, *1973. Copyright © 1973 by Scientific American, Inc. All rights reserved.*

though you were perplexed about what was happening. Perhaps your parents no longer perceived you as someone they could sit in bed with and watch television or as someone who should be kissed good night. Developmentalists pose intriguing questions about puberty's psychological dimensions, among them: With what parts of their body image are adolescents preoccupied the most? What are the effects of early and late maturation on adolescent development? How can health care improve the lives of early and late maturers?

Body Image

One thing is certain about the psychological aspects of physical change in adolescence: Adolescents are preoccupied with their bodies and develop individual images of what their bodies are like. Perhaps you looked in the mirror daily or even hourly to see if you could detect anything different about your changing body. Preoccupation with one's body image is strong throughout adolescence, but it is especially acute during puberty, a time when adolescents are more dissatisfied with their bodies than in late adolescence (Wright, 1989).

Being physically attractive and having a positive body image are associated with an overall positive conception of one's self. In one investigation, girls who were judged as being physically attractive and who generally had a positive body image had higher opinions of themselves in general (Lerner & Karabenick, 1974). In another investigation, breast growth in girls 9 to 11 years old was associated with a positive body image, positive peer relationships, and superior adjustment (Brooks-Gunn & Warren, in press).

Was there a certain part of your body with which you were preoccupied the most during puberty? In one study, boys and girls did not differ much in their preoccupation with various body characteristics (Lerner & Karabenick, 1974). For both

males and females, general appearance, the face, facial complexion, and body build were thought to be the most important characteristics in physical attractiveness. Ankles and ears were thought to be the least important.

Early and Late Maturation

Some of you entered puberty early, others late, and yet others on time. When adolescents mature earlier or later than their peers, might they perceive themselves differently? Some years ago, in the California Longitudinal Study, early-maturing boys perceived themselves more positively and had more successful peer relations than did their late-maturing counterparts (Jones, 1965). The findings for early-maturing girls were similar but not as strong as for boys. When the late-maturing boys were in their thirties, however, they had developed a stronger sense of identity than the early-maturing boys (Peskin, 1967). Possibly this occurred because the late-maturing boys had more time to explore life's options or because the early-maturing boys continued to focus on their advantageous physical status instead of on career development and achievement.

More recent research confirms, though, that at least during adolescence, it is advantageous to be an early-maturing rather than a late-maturing boy (Blyth, Bulcroft, & Simmons, 1981; Simmons & Blyth, 1987). The more recent findings for girls suggest that early maturation is a mixed blessing: These girls experience more problems in school but also more independence and popularity with boys. The time that maturation is assessed also is a factor. In the sixth grade, early-maturing girls showed greater satisfaction with their figures than late-maturing girls, but by the tenth grade, late-maturing girls were more satisfied (Figure 14.5). The reason for this is that by late adolescence, early-maturing girls are shorter and stockier, while late-maturing girls are taller and thinner. The late-maturing girls in late adolescence have bodies that more closely approximate the current American ideal of feminine beauty—tall and thin.

Adolescence

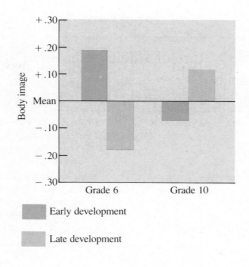

FIGURE 14.5 Early-and late-maturing adolescent girls' perceptions of body image in early and late adolescence (Blythe & others).

Pubertal Timing and Health Care

What can be done to identify off-time maturers who are at risk for problems? Many adolescents whose development is extremely early or extremely late are likely to come to the attention of a physician—such as a boy who has not had a spurt in height by the age of 16 or a girl who has not menstruated by the age of 15. Girls and boys who are early or late maturers but well within the normal range are less likely to be taken to a physician because of their maturational status. Nonetheless, these boys and girls may have fears and doubts about being normal that they do not raise unless the physician, counselor, or some other health-care provider takes the initiative. A brief discussion outlining the sequence and timing of events and the large individual variations in them may be all that is required to reassure many adolescents who are maturing very early or very late.

Health-care providers may want to discuss the adolescent's off-time development with parents as well as the adolescent. Information about the peer pressures of off-time development can be beneficial. Especially helpful to early-maturing girls is a discussion of peer pressures to date and to engage in adultlike behavior at early ages. The transition to middle school, junior high school, or high school may be more stressful for girls and boys who are in the midst of puberty than for those who are not (Brooks-Gunn, 1988).

If pubertal development is extremely late, a physician may recommend hormonal treatment. In one investigation of extended pubertal delay in boys, hormonal treatment worked to increase the height, dating interest, and peer relations in several boys, but resulted in little or no improvement in other boys (Lewis, Money, & Bobrow, 1977).

In sum, most early- and late-maturing individuals weather puberty's challenges and stresses competently. For those who do not, discussions with sensitive and knowledgeable health-care providers and parents can improve the off-time maturing adolescent's coping abilities.

Thus far, we have discussed several ideas about the nature of adolescence and puberty. These ideas are summarized in Concept Table 14.1. Next, we will turn to a discussion of adolescent sexuality.

The Nature of Adolescence and Puberty

Concept	Processes and Related Ideas	Characteristics and Description
The Nature of Adolescence	Storm and stress view	G. Stanley Hall's book *Adolescence* marked the beginning of the scientific study of adolescence. Hall is known for his storm and stress view and for the belief that biology plays a prominent role in development.
	Inventionist view	Many scholars argue that adolescence is a sociohistorical invention. They believe that legislation ensured the dependency of youth and made their move into the economic sphere more manageable early in the twentieth century.
	Stereotyping adolescents	Many stereotypes about adolescents are inaccurate. It is not unusual for widespread generalizations about adolescents to be formed based on a limited group of highly visible adolescents. An accurate vision of adolescence is a time of evaluation, a time of decision making, and a time of commitment as youth carve out their place in the world.
Puberty	Boundaries and determinants	Puberty is a rapid change to physical maturation involving hormonal and body changes that takes place primarily in early adolescence. Its determinants include nutrition, health, heredity, and body mass.
	Hormonal changes	The endocrine system is made up of endocrine glands and their secretions. The secretions of these ductless glands are called hormones, powerful chemicals that regulate organs. The hypothalamic-pituitary-gonadal axis is an important aspect of the complex hormonal system that contributes to pubertal change. Testosterone, an androgen, plays a key role in male pubertal development; estradiol, an estrogen, plays a key role in female pubertal development. Recent research has documented a link between hormonal levels and the adolescent's behavior.
	Physical changes	The growth spurt for boys occurs about two years later than for girls, with 12½ being the average age of onset for boys, and 10½ for girls. Sexual maturation is a predominant feature of pubertal change. Individual maturation in pubertal change is extensive.
	Psychological dimensions of puberty	Adolescents show a heightened interest in their body image. Young adolescents are more preoccupied and less satisfied with their body image than are late adolescents. Early maturation favors boys, at least during adolescence. As adults, though, late-maturing boys achieve more successful identities. The results for girls are more mixed than for boys. Of special concern is the health care of early- and late-maturing adolescents.

Sexuality

I am 16 years old and I really like this one girl. She wants to be a virgin until she marries. We went out last night and she let me go pretty far, but not all the way. I know she really likes me too, but she always stops me when things start getting hot and heavy. It is getting hard for me to handle. She doesn't know it but I'm a virgin too. I feel I am ready to have sex. I have to admit I think about having sex with other girls too. Maybe I should be dating other girls.

—Frank C.

The sexual fantasies of adolescent boys focus specifically on sexual activity.

I'm 14 years old. I have a lot of sexy thoughts. Sometimes just before I drift off to sleep at night I think about this hunk who is 16 years old and plays on the football team. He is so gorgeous and I can feel him holding me in his arms and kissing and hugging me. When I'm walking down the hall between classes at school, I sometimes start daydreaming about guys I have met, and wonder what it would be like to have sex with them. Last year I had this crush on the men's track coach. I'm on the girls' track team so I saw him a lot during the year. He hardly knew I thought about him the way I did, although I tried to flirt with him several times.

—Amy S.

During adolescence, the lives of males and females become wrapped in sexuality. Adolescence is a time of sexual exploration and experimentation, of sexual fantasies and sexual realities, of incorporating sexuality into one's identity. At a time when sexual identity is an important developmental task of adolescence, the adolescent is confronted with conflicting sexual values and messages. The majority of adolescents eventually manage to develop a mature sexual identity, but most have periods of vulnerability and confusion along life's sexual journey. Our coverage of adolescent sexuality focuses on sexual attitudes and behavior, sexually transmitted diseases, and adolescent pregnancy.

Sexual Attitudes and Behavior

How extensively have heterosexual attitudes and behaviors changed in the twentieth century? What sexual scripts do adolescents follow? How extensive is homosexual behavior in adolescence? We will consider each of these questions in turn.

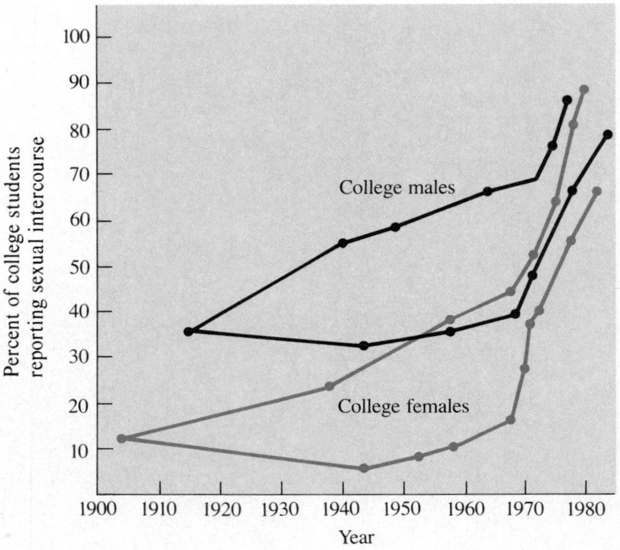

FIGURE 14.6   Percentage of college youth reporting having sexual intercourse at different points in the twentieth century. Two lines are drawn for males and two for females. The lines represent the best two fits through the data for males and the data for females of the many studies surveyed (Darling & others, 1984).

TABLE 14.1   *Percentages of Young People Sexually Active at Specific Ages*

Age	Women (%)	Men (%)
15	5.4	16.6
16	12.6	28.7
17	27.1	47.9
18	44.0	64.0
19	62.9	77.6
20	73.6	83.0

National Research Council, *Risking the Future: Adolescent Sexuality, Pregnancy, and Childbearing.* © 1987 by The National Academy of Sciences.

Adolescent Heterosexual Behavior—Trends and Incidence

Had you been in high school or college in 1940, you probably would have had a different attitude toward many aspects of sexuality than you do today, especially if you are a female. A review of students' sexual practices and attitudes from 1900 to 1980 reveal two important trends (Darling, Kallen, & VanDusen, 1984). First, the percentage of youth reporting that they have had sexual intercourse has increased dramatically. Second, the percentage of females reporting that they have had sexual intercourse has increased more rapidly than for males, although the initial base for males was greater (Figure 14.6). These changes suggest movement away from a double standard that says it is more appropriate for males than females to have sexual intercourse.

Large numbers of American adolescents are sexually active. Table 14.1 shows that by age 18, 44 percent of adolescent females and 64 percent of adolescent males are sexually experienced (National Research Council, 1987). Other surveys indicate that almost four of five adolescents from 17 to 19 years old have experienced sexual intercourse at least once (Zelnik & Kantner, 1980). While the gap is closing,

If we listen to boys and girls at the very moment when they seem most pimply, awkward and disagreeable, we can partly penetrate a mystery most of us once felt heavily within us, and have now forgotten. This mystery is the very process of creation of man and woman.

Colin Macinnes, The World of Children

males still are more sexually experienced at an earlier age than females. Black adolescent females are more sexually active than their white counterparts, with approximately two of three black adolescent females, but slightly less than one of two white adolescent females, reporting having sexual intercourse at least once.

Among younger adolescents, surveys indicate that between 5 and 17 percent of girls 15 years old and younger have had sexual intercourse. Among boys the same age, the range is 16 to 38 percent (Gilgun, 1984; Jessor & Jessor, 1975; National Research Council, 1987; Ostrov & others, 1985). At age 13, boys also show earlier experience with sexual intercourse than girls—12 percent versus 5 percent (Dreyer, 1982). The pressure on adolescent males to have sexual intercourse is reflected in these figures, even though, on the average, adolescent males enter puberty two years later than adolescent females.

Recent data indicate that in some areas of the country, sexual experiences of young adolescents may even be greater than these figures indicate. In inner-city Baltimore, 81 percent of 14-year-old males said they had already engaged in sexual intercourse. Other surveys in inner-city, low-income areas also reveal a high incidence of early sexual intercourse (Clark, Zabin, & Hardy, 1984).

Clearly, large numbers of America's adolescents are sexually active, but there is a positive note in the most recent data collected about adolescent sexual behavior. While the rate of sexual activity among adolescents increased dramatically in the 1970s, it appears to be stabilizing or decreasing as we enter the last decade of the twentieth century (National Research Council, 1987).

Adolescent Female and Male Sexual Scripts

As adolescents explore their sexual identities, they engage in sexual scripts (Gagnon & Simon, 1973; Gordon & Gilgun, 1987). A **sexual script** is a stereotyped pattern of role prescriptions for how individuals should behave sexually. Differences in the way females and males are socialized are wrapped up in the sexual scripts adolescents follow. Discrepancies in male-female scripting can cause problems and confusion for adolescents as they work out their sexual identities. Adolescent girls have learned to link sexual intercourse with love. Female adolescents often rationalize their sexual behavior by telling themselves that they were swept away by love. A number of investigators have reported that adolescent females, more than adolescent males, report being in love as the main reason for being sexually active (Cassell, 1984). Far more females than males have intercourse with partners they love and would like to marry. Other reasons for females having sexual intercourse include giving in to male pressure, gambling that sex is a way to get a boyfriend, curiosity, and sexual desire unrelated to loving and caring. Adolescent males may be aware that their female counterparts have been socialized into a love ethic. They also may understand the pressure many of them feel to have a boyfriend. A classic male line shows how males understand female thinking about sex and love: "If you really loved me, you would have sex with me." The female adolescent who says, "If you really loved me, you would not put so much pressure on me," reflects insight about male sexual motivation.

Some experts on adolescent sexuality believe that we are moving toward a new norm suggesting that sexual intercourse is acceptable, but mainly within the boundary of a loving and affectionate relationship (Dreyer, 1982). As part of this new norm, promiscuity, exploitation, and unprotected sexual intercourse are more often perceived as unacceptable by adolescents. One variation of the new norm is that intercourse is acceptable in a nonlove relationship, but physical or emotional

Female adolescents, more than adolescent males, report being in love as the main reason for being sexually active.

exploitation of the partner is not (Cassell, 1984). The new norm suggests that the double standard that previously existed does not operate as it once did. That is, physical and emotional exploitation of adolescent females by males is not as strong today as in prior decades.

Other experts on adolescent sexuality are not so sure that the new norm has arrived (Gordon & Gilgun, 1987; Morrison, 1985). They argue that remnants of the double standard are unfortunately still flourishing. In most investigations, about twice as many boys as girls report having positive feelings about sexual intercourse. Females are more likely to report guilt, fear, and hurt. Adolescent males feel considerable pressure from their peers to have experienced sexual intercourse and to be sexually active. I remember vividly the raunchy conversations that filled our basketball locker room in junior high school. By the end of the ninth grade, I was sure that I was the only virgin on the 15-member team, but of course, there was no way I let my teammates know that. As one young adolescent recently remarked, "Look, I feel a lot of pressure from my buddies to go for the score." Further evidence for the male's physical and emotional exploitation of females was found in a survey of 432 14- to 18-year-olds (Goodchilds & Zellman, 1984). Both male and female adolescents accepted the right of the male adolescent to be sexually aggressive but left matters up to the female to set the limits for the male's sexual overtures. Another attitude related to the double standard was the belief that females should not plan ahead to have sexual intercourse but should be swept up in the passion of the moment, not taking contraceptive precautions. Unfortunately, while we may have chipped away at some parts of the sexual double standard, other aspects still remain.

Homosexual Attitudes and Behavior

Both early and more recent surveys of sexual choice indicate that about 4 percent of males and about 3 percent of females are exclusively homosexual (Hunt, 1974; Kinsey, Pomeroy, & Martin, 1948). As many as 10 percent of adolescents worry about whether they are lesbian or gay (Gordon & Gilgun, 1987). At least until several years ago, attitudes toward homosexuality were becoming increasingly permissive. But with the threat of AIDS, future surveys probably will indicate reduced acceptance of homosexuality.

Adolescence may play an important role in the development of homosexuality. In one investigation, participation in homosexual behavior and sexual arousal by same-sex peers in adolescence was strongly related to an adult homosexual orientation (Bell & others, 1981). When interest in the same sex is intense and compelling, an adolescent often experiences severe conflict (Boxer, 1988; Irvin, 1988). The American culture stigmatizes homosexuality; negative labels such as "fag" and "queer" are given to male homosexuals, and "lessie" and "dyke" are given to female homosexuals. The sexual socialization of adolescent homosexuals becomes a process of learning to hide (Herdt, 1988). Some gay males wait out their entire adolescence, hoping that heterosexual feelings will develop. Many female adolescent homosexuals have similar experiences, although same-sex genital contact is not as common as among males. Many adult females who identify themselves as homosexuals considered themselves predominantly heterosexual during adolescence (Bell & others, 1981).

Sexually Transmitted Diseases

Tammy, age 15, has just finished listening to an expert lecture in her health class. We overhear her talking to one of her girlfriends as she walks down the school corridor. "That was a disgusting lecture. I can't believe all the diseases you can get by having sex. I think she was probably trying to scare us. She spent a lot of time talking about AIDS, which I have heard that normal people do not get. Right? I've heard that only homosexuals and drug addicts get AIDS. And I've also heard that gonorrhea and most other sexual diseases can be cured, so what is the big deal if you get something like that?" Tammy's view of sexually transmitted diseases (formerly called veneral disease, or VD) is common among adolescents. Teenagers tend to believe that sexually transmitted diseases always happen to someone else, can be easily cured without any harm done, and are too disgusting for a nice young person to even hear about, let alone get. This view is wrong. Adolescents who are having sex *do* run the risk of getting sexually transmitted diseases. Sexually transmitted diseases are fairly common among today's adolescents.

Sexually transmitted diseases are primarily transmitted through sexual intercourse, although they can be transmitted orally. Chlamydia and herpes are among the most common sexually transmitted diseases. **Chlamydia** affects as many as 10 percent of all college students. The disease, which is named for the tiny bacteria

The AIDS advertisement indicates how vulnerable our nation's population is to the epidemic of AIDS, and the disease's lethal consequences.

that cause it, appears in both males and females. Males experience a burning sensation during urination and a mucoid discharge. Females experience painful urination or a vaginal discharge. These signs often mimic those of gonorrhea. However, when penicillin is prescribed for gonorrhealike symptoms, the problem does not go away, as it would if gonorrhea were the culprit. If left untreated, the disease can affect the entire reproductive tract. This can lead to problems left by scar tissue that can prevent the female from becoming pregnant. Effective drugs have been developed that treat this common sexually transmitted disease.

In recent years, an alarming increase has occurred in another sexually transmitted disease: **herpes simplex virus II.** While this disease is more common among young adults (estimates range to as high as 1 in 5 sexually active adults), as many as 1 in 35 adolescents have genital herpes (Oppenheimer, 1982). Its symptoms include irregular cycles of sores and blisters in the genital area. The herpes virus is potentially dangerous. If babies are exposed to the active virus during birth, they are vulnerable to brain damage or even death. And women with herpes are eight times more likely than unaffected women to develop cervical cancer (Harvard Medical School Newsletter, 1981). At present, herpes is incurable.

Another sexually transmitted disease—AIDS—is causing even greater fear among the American population. **AIDS** (acquired immune deficiency syndrome) is unrivaled in the fear it has generated among the American public. AIDS is caused by a virus that destroys the body's immune system. Consequently, many germs that would usually not harm a person with a normal immune system can produce devastating results and ultimately death.

In 1981, when AIDS was first recognized in the United States, there were fewer than 60 cases. By November, 1986, there were 27,000 cases of AIDS and 15,000 deaths from the disease. By March 1987, there were more than 32,000 cases of AIDS and 20,000 deaths from the disease. Beginning in 1990, according to Dr. Frank Press, president of the National Academy of Sciences, "We will lose as many Americans each year to AIDS as we lost in the entire Vietnam War." Almost 60,000 Americans died in that war. According to federal health officials, 1 to 1.5 million Americans are now asymptomatic carriers of AIDS; they are infected with the virus and are presumably capable of infecting others, but they show no clinical symptoms of AIDS.

In 1989, the first attempt to assess AIDS among college students was made. Testing of 16,861 students found 30 students infected with the virus (American College Health Association, 1989). If the 12.5 million students attending college were infected at the same rate, 25,000 students would have the AIDS virus.

In a recent survey of 35,239 high school students in 11 states by the Centers for Disease Control in Atlanta, it was revealed that many adolescents are misinformed about AIDS. More than 50 percent of the adolescents believed that a person can get AIDS from a blood test. About the same percentage said that AIDS can be contracted from a public toilet. Experts say the disease can be transmitted only by sexual contact, sharing needles, or blood transfusions. More than 90 percent of the adolescents did know that AIDS can be transmitted through sex and through sharing drug needles. A recent survey of 38,000 Canadian adolescents revealed that the adolescents felt the media is doing a poor job of providing easy-to-understand information about AIDS (King & others, 1989).

While 90 percent of AIDS cases continue to occur among homosexual males or intravenous drug users, a disproportionate increase among females who are heterosexual partners of bisexual males or of intravenous drug users was noted from 1985 to 1988. This increase suggests that the risk of AIDS may be rising among heterosexual individuals who have multiple sexual partners (Hein, 1989).

Of special interest to children and adolescents is the controversy surrounding individuals who have contracted the AIDS virus. For example, one 13-year-old hemophiliac contracted AIDS while receiving injections of a clotting agent. He was barred from his seventh-grade classes. In another case in another school district, school officials and doctors met with more than 800 concerned parents to defend their decision to admit a 14-year-old AIDS patient to school. Some parents will not let their children attend schools where an identified AIDS patient is enrolled. Others believe that children with the disease should not be society's outcasts, based on our current knowledge of how the disease spreads (Prothrow-Stith, 1989; Task Force on Pediatric Aids, 1989).

AIDS is a lethal threat to adolescents whose sexual activities put them at risk for contracting the disease—especially those who are sexually active with more than one partner and those who are intravenous drug users. Sexually active adolescents—both homosexual and heterosexual—can reduce the probability they will contract AIDS by following certain precautions (Bingham, 1989). First, sex with strangers or sex with individuals living in metropolitan locations where AIDS is most prevalent should be engaged in with extreme caution. Second, condoms may provide some protection against the virus, but data on this are inconclusive at this time. Third, a test is now available to determine whether an individual has AIDS. Not everyone exposed to the AIDS virus contracts AIDS, but adolescents who test positive for the AIDS virus should refrain from further sexual contact until their physician informs them otherwise.

Adolescent Pregnancy

Angela is 15 years old and pregnant. She reflects, "I'm three months pregnant. This could ruin my whole life. I've made all of these plans for the future and now they are down the drain. I don't have anybody to talk to about my problem. I can't talk to my parents. There is no way they can understand." Pregnant adolescents were once practically invisible and unmentionable. But yesterday's secret has become today's national dilemma.

They are of different races and from different places, but their circumstances have a distressing sameness. Each year more than 1 million American teenagers will become pregnant, four out of five of them unmarried. They represent a flaw in our nation's social fabric. Like Angela, many become pregnant in their early or middle adolescent years, 30,000 of them under the age of 15. In all, this means that 1 of every 10 adolescent females in the United States becomes pregnant each year, with 8 of the 10 pregnancies unintended (National Research Council, 1987). As one 17-year-old Los Angeles mother of a 1-year-old boy said, "We are children having children." The only bright spot in the adolescent pregnancy statistics is that the adolescent pregnancy rate, after increasing during the 1970s, has leveled off and may even be beginning to decline (National Research Council, 1987).

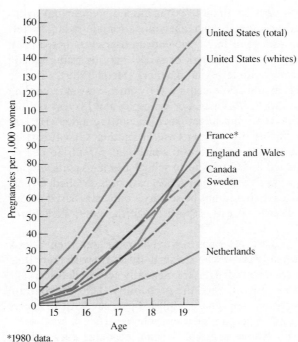

FIGURE 14.7   Pregnancy rates per 1,000 women by women's age, 1981 (Jones & others, 1985).

*1980 data.

Note: pregnancies are defined here as births plus abortions; age is the age at outcome.

The adolescent pregnancy rate in the United States is the highest of any in the Western world. It is more than twice the rates in England, France, or Canada, almost three times the rate in Sweden, and seven times the rate in the Netherlands (Alan Guttmacher Institute, 1981; Jones & others, 1985) (Figure 14.7). Although American adolescents are no more sexually active than their counterparts in these other nations, they are many more times likely to become pregnant.

Adolescent pregnancy is a complex American problem, one that strikes many nerves. The subject of adolescent pregnancy touches on many explosive social issues: the battle over abortion rights, contraceptives and the delicate question of whether adolescents should have easy access to them, and the perennially touchy subject of sex education in the public schools.

Dramatic changes involving sexual attitudes and social morals have swept through the American culture in the last three decades. Adolescents actually gave birth at a higher rate in 1957 than they do today, but that was a time of early marriage, with almost 25 percent of 18- and 19-year-olds married. The overwhelming majority of births to adolescent mothers in the 1950s occurred within a marriage and mainly involved females 17 years of age and older. Two or three decades ago, if an unwed adolescent girl became pregnant, in most instances her parents had her swiftly married off in a shotgun wedding. If marriage was impractical, the girl would discreetly disappear, the child would be put up for adoption, and the predicament would never be discussed again. Abortion was not a real option for most adolescent females until 1973, when the Supreme Court ruled it could not be outlawed.

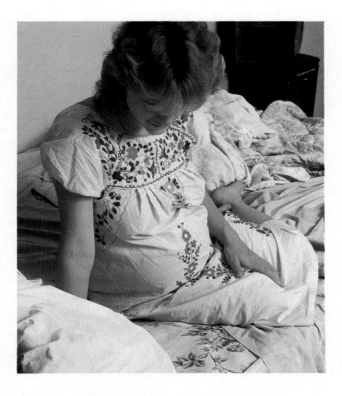

A 14-year-old mother just before giving birth. What are some of the hurdles the adolescent mother and her offspring face as they try to cope with their lives?

In today's world of adolescent pregnancies, a different scenario unfolds. If the girl does not choose to have an abortion (some 45 percent of pregnant adolescent girls do), she usually keeps the baby and raises it without the traditional involvement of marriage. With the stigma of illegitimacy largely absent, girls are less likely to give up their babies for adoption. Fewer than 5 percent do, compared with about 35 percent in the early 1960s. But while the stigma of illegitimacy has waned, the lives of most pregnant teenagers is anything but rosy.

The consequences of our nation's high adolescent pregnancy rate are of great concern. Adolescent pregnancy increases the health risks of both the child and the mother. Infants born to adolescent mothers are more likely to have low birth weights (a prominent cause of infant mortality), as well as neurological problems and childhood illnesses (Furstenberg, Brooks-Gunn, & Chase-Lansdale, 1989). Adolescent mothers often drop out of school, fail to gain employment, and become dependent on welfare. Although many adolescent mothers resume their education later in life, they generally do not catch up with women who postpone childbearing. In the National Longitudinal Survey of Work Experience of Youth, it was found that only half of the women 20 to 26 years old who first gave birth at age 17 had completed high school by their twenties. The percentage was even lower for those who gave birth at a younger age (Table 14.2) (Mott & Marsiglio, 1985). By contrast, among young females who waited until age 20 to have a baby, more than 90 percent had obtained a high school education. Among the younger adolescent mothers, almost half had obtained a General Equivalency Diploma (GED), which does not often open up good employment opportunities.

TABLE 14.2	*Percentage Distribution of Women, Aged 20–26 in 1983, by Type of High School Completion, According to Age at First Birth*		
		High School Completion by 1983	
Age at First Birth	Total (%)	Diploma (%)	GED(%)
15	45	24	21
16	49	28	21
17	53	38	15
18	62	52	10
19	77	68	9
Under 20	90	86	4

From Frank L. Mott and William Marsiglio, "Early Childbearing and Completion of High School" in *Family Planning Perspectives*, September/October 1985. Copyright © 1985 Alan Guttmacher Institute, New York, New York.

THE CULTURAL WORLDS OF CHILDREN

Adolescent Sexual Orientation in Holland and Sweden

In Holland, as well as in other European countries, such as Sweden, sex does not carry the mystery and conflict it does in American society. Holland does not have a mandated sex-education program, but adolescents can obtain contraceptive counseling at government-sponsored clinics for a small fee. The Dutch media also have played an important role in educating the public about sex through frequent broadcasts focused on birth control, abortion, and related matters. Most Dutch adolescents do not consider having sex without birth control.

Swedish adolescents are sexually active at an earlier age than are American adolescents, and they are exposed to even more explicit sex on television. However, the Swedish National Board of Education has developed a curriculum that ensures that every child in the country, beginning at age 7, will experience a thorough grounding in reproductive biology and by the ages of 10 or 12 will have been introduced to information about various forms of contraceptives. Teachers are expected to handle the subject of sex whenever it becomes relevant, regardless of the subject they are teaching. The idea is to dedramatize and demystify sex so that familiarity will make the individual less vulnerable to unwanted pregnancy and sexually transmitted diseases (Wallis, 1985). American society is not nearly so open about sex education. ◆

These educational deficits have negative consequences for the young women themselves and for their children (Kenney, 1987). Adolescent parents are more likely than those who delay childbearing to have low-paying, low-status jobs or to be unemployed. The mean family income of white females who give birth before age 17 is approximately half that of families in which the mother delays birth until her mid- or late twenties. The difficulties faced by adolescent mothers is clear in the descriptions of three girls in Children 14.1.

Angela, Michelle, and Stephanie: Three Adolescent Mothers

Before the baby arrived, her bedroom was a dimly lit shrine to the idols of rock music. Now the rock posters have been removed and the walls painted stark white. Angela's room has become a nursery for her 6-week-old son. Angela, who just turned 15, has difficulty thinking of herself as a mother. She still feels as young as she did before the baby was born; she also feels that she hasn't grown up any faster. She looks like a typical adolescent girl as she sits in her parents' living room, asking her mother for permission to attend a rock concert, asking if she can buy a puppy, and complaining that she isn't allowed to do anything. She mentions that last night she couldn't get her homework done because it took her so long to feed the baby. She commented, "When I laid him down, he wanted me to pick him back up." She ponders, "Babies are a giant step in life. I should have thought more about what I was doing. I had no idea what this was going to be like."

It is a hot summer day in San Francisco. Michelle, a 14-year-old black girl is typing away, practicing her office skills with fervor as beads of sweat trickle down her forehead. She is worried about her future. She feels that she has to learn some skills so she can make some money. She is right. In three weeks, Michelle is going to have a baby. She comes from a low-income family. She doesn't know her father's whereabouts, and her mother barely can make ends meet. She says that she used to think, "In 10 years I will be 24. Now I think, I'll be 24 and my child will be 10."

In the early afternoon, the smells of dirty diapers and grease fill the air in a bleak Minneapolis apartment. The television is turned to *All My Children*. Seventeen-year-old Stephanie has collapsed on the sofa. A few minutes later, over the sounds of the voices on the television, she hears a loud wail. Her 1-month-old baby is hungry. In an adjacent bedroom, her other child, 1½-year-old Joey is recovering from the flu. Stephanie is one of 10 children herself. She first became pregnant at age 15. She says it was an accident. So was her second baby, she says. Stephanie complains that she always feels tired. Before Joey was born, she dropped out of school. She dreamed of being an airline stewardess. Now her hopes are more down to earth. She would like to pay her bills, buy groceries, and be able to live in a house with her own furniture. Says Stephanie, "It has been a long, long time since I had a good time" (Wallis, 1985). ◆

Serious, extensive efforts need to be developed to help pregnant adolescents and young mothers enhance their educational and occupational opportunities. Adolescent mothers also need extensive help in obtaining competent day care and in planning for the future (Edleman, 1987; Furstenberg, Brooks-Gunn, & Morgan, 1987). Experts recommend that to reduce the high rate of teen pregnancy, adolescents need improved sex-education and family-planning information, greater access to contraception, and broad community involvement and support (Conger, 1988; Wallace & Vienonen, 1989).

Thinking Critically
You have been asked to design a community program to reduce the rate of adolescent pregnancy in your community. What would the program be like?

Problems and Disturbances

We have already discussed several major problems in adolescence—sexually transmitted diseases and pregnancy, for example. But there are other problems that adolescents confront. Among the main ones are drug and alcohol abuse, suicide, and eating disorders, each of which we will consider in turn.

Whatever is formed for long duration arrives slowly to its maturity.

Samuel Johnson, The Rambler, *1750*

Drugs and Alcohol

The 1960s and 1970s were a time of marked increases in the use of illicit drugs. During the social and political unrest of those years, many youth turned to marijuana, stimulants, and hallucinogens. Increases in alcohol consumption by adolescents also were noted (Robinson & Greene, 1988). More precise data about drug

What is the pattern of alcohol consumption among adolescents?

use by adolescents have been collected in recent years. Each year since 1975, Lloyd Johnston, Patrick O'Malley, and Gerald Bachman (1988, 1989), working at the Institute of Social Research at the University of Michigan, have carefully monitored drug use by America's high school seniors in a wide range of public and private high schools. From time to time, they also sample the drug use of younger adolescents and adults as well.

An encouraging finding from the most recent survey (conducted in 1988) of 16,300 high school seniors is the continued gradual decrease in the use of illicit drugs (Johnston, O'Malley, & Bachman, 1989). Nonetheless, the United States still has the highest rate of drug use among the world's industrialized nations. In 1987, 57 percent of the nation's high school seniors tried an illicit drug other than marijuana. A special concern is the use of alcohol and cocaine by adolescents, each of which we will consider in turn.

Alcohol

Some mornings, 15-year-old Annie was too drunk to go to school. Other days, she'd stop for a couple of beers or a screwdriver on the way to school. She was tall, blonde, and good looking, and no one who sold her liquor, even at 8:00 in the morning, questioned her age. Where did she get her money? From babysitting and from what her mother gave her to buy lunch. Annie used to be a cheerleader, but no longer; she was kicked off the squad for missing practice so often. Soon, she and several of her peers were drinking almost every morning. Sometimes, they skipped school and went to the woods to drink. Annie's whole life began to revolve around her drinking.

This routine went on for two years, and during the last summer, any time she saw anybody, she was drunk. After a while, Annie's parents discovered her problem. But even though they punished her, it did not stop her drinking. Finally, this year, Annie started dating a boy she really liked and who would not put up with her drinking. She agreed to go to Alcoholics Anonymous and has just successfully completed treatment. She has stopped drinking for four consecutive months now, and she hopes that her abstinence will continue.

Alcohol is the drug most widely used by adolescents in our society. For them, it has produced many enjoyable moments and many sad ones as well. Alcoholism is the third-leading killer in the United States, with more than 13 million people classified as alcoholics, many of whom established their drinking habits during adolescence. Each year, approximately 25,000 people are killed and 1.5 million injured by drunk drivers. In 65 percent of the aggressive male acts against females, the offender has been under the influence of alcohol (Goodman & others, 1986). In numerous instances of drunk driving and assaults on females, the offenders have been adolescents.

How extensive is alcohol use by adolescents? Although the use of marijuana and other drugs among adolescents has declined recently, adolescents do not seem to be drinking more to offset their reduced intake of other drugs. Alcohol use by high school seniors has gradually declined. Monthly use declined from 72 percent in 1980 to 64 percent in 1988. The prevalence of drinking five or more drinks in a row during the prior two-week interval fell from 41 percent in 1983 to 35 percent in 1988. There remains a substantial sex difference in heavy adolescent drinking: 28 percent for females versus 46 percent for males in 1986, although this difference diminished gradually during the 1980s. However, data from college students show little drop in alcohol use and an increase in heavy drinking: Forty-five percent in 1986, up 2 percent from the previous year. Heavy drinking at parties among college males is common and is becoming more common (Johnston, O'Malley, & Bachman, 1988, 1989).

Thinking Critically
Why do you think alcohol use has remained so high during adolescence?

Cocaine

Did you know that cocaine was once an ingredient in Coca-Cola? Of course, it has long since been removed from the soft drink. **Cocaine** comes from the coca plant, native to Bolivia and Peru. For many years Bolivians and Peruvians chewed the plant to increase their stamina. Today cocaine is usually snorted, smoked, or injected in the form of crystals or powder. The effect is a rush of euphoric feelings, which eventually wear off, followed by depressive feelings, lethargy, insomnia, and irritability.

Cocaine is a highly controversial drug. Users claim it is exciting, makes them feel good, and increases their confidence. Yet it is clear that cocaine has potent cardiovascular effects and is potentially addictive. The recent deaths of sports stars, such as University of Maryland basketball player Len Bias, demonstrate how lethal cocaine can be. When the drug's effects are extreme, it can produce heart attack, a stroke, or a brain seizure. The increase in cocaine-related deaths often is traced to very pure or tainted forms of the drug, (Gold, Gallanter, & Stimmel, 1987).

How many people use cocaine? Figures vary, but estimates range as high as 5 million regular users and 20 million casual users (Smith, 1986). One encouraging fact is that in 1987, for the first time in eight years, cocaine use showed a significant drop among high school seniors and college students. Eight percent of high school seniors used cocaine at least once a year in 1988, down from 13 percent in 1986.

Alcohol Abuse in Native American Youth

The problem of alcohol abuse in native American youth has grown in recent years. In one national survey, native American youth had a 42 percent problem-drinking rate compared to 34 percent for Anglo youth (Donovan & Jessor, 1978). There is not one single, concise answer to the problem of alcohol abuse in native American youth (Watts & Lewis, 1988). It is a complex problem, involving cultural, historical, educational, and economic circumstances. Proposed solutions involve elements such as alcohol education and prevention programs that truly involve the local tribal community, programs that involve parents and youth, and economic development programs. Both family and community involvement are especially recommended for further examination (Edwards & Edwards, 1988; Oetting, Beauvais, & Edwards, 1988). ◆

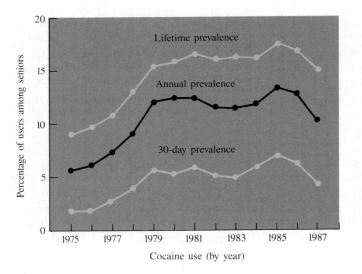

FIGURE 14.8   Trends in lifetime, annual, and 30-day prevalence of cocaine among all high school seniors.

Source: L. D. Johnston, et al. (1988) "Illicit Drug Use, Smoking, and Drinking by America's High School Students, College Students, and Young Adults, 1975–1987." Washington, D.C.: National Institute of Drug Abuse.

Cocaine use by college students also declined from 17.1 percent annual prevalence in 1986 to 10 percent in 1987. A growing proportion of high school seniors and college students are reaching the conclusion that cocaine use holds considerable, unpredictable risk for the user. Still, the percentage of adolescents and young adults who use cocaine is precariously high. About 1 of every 6 high school seniors has tried cocaine at least once, and 1 in 18 has tried crack cocaine. The trends in lifetime, annual, and 30-day prevalence of cocaine use by high school seniors from 1975 to 1987 are shown in Figure 14.8. As can be seen, while cocaine use dropped in 1987, prevalence of use is still very high in comparison to use in the 1970s. For students who drop out of high school, cocaine use is estimated to be higher.

The Anabolic Steroid Crisis

Anabolic steroids are synthetic derivatives of male hormones. Initially, anabolic steroids were prescribed by doctors to help rehabilitate muscles, but more recently they have been prescribed for treating anemia. The current controversy about anabolic steroids focuses on their widespread use to improve athletic performance and to develop a better body build.

In a recent investigation of 3,403 male seniors in 46 high schools, 6.6 percent reported that they had used anabolic steroids (Buckley & others, 1988). That figure translates to an estimated half a million adolescent boys using anabolic steroids in the United States. Nearly half of the boys who admitted using steroids said they did so to improve their athletic performance. About 10 percent said they used steroids to treat sports-related injuries. However, 35 percent of the users said they did not participate in school sports. And 27 percent said they took pills or injected the drugs to improve muscular appearance. Almost half of the boys "stacked" the drugs—that is, they used more than one steroid at a time. More than one-third started using the drugs by age 15, another one-third by age 16. Approximately 20 percent got the drugs from a doctor, pharmacist, or a veterinarian; 65 percent got them from black market sources such as athletes and coaches.

Why are health experts so concerned about the increase in anabolic steroid use? A number of negative side effects are associated with the drugs:

The current controversy focused on anabolic steroids involves their widespread use to improve athletic performance and develop a better body build. It is estimated that about 500,000 adolescent boys in the United States are currently using anabolic steroids.

—hair growth or baldness in females
—acne in males and females
—high blood pressure; clogging of arteries
—liver cancer in males and females; prostate cancer in males

—increased hostility, aggressiveness, hypertension
—breast growth in males; breast cancer and decreased breast size in females
—sterility or atrophied testicles in males; menstrual irregularities, enlarged genitals in females ◆

A troublesome part of the cocaine story rests in the dangerous shift in the mode of administration being used, due in large part to the advent of crack cocaine, an inexpensive, purified, smokeable form of the drug. The proportion of high school seniors who said they had smoked cocaine more than doubled between 1983 and 1986, from 2.5 percent to 6 percent. In 1986, for the first time, seniors were asked specifically about crack use. In 1986 and 1987, 4 percent said they had used crack cocaine in the previous 12 months. Crack use was especially heavy among non-college-bound youths in urban settings. Some good news about crack use appeared in the 1988 national survey by Johnston, O'Malley, & Bachman (1989). Use of crack cocaine by high school seniors began to decline—from 4 percent annual use in 1987 to 3 percent annual use in 1988. Another recent crisis in drug use that has surfaced among adolescents—anabolic steroid use—is described in Children 14.2.

The Role of Parents, Peers, and Schools in Adolescent Drug Use

Most adolescents become drug users at some point in their development, whether their use is limited to alcohol, caffeine, and cigarettes or extended to marijuana, cocaine, and hard drugs. A special concern occurs when adolescents use drugs as a way of coping with stress, a practice that can interfere with the development of competent coping skills and responsible decision making. Researchers have found that when drug use occurs initially in childhood or in early adolescence, it has more detrimental long-term effects on the development of responsible, competent behavior than when drug use occurs initially in late adolescence (Newcomb & Bentler, 1989). By using drugs to cope with stress, young adolescents often enter adult roles of marriage and work prematurely without adequate socioemotional growth, and they experience greater failure in adult roles.

A special concern in the use of drugs by adolescents is the role parents, peers, and schools play in preventing and reducing the drug use. Families play an important role in adolescent drug use. In one recent longitudinal investigation, boys' poor self-control at age 4 was related to their drug use in adolescence, and permissive parenting in the families of girls at age 4 was related to their drug use in adolescence (Block & Block, 1988). In another recent investigation, social support during adolescence substantially reduced drug use (Newcomb & Bentler, 1988). In this study, social support included good relationships with parents, other adults, siblings, and peers. Another researcher found that the greatest use of drugs by adolescents takes place when both the adolescent's parents take drugs (such as tranquilizers, amphetamines, alcohol, or nicotine) and the adolescent's peers take drugs (Kandel, 1974).

Schools are involved in drug use because they frequently are the place where peers initiate and maintain drug use. Schools can play an important role in preventing or reducing drug use; there are few other settings where the adolescent population congregates on such a frequent basis. Although most schools have established policies on drug use, some have gone further and developed drug prevention or intervention programs (Bailey, 1989; Minuchin & Shapiro, 1983). The most promising school programs have been those involving comprehensive long-term approaches, not only providing specific information and services, but dealing with the social organization of the school as a whole as well. Programs that have emphasized detection, discipline, and scare tactics have been the least effective in preventing or reducing drug use by adolescents.

Juvenile Delinquency

Arnie is 13 years old. His history includes a string of thefts and physical assaults. The first theft occurred when Arnie was 8; he stole a SONY walkman from an electronics store. The first physical assault took place a year later when he shoved his 7-year-old brother up against the wall, bloodied his face, and then threatened to kill him with a butcher knife. Recently, the thefts and physical assaults have increased. In the last week, he stole a television set and struck his mother repeatedly and threatened to kill her. He also broke some neighborhood street lights and threatened some youths with a wrench and a hammer. Arnie's father left home when Arnie was 3 years old. Until the father left, his parents argued extensively and his father often beat up his mother. Arnie's mother indicates that when Arnie was younger, she was able to control his behavior; but in the last several years she has not been

Juvenile delinquents shown vandalizing a property. What causes juvenile delinquency?

able to enforce any sanctions on his antisocial behavior. Because of Arnie's volatility and dangerous behavior, it was recommended that he be placed in a group home with other juvenile delinquents.

The label **juvenile delinquent** is applied to an adolescent who breaks the law or engages in behavior that is considered illegal. Like other categories of disturbance, juvenile delinquency is a broad concept; legal infractions range from littering to murder. Because the adolescent technically only becomes a juvenile delinquent after being judged guilty of a crime by a court of law, official records do not accurately reflect the number of illegal acts juvenile delinquents commit. Nevertheless, there is every indication that in the last 10 to 15 years, juvenile delinquency has increased in relation to the number of crimes committed by adults. Estimates regarding the number of juvenile delinquents in the United States are sketchy, but FBI statistics indicate that at least 2 percent of all youths are involved in juvenile court cases. The number of girls found guilty of juvenile delinquency has increased substantially in recent years. Delinquency rates among blacks, other minority groups, and the lower class are especially high in proportion to the overall population of these groups. However, such groups have less influence over the judicial decision-making process in the United States and therefore may be judged delinquent more readily than their white, middle-class counterparts (Binder, 1987; Gold, 1987; Polier, in press).

What causes delinquency? Many causes have been proposed, including heredity, identity problems, community influences, and family experiences. Erik Erikson (1968), for example, believes that adolescents whose development has restricted them from acceptable social roles or made them feel that they cannot measure up to the demands placed on them may choose a negative identity. The adolescent with a negative identity may find support for his delinquent image among peers, reinforcing the negative identity. For Erikson, delinquency is an attempt to establish an identity, although it is a negative identity.

Although delinquency is less exclusively a lower-class phenomena than it was in the past, some characteristics of the lower-class culture may promote delinquency (Simons & Gray, 1989). The norms of many lower-class peer groups and gangs are antisocial, or counterproductive, to the goals and norms of society at large. Getting into and staying out of trouble become prominent features of life for some adolescents in low-income neighborhoods. Adolescents from low-income backgrounds may sense that they can gain attention and status by performing antisocial actions. Being "tough" and "masculine" are high-status traits for lower-class boys, and these traits often are measured by the adolescent's success in performing and getting away with delinquent acts. A community with a high crime rate also lets the adolescent observe many models who engage in criminal activities. These communities may be characterized by poverty, unemployment, and feelings of alienation toward the middle class. Quality schooling, educational funding, and organized neighborhood activities may be lacking in these communities (Chesney-Lind, 1989).

Family support systems are also associated with delinquency. Parents of delinquents are less skilled in discouraging antisocial behavior and in encouraging skilled behavior than are parents of nondelinquents. Parental monitoring of adolescents is especially important in determining whether an adolescent becomes a delinquent (Dishion, Patterson, & Skinner, 1989; Patterson, DeBarsyhe, & Ramsey, 1989). "It's 10 P.M., do you know where your children are?" seems to be an important question for parents to answer affirmatively. Family discord and inconsistent and inappropriate discipline are also associated with delinquency.

A special concern in delinquency has surfaced recently: escalating gang violence, which is being waged on a level more lethal than ever before. Knives and clubs have been replaced by grenades and automatic weapons, frequently purchased with money made from selling drugs. The lure of gang membership is powerful, especially for children and adolescents who are disconnected from family, school, work, and the community. Children as young as 9 years of age cling to the fringes of neighborhood gangs, eager to prove themselves worthy of membership by the age of 12. Once children are members of a gang, it is difficult to get them to leave. Recommendations for prevention of gang violence involve identification of disconnected children in elementary schools and initiation of counseling with the children and their families (Calhoun, 1988). More about life in gangs and an effort in Detroit, Michigan, that has made a difference in reducing gang participation appears in Children 14.3.

Frog and Dolores

He goes by the name of Frog. He is the cocky prince of the barrio in East Los Angeles. He has street smarts. Frog happily smiles as he talks about raking in $200 a week selling crack cocaine. He proudly details his newly acquired membership in a violent street gang, the Crips. Frog brags about using his drug money to rent a convertible on weekends, even though at less than 5 feet in height, he can barely see over the dashboard. Frog is 13 years old.

With the advent of crack, juvenile arrests in New York City tripled from 1983 to 1987 and almost quadrupled in the same time frame in Washington, D.C. Adults who founded the crack trade recognized early on that young adolescents do not run the risk of the mandatory jail sentence that courts hand out to adults. Being a lookout is the entry-level position for 9- and 10-year-olds. They can make as much as $100 a day warning dealers that police are in the area. The next step up the ladder is runner, a job that can pay as much as $300 a day. A runner transports drugs to the dealers on the street from makeshift factories where cocaine powder is cooked into rock-hard crack. At the next level, an older adolescent can reach the status of dealer; in a hot market like New York City, a dealer can make over $1,000 a day.

The escalating drug-related gang violence is difficult to either contain or reduce. Police crackdowns across the country seem to have had a minimal impact. In a recent weekend-long raid of drug-dealing gangs in Los Angeles, police arrested 1,453 persons, including 315 adolescents. Half had to be released for lack of evidence. The Los Angeles County juvenile facilities are designed to house 1,317. Today more than 2,000 adolescents are crammed into their facilities.

Counselors, school officials, and community workers report that it is extremely difficult to turn around the lives of children and adolescents involved in drug-related gang violence. When impoverished children can make $100 a day, it is hard to wean them from gangs. Federal budgets for training and employment programs, which provide crucial assistance to disadvantaged youth, have been reduced dramatically.

In Detroit, Michigan, Dolores Bennett, though, has made a difference. For 25 years, she has worked long hours trying to find things to keep children from low-income families busy. Her activities have led to the creation of neighborhood sports teams, regular fairs and picnics, and an informal job-referral service for the children in her neighborhood. She also holds many casual get-togethers for the youths in her small, tidy yellow frame house. The youth talk openly and freely about their problems and their hopes, knowing that Dolores will listen. Dolores says that she has found being a volunteer to be a priceless job. On the mantel in her living room are hundreds of pictures of children and adolescents she has worked with. She points out that most of them did not have someone in their homes who would listen to them and give them love. Our nation needs more Dolores Bennetts. ♦

Dolores Bennett, volunteer in a low-income area of Detroit, Michigan, shown here talking with and listening to two of her "children."

Suicide

Suicide is a common problem in our society. Its rate has quadrupled during the last 30 years in the United States; each year about 25,000 people take their own lives. Beginning at about the age of 15, the rate of suicide begins to rise rapidly. Suicide accounts for about 12 percent of the mortality in the adolescent and young adult age group (Brent, 1989). Males are about three times as likely to commit suicide as females; this may be because of their more active methods for attempting suicide—shooting, for example. By contrast, females are more likely to use passive methods such as sleeping pills, which are less likely to produce death. While males commit suicide more frequently, females attempt it more frequently (Maltsberger, 1988).

Estimates indicate that for every suicide in the general population, 6 to 10 suicide attempts are made. For adolescents the figure is as high as 50 attempts for every life taken. As many as two in every three college students has thought about suicide on at least one occasion; their methods range from drugs to crashing into the White House in an airplane.

Why do adolescents attempt suicide? There is no simple answer to this important question. It is helpful to think of suicide in terms of proximal and distal factors. Proximal, or immediate, factors can trigger a suicide attempt. Highly stressful circumstances such as the loss of a boyfriend or a girlfriend, failing a class at school, or an unwanted pregnancy can produce a suicide attempt (Blumenthal & Kupfer, 1988; Neiger & Hopkins, 1988). Drugs also have been involved more often in recent suicide attempts than in attempts in the past (Rich, Young, & Fowler, 1986).

But distal, or earlier, experiences often are involved in suicide attempts as well. A longstanding history of family instability and unhappiness may be present (Shapiro & Freedman, 1989). Just as a lack of affection and emotional support, high control, and pressure for achievement by parents during childhood are related to adolescent depression, so are such combinations of family experiences likely to show up as distal factors in suicide attempts. Lack of supportive friendships also may be present (Rubenstein & others, 1989). In an investigation of suicide among gifted women, previous suicide attempts, anxiety, conspicuous instability in work and in relationships, depression, or alcoholism also were present in the women's lives (Tomlinson-Keasey, Warren, & Elliott, 1986). These factors are similar to those found to predict suicide among gifted men (Shneidman, 1971).

Just as genetic factors are associated with depression, so are they associated with suicide. The closer the genetic relationship a person has to someone who has committed suicide, the more likely that person is to commit suicide (Wender & others, 1986). The advice offered in Table 14.3 provides valuable information about what to do and what not to do when you suspect an adolescent is contemplating suicide.

Eating Disorders

Fifteen-year-old Jane gradually eliminated foods from her diet to the point where she subsisted by eating *only* applesauce and eggnog. She spent hours observing her own body, wrapping her fingers around her waist to see if it was getting any thinner. She fantasized about becoming a beautiful fashion model who would wear designer

TABLE 14.3   *What to Do and What Not to Do When You Suspect an Adolescent Is Likely to Attempt Suicide*

What to do
1. Ask direct, straightforward questions in a calm manner. "Are you thinking about hurting yourself?"
2. Assess the seriousness of the suicidal intent by asking questions about feelings, important relationships, who else the person has talked with, and the amount of thought given to the means to be used. If a gun, pills, rope, or other means have been obtained and a precise plan developed, clearly the situation is dangerous. Stay with the person until some type of help arrives.
3. Be a good listener and be very supportive without being falsely reassuring.
4. Try to persuade the adolescent to obtain professional help and assist him or her in getting this help.

What Not to Do
1. Do not ignore the warning signs.
2. Do not refuse to talk about suicide if an adolescent approaches you about the topic.
3. Do not react with horror, disapproval, or repulsion.
4. Do not give false reassurances by saying things like, "Everything is going to be okay." Also don't give out simple answers or platitudes like "You have everything to be thankful for."
5. Do not abandon the adolescent after the crisis has gone by or after professional help has commenced.

After information presented in *Living with 10–15-Year-Olds: A Parent Education Curriculum* by Gayle Dorman, et al., 1982. Reprinted with permission from The Center For Early Adolescence, Carrboro, NC.

bathing suits. But even when she reached 85 pounds, Jane still felt fat. She continued to lose weight, eventually emaciating herself. She was hospitalized and treated for **anorexia nervosa,** an eating disorder that involves the relentless pursuit of thinness through starvation. Eventually anorexia nervosa can lead to death, as it did for popular singer Karen Carpenter (Casper, 1989; Schlundt & Johnson, 1990).

Anorexia nervosa afflicts primarily females during adolescence and early adulthood (only about 5 percent of anorexics are male). Most individuals with this disorder are white and from well-educated middle- and upper-income families. Although anorexics avoid eating, they have an intense interest in food, they cook for others, they talk about food, and they insist on watching others eat. Anorexics have a distorted body image, perceiving themselves as beautiful even when they have become skeletal in appearance. As self-starvation continues and the fat content of the body drops to a bare minimum, menstruation usually stops. Behavior is often hyperactive (Polivy & Thomsen, 1987).

Numerous causes of anorexia nervosa have been proposed. They include societal, psychological, and physiological factors (Attie & Brooks-Gunn, in press; Brumberg, 1988; Stern & others, 1989). The societal factor most often held responsible is the current fashion of thinness. Psychological factors include motivation for attention, desire for individuality, denial of sexuality, and a way of coping with overcontrolling parents. Anorexics sometimes have families that place high demands for achievement on them. Unable to meet their parents' high standards, anorexics feel unable to control their own lives. By limiting their food intake, anorexics gain some sense of self-control. Physiological causes focus on the hypothalamus, which becomes abnormal in a number of ways when the individual is anorexic (Brumberg, 1988). At this time, however, we are not exactly certain what causes anorexia nervosa.

Anorexia nervosa has become an increasingly frequent problem among adolescent females.

An eating disorder related to anorexia nervosa is **bulimia.** Anorexics occasionally binge and purge, but bulimics do this on a regular basis. The bulimic binges on large amounts of food and then purges by self-induced vomiting or use or a laxative. The binges sometimes alternate with fasting; at other times they alternate with normal eating behavior. Like anorexia nervosa, bulimia is primarily a female disorder. Bulimia has become prevalent among college women. Some estimates suggest that one in two college women binge and purge at least some of the time. However, recent estimates suggest that true bulimics—those who binge and purge on a regular basis—make up less than 2 percent of the college female population (Stunkard, 1987). While anorexics can control their eating, bulimics cannot. Depression is a common characteristic of bulimics (Levy, Dixon, & Stern, 1989). Many of the same causes proposed for anorexia nervosa are offered for bulimia.

Thus far, we have discussed a number of ideas about sexuality and problems and disturbances in adolescence. These ideas are summarized in Concept Table 14.2. In the next chapter, we will turn our attention to the adolescent's cognitive development.

Summary

I. **The Nature of Adolescence**
G. Stanley Hall's book *Adolescence* marked the beginning of the scientific study of adolescence. Hall is known for his storm and stress view and for the belief that biology plays a prominent role in development. Many scholars argue that adolescence is a sociohistorical invention. They believe that legislation ensured the dependency of youth and made their move into the economic sphere more manageable early in the twentieth century. Many stereotypes of adolescents are inaccurate. It is not unusual for widespread generalizations about adolescents to be based on a limited group of highly visible adolescents. An accurate vision of adolescence is a time of evaluation, a time of decision making, and a time of commitment as youth carve out their place in the world.

II. **Puberty's Boundaries, Determinants, and Hormonal Changes**
Puberty is a rapid change to physical maturation involving hormonal and body changes that take place primarily in early adolescence. Its determinants include nutrition, health, heredity, and body mass. The endocrine system is made up of endocrine glands and their secretions. The secretions of these ductless glands are called hormones, powerful chemicals that regulate organs. The hypothalamic-pituitary-gonadal axis is an important aspect of the complex hormonal system that contributes to pubertal change. Testosterone, an androgen, plays a key role in male pubertal development; estradiol, an estrogen, plays a key role in female pubertal development. Recent research has documented a link between hormonal levels and the adolescent's behavior.

III. **Physical Changes**
The growth spurt for boys occurs about two years later than for girls, with 12½ being the average age of onset for boys, 10½ for girls. Sexual maturation is a predominant feature of pubertal change. Individual differences in pubertal change are extensive.

IV. **Psychological Dimensions of Puberty**
Adolescents show a heightened interest in their body image. Young adolescents are more preoccupied and less satisfied with their body image than late adolescents are. Early maturation favors boys, at least during adolescence. As adults, though, late-maturing boys achieve more successful identities. The results for girls are more mixed than for boys. A special concern is the health care of early- and late-maturing adolescents.

Sexuality, and Problems and Disturbances

Concept	Processes and Related Ideas	Characteristics and Description
Sexuality	Sexual attitudes and behavior	There has been a major increase in the number of adolescents reporting intercourse. The proportion of females reporting intercourse has increased more rapidly than the proportion of males. National data indicate that by age 18, 44 percent of females and 64 percent of males are sexually experienced. Urban inner-city adolescents have even higher incidences. As we develop our sexual attitudes, we follow certain sexual scripts, which are different for males and females. About 4 percent of males and 3 percent of females choose to be exclusively homosexual. About 10 percent of adolescents worry about whether they are lesbian or gay.
	Sexually transmitted diseases	Any adolescent who has sex runs the risk of getting a sexually transmitted disease, although many adolescents underestimate their own risk. Among the sexually transmitted diseases adolescents may get are chlamydia, herpes, and AIDS.
	Adolescent pregnancy	More than 1 million American adolescents become pregnant each year. Eight of 10 adolescent pregnancies are unintended. Our nation's adolescent pregnancy rate is the highest in the Western world. Dramatic changes have swept through the American culture in the last three decades regarding adolescent sexuality and pregnancy. The consequences of adolescent pregnancy include health risks for the mother and the offspring. Adolescent mothers often drop out of school, fail to gain employment, and become dependent on welfare. Experts are calling for increased sex education and family planning, access to contraceptive methods, and broad community involvement and support.
Problems and Disturbances	Drugs and alcohol	The United States has the highest adolescent drug use rate of any industrialized nation. The 1960s and 1970s were a time of marked increase in adolescent drug use. Since the mid-1980s there has been a slight overall downturn in drug use among adolescents. Alcohol is the drug most widely used by adolescents; alcohol abuse by adolescents is a major problem. Heavy drinking is common. Cocaine is a highly controversial drug. Its use by high school seniors dropped off for the first time in eight years in 1987, but a dangerous form of the drug, crack cocaine, which is smoked, is increasingly used. Parents, peers, and schools play important roles in adolescent drug use.
	Juvenile delinquency	A juvenile delinquent is an adolescent who breaks the law or engages in conduct that is considered illegal. Heredity, identity problems, community influences, and family experiences have been proposed as causes of delinquency. Parents' failure to discourage antisocial behavior and encourage skilled behavior, as well as parents' lack of monitoring of the adolescent's whereabouts, are related to delinquency.
	Suicide	The rate of suicide has increased; suicide increases dramatically at about the age of 15. Both proximal and distal factors are involved in suicide's causes.
	Eating disorders	Anorexia nervosa and bulimia have become increasing problems for adolescent females. Societal, psychological, and physiological causes of these disorders have been proposed.

V. Sexual Attitudes and Behavior

There has been a major increase in the number of adolescents reporting intercourse. The proportion of females reporting intercourse has increased more rapidly than the proportion of males. National data indicate that by age 18, 44 percent of females and 64 percent of males are sexually experienced. Urban inner-city adolescents have even higher incidences. As we develop our sexual identities, we follow certain sexual scripts, which are different for males and females. About 4 percent of males and 3 percent of females choose to be exclusively homosexual. About 10 percent of adolescents worry about whether they are lesbian or gay.

VI. Sexually Transmitted Diseases

Any adolescent who has sex runs the risk of getting a sexually transmitted disease, although many adolescents underestimate their own risk. Among the sexually transmitted diseases adolescents may get are chlamydia, herpes, and AIDS.

VII. Adolescent Pregnancy

More than 1 million American adolescents become pregnant each year. Eight of 10 adolescent pregnancies are unintended. Our nation's adolescent pregnancy rate is the highest in the Western world. Dramatic changes have swept through the American culture in the last three decades regarding adolescent sexuality and pregnancy. The consequences of adolescent pregnancy include health risks for the mother and the offspring. Adolescent mothers often drop out of school, fail to gain employment, and become dependent on welfare. Experts are calling for increased sex education and family planning, access to contraceptive methods, and broad community involvement and support.

VIII. Drugs and Alcohol

The United States has the highest adolescent drug use rate of any industrialized nation. The 1960s and 1970s were a time of marked increase in adolescent drug use. Since the mid-1980s, there has been a slight downturn in drug use among adolescents. Alcohol is the drug most widely used by adolescents; alcohol abuse by adolescents is a major problem. Heavy drinking is common. Cocaine is a highly controversial drug. Its use by high school seniors dropped off for the first time in eight years in 1987, but a dangerous form of the drug—crack cocaine, which is smoked—is increasingly used. Parents, peers, and school play important roles in adolescent drug use.

IX. Juvenile Delinquency

A juvenile delinquent is an adolescent who breaks the law or engages in illegal conduct. Heredity, identity problems, community influences, and family experiences have been proposed as delinquency's causes. Parents' failure to discourage antisocial behavior and encourage skilled behavior, as well as parents' lack of monitoring of the adolescent's whereabouts, are related to delinquency.

X. Suicide and Eating Disorders

The rate of suicide has increased; suicide increases dramatically at about the age of 15. Both proximal and distal factors are involved in suicide's causes. Anorexia nervosa and bulimia have become increasing problems for adolescents. Societal, psychological, and physiological causes of these disorders have been proposed.

Key Terms

storm and stress view 457
adolescent generalization
   gap 458
menarche 459
hormones 460
hypothalamic-pituitary-
   gonadal axis 460

testosterone 461
estradiol 461
sexual script 469
chlamydia 471
herpes simplex virus II 472

AIDS 472
cocaine 479
juvenile delinquent 483
anorexia nervosa 487
bulimia 488

Suggested Readings

Coleman, J. (Ed.). (1987). *Working with troubled adolescents.* Orlando, FL: Academic
   Press
   Includes chapters on adolescent intervention and family therapy, social skills training
   for adolescents, helping adolescents improve their identity, and suicide.
Gordon, S., & Gilgun, J. F. (1987). Adolescent Sexuality. In V. B. Van Hasselt & M.
   Hersen (Eds.), *Handbook of adolescent psychology.* New York: Pergamon.
   An excellent chapter on adolescent's sexual choices and what sexuality means to
   adolescents.
Lerner, R. M., & Foch, T. T. (Eds.). (1987). *Biological-psychological interaction in early
   adolescence.* Hillsdale, NJ: Erlbaum.
   Includes articles on a wide range of topics related to pubertal changes and their
   effects on development.
McAnarney, E. R. (1988). Early adolescent motherhood: Crisis in the making? In M. D.
   Levine & E. R. McAnarney (Eds.), *Early adolescent transitions.* Lexington, MA:
   D. C. Heath.
   Provides recent information about adolescent mothers, including potential intervention
   strategies.
Pierce, C., & VanDeVeer, D. (1988). *AIDS.* Belmont, CA: Wadsworth.
   An excellent collection of essays on AIDS is presented, including a general overview
   of what is known about AIDS and information about ethical issues and public policy
   involved in AIDS.

The thoughts of youth are long, long thoughts.

Henry Wadsworth Longfellow

15

Cognitive Development

C leveland Wilkes's family lives in Providence, Rhode Island. They never have had much money. He and his parents know what unemployment can do to a family. Nonetheless, Cleveland, who is 17 years old, is known as "the dresser" to his friends because of his penchant for flamboyant clothes, especially shoes. What little money Cleveland manages to scrape together is all channeled into maintaining a wardrobe. In Cleveland's own words:

> Whole world floats by around here. There ain't nothing you can't see on these streets. See more in a month here than a lifetime where the rich folks live, all protected from the bad world. I ain't saying it's so great here. Only thing we don't have is the thing we need most of: jobs. Ain't no jobs for us here. Not a one, man, and I know, too, 'cause I been looking for three years, and I ain't all that old.
>
> Country got no use for me, folks around here neither. Ain't nobody care too much what happens to us. Tell us, "Ain't you boys got nothing better to do than stand around all day? What you find to talk about all these hours? And ain't you supposed to be in school? Ain't you supposed to be doing this or doing that?"
>
> If you want to know what the teenagers are doing on this side of town to pass the time of day, now you got it. We got so many folks out of work it's enough to blow your mind. I can hear my brain rotting it's been so long since I done anything. How they let this happen in a country like this, having all these kids walking around the streets, got their hands jammed in their pockets, got their head down? What do folks think these kids gonna do, when they go month after month, year after year without nothing that even smells like a job? (*Psychology Today*, 1979)

Cleveland Wilkes is a high school dropout. Unemployed, he is described by some as one of the forgotten half of America—those who are poor, lack a high school diploma, and do not have a job. Later in the chapter we will focus on high school dropouts and consider ways that our nation can improve their circumstances. We will also study adolescents' values and religion, schools, and career development. But to begin, we will evaluate some of the basic cognitive developmental changes that characterize adolescents.

Cognitive Developmental Changes

Adolescents' developing power of thought opens up new cognitive and social horizons. Their thought becomes more abstract, logical, and idealistic; more capable of examining one's own thoughts, others' thoughts, and what others are thinking about one's self; and more likely to interpret and monitor the social world. First, we evaluate Piaget's ideas about adolescent thought and, second, about social cognition in adolescence.

Formal Operational Thought

Piaget believed that formal operational thought comes into play between the ages of 11 and 15. Formal operational thought is more *abstract* than a child's thinking. The adolescent is no longer limited to actual concrete experience as the anchor of thought. Instead, she may conjure up make-believe situations, hypothetical possibilities, or purely abstract propositions and reason about them. The adolescent increasingly thinks about thought itself. One adolescent pondered, "I began thinking about why I was thinking what I was. Then I began thinking about why I was thinking about why I was thinking about what I was." If this sounds abstract, it is, and it characterizes the adolescent's increased interest on thought itself and the abstractness of thought.

Accompanying the abstract nature of adolescent thought is the quality of idealism. Adolescents begin to think about ideal characteristics for themselves and others and to compare themselves and others to these ideal standards. In contrast, children think more in terms of what is real and what is limited. During adolescence, thoughts often take fantasy flights into the future. It is not unusual for the adolescent to become impatient with these newfound ideal standards and to be perplexed over which of many ideal standards to adopt.

At the same time an adolescent thinks more abstractly and idealistically than a child, she also thinks more logically. The adolescent begins to think like a scientist, in devising plans to solve problems and systematically testing solutions. This kind of problem solving has an imposing name: **hypothetical deductive reasoning.** The adolescent develops hypotheses, or best guesses, about ways to solve a problem, such as an algebraic equation. She then deduces, or concludes, which is the best path to follow in solving the equation. By contrast, a child is more likely to solve the problem in a trial-and-error fashion.

As the adolescent's thought becomes more abstract and logical, the use of language also changes. This development includes changes in the use of satire and metaphor, in writing skills, and in conversational skills.

A junior high school student is sitting in school making up satirical labels for his teachers. One he calls "the walking wilt Wilkie and his wilking waste." Another he describes as "the magnificent Manifred and his manifest morbidity." The use of nicknames increases during early adolescence, as does their abstractness—"stilt," "spaz," "nerd," and "marshmallow mouth," for example. These examples reflect the aspect of language known as **satire,** which refers to irony, wit, or derision used to expose folly or wickedness. Adolescents use and understand satire more than children do (Demorest & others, 1984). The satire of *Mad* magazine, which relies on double meaning, exaggeration, and parody to highlight absurd circumstances and contradictory happenings, finds a more receptive audience among 12- and 13-year-olds than among 7- to 8-year olds (Figure 15.1).

Another aspect of language that comes into use in adolescence is **metaphor.** A metaphor is an implied comparison between two ideas that is conveyed by the abstract meaning contained in the words used. For example, a person's faith and a piece of glass are alike in that both can be shattered. A runner's performance and a politician's speech are alike in that both are predictable. Children have a difficult time understanding metaphorical comparisons; adolescents are better able to understand their meaning.

The increased abstractness and logical reasoning of the adolescent's cognition can be witnessed in improved writing ability (Scardamalia, Bereiter, & Goelman, 1982; Englert, Stewart, & Hiebert, 1988). Organizing ideas is critical to good writing. Logical thinking helps the writer develop a hierarchical structure, which helps the reader understand which ideas are general, which are specific, and which are more important than others. Researchers have discovered that children are poor at organizing their ideas before writing and have difficulty detecting the salient points in prose passages (Brown & Smiley, 1977). While adolescents are not yet Pulitzer Prize–winning novelists, they are better than children at recognizing the need for making both general and specific points in their writing. The sentences adolescents

FIGURE 15.1   I was 12 years old the first time I read *Mad* magazine. It was a time when my best friend and I were already starting to make up crazy nicknames for our teachers and peers. Think back to when you were a young adolescent—were you intrigued by absurdities and contradictory happenings?

string together make more sense than those constructed by children. And adolescents are more likely than children to include an introduction, several paragraphs that represent a body, and concluding remarks when writing an essay (Fischer & Lazerson, 1984).

Most adolescents are also better conversationalists than children are. Adolescents are better at taking turns in conversations, using questions to convey commands ("Why is it so noisy in here?"), using words like *the* and *a* in ways that enhance understanding ("He is *the* living end! He is not just *a* person."), using polite language in appropriate situations (when a guest comes to the house, for example), and telling stories that are interesting, jokes that are funny, and lies that are convincing.

Some of Piaget's ideas on formal operational thought are currently being challenged (Byrnes, 1988; Danner, 1989; Keating, in press; Lapsley, 1989; Small, 1990). There is much more individual variation in formal operational thought than Piaget envisioned. Only about 1 in 3 young adolescents is a formal operational thinker. Many adults never reach formal operational thought. Many young adolescents are at the point of consolidating their concrete operational thought, using it more consistently than in childhood. At the same time, many young adolescents are just beginning to think in formal operational ways. As formal operational thought begins to be used, there is an excess of assimilation (incorporating new information into existing knowledge) as the world is perceived too subjectively and idealistically. Later in adolescence, as intellectual balance is restored, the individual accommodates (adjusts to new information) to the cognitive upheaval that has occurred.

Social Cognition

Impressive changes in social cognition characterize adolescent development. Adolescents develop a special type of egocentrism, begin to think about personality not unlike the way personality theorists do, and monitor their social world in sophisticated ways.

Adolescent thought is egocentric. David Elkind (1976) believes that **adolescent egocentrism** has two parts: an imaginary audience and a personal fable. The **imaginary audience** is the adolescent's belief that others are as preoccupied with her as she herself is. Attention-getting behavior, so common in adolescence, reflects egocentrism and the desire to be on stage, noticed, and visible. Imagine the eighth-grade boy who thinks he is an actor and all others the audience as he stares at the small spot on his trousers. Imagine the seventh-grade girl who thinks that all eyes are riveted on her complexion because of the tiny blemish she has. Current controversy about the nature of egocentrism focuses on whether it emerges because of formal operational thought (Elkind, 1985) or because of perspective taking and interpersonal understanding (Lapsley & Murphy, 1985, 1989, in press).

Jennifer talks with her best friend, Anne, about something she has just heard. "Anne, did you hear about Barbara. You know she fools around a lot. Well, the word is that she is pregnant. Can you believe it? That would never happen to me." Later in the conversation, Anne tells Jennifer, "I really like Bob, but sometimes he is a jerk. He just can't understand me. He has no clue about what my personal feelings are." The **personal fable** refers to the adolescent's sense of personal uniqueness and indestructibility, reflected respectively in Jennifer's and Anne's comments.

The error of youth is to believe that intelligence is a substitute for experience, while the error of age is to believe that experience is a substitute for intelligence.

Slyman Bryson

The junior high school girl shown here has been left out of a game because of an injury. She may develop the imaginary audience sense that all others are as preoccupied with her injury and being left out of the game as she herself is.

THE CULTURAL WORLDS OF CHILDREN

Culture and Formal Operational Thought

The ability to think in scientific ways—to develop hypotheses, systematically evaluate possible solutions, deduce a correct answer to a difficult problem—is an important dimension of formal operational thought. A majority of adolescents in the United States do not think in formal operational ways when presented with scientific reasoning problems, and in developing countries an even smaller percentage of individuals do so (Neimark, 1982). In one cross-cultural investigation including the countries of the United States, Germany, Austria, and Italy, only 7 percent of the eighth-grade students reasoned in formal operational ways (Karplus, 1981). In one Italian group, the adolescents did especially well. Closer observation revealed that these adolescents have been with the same outstanding teacher for three years, indicating the role education may play in improving formal operational thought. According to observers, in many third-world, developing countries formal operational thought in the form of scientific thinking is a rare occurrence. ♦

In their efforts to maintain a sense of uniqueness and indestructibility, adolescents sometimes create a fictitious story, or a fable. Imagine a girl who is having difficulty getting a date. She may develop a fictitious account of a handsome young man living in another part of the country who is madly in love with her. More about the personal fable appears in Children 15.1, where its application to understanding adolescent sexuality is examined.

Adolescents also begin to interpret personality not unlike the way personality theorists do (Barenboim, 1981, 1985). First, when adolescents are given information about another person, they consider previously acquired information and current information and do not rely solely on the concrete information at hand, as children do. Second, adolescents are more likely to detect the contextual or situational variability in the behavior of themselves and others, rather than thinking that they and others always behave consistently. Third, rather than merely accepting surface traits as a valid description of another person or themselves, adolescents begin to look for deeper, more complex—even hidden—causes of personality.

As part of their increased awareness of others—including what others are doing and thinking—adolescents engage in social monitoring. For example, Bob, a 16-year-old, feels he does not know as much as he wants or needs to know about Sally, another 16-year-old. He also wants to know more about Sally's relationship with Brian, a 17-year-old. Bob decides that he wants to know more about the groups Sally belongs to—her student council friends, the clique she is in, and so on. Adolescents use a number of social monitoring methods on a daily basis. For example, an adolescent may check incoming information about an organization (school, club, or group of friends) to determine if it is consistent with the adolescent's impression of the group. Still another adolescent may question someone or paraphrase what that person has just said about her feelings to ensure that he has understood them correctly. Yet another adolescent may meet someone new and quickly think, "It's going to be hard to really get to know him" (Flavell, 1979).

Values, Religion, and Cults

What are adolescents' values like today? What is their spiritual orientation, and what is the church's influence? Why do some adolescents run away to join cults? We will consider each of these questions in turn.

Values

Adolescents carry with them a set of values that influence their thoughts, feelings, and actions. What were your values like when you were an adolescent? Are the values of today's adolescents changing?

Over the last two decades, although the shift has sometimes been exaggerated, adolescents show an increased concern for personal well-being and a decreased concern for the welfare of others, especially the disadvantaged (Astin, Green, & Korn, 1987; Conger, 1981, 1988). As shown in Figure 15.2, today's college freshmen are much more strongly motivated to be very well off financially and much less motivated to develop a meaningful philosophy of life than their counterparts from 20 or even 10 years ago. Increasing numbers of high school seniors are motivated by the chance to earn a considerable amount of money (Johnston, Bachman, & O'Malley,

Personal Fables and Pregnancies

With their developing idealism and ability to think in more abstract and hypothetical ways, young adolescents often get caught up in a mental world far removed from reality, one that may involve a belief that things can't or won't happen to them and that they are omnipotent and indestructible. These cognitive changes, as well as others, have intriguing implications for the sex education of adolescents. Joan Lipsitz (1980) points out that having information about contraceptives is not enough. What seems to predict whether adolescents will use contraceptives or not depends on their acceptance of themselves and their sexuality. Such acceptance probably requires not only emotional maturity, but cognitive maturity as well.

Most discussions of adolescent pregnancy and its prevention assume that adolescents have the ability to anticipate consequences, to weigh the probable outcome of behavior, and to project into the future what will happen if they engage in certain acts, such as sexual intercourse. That is, prevention is based on the belief that adolescents have the cognitive ability to approach problem solving in a planned, organized, and analytical manner. However, many adolescents are just beginning to develop such capacities, and others have not developed them at all.

Lipsitz, in addressing the American Association of Sex Educators, Counselors, and Therapists, described the personal fable and how it may be associated with adolescent pregnancy. The young adolescent may say, "Hey, it won't happen to me." If the adolescent is locked into this personal fable, she may not respond well to a course on sex education that preaches prevention. Lipsitz points out that the best of what we know about prevention is not appropriate for young adolescents. A developmental perspective on cognition may provide some insight into what can be taught in sex education courses for early adolescents.

Late adolescents (those 18 to 19 years of age) are, at least to some degree, realistic and future-oriented about sexual experiences, just as they are about careers and marriage. Middle adolescents (those 15 to 17 years of age) often romanticize sexuality. However, young adolescents (those 10 to 15 years of age) appear to experience sex in a depersonalized way that is filled with anxiety and denial. This depersonalized orientation to sex is not likely to lead to preventive behavior.

Consider the outcome if the following are combined: the nature of early adolescent cognition, the personal fable, anxiety about sex, gender-role definitions about what is masculine and what is feminine, the sexual themes of music in the adolescent culture, the sexual overtones that are rampant in magazines and on television, and a societal standard that says sex is appropriate for adults but promiscuous for adolescents. That is, our society tells adolescents: Sex is fun, harmless, adult, and forbidden. Add to this the growing need for adolescents to develop a commitment, especially in a career. Yet youth face a huge unemployment rate, which can turn them away from the future and intensively toward the present. Piece together early adolescent development, America's sexual ambivalence, and adolescents' vulnerability to economic forces, and the result is social dynamite. ♦

Our society has not handled adolescent sex very effectively. We tell adolescents that sex is fun, harmless, adult, and forbidden. Adolescents 13 years old going on 21 want to try out new things and take risks. They see themselves as unique and indestructible—pregnancy couldn't happen to them, they think. Add to this the adolescent's increasing need for love and commitment, and the result all too often is social dynamite.

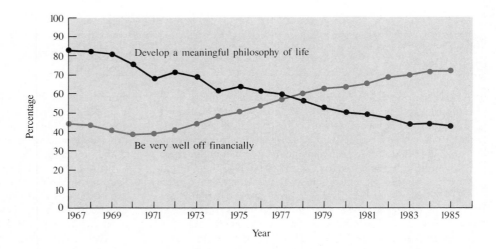

As reflected by their participation in exercise classes and other self-improvement activities, today's adolescents show an increased concern for their physical health and well-being.

FIGURE 15.2   Changing freshman life goals, 1967 to 1985.

1986). College and high school students show less interest in the nation's social problems and how they might be resolved than did their peers of a decade earlier (Bachman & others, 1987; Astin & others, 1987).

Two aspects of the new values that increased during the 1960s, however, continue to characterize today's youth: self-fulfillment and the opportunity for self-expression (Conger, 1981, 1988). As part of this interest in self, many youth show an increased interest in their physical health and well-being. Greater self-fulfillment and self-expression can be laudable goals for youth, but if they become the only goals, self-destruction, loneliness, or alienation may result. Youth also need to have a corresponding sense of commitment to others' welfare. Encouraging adolescents to develop a stronger commitment to others, in concert with an interest in self-fulfillment, is a major task for our nation as we draw near the end of the twentieth century.

Religious Beliefs and the Church

Adolescents are more interested in religion and spiritual beliefs than are children. Their increasing abstract and idealistic thoughts, as well as their increasing interest in identity, make religion and spiritual matters attractive concerns.

The Development of Religious Concepts

In a series of studies, David Elkind (1978) tested several hundred Jewish, Catholic, and Protestant boys and girls from 5 to 14 years of age. He asked questions such as "Are you a Catholic?" "Is your family Jewish?" "Are all boys and girls in the world Christians?" He also asked questions like "What is a Jew?" "How do you become a Catholic?" and "Can you be an American and a Protestant (or Jew, or Catholic) at the same time?" The formal-operational thinkers—those who were in early adolescence—had a different way of thinking about religious concepts than did the concrete-operational thinkers—those in childhood. The formal-operational thinkers were more reflective than their younger counterparts. They no longer looked for manifestations of religious identity in an individual's outward behavior, but instead sought it in the evidence of inner beliefs and convictions. For example, one concrete-operational thinker said that the way you can tell an individual is a Catholic is by whether the person goes to church or not. By contrast, one formal operational thinker said that you can tell if a person is a Protestant because the person is free to repent and pray to God.

Another perspective on the development of religious concepts was proposed by James Fowler (1976). He believes that late adolescence is especially important in developing a religious identity. Beginning at about age 18, says Fowler, individuals enter a stage called **individuating-reflective faith.** For the first time in their lives, individuals take full responsibility for their religious beliefs. Earlier they relied heavily on their parents' beliefs. During late adolescence, individuals come face to face with personal decisions, evaluating such questions as "Should I consider myself first, or should I consider the welfare of others first?" "Are the doctrines that have been taught to me absolute or are they more relative than I have been led to believe?"

Fowler believes there is a close relationship between the adolescent's development of moral values and religious values. He also acknowledges that this stage of individuating-reflective faith is closely aligned with Kohlberg's level of postconventional morality. In both instances, the individual makes the transition from conventional to more individualized reflective thinking about religious values.

Spiritual Interest and Church Influences

The sociocultural conditions in which adolescents grow up combine with their developing cognitive capacities to influence their religious identities. The formal operational characteristics of abstract thought and idealism contribute to the adolescent's interest in spiritual matters. And adolescents do show a strong interest in spiritual matters. For example, in one national survey, almost 9 of 10 adolescents

Shown here are adolescents at San Fernando parish in San Antonio, Texas. Adolescents show a strong interest in spiritual matters. In one national survey, almost nine of ten adolescents said they pray, for example.

THE CULTURAL WORLDS OF CHILDREN

Religious Influences on Chicano Adolescents

The lives of Chicano adolescents can become complicated. Chicano adolescents believe in the New Testament promise that for the poor there will be another chance—after death. And death is no stranger to them. They often see people get sick and die. They often are born at home and die at home themselves. They may never see a doctor in their lives. The sight of a priest praying near a sick person, or near a mother giving birth to a child, or near an infant who has never really lived, impresses upon adolescents a grave and guarded view of life and its possibilities. The adolescents have double the reason to be philosophical: because they are taught in church to think about God's abstract presence, and because in their daily lives they live so close to tragedy, including extreme poverty, serious illness, and unpredictable death (Coles, 1977). ♦

said they pray, an even higher percentage said they believe in God or a universal spirit, and only 1 in 100 says that she does not have some type of religious preference or affiliation (Gallup & Poling, 1980). But at the same time, many adolescents say that organized religion has little meaning for them and that the church's doctrines are outmoded. Only 25 percent say that they have a high degree of confidence in organized religion. About 40 percent say that honesty and the personal ethics of the clergy are average to very low. As we will see next, the ethical standards of many cult leaders also is seriously questioned.

The Hare Krishna, shown here, are one of specific religious cults that have attracted the attention of youth.

Cults

Barb is 17 years old. She grew up in an affluent family and was given all the material things she wanted. When she was 15, her parents paid her way to Europe and for the last three years she had been attending a private boarding school. Her parents attended a Protestant church on a regular basis, and when Barb was home they took her with them. Six months ago, Barb shocked her parents by joining the "Moonies."

There are six unorthodox religious movements that have attracted attention from America's youth: Transcendental Meditation (TM), yoga, the charismatic movement, mysticism, faith healing, and various Eastern religions (Gallup & Poling, 1980). More than 27 million Americans have been touched by these religions, either superficially or deeply. In all, there are more than 2,500 cults in the United States. Two to three million youth and young adults are cult members (Levine, 1984; Swope, 1950). Among the more specific religious cults that have attracted the attention of youth are the Unification Church of Sun Myung Moon (the Moonies), the Divine Light Mission of Maharaj Ji, the Institute of Krishna Consciousness, the Children of God, and the Church of Scientology.

The most recent concerns about cults focus on satanism, or devil worship. The nightmarish tale of human sacrifice that unfolded in the spring of 1989 in Matamoros, Mexico, brought national attention to the increasing prevalence of devil worship. Some of the bodies in the mass grave had been decapitated. Investigation of the Satanic cult revealed its ties to drugs. The cult's ringleader, Adolpho de Jesus Constanzo, controlled members' lives, getting them to believe that the devil has supernatural powers.

Critics of the cults argue that the cult leaders are hypocritical, exploit members to gain wealth, brainwash youth, and cast a hypnotic spell over their lives. In some cases, cults have been accused of kidnapping youth and placing them in deprived circumstances to gain control over their minds. Most cults have elaborate training programs in which the cult's teachings are memorized. Cult members are usually required to turn over their wealth to the cult leaders. And cult members are often told that they can associate with or marry only other members of the cult (Galanter, 1989).

Cognitive Developmental Changes and Values, Religion, and Cults

Concept	Processes and Related Ideas	Characteristics and Description
Cognitive Developmental Changes	Formal operational thought	Piaget believed that formal operational thought comes into play between 11 and 15 years of age. Formal operational thought is more abstract, idealistic, and logical than concrete operational thought. Piaget believed that adolescents become capable of using hypothetical deductive reasoning. Language changes that accompany formal operational thought involve an increased understanding of satire and metaphor, improved writing ability, and superior conversational skills. Some of Piaget's ideas on formal operational thought are being challenged.
	Social cognition	Impressive changes in social cognition characterize adolescent development. Adolescents develop a special type of egocentrism that involves an imaginary audience and a personal fable about being unique and indestructible. They begin to think about personality not unlike the way personality theorists do, and they monitor their social world in more sophisticated ways.
Values, Religion, and Cults	Values	Over the last two decades adolescents have shown an increased concern for personal well-being and a decreased concern for the welfare of others.
	Religious beliefs and the church	Both Elkind's and Fowler's views illustrate the increased abstractness in adolescent's thinking that provides them with improved understanding of the nature of religion. Adolescents show a strong interest in spiritual matters, but they believe organized religion has not provided them with the spiritual understanding they seek.
	Cults	Cult membership in the United States is extensive among youth. Cults may appeal to adolescents because of weaknesses in organized religion and families.

Why do some adolescents leave home and become members of a cult? Some experts believe that the failure of organized religion and the church, as well as a weakening of family life, may be the culprits (Gallup & Poling, 1980; Levine, 1984).

Thus far, we have discussed a number of ideas about cognitive developmental changes and values, religion, and cults. These ideas are summarized in Concept Table 15.1. Next, we will turn our attention to the nature of adolescents' schooling.

Schools

The impressive changes in adolescents' cognition lead us to examine the nature of schools for adolescents. In Chapter 13, we discussed different ideas about the effects of schools on children's development. Here we will focus more exclusively on the nature of secondary schools. Among the questions we try to answer are the following: What should be the function of secondary schools? What is the nature of the transition from elementary to middle or junior high school? What is the nature of high school dropouts, and how can we reduce the number of dropouts?

The Controversy Surrounding Secondary Schools

During the twentieth century, schools have assumed a more prominent role in the lives of adolescents. From 1890 to 1920, virtually every state developed laws that excluded youth from work and required them to attend school. In this time frame, the number of high school graduates increased 600 percent (Tyack, 1976). By making secondary education compulsory, the adult power structure placed adolescents in a submissive position and made their move into the adult world of work more manageable. In the nineteenth century, high schools were mainly for the elite, with the main educational emphasis on classical liberal arts courses. By the 1920s, educators perceived that the secondary school curriculum needed to be changed. Schools for the masses, it was thought, should not just involve intellectual training, but should also involve training for work and citizenship (Murphy, 1987). The curriculum of secondary schools became more comprehensive and grew to include general education, college preparatory, and vocational education courses. As the twentieth century unfolded, secondary schools continued to expand their orientation, adding courses in music, art, health, physical education, and other topics. By the middle of the twentieth century, schools had moved further toward preparing students for comprehensive roles in life (Conant, 1959). Today, secondary schools have retained their comprehensive orientation, designed to train adolescents intellectually; but they now also train students in many other ways as well, such as vocationally and socially.

While there has been a consistent trend of increased school attendance for more than 150 years, the distress over alienated and rebellious youth led some social scientists to question whether secondary schools actually benefit adolescents. During the early 1970s, three independent panels agreed that high schools contribute to adolescent alienation and actually restrict the transition to adulthood (Brown, 1973; Coleman & others, 1974; Martin, 1976). These prestigious panels argued that adolescents should be given educational alternatives to the comprehensive high school, such as on-the-job community work, to increase their exposure to adult roles and to decrease their sense of isolation from adults. To some degree in response to these reports, a number of states lowered the age at which adolescents could leave school from 16 to 14.

As we enter the last decade of the twentieth century, the back-to-basics movement has gained momentum, with proponents arguing that the main function of schools should be rigorous training of intellectual skills through subjects like English, math, and science (Kearns, 1988). Advocates of the back-to-basics movement point to the excessive fluff in secondary school curricula, with students being allowed to select from many alternatives that will not give them a basic education in intellectual subjects. Some critics also point to the extensive time students spend in extracurricular activities. They argue that schools should be in the business of imparting knowledge to adolescents and not be so concerned about their social and emotional lives. Related to the proverbial dilemma of schools' functions is whether schools should include a vocational curriculum in addition to training in basic subjects such as English, math, and science. Some critics of the fluff in secondary schools argue that the school day should be longer and that the school year should be extended into the summer months. Such arguments are made by critics who believe that the main function of schools should be the training of intellectual skills. Little concern for adolescents' social and emotional development appear in these arguments.

Should the main—and perhaps only—major goal of schooling for adolescents be the development of an intellectually mature individual? Or should schools also focus on the adolescent's maturity in social and emotional development? Should

In youth we learn, in age we understand.

Marie Ebner von Eschenbach,
Aphorism, 1904

A drill team shown performing at the Winchester, Virginia, Apple Blossom festival parade. Some critics believe students spend too much time in activities such as drill team, football, and clubs. They argue that school should be in the business of imparting knowledge and not be so concerned about student's social and emotional lives. Where do you stand on this controversy?

schools be comprehensive, providing a multifaceted curriculum that includes many electives and alternative subjects to basic core courses? These are provocative questions, and they continue to be heatedly debated in educational and community circles (Bloome, 1989; Goodlad, 1983; Sizer, 1984; Tharp & Gallimore, 1989).

Tension may always characterize debate about the function of schools. Should intellectual development be emphasized more than it is even today? Or, should intellectual development be only one of school's functions? Should preparation of the individual for work, a thirst for lifelong learning in many areas of life, and social and emotional development also be part of the schooling equation? Patricia Cross (1984) argues that tension produces shifts of emphases much like a swinging pendulum, moving toward basic skills at one point in time, and toward options, frills, or comprehensive training for life at another, and so on back and forth. What we should strive for is not a swinging pendulum, but rather something like a spiral staircase. That is, we might continually be developing more sophisticated ways of fulfilling the varied and changing functions of schools (Figure 15.3).

Transition to Middle or Junior High School

The emergence of junior high schools in the 1920s and 1930s was justified on the basis of physical, cognitive, and social changes that characterize early adolescence, as well as the need for more schools for the growing student population. Old high

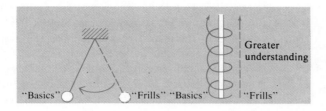

FIGURE 15.3 There may always be tension between two functions of schooling—cognitive development versus the more social enterprises such as athletics, band, and drivers' education. Undoubtedly this tension will produce shifts of emphasis, as with a swinging pendulum. But if we are successful in developing an instructional psychology, we might achieve something similar to a spiral staircase, as opposed to a pendulum that just swings back and forth. That is, we might continually develop more sophisticated ways of fulfilling the varied and changing functions of schooling.

The transition from elementary to middle or junior high school occurs at the same time a number of other changes are taking place in development. Biological, cognitive, and social changes converge with this schooling transition to make it a time of considerable adaptation.

schools became junior high schools and new, regional high schools were built. In most systems, the ninth grade remained a part of the high school in content, although physically separated from it in a 6-3-3 system. Gradually, the ninth grade has been restored to the high school as many school systems have developed middle schools that include the seventh and eighth grades, or sixth, seventh, and eighth grades. The creation of middle schools has been influenced by the earlier onset of puberty in recent decades.

One worry of educators and psychologists is that junior high and middle schools have simply become watered-down versions of high schools, mimicking their curricular and extracurricular schedules (Hill, 1980). The critics argue that unique curricular and extracurricular activities reflecting a wide range of individual differences in biological and psychological development in early adolescence should be incorporated into our junior high and middle schools. The critics also stress that many high schools foster passivity rather than autonomy, and that schools should create a variety of pathways for students to achieve an identity.

As shown in this situation of an eighth-grade boy teasing a seventh-grade boy, the transition from elementary to middle school can be difficult. Elementary schoolchildren move from being the "top dog" to being the "underdog."

The transition to middle school or junior high school from elementary school interests developmentalists because, even though it is a normative experience for almost all children, the transition can be stressful. The transition takes place at a time when simultaneous changes are occurring, including changes in the individual, the family, and the school (Eccles & others, 1989; Hawkins & Berndt, 1985; Hirsch, 1989; Simmons & others, 1987). These changes include puberty and related concerns about body image, the emergence of at least some aspects of formal operational thought, and increased responsibility and independence in association with decreased dependency on parents. The changes also include movement from a small, contained classroom structure to a larger, more impersonal school structure, from one teacher to many teachers and from a small, homogeneous set of peers to a larger, more heterogeneous set of peers. Increased focus on achievement and its assessment also occurs. This list includes a number of negative, stressful features, but the transition can also have positive aspects. Students are more likely to feel grown up, have more subjects from which to select, have more opportunities to spend time with peers and more opportunities to locate compatible friends, enjoy increased independence from direct parental monitoring, and be more challenged intellectually by academic work (Hawkins & Berndt, 1985).

When students make the transition from elementary school to middle school or junior high school, they experience the **top-dog phenomenon.** Moving from the top position (in elementary school, as the oldest, biggest, and most powerful students in the school) to the bottom or lowest position (in middle or junior high school, the youngest, smallest, and least powerful students in the school) may create a number of difficulties for the student.

Researchers who have charted the transition from elementary to middle or junior high school find that the first year of middle school or junior high school can be difficult for many students (Hawkins & Berndt, 1985; Hirsch & Rapkin, 1987; Simmons & Blyth, 1987). For example, in one investigation of the transition from sixth grade in an elementary school to the seventh grade in a junior high school, adolescents' perceptions of the quality of school life plunged in the seventh grade (Hirsch & Rapkin, 1987). In the seventh grade, students were less satisfied with school, were less commited to school, and liked their teachers less. This drop in school satisfaction occurred regardless of how academically competent the students were.

What kind of experiences might ease the transition from elementary school to middle or junior high school? Schools that provide more support, less anonymity, more stability, and less complexity improve student adjustment during the transition from elementary school to middle or junior high school. For example, in one investigation, 101 students were studied at three points in time: spring of the sixth grade (pretransition), fall of the seventh grade (early transition), and spring of the seventh grade (late transition). Two different schools were sampled—one a traditional junior high school, the other a junior high in which the students were grouped into small teams (100 students, four teachers). The students' adjustment was assessed through self-reports, peer ratings, and teacher ratings. Adjustment dropped during the post-transition. For example, the self-esteem of students was lower in the seventh grade than in the sixth grade. More teacher support was reported by students in the team-oriented junior high school, and the nature of friendship also was related to the students' adjustment. Students with greater friendship contact and higher quality of friendship had a more positive perception of themselves and of their junior high school. These data indicate that a supportive, more intimate school environment and friendship can ease the students' stressful school transitions.

What makes a successful middle school? Joan Lipsitz (1984) and her colleagues searched the nation for the best middle schools. Extensive contacts and observations were made. Based on the recommendations of education experts and observations in schools in different parts of the United States, four middle schools were chosen for their outstanding ability to educate young adolescents. What were these middle schools like? The most striking feature was their willingness and ability to adapt all school practices to the individual differences in physical, cognitive, and social development of their students. The schools took seriously the knowledge we have developed about young adolescents. This seriousness was reflected in decisions about different aspects of school life. For example, one middle school fought to keep its schedule of minicourses on Friday so that every student could be with friends and pursue personal interests. Two other middle schools expended considerable energy on a complex school organization so that small groups of students worked with small groups of teachers who could vary the tone and pace of the school day, depending on students' needs. Another middle school developed an advisory scheme so that each student had daily contact with an adult who was willing to listen, explain, comfort, and prod the adolescent. Such school policies reflect thoughtfulness and personal concern about individuals who have compelling developmental needs.

Another aspect of the effective middle schools was that, early in their existence—the first year in three of the schools and the second year in the fourth school—they emphasized the importance of creating an environment that was positive for the adolescent's social and emotional development. This goal was established not only because such environments contribute to academic excellence, but also because social and emotional development are intrinsically valued as important in themselves in adolescents' schooling. More information about effective and ineffective middle schools appears in Children 15.2.

Thinking Critically
Analyze your own middle school or junior high school. How did it measure up to Lipsitz's criteria for effective schools for young adolescents?

Recognizing that the vast majority of middle schools do not approach the excellent schools described by Joan Lipsitz (1984), in 1989 the Carnegie Corporation issued an extremely negative evaluation of our nation's middle schools. In the report, "Turning Points: Preparing American Youth for the 21st Century," the conclusion was reached that most young adolescents attend massive, impersonal schools, learn from seemingly irrelevant curricula, trust few adults in school, and lack access to health care and counseling. The Carnegie report recommends the following:

—Divide large schools into units of 200 to 500 students so adolescents can get to know each other and their teachers better.
—Give teachers and administrators more creative power and hire teachers who specialize in working with young adolescents.
—Involve parents and community leaders in middle schools.
—Teach a core academic program aimed at producing students who are literate, understand the sciences, and have a sense of health, ethics, and citizenship.
—Boost students' health and fitness with more in-school programs and help students who need public health care to get it.

In sum, middle schools need a major overhaul if they are to be effective in educating young adolescents for becoming competent adults in the twenty-first century.

Beyond the Zoo

When teachers complain about young adolescents, animal imagery is pervasive: "This school is a zoo," "Those students are like animals," "It is a jungle in the classroom." In schools that seem like "zoos," students usually do not learn effectively and often are not very happy. Consider these vignettes about four ineffective middle schools:

> A teacher sits in the back of the room, her legs up on her desk, asking students questions from the textbook. The students, bored and listless, sit in straight rows facing no one in the front of the room, answering laconically to a blank blackboard. When the principal enters the room, the teacher lowers her legs to the floor. Nothing else changes.
>
> A teacher drills students for a seemingly endless amount of time on prime numbers. After the lesson, not one of them can say why it is important to learn prime numbers.
>
> A visitor asks a teacher if hers is an eighth-grade class. "It's called eighth grade," she answers archly, "but we know it's really kindergarten—right, class?"
>
> In a predominantly Hispanic school, only the one adult hired as a bilingual teacher speaks Spanish.
>
> In a biracial school, the principal and the guidance counselor cite test scores with pride. They are asked if the difference between the test scores of black and white students is narrowing. "Oh, that's an interesting question!" the guidance counselor says in surprise. The principal agrees. It has never been asked by or of them before.
>
> A teacher in a social studies class squelches several imaginative questions, exclaiming, "You're always asking 'what if' questions. Stop asking 'what if'!" When a visitor asks who will become president if the president-elect dies before the electoral college meets, the teacher explodes: "You're as bad as they are! That's another 'what if' question!" (Lipsitz, 1984, pp. 169–170)

By contrast, consider the following circumstances in effective middle schools:

> Everything is peaceful. There are open cubbies instead of locked lockers. There is no theft. Students walk quietly in the corridor. "Why?" they are asked. "So as not to disturb the media center," they answer, which is self-evident to them but not the visitor who is left wondering. . . . When asked,

"Do you like this school?" (They) answer: "No, we don't like it. We love it!" (Lipsitz, 1984, p. 27)

> When asked how the school feels, one student answered, "It feels smart. We're smart. Look at our test scores." Comments from one of the parents of a student at the school are revealing: "My child would have been a dropout. In elementary school, his teacher said to me: 'That child isn't going to give you anything but heartaches.' He had perfect attendance here. He didn't want to miss a day. Summer vacation was too long and boring. Now he's majoring in communications at the University of Texas. He got here and all of a sudden someone cared for him. I had been getting notes about Roger every other day, with threats about expulsion. Here, the first note said: 'It's just a joy to have him in the classroom.' " (Lipsitz, 1984, p. 84)

> The humane environment that encourages teachers' growth . . . is translated by the teachers . . . into a humane environment that encourages students' growth. The school feels cold when one first enters. It has the institutional feeling of any large school building with metal lockers and impersonal halls. Then one opens the door to a team area, and it is filled with energy, movement, productivity, doing. There is a lot of informal relating among students and between students and teachers. Visible from one vantage point are students working on written projects, putting the last touches on posters, watching a film, and working independently from reading kits. . . . Most know what they are doing, can say why it is important, and go back to work immediately after being interrupted. (Lipsitz, 1984, p. 109)

> Authors' Week is yet another special activity built into the school's curriculum that entices students to consider themselves in relation to the rich variety of making and doing in people's lives. Based on student interest, availability, and diversity, authors are invited . . . to discuss their craft. Students sign up to meet with individual authors. They must have read one individual book by the author. . . . Students prepare questions for their sessions with the authors. . . . Sometimes, an author stays several days to work with a group of students on his or her manuscript. (Lipsitz, 1984, p. 141)

These excerpts about a variety of schools in different areas of the United States reveal the great diversity among schools for adolescents. They also tell us that, despite the ineffectiveness of many schools for adolescents, others are very effective. Secondary schools can be breeding grounds for competent academic *and* social development. ◆

Excerpted by permission of Transaction Publishers, from Successful Schools for Young Adolescents, *by Joan Lipsitz. Copyright © 1983 by Transaction Publishers.*

High School Dropouts and Non-College-Bound Youth

For many decades, dropping out of high school has been viewed as a serious educational and societal problem. By leaving high school before graduating, many dropouts take with them educational deficiencies that severely curtail their economic and social well-being throughout their adult lives (Rumberger, 1987). We will study the scope of the problem, the causes of dropping out, and ways to reduce dropout rates.

High School Dropout Rates

While dropping out of high school often has negative consequences for youth, the picture is not entirely bleak (William T. Grant Foundation Commission on Work, Family, and Citizenship, 1988). Over the last 40 years, the proportion of adolescents who have not finished high school has decreased considerably. In 1940, more than 60 percent of all individuals 25 to 29 years of age had not completed high school. By 1986, this proportion had dropped to less than 14 percent. From 1973 to 1983, the annual dropout rate nationwide fell by almost 20 percent, from 6.3 to 5.2 percent.

Despite the decline in overall high school dropout rates, a major concern remains the higher dropout rate of minority group and low-income students, especially in large cities. While the dropout rates of most minority-group students have also been declining, they remain substantially above those of white students. Note in Table 15.1 that Hispanic dropout rates are the highest and have declined little, if at all. Note also that the dropout rate for black students has improved considerably, although, overall, it still is above that of white students. Dropout rates also are high for Native Americans (American Indians) (fewer than 10 percent graduate from high school) and certain Hispanic subgroups, especially Cubans and Mexican Americans (LaFromboise & Rudes, 1983). The dropout problem is acute for low-income, minority-group students in large cities, such as Newark, Atlanta, and San Antonio, where minority-group students make up more than 90 percent of the student population. In Chicago, the dropout rate recently was computed to be 50.7 percent (Hahn, 1987).

Other concerns about problems for high school dropouts focus on increased academic demands by schools and increased educational requirements for jobs. Many states have recently passed legislation to raise academic standards in schools, which can benefit some students, but for those whose commitment to school is weak, the more rigorous requirements could push the dropout rate higher. Also the increase of new technologies and structural changes in jobs mean that more educational skills will be needed to get these jobs (Levin & Rumberger, in press).

The Causes of Dropping Out

Students drop out of school for many different reasons. In one investigation, almost 50 percent of the dropouts cited school-related reasons for leaving school, such as not liking school or being expelled or suspended (Rumberger, 1983). Twenty percent of the dropouts (but 40 percent of the Hispanic students) cited economic reasons for leaving school. One-third of female students dropped out for personal reasons, such as pregnancy or marriage. What are some other factors associated with dropping out of school? They include the demographic factors cited earlier, family-related,

TABLE 15.1	Dropout Rates by Age, Sex, Race, and Ethnicity, 1968–1984 (percentages)				
Group	**1968**	**1978**	**1980**	**1982**	**1984**
33-to-34-year-olds	18.3	12.9	12.7	12.7	12.6
White males	17.1	12.2	12.2	12.4	12.5
White females	17.3	12.4	11.9	11.9	11.7
Black males	25.8	17.2	16.5	16.7	15.7
Black females	25.6	16.2	16.2	14.9	15.0
Hispanic males	—	28.1	28.3	26.9	27.0
Hispanic females	—	29.0	27.3	27.3	26.7
18-to-19-year-olds	15.7	16.7	15.7	16.7	15.2
White males	14.3	16.3	16.1	16.6	15.8
White females	14.6	15.0	13.8	14.9	14.0
Black males	23.8	25.8	22.7	26.4	19.7
Black females	24.7	22.8	19.8	18.1	14.5
Hispanic males	—	36.6	43.1	34.9	26.2
Hispanic females	—	39.6	34.6	31.1	26.0
16-to-17-year-olds	7.8	8.8	8.8	7.3	6.8
White males	6.9	9.6	9.3	7.3	7.3
White females	7.6	8.7	9.2	8.0	6.9
Black males	10.1	5.2	7.2	6.4	5.5
Black females	14.2	9.4	6.6	5.5	4.9
Hispanic males	—	15.6	18.1	12.2	13.6
Hispanic females	—	12.2	15.0	15.9	12.7

Source: U.S. Department of the Census, *School Enrollment, Current Population Reports, Series P-20,* various issues (Washington, D.C.: U.S. Government Printing Office, various years).

Note: Dropout rates represent the percent of each group who are dropouts. Dropouts are defined as persons of a given group who are not enrolled in school in October of the year in question and have not received a high school diploma or an equivalent high school certificate.

Among the reasons students drop out of school are school-related matters, such as not liking school or being expelled, economic problems, and personal circumstances, as when adolescent females become pregnant. Males are more likely to drop out than females.

peer-related, school-related, economic, and individual factors. Ethnic and minority-group students are more likely to drop out of school than are white students. Males also are more likely to drop out than are females. The factor in family background that is related most strongly to dropping out of school is socioeconomic status; students from low-income families are much more likely to drop out than are those from more socioeconomically advantaged families. Peers have not been given much attention in dropout rates, but many dropouts have friends who also are dropouts. School-related factors, such as poor grades, inferior test scores, and grade retention, are associated with dropping out, as are behavior problems such as truancy and discipline difficulties (Wehlage & Rutter, 1986). Economic factors also influence a student's decision to quit school. In the investigation by Russell Rumberger (1983), about 20 percent left school because they wanted to or felt they had to work to support their families.

There are many individual reasons for dropping out of school. Dropouts have lower self-esteem and a lesser sense of control over their lives than do nondropouts. They have poor attitudes toward school and low educational and occupational aspirations. A number of dropouts also leave school to marry or because they are pregnant. A comprehensive model of dropouts needs to address the different types of dropouts who leave school for different reasons.

Adolescence

Literacy and Secondary School Attendance around the World

The rate of literacy (the ability to read and write) in developing countries more than doubled from 1950 to 1985, increasing from 26 to 62 percent. However, compared to the 98 percent literacy rate of industrialized nations, these figures show that developing countries face a major task in improving the literacy of their inhabitants. Not only are literacy rates low in developing countries, so is secondary school attendance. Only 36 percent of adolescents attend secondary schools in developing countries, while 87 percent of adolescents attend secondary schools in industrialized countries. The improvements that have taken place in literacy and schooling have been uneven in developing countries. Illiteracy rates are much higher in rural areas than in urban areas, and are much higher among females than among males. More than two-thirds of the world's illiterate people are female. Consider the situation in India: Less than half of the population can read and write. In some of India's states, the female literacy rate is as low as 11 percent (MacPherson, 1987; UNICEF, 1986). ◆

Reducing the Dropout Rate and Improving the Lives of Non-College-Bound Youth

In a recent report, "The Forgotten Half: Non-College Youth in America," the William T. Grant Foundation Commission on Work, Family, and Citizenship (1988) recommended that reducing the dropout rate and improving the lives of non-college youth could be accomplished by strengthening schools and bridging the gap between school and work.

Part of the solution lies within schools. Students may work hard through 12 grades of school, attain adequate records, learn basic academic skills, graduate in good standing, and still experience problems in getting started in a productive career. Others may drop out of school because they see little benefit from the type of education they are getting. Although not a complete cure-all, strengthening schools is an important dimension of reducing dropout rates. While the education reform movements of the 1980s have encouraged schools to set higher standards for students and teachers, most of the focus has been on college-bound students. But students who will not go to college should not be penalized. One way non-college-bound youth are being helped is through Chapter 1 of the Education Consolidation and Improvement Act, which provides extra services for low-achieving students. States and communities need to establish clear goals for school completion, youth employment, parental involvement, and youth community service. For example, the goal of every state should be to reduce the dropout rate to 10 percent or less by the year 2000.

Among the experiences required to help adolescents stay on the education ladder until they reach the career level they desire is career counseling like that involved here in an advisory period at an alternative school.

Community institutions, especially schools, need to break down the barriers between work and school. Many youth step off the education ladder long before reaching the level of a professional career, often with nowhere to step next, left to their own devices to search for work. These youth need more assistance than they are now receiving. Among the approaches worth considering are:

—monitored work experiences, such as through cooperative education, apprenticeships, internships, preemployment training, and youth-operated enterprises.
—community and neighborhood services, including voluntary service and youth-guided services.
—redirected vocational education, the principal thrust of which should not be preparation for specific jobs but acquisition of basic skills needed for a wide range of jobs.

Sandy Bonds

Sandy Bonds was 14 when she first left her mother's home in Maryland. She hitched a ride to Phoenix, where she planned to live with her father and finish high school. When things did not work out there, she moved on to Albuquerque. By the time she decided to settle down in Oregon, Sandy had lived in five different states in four years. She was 18 when she came to a city-operated youth center in Portland looking for help to find a job. Sandy had been out of school for more than two years, but she did not know much about the world of work:

> I've traveled around, but I haven't worked much, you know? 'Cause most of the time, I was livin' with a foster parent or with friends, and they were always tryin' to get me back in school. The only job I can really say I ever had was bein' like a housekeeper for five months for this one family I lived with in Washington. And I worked at Burgerville once for about two days. I always had it in my mind to work, but I didn't have any skills, didn't know what I wanted to work at, you know? I learned how to get by out on the street. But working—I just plain don't know much about it. I don't know what I could do with myself once I had the skills. (Snedeker, 1982). ◆

—guarantees of continuing education, employment, or training, especially in conjunction with mentor programs.
—career information and counseling to expose youth to job opportunities and career options as well as to successful role models.
—school volunteer programs, not only for tutoring but to provide access to adult friends and mentors.

For more information about improving our nation's education of minority-group adolescents, turn to Children 15.3, where you will find a discussion of ways to help Hispanic youth stay in school and go to college.

Careers and Work

What are the future occupations of today's adolescents? What roles do exploration, planning, and decision making play in career development? What changes have taken place in the career development of females? What is the nature of work in adolescence? We will consider each of these questions in turn.

Helping Hispanic Youth Stay in School and Go to College

The Hispanic population in the United States is increasing more rapidly than any other ethnic minority. Educators are increasingly interested in helping Hispanic adolescents stay in school and succeed in the courses needed for educational and occupational success. As colleges compete to recruit seniors from the small pool of college-eligible and college-ready Hispanics, it is apparent that the pool itself needs to be greatly expanded. Gloria De Necochea (1988) recently described seven strategies to help keep Hispanic adolescents in school and get them ready to go to college:

1. Identify students early for a college preparatory curriculum. As early as the sixth grade, both students and parents need to know about the college preparatory curriculum and the long-term consequences of choices.
2. Give more attention to math and science. Mathematics and science are critical for both college admissions and a range of career options, but these subjects pose big barriers for Hispanic students. Success can be increased by teaching the complex academic language necessary to tackle these subjects effectively. This is especially important in grades 7 through 9, where the gatekeeping course—algebra—for future scientific and technical courses is taught.
3. Increase school participation. Counselors and teachers can make college-related information more visible throughout the school. Precollege clubs can be developed. Administrators can invite college representatives, alumni, and individuals in different careers to address students. Critical-thinking skills can be stressed. And teachers can occasionally tailor the structure of exams to be more like the SAT and the ACT.
4. Expose students to the world of college. College recruiters, faculty, and financial-aid officers are important role models and sources of current information. Visits to colleges enable youth to gain firsthand knowledge about campus life (Justiz & Rendon, 1989).
5. Increase workshops. Study skills, assertiveness training, and survival tips can be taught. College-related topics such as "How to choose a college" and "What to say to college admissions officers" should be offered during the senior year.
6. Involve parents. Invitations to all activities should be bilingual and mailed home well in advance of the event. To increase attendance, students can provide child care. Parents should be encouraged to come to workshops and to participate in planning activities.
7. Organize outside support. Better coordination between community organizations and schools could provide a central source for descriptions of available programs at the school and in the community. ◆

These Hispanic youth leaders, participating in a mock legislation session, are positive examples of the increased concern for helping Hispanic youth stay in school and go to college.

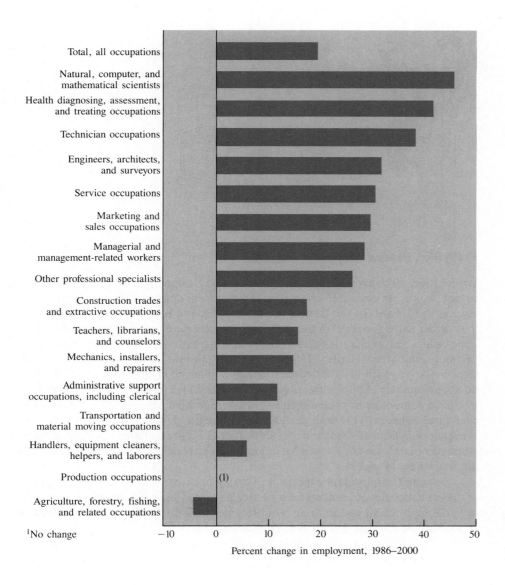

FIGURE 15.4   Employment growth in the future.

Source: Occupational Outlook Handbook. *U.S. Department of Labor, Bureau of Labor Statistics, April, 1988, Bulletin 2300, p. 12.*

Tomorrow's Jobs for Today's Adolescents

For nearly 40 years, the United States Bureau of Labor Statistics has published the *Occupational Outlook Handbook,* a valuable source of career information that is revised every two years. The following information comes from the 1988–1989 edition. The long-term shift from goods-producing to service-producing employment will continue. By the year 2000, nearly four out of five jobs will be in industries that provide services—industries such as banking, insurance, health care, education, data processing, and management consulting. Continued expansion of the service-producing sector generates an image of a work force dominated by cashiers, retail sales workers, and waiters. However, while growth in the service sector will create millions of clerical, sales, and service jobs, it also will create jobs for engineers, accountants, lawyers, nurses, and many other managerial, professional, and technical workers. In fact, the fastest-growing careers will be those that require the most educational preparation (Figure 15.4).

Whatever you can do, or dream you can, begin it. Boldness has genius, power and magic in it.

Johann Wolfgang Goethe

"Your son has made a career choice, Mildred. He's going to win the lottery and travel a lot."

Exploration, Decision Making, and Planning

Exploration, decision making, and planning play important roles in adolescents' career choices. In countries where equal employment opportunities have emerged—such as the United States, Canada, Great Britain, and France—exploration of various career paths is critical in the adolescent's career development. Adolescents often approach career exploration and decision making with considerable ambiguity, uncertainty, and stress (Crites, 1989; Schulenberg, 1988). Many of the career decisions made by youth involve floundering and unplanned changes. Many adolescents do not adequately explore careers on their own and also receive little direction from guidance counselors at their schools. The average high school student spends less than three hours per year with guidance counselors; and in some schools, the amount is even less (National Assessment of Educational Progress, 1976). In many schools, students not only do not know what information to seek about careers, they also do not know how to seek it.

Among the important aspects of planning in career development is awareness of the educational requirements for a particular career. In one investigation, a sample of 6,029 high school seniors from 57 different school districts in Texas was studied (Grotevant & Durrett, 1980). Students lacked knowledge about two aspects of careers: (1) accurate information about the educational requirements of careers they desired; and (2) information about the vocational interests predominantly associated with their career choices.

Career Development and Gender

The number of females entering careers previously thought to be appropriate only for males has increased significantly. Yet discrimination and inadequate opportunities for education are prominent issues affecting the achievement levels of females (Eccles, 1987; Gutek, 1988; Tittle, 1988). Females diminished the gap between male and female earnings in the 1980s, but significant disparities still exist. The gap is smallest for workers in their twenties, probably because females and males have had similar access to education and job opportunities in recent years. Overall, the earnings for females who worked full time were 70 percent of those for males in 1986, up from 62 percent in 1979. More than half the remaining gap is explained by differences in such factors as education and work experience. Females are more

Thinking Critically

Imagine that you have been hired as the new director of career development for a school system. How would you get career development to become a more central feature of the school system's curriculum? What would your career education program feature? What developmental considerations would you make?

A special concern is to provide opportunities for females to enter professions dominated by males. By encouraging young female adolescents to take more science courses and become involved in science-related activities, such as the science fair for which this young adolescent girl has developed a project, it is hoped that male-female imbalance in science careers will be lessened.

than three times as likely as males to have had interruptions in their work experience. Forty-seven percent of females between the ages of 21 and 64 had spent six months or more without a job since their twenty-first birthday; only 13 percent of the males had experienced this gap. Reasons for interruptions included childbearing, child care, illness, disability, and unemployment.

How much progress have females made in moving into professions dominated by males? They made some progress in the 1980s, but fields such as computer systems analysis, computer programming, electrical engineering, accounting, and law are still male dominated.

Because females have been socialized to adopt nurturing roles rather than career or achieving roles, traditionally they have not planned seriously for careers, have not explored career options extensively, and have restricted their career choices to those that are gender stereotyped (Diamond, 1988). However, the motivation for work is the same for both sexes. Females and males, though, make different choices because of their socialization experiences (Astin, 1984).

As growing numbers of females pursue careers, they are faced with issues involving career and family. Should they delay marriage and childbearing and establish their career first? Or should they combine their career, marriage, and childbearing in their twenties. Some women in recent years have embraced the domestic patterns of an earlier historical period: They have married, borne children, and committed themselves to full-time mothering. These "traditional" females have worked outside the home only intermittently, if at all, and have subordinated the work role to the family role.

Many other females, though, have veered from this time-honored path. They have postponed, and even forgone, motherhood. They have developed committed, permanent ties to the work place that resemble the pattern once reserved only for males. When they have had children, they have strived to combine a career and motherhood. While there have always been "career" females, today their numbers are growing at an unprecedented rate. Recent research reveals that high-ability juniors and seniors in college show a strong interest in combining career and family (Fassinger, 1985).

Yes, I am wise but it is wisdom for the pain. Yes, I've paid the price but look how much I've gained. If I have to I can do anything. I am strong, I am invincible, I am woman . . .

Helen Reddy

Some of the brightest and most gifted females do not have achievement and career aspirations that match their talents. In one investigation, high-achieving females had much lower expectations for success than high-achieving males (Stipak & Hoffman, 1980). In the gifted research program at Johns Hopkins University, many mathematically precocious females did select scientific and medical careers, although only 46 percent aspired to a full-time career compared to 98 percent of the males (Fox, Brody, & Tobin, 1979).

To help talented females redirect their life paths, some high schools are using programs developed by colleges and universities. Project CHOICE (Creating Her Options in Career Education) was designed by Case Western University to detect barriers in reaching one's potential. Gifted eleventh-grade females received individualized counseling that included interviews with female role models, referral to appropriate occupational groups, and information about career workshops. A program at the University of Nebraska (Kerr, 1983) was successful in encouraging talented female high school students to pursue more prestigious careers. This was accomplished through individual counseling and participation in a "Perfect Future Day," a day in which girls shared their career fantasies and discussed barriers that might impede their success. Internal and external constraints were evaluated, gender-role stereotypes were discouraged, and high aspirations were applauded. While these programs have short-term success in redirecting the career paths of high-ability females, in some instances the effects fade over time—six months or more, for example. It is important to be concerned about improving the career alternatives for all female youth, however, not just those of high ability.

Thinking Critically

As the achievement orientation of females has changed, what adaptations have schools—especially males in schools—been forced to make?

Work

One of the greatest changes in adolescents' lives in recent years has been the increased number of adolescents who work in some part-time capacity and still regularly attend school. Our coverage of adolescents and work includes information about the sociohistorical context of adolescent work, the advantages and disadvantages of part-time work, and bridging the gap between school and work.

Sociohistorical Context of Work

Over the past century, the percentage of youth who work full time as opposed to those who are in school has decreased dramatically. In the late 1800s, less than 1 of every 20 high school-aged adolescents was in school. Today more than 9 of every 10 adolescents receive high school diplomas. In the nineteenth century, many adolescents learned a trade from their father or some other adult member of the community.

While prolonged education has kept many contemporary youth from holding full-time jobs, it has not prevented them from working part time while going to school. Most high school seniors have had some work experience. In a national survey of 17,000 high school seniors, 3 of 4 reported some income from a job during the average school week (Bachman, 1982). For 41 percent of the males and 30 percent of the females, this income exceeded 50 dollars a week. The typical part-time job for high school seniors involves 16 to 20 hours of work per week, although 10 percent work 30 hours a week or more.

In 1940, only 1 of 25 tenth-grade males attended school while working part time. In the 1970s, the number had increased to more than 1 of every 4. And, in the 1980s, as just indicated, 3 of 4 combined school and part-time work. Adolescents also are working longer hours now than in the past. For example, the number of 14- and 15-year-olds who work more than 14 hours per week has increased substantially since 1960. A similar picture emerges for 16-year-olds. In 1960, 44 percent of 16-year-old males who attended school worked more than 14 hours a week, but by the 1980s, the figure had increased to more than 60 percent.

What kinds of jobs are adolescents working at today? About 17 percent who work do so in restaurants, such as McDonald's, Burger King, and the like, waiting on customers, cleaning up, and so on. Other adolescents work in retail stores as cashiers or salespeople (about 20%), in offices as clerical assistants (about 10%), or as unskilled laborers (about 10%) (Cole, 1981).

Do male and female adolescents take the same type of jobs and are they paid equally? Some jobs are held almost exclusively by male adolescents—busboys, gardeners, manual laborers, and newspaper carriers—while other jobs are held almost exclusively by female adolescents—babysitters and maids. Male adolescents work longer hours and are paid more per hour than female adolescents (Helson, Elliott, & Leigh, 1989).

Advantages and Disadvantages of Part-Time Work in Adolescence

Does the increase in work have benefits for adolescents? In some cases, yes; in others, no. Ellen Greenberger and Laurence Steinberg (1981) examined the work experiences of students in four California high schools. Their findings disproved some common myths. For example, generally it is assumed that adolescents get extensive on-the-job training when they are hired for work; the reality is that they get little training at all. Also, it is assumed that youths, through work experiences, learn to get along better with adults. However, adolescents reported that they rarely felt close to the adults with whom they worked. The work experiences of the adolescents did help them to understand how the business world works, how to get and keep a job, and how to manage money. Working also helped adolescents learn to budget their time, to take pride in their accomplishments, and to evaluate their goals. But working adolescents often have to give up sports, social affairs with peers, and sometimes sleep. And they have to balance the demands of work, school, family, and peers.

Greenberger and Steinberg asked students about their grade-point averages, school attendance, satisfaction from school, and the number of hours spent studying and participating in extracurricular activities since they began working. They found that working adolescents have lower grade-point averages than nonworking adolescents. More than one of four students reported that their grades dropped when they began working; only one of nine said that their grades improved. But it was not just working that affected adolescents' grades; more importantly, it was *how long* they worked. Tenth-graders who worked more than 14 hours a week suffered a drop in grades. Eleventh-graders worked up to 20 hours a week before their grades dropped. When adolescents work more than 20 hours per week, they have little time to study for tests and to complete homework assignments.

In addition to the effects of work on grades, working adolescents felt less involved in school, were absent more often, and said they did not enjoy school as much as their nonworking counterparts. Adolescents who worked also spent less time with their families than did their nonworking counterparts, but they spent just as much time with their peers. Adolescents who worked long hours also were more frequent users of alcohol and marijuana.

Some states have responded to these findings by limiting the number of hours adolescents can work while they are attending secondary school. In 1986, in Pinellas County, Florida, a law was enacted that placed a cap on the previously unregulated hours that adolescents could work while school is in session. The allowable limit was set at 30 hours, which research evidence suggests is still too high (Greenberger, 1987).

The Transition from School to Work

In some cases, the media have exaggerated the degree of adolescent unemployment. For example, based on data collected by the U.S. Department of Labor, 9 of 10 adolescents are in school, are working at a job, or both. Only 5 percent are out of school, have no job, and are looking for full-time employment. Most adolescents who are unemployed are not unemployed for long periods of time. Only 10 percent are without a job for six months or longer. The major portion of adolescents who are unemployed are individuals who have dropped out of school.

Certain segments of the adolescent population, however, are more likely to be unemployed than others. A disproportionate percentage of unemployed adolescents are black, for example. As indicated in Table 15.2, the unemployment situation is especially acute for blacks and other minorities between the ages of 16 and 19. The job situation has improved for black adolescents: In 1969, 44 percent of black adolescents were unemployed; today's figures indicate that about 65 percent are unemployed.

How can adolescents be helped to bridge the gap between school and work? For the adolescent bound for higher education and a professional degree, the education system provides connections from school to career. Most youth, though, step off the education ladder before reaching the level of a professional career. Often they are on their own in their search for work.

TABLE 15.2	Percentages of Unemployed Youths and Adults	
	Whites	**Blacks and Other Minorities**
Men 20 years and older	5.1	8.3
Women 20 years and older	3.5	10.2
Men 16 to 19 years old	14.1	34.8
Women 16 to 19 years old	13.9	35.9

Source: U.S. Department of Labor, *Special Labor Force Report No. 218.* Washington, D.C.: U.S. Government Printing Office, 1979, p. 9.

How can the gap from school to work be bridged? Monitored work experiences should be implemented. This includes cooperative education, internships, apprenticeships, preemployment training, and youth-operated enterprises. These efforts feature opportunities for youth to gain work experience, to be exposed to adult supervisors and models in the workplace, and to relate their academic training to the work place.

Community and neighborhood services should be expanded. This includes individual voluntary service and youth-guided services. Youth need experiences not only as workers, but also as citizens. Service programs not only expose youth to the adult world, but also provide them with a sense of the obligations of citizenship in building a more caring and competent society.

Vocational education should be redirected. With few exceptions, the vocational education adolescents experienced in the 1980s does not prepare youth adequately for specific jobs. However, its hands-on methods can provide students with valuable and effective ways of acquiring skills they will need to be successful in a number of jobs.

Incentives need to be introduced. Low motivation and low expectations for success in the workplace often restrict adolescents' educational achievement. Recent efforts to guarantee postsecondary and continuing education, guaranteed employment, and guaranteed work-related training for students who do well show promise of encouraging adolescents to work harder and be more successful in school.

Career information and counseling need to be improved. A variety of information and counseling approaches can be implemented to expose adolescents to job opportunities and career options. These services can be offered both in school and in community settings. They include setting up career-information centers, developing the capacity of parents as career educators, and expanding the work of community-based organizations.

More school volunteers should be used. Tutoring is the most common form of school volunteer activity. However, adults are needed even more generally—as friends, as mentors for opening up career opportunities, and as guides for assisting youth in mastering the dilemmas of living in a stressful time.

Improving education, elevating skill levels, and providing hands-on experience will help adolescents bridge the gap between school and work. We need to address the needs of youth if we are to retain the confidence of youth who have been brought up to believe in the promise of the American Dream (Grubb, 1989; William T. Grant Foundation Commission, 1988; Wilson, 1989).

Thus far, we have discussed a number of ideas about schools, careers, and work in adolescence. These ideas are summarized in Concept Table 15.2. In the next chapter, we will turn our attention to the nature of social development in adolescence.

Schools, Careers, and Work

Concept	Processes and Related Ideas	Characteristics and Description
Schools	Function of schools	In the nineteenth century, secondary schools were for the elite. By the 1920s, they had changed, becoming more comprehensive and training adolescents for work and citizenship, as well as improving their intellect. The comprehensive high school remains today, but the function of secondary schools continues to be debated. Some maintain that the function should be intellectual development; others argue for more comprehensive functions.
	Transition to middle or junior high school	The emergence of junior high schools in the 1920s and 1930s was justified on the basis of physical, cognitive, and social changes in early adolescence and the need for more schools in response to a growing student population. Middle schools have become more popular in recent years, coinciding with puberty's earlier arrival. The transition to middle or junior high school coincides with many social, familial, and individual changes in the adolescent's life. The transition involves moving from the top-dog to the bottom-dog position. Successful schools for young adolescents take individual differences in development seriously, show a deep concern for what is known about early adolescence, and emphasize social and emotional development as much as intellectual development.
	High school dropouts and non-college youth	Dropping out has been a serious problem for decades. Many dropouts have educational deficiencies that curtail their economic and social well-being for much of their adult lives. Some progress has been made; dropout rates for most ethnic-minority groups have declined in recent decades, although dropout rates for inner-city, low-income minorities are still precariously high. Dropping out of school is associated with demographic, family-related, peer-related, school-related, economic, and individual factors. Reducing the dropout rate and improving the lives of non-college youth could be accomplished by strengthening schools and bridging the gap between school and work.

Summary

I. Formal Operational Thought
Piaget believed that formal operational thought comes into play between 11 and 15 years of age. Formal operational thought is more abstract, idealistic, and logical than concrete operational thought. Piaget believed that adolescents are capable of using hypothetical deductive reasoning. Language changes that accompany formal operational thought involve an increased understanding of satire and metaphor, improved writing ability, and superior conversational skills. Some of Piaget's ideas in formal operational thought are being challenged.

II. Social Cognition
Impressive changes in social cognition characterize adolescent development. Adolescents develop a special type of egocentrism that involves an imaginary audience and a personal fable about being unique and indestructible. They begin to think about personality not unlike personality theorists do, and they monitor their social world in more sophisticated ways.

Concept	Processes and Related Ideas	Characteristics and Description
Careers and Work	Tomorrow's jobs for today's adolescents	The long-term shift from goods-producing to service-producing employment will continue. In the year 2000, nearly four of five jobs will be in industries that provide services.
	Exploration, decision making, and planning	Exploration of career options is a critical aspect of career development in countries where equal employment opportunities exist. Many youth flounder and make unplanned career-choice changes. Students also need more knowledge about education and ability requirements of various careers.
	Career development and gender	There has been a tremendous influx of females into the labor force in recent years. Females diminished the pay gap in the 1980s, but a gap still exists. Females also have increased their presence in occupations previously dominated by males. As greater numbers of females pursue careers, they are faced by issues involving both family and career. Special attention needs to be given to the career paths of the brightest and most gifted female adolescents, but not to the exclusion of promoting career exploration and options for all female adolescents.
	Work	Adolescents are not as likely to hold full-time jobs today as their adolescent counterparts from the nineteenth century. There has been a tremendous increase in the number of adolescents who work part time and go to school, which has both advantages and disadvantages. In some cases, adolescent unemployment has been exaggerated; however, for many minority-group adolescents, unemployment is a major problem. We should monitor work experiences of adolescents, expand community and neighborhood services, redirect vocational education, introduce incentives, improve career information and counseling, and use more school volunteers.

III. **Values, Religious Beliefs, and Cults**

Over the last two decades, adolescents have shown an increased concern for personal well-being and a decreased concern for the welfare of others. Both Elkind's and Fowler's views illustrate the increased abstractness in adolescents' thinking that provides them with improved understanding of the nature of religion. Adolescents show a strong interest in spiritual matters, but they believe organized religion has not provided them with the spiritual understanding they seek. Cult membership in the United States is extensive among youth. It may appeal to adolescents because of weaknesses in organized religion and in families.

IV. **Function of Schools**

In the nineteenth century, secondary schools were for the elite. By the 1920s, they had changed, becoming more comprehensive and training adolescents for work and citizenship, as well as intellect. The comprehensive high school remains today, but the function of secondary schools continues to be debated. Some maintain that the function of secondary schools should be intellectual development; others argue for more comprehensive functions.

Cognitive Development 525

V. Transition to Middle or Junior High School

The emergence of junior high schools in the 1920s and the 1930s was justified on the basis of physical, cognitive, and social changes in early adolescence and the need for more schools in response to a growing student population. Middle schools have become more popular in recent years, coinciding with the earlier arrival of puberty. The transition to middle or junior high school coincides with many social, familial, and individual changes in the adolescent's life. The transition involves moving from the top-dog to the bottom-dog position. Successful schools for young adolescents take individual differences in development seriously, show a deep concern for what is known about early adolescence, and emphasize social and emotional development as much as intellectual development.

VI. High School Dropouts and Non-College-Bound Youth

Dropping out of school has been a serious problem for decades. Many dropouts have educational deficiencies that curtail their economic and social well-being for much of their adult lives. Some progress has been made, however; dropout rates for most ethnic-minority groups have declined in recent decades, although the dropout rates for inner-city, low-income minorities are still precariously high. Dropping out of school is associated with demographic, family-related, peer-related, school-related, economic, and individual factors. Reducing the dropout rate and improving the lives of non-college-bound youth could be accomplished by strengthening schools and bridging the gap between school and work.

VII. Tomorrow's Jobs for Today's Adolescents and Exploration, Decision Making, and Planning

The long-term shift from goods-producing to service-producing employment will continue. In the year 2000, nearly four of five jobs will be in industries that provide services. Exploration of career options is a critical aspect of career development in countries where equal employment opportunities exist. Many youth flounder and make unplanned career-choice changes. Students also need more knowledge about education and ability requirements of various careers.

VIII. Career Development and Gender

There has been a tremendous influx of females into the labor force in recent years. Females diminished the pay gap in the 1980s, but a gap still exists. Females also have increased their presence in occupations that once were dominated by males. As greater numbers of females pursue careers, they face issues involving both family and career. Special attention needs to be given to the career paths of the brightest and most gifted female adolescents, but not to the exclusion of promoting career exploration and options for all female adolescents.

IX. Work

Adolescents are not as likely to hold full-time jobs today as their counterparts from the nineteenth century. The number of adolescents who work part time and go to school has increased tremendously; this has both advantages and disadvantages. In some cases, adolescent unemployment has been exaggerated, however, for many minority-group adolescents, unemployment is a major problem. We should monitor work experiences of adolescents, expand community and neighborhood services, redirect vocational education, introduce incentives, improve career information and counseling, and use more school volunteers.

Key Terms

hypothetical deductive
    reasoning 495
satire 495
metaphor 495

adolescent egocentrism 496
imaginary audience 496
personal fable 496

individuating-reflective
    faith 501
top-dog phenomenon 508

Suggested Readings

Elkind, D. (1976). *Child development and education.* New York: Oxford University Press.
    An excellent application of Piaget's view to education with many examples of
    adolescent cognition.
Levine, S. V. (1984, August). Radical departures. *Psychology Today,* 18–27.
    An in-depth discussion of cults. Includes discussion of how families should deal with
    cults and strategies for helping adolescents who have joined cults.
Lipsitz, J. (1984). *Successful schools for young adolescents.* New Brunswick, NJ:
    Transaction Books.
    Important reading for anyone interested in better schools for young adolescents. Filled
    with rich examples of adolescents in schools.
Phi Delta Kappan. A leading educational journal. Leaf through the issues of the 1980s to
    get a feel for controversial, widely debated ideas in secondary education.
The William T. Grant Foundation Commission on Work, Family and Citizenship. (1980).
    The forgotten half: Non-college youth in America. New York.
    This excellent report on the status of non-college youth in America calls attention to
    ways our society can help these individuals more effectively make the transition to
    work.

16

Social Development

A s soon as the last bell rings at West High School, Rob rushes to the parking lot, hops into his Mustang convertible, flips the knob on the radio to a high pitch, and peels out of the school lot, leaving a trail of rubber. Rob heads for McDonald's, where he works 25 hours a week so that he can have his own spending money. He is saving to buy a tape deck for his car. Not all high school students drive their own cars, and not all of them are as materially oriented as Rob, but for many adolescents, money and cars are highly desired commodities.

Among other material items, money, cars, and clothes play important roles in the need system of many adolescents. They contribute to the adolescent's self-identity and self-esteem. Adolescents with their own cars or motorcycles achieve a status level in the youth culture beyond that of adolescents without these material goods.

Social scientists suggest that material goods can reflect the adolescent's personality. For example, an adolescent male who dresses casually, lets his hair grow long, and buys a motorcycle probably has a different personality than an adolescent male who dresses conservatively, trims and neatly parts his hair, and drives his mother's car when it is available. The appearances of these two adolescents also are likely to elicit different expectations from their peers and from adults.

Think about your own adolescent years, about the material aspects of the culture . . . wishing for the day you could get your driver's license . . . trying to convince your parents you needed a car, or at least needed ready access to their car . . . or if all else failed, at least having a good friend who owned a car so you could cruise around and get where you wanted to go. Think about how much time you spent looking at and trying on clothes. According to *Seventeen* magazine, adolescent girls spend more than $9 billion dollars just on back-to-school clothes. In 1987, adolescents spent $34 billion dollars of their own money, an increase of $4 billion dollars from 1985 levels. Adolescent girls aged 13 to 15 years had $31 a week in allowance and job earnings to spend in 1988 (Rand Youth Poll, 1988). In the same survey, girls 16 to 19 years old had $68 a week in pocket money. Because adolescents have few overhead expenses, with the possible exception of an occasional school lunch or bus fare, they spend most of their money on themselves—clothes, cosmetics, snack food, gasoline, cars, and entertainment. Some money may go into savings, but the savings usually goes toward the purchase of a large item. Today's adolescents are a very consumer-oriented group, perhaps the most consumer-oriented group ever (Carton, 1988).

There are other aspects of the adolescent's culture to consider—the telephone, for one. The caricature of a phone growing out of an adolescent's ear is not too far-fetched. The telephone plays a special role in the social network of young adolescents, who are not yet old enough to drive. At the time I wrote the first edition of this text, my oldest daughter, Tracy, was 13. Her telephone use went up dramatically at this time. One night I came home about 11 P.M. and asked my wife how her evening had gone. She replied, "Your daughter was on the phone from 7:30 to 10:00—either she was calling her friends, or they were calling her." Many young adolescents spend long hours talking with each other about school, about members of the opposite sex, about friends, about parents, about music, and about clothes. And the

telephone comes in handy when the moment comes to ask someone out for a first date; adolescents use the telephone as a "long-distance" communication system to avoid the anxiety of asking in person.

The social worlds of adolescents are many and fascinating. Through experiences with parents, siblings, peers, friends, clique members, teachers, and other adults, adolescents make the transition from being a child to being an adult. There are many hills and valleys in this transition, and there are times when parent-child relationships become strained. But a large majority of adolescents make the transition from childhood to adulthood completely, continuing to be attached to their parents and exploring an ever-widening social world as they move toward more autonomous behavior and decision making. As they make the transition from child to adult, a major concern of adolescents is the development of an identity: Who am I, What am I all about, and Where am I headed in life? In this chapter, we explore the social worlds of adolescents and the adolescent's concern with identity.

The telephone is a prominent object in the cultural lives of many adolescents, serving as a contact with the wider social world, especially in terms of friendship, peer popularity, and dating.

Families

In Chapter 13, we discussed how parents spend less time with their children during middle and late childhood than in early childhood, how discipline involves an increased use of reasoning and deprivation of privileges, how there is a gradual transfer of control from parents to children but still within the boundary of coregulation, and how parents and children increasingly respond to each other on the basis of labels. What are some of the most important issues and questions that need to be raised about family relationships in adolescence? They include: What is the nature of autonomy and attachment in adolescence? How extensive is parent-adolescent conflict and how does it influence the adolescent's development? Do maturation of the adolescent and maturation of parents contribute to understanding parent-adolescent relationships? What are the effects of divorce on adolescents?

Autonomy and Attachment

The adolescent's push for autonomy and a sense of responsibility puzzles and angers many parents. Parents see their teenager slipping from their grasp. They may have an urge to take stronger control as the adolescent seeks autonomy and responsibility. Heated emotional exchanges may ensue, with either side calling names, making threats, and doing whatever seems necessary to gain control. Parents may seem frustrated because they *expect* their teenager to heed their advice, to want to spend time with the family, and to grow up to do what is right. Most parents anticipate that their teenager will have some difficulty adjusting to the changes that adolescence brings, but few parents can imagine and predict just how strong an adolescent's desires will be to spend time with peers and how adolescents want to show that it is they—not their parents—who are responsible for their successes and failures.

The ability to attain autonomy and gain control over one's behavior in adolescence is acquired through appropriate adult reactions to the adolescent's desire for control. At the onset of adolescence, the average individual does not have the knowledge to make appropriate or mature decisions in all areas of life. As the adolescent pushes for autonomy, the wise adult relinquishes control in those areas in which the adolescent can make reasonable decisions and continues to guide the adolescent to make reasonable decisions in areas in which the adolescent's knowledge is more limited. Gradually, adolescents acquire the ability to make mature decisions on their own.

But adolescents do not simply move away from parental influence into a decision-making process all their own. There is continued connectedness to parents as adolescents move toward and gain autonomy. Attachment to parents increases the probability that the adolescent will be a competent adolescent and become a competent adult. Just as in childhood, parents provide an important support system that helps the adolescent to explore in a healthy way a wider, more complex social world full of uncertainties, challenges, and stresses (Hill & Holmbeck, 1986; Santrock, 1990). Although adolescents show a strong desire to spend more time with peers, they do not move into a world isolated from parents. For example, in one investigation, adolescent girls who had the best relationships with their girlfriends showed a strong identification with their mothers, indicating that they would like to be like their mothers (Gold & Yanof, 1985). Of course, there are times when

The adolescent's push for autonomy and a sense of self-responsibility is strong. As the adolescent pushes for autonomy, the wise parent relinquishes control in those areas where the adolescent can make reasonable decisions and continues to closely monitor those situations where the adolescent's behavior is not yet mature.

adolescents reject this closeness as they try to assert their own ability to make decisions and develop an identity. But, for the most part, the worlds of parent-adolescent and adolescent-peer relationships are coordinated and connected, not uncoordinated and disconnected.

Parent-Adolescent Conflict

While attachment and connectedness to parents remains strong during adolescence, the attachment and connectedness is not always smooth. Early adolescence is a time when conflict with parents escalates beyond childhood levels (Montemayor & Hanson, 1985; Steinberg, 1987). This increase may be due to a number of factors: the biological changes of puberty, cognitive changes involving increased idealism and logical reasoning, social changes focused on independence and identity, maturational changes in parents, and violated expectations on the part of parents and adolescents. The adolescent compares her parents to an ideal standard and then

Early adolescence is a time when conflict with parents escalates beyond childhood levels. Might a moderate degree of conflict with parents have a positive developmental function? If so, how?

criticizes the flaws. A 13-year-old girl tells her mother, "That is the tackiest-looking dress I have ever seen. Nobody would be caught dead wearing that." The adolescent demands logical explanations for comments and discipline. A 14-year-old boy tells his mother, "What do you mean I have to be home at 10 P.M. because it's the way we do things around here? Why do we do things around here that way? It doesn't make sense to me."

Many parents see their adolescent changing from a compliant child to someone who is noncompliant, oppositional, and resistant to parental standards. When this happens, parents tend to clamp down and put more pressure on the adolescent to conform to parental standards (Collins, 1989). Parents often expect their adolescents to become mature adults overnight instead of understanding that the journey takes 10 to 15 years. Parents who recognize that this transition takes time handle their youth more competently and calmly than those who demand immediate conformity to adult standards. The opposite tactic—letting adolescents do as they please without supervision—also is unwise.

While conflict with parents does increase in early adolescence, it does not reach the tumultuous proportions G. Stanley Hall envisioned at the beginning of the twentieth century. Rather, much of the conflict involves the everyday events of family life such as keeping a bedroom clean, dressing neatly, getting home by a certain time, not talking forever on the phone, and so on. The conflicts rarely involve major dilemmas like drugs and delinquency.

It is not unusual to talk to parents of young adolescents and hear them ask, "Is it ever going to get better?" Things usually do get better as adolescents move from early to late adolescence. Conflict between parents usually escalates during early adolescence, remains somewhat stable during the high school years, and then lessens as the adolescent reaches 17 to 20 years of age. Parent-adolescent relationships become more positive if adolescents go away to college than if they stay at home and go to college (Sullivan & Sullivan, 1980).

The everyday conflicts that characterize parent-adolescent relationships may serve a positive developmental function (Blos, 1989; Hill, 1983). These minor disputes and negotiations facilitate the adolescent's transition from being dependent on parents to becoming an autonomous individual. For example, in one investigation, adolescents who expressed disagreement with parents explored identity development more actively than adolescents who did not express disagreement with their parents (Cooper & others, 1982).

As suggested earlier, one way for parents to cope with the adolescent's push for independence and identity is to recognize that adolescence is a 10-to-15-year transition period rather than an overnight accomplishment. Recognizing that conflict and negotiation can serve a positive developmental function can tone down parental hostility, too. Understanding parent-adolescent conflict, though, is not simple. As we will observe next, both the maturation of the adolescent and the maturation of parents probably are wrapped up in this conflict.

The Maturation of the Adolescent and Parents

Physical, cognitive, and social changes in the adolescent's development influence the nature of parent-adolescent relationships. Parental changes also influence the nature of these relationships. Among the changes in the adolescent are puberty, expanded logical reasoning and increased idealistic and egocentric thought, violated expectations, changes in schooling, peers, friendship, and dating, and movement toward independence. Several recent investigations have shown that conflict between parents and adolescents, especially between mothers and sons, during the apex of pubertal growth, is the most stressful (Hill & others, 1985; Steinberg, 1981, 1988).

Parental changes include those involving marital dissatisfaction, economic burdens, career reevaluation and time perspective, and health and body concerns. Marital dissatisfaction is greater when the offspring is an adolescent rather than a child or an adult. A greater economic burden is placed on parents during the rearing of their adolescents. Parents may reevaluate their occupational achievement, deciding whether they have met their youthful aspirations for success. Parents may look to the future and think about how much time they have remaining to accomplish what they want. Adolescents, however, look to the future with unbounded optimism, sensing that they have an unlimited amount of time to accomplish what they desire. Health concerns and an interest in body integrity and sexual attractiveness become prominent themes of adolescents' parents. Even when their body and sexual attractiveness are not deteriorating, many parents of adolescents perceive that they are. By contrast, adolescents are beginning to reach the peak of their physical attractiveness, strength, and health. While both adolescents and their parents show a heightened preoccupation with their bodies, the adolescent's outcome probably is more positive. More about the developmental aspects of adolescents' parents appears in Children 16.1, where we discuss the increase in delayed childbearing.

It is not enough for parents to understand children. They must accord children the privilege of understanding them.

Milton Sapirstein, Paradoxes of Everyday Life, *1955*

Thinking Critically
As the parents of adolescents will become increasingly older in the future because of delayed marriage and childbearing, how do you think this will influence the nature of parent-adolescent relationships?

In case you're worried about what's going to become of the younger generation, it's going to grow up and start worrying about the younger generation.

Roger Allen

Changing Developmental Trajectories: Delayed Childbearing

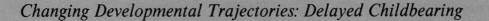

The changes in adolescents' parents we have described are those that characterize development in middle adulthood. The majority of adolescents' parents either are in middle adulthood or are rapidly approaching middle adulthood. However, in the last two decades, the timing of parenthood has undergone some dramatic shifts. Parenthood is taking place earlier for some, and later for others than in previous decades. First, the number of adolescent pregnancies during the 1980s increased dramatically. Second, there has been a simultaneous increase in the number of women who postpone childbearing until their thirties and early forties. Table 16.A shows another increasing trend related to later childbearing—the postponement in marriage.

There are many contrasts between becoming a parent in adolescence and becoming a parent 15 or 30 years later. When

childbearing is delayed, considerable progress in occupational and educational domains often has taken place. Both males and females will usually have completed their education and have well-established careers (Parke, 1988).

The marital relationship varies with the timing of parenthood onset. In one investigation, couples who began childbearing in their early twenties were compared with those who began in their early thirties (Walter, 1986). The late-timed couples had more egalitarian relationships, with men participating in child care and household tasks more often.

Is parent-child interaction different for families who delay having their children until their thirties or forties? Investigators have found that older fathers are warmer, communicate better, encourage more achievement, and show less rejection with their children than younger fathers. However, older fathers are less likely to place demands on children, are less likely to enforce rules, and are less likely to engage in physical play or sports with their children (MacDonald, 1987; Parke & others, 1988). These findings suggest that sociohistorical changes are resulting in different developmental trajectories for many families, trajectories that involve changes in the way marital partners and parents and adolescents interact. ◆

TABLE 16.A	*Median Age at First Marriage*	
	1970	**1984**
Men	23.2	25.4
Women	20.8	23.0

Peers

In Chapter 13, we discussed how children spend more time with their peers in middle and late childhood than in early childhood. We also found that friendships become more important in middle and late childhood and that popularity with peers is a strong motivation for most children. Advances in cognitive development during middle and late childhood also allow children to take the perspective of their peers and friends more readily, and their social knowledge of how to make and keep friends increases.

Imagine you are back in junior or senior high school, especially during one of your good times. Peers, friends, cliques, dates, parties, and clubs probably come to mind. Adolescents spend huge chunks of time with peers, more than in middle and late childhood. Among the important issues and questions to be asked about peer relations in adolescents are: What is the nature of peer pressure and conformity? How important are cliques in adolescence? How do children and adolescent groups differ? What is the nature of dating in adolescence?

Peer Pressure and Conformity

Consider the following statement made by an adolescent girl:

> Peer pressure is extremely influential in my life. I have never had very many friends, and I spend quite a bit of time alone. The friends I have are older. . . . The closest friend I have had is a lot like me in that we are both sad and depressed a lot. I began to act even more depressed than before when I was with her. I would call her up and try to act even more depressed than I was because that is what I thought she liked. In that relationship, I felt pressure to be like her. . . .

During adolescence, especially early adolescence, we conformed more to peer standards than we did in childhood. Investigators have found that around the eighth and ninth grades, conformity to peers—especially to their antisocial standards—peaks (Berndt, 1979; Berndt & Perry, 1990). At this point in adolescence, a person is most likely to go along with a peer to steal hubcaps off a car, draw grafitti on a wall, or steal cosmetics from a store counter.

Cliques and Crowds

Most peer-group relationships in adolescence can be categorized in one of three ways: The crowd, the clique, or individual friendships. The largest and least personal of these is the **crowd.** Members of the crowd meet because of their mutual interest in activities, not because they are mutually attracted to each other. By contrast, the members of cliques and friendships are attracted to each other on the basis of similar interests and social ideals. **Cliques** are smaller, involve greater intimacy among members, and have more group cohesion than crowds.

Allegiance to cliques, clubs, organizations, and teams exerts powerful control over the lives of many adolescents. Group identity often overrides personal identity. The leader of a group may place a member in a position of considerable moral conflict by asking, in effect, "What's more important, our code or your parents'?" or "Are you looking out for yourself, or the members of the group?" Labels like "brother" and "sister" sometimes are adopted and used in the members' conversations with each other. These labels symbolize the bond between the members and suggest the high status of group membership.

One of the most widely cited studies of adolescent cliques and crowds is that of James Coleman (1961). Students from 10 different high schools were asked to identify the leading crowds in their schools. They also were asked to identify the students who were the most outstanding in athletics, popularity, and different school activities. Regardless of the school sampled, the leading crowds were composed of athletes and popular girls. Much less power in the leading crowd was attributed to the bright student. Coleman's finding that being an athlete contributes to popularity for adolescent boys was reconfirmed in a more recent investigation (Eitzen, 1975).

Think about your high school years. What were the cliques, and which one were you in? While the names of the cliques change, we could go to almost any high school in the United States and find three to six well-defined cliques or crowds. In one recent investigation, six peer group structures emerged: populars, unpopulars,

(a)

(b)

Among the common cliques in secondary schools are (a) populars, such as the cheerleaders shown here, who are well-known students who lead social activities, and (b) druggies/toughs, who are known for their illicit drug use or delinquent activities.

jocks, brains, druggies, and average students (Brown & Mounts, 1989). The proportion of students placed in these cliques was much lower in multiethnic schools because of the additional existence of ethnically based crowds.

A recent investigation revealed that clique membership is associated with the adolescent's self-esteem (Brown & Lohr, 1987). Cliques included jocks (athletically oriented), populars (well-known students who lead social activities), normals (middle-of-the-road students who make up the masses), druggies or toughs (known for illicit drug use or other delinquent activities), and nobodies (low in social skills or intellectual abilities). The self-esteem of the jocks and the populars was highest while that of the nobodies was the lowest. But one group of adolescents not in a clique had self-esteem equivalent to that of the jocks and the populars; this group was the independents, who indicated that clique membership was not important to them. Keep in mind that these data are correlational; self-esteem could increase an adolescent's probability of becoming a clique member just as clique membership could increase the adolescent's self-esteem.

Children and Adolescent Groups

Children groups differ from adolescent groups in several important ways. The members of children groups often are friends or neighborhood acquaintances. Their groups usually are not as formalized as many adolescent groups. During the adolescent years, groups tend to include a broader array of members. In other words, adolescents other than friends or neighborhood acquaintances often are members of adolescent groups. Try to recall the student council, honor society, or football team at your junior high school. If you were a member of any of these organizations, you probably remember that they were made up of many people you had not met before and that they were a more heterogeneous group than your childhood peer groups. Rules and regulations were probably well defined, and captains or leaders were formally elected or appointed in the adolescent groups.

Ethnic-Minority Adolescents' Peer Relations

As ethnic-minority children move into adolescence and enter schools with more heterogeneous school populations, they become more aware of their ethnic-minority status. Ethnic-minority adolescents may have difficulty joining peer groups and clubs in predominantly white schools. However, schools are only one setting in which peer relations take place.

Adolescent peer relations take place in diverse settings—at school, in the neighborhood, and in the community. Ethnic-minority adolescents often have two sets of peer relationships—one at school, the other in the community. Community peers are more likely to be from their own ethnic group in their immediate neighborhood. Sometimes they go to the same church and participate in activities together such as Black History Week, Chinese New Year's, or Cinco de Mayo Festival. Because ethnic-group adolescents usually have two sets of peers and friends, researchers asking about their peers and friends should focus on relationships both at school and in the neighborhood and community. Ethnic-minority group adolescents who are social isolates at school may be sociometric stars in their segregated neighborhood. Also, because adolescents are more mobile than children, inquiries should be made about the scope of their social networks (Gibbs & Huang, 1989). ◆

A well-known observational study by Dexter Dunphy (1963) supports the notion that opposite-sex participation in groups increases during adolescence. In late childhood, boys and girls participate in small, same-sex cliques. As they move into the early adolescent years, the same-sex cliques begin to interact with each other. Gradually, the leaders and high-status members form further cliques based on heterosexual relationships. Eventually, the newly created heterosexual cliques replace the same-sex cliques. The heterosexual cliques interact with each other in large crowd activities, too—at dances and athletic events, for example. In late adolescence, the crowd begins to dissolve as couples develop more serious relationships and make long-range plans that may include engagement and marriage. Dunphy's ideas are summarized in Figure 16.1.

Dating

Dating takes on added importance during adolescence. As Dick Cavett (1974) remembers, the thought of an upcoming dance or sock hop was absolute agony: "I knew I'd never get a date. There seemed to be only this limited set of girls I could and should be seen with, and they were all taken by the jocks." Adolescents spend considerable time either dating or thinking about dating, which has gone far beyond its original courtship function to a form of recreation, a source of status and achievement, and a setting for learning about close relationships.

He who would learn to fly one day must first learn to stand and walk and climb and dance: One cannot fly into flying.

Friedrich Nietzche, Thus Spoke Zarathustra, *1883*

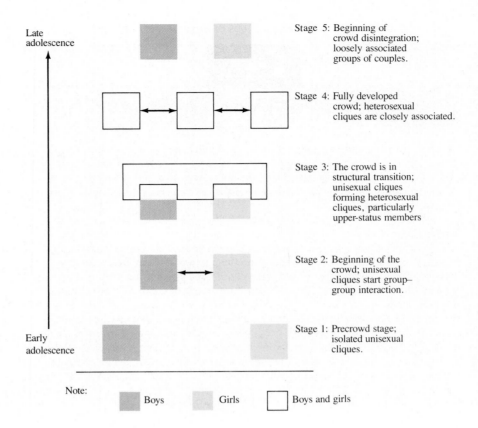

Late
adolescence

Stage 5: Beginning of
crowd disintegration;
loosely associated
groups of couples.

Stage 4: Fully developed
crowd; heterosexual
cliques are closely associated.

Stage 3: The crowd is in
structural transition;
unisexual cliques
forming heterosexual
cliques, particularly
upper-status members

Stage 2: Beginning of the
crowd; unisexual
cliques start group–
group interaction.

Early
adolescence

Stage 1: Precrowd stage;
isolated unisexual
cliques.

Note:

Boys   Girls   Boys and girls

FIGURE 16.1   Dunphy's stages of group
development (Dunphy, 1963).

Most girls in the United States begin dating at the age of 14, while most boys begin sometime between the ages of 14 and 15 (Douvan & Adelson, 1966; Sorenson, 1973). The majority of adolescents have their first date between the ages of 12 and 16. Fewer than 10 percent have a first date before the age of 10, and by the age of 16, more than 90 percent have had at least one date. More than 50 percent of high school students average one or more dates per week (Dickinson, 1975). About 15 percent date less than once per month, and about three of every four students have gone steady at least once by the end of high school.

Female adolescents bring a stronger desire for intimacy and personality exploration to dating than do male adolescents (Duck, 1975). Adolescent dating is a context in which gender-related role expectations intensify. Males feel pressured to perform in "masculine" ways and females feel pressured to perform in "feminine" ways. Especially in early adolescence when pubertal changes are occurring, the adolescent male wants to show that he is the very best male possible, and the adolescent female wants to show that she is the very best female possible.

Thus far, we have discussed a number of ideas about families and peers during adolescence. These ideas are summarized in Concept Table 16.1. We turn next to the powerful motivation of the adolescent to develop an identity.

Thinking Critically
How do you think variations in adolescents' observations of their parents' marital lives and relationships with their parents influence dating relationships in adolescence?

Families and Peers

Concept	Processes and Related Ideas	Characteristics and Description
Families	Autonomy and attachment	Many parents have a difficult time handling the adolescent's push for autonomy, even though this push is one of the hallmarks of adolescent development. Adolescents do not simply move into a world isolated from parents; attachment to parents increases the probability that the adolescent will be socially competent and explore a widening social world in healthy ways.
	Parent-adolescent conflict	Conflict with parents does seem to increase in early adolescence. Such conflict usually is moderate. The increase in conflict probably serves the positive developmental function of promoting autonomy and identity.
	The maturation of the adolescent and parents	Physical, cognitive, and social changes in the adolescent's development influence parent-adolescent relationships. Parental changes— marital dissatisfaction, economic burdens, career reevaluation and time perspective, and health and body concerns—also influence parent-adolescent relationships.
Peers	Peer pressure and conformity	The pressure to conform to peers is strong during adolescence, especially during the eighth and ninth grades.
	Cliques and crowds	There usually are three to six well-defined cliques in every secondary school. Membership in certain cliques—especially jocks and populars—is associated with increased self-esteem. Independents also show high self-esteem.
	Children and adolescent groups	Children groups are less formal, less heterogeneous, and less heterosexual than adolescent groups. Dunphy found that the development of adolescent groups moves through five stages.
	Dating	Dating can be a form of recreation, a source of status and achievement, and a setting for learning about close relationships. Most adolescents are involved in dating. Adolescent females appear to be more interested in intimacy and personality exploration than adolescent males are.

Identity

By far the most comprehensive and provocative story of identity development has been told by Erik Erikson. As you may remember from Chapter 2, identity versus identity confusion (diffusion) is the fifth stage in Erikson's eight stages of the life cycle, occurring at about the same time as adolescence. It is a time of interest in finding out who one is, what one is all about, and where one is headed in life.

During adolescence, world views become important to the individual, who enters what Erikson (1968) calls a "psychological moratorium," a gap between the security of childhood and the autonomy of adulthood. Adolescents experiment with numerous roles and identities they draw from the surrounding culture. The youth who successfully copes with these conflicting identities during adolescence emerges

Identity versus identity confusion is Erik Erikson's fifth stage in the human life cycle. Developing an identity is about finding out who we are and where we are going in life.

During adolescence, we enter a psychological moratorium during which we seek to understand who we are and what we are going to do with our lives.

with a new sense of self that is both refreshing and acceptable. The adolescent who does not successfully resolve this identity crisis is confused, suffering what Erikson calls identity confusion. This confusion takes one of two courses: The individual withdraws, isolating himself from peers and family; or he may lose his identity in the crowd.

The Four Statuses of Identity

James Marcia (1966, 1980) analyzed Erikson's theory of identity development and concluded that four identity statuses, or modes of resolution, appear in the theory: identity diffusion, identity foreclosure, identity moratorium, and identity achievement. The extent of an adolescent's commitment and crisis is used to classify the individual according to one of the four identity statuses. **Crisis** is defined as a period during which the adolescent is choosing among meaningful alternatives. Most researchers now use the term *exploration* rather than *crisis,* although in the spirit of Marcia's original formulation, we will use *crisis.* **Commitment** is defined as the extent to which the adolescent shows a personal investment in what she is going to do.

In **identity diffusion,** adolescents have not yet experienced a crisis (that is, they have not explored meaningful alternatives) or made any commitments. Not only are they undecided about occupational or ideological choices, they also are likely to show little interest in such matters. In **identity foreclosure,** adolescents have made

The American Indian's Quest for Identity

The Hopi Indians are a quiet, thoughtful people who go to great lengths not to offend anyone. In a pueblo north of Albuquerque, a 12-year-old boy speaks: "I've been living in Albuquerque for a year. The Anglos I've met, they're different. I don't know why. In school, I drew a picture of my father's horse. One of the other kids wouldn't believe that it was ours. He said, 'You don't really own that horse.' I said, 'It's a horse my father rides, and I feed it every morning.' He said, 'How come?' I said, 'My uncle and my father are good riders, and I'm pretty good.' He said, 'I can ride a horse better than you, and I'd rather be a pilot.' I told him I never thought of being a pilot."

The 12-year-old Indian boy continues, "Anglo kids, they won't let you get away with anything. Tell them something, and fast as lightning and loud as thunder, they'll say, 'I'm better than you, so there!' My father says it's always been like that."

The Indian adolescent is not really angry or envious of the white adolescent. Maybe he is in awe of his future power, maybe he fears it. And the white adolescent can't keep from wondering somehow, in some way, that he has missed out on something, and may end up "losing" (Coles, 1986). ◆

The American Indian adolescent's quest for identity involves a cultural meshing of tribal customs and the technological, educational demands of modern society.

TABLE 16.1 *The Four Statuses of Identity*

Position on Occupation and Ideology	Identity Status			
	Identity Moratorium	**Identity Foreclosure**	**Identity Diffusion**	**Identity Achievement**
Crisis	Present	Absent	Absent	Present
Commitment	Absent	Present	Absent	Present

a commitment but have not experienced a crisis. This occurs most often when parents simply hand down commitments to their adolescents, more often than not in an authoritarian way. In these circumstances, adolescents have not had adequate opportunities to explore different approaches, ideologies, and vocations on their own. In **identity moratorium,** adolescents are in the midst of a crisis, but their commitments either are absent or are only vaguely defined. These adolescents are searching for commitments by actively questioning alternatives. In **identity achievement,** adolescents have undergone a crisis and have made a commitment. Marcia's four statuses of identity are summarized in Table 16.1.

Family Influences on Identity

Parents are important figures in the adolescent's development of identity. Catherine Cooper and Harold Grotevant (1989; Grotevant & Cooper, 1985) believe both connectedness to parents and the presence of a family atmosphere promote individuation in the adolescent's identity development. **Connectedness** is reflected in mutuality and permeability. *Mutuality* refers to the adolescent's sensitivity to and respect for others' views. *Permeability* refers to openness and responsiveness to others' views. Mutuality provides adolescents with support, acknowledgment, and respect for their own beliefs; permeability lets the adolescent sense how to manage the boundaries between the self and others. **Individuation** has two main components: separateness and self-assertion. *Separateness* is seen in the expressions of how distinctive the self is from others. *Self-assertion* is involved in the adolescent's expression of her personal point of view and in taking responsibility for communicating this clearly. Parents who have both a connectedness with their adolescents and who promote individuation encourage the adolescent's development of identity. With identity, as with social competence, we see the importance of thinking about both an individual orientation and a social or relationship orientation (Allen & Hauser, 1989; Powers, Hauser, & Kilner, 1989).

Some Contemporary Thoughts About Identity

Contemporary views of identity development suggest several important considerations. First, identity development is a lengthy process—in many instances a more gradual, less cataclysmic transition than Erikson's term *crisis* implies. Second, identity development is extraordinarily complex (Marcia, 1980, 1987). Identity formation neither begins nor ends with adolescence. It begins with the appearance of attachment, the development of a sense of self, and the emergence of independence in infancy and reaches its final phase with a life review and integration in old age.

Reprinted with special permission of King Features Syndicate, Inc.

What is important about identity in adolescence, especially late adolescence, is that for the first time physical development, cognitive development, and social development advance to the point at which the individual can sort through and synthesize childhood identities and identifications to construct a viable pathway toward adult maturity. Resolution of the identity issue at adolescence does not mean identity will be stable through the remainder of one's life. A person who develops a healthy identity is flexible, adaptive, and open to changes in society, in relationships, and in careers. This openness assures numerous reorganizations of identity features throughout the identity-achieved person's life.

Identity formation does not happen neatly, and it usually does not happen cataclysmically. At the bare minimum, it involves commitment to a vocational direction, an ideological stance, and a sexual orientation. Synthesizing the identity components can be a long, drawn-out process with many negations and affirmations of various roles and faces. Identities are developed in bits and pieces. Decisions are not made once and for all, but have to be made again and again. And the decisions may seem trivial at the time: whom to date, whether or not to break up, whether or not to have intercourse, whether or not to take drugs, whether to go to college or finish high school and get a job, which major to choose, whether to study or whether to play, whether or not to be politically active, and so on. Over the years of adolescence, the decisions begin to form a core of what the individual is all about as a person—what is called identity (Archer, 1989; Papini & others, 1989).

Culture

Think about the community you grew up in. What was it like? Was it rural or urban? Were the schools traditional or progressive? What kind of community organizations for youth existed? How much did the townspeople support the school and its athletic teams? What values were emphasized in the community? Were community leaders oriented toward a conservative or a liberal political philosophy? What kinds of goals were promoted for adolescents? Was going to college standard, or was the orientation toward finishing high school and then taking a job? Did most people have two cars, take expensive vacations, and send their youth off to summer camps? By thinking about and responding to questions such as these, you can get a feel for what the cultural world of the adolescent is like. Ideas about the nature of adolescents and orientation toward adolescents may vary from culture to culture and within the

Music is a prominent feature of most adolescent's worlds. Listening to music on the radio and on tapes, and watching music videos on television, are common everyday occurrences in most adolescents' lives.

same culture over different time periods (Valsiner, 1988; Whiting, 1989). For example, there are cultures that have more permissive attitudes toward adolescent sexuality than the American culture (the Mangaian culture in the South Sea islands, for example), and there are cultures that have more conservative attitudes toward adolescent sexuality than the American culture (the Ines Beag culture off the coast of Ireland, for example). Over the course of the twentieth century, attitudes toward sexuality—especially for females—have become more permissive in the American culture. How can we define something as broad as *culture*? One definition is "A broad concept referring to the behavior patterns, beliefs, values, and other products of humans that are learned and shared by a particular group of people and passed on from one generation to the next." Our further coverage of culture will focus on the media and musical interests of adolescents, poverty, ethnicity, and rites of passage.

Media and Music

Anyone who has been around adolescents very long knows that many of them spend huge chunks of time listening to music on the radio, playing records or tapes of their favorite music, or watching music videos on television. Approximately two-thirds of all records and tapes are purchased by the 10-to-24 age group. And one-third of the nation's 8,200 radio stations aim their broadcast rock music at the pool of adolescent listeners.

The music adolescents enjoy on records, tapes, radio, and television is an important dimension of their culture. Rock music does not seem to be a passing fad; it has now been around for more than 35 years. Recently it has had its share of controversy. Starting in 1983, MTV (the first music video television channel) and music videos in general were targets of debate in the media. About a year later, rock music's lyrics were attacked by the Parents Music Resource Center (PMRC). This group charged in a congressional hearing that rock music lyrics were dangerously shaping the minds of adolescents in the areas of sexual morality, violence, drugs, and satanism. The national Parent Teacher Association agreed. And recently Tipper Gore (1987), a PMRC founder, voiced her views about the dangers of rock music lyrics in a book.

How pervasively does rock music affect adolescents? In one investigation, a group of young people waiting in line to attend a punk rock concert by the group *Dead Kennedys* were interviewed (Rosenthal, 1985). More than 90 percent agreed with the rebellious sentiments expressed in the *Dead Kennedys'* songs, clearly higher than the percentage in the population as a whole. However, direction of influence cannot be assessed in this case. That is, young people with particular views are attracted to a particular kind of music such as punk. At the same time, it may be these young people, in particular, who pay attention to, comprehend, and are vulnerable to the lyrics' influence.

Motivation, experience, and knowledge are factors involved in the interpretation of lyrics. In one investigation, preadolescents and adolescents often missed sexual themes in lyrics (Prinsky & Rosenbaum, 1987). Adult organizations such as the PMRC interpret rock music lyrics in terms of sex, violence, drugs, and satanism more than adolescents themselves do. In this investigation, it was found that in contrast to these adult groups, adolescents interpreted their favorite songs in terms of love, friendship, growing up, life's struggles, having fun, cars, religion, and other topics in teenage life.

Other recent research has focused on the medium of music video in comparison with other presentations of music (Greenfield & others, 1987). Music videos generate less imaginative responses by adolescents than do audio songs (Greenfield & Beagles-Roos, in press). It also has been found, as some rock singers have complained, that music videos detract attention away from a song's lyrics (Beagles-Roos & Gat, 1983; Greenfield & Beagles-Roos, in press).

Poverty

Of special concern to psychologists and educators who work with adolescents is the subculture of the poor—those adolescents from the lower strata of working-class families. Although the most noticeable aspect of the poor is their economic poverty, other psychological and social characteristics are present as well. First, the poor are often powerless. In occupations, they rarely are the decision makers. Rules are handed down to them in an authoritarian way. Second, the poor are vulnerable to disaster. They are not likely to be given advance notice when they are laid off from work and usually do not have financial resources to fall back on when problems arise. Third, their range of alternatives is restricted; a limited range of jobs is open to them. Even when alternatives are available, they may not know about them or be prepared to make a wise decision because of inadequate education and an inability to read well. Fourth, there is less prestige in being poor. This lack of prestige is transmitted to children early in life. The poor child observes other children who wear nicer clothes and live in more attractive houses.

Currently, one in four children and one in five adolescents is living in poverty. The poverty rate for youth in single-parent, female-headed households is much higher (54%) than for youth in other families (12.5%) (U.S. Bureau of the Census, 1986). In the words of Marian Wright Edelman (1987), president of the Children's Defense Fund:

> The America of the 1980s presents a cruel paradox: While the rich are getting richer and often getting more government help, the poor are getting poorer and receiving less help. The decline in federal assistance for children has made living in poverty a harsher existence for 13 million children, and it has crippled the efforts of families to struggle back up out of poverty (p. 40).

Any society that aspires to be great cannot continue to slash billions of dollars from essential programs for adolescents and their families while poverty rises and nearly half of minority adolescents are unemployed and seeking work. We owe all adolescents, both rich *and* poor, the best we have to give (Conger, 1988; Schorr, 1989).

Ethnicity

One social identity we become acutely aware of during adolescence is our ethnic identity (Phinney, 1989). **Ethnicity** refers to membership in a particular ethnic group. Each of you is a member of one or more ethnic groups, and so is every adolescent. Membership in an ethnic group is based on racial, religious, national, and ancestral background. As shown in Table 16.2, adolescents in the United States are members of many different ethnic backgrounds. Notice that black and Hispanic adolescents make up the largest portion of minority-group adolescents in the United States. Overall, the percentage of ethnic minority-group adolescents has increased in recent decades. In 1970, 11.8 percent of adolescents were black. By 1980, the figure had reached 13.7 percent. In 1970, 4.7 percent of adolescents were of Hispanic origin. By 1980, 7.5 percent were of Hispanic origin. In 1970, 87 percent of adolescents were Caucasian. By 1980, that figure decreased to 76.5 percent. Let's look more closely at adolescents from ethnic-minority backgrounds.

Black Adolescents

Black adolescents make up the largest easily visible ethnic-minority group. Black adolescents are distributed throughout the social class structure, although they comprise a larger portion of poor and lower-class individuals than does the majority white group (McLloyd, 1989). No cultural characteristic is common to all or nearly all blacks and absent in whites, unless it is the experience of being black and the ideology that develops from that experience (Gibbs, 1989; Havighurst, 1987).

The majority of black youth stay in school, do not take drugs, do not get married prematurely and become parents, are employed and eager to work, are not involved in crime, and grow up to lead productive lives in spite of social and economic disadvantage. While much of the writing and research about black adolescents has focused on low-income youth from families mainly residing in inner cities, the majority of black youth do not reside in the ghettos of inner cities. At the heart of the new model of studying black youth is recognition of the growing diversity within black communities in the United States (Bell-Scott & Taylor, 1989).

While prejudice against blacks in some occupations still persists, the proportion of males and females in middle-class occupations has been increasing since 1940. A substantial and increasing proportion of black adolescents are growing up in middle-class families and share middle-class values and attitudes with white, middle-class adolescents. Nonetheless, society's economic structure has changed so that a large underclass of black adolescents now lives in poverty enshrouded ghettos (Heath, 1989; Wilson, 1989). Thus, two contrasting black subcultures have emerged, one middle class and one characteristic of individuals below working class, which is sometimes referred to as *underclass*. In the words of Julius Wilson (1978):

> A history of discrimination and oppression created a huge black underclass, and the recent technological and economic revolutions have combined to insure it a permanent status. As the black middle class rides on the wave of political and social changes, benefitting from the growth of employment opportunities in the growing corporate and government sectors of the economy, the black underclass falls behind the larger society in every conceivable respect (p. 21).

TABLE 16.2 *Percentage of Adolescents Aged 10–19 from Different Ethnic Backgrounds*

Ethnic Group	Percentage Adolescent Population
Caucasian	
Age 10–19	76.5
Age 10–14	35.2
Age 15–19	41.3
Black	
Age 10–19	13.7
Age 10–14	6.5
Age 15–19	7.2
Hispanic origin	
Age 10–19	7.5
Age 10–14	3.6
Age 15–19	3.9
Asian and Pacific islander	
Age 10–19	1.5
Age 10–14	.7
Age 15–19	.8
American Indian, Eskimo, and Aleut	
Age 10–19	.8
Age 10–14	.4
Age 15–19	.4

Source: United States Bureau of the Census, 1980, *Detailed Population Characteristics of the United States,* Table 253.

The black middle-class subculture graduates from high school and enrolls in college to almost the degree white youth do. The concerns of many middle-class black youth reflect the theme that blacks must continue to fight against racial discrimination. Some of these youth may favor "black studies" programs that have developed in secondary and college curricula. A number of black youth look to their African heritage to develop a sense of racial and cultural identity. Erik Erikson (1968) believes, though, that this positive sense of identity needs to be integrated into the larger culture in which black adolescents participate, a culture dominated by nonblack elements. Erikson believes that for young blacks to achieve a positive, healthy integration into American culture, they should avoid antisocial, angry protests and work toward vocational competence and moral commitment. In this way, black adolescents can earn their rightful place in American society while maintaining their cultural and racial identity. These ideas of Erikson apply to virtually any ethnic minority group, not just blacks.

In the 1960s, black adolescents were described as having a more negative self-concept than white adolescents had (Coopersmith, 1967). However, more recent investigations find this not to be true, and in some instances black adolescents perceive themselves more positively than white adolescents (Iheanacho, 1987; Simmons & others, 1978).

The black middle-class graduates from high school and enrolls in college to almost the degree that white youth do.

The Hispanic adolescent girl, shown here in a California junior high school art class, is a member of the fastest growing ethnic group in America.

Hispanic Adolescents

The number of Hispanics in the United States has increased 30 percent since 1980 to 19 million (Lacayo, 1988). They now account for almost 8 percent of the United States population. Most trace their roots to Mexico (63%), Puerto Rico (12%), and Cuba (5%), the rest to Central and South American countries and the Caribbean (Laosa, 1989). By the year 2000 their numbers are expected to swell to 30 million, 15 percent of the U.S. population. Roughly one-third of all Hispanics in the United States marry non-Hispanics, promising the day when the two cultures will be more intertwined.

By far the largest group of Hispanic adolescents are those who identify themselves as having a Mexican origin, although many of them were born in the United States (Ramirez, 1989). Their largest concentration is in the Southwest. They represent more than 50 percent of the student population in the schools of San Antonio and close to that percentage in the schools of Los Angeles. Mexican-Americans have a variety of life-styles and come from a range of socioeconomic statuses—from affluent professional and managerial to migrant farm worker and welfare recipient in big-city barrios. The life of one Mexican-American adolescent, described in Children 16.2, vividly portrays the ethnic minority-group adolescent's dreams and struggles. While coming from families with diverse backgrounds, Hispanic adolescents have one of the lowest educational levels of any ethnic group in the United States.

The Dreams and Struggles of John David Gutierrez

John David Gutierrez lives in a comfortable house on a tree-lined street in Austin, Texas. His black hair, olive skin, and dark eyes reveal the Mexican heritage his grandparents brought to America. His American-born mother and father, fluent in Spanish and English, describe themselves as Mexican-Americans. John David, now 13 years old, speaks only English. He says that he is not sure who he is. "I guess I'm Tex-Mex," he says. "Or, I would be happy if you call me American," he quickly follows.

John David has achieved an identity through sports. He has quick reflexes, good speed, and a trim build. At 5'6" he is still growing. He plays basketball for a community team, baseball for another community team, and football for his school team. John David says, "I dream a lot. I want to become a pro baseball player. I try to do the best I can."

John David is still young enough to dream, but he has seen the dreams of his two older brothers fail. Abelardo, 24, and Xavier, 20, lost their way during adolescence. John David says that they had a chance but didn't hang tough enough. Abelardo was a good pitcher and had a chance to go to college, but he didn't. He feels he could have made it to the big leagues too. Xavier recently told John David not to mess up like he did. From his brothers, John David has learned how difficult it is to take on adult responsibilities. He reflects, "I don't want to have a family at an early age like my brother has now. Not that soon."

John David also has a different perspective than his parents. They were kept out of the Anglo world as children and adolescents. John David has not grown up as an outsider. His grandparents were poor and powerless, but they had the rich hope that America would be better for their children and their grandchildren. That wish came true. The Gutierrez family has the comforts of a middle-class life, but the parents still worry about the hurdles John David must still clear, temptations he needs to resist: the prevalence of drugs and alcohol, the growing problem of early sex. His parents hope that the family security they have provided will give him the strength to resist the intense pressures he faces in his effort to reach his dreams (Ludtke, 1988). ◆

Thirteen-year-old John David Gutierrez, shown here playing baseball for his community team in Austin, Texas, struggles to find his identity and dreams of becoming a professional baseball player.

Many Hispanic adolescents have developed a new political consciousness and pride in their cultural heritage. Some have fused strong cultural links to Mexican and Indian cultures with the economic limitations and restricted opportunities in the barrio. The politically conscious Mexican-American adolescents call themselves **Chicanos,** individuals who are a product of Spanish-Mexican-Indian heritage and Anglo influences.

Chinese-American and Japanese-American adolescents can be found in virtually every large American city. Both groups have been very successful in schools.

Asian-American Adolescents

Asian-American adolescents also are a fast-growing segment of the adolescent population. They too show considerable diversity. In the 1970 census, only three Asian-American groups were prominent: Japanese, Chinese, and Philippino. But in the last two decades, rapid growth has occurred in three other groups: Koreans, Pacific Islanders (Guam and Samoa), and Vietnamese (Huang, 1989).

Adolescents of Japanese or Chinese origin can be found in nearly every large city. While their grasp of the English language is usually good, they have been raised in a subculture in which family loyalty and family influence are powerful. This has tended to maintain their separate subcultures. The Japanese-American adolescents are somewhat more integrated into the Anglo life-style than are the Chinese-American adolescents. However, both groups have been very successful in school. They tend to take considerable advantage of educational opportunities.

A Choctaw Indian girl in Philadelphia, Mississippi. Native American adolescents cope with retaining an identity to their Indian cultural heritage and with developing an identity in the contemporary American culture.

Native American Adolescents

Approximately 100,000 American Indian and Eskimo adolescents are scattered in 30 or more tribal groups in about 20 states. About 90 percent are enrolled in schools. About 15,000 are in boarding schools, many of which are maintained by the federal government's Bureau of Indian Affairs. Another 45,000 are in public schools on or near Indian reservations. In these schools, the Native American adolescents make up more than 50 percent of the students. The remaining 30,000 are in public schools where they are an ethnic minority. A growing proportion of Native American adolescents have moved to large cities (Havighurst, 1987).

The Native American (American Indian) adolescents have experienced an inordinate amount of discrimination (Locust, 1988). While virtually any minority group experiences some discrimination in being a member of a larger, majority-group culture, in the early years of our country Native Americans were the victims of terrible physical abuse and punishment. Injustices that these 800,000 individuals have experienced are reflected in the lowest standard of living of any ethnic group, the highest teenage pregnancy rate, the highest suicide rate, and the highest school dropout rate of any ethnic group (LaFromboise & Low, 1989).

American: A Nation of Blended Cultures

America has been a great receiver of ethnic groups and continues to be a great receiver of ethnic groups. From many cultures, it has embraced new ingredients. The cultures often collide and commingle, mixing their ideologies and identities. Some of the culture of origin is retained, some of it is lost, some of it is mixed with the American culture. One after another, immigrants have come to America and been exposed to new channels of awareness and exposed Americans to new channels of awareness. Black, Hispanic, Asian-American, Native American, and other cultural heritages mix with the mainstream, receiving a new content, giving a new content (Gibbs & Huang, 1989).

Rivers flow.
The sea sings.
Oceans roar.
Tides rise.
Who am I?
A small pebble
on a giant shore;
who am I
to ask who I am?
Isn't it enough to be?

American Indian

Canada

Adolescents in Canada are exposed to some cultural dimensions similar to those of their counterparts in the United States. Canada has long been economically and culturally tied to the United States. For example, Canadian adolescents are inundated with American mass media: popular magazines, radio, and television. However, the cultural worlds of Canadian adolescents differ in certain ways from the cultural worlds of United States adolescents. In 1971, Canada was officially redefined by the federal government as bilingual (English/French), yet multicultural. Primarily French-speaking individuals reside mainly in Quebec, primarily English-speaking individuals in the other Canadian provinces. While officially Canada is a bilingual nation, it is predominantly the French Canadians who are bilingual. Canada's main ethnic ties are British and French, yet a number of ethnic minorities live in Canada: German (6%), Italian (3%), Ukranian (3%), Scandinavian (2%), Dutch (2%), Indian and Eskimo (1%), and Jewish (1%), for example. While Canada has become more of a multicultural mosaic, it does not approach the ethnic melting pot of the United States culture (Anderson & Frideres, 1981).   ♦

To describe the way cultures mix, two concepts have been developed. **Acculturation** occurs when members of different cultures interact and the process produces changes in one or both of the cultures. While each culture may retain its "personality," both cultures change through reformulation of the cultures' elements. **Assimilation** (the term has another meaning in Piaget's theory) occurs when the members of one culture become completely absorbed into a more dominant culture. Assimilation has been common in the "melting pot" of American society for many years. More recently, though, many minority cultures have sought to maintain their own identities and standards, yielding an increasing amount of acculturation.

Rites of Passage

Some societies have elaborate ceremonies that signal the adolescent's move to maturity and achievement of adult status. A ceremony or ritual that marks an individual's transition from one status to another, especially into adulthood, is called a **rite of passage.** In many primitive cultures, rites of passage are the avenue through which adolescents gain access to sacred adult practices, to knowledge, and to sexuality (Sommer, 1978). These rites often involve dramatic practices intended to facilitate the adolescent's separation from the immediate family, especially the mother. The transformation usually is characterized by some form of ritual death and rebirth, or by means of contact with the spiritual world. Bonds are forged between the adolescent and the adult instructors through shared rituals, hazards, and secrets to allow the adolescent to enter the adult world. This kind of ritual provides a forceful and discontinuous entry into the adult world at a time when the adolescent is perceived to be ready for the change.

In Kenya, Africa, the Turkana tribe is shown running as they begin an initiation ceremony in which the adolescent goes through a rite of passage to adult status.

Africa has been the location of many rites of passage for adolescents, especially Sub-Saharan Africa. Under the influence of Western culture, many of the rites are disappearing today, although some vestiges remain. In locations where formal education is not readily available, rites of passage are still prevalent.

Do we have such rites of passage for American adolescents? We certainly do not have universal formal ceremonies that mark the passage from adolescence to adulthood. Certain religious and social groups do go through initiation ceremonies that indicate an advance in maturity has been reached—the Jewish Bar Mitzvah, the Catholic Confirmation, and social debuts, for example. School graduation ceremonies come the closest to being rites of passages in today's world. The high school graduation ceremony is especially noteworthy, becoming nearly universal for middle-class adolescents and increasing numbers of adolescents from low-income families (Fasick, 1988). Nonetheless, high school graduation does not result in universal changes; many high school graduates continue to live with their parents, continue to be economically dependent on them, and continue to be undecided about career and life-style directions.

Josh Maisel's Bar Mitzvah

Aunts, uncles, and cousins from many places came to celebrate Josh Maisel's Bar Mitzvah. That morning Josh entered Beth Israel Congregation in Waterville, Maine, as a child. He emerged, in the eyes of his faith, a man. Serious duties will replace the weightlessness of his younger years. As a child, Josh had listened to the Scripture and learned. As an adult, Josh is allowed to read from the Torah so that he can pass on his family's faith to a new generation.

Childhood has not been an easy path for Josh. He will never forget the night almost 9 years ago when his parents told him they were going to get a divorce. When asked about his greatest worry as a child, Josh replies, "War. It is scary to think what would happen." But at the mention of his parents' divorce, Josh adds, "Now that I think about it, war looks really small compared to that."

At times Josh imagines what it would be like to be an adult. "I will have to really look after myself and not have somebody looking over my shoulder to be sure I'm doing the right thing," he says. "And I'll have to teach my kids the things I've been taught." (Ludtke, 1988). ♦

Josh Maisel, shown here, recently completed his bar mitzvah, emerging in the eyes of his faith, a man.

Thinking Critically
Can you think of any rites of passage for adolescents other than those we have discussed? Does the lack of formal rites of passage for adolescents in the American culture make the development of adolescents' identity more difficult? Explain.

The absence of clear-cut rites of passage make the attainment of adult status ambiguous. Many individuals are unsure whether they have reached adult status or not. In Texas, the age for beginning employment is 15, but there are many younger adolescents and even children who are employed, especially Mexican immigrants. The age for driving is 16, but when emergency need is demonstrated, a driver's license can be obtained at 15. Even at age 16, some parents may not allow their son or daughter to obtain a driver's license, believing they are too young for this responsibility. The age for voting is 18; the age for drinking recently has been raised to 21. Exactly when adolescents become adults in America has not been clearly delineated as it has been in some primitive cultures, where rites of passage are universal in the culture.

Thus far, we have discussed a number of ideas about identity and culture. These ideas are summarized in Concept Table 16.2.

Identity and Culture

Concept	Processes and Related Ideas	Characteristics and Description
Identity	Erikson's theory	The most comprehensive and provocative view of identity development. Identity versus identity confusion is the fifth stage in Erikson's life-cycle theory. During adolescence, world views become important and the adolescent enters a psychological moratorium, a gap between childhood security and adult autonomy.
	The four statuses of identity	Marcia proposed that four statuses of identity exist, based on a combination of conflict and commitment: identity diffusion, identity foreclosure, identity moratorium, and identity achievement.
	Family influences	Both connectedness to parents and the presence of a family atmosphere that promotes individuation are related to the adolescent's identity development.
	Some contemporary thoughts about identity	Identity development is extraordinarily complex. It is done in bits and pieces. For the first time in development, during adolescence, individuals are physically, cognitively, and socially mature enough to synthesize their lives and pursue a viable path toward adult maturity.
Culture	Its nature	A broad concept referring to the behavior patterns, beliefs, values, and other products of humans that are learned and shared by a particular group of people and passed on from one generation to the next.
	Media and music	Adolescents are heavy consumers of records, tapes, and live rock music. Rock music's lyrics have been controversial. A number of factors influence the power of rock music over adolescent's thoughts and behavior. The degree of this power has not been determined. Music video is a compelling medium. It is attention grabbing and may produce less imaginative responses than audio versions of songs. Rock music does not seem to be a passing fad, and it is an important dimension of the youth culture.
	Poverty	The subculture of the poor is characterized not only by economic poverty, but also by social and psychological handicaps. Currently, one in five adolescents grows up in poverty. Government assistance to the poor has been reduced.
	Ethnicity	Refers to membership in a particular ethnic group based on racial, religious, national, and ancestral background. Black and Hispanic adolescents make up the largest ethnic-minority groups in the United States. Other important ethnic minority groups include Asian-American and Native American adolescents. Black, Hispanic, Asian-American, and Native American adolescents mix with the mainstream, receiving a new content, giving a new content. Two concepts describing how cultures mix are acculturation and assimilation.
	Rites of passage	Ceremonies that mark an individual's transition from one status to another, especially into adulthood. In primitive cultures, rites of passage are often well defined. In contemporary America, rites of passage to adulthood are ill defined.

Summary

I. Autonomy and Attachment

Many parents have a difficult time handling the adolescent's push for autonomy, even though this push is one of the hallmarks of adolescent development. Adolescents do not simply move into a peer world isolated from parents. Attachment to parents increases the likelihood the adolescent will be socially competent and explore a widening social world in healthy ways.

II. Parent-Adolescent Conflict and the Maturation of the Adolescent and Parents

Conflict with parents usually does increase in early adolescence. This conflict often is of the moderate variety. The increase in conflict probably serves a positive developmental function of promoting autonomy and identity. Physical, cognitive, and social changes in the adolescent's development influence parent-adolescent relationships. Parental changes—marital dissatisfaction, economic burdens, career reevaluation and time perspective, and health and body concerns—also influence parent-adolescent relationships.

III. Peer Pressure and Conformity, Cliques and Crowds

The pressure to conform to peers is strong in adolescence, especially during the eighth and ninth grades. There usually are three to six well-defined cliques in every secondary school. Membership in certain cliques—especially jocks and populars—is associated with increased self-esteem. Independents also show high self-esteem.

IV. Children and Adolescent Groups, and Dating

Children groups are less formal, less heterogeneous, and less heterosexual than adolescent groups. Dunphy found that the development of adolescent groups moves through five stages. Dating can be a form of recreation, a source of status and achievement, and a setting for learning about close relationships. Most adolescents are involved in dating. It appears that adolescent females are more interested in intimacy and personality exploration than adolescent males are.

V. Erikson's Theory and the Four Statuses of Identity

Erikson's theory is the most comprehensive and provocative view of identity development. Identity versus identity confusion is the fifth stage in Erikson's life-cycle theory. During adolescence, world views become important, and the adolescent enters a psychological moratorium, a gap between childhood security and adult autonomy. Marcia proposed that four statuses of identity exist, based on a combination of conflict and commitment: identity diffusion, identity foreclosure, identity moratorium, and identity achievement.

VI. Family Influences and Contemporary Thoughts About Identity

Both connectedness to parents and the presence of a family atmosphere that promotes individuation are related to the adolescent's development. Identity development is extraordinarily complex. It is done in bits and pieces. For the first time in development, during adolescence, individuals are physically, cognitively, and socially mature enough to synthesize their lives and pursue a viable path toward adult maturity.

VII. The Nature of Culture, and Media and Music

Culture is a broad concept referring to the behavior patterns, beliefs, values, and other products of human beings that are learned and shared by a particular group of people and passed on from one generation to the next. Music, especially rock music, is a prominent feature of adolescent culture. Adolescents are heavy consumers of records, tapes, and live rock music. Rock music's lyrics have been controversial. A number of factors influence the power of rock music over adolescents' thoughts and behavior. The degree of this power has not yet been determined. Music video is a compelling medium. It is attention grabbing and may produce less imaginative responses than audio versions of songs. Rock music does not seem to be a passing fad, and it is an important dimension of the youth culture.

VIII. **Poverty and Ethnicity**

The subculture of the poor is characterized not only by economic poverty, but also by social and psychological handicaps. Currently, one in five adolescents grows up in poverty. Government assistance to the poor has been reduced. Ethnicity refers to membership in a particular ethnic group based on racial, religious, national, and ancestral background. Black and Hispanic adolescents make up the largest ethnic minority groups in the United States. Other important ethnic minority groups include Asian-American and Native American adolescents. Black, Hispanic, Asian-American, and Native American adolescents mix with the mainstream, receiving a new content, giving a new content. Two concepts describing how cultures mix are acculturation and assimilation.

IX. **Rites of Passage**

Rites of passage are ceremonies that mark an individual's transition from one status to another, especially into adulthood. In primitive cultures, rites of passage are often well defined. In contemporary America, rites of passage to adulthood are ill-defined.

Key Terms

crowd 537	identity foreclosure 542	ethnicity 548
cliques 537	identity moratorium 544	Chicanos 551
crisis 542	identity achievement 544	acculturation 554
commitment 542	connectedness 544	assimilation 554
identity diffusion 542	individuation 544	rites of passage 554

Suggested Readings

Berndt, T. J., & Ladd, G. W. (1989). *Peer relationships in child development*. New York: John Wiley.

Very up-to-date, authoritative information about the nature of peer relations in childhood and adolescence.

Erikson, E. H. (1969). *Gandhi's truth*. New York: Norton.

In this Pulitzer prize-winning novel, Erikson weaves an insightful picture of Gandhi's identity development.

Gibbs, J. T., & Huang, L. N. (Eds.). (1989). *Children of color*. San Francisco: Jossey-Bass.

An excellent collection of articles about the cultural and ethnic worlds of children and adolescents.

Journal of Early Adolescence, Spring, 1985 (Vol. 5, no. 1).

The entire issue is devoted to contemporary approaches to the study of families with adolescents.

Lapsley, D., & Power, F. C. (1988). *Self, ego, and identity*. New York: Springer.

A penetrating look at the nature of identity development.

Schorr, L. B. (1988). *Within our reach: Breaking the cycle of disadvantage and despair*. New York: Doubleday/Anchor.

A thought-provoking, extensive examination of poverty in America and the difficulties adolescents from low-income families face.

Epilogue

Children: The Future of Society

W e have arrived at the end of this book. I hope you can look back and say that you learned a lot about children, not only other children, but yourself as a child and how your childhood contributed to who you are today. The insightful words of philosopher Sören Kierkegaard capture the importance of looking back to understand ourselves: "Life is lived forward but understood backwards." I also hope that those of you who become the parents of children or who work with children in some capacity—whether as a teacher, counselor, or community leader—feel that you have a better grasp of what children's development is all about.

As the twenty-first century approaches, the well-being of children is one of America's foremost concerns. We all cherish the future of our children, because they are the future of any society. Children who do not reach their potential, who are destined to make fewer contributions to society than society needs, and who do not take their place as productive adults diminish the power of that society's future (Horowitz & O'Brien, 1989).

Future generations depend on our ability to face our children. At some point in our adult lives, each one of us needs to examine the shape of our life and ask whether we have met the responsibility of competently and caringly carving out a better world for our children. Twenty-one centuries ago, the Roman poet and philosopher Lucretius described one of adult life's richest meanings: grasping that the generations of living things pass in a short while, and like runners, pass on the torch of life. More than twenty centuries later, the American writer James Agee captured yet another of life's richest meanings: In every child who is born the potentiality of the human race is born again.

John W. Santrock

561

Glossary

ABC method A technique for learning to read that emphasizes memorization of the names of the letters of the alphabet. (p. 399)

accommodation Occurs when we have to adjust to new information; Piagetian concept. (p. 51)

acculturation When members of different cultures interact, and the process produces changes in one or both of the cultures. (p. 554)

adolescence The period of transition from childhood to early adulthood, entered at approximately 11 to 13 years of age and ending at age 18 to 22. This period is characterized by the onset of physical, cognitive, and social changes. (p. 19)

adolescent egocentrism A cognitive change in adolescence that consists of two main parts—the imaginary audience and the personal fable. (p. 496)

adolescent generalization gap The development of widespread generalizations based on information about a limited set of adolescents due to a weak research base. (p. 458)

adoption study A strategy of research used to assess the role of heredity in behavior by comparing an adopted child's similarity to his or her biological parents and to his or her adopted parents. (p. 90)

afterbirth The third birth stage; involves the detachment and expelling of the placenta, fetal membranes, and umbilical cord after delivery. (p. 119)

AIDS (acquired immune deficiency syndrome) A sexually transmitted disease caused by a virus that destroys the body's immune system; produces devastating results and ultimately death. (p. 472)

altruism An unselfish interest in helping someone else. (p. 334)

amniocentesis A procedure by which cells of the fetus are removed from the amniotic sac to test for the presence of certain chromosomal and metabolic disorders. (p. 87)

amnion A sort of bag or envelope that contains clear fluid in which the developing embryo floats. (p. 105)

anal stage Freud's second stage of development, lasting from about 1½ to 3 years of age; pleasure involves the anus. (p. 44)

androgen Sex hormones that are primarily involved in the development of male sex characteristics. (p. 327)

androgyny A term that describes the existence of masculine and feminine characteristics in both males and females. (p. 435)

animism The belief that inanimate objects have lifelike qualities and are capable of action. (p. 271)

anorexia nervosa An eating disorder that leads to self-starvation; occurs primarily in females. (p. 487)

anoxia Lack of sufficient oxygen to the brain, causing neurological damage or death. (p. 119)

Apgar Scale Method used to assess the health of a newborn one and five minutes after birth. Evaluates heart rate, respiratory effort, muscle tone, body color, and reflex irritability. (p. 124)

aptitude-treatment interaction (ATI) A field of educational research that determines the best learning conditions for a particular student's abilities and various teaching methods. (p. 428)

assimilation In culture, the process whereby a group gradually merges with another group, losing its separate identity. (p. 544)

assimilation Incorporation of new information into our existing knowledge; Piagetian concept. (p. 51)

associative play Social interaction with little or no organization. In this type of play, children seem to be more interested in associating with each other than in the tasks they are performing. (p. 316)

attachment A relationship between two persons in which they feel strongly about each other and try to ensure the continuation of the relationship. (p. 207)

attention-deficit disorder Sometimes called hyperactivity; children are characterized as being extremely active, impulsive, distractible, and excitable and have great difficulty concentrating on what they are doing. (p. 354)

authoritarian parenting A restrictive, cold punitive style of parenting with little verbal give-and-take between the parent and child; Baumrind's category associated with social incompetence on the part of children. (p. 301)

authoritative parenting Baumrind's style of parenting that encourages a child to be independent but still places limits and controls on the child's actions. Extensive verbal give and take occurs between parent and child. This style of parenting is associated with social competence among the children. (p. 302)

autonomous morality The second stage of moral development in Piaget's theory. The child becomes aware that rules and laws are created by people and that, in judging an action, one should consider the actor's intentions as well as the act's consequences. (p. 332)

autonomy versus shame and doubt Erikson's second stage of development, corresponding approximately to the second year of life; the bipolar conflict is between developing a sense of autonomy and a sense of doubt. (p. 46)

baby-talk register A characteristic way of talking to young language learners. (p. 190)

basal metabolism rate (BMR) The minimum amount of energy an individual uses in a resting state. (p. 253)

Bayley Scales of Infant Development Measure used in the assessment of infant development. The most current version has three components: a Mental scale, a Motor scale, and an Infant Behavior Profile. (p. 180)

behavior genetics The discipline concerned with the degree and nature of the heredity basis of behavior. (p. 90)

bimodal perception The ability to relate and integrate information about two sensory modalities, such as vision and hearing. (p. 160)

biological processes The influences of evolution, genetics, neurological development, and physical growth on development. (p. 17)

blastocyst The inner layer of blastula that later develop into the embryo. (p. 104)

blastula An early embryo form typically having the form of a hollow, fluid-filled, rounded cavity bounded by a single layer of cells. (p. 104)

bonding A close, personal relationship (as between mother and child), especially through frequent or constant association. (p. 126)

Brazelton Neonatal Behavioral Assessment Scale A test that detects an infant's neurological integrity; includes an evaluation of the infant's reaction to people along with the assessment of 20 reflexes and the infant's reaction to various circumstances. (p. 124)

Brazelton training Involves using the Brazelton scale to show parents how their newborn responds to people. Parents are shown how the neonate can respond positively to people and how such responses can be stimulated. Brazelton training has been shown to improve an infant's social skills. (p. 126)

breech position The baby's position in the uterus that would cause the buttocks to be the first part to emerge from the vagina. (p. 119)

bulimia A binge-and-purge syndrome that is marked by periods of very heavy eating followed by self-induced vomiting; occurs primarily in females. (p. 488)

canalization A term used to describe the narrow path or developmental course that certain characteristics take. (p. 90)

care perspective A focus on interpersonal communication and a connectedness with others; vastly underplayed in Kolhberg's theory, according to Carol Gilligan. (p. 443)

case study An in-depth look at a person that provides information that helps the psychologist understand the person. (p. 27)

centration The focusing of attention on one characteristic to the exclusion of all others. (p. 273)

cephalocaudal pattern A general pattern of physical growth that suggests that the greatest growth in anatomical differentiation occurs first in the head and later in the lower regions. (p. 144)

Chicanos Individuals who are a product of Spanish-Mexican-Indian heritage and Anglo influences. (p. 551)

child-centered kindergarten A form of education that encompasses all aspects—physical, cognitive, and social—of a child's development; instruction is centered on each child's needs, interests, and learning styles; and the process of learning is emphasized rather than the finished product. (p. 289)

chlamydia A sexually transmitted disease. The symptoms mimic gonorrhea and can infect the entire reproductive tract if left untreated. (p. 471)

chorionic villus test A procedure by which a small sample of the placenta is removed during the first trimester, between the ninth and tenth weeks; diagnosis usually takes two to three weeks. (p. 87)

chromosomes Threadlike structures in each human cell that come in structurally similar pairs (23 pairs in human beings). (p. 81)

cliques Peer groups that are smaller in size than a crowd, involve greater intimacy among members, and have more group cohesion. Members of a clique are attracted to one another on the basis of similar interests and social ideals. (p. 537)

cocaine A stimulant, taken in the form of either crystals or powder, which provides increased feelings of stamina, enhanced mental capacities, excitability, and occasionally hallucinations. (p. 479)

cognitive processes Mental activities, such as thought, perception, attention, problem solving, and language, that influence development. (p. 17)

cohort effects Effects that are due to a subject's time of birth or generation but not actually to his or her age. (p. 32)

commitment In identity formation, the extent to which the adolescent shows a personal investment in what she is going to do. (p. 542)

community rights versus individual rights Kohlberg's fifth stage of moral reasoning. The individual understands that values and laws are relative and that standards may vary from one individual to another. (p. 441)

concrete operational stage Piaget's stage that roughly corresponds to the 7-to-11-year period. The child can think operationally and can reason about anything he or she can perceive. The ability to classify objects improves dramatically during this period. (p. 52)

conditional positive regard Love and praise are not given without certain restrictions, such as conforming to parental rules or social standards; a Rogerian concept. (p. 62)

connectedness Reflected in mutuality and permeability. Mutuality refers to the adolescent's sensitivity to and respect for others' views. *Permeability* refers to openness and responsiveness to others' views. (p. 544)

conservation The idea that amount stays the same or is conserved, regardless of how shape changes. (p. 273)

constructivist view The belief that what one experiences is a cognitive process based on sensory input plus information retrieved from memory; a kind of representation of the world one builds up in one's mind. (p. 161)

continuity in development A gradual, cumulative change from conception to death. (p. 21)

control group The group in psychological experiments that is exposed to all experimental conditions except the independent variable; the comparison or baseline group. (p. 30)

control processes Learning and memory strategies that draw heavily on information-processing capacities and are under the learner's conscious control. (p. 380)

conventional reasoning At this level of morality, internalization is intermediate. The individual abides by certain standards, but they are the standards of others (external). Kohlberg's second and middle level of moral judgment. (p. 441)

convergent thinking Thinking that goes toward one correct answer, characteristic of the thinking that most intelligence tests elicit. (p. 397)

cooperative play Social interaction in a group with a sense of group identity and organized activity. (p. 316)

coordination of secondary reactions Develops between 8 and 12 months of age; the infant readily combines and recombines previously learned schemes in a coordinated way. (p. 171)

coregulation A gradual transfer of control from parent to child; a transition period between the strong parental control of the preschool years and the increased relinquishment of general supervision that occurs during adolescence. (p. 418)

correlation coefficient A measure of the degree of the relationship between two distributions (samples) that range from −1.00 to 1.00. A positive coefficient means that the distribution increases together; a negative coefficient means that as one increases, the other decreases; and a zero coefficient means that no correlation exists. (p. 29)

correlational strategy A research strategy in which the investigator observes whether and how two factors are associated but does not systematically change characteristics in the child's environment. From research using a correlational strategy, one cannot infer causal relationships. (p. 29)

creativity The ability to think about something in a novel way and to come up with unique solutions to problems. (p. 398)

crisis In identity formation, a period during which an adolescent is choosing among meaningful alternatives. (p. 542)

critical period A fixed time period very early in development during which certain behaviors optimally emerge. (p. 65)

cross-sectional approach A method used to study a large number of representative persons or variables at a given period in time; frequently employed in the establishment of normative data. (p. 31)

crowd The largest and least personal of peer group relationships. The members of the crowd meet because of their mutual interest in activities, not because of mutual attraction to each other. (p. 537)

cultural-familial retardation Persons who make up the majority of the mentally retarded population; they have no evidence of organic damage or brain dysfunction. (p. 395)

culture-fair tests Tests designed to reduce cultural bias in intelligence tests. (p. 390)

deep structure The syntactic relation of the words in a sentence. (p. 184)

defense mechanisms Means by which the ego resolves conflicts between its demands for reality and the id's wishes; defense mechanisms protect the ego and reduce conflict. (p. 42)

Denver Developmental Screening Test A widely used measure devised to diagnose developmental delay in children from birth through 6 years of age. (p. 247)

dependent variable The variable that is measured or recorded by the experimenter for changes that are presumed to be under the control of the independent or manipulated variable. (p. 30)

deprivation dwarfism A type of growth retardation caused by emotional deprivation; children are deprived of affection, which causes stress and alters the release of hormones by the pituitary gland. (p. 242)

design stage The stage, occurring rather quickly after the shape stage, when children mix two basic shapes into a more complex design. (p. 250)

development A pattern of change or movement that begins at conception and continues throughout the entire life span. (p. 17)

developmental quotient (DQ) An overall developmental score in such domains as motor, language, adaptive, and personal-social; used on the Gessell measure of development. (p. 180)

direct perception view The view that the infant is biologically equipped to pick up perceptual information from the environment. No cognitive construction of information is needed for perception to take place. (p. 161)

discontinuity in development Stresses distinct changes in the life span; emphasizes change. (p. 21)

dishabituation An infant's renewed interest in a stimulus. (p. 175)

displacement The characteristic of language that enables us to communicate information about another place and time. (p. 183)

divergent thinking Thinking that produces many different answers to the same question. Guilford believes that this form of thinking is closely related to creativity. (p. 397)

dizygotic A term that refers to fraternal twins who come from two different eggs and are therefore genetically more different than identical twins. (p. 90)

DNA (deoxyribonucleic acid) A complex molecule running along the length of each chromosome: forms the basis for genetic structure in humans beings. (p. 81)

dominant-recessive genes In the process of genetic transmission, a dominant gene is one that exerts its full characteristic effect regardless of its gene partner; a recessive gene is one whose code is masked by a dominant gene and is expressed only when paired with another recessive gene. (p. 86)

Down syndrome A disorder characterized by physical and mental retardation and a rather typical appearance. In the most common cases, individuals have 47 instead of 46 chromosomes, with 3 rather than 2 chromosomes in the twenty-first set. (p. 84)

early childhood Also called the preschool years. This period extends from the end of infancy to about 5 or 6 years of age, roughly corresponding to the period when the child prepares for formal schooling. (p. 19)

echoing Repeating what the child says to you, especially if it is an incomplete phrase or sentence. (p. 190)

echolalia Speech disorder associated with autistic children in which the children echo what they hear. (p. 230)

ectoderm The outermost layer of the embryo; becomes the nervous system, sensory receptors, and skin parts. (p. 105)

ego The executive branch of personality, according to Freud; the structure of personality that operates according to the demands and constraints of society; it includes our higher cognitive processes, such as reasoning and problem solving. (p. 41)

egocentrism Piaget's term for the preoperational child's inability to distinguish between his or her own and another's perspectives. (p. 267)

embryonic period A period lasting from about two to eight weeks after conception, during which the endoderm, mesoderm, and ectoderm develop and primitive human form takes shape. (p. 104)

empathy The ability to understand the feelings of another person; it is believed to be an important aspect of a child's altruism. (p. 334)

endoderm The inner layer of the embryo; develops into the digestive system, lungs, pancreas, and liver. (p. 105)

epigenetic principle Erikson's concept that anything that grows has a ground plan, out of which the parts arise, each having a special time of ascendency, until all of the parts have arisen to form a functioning whole. (p. 46)

erogenous zones Freud's concept that at each stage of development, pleasure is experienced in one part of the body more than in others. (p. 43)

estradiol Important hormone responsible for pubertal development in females; one hormone in a complex hormonal system associated with the physical changes of puberty in females. (p. 461)

estrogen Sex hormones that are primarily involved in the development of female sex characteristics. (p. 327)

ethnicity The condition of belonging to a particular ethnic group, membership being based on racial, religious, national, and ancestral background. (p. 548)

ethology The view that stresses that behavior is biologically determined. Special emphasis is given to the evolutionary basis of behavior and critical or sensitive periods. (p. 64)

eustress Selye's term for the positive features of stress. (p. 362)

exosystem Settings in which the child does not participate, although important decisions that affect the child's life are made in these settings. (p. 202)

expanding Restating what the child has said in a linguistically sophisticated form. (p. 190)

experimental group The group of subjects in an experiment; this group is exposed to the independent variable. (p. 29)

experimental strategy A research strategy in which the experimenter introduces a change into the child's environment and then measures the effects of that change on the child's subsequent behavior. The experimental strategy allows for the inference of causal relationships. (p. 29)

expressive orientation Describes the feminine dimension of gender roles; emphasis on expression of emotion in social relationships. (p. 437)

extrinsic motivation Motivation because of external factors in the environment, especially rewards. (p. 406)

father absence tradition Children from father-absent and father-present families are compared, and differences in their development are attributed to the absence of the father. (p. 308)

fetal alcohol syndrome (FAS) A cluster of characteristics identified in children born to mothers who are heavy drinkers. Children may show abnormal behavior, such as hyperactivity or seizures, and the majority of FAS children score below average on intelligence tests, with a number of them in the mentally retarded range. (p. 113)

fetal period The period of prenatal development that begins eight weeks after conception and lasts, on the average, for seven months. (p. 106)

fine motor skills Skills involving finer movements, such as finger dexterity. (p. 146)

first habits and primary circular reactions Develops between 1 and 4 months of age; the infant learns to coordinate sensation and types of schemes or structures. (p. 170)

fixation Occurs when an individual becomes stuck at a particular stage of development because his or her needs are under- or overgratified. (p. 44)

formal operational stage The stage that Piaget believed individuals enter between the ages of 11 and 15. Thought becomes more abstract, more logical, and more idealistic. (p. 52)

functional amblyopia Also called the "lazy eye"; usually results from not using one eye enough to avoid the discomfort of double vision produced by imbalanced eye muscles. (p. 243)

gametes The sex cells; the means by which genes are transmitted from parents to offspring. (p. 81)

gender roles Social expectations of how we should act, think, and feel as males and females. (p. 327)

gender schema A cognitive structure that organizes the world in terms of female and male. (p. 328)

general adaptation syndrome A concept proposed by Selye that explains how an individual's body responds to the demands placed on it by stress. Three stages are involved: the alarm reaction stage, the resistance stage, and the exhaustion stage. (p. 362)

generativity versus stagnation Erikson's seventh stage, corresponding approximately to middle adulthood. *Generativity* refers to helping the younger generation in developing and leading useful lives. Stagnation refers to the feeling of not having helped the younger generation. (p. 47)

genes Segments of chromosomes comprised of DNA. (p. 81)

genetic epistemology Refers to how knowledge changes over the course of child's development. (p. 16)

genital stage Freud's fifth stage of development, lasting from the onset of puberty through adulthood; a time of sexual reawakening. The source of pleasure now becomes someone outside the family. (p. 44)

genotype The unique combination of genes that forms the genetic structure of each person. (p. 88)

germinal period The period from conception until about 12 to 14 days later. (p. 104)

gifted A person with well-above-average intelligence, a superior talent for something, or both. (p. 396)

grammar Closely related to syntax. Refers to the formal description of syntactic rules. (p. 184)

grasping reflex An infantile response that occurs when something touches the infant's palm. The infant will grasp the object tightly. This reflex diminishes by the third month, when the infant grasps more voluntarily. (p. 139)

gross motor skills Skills involving large muscle activities, like moving one's arms or walking. (p. 146)

habituation Technique used to study an infant's perceptual world. Repeated presentation of the same stimulus causes a drop in the infant's interest. Similar to getting bored with a stimulus. (p. 175)

heritability A mathematical estimate of the degree to which a particular characteristic is genetically determined. (p. 90)

hermaphrodite A person with genitals that are intermediate between male and female. (p. 327)

herpes simplex II A sexually transmitted disease whose symptoms include irregular cycles of sores and blisters in the genital area. (p. 472)

heteronomous morality The first stage of moral development in Piaget's theory. Justice and rules are conceived of as unchangeable properties of the world, removed from the control of people. (p. 332)

holistic health A new approach to preventing illness and promoting health in which the psychological factors as well as the physical factors of a person are understood; it is a multidimensional and complex approach to the nature of illness and health. (p. 358)

holophrase hypothesis A single word used to imply a complete sentence. (p. 191)

hormones The secretion of endocrine glands; powerful chemical substances that regulate bodily organs. (p. 460)

humanistic theory Theory that stresses the importance of self-perceptions, inner experiences, self-determination, and self-confidence in explaining behavior. (p. 61)

hypothalamic-pituitary-gonadal axis Aspect of the endocrine system that is important in puberty and involves the interaction of the hypothalamus, the pituitary gland, and the sex glands. (p. 460)

hypotheses Assumptions that can be tested to determine their accuracy. (p. 24)

hypothetical deductive reasoning Reasoning that occurs for the first time during adolescence; the person develops hypotheses about ways to solve a problem and then deduces or concludes which is the best path to follow. Piaget's concept. (p. 495)

id A structure of personality in Freud's theory; the reservoir of psychic energy and instincts that perpetually press us to satisfy our basic needs. (p. 41)

identity achievement Period in which adolescents have undergone a crisis and have made a commitment. (p. 544)

identity diffusion Adolescents who have not experienced any crisis (explored any meaningful alternatives) or made any commitments. (p. 542)

identity foreclosure Adolescents who have made a commitment but have not experienced a crisis. (p. 542)

identity moratorium Adolescents in the midst of a crisis, but their commitments are either absent or only vaguely defined. (p. 544)

identity versus identity confusion Erikson's fifth stage, which corresponds approximately to adolescence. Adolescents seek to know who they are, what they are all about, and where they are headed in life. (p. 47)

imaginary audience The belief of adolescents that others are preoccupied with their behavior as they are. (p. 496)

immanent justice If a rule is broken, punishment will be meted out immediately; a Piagetian concept. (p. 332)

implantation The firm attachment of the zygote to the uterine wall, which occurs about 10 days after conception. (p. 104)

imprinting Lorenz's term for the rapid, innate learning within a critical period of time that involves attachment to the first moving object seen. (p. 65)

independent variable The factor in an experiment that is manipulated or controlled by the experimenter to determine its effect on the subject's behavior. (p. 30)

individualism and purpose Kohlberg's second stage of moral reasoning. Moral thinking is based on rewards and self-interest; children obey when they want to obey and when it is in their best interest to do so. (p. 441)

individuating-reflexive faith Stage in the development of religious beliefs proposed by Fowler, during which the late adolescent makes the transition from a conventional perspective on values to an individualized perspective. (p. 501)

individuation Comprised to two components—separateness and self-assertion. Separateness is seen in the expressions of how distinctive the self is from others. Self-assertion is involved in the adolescent's expression of her personal point of view and in taking responsibility for communicating this clearly. (p. 544)

industry versus inferiority Erikson's fourth stage, corresponding approximately to the elementary school years; children develop either a sense of industry and work or a feeling of inferiority. (p. 46)

infancy This period begins at birth and extends through the eighteenth to the twenty-fourth months: a time of extensive dependency on adults and development of abilities such as thought and language. (p. 19)

infantile amnesia Little or no memory of events experienced before 3 years of age. (p. 177)

infantile autism A very severe developmental disturbance that includes deficiencies in social relationships, abnormalities in communication, and restricted, repetitive, and stereotyped patterns of behavior. (p. 229)

infinite generativity A person's ability to generate an infinite number of meaningful sentences from a finite set of words and rules. (p. 183)

information-processing theory Theory of cognition that is concerned with the processing of information; involves such processes as attention, perception, memory, and problem solving. (p. 53)

initiative versus guilt Erikson's third stage, corresponding approximately to early childhood; children develop either a sense of initiative or a sense of guilt in this period. (p. 46)

innate goodness Eighteenth-century belief that children are basically good and should be permitted to grow naturally with little parental monitoring. (p. 14)

instrumental orientation Describes the masculine dimension of gender roles. It is concerned with the attainment of goals and an emphasis on the person's accomplishments. (p. 437)

integrity versus despair Erikson's final stage of development, corresponding to late adulthood; involves looking back and evaluating what we have accomplished in our lives. (p. 47)

intelligence Verbal ability, problem-solving skills, and the ability to learn from and adapt to the experiences of everyday life. (p. 384)

intelligence quotient (IQ) A term devised in 1912 by William Stern. IQ consists of a child's normal age, divided by chronological age, multiplied by 100. (p. 385)

internalization of schemes In Piaget's theory, this develops between 18 and 24 months; the infant's mental functioning shifts from a purely sensorimotor plane to a symbolic plane, and the infant develops the ability to use primitive symbols. (p. 173)

interpersonal norms Stage three of Kohlberg's moral reasoning. Moral judgments are based on trust, caring, and loyalty to others; children often adopt their parents' moral standards, seeking to be thought of as a "good girl" or a "good boy." (p. 441)

interviews A method of study in which the researcher asks questions of a person and records that person's responses. (p. 26)

intimacy Intimate self-disclosure and the sharing of private thoughts; private and personal knowledge. (p. 424)

intimacy versus isolation Erikson's sixth stage, corresponding approximately to early adulthood; the individual develops either a sense of intimacy or a sense of isolation. (p. 47)

intrinsic motivation An underlying need for competence and self-determination; internal motivation. (p. 406)

intuitive thought substage In Piaget's theory, stretches from approximately 4 to 7 years of age; the child begins to reason primitively and wants to know the answers to all sorts of questions. (p. 272)

in vitro fertilization A procedure in which the mother's ovum is removed surgically and fertilized in a laboratory medium with live sperm cells obtained from the father or male donor. Then the fertilized egg is stored in a laboratory solution that substitutes for the uterine environment and is finally implanted in the mother's uterus. (p. 83)

jigsaw classroom Aronson's technique emphasizing cooperation to improve ethnic interpersonal relations and learning in racially mixed classrooms. (p. 430)

justice perspective A focus on the rights of the individual when making moral decisions. People are seen as standing alone when making moral decisions. Proposed by Carol Gilligan, who argued that it characterizes Kohlberg's theory. (p. 443)

juvenile delinquent An adolescent who breaks the law or engages in conduct that is considered illegal. Heredity, identity problems, community influences, and family experiences have been proposed as causes. (p. 483)

Klinefelter's syndrome A genetic disease in which males have an extra X chromosome, making them XXY instead of XYY. (p. 86)

labeling Identifying objects by name. (p. 190)

laboratory A controlled setting in which many of the complex factors of the real world are removed. (p. 25)

Lamaze method A form of prepared or natural childbirth that allows the pregnant mother to cope with the pain of childbirth in an active way to avoid or reduce medication. (p. 116)

language A set of sequences of words that convey information. (p. 183)

language acquisition device (LAD) The natural ability to detect certain categories of language (phonological, syntactic, and semantic); emphasizes the biological basis of language. (p. 185)

latency stage Freud's fourth stage of development, corresponding approximately to the elementary school years; the child represses sexual urges and focuses on intellectual and social skills. (p. 44)

learning disabilities Within the global concept of learning disabilities fall problems in listening, thinking, memory, reading, writing, spelling, and math. Children with learning disabilities are of normal intelligence or above, they have difficulties in several academic areas but usually do not show deficits in others, and they are not suffering from some other condition or disorder that could explain their learning problems. (p. 354)

least restrictive environment A provision of Public Law 94–142, which requires that all states ensure that all handicapped students are educated with students who are not handicapped. (p. 352)

Leboyer method A birth procedure developed to make the birth experience less stressful for the infant; "birth without violence." (p. 116)

longitudinal approach A method of study in which the same subject or group of subjects is tested repeatedly over a significant period of time. (p. 32)

long-term memory The retention of information for an indefinite period of time. (p. 380)

low-birth-weight infants Infants born after a regular gestation period of 38 to 42 weeks, but who weigh less than 5½ pounds. (p. 120)

macrosystem The attitudes and ideologies of the culture. (p. 202)

mainstreaming Handicapped children attend regular school classes with nonhandicapped children; they enter the "mainstream" of education in the school and are not separated from the nonhandicapped students. (p. 352)

marasmus A wasting away of body tissues in the infant's first year of life; it is the result of a severe protein-calorie deficiency. The infant becomes grossly underweight and the muscles atrophy. (p. 153)

maturation The orderly sequence of changes dictated by the genetic blueprint each of us has. (p. 20)

MAX Maximally Discriminative Facial Movement Coding System; a measure devised by Izard to analyze facial reactions of infants to stimuli or circumstances. (p. 221)

mean length of utterance (MLU) Estimation of the number of words per sentence that a child produces in a sample of about 50 to 100 sentences. Is a good index of a child's language maturity. Proposed by Roger Brown. (p. 193)

meiosis The process by which gametes reproduce, which allows for the mixing of genetic material. (p. 81)

memory The retention of information over time. (p. 176)

menarche The first menstruation in pubertal females. (p. 459)

mental age (MA) An individual's level of mental development relative to that of others. (p. 385)

mental retardation Refers to a person who has a low IQ, usually below 70 on a traditional intelligence test, and who has difficulty adapting to everyday life. (p. 395)

mesoderm The middle layer of cell in the embryo; becomes the circulatory system, bones, muscle, excretory system, and reproductive system. (p. 105)

mesosystem Linkages between microsystems or connectedness between contexts—for example, relation of family experiences to school experiences. (p. 202)

metamemory Knowledge of one's own memory; includes knowledge of how to monitor memory during the course of learning. (p. 381)

metaphor An implied comparison between two ideas that is conveyed by the abstract meaning contained in the words used. (p. 495)

microsystem Contexts in which the child has face-to-face interactions with others who are influential in his or her life. (p. 201)

middle and late childhood This period extends from about 6 to 11 years of age and is sometimes called the elementary school years; a time when a sense of industry is developed. (p. 19)

monozygotic A term that refers to identical twins, meaning that they come from the same egg. (p. 90)

Montessori approach A philosophy of education in which children are given considerable freedom and spontaneity in choosing activities, and they move from one activity to another as they desire. The teacher acts as a facilitator rather than as a director of learning and allows the child to work independently to complete tasks in a prescribed manner; the teacher can offer assistance if asked by the child. (p. 266)

moral development The acquisition of rules and conventions about what people should do in their interactions with others. (p. 331)

Moro reflex An infantile startle response that is common to all neonates but disappears by about 3 to 4 months of age. When startled, the neonate arches its back, throws its head back, and flings out its arms and legs. The neonate then rapidly closes its arms and legs to the center of the body. (p. 139)

morphology The rules for combining morphemes. (p. 183)

myelination A process in which nerve cells are covered and insulated with a layer of fat cells; this increases the speed of information traveling through the nervous system. (p. 243)

n **achievement (need for achievement)** A term proposed by McClelland to explain the varying achievement motivation between individuals; the differences in achievement motivation can be measured. (p. 404)

naturalistic observation Research conducted in real-world or natural settings—for example, observing a child at home, in school, or on the playground. (p. 26)

nature-nurture controversy The "nature" proponents claim that biological and genetic factors are the most important determinants of development; the "nurture" proponents claim that environment and experiences are more important. (p. 21)

neglected children Children who receive little attention from their peers but who are not necessarily disliked by their peers even though they often do not have many friends. (p. 422)

nonnutritive sucking Sucking behavior by the child that is unrelated to the child's feeding. (p. 140)

normal distribution Also called the normal curve; a symmetrical distribution of scores on a graph, in which a majority of the cases fall in the middle range of possible scores and fewer scores appear toward the ends of this range. (p. 385)

object permanence Piaget's concept for the infant's ability to understand that objects and events still exist, even though the infant is not in direct contact with them. (p. 173)

Oedipus complex A condition that exists when a young child develops an intense desire to replace the parent of the same sex and enjoy the affections of the opposite-sex parent. (p. 44)

onlooker play The child watches other children playing. He or she may talk with them and ask questions but does not enter into their play behavior. (p. 316)

568   Glossary

operant conditioning A form of learning in which the consequences of behavior lead to changes in the probability of that behavior's occurrence; the form of learning stressed by Skinner. (p. 58)

operations Mental representations that are reversible; a Piagetian concept. (p. 267)

oral rehydration therapy (ORT) Type of treatment that involves techniques designed to prevent dehydration during episodes of diarrhea by giving the child fluids by mouth. (p. 254)

oral stage Freud's first stage of development, corresponding approximately to the first year of life; pleasure focuses on the mouth. (p. 44)

organic retardation Retardation caused by a genetic disorder or brain damage. (p. 395)

organogenesis The first two months of prenatal development when the organ systems are formed; may be adversely influenced by environmental events. (p. 106)

original sin In the Middle Ages, the catholic and Puritan concept of children reflecting the philosophical perspective that children are basically evil. (p. 14)

overextension The tendency of children to misuse words by extending one word's meaning to include a whole set of objects that are not related to or are inappropriate for the word's meaning. (p. 192)

overgeneralizations The extension of morphological rules to all words such that some of the rules are violated; for example, such as saying *foots* instead of *feet* or *goed* instead of *went*. (p. 280)

oxytocin A hormone that stimulates uterine contractions and is widely used to speed delivery. (p. 119)

parallel play Parten's term for play in which the child plays separately from others, but with toys like those the others are using or in a manner that mimics their play. (p. 316)

peers Refers to children who are about the same age or at the same behavioral level. (p. 311)

Perceived Competence Scale for Children Harter's measure that assesses general self-worth, as well as perceived competence in three skill domains: physical, cognitive, and social. (p. 433)

perception The interpretation of what is sensed. (p. 156)

permissive indifferent parenting A parenting style in which the parent is very uninvolved with the child; associated with social incompetence on the part of the child, especially a lack of self-control. (p. 302)

permissive indulgent parenting A parenting style in which parents are involved with their children but place few demands or limits on them; associated with a lack of self-control on the part of children. (p. 302)

personal fable A story or fable that the adolescent may make up to protect his or her sense of uniqueness and indestructibility. Part of adolescent egocentrism. (p. 496)

phallic stage Freud's third stage, corresponding to the preschool years; pleasure focuses on the genitals. (p. 44)

phenomenological theory Theory that stresses the importance of people's perceptions of themselves and their world in understanding their development. (p. 61)

phenotype The observed and measurable characteristics of persons, including physical characteristics, such as height, weight, eye color, and skin pigmentation, and psychological characteristics, such as intelligence, creativity, personality, and social tendencies. (p. 89)

phonics method A technique for learning to read that stresses the sounds that letters have when in words. Such sounds can differ from the names of these letters. (p. 399)

phonology The study of the sound system of language. (p. 183)

pictorial stage Stage in which children's drawings begin to look like objects that adults can recognize; usually occurs between the ages of 4 and 5. (p. 250)

PKU syndrome (phenylketonuria) A disorder, caused by a recessive gene, that leads to the absence of an enzyme necessary to convert phenylalanine into tyrosine. This leads to an accumulation of phenylpyruvic acid, which has a damaging effect on the nervous system of a child. (p. 84)

placement stage Stage in which earliest drawings of children are drawn in placement patterns and not at random on a page. (p. 250)

placenta A disk-shaped group of tissues in which small blood cells from the mother and the offspring intertwine but do not join. (p. 105)

play therapy Therapy that allows the child to work off frustrations through play and is a medium through which the therapist can analyze the child's conflicts and ways of coping with them. (p. 314)

pleasure principle Always seeking pleasure and avoiding pain; the way the id works. (p. 41)

polygenic inheritance A complex form of genetic transmission involving the interaction of many different genes to produce certain traits. (p. 88)

postconventional reasoning This is the highest level of moral reasoning in Kohlberg's theory. Morality is completely internalized and not based on others' standards. (p. 441)

pragmatics The ability to engage in appropriate conversation. (p. 184)

precipitate A delivery that takes the baby less than 10 minutes to be squeezed through the birth canal. The rapidity of this delivery may disturb the normal flow of blood in the infant, and the pressure on the head may lead to hemorrhaging. (p. 110)

preconventional reasoning The level at which the person shows no internalization of moral values. Morality is truly external to the individual. The lowest level in Kohlberg's theory. (p. 441)

prenatal period The period from conception to birth. (p. 19)

preoperational stage In Piaget's theory, the stage at which a child develops stronger symbolic representations of the world but still cannot perform operations; corresponds approximately to the period from 2 to 7 years of age. (p. 52)

pretend play When children engage in pretend play, they transform the physical environment into a symbol. (p. 316)

preterm infants Refers to babies born before 38 weeks in the womb. (p. 120)

primary circular reactions A scheme based on the infant's attempt to reproduce an interesting or pleasurable event that initially occurred by chance. (p. 170)

Project Follow Through A program instituted in 1967 as an adjunct to Project Head Start. Under this program, different kinds of educational programs were devised to see whether specific programs were effective. (p. 290)

Project Head Start Compensatory education program designed to provide children from low-income families with an opportunity to experience an enriched early environment and to acquire the skills and experience considered important for success in school. (p. 290)

proximodistal pattern A general pattern of physical growth and development that suggests that growth starts at the center of the body and moves toward the extremities. (p. 145)

Public Law 94–142 The Education for All Handicapped Children Act, passed in 1975, which requires all states to ensure a free, appropriate eduction for all handicapped children. (p. 352)

punishment A consequence that decreases the probability that a behavior will occur. (p. 59)

punishment and obedience orientation Kohlberg's first stage of moral reasoning. Moral thinking is based on punishments; children obey because parents tell them to obey. (p. 441)

questionnaires Similar to a highly structured interview, except that the respondent reads the question and marks his or her answer on paper rather than responding verbally to the interview. (p. 26)

reaction formation A defense mechanism by which we express an unacceptable impulse by transforming it into its opposite. (p. 42)

reaction range A range of one's potential phenotypical outcomes, given one's genotype and the influences of environmental conditions. The reaction range limits how much environmental change can modify a person's behavioral characteristics. (p. 89)

reality principle The way the ego operates, taking into account the constraints and demands of reality. (p. 41)

recasting Phrasing the same meaning or a similar meaning of a sentence in a different way. (p. 190)

reciprocal socialization The view that socialization is a bidirectional process; children socialize parents, just as parents socialize children. (p. 205)

reflexive smile A smile that does not occur in response to external stimuli. (p. 142)

regression A defense mechanism by which we behave in a way that characterizes a previous developmental level. (p. 42)

rehearsal The extended processing of to-be-remembered material after it has been presented; a control process used to facilitate long-term memory. (p. 380)

reinforcement Stimulation following a response that increases the probability that the same response will occur again in the same situation. (p. 59)

rejected children Children who are overtly disliked by their peers and who often have more long-term maladjustment than neglected children. (p. 422)

REM sleep Rapid eye movement sleep. (p. 143)

repression The most powerful and pervasive defense mechanism, according to Freud; it works to push unacceptable id impulses out of awareness and back into our unconscious mind. (p. 42)

reproduction A process that involves the fertilization of a female gamete (ovum) by a male gamete (sperm) to create a single-celled zygote. (p. 81)

rhythmic motor behavior Rapid, repetitive movement of the limbs, torso, and head during the first year of life. These motor behaviors occur frequently and appear to be a source of pleasure for the infant. (p. 146)

rites of passage Pubertal rites that are the avenue through which adolescents gain access to sacred adult practices, to knowledge, and to sexuality. The formal initiation ceremony associated with entry into adolescence in some cultures. (p. 554)

satire Refers to irony, wit, or derision used to expose folly or wickedness. (p. 495)

scaffolding Term used to describe an important caregiver's role in early parent-child interactions. Through their attention and choice of behaviors, caregivers provide a framework around which they and their infants interact. (p. 205)

schemata The existing set of information we have about various concepts, events, and knowledge. (p. 381)

scheme Behaviors or existing cognitive structures that characterize the substages in Piaget's theory of cognitive development; schemes change in organization from one substage to the next. (p. 169)

scientific method A series of steps used to obtain accurate information, identify and analyze the problem, collect data, draw conclusions, and revise theories. (p. 24)

scripts Schemata for events. (p. 381)

secondary circular reactions In Piaget's theory, develops between 4 and 8 months of age; the infant becomes more object oriented or focused on the world, moving beyond preoccupation with the self in sensorimotor interactions. (p. 170)

secure attachment The infant uses the caregiver, usually the mother, as a secure base from which to explore the environment. Ainsworth believes secure attachment is enhanced by the caregiver's sensitivity to the infant's signals. (p. 210)

self-actualization A process by which a person becomes a fully functioning human being; he or she is open to experience, not defensive, aware of and sensitive to the self and the external world, and for the most part has a harmonious relationship with others. (p. 63)

semantics Refers to the meaning of words and sentences. (p. 184)

sensation The detection of the environment through stimulation of receptors in the sense organs. (p. 156)

sensitive period Concept that emphasizes a more flexible band of time for a behavior to emerge optimally; sensitive periods last for months and even years rather than days or weeks. (p. 66)

sensorimotor stage The Piagetian stage lasting from birth to about 2 years of age. The infant constructs an understanding of the world by coordinating sensory experiences with physical motoric actions. (p. 51)

separation anxiety Behavior in which an infant may protest the departure of a caregiver by whining, crying, thrashing about, or otherwise indicating displeasure. (p. 207)

sequential approach A research approach that combines the features of cross-sectional and longitudinal designs in a search for more effective ways to study development. This approach allows researchers to see whether the same pattern of development is produced by each of the research strategies. (p. 33)

sexual script A stereotyped pattern of role prescriptions for how individuals should behave sexually. (p. 469)

shape stage Stage in which children can draw diagrams in different shapes; usually occurs by their third birthday. (p. 250)

short-term memory The retention of recently encountered information or information retrieved from long-term memory for a brief period of time, usually about 15 to 30 seconds. (p. 278)

sickle-cell anemia A genetic disease of the red blood cells. This is a common disorder among black individuals. A red blood cell is usually shaped like a disk, but a change in a recessive gene modifies its shape to that of a hook-shaped "sickle." (p. 84)

simple reflexes The basic means of coordinating sensation and action is through reflexive behaviors—such as rooting and sucking—which the infant has at birth. (p. 170)

social learning theory A theory with behavioral ties that emphasizes the environment's role in behavior. The most recent version, cognitive social learning theory, stresses the role of cognition and environment in determining behavior. (p. 59)

social processes A person's interaction with other persons in the environment and the effect of these interactions on development. (p. 19)

social smile A smile that occurs in response to a face. (p. 142)

social systems morality Kohlberg's fourth stage of moral reasoning. Moral judgments are based on understanding the social order, law, justice, and duty. (p. 441)

solitary play The child plays alone and independently of others. The child seems engrossed in what he or she is doing and does not care much about anything else that is happening. Usually seen in 2-to-3-year-olds. (p. 316)

stability-change issue How consistent individual differences are over time. Addresses the degree to which we become older versions of our early selves or whether we can develop into someone different from who we were at an earlier point in development. (p. 22)

standardized tests Questionnaires, structured interviews, or behavioral tests that are developed to identify a person's characteristics or abilities, relative to those of a large group of similar persons. (p. 27)

storm and stress view View proposed by Hall that sees adolescence as a turbulent time charged with conflict and full of contradiction and wide swings in mood and emotion. (p. 457)

stranger anxiety An infant's fear of strangers. (p. 208)

structure-process dilemma The basic issue of what the mechanisms of intelligence are and how they develop, whether by expanding information-processing abilities (process), growing knowledge and expertise (structure), or both. (p. 392)

sublimation A defense mechanism by which a socially useful course of action replaces a distasteful one. (p. 42)

sucking reflex A reflex that enables a newborn to get food before he or she has associated a nipple with food. (p. 138)

superego The moral branch of personality, according to Freud; much like our "conscience." (p. 42)

surface structure The actual order of words in a sentence. (p. 184)

symbolic function substage In Piaget's theory, occurs roughly between the ages of 2 and 4; the child has the ability to mentally represent an object. (p. 267)

syntax The way words are combined to form acceptable phrases and sentences. (p. 184)

tabula rasa Locke's view that children are not innately evil but instead are like a blank tablet, becoming a particular kind of child or adult because of particular life experiences. (p. 14)

telegraphic speech Speech that includes content words, such as nouns and verbs, but omits the extra words that serve only a grammatical function, such as prepositions and articles. (p. 193)

teratology The field of study that investigates the causes of congenital (birth) defects. (p. 110)

tertiary circular reactions Schemes in which the infant purposely explores new possibilities with objects, continually changing what is done to them and exploring the results. (p. 171)

tertiary circular reactions, novelty, and curiosity Develops between 12 and 18 months of age; the infant becomes intrigued by the variety of properties that objects possess and by the multiplicity of things he or she can make happen to objects. Piagetian concept. (p. 171)

testis determining factor (TDF) Genes carried on the twenty-third chromosome pair, believed to determine a person's sex. (p. 88)

testosterone A male sex hormone important in the development of sexual characteristics and behavior. (p. 461)

theories General beliefs that help us to explain the data or facts we have observed and to make predictions. (p. 24)

top-dog phenomenon Moving from the top position (in elementary school, as the oldest, biggest, and most powerful students in the school) to the lowest position (in middle or junior high school, the youngest, smallest, and the least powerful group of students). (p. 508)

triarchic theory of intelligence R. J. Sternberg's belief that every child has three types of intelligence: componential, experiential, and contextual. (p. 393)

trophoblast The outer layer of the blastula that provides nutrition and support for the embryo. (p. 104)

trust versus mistrust Erikson's first stage of development, corresponding approximately to the first year of life. In this bipolar conflict, infants develop either a trust in themselves and the world or a sense of mistrust. (p. 46)

Turner's syndrome A genetic disease in which females are missing an X chromosome, making them XO instead of XX. (p. 86)

twin study A strategy of research that focuses on the genetic relationship between identical (monozygotic) twins and fraternal (dizygotic) twins. (p. 90)

two-factor theory Spearman's view that we have both general intelligence and a number of specific intelligences. (p. 389)

type A babies These babies exhibit insecurity by avoiding the mother—for example, ignoring her, averting her gaze, and failing to seek proximity. (p. 210)

Type A behavioral pattern A cluster of characteristics—excessively competitive, an accelerated pace of ordinary activities, impatience, thinking about doing several things at once, hostility, and an inability to hide the fact that life is a struggle—thought to be related to the incidence of heart disease. (p. 364)

type B babies A positive bond develops between the infant and the caregiver; this promotes the healthy exploration of the world because the caregiver provides a secure base to which the infant can return if stressors are encountered. (p. 210)

type C babies These babies exhibit insecurity by resisting the mother—for example, clinging to her but at the same time fighting against the closeness, perhaps by kicking and pushing away. (p. 210)

ultrasound sonography A test in which high-frequency sound waves are directed into the pregnant woman's abdomen. The echo from the sounds is transformed into a visual representation of the fetus's inner structures. (p. 87)

umbilical cord Contains two arteries and one vein and connects the baby to the placenta. (p. 105)

unconditional positive regard Positive behaviors, love, and praise are given without contingency; a Rogerian concept. (p. 62)

underextension The tendency of children to misuse words by not extending one word's meaning to other appropriate contexts for the word. (p. 192)

undifferentiated The category that describes a person who has neither masculine nor feminine characteristics. (p. 435)

universal ethical principles Kohlberg's sixth stage of moral reasoning. The individual has developed a moral standard based on universal human rights; when faced with a conflict involving law and conscience, the person will follow his or her conscience even though the decision might involve personal risk. (p. 441)

unoccupied play The child is not engaging in play as it is commonly understood and may stand in one spot, look around the room, or perform random movements that do not seem to have a goal. (p. 315)

Wechsler Scales Widely used individual intelligence tests developed by David Wechsler. (p. 386)

whole-word method A technique for learning to read that focuses on learning direct associations between whole words and their meanings. (p. 399)

XYY syndrome A genetic disease in which the male has an extra Y chromosome. (p. 86)

zone of proximal development (ZPD) In Vygotsky's theory, ZPD is conceptualized as a measure of learning potential; it has an upper and a lower limit. (p. 286)

zygote A singe-celled fertilized ovum (egg) created in the reproductive process. (pp. 81, 104)

References

Abramovitch, R., Corter, C., Pepler, D. J., & Stanhope, L. (1986). Sibling and peer interaction: A final follow-up and comparison. *Child Development, 47,* 217–229.

Achenbach, T. M., & Edelbrock, C. S. (1981). Behavioral problems and competencies reported by parents of normal and disturbed children aged four through sixteen. *Monographs of the Society for Research in Child Development, 46,* (1, Serial No. 188).

Acredolo, L. P., & Hake, J. L. (1982). Infant perception. In B. B. Wolman (Ed.), *Handbook of developmental psychology.* Englewood Cliffs, NJ: Prentice-Hall.

Adelson, J. (1979, January). Adolescence and the generalization gap. *Psychology Today,* pp. 33–37.

Agnew, N., McK., & Pyke, S. W. (1987). *The science game* (4th ed.). Englewood Cliffs, NJ: Prentice-Hall.

Ainsworth, M. D. S. (1979). Infant-mother attachment. *American Psychologist, 34,* 932–937.

Alan Guttmacher Institute (1981). *Teenage pregnancy: The problem that has not gone away.* New York: Author.

Alexander, K. L., & Entwisle, D. R. (1988). Achievement in the first two years of school: Patterns and processes. *Monographs of the Society for Research in Child Development, 53,* (2, Serial No. 218).

Allen, J. P., & Hauser, S. T. (1989, April). *Autonomy and relatedness in adolescent-family interactions as predictors of adolescent ego development.* Paper presented at the Society for Research in Child Development, Kansas City.

Als, H. (1988, November). *Intensive care unit stress for the high-risk preterm infant: Neurofunctional and emotional sequelae.* Paper presented at the Developmental Interventions in Neonatal Care Conference, San Diego, CA.

Altshuler, J. L., & Ruble, D. N. (in press). Developmental changes in children's awareness of strategies for coping with uncontrollable stress. *Child Development.*

American Association for Protecting Children (1986). *Highlights of Official Child Neglect and Abuse Reporting:* 1984, American Humane Association, Denver, CO.

American College Health Association (1989, May). *Survey of AIDS on college on American college and university campuses.* Washington, DC: American College Health Association.

Ames, C., & Ames, R. (Eds.). (1989). *Research on motivation in education.* (Vol. 3) *Goals and cognitions.* San Diego: Academic Press.

Amsterdam, B. K. (1968). *Mirror behavior in children under two years of age.* Unpublished doctoral dissertation, University of North Carolina, Chapel Hill.

Anastasi, A. (1988). *Psychological testing* (6th ed.). New York: Macmillan.

Anderson, A. B., & Frideres, J. S. (1981). *Ethnicity in Canada.* Toronto: Butterworths.

Anderson, D. R., Lorch, E. P., Field, D. E., Collins, P. A., & Nathan, J. G. (1985, April). *Television viewing at home: Age trends in visual attention and time with TV.* Paper presented at the biennial meeting of the Society for Research in Child Development, Toronto.

Anderson, L. W. (1989, April). The impact of sex and age on the resolutions of preschool children's conversational disagreements. Paper presented at the biennial meeting of the Society for Research in Child Development, Kansas City.

Angoff, W. (1989, August). *Perspectives on bias in mental testing.* Paper presented at the meeting of the American Psychological Association, New Orleans.

Archer, S. L. (1989). Gender differences in identity development: Issues of process, domain, and timing. *Journal of Adolescence, 12,* 117–138.

Aries, P. (1962). *Centuries of childhood* (R. Baldrick, Trans.). New York: Knopf.

Arman-Nolley, S. (1989, April). *Vygotsky's perspective on development of creativity and imagination.* Paper presented at the biennial meeting of the Society for Research on Child Development, Kansas City.

Aronson, E. (1986, August). *Teaching students things they think they already know about: The case of prejudice and desegregation.* Paper presented at the meeting of the American Psychological Association, Washington, DC.

Asarnow, J. R., & Callan, J. W. (1985). Boys with peer adjustment problems: Social cognitive processes. *Journal of Consulting and Clinical Psychology, 53,* 80–87.

Ashburn, S. S. (1986). Biophysical development of the toddler and preschooler. In C. S. Schuster & S. S. Ashburn (Eds.), *The process of human development.* Boston: Little, Brown.

Asher, J. (1987). Born to be shy? *Psychology Today, April,* 56–64.

Asher, J., & Garcia, R. (1969). The optimal age to learn a foreign language. *Modern Language Journal, 53,* 334–341.

Asher, S. R., & Parker, J. G. (in press). The significance of peer relationship problems in childhood. In B. H. Schneider, G. Attili, J. Nadel, & R. P. Weisberg (Eds.), *Social competence in developmental perspective.* Amsterdam: Kluwer Academic Publishing.

Ashmead, D. H., & Perlmutter, M. (1979, August). *Infant memory in everyday life.* Paper presented at the meeting of the American Psychological Association, New York City.

Aslin, R. N. (1987). Visual and auditory development in infancy. In J. D. Osofsky (Ed.), *Handbook of infant development* (2nd ed.). New York: Wiley.

Astin, A. W., Green, K. C., & Korn, W. S. (1987). *The American freshman: Twenty-year trends.* Los Angeles: UCLA Higher Education Research Institute.

Astin, H. S. (1984). The meaning of work in women's lives: A sociopsychological model of career choice and work behavior. *The Counseling Psychologist, 12,* 117–126.

Atkinson, J. W., & Raynor, I. O. (1974). *Motivation and achievement.* New York: Wiley.

Attie, I., & Brooks-Gunn, J. (in press). The emergence of eating disorders and eating problems in adolescence: A developmental perspective. *Journal of Child Psychology and Psychiatry, and Allied Disciplines.*

Bachman, J. G. (1982, June). *The American high school student: A profile based on national survey data.* Paper presented at conference on "The American High School Today and Tomorrow," Berkeley, CA.

Bachman, J. G., Johnston, L. P., & O'Malley, P. M. (1987). *Monitoring the future.* Ann Arbor: University of Michigan, Institute of Social Research.

Baer, D. M. (1989, April). *Behavior analysis of human development.* Paper presented at the biennial meeting of the Society for Research in Child Development, Kansas City.

Bahrick, L. E. (1988). Intermodal learning in infancy: Learning on the basis of two kinds of invariant relations in audible and visible events. *Child Development, 59,* 197–209.

Bailey, G. W. (1989). Current perspectives on substance abuse in youth. *Journal of the American Academy of Child and Adolescent Psychiatry, 28,* 151–162.

Bakeman, R., & Brown, J. V. (1980). Early interaction: Consequences for social and mental development at three years. *Child Development, 51,* 437–447.

Baker, K. (1987). Comment on Willig's "A meta-analysis of selected studies in the effectiveness of bilingual education. *Review of Educational Research, 57,* 351–362.

Ballenger, M. (1983). Reading in the kindergarten: Comment. *Childhood Education, 59,* 187.

Baltes, P. B. (1973). Prototypical paradigms and questions in life-span research on development and aging. *The Gerontologist, 113,* 458–467.

Bandura, A. (1965). Influence of models' reinforcement contingencies on the acquisition of imitative responses. *Journal of Personality and Social Psychology, 1,* 589–595.

Bandura, A. (1977). *Social learning theory.* Englewood Cliffs, NJ: Prentice-Hall.

Bandura, A. (1989). Social cognitive theory. In R. Vasta (Ed.), *Six theories of child development: Revised formulations and current issues.* Greenwich, CT: JAI Press.

Bane, M. J. (1978). *HEW policy toward children, youth, and families.* Office of the Assistant Secretary for Planning and Evaluation, Cambridge, MA.

Banks, M. S., & Salapatek, P. (1983). Infant visual perception. In P. H. Mussen (Ed.), *Handbook of child psychology* (4th ed., Vol. 2). New York: Wiley.

Barcus, F. E. (1978). *Commercial children's television on weekends and weekday afternoons.* Newtonville, MA: Action for Children's Television.

Barenboim, C. (1981). The development of person perception in childhood and adolescence: From behavioral comparisons to psychological constructs to psychological comparisons. *Child Development, 52,* 129–144.

Barenboim, C. (1985, April). *Person perception and interpersonal behavior.* Paper presented at the biennial meeting of the Society for Research in Child Development, Toronto.

Barkeley, R. (in press). Attention deficit disorders: History, definition, diagnosis. In M. Lewis & S. Miller (Eds.), *Handbook of developmental psychopathology.* New York: Plenum.

Barker, R., & Wright, H. F. (1951). *One boy's day.* New York: Harper & Row.

Barnes, K. E. (1971). Preschool play norms: A Replication. *Developmental Psychology, 4,* 99–103.

Baron, J. B., & Sternberg, R. J. (Eds.). (1987). *Teaching thinking skills.* New York: W. H. Freeman.

Barrett, D. E., Radke-Yarrow, M., & Klein, R. E. (1982). Chronic malnutrition and child behavior: Effects of calorie supplementation on social and emotional functioning at school age. *Developmental Psychology, 18,* 541–556.

Barrett, K. C., & Campos, J. J. (1987). A functionalist approach to emotions. In J. D. Osofsky (Ed.), *Handbook of infant development.* New York: Wiley.

Baskett, L. M., & Johnston, S. M. (1982). The young child's interaction with parents verus siblings. *Child Development, 53,* 643–650.

Bates, E., O'Connell, B., & Shore, C. (1987). Language and communication in infancy. In J. D. Osofsky (Ed.), *Handbook of infant development.* New York: Wiley.

Batshaw, M. L., & Perret, Y. M. (1986). *Children with handicaps.* Baltimore: Brookes.

Batson, C. D. (1989). Personal values, moral principles, and the three path model of prosocial motivation. In N. Eisenberg & J. Reykowski (Eds.). *Social and moral values.* Hillsdale, NJ: Erlbaum.

Baumeiser, A. A. (1987). Mental retardation: Some conceptions and dilemmas. *American Psychologist, 42,* 796–800.

Baumrind, D. (1971). Current patterns of parental authority. *Developmental Psychology Monographs, 4* (1, Pt. 2).

Bayley, N. (1969). *Manual for the Bayley Scales of infant development.* New York: The Psychological Corporation.

Bayley, N. (1970). Development of mental abilities. In P. H. Mussen (Ed.), *Manual of child psychology* (3rd ed. Vol. 1). New York: Wiley.

Beagles-Roos, J., & Gat, I. (1983). Specific impact of radio and television on children's story comprehension. *Journal of Educational Psychology, 75,* 128–135.

Behrman, R. E., & Vaughan, V. C. (Eds.) (1983). *Nelson textbook of pediatrics* (12th ed.). Philadelphia: Saunders.

Beilin, H. (1989). Piagetian theory. In R. Vasta (Ed.), *Six theories of child development: Revised formulations and current issues.* Greenwich, CT: JAI Press.

Bell, A. P., Weinberg, M. S., & Mammersmith, S. K. (1981). *Sexual preference: Its development in men and women.* New York: Simon & Schuster.

Bell, S. M., & Ainsworth, M. D. S. (1972). Infant crying and maternal responsiveness. *Child Development, 43,* 1171–1190.

Bell-Scott, P., & Taylor, R. L. (1989). Introduction: The multiple ecologies of black adolescent development. *Journal of Adolescent Research, 4,* 117–118.

Belmont, J. M. (1989). Cognitive strategies and strategic learning: The socio-instructional approach. *American Psychologist, 44,* 142–148.

Belsky, J. (1981). Early human experience: A family perspective. *Developmental Psychology, 17,* 3–23.

Belsky, J. (1987, April). *Science, social policy, and day care: A personal odyssey.* Paper presented at the biennial meeting of the Society for Research in Child Development, Baltimore.

Belsky, J. (1988, October). *Day care.* Paper presented at the meeting of the American Academy of Pediatrics, San Francisco.

Belsky, J. (1989, Apr. 2). *Conversation hour: Day care research today.* Biennial meeting of the Society for Research in Child Development, Kansas City.

Belsky, J., & Rovine, M. J. (1988). Nonmaternal care in the first year of life and infant-parent attachment security. *Child Development.*

Belsky, J., Rovine, M., & Fish, M. (1989). The developing family system. In M. R. Gunnar & E. Thelen (Eds.), *Systems and development: The Minnesota Symposia on Child Psychology Series* (Vol. 22). Hillsdale, NJ: Erlbaum.

Belson, W. (1978). *Television violence and the adolescent boy.* London: Saxon House.

Bem, S. L. (1977). On the utility of alternative procedures for assessing psychological androgyny. *Journal of Consulting and Clinical Psychology, 45,* 196–205.

Bem, S. L. (1985). Androgyny and gender schema theory: Conceptual and empirical integration. In T. B. Sonderegger (Ed.), *Nebraska Symposium on Motivation.* Lincoln, NE: University of Nebraska Press.

Berensen, G. (1989, February). *The Bogalusa heart study.* Paper presented at the science forum, American Heart Association, Monterey, CA.

Berg, W. K., & Berg, K. M. (1987). Psychophysiological development in infancy: State, startle, & attention. In J. D. Osofsky (Ed.), *Handbook of infant development* (2nd ed.). New York: Wiley.

Berko, J. (1958). The child's learning of English morphology. *Word, 14,* 150–177.

Berlyne, D. E. (1960). *Conflict, arousal, and curiosity.* New York: McGraw-Hill.

Berndt, T. J. (1979). Developmental changes in conformity to peers and parents. *Developmental Psychology, 15,* 608–616.

Berndt, T. J. (1982). The features and effects of friendships in early adolescence. *Child Development, 53,* 1447–1460.

Berndt, T. J., & Perry, T. B. (1990). Distinctive features and effects of early adolescent friendships. In R. Montemayor (Ed.), *Advances in adolescent research.* Greenwich, CT: JAI Press.

Bijou, S. W. (1989). Behavior analysis. In R. Vasta (Ed.), *Six theories of child development: Revised formulations and current issues.* Greenwich, CT: JAI Press.

Binder, A. (1987). An historical and theoretical introduction. In H. C. Quay (Ed.), *Handbook of juvenile delinquency.* New York: Wiley.

Bingham, C. R. (1989). AIDS and adolescents: Threat of infection and approaches for prevention. *Journal of Early Adolescence, 9,* 50–66.

Bjorklund, D. F. (1989). *Children's thinking.* Belmont, CA: Brooks/Cole.

Bloch, M. N., & Pellegrini, A. D. (Eds.). (1989). *The ecological context of children's play.* Norwood, NJ: Ablex.

Block, J., & Block, J. H. (1988). Longitudinally foretelling drug usage in adolescence: Early childhood personality and environmental precursors. *Child Development, 59,* 336–355.

Block, J. H., Block, J., & Gjerde, P. F. (1986). The personality of children prior to divorce. *Child Development, 57,* 827–840.

Bloom, B. S. (1983, April). *The development of exceptional talent.* Paper presented at the biennial meeting of the Society for Research in Child Development, Detroit.

Bloom, L. (1973). *One word at a time.* The Hague, Netherlands: Mouton.

Bloome, D. (1989). *Classrooms and literacy.* Norwood, NJ: Ablex.

Bloome, D. (Ed.). (in press). *Classrooms and literacy.* Norwood, NJ: Ablex.

Blos, P. (1989). The inner world of the adolescent. In A. H. Esman (Ed.), *International Annals of Adolescent Psychiatry.* Chicago: University of Chicago Press.

Blum, R. W., Goldhagen, J. (1981). Teenage pregnancy in perspective. *Clinical Pediatrics, 20,* 335–340.

Blumberg, M. L. (1974). Psychopathology of the abusing parent. *American Journal of Psychotherapy, 28,* 1121–1129.

Blumenfeld, P. C., Pintrich, P. R., Wessles, K., & Meece, J. (1981, April). *Age, and sex differences in the impact of classroom experiences on self perceptions.* Paper presented at the biennial meeting of the Society for Research in Child Development, Boston.

Blumenthal, S. J., & Kupfer, D. J. (1988). Overview of early detection and treatment strategies for suicidal behavior in young people. *Journal of Youth and Adolescence, 17,* 1–14.

Blurton-Jones, N. (1972). Categories of child-child interaction. In N. Blurton-Jones (Ed.), *Ethological studies of child behavior.* Cambridge, England: Cambridge University Press.

Blyth, D. A., Bulcroft, R., & Simmons, R. G. (1981, August). *The impact of puberty on adolescents: A longitudinal study.* Paper presented at the meeting of the American Psychological Association, Los Angeles.

Bogin, B., & MacVean, R. B. (1983). The relationship of socioeconomic status and sex to body size, skeletal maturation, and cognitive status of Guatemala City schoolchildren. *Child Development, 54,* 115–128.

Bohannon, J. N., III, & Stanowicz, L. (1988). The issue of negative evidence. Adult responses to children's language errors. *Developmental Psychology, 24,* 684–689.

Bolter, J. D. (1984). *Turing's man.* Chapel Hill, NC: University of North Carolina Press.

Bornstein, M. H. (1988). Perceptual development across the life cycle. In M. H. Bornstein & M. E. Lamb (Eds.), *Developmental Psychology* (2nd ed.). Hillsdale, NJ: Erlbaum.

Bornstein, M. H. (1989). Stability in early mental development. In M. H. Bornstein & N. A. Krasnegor (Eds.), *Stability and continuity in mental development.* Hillsdale, NJ: Erlbaum.

Bornstein, M. H. (Ed.). (1987). *Sensitive periods in development,* Hillsdale, NJ: Erlbaum.

Bornstein, M. H., & Krasnegor, N. A. (1989). *Stability and continuity in mental development.* Hillsdale, NJ: Erlbaum.

Bornstein, M. H., & Sigman, M. D. (1986). Continuity in mental development from infancy. *Child Development, 57,* 251–274.

Bornstein, M. W. (1989). Cross-cultural developmental comparisons: The case of Japanese-American infant and mother activities and interactions. What we know, what we need to know, and why we need to know. *Developmental Review, 9,* 171–204.

Borovsky, D., Hill, W., & Rovee-Collier, C. (1987, April). *Developmental changes in infant long-term memory.* Paper presented at the biennial meeting of the Society for Research in Child Development, Baltimore.

Borstelmann, L. J. (1983). Children before psychology: Ideas about children from antiquity to the late 1800s. In P. H. Mussen (Ed.), *Handbook of child psychology* (4th ed., Vol. 1). New York: Wiley.

Bouchard, T. J., Heston, L., Eckert, E., Keyes, M., & Resnick, S. (1981). The Minnesota study of twins reared apart: Project description and sample results in the developmental domain. *Twin Research, 3,* 227–233.

Bower, B. (1985). The left hand of math and verbal talent. *Science News, 127,* 263.

Bowlby, J. (1969). *Attachment and loss* (Vol. 1). London: Hogarth.

Bowlby, J. (1980). *Attachment and loss* (Vol. 3). London: Hogarth.

Bowlby, J. (1989). *Secure attachment.* New York: Basic Books.

Boxer, A. M. (1988, August). *Developmental continuities of gay and lesbian youth.* Paper presented at the meeting of the American Psychological Association, Atlanta, GA.

Brackbill, Y. (1979). Obstetric medication and infant behavior. In J. D. Osofsky (Ed.), *Handbook of infant development.* New York: Wiley.

Brady, M. P., Swank, P. R., Taylor, R. D., & Freiberg, H. J. (1988). Teacher-student interactions in middle school mainstreamed classes: Differences with special and regular students. *Journal of Educational Research, 81,* 332–340.

Bray, J. H. (1988). The effects of early remarriage on children's development: Preliminary analyses of the developmental issues in stepfamily research project. In E. M. Hetherington & J. D. Arasteh (Eds.), *Impact of divorce, single-parenting, and stepparenting on children.* Hillsdale, NJ: Erlbaum.

Brazelton, T. B. (1956). Sucking in infancy. *Pediatrics, 17,* 400–404.

Brazelton, T. B. (1973). *Neonatal Behavioral Assessment Scale.* London: Heinemann Medical Books.

Brazelton, T. B. (1979). Behavioral competence in the newborn infant. *Seminars in Perinatology, 3,* 35–44.

Brazelton, T. B. (1984) *Neonatal Behavioral Assessment Scale* (2nd ed.). Philadelphia: Lippincott.

Brazelton, T. B. (1987, August). *Opportunities for intervention with infants at risk.* Paper presented at the meeting of the American Psychological Association, New York City.

Brazelton, T. B. (1988, November). *Family stresses and emotional issues of parents during NICU hospitalization.* Paper presented at conference of Developmental Interventions in Neonatal Care, San Diego, CA.

Brazelton, T. B. (1989). Observations of the neonate. In C. Rovee-Collier & L. P. Lipsitt (Eds.), *Advances in infancy* (Vol. 6). Norwood, NJ: Ablex.

Brazelton, T. B., Nugent, J. K., & Lester, B. M. (1987). Neonatal Behavioral Assessment Scale. In J. D. Osofsky (Ed.), *Handbook of infant development* (2nd ed.). New York: Wiley.

Bredekamp, S., & Shepard, L. (1989). How to best protect children from inappropriate school expectations, practices, and policies. *Young Children, 44,* 14–24.

Brenner, A. (1984). *Helping children cope with stress.* Lexington, MA: D. C. Heath.

Brent, D. A. (1989). Suicide and suicidal behavior in children and adolescents. *Pediatrics in Review, 10,* 269–275.

Bretherton, I., Fritz, J., Zahn-Waxler, C., & Ridgeway, D. (1986). Learning to talk about emotions. *Child Development, 57,* 529–548.

Bronfenbrenner, U. (1979). Contexts of child rearing: Problems and prospect. *American Psychologist, 34,* 844–850.

Bronfenbrenner, U. (1989, April). *The developing ecology of human development*. Paper presented at the biennial meeting of the Society for Research in Child Development, Kansas City.

Bronstein, P. (1988). Marital and parenting roles in transition. In P. Bronstein & C. P. Cowen (Eds.), *Contemporary fatherhood*. New York: Wiley.

Bronstein, P. A., & Quina, K. (Eds.) (1988). *Teaching a psychology of people*. Washington, DC: American Psychological Association.

Brooks-Gunn, J. (1988). Antecedents and consequences of variations in girls' maturational timing. In M. D. Levine & E. R. McAnarney (Eds.), *Early adolescent transitions*. Lexington, MA: Lexington Books.

Brooks-Gunn, J., & Warren, M. P. (1989, April). *How important are pubertal and social events for different problem behaviors and contexts?* Paper presented at the biennial meeting of the Society for Research in Child Development, Kansas City.

Brooks-Gunn, J., & Warren, M. P. (in press). The psychological significance of secondary sexual characteristics in 9- to 11-year-old girls. *Child Development*.

Brown, A. L., Bransford, J. D., Ferrara, R. A., & Campione, J. C. (1983). Learning, remembering and understanding. In P. H. Mussen (Ed.), *Handbook of child psychology* (4th ed., Vol. 3). New York: Wiley.

Brown, A. L., & Smiley, S. S. (1977). Rating the importance of structural units of prose passages: A problem of metacognitive development. *Child Development, 48,* 1–8.

Brown, B. B., & Lohr, M. J. (1987). Peer group affiliation and adolescent self-esteem: An integration of ego identity and symbolic interaction theories. *Journal of Personality and Social Psychology, 52,* 47–55.

Brown, B. B., & Mounts, N. (1989, April). *Peer group structures in single versus multiethnic high schools*. Paper presented at the biennial meeting of the Society for Research in Child Development, Kansas City.

Brown, F. (1973). *The reform of secondary education: Report of the national commission on the reform of secondary education*. New York: McGraw-Hill.

Brown, J. L. (1964). States in newborn infants. *Merrill-Palmer Quarterly, 10,* 313–327.

Brown, J. L., & Pizer, H. F. (1987). *Living hungry in America*. New York: Macmillan.

Brown, R. (1973). *A first language: The early stages*. Cambridge, MA: Harvard University Press.

Brown, R. (1986). *Social psychology* (2nd ed.). New York: The Free Press.

Brumberg, J. J. (1988). *Fasting girls*. Cambridge, MA: Harvard University Press.

Bruner, J. S. (1989, April). *The state of developmental psychology*. Paper presented at the biennial meeting of the Society for Research in Child Development, Kansas City.

Bryant, B. K. (1985). The neighborhood walk: Sources of support in middle childhood. *Monographs of the Society for Research in Child Development, 50* (3, Serial No. 210).

Buckley, W. E., Yesalis, C. E., Friedl, K. E., Anderson, W. A., Streit, A. L., & Wright, J. E. (1988). Estimated prevalence of anabolic steroid use among male high school students. *Journal of the American Medical Association, 260,* 3441–3445.

Buhrmester, D. (1989). *Changes in friendship, interpersonal competence, and social adaptation during early adolescence*. Unpublished manuscript, Department of Psychology, UCLA, Los Angeles.

Bullock, M. (1985). Animism in childhood thinking: A new look at an old question. *Developmental Psychology, 21,* 217–225.

Burkett, C. L. (1985, April). *Childrearing behaviors and the self-esteem of preschool-age children*. Paper presented at the biennial meeting of the Society for Research in Child Development, Toronto.

Burtchaell, J. (in press). University policy on experimental use of aborted fetal tissue. *IRB, A Review of Human Subjects*.

Buss, A. H., & Plomin, R. (1984). *A temperament theory of personality development*. New York: Wiley-Interscience.

Buss, A. H., & Plomin, R. (1987). Commentary. In H. H., Goldsmith, A. H. Buss, R. Plomin, M. K. Rothbart, A. Thomas, A. Chess, R. R. Hinde, & R. B. McCall. Roundtable: What is temperament? Four approaches. *Child Development, 58,* 505–529.

Byrnes, J. P. (1988). Formal operations: A systematic reformulation. *Developmental Review, 8,* 66–87.

Cairns, R. B. (1983). The emergence of developmental psychology. In P. H. Mussen (Ed.), *Handbook of child psychology* (4th ed., Vol. 1). New York: Wiley.

Cairns, R. B., & Cairns, B. D. (in press). Social cognition and social networks. A developmental perspective. In D. Pepler & K. Rubin (Eds.), *Aggression in childhood*. Hillsdale, NJ: Erlbaum.

Calhoun, J. A. (1988, March). *Gang violence*. Testimony to the House Select Committee on Children, Youth, and Families, Washington, D.C.

Camara, K. A., & Resnick, G. (1988). Interparental conflict and cooperation: Factors moderating children's post-divorce adjustment. In E. M. Hetherington & J. D. Arasteh (Eds.). *Impact of divorce, single-parenting, and stepparenting on children*. Hillsdale, NJ: Erlbaum.

Cameron, D. (1988, February). Soviet schools. *NEA Today,* p. 15.

Campos, J. J., Barrett, K. C., Lamb, M. E., Goldsmith, H. H., & Stenberg, C. (1983). Socioemotional development. In P. H. Mussen (Ed.), *Handbook of child psychology* (4th ed., Vol. 2). New York: Wiley.

Campos, J. J., Langer, A., & Krowitz, A. (1970). Cardiac responses on the visual cliff in prelocomotor human infants. *Science, 170,* 196–197.

Carbo, M. (1987). Reading styles research: "What works" isn't always phonics. *Phi Delta Kappan, 68,* 431–435.

Carey, S. (1977). The child as word learner. In M. Halle, J. Bresman, & G. A. Miller (Eds.), *Linguistic theory and psychological reality*. Cambridge, MA: MIT Press.

Carnegie Corporation (1989). *Turning points: Preparing youth for the 21st century*. New York City: Carnegie Corporation.

Carper, L. (1978, April). Sex roles in the nursery. *Harper's*.

Carroll, J. B. (1989). Intellectual abilities and aptitudes. In A. Lesgold & R. Glaser (Eds.), *Foundations for a psychology of education*. Hillsdale, NJ: Erlbaum.

Carskadon, M. A., & Dement, W. C. (1989). Normal human sleep: An overview. In M. H. Kryger, T. Roth, & W. C. Dement (Eds.), *Principles and practices of sleep medicine.* San Diego: Harcourt Brace Jovanovich.

Carter, D. B. (1989, April). *Gender identity and gender constancy.* Paper presented at the biennial meeting of the Society for Research in Child Development, Kansas City.

Carter-Saltzman, L. (1980). Biological and sociocultural effects on handedness: Comparison between biological and adoptive families. *Science, 209,* 1263–1265.

Carton, B. (1988, July 27). Teen buyers: Tracking what's hot. *The Boston Globe,* A1, A13.

Case, R., Kurland, D. M., & Goldberg, J. (1982). Operational efficiency and the growth of short-term memory span. *Journal of Experimental Child Psychology, 33,* 386–404.

Casper, R. (1989). Psychodynamic psychotherapy in acute anorexia nervosa and acute bulimia nervosa. In A. H. Esman (Ed.), *International Annals of Adolescent Psychiatry.* Chicago: University of Chicago Press.

Cassell, C. (1984). *Swept away: Why women fear their own sexuality.* New York: Simon & Schuster.

Cavett, D. (1974). *Cavett.* San Diego: Harcourt Brace Jovanovich.

Chalfant, J. C. (1989). Learning disabilities: Policy issues and promising approaches. *American Psychologist, 44,* 392–398.

Charlesworth, R. (1989). "Behind" before they start? *Young Children, 44,* 5–13.

Chase-Lansdale, P. L., & Hetherington, E. M. (in press). The impact of divorce on life-span development: Short and longterm effects. In P. B. Baltes, D. L. Featherman, & R. M. Lerner (Eds.), *Life-span development and behavior.* Hillsdale, NJ: Erlbaum.

Chasnoff, I. J., Burns, K. A., & Burns, W. J. (1987, April). *Cocaine and Pregnancy.* Paper presented at the Society for Research in Child Development, Baltimore.

Chen, C., & Stevenson, H. W. (1989). Homework: A cross-cultural examination. *Child Development, 60,* 551–561.

Chesney-Lind, M. (1989). Girls' crime and woman's place: Toward a feminist model of female delinquency. *Crime and Delinquency, 35,* 5–30.

Chess, S., & Thomas, A. (1977). Temperamental individuality from childhood to adolescence. *Journal of Child Psychiatry, 16,* 218–226.

Chess, S., & Thomas, A. (1986). *Temperament in clinical practice.* New York: Guilford.

Chi, M. T. (1978). Knowledge structures and memory development. In R. S. Siegler (Ed.), *Children's thinking: What develops?* Hillsdale, NJ: Erlbaum.

Children's Defense Fund (1985). *Black and white children in America: Key facts.* Washington, D.C.: United States Public Health Service.

Chivian, E., Mack, J., Waletzky, J., Lazaroff, C., Doctor, R., & Goldening, J. (1985). Soviet children and the threat of nuclear war: A preliminary study, *Journal of Orthopsychiatry, 55,* 484–502.

Chomsky, N. (1957). *Syntactic structures.* The Hague: Mouton.

Cicirelli, V. (1977). Family structure and interaction: Sibling effects on socialization. In M. McMillan & M. Sergio (Eds.), *Child psychiatry: Treatment and research.* New York: Brunner/Mazel.

Clark, E. V., (1983). Meanings and concepts. In P. H. Mussen (Ed.), *Handbook of child psychology* (4th ed., Vol. 4). New York: Wiley.

Clark, H. H., & Clark, E. V. (1977). *Psychology and language.* New York: Harcourt Brace Jovanovich.

Clark, S. D., Zabin, L. S., & Hardy, J. B. (1984). Sex, contraception, and parenthood: Experience and attitudes among urban black young men. *Family Planning Perspectives, 16,* 77–82.

Clarke-Stewart, A., & Fein, G. (1983). Early childhood programs. In P. H. Mussen (Ed.), *Handbook of child psychology* (4th ed., Vol. 2). New York: Wiley.

Clarke-Stewart, K. (1989). Infant day care: Maligned or malignant? *American Psychologist, 44,* 266–273.

Clarke-Stewart, K. A. (1978). Recasting the lone stranger. In J. Glick & K. A. Clarke-Stewart (Eds.), *The development of social understanding.* New York: Gardner Press.

Clarke-Stewart, K. A., & Fein, G. G. (1983). Early childhood programs. In P. H. Mussen (Ed.), *Handbook of child psychology* (4th ed., Vol. 2). New York: Wiley.

Cohen, P., Velez, C. N., Brook, J., & Smith, J. (1989). Mechanisms of the relation between perinatal problems, early childhood illness, and psychopathology in late childhood and adolescence. *Child Development, 60,* 701–709.

Cohn, J. F., & Tronick, E. Z. (1988). Mother-infant face-to-face interaction. Influence is bidirectional and unrelated to periodic cycles in either partner's behavior. *Developmental Psychology, 24,* 396–397.

Colby, A., & Kohlberg, L. (1987). *The measurement of moral judgment.* (Vols. 1 and 2). Cambridge, England: Cambridge University Press.

Colby, A., Kohlberg, L., Gibbs, J., & Lieberman, M. (1983). A longitudinal study of moral judgment. *Monographs of the Society for Research in Child Development* (Serial No. 201).

Cole, S. (1981). *Working kids on working,* New York: Lothrop, Lee, & Shepard.

Coleman, J. S. (1961). *The adolescent society.* New York: Free Press.

Coleman, J. S., et. al. (1974). *Youth: Transition to adulthood.* Report of the Panel on Youth of the President's Science Advisory Committee. Chicago: University of Chicago Press.

Coles, R. (1977). *Eskimos, Chicanos, and Indians.* Boston: Little, Brown.

Coletta, N. D. (1978). *Divorced mothers at two income levels: Stress, support, and child rearing practices.* Unpublished thesis, Ithaca, NY: Cornell University.

Collins, W. A. (1989, April). *Parents' relational cognitions and developmental changes in relationships during adolescence.* Paper presented at the biennial meeting of the Society for Research in Child Development, Kansas City.

Colombo, J., Moss, M., & Horowitz, F. D. (in press). Neonatal state profiles: Reliability and short-term prediction of neurobehavioral status. *Child Development.*

Compas, B. (1989, April). *Vulnerability to stress in childhood and adolescence.* Paper presented at the biennial meeting of the Society for Research in Child Development, Kansas City.

Conant, J. B. (1959). *The American high school today.* New York: McGraw-Hill.

Condry, J., Bence, P., & Scheibe, C. (1988). Nonprogram content of children's television. *Journal of Broadcasting and Electronic Media, 32,* 255–270.

Condry, J. C. (1989). *The psychology of television.* Hillsdale, NJ: Erlbaum.

Conger, J. J. (1981). Freedom and commitment: Families, Youth, and Social Change. *American Psychologist, 36,* 1475–1484.

Conger, J. J. (1988). Hostages to fortune: Youth, values, and the public interest. *American Psychologist, 43,* 291–300.

Conger, R. D., Elder, G. H., Lasley, P., Lorenz, F., Norem, R., & Simons, R. L. (1989). *Preliminary findings from the Iowa Youth and Families Project.* Paper presented at the biennial meeting of the Society for Research in Child Development, Kansas City.

Coons, S., & Guilleminault, C. (1984). Development of consolidated sleep and wakeful periods in relation to the day/night cycle of infancy. *Developmental Medicine and Child Neurology, 26,* 169–176.

Cooper, C. R., & Ayers-Lopez, S. (1985). Family and peer systems in early adolescence: New models of the role of relationships in development. *Journal of Early Adolescence, 5,* 9–22.

Cooper, C. R., & Grotevant, H. D. (1989, April). *Individuality and connectedness in the family and adolescents' self and relational competence.* Paper presented at the biennial meeting of the Society for Research in Child Development, Kansas City.

Cooper, C. R., Grotevant, H. D., Moore, M. S., & Condon, S. M. (1982, August). *Family support and conflict: Both foster adolescent identity and role taking.* Paper presented at the meeting of the American Psychological Association, Washington, DC.

Coopersmith, S. (1967). *The antecedents of self-esteem.* San Francisco: W. H. Freeman.

Corrigan, R. (1981). The effects of task and practice on search for invisibly displaced objects. *Developmental Review, 11,* 1–17.

Corwin, V. (1989, March). *Sesame Street abroad. Sesame Street Magazine Parent's Guide,* pp. 24, 26.

Cowan, P. A. (1988). Becoming a father: A time of change, an opportunity for development. In P. Bronstein & C. P. Cowan (Eds.), *Fatherhood today.* New York: Wiley.

Cowan, P. A., & Cowan, C. P. (1989, April). *From parent adaptation pregnancy to child adaptation in kindergarten.* Paper presented at the biennial meeting of the Society for Research in Child Development, Kansas City.

Cowan, P. A., & Cowan, C. P. (in press). Becoming a family: Research and intervention. In I. E. Sigel & G. Brody (Eds.), *Methods of family research* (Vol. 1). Hillsdale, NJ: Erlbaum.

Crites, J. O. (1989). Career differentiation in adolescence. In D. Stern & D. Eichorn (Eds.), *Adolescence and work.* Hillsdale, NJ: Erlbaum.

Crittenden, P. (1988a). Family and dyadic patterns of functioning in maltreating families. In K. Browne, C. Davies, & P. Stratton (Eds.), *Early prediction and prevention of child abuse.* New York: John Wiley.

Crittenden, P. (1988b). Relationships at risk. In J. Belsky & T. Nezworski (Eds.), *The clinical implications for attachment.* Hillsdale, NJ: Erlbaum.

Cronbach, L. J., & Snow, R. E. (1977). *Aptitudes and instructional methods.* New York: Irvington Books.

Cross, K. P. (1984, November). The rising tide of school reform reports. *Phi Delta Kappan,* pp. 167–172.

Crowder, R. G. (1982). *The psychology of reading.* New York: Oxford University Press.

Csapo, M. (1986). Education and special education in Vietnam. In K. Marfo, S. Walker, & B. Charles (Eds.), *Childhood disability in developing countries.* New York: Praeger.

Cuban, L. (1988, April). You're on the right track, David. *Phi Delta Kappan,* 565–570.

Culp, R. E., & Osofsky, J. D. (1987, April). *Transition to parenthood in the early postpartum period.* Paper presented at the biennial meeting of the Society for Research in Child Development, Baltimore.

Curtiss, S. (1977). *Genie.* New York: Academic Press.

Danner, F. (1989). Cognitive development in adolescence. In J. Worrell & F. Danner (Eds.), *The adolescent as decision maker.* New York: Academic Press.

Darling, C. A., Kallen, D. J., & VanDusen, J. E. (1984). Sex in transition, 1900–1984. *Journal of Youth and Adolescence, 13,* 385–399.

Daro, D. (1988). *Confronting child abuse.* New York: The Free Press.

Dawson, G. (Ed.). (1989). *Autism: Nature, diagnosis, and treatment.* New York: Guilford.

Deci, E. L. (1975). *Intrinsic motivation.* New York: Plenum.

DeFries, J. C., Plomin, R., Vandenberg, S. G., & Kuse, A. R. (1981). Parent-offspring resemblance in cognitive abilities in the Colorado adoption project: Biological, adoption, and control parents and one-year-old children. *Intelligence, 5,* 245–277.

DeLoache, J. S., Cassidy, D. J., & Carpenter, C. J. (1987). The Three Bears are all boys: Mother's gender labeling of neutral picture book characters. *Sex Roles, 17,* 163–178.

Dembrowski, T., & Czajkowski, S. M. (1989). Historical and current developments in coronary-prone behavior. In A. W. Siegman & T. Dembrowski (Eds.), *In search of coronary-prone behavior: Beyond Type A.* Hillsdale, NJ: Erlbaum.

Demorest, A., Meyer, C., Phelps, E., Gardner, H., & Winner, E. (1984). Words speak louder than actions: Understanding deliberately false remarks. *Child Development, 55,* 1527–1534.

Dempster, F. N. (1981). Memory span: Sources of individual and developmental differences. *Psychological Bulletin, 80,* 63–100.

De Necochea, G. (1988, May). Expanding the Hispanic college pool. *Change,* pp. 61–62.

Denham, S. A. (1986). Social cognition, prosocial behavior, and emotion in preschoolers: Contextual validation. *Child Development, 57,* 194–201.

de Souza, A. (1979). *Children in India.* New Delhi: Manohar.

de Villiers, J. G., & de Villiers, P. A. (1978). *Language acquisition.* Cambridge, MA: Harvard University Press.

Diamond, A. (1989, April). Behavioral and anatomical approaches to the study of frontal and hippocampal functions in infants and toddlers. Paper presented at the biennial meeting of the Society for Research in Child Development, Kansas City.

Diamond, E. E. (1988). Women's occupational plans and decisions: An introduction. *Applied Psychology: An International Review, 37,* 97–102.

Dickerscheid, J. D., Schwarz, P. M., Noir, S., & El-Taliawy, T. (1988). Gender concept development of preschool-aged children in the United States and Egypt. *Sex Roles, 18,* 669–677.

Dickinson, G. E. (1975). Dating behavior of black and white adolescents before and after desegregation. *Journal of Marriage and the Family, 37,* 602–608.

Dillon, R. S. (1980) *Diagnosis and management of endocrine and metabolic disorders* (2nd ed.). Philadelphia: Lea & Febiger.

DiPietro, J. A. (1981). Rough and tumble play: A function of gender. *Developmental Psychology, 17,* 50–58.

Dishion, T. J., Patterson, G. R., & Skinner, M. L. (1989, April). *Parent monitoring and peer relations in the drift to deviant peers.* Paper presented at the biennial meeting of the Society for Research in Child Development, Kansas City.

Dodge, K. A. (1983). Behavioral antecedents of peer social status. *Child Development, 54,* 1386–1399.

Dodge, K. A., Petit, G. S., McClaskey, C. L., & Brown, M. M. (1986). Social competence in children. *Monographs of the Society for Research in Child Development, 51* (2, Serial No. 213).

Dolgin, K. G., & Behrend, D. A. (1984). Children's knowledge about animates and inanimates. *Child Development, 55,* 1646–1650.

Doll, G. (1988, Spring). Day care. *Vanderbilt Magazine,* p. 29.

Donovan, J. E., & Jessor, R. (1978). Adolescent problem drinking. Psychosocial correlates in a national sample study. *Journal of Studies on Alcohol, 39,* 1506, 1524.

Douvan, E., & Adelson, J. (1966). *The adolescent experience.* New York: John Wiley.

Downey, A. M., Frank, G. C., Webber, L. S., Harsha, D. W., Virgilio, S. J., Franklin, F. A., & Berenson, G. S. (1987). Implementation of "Heart Smart": A cardiovascular school health promotion program. *Journal of School Health, 57,* 98–104.

Downs, A. C., & Langlois, J. H. (1988). Sex typing: Construct and measurement issues. *Sex Roles, 18,* 87–100.

Dreyer, P. H. (1982). Sexuality during adolescence. In B. B. Wolman (Ed.), *Handbook of developmental psychology.* Englewood Cliffs, NJ: Prentice-Hall.

Dubow, E. F., & Tisak, J. (in press). The relation between stressful life events and adjustment in elementary school children: The role of social support and social problems solving skills. *Child Development.*

Ducey, S. (1989, April). *Gender differences in mathematics: Beyond description.* Paper presented at the biennial meeting of the Society for Research in Child Development, Kansas City.

Duck, S. W. (1975). Personality similarity and friendship choices by adolescents. *European Journal of Social Psychology, 5,* 351–365.

Dugdale, S., & Kibbey, D. (1980). *Fractions curriculum of the PLATO elementary mathematical project.* Urbana-Champaign, IL: Computer-based Education Research Laboratory.

Dumtschin, J. U. (1988, March). Recognize language development and delay in early childhood. *Young Children,* pp. 16–24.

Dunn, J., & Kendrick, C. (1982). *Siblings.* Cambridge, MA: Harvard University Press.

Dunn, J. (1988). *The beginnings of social understanding.* Cambridge, MA: Harvard University Press.

Dunphy, D. C. (1963). The social structure of urban adolescent peer groups. *Society, 26,* 230–246.

Durand, V. M., & Crimmins, D. B. (1987). Assessment and treatment of psychotic speech in an autistic child. *Journal of Autism and Developmental Disorders, 17,* 17–28.

Durden-Smith, J., & Desimone, D. (1983). *Sex and the brain,* New York: Arbor House.

Durkin, D. (1987). *Teaching young children how to read* (4th ed) Boston: Allyn & Bacon.

Eagleston, J. R., Kirmil-Gray, K., Thoresen, C. E., Wiedenfield, S. A., Bracke, P., Heft, L., & Arnow, B. (in press). Physical health correlates of Type A behavior in children and adolescents. *Journal of Behavioral Medicine.*

Early Childhood and Literacy Development Committee of the International Reading Association (1986). Literacy development and pre-first grade. *Young Children, 41,* 10–13.

Eccles, J. S. (1987). Gender roles and achievement patterns: An expectancy value perspective. In J. M. Reinisch, L. A. Rosenblum, & S. A. Sanders (Eds.), *Masculinity/Femininity.* New York: Oxford University Press.

Eccles, J. S., Midgley, C., Feldlaufer, H., Reuman, D., Wigfield, A., & MacIver, D. (1989, April). *Junior high transition: Evidence of a developmental mismatch.* Paper presented at the biennial meeting of the Society for Research in Child Development, Kansas City.

Edelman, M. W. (1987). *Families in peril.* Cambridge, MA: Harvard University Press.

Edelman, M. W. (1987). *Families in peril: An agenda for social change.* New York: Alan Guttmacher Institute.

Edwards, E. D., & Edwards, M. E. (1988). Alcoholism prevention/ treatment and native American youth: A community approach. *Journal of Drug Issues, 18,* 103–114.

Egeland, B. (1989, January). *Secure attachment in infancy and competence in the third grade.* Paper presented at the meeting of the American Association for the Advancement of Science, San Francisco.

Egeland, B., Jacobvitz, D., & Papatola, K. (in press). Intergenerational continuity of parental abuse. In J. Lancaster & R. Gelles (Eds.), *Biosocial aspects of child abuse.* New York: Jossey-Bass.

Egeland, B., Jacobvitz, D., & Sroufe, L. A. (1987). *Breaking the cycle of abuse: Relationship predictors.* University of Minnesota, Minneapolis.

Eibl-Eibesfeldt, I. (1989). *Human ethology.* Hawthorne, NY: Aldine.

Eisenberg, N. (1987). The relation of altruism and other moral behaviors to moral cognition: Methodological and conceptual issues. In N. Eisenberg (Ed.), *Contemporary topics in developmental psychology*. New York: Wiley.

Eisenberg, N. (1989). The development of prosocial values. In N. Eisenberg & J. Reykowski (Eds.), *Social and moral values*. Hillsdale, NJ: Erlbaum.

Eitzen, D. S. (1975). Athletics in the status system of male adolescents. A replication of Coleman's *The Adolescent Society*. *Adolescence, 10*, 267–276.

Elder, G. H., & Caspi, A. (in press). Studying lives in a changing society. In A. I. Rabin, R. A. Zucker, S. Frank, & R. Emmons (Eds.), *Study in persons and lives*. New York: Springer.

Elder, G. H, Caspi, A., & Downey, G. (1986). Problem behavior and family relationships: A multigenerational analysis. In A. Sorensen, F. Weinert, & L. Sherrod (Eds.), *Human development and the life course*. Hillsdale, NJ: Erlbaum.

Elkind, D. (1970, April 5). Erik Erikson's eight ages of man. *New York Times Magazine*.

Elkind, D. (1976). *Child development and education*. New York: Oxford University Press.

Elkind, D. (1976). *Child development and education: A Piagetian perspective*. New York: Oxford University Press.

Elkind, D. (1978). Understanding the young adolescent. *Adolescence, 13*, 127, 134.

Elkind, D. (1981). *The hurried child*. Reading, MA: Addison-Wesley.

Elkind, D. (1987). *Miseducation: Preschoolers at risk*. New York: Knopf.

Elkind, D. (1988, January). Educating the very young: A call for clear thinking. *NEA Today*, pp. 22–27.

Emde, R. N., Gaensbauer, T. G., & Harmon, R. J. (1976). Emotional expression in infancy: A biobehavioral study. *Psychological Issues, Monograph Series, 10* (37).

Emery, R. E. (1989). Family violence. *American Psychologist, 44*, 321–328.

Englert, C. S., Stewart, S. R., & E. H. Hiebert (1988). Young writers' use of text structure in expository text generation. *Journal of Educational Psychology, 80*, 143–151.

Ensher, G., & Miller, P. (1989, April). The Syracuse Scales of Infant Development and Home Observation: A standardized measure for high risk and handicapped babies, birth to 12 months. Paper presented at the biennial meeting of the Society for Research in Child Development, Kansas City.

Epstein, S. (1973). The self-concept revisited. *American Psychologist, 28*, 404–416.

Erikson, E. H. (1950). *Childhood and society*. New York: Norton.

Erikson, E. H. (1968). *Identity: Youth and crisis*. New York: Norton.

Eron, L. D. (1987). The development of aggression from the perspective of a developing behaviorism. *American Psychologist. 42*, 435–442.

Escalona, S. (1988). Cognition in its relationship to total development in the first year. In B. Inhelder, D. DeCaprona, & A. Cornu-Wells (Eds.), *Piaget Today*. Hillsdale, NJ: Erlbaum.

Etzel, R. (1988, October). *Children of smokers*. Paper presented at the American Academy of Pediatrics meeting, New Orleans.

Fagan, J. F., & Knevel, C. R. (1989, April). The prediction of above average intelligence from infancy. Paper presented at the biennial meeting of the Society for Research in Child Development, Kansas City.

Fagot, B. (1975, April). *Teacher reinforcement of feminine-preferred behavior revisited*. Paper presented at the biennial meeting of the Society for Research in Child Development, Denver.

Falbo, T., & Polit, D. F. (1986). A quantitative review of the only-child literature. Research evidence and theory development. *Psychological Bulletin, 100*, 176–189.

Fantz, R. L. (1958). Pattern vision in young infants. *Psychological Record, 8*, 43–49.

Fantz, R. L. (1961). The origin of form perception. *Scientific American, 204*, 66–72.

Farmer, J. E., Peterson, L., & Kashani, J. H. (1989, April). *Injury risk, parent and child psychopathology*. Paper presented at the biennial meeting of the Society for Research in Child Development, Kansas City.

Fasick, F. A. (1988). Patterns of formal education in high school as rites of passage. *Adolescence, 23*, 457–468.

Fassinger, K. E. (1985). A causal model of college women's career choice. *Journal of Vocational Behavior, 27*, 123–153.

Fein, G. G. (1986). Pretend play. In D. Görlitz & J. F. Wohlwill (Eds.), *Curiosity, imagination, and play*. Hillsdale, NJ: Erlbaum.

Feingold, A. (1988). Cognitive gender differences are disappearing. *American Psychologist, 43*, 95–103.

Feiring, C., & Lewis, M. (1978). The child as a member of the family system. *Behavioral Science, 23*, 225–233.

Feldman, D. H. (1989). Creativity: Proof that development occurs. In W. Damon (Ed.), *Child development today and tomorrow*. San Francisco: Jossey-Bass.

Ferber, R. (1989). Sleeplessness in the child. In M. H. Kryger, T. Roth, & W. C. Dement (Eds.), *Principles and practices of sleep medicine*. San Diego: Harcourt Brace Jovanovich.

Ferguson, K. J., Yesalis, C. E., Pomrehn, P. R., & Kirkpatrick, M. B. (1989). Attitudes, knowledge, and beliefs as predictors of exercise intent and behavior in schoolchildren. *Journal of School Health, 59*, 112–115.

Field, T. (1987, January). Interview. *Psychology Today*, p. 31.

Field, T., Scafidi, F., & Schanberg, S. (1987). Massage of preterm newborns to improve growth and development. *Pediatric Nursing, 13*, 385–387.

Field, T. M. (1979). Visual and cardiac responses to animate and inanimate faces by young term and preterm infants. *Child Development, 50*, 188–194.

Field, T. M., Woodson, R., Greenberg, R., & Cohen, D. (1982). Discrimination and imitation of facial expressions by neonates. *Science, 218*, 179–181.

Fincher, J. (1982). Before their time. *Science*, '82.

Firush, R., & Cobb, P. A. (1989, April). *Developing scripts*. Paper presented at the biennial meeting of the Society for Research in Child Development, Kansas City.

Fischer, K. W., & Lazerson, A. (1984). *Human development*. San Francisco: W. H. Freeman.

Fischman, S. H. (1987, February). Type A on trial. *Psychology Today*, pp. 42–50.

Fish, M. (1989, April) *Temperament and attachment of separation intolerance at three years*. Paper presented at the biennial meeting of the Society for Research in Child Development, Kansas City.

Flannagan, D. A., & Tate, C. S. (1989, April). *The effects of children's script knowledge on their communication and recall of scenes*. Paper presented at the biennial meeting of the Society for Research in Child Development, Kansas City.

Flavell, J. H. (1979). Metacognition and cognitive monitoring: A new area of psychological inquiry. *American Psychologist, 34*, 906–911.

Flavell, J. H. (1985). *Cognitive development* (2nd ed.). Englewood Cliffs, NJ: Prentice-Hall.

Flavell, J. H., Beach, D. R., & Chinsky, J. M. (1966). Spontaneous verbal rehearsal in a memory task as a function of age. *Child Development, 37*, 283–299.

Flavell, J. H., Friedrichs, A. G., & Hoyt, J. D. (1970). Developmental changes in memorization processes. *Cognitive Psychology, 1*, 324–340.

Flavell, J. H., Shipstead, S. G., & Croft, K. (1978). *What young children think you see when their eyes are closed*. Unpublished manuscript, Stanford University, Palo Alto, CA.

Flavell, J. H., & Wellman, H. M. (1977). Metamemory. In R. V. Kail & J. W. Hagen (Eds.), *Perspectives on the development of memory and cognition*. Hillsdale, NJ: Erlbaum.

Fleming, A. S., Ruble, D. N., Flett, G. L., & Shaul, D. L. (1988). Postpartum adjustment in first-time mothers: relations between mood, maternal attitudes, and mother-infant interactions. *Developmental Psychology, 24*, 71–81.

Fogel, A. (1988). Cyclicity and stability in mother-infant face-to-face interaction: A comment on Cohn & Tronick (1988). *Developmental Psychology, 24*, 393–395.

Fogel, A., & Melson, G. F. (Eds.) (1987). *Origins of nurturance*. Hillsdale, NJ: Erlbaum.

Fogel, A., Toda, S., & Kawai, M. (1988). Mother-infant face-to-face interaction in Japan and the United States: A laboratory comparison using 3-month-old infants. *Developmental Psychology, 24*, 398–406.

Fontana, V. J. (1988, February). Detection and management of child sexual abuse. *Medical Aspects of Human Sexuality*, pp. 126–142.

Ford, M. E. (1986). *Androgyny as self-assertion and integration: Implications for psychological and social competence*. Unpublished manuscript, Stanford University School of Education, Stanford, CA.

Foulkes, D. (1982). *Children's dreams: Longitudinal studies*. New York: Wiley.

Fowler, J. W. (1976). Stages in faith: The structural developmental approach. In T. Hennessy (Ed.), *Values and moral development*. New York: Paulist Press.

Fox, B. (1987). Literacy and state funded prekindergarten programs: Speaking out on the issues. *The Reading Teacher, 41*, 58–65.

Fox, L. H., Brody, L., & Tobin, D. (1979). *Women and mathematics*. Baltimore, MD: Intellectually Gifted Study Group, Johns Hopkins University.

Fox, N., Kagan, J., & Weiskopf, F. (1979). The growth of memory during infancy. *Genetic Psychology Monographs, 99*, 91–130.

Fox, N. A., Sutton, B., Aaron, N., & Luebering, A. (1989, April). *Infant temperament and attachment: A new look at an old issue*. Paper presented at the biennial meeting of the Society for Research in Child Development, Kansas City.

Fraiberg, S. (1977). *Insights from the blind: Comparative Studies of blind and sighted infants*. New York: Basic Books.

Frank, A. (1952). *Diary of a Young Girl*. Garden City, NY: Doubleday.

Freedman, D. G. (1971). Genetic influences on development of behavior. In G. B. A. Stoelinga & J. J. Van Der Werff Ten Bosch (Eds.), *Normal and abnormal development of behavior*. Leiden: Leiden University Press.

Freedman, D. G., & Freedman, N. (1969). Behavioral differences between Chinese-American and European-American newborns. *Nature, 224*, 1127.

Freedman, J. L. (1984). Effects of television violence on aggressiveness. *Psychological Bulletin, 96*, 227–246.

Freud, A., & Dann, S. (1951). Instinctual anxiety during puberty. In A. Freud (Ed.), *The ego and its mechanisms of defense*. New York: International Universities Press.

Freud, S. (1924). *A general introduction to psychoanalysis*. New York: Boni and Liveright.

Friedman, M. & Rosenman, R. (1974). *Type A behavior and your heart*. New York: Knopf.

Friedrich, L. K., & Stein, A. H. (1973). Aggressive and prosocial TV programs and the natural behavior of preschool children. *Monographs of the Society for Research in Child Development, 38* (4, Serial No. 151).

Frost, J. L., & Wortham, S. C. (1988, July). The evolution of American playgrounds. *Young Children*, 19–28.

Furman, L. N., & Walden, T. A. (1989, April). *The effect of script knowledge on children's communicative interactions*. Paper presented at the biennial meeting of the Society for Research in Child Development, Kansas City.

Furstenberg, F. F. (1988). Child care after divorce and remarriage. In E. M. Hetherington & J. Arasteh (Eds.), *Impact of divorce, single-parenting, and stepparenting on children*. Hillsdale, NJ: Erlbaum.

Furstenberg, F. F., Brooks-Gunn, J., & Chase-Lansdale, L. (1989). Teenaged pregnancy and childbearing. *American Psychologist, 44*, 313–320.

Furstenberg, J. J., Brooks-Gunn, J., & Morgan, S. P. (1987). Adolescent mothers in later life. New York: Cambridge University Press.

Furth, H. G., & Wachs, H. (1975). *Thinking goes to school*. New York: Oxford University Press.

Gage, N. L. (1965). Desirable behaviors of teachers. *Urban Education, 1*, 85–96.

Gagne, E. D. (1985). *The cognitive psychology of school learning*. Boston: Little, Brown.

Gagne, E. D., Weidemann, C., Bell, M. S., & Ander, T. D. (in press). Training thirteen-year-olds to elaborate while studying text. *Journal of Human Learning*.

Gagnon, J. H., & Simon, W. (1973). *Sexual conduct*. New York: Aldine.

Galambos, N. L., & Maggs, J. L. (1989, April). *The after-school ecology of young adolescents and self-reported behavior*. Paper presented at the biennial meeting of the Society for Research in Child Development, Kansas City.

Galanter, M. (1989). *Cults: Faith, healing, and coercion.* New York: Oxford University Press.

Gallagher, J. J., Trohanis, P. L., & Clifford, R. M. (1989). *Policy implementation and PL 99–457.* Baltimore, MD: Brookes.

Gallup, G., & Poling, D. (1980). *The search for America's faith.* New York: Abington.

Galst, J. P. (1980). Television food commercials and pronutritional public service announcements as determinants of young children's snack choices. *Child Development, 51,* 935–938.

Garbarino, J. (1976). The ecological correlates of child abuse: The impact of socioeconomic stress on mothers. *Child Development, 47,* 178–185.

Garbarino, J. (1989). *The psychologically battered child.* San Francisco: Jossey-Bass.

Garbarino, J., & Bronfenbrenner, U. (1976). The socialization of moral judgment and behavior in cross-cultural perspective. In T. Lickona (Ed.), *Moral development and behavior.* New York: Holt, Rinehart & Winston.

Garber, H. L. (1988). *The Milwaukee project.* Washington, DC: American Association of Mental Retardation.

Gardner, B. T., & Gardner, R. A. (1971). Two-way communication with an infant chimpanzee. In A. Schrier & F. Stollnitz (Eds.), *Behavior of nonhuman primates* (Vol. 4), New York: Academic Press.

Gardner, B. T. & Gardner, R. A. (1986). Discovering the meaning of primate signals. *British Journal for the Philosophy of Science, 37,* 477–495.

Gardner, H. (1983). *Frames of mind.* New York: Basic Books.

Gardner, H. (1989). Beyond a modular view of mind. In W. Damon (Ed.), *Child development today and tomorrow.* San Francisco: Jossey-Bass.

Gardner, H., & Perkins, D. (Eds.) (1989). *Art, mind, and education.* Ithaca, NY: University of Illinois Press.

Gardner, L. I. (1972). Deprivation dwarfism. *Scientific American, 227,* 76–82.

Garelik, G. (1985, October). Are the progeny prodigies? *Discover Magazine, 6,* 45–47, 78–84.

Garmezy, N. (1983). Stressors of childhood. In N. Garmezy & M. Rutter (Eds.), *Stress, coping, and development in children.* New York: McGraw-Hill.

Garrison, W. T., & McQuiston, S. (1989). *Chronic illness during childhood and adolescence.* Newbury Park, CA: Sage.

Garton, A. F., & Pratt, C. (1989). *Learning to be literate.* New York: Basil Blackwell.

Garvey, C. (1977). *Play.* Cambridge, MA: Harvard University Press.

Gaylord-Ross, R. (Ed.). (1989). *Integration strategies for students with handicaps.* Baltimore, MD: Brookes.

Gelman, R. (1969). Conservation acquisition: A problem of learning to attend to relevant attributes. *Journal of Experimental Child Psychology, 7,* 67–87.

Gelman, R. (1972). Logical capacity of very young children: Number invariance rules. *Child Development, 43,* 75–90.

Gelman, R. (1979). Preschool thought. *American Psychologist, 34,* 900–905.

Gelman, R., & Baillargeon, R. (1983). A review of some Piagetian concepts. In P. H. Mussen (Ed.), *Handbook of child psychology* (4th ed., Vol. 3). New York: Wiley.

Gesell, A. (1934). *An atlas of infant behavior.* New Haven, CT: Yale University Press.

Gesell, A. (1954). The ontogenesis of infant behavior. In L. Carmichael (Ed.), *Manual of child psychology.* New York: Wiley.

Gesell, A. L. (1928). *Infancy and human growth.* New York: Macmillan.

Gewirtz, J. (1977). Maternal responding and the conditioning of infant crying: Directions of influence within the attachment-acquisition process. In B. C. Etzel, J. M. LeBlanc, & D. M. Baer (Eds.), *New developments in behavioral research.* Hillsdale, NJ: Erlbaum.

Gibbs, J. T. (1989). Black American adolescents. In J. T. Gibbs & L. N. Huang (Eds.), *Children of color.* San Francisco: Jossey-Bass.

Gibbs, J. T., & Huang, L. N. (1989). A conceptual framework for assessing and treating minority youth. In J. T. Gibbs & L. N. Huang (Eds.), *Children of color.* San Francisco, CA: Jossey-Bass.

Gibson, E. J. (1969). *The principles of perceptual learning and development.* New York: Appleton-Century-Crofts.

Gibson, E. J. (1986, October). *The concept of affordance in development.* Paper presented at the Symposium on Human Development and Communication Sciences, University of Texas at Dallas, Richardson, TX.

Gibson, E. J. (in press). Exploratory behavior in the development of perceiving, acting, and acquiring of knowledge. *Annual Review of Psychology.*

Gibson, E. J., & Spelke, E. S. (1983). The development of perception. In P. H. Mussen (Ed.), *Handbook of child psychology* (4th ed., Vol. 3). New York: Wiley.

Gibson, E. J., & Walk, R. D. (1960). The "visual cliff." *Scientific American, 202,* 64–71.

Gibson, J. J. (1979). *The ecological approach to visual perception.* Boston: Houghton Mifflin.

Gilgun, J. F. (1984). Sexual abuse of the young female in life course persective. *Dissertations Abstracts International, 45,* 3058.

Gill, S., Stockard, J., Johnson, M., & Williams, S. (1987). Measuring gender differences: The expressive dimension and critique of the androgyny scales. *Sex Roles, 17,* 375–400.

Gilligan, C. (1982). *In a different voice.* Cambridge, MA: Harvard University Press.

Gilligan, C. (1985, April). *Response to critics.* Paper presented at the biennial meeting of the Society for Research in Child Development, Toronto.

Ginsburg, H., & Opper, S. (1988). *Piaget's theory of intellectual development.* Englewood Cliffs, NJ: Prentice-Hall.

Glasser, R., & Bassok, A. (1989). Learning theory and the study of instruction. *Annual Review of Psychology, 40,* Palo Alto, CA: Annual Reviews.

Glazer, R., & Bassok, M. (1989). Learning theory and the study of instruction. *Annual Review of Psychology, 40.* Palo Alto, CA: Annual Reviews.

Gleason, J. B. (1988). Language and socialization. In F. Kessel (Ed.), *The development of language and language researchers.* Hillsdale, NJ: Erlbaum.

Glick, J. (1975). Cognitive development in cross-cultural perspective. In F. Horowitz (Ed.), *Review of Child Development Research* (Vol. 4). Chicago: University of Chicago Press.

Gold, M. (1987). Social ecology. In H. C. Quay (Ed.), *Handbook of juvenile delinquency.* New York: Wiley.

Gold, M., & Yanof, D. S. (1985). Mothers, daughters, and girlfriends. *Journal of Personality and Social Psychology, 49,* 654–659.

Gold, M. S., Gallanter, M., & Stimmel, B. (1987). *Cocaine.* New York: Haworth Press.

Goldman, J. A., Fujimura, J. B., Contois, J. H., & Lerman, R. H. (1987, April). *Interactions among preschool children following the ingestion of sucrose.* Paper presented at the biennial meeting of the Society for Research in Child Development, Baltimore.

Goldman, J. A., Lerman, R. H., Contois, J. H., & Udall, J. N. (1986). Behavioral effects of sucrose on preschool children. *Journal of Abnormal Child Psychology, 14,* 565–577.

Goldman-Rakic, P. S., Isseroff, A., Schwartz, M. L., & Bugbee, N. M. (1983). The neurobiology of cognitive development. In P. H. Mussen (Ed.), *Handbook of child psychology* (4th ed., Vol. 2). New York: Wiley.

Goldsmith, H. H. (1988, August). *Does early temperament predict late development?* Paper presented at the meeting of the American Psychological Association, Atlanta, GA.

Goldsmith, H. H., Buss, A. H., Plomin, R., Rothbart, R., Thomas, A., Chess, S., Hinde, R. A., & McCall, R. B. (1987). Roundtable: What is temperament? Four approaches. *Child Development, 58,* 505–529.

Goldsmith, H. H., & Gottesman, I. I. (1981). Origins of variation in behavioral style: A longitudinal study of temperament in young twins. *Child Development, 52,* 91–103.

Goodchilds, J. D., & Zellman, G. L. (1984). Sexual signalling and sexual aggression in adolescent relationship. In N. M. Malamuth & E. D. Donnerstein (Eds.), *Pornography and sexual aggression.* New York: Academic Press.

Goodlad, J. (1983). *A place called school.* New York: McGraw-Hill.

Goodman, R. A., Mercy, J. A., Loya, F., Rosenberg, M. L. Smith, J. C., Allen, N. H. Vargas, L., & Kolts, R. (1986). Alcohol use and interpersonal violence. Alcohol detected in homicide victims. *American Journal of Public Health, 76.* 144–149.

Goodman, S. (1979). *You and your child: From birth to adolescence.* Chicago: Rand McNally.

Gordon, S., & Gilgun, J. F. (1987). Adolescent sexuality. In V. B. Van Hasselt & M. Hersen (Eds.), *Handbook of adolescent psychology.* New York: Pergamon.

Gore, T. (1987). *Raising PG kids in an X-rated society.* Nashville, TN: Abingdon Press.

Görlitz, D., & Wohlwill, J. F. (Eds.) (1986). *Curiosity, imagination, and play.* Hillsdale, NJ: Erlbaum.

Gorski, P. A. (1988, November). *Iatrogenic stressors: Progress, plight, and promise.* Paper presented at the Developmental Interventions in Neonatal Care Conference, San Diego, CA.

Gotowiec, A., & Ames, E. W. (1989, April). *Crying and behavioral state organization in six- to eight-week-old infants.* Paper presented at the biennial meeting of the Society for Research in Child Development, Kansas City.

Gottfried, A. W., & Bathurst, K. (1989, April). Infant predictors of IQ and achievement: A comparative analysis. Paper presented at the biennial meeting of the Society for Research in Child Development, Kansas City.

Gottlieb, D. (1966). Teaching and students: The views of Negro and white teachers. *Sociology of Education, 37,* 345–353.

Gottman, J. M., & Parker, J. G. (Eds.). (1987). *Conversations of friends.* New York: Cambridge University Press.

Graddol, D., & Swann, J. (1989). *Gender voices.* New York: Basil Blackwell.

Graham, D. (1981). The obstetric and neonatal consequences of adolescent pregancy. In E. R. McAnarney & G. Stickle (Eds.), *Pregnancy and childbearing during adolescence: Research priorities for the 1980s.* New York: Alan R. Liss.

Graham, S. (1984). Communicating sympathy and anger to black and white students: The cognitive (attributional) antecedents of affective cues. *Journal of Personality and Social Psychology, 47,* 40–54.

Graham, S. (1986, August). *Can attribution theory tell us something about motivation in blacks?* Paper presented at the meeting of the American Psychological Association, Washington, DC.

Graham, S. (1987, August). *Developing relations between attributions affect, and intended social behavior.* Paper presented at the meeting of the American Psychological Association, New York.

Granrud, C. E. (1989, April). *Visual size and shape constancy in 4-month-old infants.* Paper presented at the biennial meeting of the Society for Research in Child Development, Kansas City.

Grant, J. P. (1988). *The state of the world's children.* New York: UNICEF and Oxford University Press.

Graubard, P. S., & Rosenberg, H., with Gray, F. (1974, May). Little brother is changing you. *Psychology Today,* pp. 42–46.

Graves, D. (1983). *Writing: Teachers and children at work.* Portsmouth, NH: Heinemann.

Greenberg, M. T., & Crnic, K. A. (1988). Longitudinal predictors of developmental status and social interaction in premature and full-term infants at age two. *Child Development, 59,* 554–570.

Greenberger, E. (1987, August). *Teenagers who work: Research goes to Congress and meets the media.* Paper presented at the meeting of the American Psychological Association, New York City.

Greene, B. (1988, May). The children's hour. *Esquire Magazine,* 47–49.

Greenfield, P., & Beagles-Roos, J. (in press). Television vs. radio: The cognitive impact on different socio-economic and ethnic groups. *Journal of Communication.*

Greenfield, P. M., Bruzzone, L., Koyamatsu, K., Satuloff, W., Nixon, K., Brodie, M., & Kingsdale, D. (1987). What is rock music doing to the minds of our youth? A first experimental look at the effects of the rock music lyrics and music videos. *Journal of Early Adolescence, 7,* 315–329.

Grieser, D. L., & Kuhl, P. K. (1988). Maternal speech to infants in tonal language: Support for universal prosodic features in motherese. *Developmental Psychology, 24*, 14–20.

Griffing, P. (1980). The relationship between socioeconomic status and sociodramatic play among black kindergarten children. *Genetic Psychology Monographs, 101*, 3–34.

Griffing, P. (1983, January). Encouraging dramatic play in early childhood. *Young Children*, pp. 13–23.

Grossman, F. K., Pollack, W. S., & Golding, E. (1988). Fathers and children: Predicting the quality and quantity of fathering. *Developmental Psychology, 24*, 82–91.

Grotevant, H. D., & Cooper, C. R. (1985). Patterns of interaction in family relationships and the development of identity exploration in adolescence. *Child Development, 56*, 415–428.

Grotevant, H. D., & Durrett, M. E. (1980). Occupational knowledge and career development in adolescence. *Journal of Vocational Behavior, 17*, 171–182.

Grubb, W. N. (1989). Preparing youth for work. In D. Stern & D. Eichorn (Eds.), *Adolescence and work*. Hillsdale, NJ: Erlbaum.

Guilford, J. P. (1967). *The structure of intellect*. New York: McGraw-Hill.

Gunnar, M. R., Malone, S., & Fisch, R. O. (1987). The psychobiology of stress and coping in the human neonate: Studies of the adrenocortical activity in response to stress in the first week of life. In T. Field, P. McCabe, & N. Scheiderman (Eds.), *Stress and coping*. Hillsdale, NJ: Erlbaum.

Gustafson, G. E. (1989, April). *On some common assumptions about cry perception and infant development*. Paper presented at the biennial meeting of the Society for Research in Child Development, Kansas City.

Gustafson, G. E., & Green, J. A. (1989). On the importance of fundamental frequency and other acoustic features in cry perception and infant development. *Child Development, 60*, 772–780.

Gutek, B. A. (1988). Sex segregation and women at work: A selective review. *Applied Psychology: An International Review, 37*, 103–120.

Hahn, A. (1987, December). Reaching out to America's dropouts: What to do? *Phi Delta Kappan*, 256–263.

Hakuta, K. & Garcia, E. E. (1989). Bilingualism and education. *American Psychologist, 44*, 374–379.

Hall, G. S. (1904). *Adolescence* (Vols. 1 and 2). Englewood Cliffs, NJ: Prentice-Hall.

Hall, W. S. (1989). Reading comprehension. *American Psychologist, 44*, 157–161.

Hallahan, D. P., Kauffman, J. M., Lloyd, J. W., & McKinney, J. D. (1988). Questions about the regular education initiative. *Journal of Learning Disabilities, 21*, 3–5.

Hans, S. (1989, April). *Infant behavioral effects of prenatal exposure to methadone*. Paper presented at the biennial meeting of the Society for Research in Child Development, Kansas City.

Hardyck, C., & Petrinovich, L. F. (1977). Left-handedness. *Psychological Bulletin, 84*, 385–404.

Harlow, H. F., & Zimmerman, R. R. (1959). Affectional responses in the infant monkey. *Science, 130*, 421–432.

Harris, L. (1987, September 3). The latchkey child phenomena. *Dallas Morning News*, pp. 1A, 10A.

Harter, S. (1981). A new self-report scale of intrinsic versus extrinsic motivation in the classroom: Motivational and informational components. *Developmental Psychology, 17*, 300–312.

Harter, S. (1982). The Perceived Competence Scale for Children. *Child Development, 53*, 87–97.

Harter, S., Alexander, P. C., & Neimeyer, R. A. (1988). Long-term effects of incestuous child abuse in college women: Social adjustment, social cognition, and family characteristics. *Journal of Consulting and Clinical Psychology, 56*, 5–8.

Hartshorne, H., & May, M. A. (1928–30). *Studies in the nature of character*. New York: Macmillan.

Hartup, W. W. (1983). Peer relations. In P. H. Mussen (Ed.), *Handbook of child psychology* (4th ed., Vol. 4). New York: Wiley.

Hartup, W. W. (1989). Social relationships and their developmental significance. *American Psychologist, 44*, 120–126.

Harvard Medical School Newsletter (1981, April). Cambridge, MA: Department of Continuing Education, Harvard Medical School.

Haskins, R. (1989). Beyond metaphor: The efficacy of early childhood education. *American Psychologist, 44*, 274–282.

Hathaway, B. (1984, September). Japanese question the value of IQ tests. *APA Monitor*, pp. 10–11.

Haugard, J. J., & Emery, R. E. (in press). Methodological issues in child sex abuse research. *Child Abuse and Neglect*.

Havighurst, R. J. (1987). Adolescent culture and subculture. In V. B. Van Haselt & M. Hersen (Eds.) *Handbook of adolescent psychology*. New York: Pergamon.

Hawkins, J. A., & Berndt, T. J. (1985, April). *Adjustment following the transition to junior high school*. Paper presented at the biennial meeting of the Society for Research in Child Development, Toronto.

Hayden-Thomson, L., Rubin, K. M., & Hymel, S. (1987). Sex preferences in sociometric choices. *Developmental Psychology, 23*, 558–562.

Hayes, K. J., & Hayes, C. (1951). Picture perception in a home-raised chimpanzee. *Journal of Comparative and Physiological Psychology, 46*, 470–474.

Heath, L., Bresolin, L. B., & Rinaldi, R. C. (1989). Effects of media violence on children. *Archives of General Psychiatry, 46*, 376–379.

Heath, S. B. (1989). Oral and literate traditions among Black Americans living in poverty. *American Psychologist, 44*, 367–373.

Heath, S. B. (in press). The children of Trackton's children: Spoken and written language in social change. In J. Stigler, G. Herdt, & R. A. Shweder (Eds.), *Cultural psychology: The Chicago symposia*. New York: Cambridge University Press.

Hein, K. (1989). AIDS in adolescence. *Journal of Adolescent Health Care, 10*, 105–135.

Helson, R., Elliot, T., & Leigh, J. (1989). Adolescent antecedents of women's work patterns. In D. Stern & D. Eichorn (Eds.), *Adolescence and work*. Hillsdale, NJ: Erlbaum.

Hendry, J. (1986). *Becoming Japanese: The world of the preschool child*. Honolulu: University of Hawaii Press.

Henker, B., & Whalen, C. K. (1989). Hyperactivity and attention deficits. *American Psychologist, 44,* 216–223.

Hennessey, B. A., & Amabile, T. M. (1988). The conditions of creativity. In R. J. Sternberg (Ed.), *The nature of creativity.* New York: Cambridge University Press.

Herdt, G. H. (1988, August). *Coming out processes as an anthropological rite of passage.* Paper presented at the meeting of the American Psychological Association, Atlanta, GA.

Hertzig, M., & Shapiro, T. (in press). Autism and pervasive developmental disorders. In M. E. Lewis & S. Miller (Eds.), *Handbook of developmental psychopathology.* New York: Plenum.

Hess, R. D., Kashinsagi, K., Azuma, H., Price, G. C., & Dickson, W. P. (1980). Maternal expectations for mastery of developmental tasks in Japan and the United States. *International Journal of Psychology, 15,* 259–271.

Hetherington, E. M. (1989). Coping with family transitions: Winners, losers, and survivors. *Child Development, 60,* 1–14.

Hetherington, E. M., Cox, M., & Cox, R. (1982). Effects of divorce on children and parents. In M. E. Lamb (Ed.), *Nontraditional families.* Hillsdale, NJ: Erlbaum.

Hetherington, E. M., Hagan, M. S., & Anderson, E. R. (1989). Family transitions: A child's perspective. *American Psychologist, 44,* 303–312.

Hetherington, E. M., Lerner, R. M., & Perlmutter, M. (Eds.). (1988). *Child development in life-span perspective.* Hillsdale, NJ: Erlbaum.

Hewlitt, B. S. (1987). Intimate fathers: Patterns of paternal holding among Aka pygmies. In M. E. Lamb (Ed.), *The Father's role: Cross-cultural perspectives.* Hillsdale, NJ: Erlbaum.

Hill, C. R., & Stafford, F. P. (1980). Parental care of children: Time diary estimate of quantity, predictability, and variety. *Journal of Human Resources, 15,* 219–239,

Hill, J. P. (1980). The early adolescent and the family. In M. Johnson (Ed.), *The 79th Yearbook of the National Society for the Study of Education.* Chicago: University of Chicago Press.

Hill, J. P. (1983, April). *Early adolescence: A research agenda.* Paper presented at the biennial meeting of the Society for Research in Child Development, Detroit.

Hill, J. P. & Holmbeck, G. N. (1986). Attachment and autonomy during adolescence. *Annals of Child Development.* Greenwich, CT: JAI Press.

Hill, J. P., Holmbeck, G. N., Marlow, L., Green, T. M., & Lynch, M. E. (1985). Pubertal status and parent-child relations in families of seventh-grade boys. *Journal of Early Adolescence, 5,* 31–44.

Hinde, R. (1983). Ethology and child development. In P. H. Mussen (Ed.), *Handbook of child psychology* (4th ed., Vol. 2). New York: Wiley.

Hinde, R., & Stevenson-Hinde, J. (Eds.). (1988). Relationships within families. New York: Oxford University Press.

Hinde, R. A. (1989, April). *Differential treatment of particular characteristics in boys and girls.* Paper presented at the biennial meeting of the Society for Research in Child Development, Kansas City.

Hinde, R. A. (1989). Ethological and relationship approaches. In R. Vasta (Ed.), *Six theories of child development: Revised formulations and current issues.* Greenwich, CT: JAI Press.

Hinde, R. A., & Gorebel, J. (1989). The problem of aggression. In J. Groebel & R. A. Hinde (Eds.), *Aggression and war: Their biological bases.* New York: Cambridge.

Hirsch, B. J. (1989, April). *School transitions and psychological well-being in adolescence: Comparative longitudinal analyses.* Paper presented at the biennial meeting of the Society for Research in Child Development, Kansas City.

Hirsch, B. J., & Rapkin, B. D. (1987). The transition to junior high school: A longitudinal study of self-esteem, psychological symptomatology, school life, and social support. *Child Development, 58,* 1235–1243.

Hirsch, E. D. (1987). *Cultural literacy.* Boston: Houghton Mifflin.

Ho, D. Y. F. (1987). Fatherhood in Chinese culture. In M. E. Lamb (Ed.), *The father's role: Cross-cultural perspectives.* Hillsdale, NJ: Erlbaum.

Hobbs, N. (Ed.). (1975). *Issues in the classification of children* (Vol. 1). San Francisco: Jossey-Bass.

Hoffman, L. W. (1979). Maternal employment: 1979. *American Psychologist, 34,* 859–865.

Hoffman, L. W. (1989). Effects of maternal employment in two-parent families. *American Psychologist, 44,* 283–293.

Hoge, R. D. (1987). Issues in the definition and measurement of the giftedness construct. *Educational Researcher, 17,* 12–16.

Holmes, D. L., Reich, J. N., Y Gyurke, J. S. (1989). The development of high-risk infants in low-risk families. In F. J. Morrison, C. Lord, & D. P. Keating (Eds.), *Psychological development in infancy.* San Diego: Academic Press.

Holtzmann, W. H. (1982). Cross-cultural comparisons of personality development in Mexico and the United States. In D. A. Wagner & H. W. Stevenson (Eds.), *Cultural perspectives on child development.* New York: W. H. Freeman.

Holzman, M. (1983). *The language of children: Development in home and school.* Englewood Cliffs, NJ: Prentice-Hall.

Honig, A. S. (1986, July). Stress and coping in children (Pt2): Interpersonal family relationships. *Young Children,* 47–59.

Horne, M. D. (1988). Handicapped, disabled, or exceptional: Terminological issues. *Psychology in the Schools, 25,* 419–421.

Horowitz, F. D., & O'Brien, M. (1989). In the interest of the nation: A reflective essay on the state of knowledge and the challenges before us. *American Psychologist, 44,* 441–445.

Howard, J. (1982). Counseling: A developmental approach. In E. E. Bleck & D. A. Nagel (Ed.), *Physically handicapped children.* New York: Grune & Stratton.

Howard, J. (1988, November). *Developmental and behavioral concerns of drug dependent mothers.* Paper presented at the Developmental Intervention in Neonatal Care Conference, San Diego, CA.

Howes, C. (1988, April). *Can the age of entry and the quality of infant child care predict behaviors in kindergarten?* Paper presented at the International Conference on Infant Studies, Washington, D.C.

Howes, C., Unger, O., & Seidner, L. B. (1989). Social pretend play in toddlers: Parallels with social play and solitary pretend. *Child Development, 60,* 77–84.

Huang, L. L. (1982). Planned fertility of one-couple one-child policy in the People's Republic of China. *Journal of Marriage and the Family, 44,* 775–784.

Huang, L. N. (1989). Southeast Asian refugee children and adolescents. In J. T. Gibbs & L. N. Huang (Eds.), *Children of color.* San Francisco: Jossey-Bass.

Huang, L. N., & Gibbs, J. T. (1989). Future directions: Implications for research, training, and practice. In J. T. Gibbs & L. N. Huang (Eds.), *Children of color.* San Francisco: Jossey-Bass.

Hubbard, R. (1988). Allow children's individuality to emerge in their writing: Let their voices through. *Young Children, 43,* 33–38.

Humphreys, A., & Smith, P. K. (1987). Rough-and-tumble play, friendship, and dominance in school children: Evidence for continuity and change with age. *Child Development, 58,* 201–212.

Hunt, J. V., & Cooper, B. A. (1989). Determining the risk for high-risk preterm infants. In M. Bornstein & N. A. Krasnegor (Eds.), *Stability and continuity in mental development.* Hillsdale, NJ: Erlbaum.

Hunt, M. (1974). *Sexual behavior in the 1970s.* Chicago: Playboy Press.

Hurley, L. S. (1980). *Developmental nutrition.* Englewood Cliffs, NJ: Prentice-Hall.

Hurrelmann, K. (1989). *Human development and health.* New York: Springer-Verlag.

Huston, A. C. (1983). Sex-typing. In P. H. Mussen (Ed.), *Handbook of child psychology* (4th ed., Vol. 4). New York: Wiley.

Huston, A. C., Seigle, J., & Bremer, M. (1983, April). *Family environment and television use by preschool children.* Paper presented at the biennial meeting of the Society for Research in Child Development, Detroit.

Huston, A. C., Watkins, B. A., & Kunkel, D. (1989). Public policy and children's television. *American Psychologist, 44,* 424–433.

Huston-Stein, A., & Higgens-Trenk, A. (1978). Development of females from childhood through adulthood: Career and feminine role orientations. In P. Baltes (Ed.), *Life-span development and behavior* (Vol. 1). New York: Academic Press.

Hutchings, D. E., & Fifer, W. P. (1986). Neurobehavioral effects in human and animal offspring following prenatal exposure to methadone. In E. P. Riley & C. V. Vorhees (Eds.), *Handbook of behavioral teratology.* New York Plenum.

Hutchings, N. (Ed.). (1988). *The violent family.* New York: Human Sciences Press.

Hwang, P. (1987). The changing role of Swedish fathers. In M. E. Lamb (Ed.), *The father's role: Cross-cultural perspectives.* Hillsdale, NJ: Erlbaum.

Hyde, J. S., & Linn, M. C. (Eds.). (1986). *The psychology of gender: Advances through meta-analysis.* Baltimore, MD: Johns Hopkins University Press.

Hynd, G. W., & Obrzut, J. E. (1986). Exceptionality: Historical antecedents and present positions. In R. T. Brown & C. R. Reynolds (Eds.), *Psycological perspectives on childhood exceptionality: A handbook.* New York: Wiley.

Ianni, F. A. J. (1989). *The search for structure: A report on American youth today.* New York: The Free Press.

Ianotti, R. J. (1985). Naturalistic and structured assessments of prosocial behavior in preschool children: The influence of empathy and perspective taking. *Developmental Psychology, 21,* 46–55.

Iheanacho, S. O. (1987). Minority self-concept: A research review. *Journal of Instructional Psychology, 15,* 3–11.

Inhoff-German, G., Arnold, G. S., Nottelmann, E. D., Susamn, E. J., Culter, G. B., & Chrousos, G. P. (1988). Relations between hormone levels and observational measures of aggressive behavior of young adolescents in family interactions. *Developmental Psychology, 24,* 129–139.

Irvin, F. S. (1988, August). *Clinical perspectives on resilience among gay and lesbian youth.* Paper presented at the annual meeting of the American Psychological Association, Atlanta, GA.

Isberg, R. S., Hauser, S. T., Jacobson, A. M., Powers, S. I., Noam, G., Weiss-Perry, B., & Follansbee, D. (1989). Parental contexts of adolescent self-esteem. *Journal of Youth and Adolescence, 18,* 1–23.

Isenberg, J., & Quisenberry, N. L. (1988). Play: A necessity for all children. *Childhood Education, 64,* 138–145.

Ismail, H., & Lall, P. (1981). Visual acuity of school entrants. *Child Care, Health, and Development, 7,* 127.

Izard, C. E. (1982). *Measuring emotions in infants and young children.* New York: Cambridge University Press.

Izard, C. E., & Malatesta, C. Z. (1987). Differential emotions theory of early emotional development. In J. D. Osofsky (Ed.), *Handbook of infant development.* New York: Wiley.

Jacklin, C. N. (1989). Female and male: Issues of gender. *American Psychologist, 44,* 127–133.

Jalongo, M. R., & Zeigler, S. (1987). Writing in kindergarten and first grade. *Childhood Education, 74,* 97–104.

James, W. (1890). *The principles of psychology:* New York: Dover.

Janos, P. M., & Robinson, N. M. (1985). Psychosocial development in intellectually gifted children. In F. D. Horowitz & M. O'Brien (Eds.). *The gifted and the talented.* Washington, DC: American Psychological Association.

Javernik, E. (1988, January). Johnny's not jumping: Can we help obese children? *Young Children,* 18–23.

Jeans, P. C., Smith, M. B., & Stearns, G. (1955). Incidence of prematurity in relation to maternal nutrition. *Journal of the American Dietary Association, 31,* 576–581.

Jensen, A. R. (1969). How much can we boost IQ and scholastic achievement? *Harvard Educational Review, 39,* 1–123.

Jessor, L., & Jessor, R. (1975). Transition from virginity to nonvirginity among youth: A social-psychological study over time. *Developmental Psychology, 11,* 473–484.

Johnston, L. D., Bachman, J. G., & O'Malley, P. M. (1986). *Monitoring the future.* Ann Arbor: University of Michigan, Institute of Social Research.

Johnston, L. D., O'Malley, P. M., & Bachman, J. G. (1988). *Illicit drug use, smoking, and drinking by America's high school students, college students, and young adults, 1975–1987.* Washington, DC: National Institute of Drug Abuse.

Johnston, L. D., O'Malley, P. M., & Bachman, J. G. (1989, February 24). *Teen drug use continues decline.* News Release, Institute for Social Research, University of Michigan, Ann Arbor.

Jones, B., & Idol, L. (Eds.) (1989). Dimensions of thinking and cognitive instruction. Hillsdale, NJ: Erlbaum.

Jones, E. (1953). *The life and work of Sigmund Freud* (Vol. 1). New York: Basic Books.

Jones, E. R., Forrest, J. D., Goldman, N., Henshaw, S. K., Lincoln, R., Rosoff, J. I., Westoff, C. G., & Wulf, D. (1985). Teenage pregnancy in developed countries: Determinants and policy implications. *Family Planning Perspectives, 17,* 53–63.

Jones, J. M. (1989, August). *Does ethnicity influence behavior? Biculturalism in human adaptation.* Paper presented at the meeting of the American Psychological Association, New Orleans.

Jones, M. C. (1965). Psychological correlates of somatic development. *Child Development, 36,* 899–911.

Juster, F. T. (in press). A note on recent changes in time use. In F. T. Juster & F. Stafford (Eds.), *Studies in the measurement of time allocation.* Ann Arbor, MI: Institute for Social Research.

Justiz, M. J. & Rendon, L. I. (1989). Hispanic students. In M. L. Upcraft & J. N. Gardner (Eds.), *The freshman experience.* San Francisco: Jossey-Bass.

Kagan, J. (1984). *The nature of the child.* New York: Basic Books.

Kagan, J. (1987, April). *Temperamental bases for reactions to uncertainty.* Paper presented at the biennial meeting of the Society for Research in Child Development, Baltimore.

Kagan, J. (1987). Perspectives on infancy. In J. D. Osofsky (Ed.), *Handbook on infant development.* (2nd ed.). New York: Wiley.

Kagan, J. (1988, August). *The idea of temperament categories.* Paper presented at the meeting of the American Psychological Association, Atlanta, GA.

Kagan, J. (1989). *Unstable ideas: Temperament, cognition, and self.* Cambridge, MA: Harvard University Press.

Kagan, J. (in press). Inhibited and uninhibited types of children. *Child Development.*

Kagan, J., Kearsley, R. B., & Zelazo, P. R. (1978). Infancy. Cambridge, MA: Harvard University Press.

Kagan, S. L. (1988, January). Current reforms in early childhood education: Are we addressing the issues? *Young Children, 43,* 27–38.

Kail, R., & Pellegrino, J. W. (1985). *Human intelligence,* New York: W. H. Freeman.

Kandel, D. B. (1974). The role of parents and peers in marijuana use. *Journal of Social Issues, 30,* 107–135.

Kanner, A. D., Feldman, S. S., Weinberger, D. A., & Ford, M. E. (1987). Uplifts, hassles, and adaptational outcomes in early adolescents. *Journal of Early Adolescence, 7,* 371–394.

Kaplan, P. S., Rudy, J. W., & Werner, J. S. (1989) Habituation, sensitization, and infant visual attention. In C. Rovee-Collier & L. P. Lipsitt (Eds.), *Advances in infancy research.* Norwood, NJ: Ablex.

Karlin, R., & Karlin, A. R. (1987). *Teaching elementary reading.* San Diego: Harcourt Brace Jovanovich.

Karplus, R. (1981). Education and formal thought—A modest proposal. In I. Siegel, D. Brodzinsky, & R. Golinkoff (Eds.), *Piagetian theory and research: Now directions and applications.* Hillsdale, NJ: Erlbaum.

Karr-Kaiten, K. (1989, April). *Congressional responses to new parents in the work force.* Paper presented at the biennial meeting of the Society for Research in Child Development, Kansas City.

Katz, L., & Chard, S. (in press). *Engaging the minds of young children: The project approach.* Norwood, NJ: Ablex.

Katz, P. A. (1987, August). *Children and social issues.* Paper presented at the meeting of the American Psychological Association, New York.

Kearns, D. T. (1988, April). An education recovery plan for America. *Phi Delta Kappan,* 565–570.

Keating, D. P. (in press). Structuralism, deconstruction, reconstruction: The limits of reasoning. In W. F. Overton (Ed.), *Reasoning, necessity, and logic: Developmental perspectives.* Hillsdale, NJ: Erlbaum.

Keefer, C. S., Dixon, E., Tronick, E., & Brazelton, T. B. (1978, March). *Gusii infants' neuromotor behavior: Use of the neonatal behavioral assessment scale in cross-cultural studies.* Paper presented at the International Conference on Infant Studies, Providence, RI.

Keil, F. C. (1984). Mechanisms in cognitive development and the structure of knowledge. In R. J. Sternberg (Ed.), *Mechanisms of cognitive development.* New York: W. H. Freeman.

Keith, T. Z., Cool, V. A., Novak, C. G., White, L. J., & Pottebaum, S. M. (1988). Confirmatory factor analysis of the Stanford-Binet Fourth Edition: Testing the theory-test match. *Journal of School Psychology, 26,* 253–274.

Kellogg, R. (1970). *Understanding children's art. Readings in developmental psychology today.* Del Mar, CA: CRM.

Kellogg, W. N., & Kellogg, C. A. (1933). *The ape and the child.* New York: McGraw-Hill.

Kelly, J. A., & de Armas, A. (1989). Social relationships in adolescence: Skill development and training. In J. Worell & F. Danner (Eds.), *The adolescent as decision-maker.* San Diego: Academic Press.

Kelly, J. B (1987, August). *Children of divorce: Long-term effects and clinical implications.* Paper presented at the meeting of the American Psychological Association, New York City.

Kenney, A. M. (1987, June). Teen pregnancy: An issue for schools. *Phi Delta Kappan,* 728–736.

Kerr, B. A. (1983). Raising the career aspirations of gifted girls. *Vocational Guidance Quarterly, 32,* 37–43.

Kertzer, D. I., & Schaie, K. W. (Eds.). (1989). *Age structuring in comparative perspective.* Hillsdale, NJ: Erlbaum.

Kessen, W., Haith, M. M., & Salapatek, P. (1970). Human infancy. In P. H. Mussen (Ed.), *Manual of child psychology* (3rd ed., Vol. 1). New York: Wiley.

King, J. C., Beazley, R. P., Warren, W. K., Hankins, C. A., Robertson, A. S., & Radford, J. L. (1989). Highlights from the Canada youth and AIDS study. *Journal of School Health, 59,* 139–145.

Kinsch, W. (1989). Learning from text. In L. Resnick (Ed.), *Knowing, learning, and instruction.* Hillsdale, NJ: Erlbaum.

Kinsey, A. C., Pomeroy, W. B., & Martin, C. E. (1948). *Sexual behavior in the human male.* Philadelphia: Saunders.

Klahr, D. (1989). Information-processing approaches. In R. Vasta (Ed.), *Six theories of child development: Revised formulations and current issues.* Greenwich, CT: JAI Press.

Klaus, M., & Kennell, H. H. (1976). *Maternal-infant bonding.* St. Louis: Mosby.

Klaus, M. H. (1988, November). *Recognizing and managing stress in the caregiver.* Paper presented at the Developmental Interventions in Neonatal Care Conference, San Diego, CA.

Koegel, R. L., Dyer, K., & Bell, L. K. (1987). The influence of child-preferred activities on autistic children's social behavior, *Journal of Applied Behavior Analysis, 20,* 243–252.

Kohlberg, L. (1958). *The development of modes of moral thinking and choice in the years 10 to 16.* Unpublished doctoral dissertation, University of Chicago, Chicago, IL.

Kohlberg, L. (1966). A cognitive-developmental analysis of children's role concepts and attitudes. In E. E. Maccoby (Ed.), *The development of sex differences.* Palo Alto, CA: Stanford University Press.

Kohlberg, L. (1969). Stage and sequence: The cognitive-developmental approach to socialization. In D. A. Goslin (Ed.), *Handbook of socialization theory and research.* Chicago: Rand McNally.

Kohlberg, L. (1976). Moral stages and moralization: The cognitive-development approach. In T. Lickona (Ed.), *Moral development and behavior.* New York: Holt, Rinehart, & Winston.

Kohlberg, L. (1986). A correct statement on some theoretical issues. In S. Modgil & C. Modgil (Eds.), *Lawrence Kohlberg,* Philadelphia: Falmer Press.

Kohlberg, L., & Higgings, A. (1987). School democracy and social interaction. In W. M. Kurtines & J. L. Gewirtz (Eds.), *Moral development through social interaction.* New York: Wiley.

Kohn, A. (1987). *No contest: The case against competition.* Boston: Houghton Mifflin.

Kohut, H. (1977). *The restoration of the self.* New York: Norton

Kopp, C. B. (1983). Risk factors in development. In P. H. Mussen (Ed.), *Handbook of child psychology* (4th ed., Vol. 2). New York: Wiley.

Kopp, C. B. (1987). Developmental risk: Historical reflections. In J. D. Osofsky (Ed.), *Handbook of infant development* (2nd ed.), New York: Wiley.

Kopp, C. B., & Kaler, S. R. (1989). Risk in infancy: Origins and implications *American Psychologist, 44,* 224–230.

Korner, A. F., Hutchinson, C. A., Koperski, J. A., Kraemer, H. C., & Schneider, P. A. (1981). Stability of individual differences of neonatal motor and crying responses. *Child Development, 40,* 137–141.

Kostelnik, M. J., Whiren, A. P., & Stein, L. C. (1988). Living with He-Man: Managing superhero fantasy play. *Young Children, 41,* 3–9.

Kurtines, W. M., & Gewirtz, J. (Eds.). (1989). *Moral behavior and development: Advances in theory, research, and application.* Hillsdale, NJ: Erlbaum.

La Barbera, J. D., Izard, C. E., Vietze, P., & Parisi, S. A. (1976). Four- and six-month-old infants' visual responses to joy, anger, and neutral expressions. *Child Development, 47,* 535–538.

Lacayo, R. (1988, July 11). A surging new spirit. *Time,* pp. 46–49.

LaFromboise, T., & Rudes, B. (1983). *Student attendance and retention.* Washington, DC: U.S. Department of Education.

LaFromboise, T. D., & Low, K. G. (1989). American Indian children and adolescents. In J. T. Gibbs & L. N. Huang (Eds.), *Children of color.* San Francisco: Jossey-Bass.

Lamb, M. E. (1977). The development of mother-infant and father-infant attachments in the second year of life. *Developmental Psychology, 13,* 637–648.

Lamb, M. E. (1986). *The father's role: Applied perspectives.* New York: Wiley.

Lamb, M. E. (1987). *The father's role: Cross-cultural perspectives.* Hillsdale, NJ: Erlbaum.

Lamb, M. E., Frodi, A. M., Hwang, C. P., Frodi, M., & Steinberg, J. (1982). Mother- and father-infant interaction involving play and holding in traditional and nontraditional Swedish families. *Developmental Psychology, 18,* 215–221.

Lamb, M. E., Thompson, R. A., Gardner, W. R., Charnov, E. L., & Estes, D. P. (1984). Security of infantile attachment as assessed in the "strange situation": Its study and biological interpretation. *The Behavioral and Brain Sciences, 7,* 121–171.

Lambert, N. M., & Hartsough, C. S. (1984). Contribution of predispositional factors to the diagnosis of hyperactivity. *American Journal of Orthopsychiatry, 54,* 97–109.

Landesman, S., & Ramey, C. (1989). Developmental psychology and mental retardation: Integrating scientific principles with treatment practices. *American Psychologist, 44,* 409–415.

Landesman-Dwyer, S., & Sackett, G. P. (1983, April). *Prenatal nicotine exposure and sleep-wake patterns in infancy.* Paper presented at the biennial meeting of the Society for Research in Child Development, Detroit.

Lane, H. (1976). *The wild boy of Aveyron.* Cambridge, MA: Harvard University Press.

Langer, J. (1969). *Theories of development.* New York: Holt, Rinehart, & Winston.

Laosa, L. M. (1989, April). *Current research on Hispanic immigration and children's development: Theory and Methods.* Paper presented at the biennial meeting of the Society for Research in Child Development, Kansas City.

Lapsley, D. G. (1989). Continuity and discontinuity in adolescent social cognitive development. In R. Montemayor, G. Adams, & T. Gullota (Eds.), *Advances in adolescence research* (Vol. 2), Orlando, FL: Academic Press.

Lapsley, D. K. (in press). The adolescent egocentrism theory and the "new look" at the imaginary audience and personal fable. In R. M. Lerner, A. C. Petersen, & J. Brooks-Gunn (Eds.), *The encyclopedia of adolescence.* New York: Garland.

Lapsley, D. K., Enright, R. D., & Sertin, R. C. (1985). Toward a theoretical perspective on the legislation of adolescence. *Journal of Early Adolescence, 5,* 441–446.

Lapsley, D. K., & Murphy, M. N. (1985). Another look at the theoretical assumptions of adolescent egocentrism. *Developmental Review, 5,* 201–217.

Lapsley, D. K., & Quintana, S. M. (1985). Integrative themes in social and developmental theories of self. In J. B. Pryor & J. Day (Eds.), *Social and developmental perspectives of social cognition.* New York: Springer-Verlag.

Lazar, I., Darlington, R., & Collaborators. (1982). Lasting effects of early education: A report from the consortium for longitudinal studies. *Monographs of the Society for Research in Child Development, 47.* Nos. 2–3 (Whole Number 195).

Lazarus, R. S., & Folkman, S. (1984). *Stress, appraisal, and coping.* New York: Springer.

Leboyer, F. (1975). *Birth without violence.* New York: Knopf.

Lee, V. E., Brooks-Grunn, J., & Schnur, E. (1988). Does Head Start Work? A 1-year follow-up comparison of disadvantaged children attending Head Start, no preschool, and other preschool programs. *Developmental Psychology, 24,* 210–222.

Lefkowitz, M. M., Eron, L. D., Walder, L. O., & Huesmann, L. R. (1972). Television violence and children's aggression: A follow-up study. In G. A. Comstock & E. A. Rubenstein (Eds.), *Television and social behavior* (Vol. 3). Washington, DC: U.S. Government Printing Office.

Lehrer, R., & Yussen, S. R. (1988, April). *Conceptions of computer and human intelligence.* Paper presented at the annual meeting of the American Educational Research Association, New Orleans, LA.

Leinbach, J. D., & Hurt, B. (1989, April). Bears are for boys: "Metaphorical" associations in the young child's gender schema. Paper presented at the biennial meeting of the Society for Research in Child Development, Kansas City.

Lenneberg, E. H. (1962). *Biological foundations of language.* New York: Wiley.

Lenneberg, E. H., Rebelsky, F. G., & Nichols, I. A. (1965). The vocalization of infants born to deaf and hearing parents. *Human Development, 8,* 23–37.

Lepper, M., Greene, D., & Nisbett, R. R. (1973). Undermining children's intrinsic interest with extrinsic rewards. *Journal of Personality and Social Psychology, 28,* 129–137.

Lepper, M. R. (1985). Microcomputers in education: Motivational and social issues. *American Psychologist, 40,* 1–19.

Lepper, M. R., & Gurtner, J. (1989). Children and computers: Approaching the twenty-first century. *American Psychologist, 44,* 170–178.

Lerner, J. (1988). *Learning disabilities.* Boston, MA: Houghton Mifflin.

Lerner, J. W. (1989). Educational interventions in learning disabilities. *Journal of the American Academy of Child and Adolescent Psychiatry, 28,* 326–331.

Lerner, R. M., & Karabenick, S. A. (1974). Physical attractiveness, body attitudes, and self-concept in late adolescence. *Journal of Youth and Adolescence, 3,* 307–316.

Lerner, R. M., Lerner, J. V., & Tubman, J. (1989). Organismic and contextual bases of development in adolescence: A developmental view. In G. R. Adams, R. Montemayor, & T. P. Gullotta (Eds.), Biology of adolescent behavior and development. Newbury Park, CA: Sage.

Levin, H. M., & Rumberger, R. W. (in press). Educational requirements for new technologies: Visions, possibilities, and current realities. *Educational Policy.*

Levin, J. R. (1980). *The mnemonic '80s: Keywords in the classroom.* Theoretical paper No. 86, Wisconsin Research and Development Center for Individualizing Schooling, Madison, WI.

Levine, S. V. (1984, August). Radical departures. *Psychology Today,* 18–27.

Levy, A. B., Dixon, K. N., & Stern, S. L. (1989). How are depression and bulimia related? *American Journal of Psychiatry, 146,* 162–169.

Lewin, T. (1987, August 16). The new debate over life, death. *Dallas Morning News,* pp. 1A, 19A.

Lewis, M. (1987). Social development in infancy and childhood. In J. D. Osofsky (Ed.), *Handbook of infant development* (2nd ed.). New York: Wiley.

Lewis, M. (1989). What do we mean when we say emotional development? In L. Cirillo, B. Kaplan, & S. Wapner (Eds.), *Emotions in ideal human development.* Hillsdale, NJ: Erlbaum.

Lewis, M., Sullivan, M. W., Sanger, C., & Weiss, M. (1989). Self development and self-conscious emotions. *Child Development, 60,* 146–156.

Lewis, V. G., Money, J., & Bobrow, N. A. (1977). Idiopathic pubertal delay beyond the age of fifteen: Psychological study of twelve boys. *Adolescence, 12,* 1–11.

Lewkowicz, D. J. (1988). Sensory dominance in infants: 1. Six-month-old infants' response to auditory-visual compounds. *Developmental Psychology, 24,* 155–171.

Liebert, R. M., & Spratkin, J. N. (1988). *The early window: Effects of television on children and youth* (3rd ed.). Elmsford, NY: Pergamon.

Lifshitz, F., Pugliese, M. T., Moses, N., & Weyman-Daum, M. (1987). Parental health beliefs as a cause of non-organic failure to thrive. *Pediatrics, 80,* 175–182.

Linney, J. A., & Seidman, E. (1989). The future of schooling. *American Psychologist, 44,* 336–340.

Lipsitt, L. P. (1989, January). Fetal development in the drug age. *The Brown University Child Behavior and Development Newsletter, 5,* 1–3.

Lipsitt, L. P., Engen, T., & Kaye, H. (1963). Developmental changes in the olfactory threshold of the neonate. *Child Development, 34,* 371–376.

Lipsitt, L. P., Reilly, B. M., Butcher, M. J., & Greenwood, M. M. (1976). The stability and interrelationships of newborn sucking and heart rate. *Developmental Psychology, 9,* 305–310.

Lipsitz, J. (1980, March). *Sexual development in young adolescents.* Invited speech given at the American Association of Sex Educators, Counselors, and Therapists.

Lipsitz, J. (1983, October). *Making it the hard way: Adolescents in the 1980s.* Testimony prepared for the Crisis Intervention Task Force, House Select Committee on Children, Youth, and Families, Washington, DC.

Lipsitz, J. (1984). *Successful schools for young adolescents.* New Brunswick, NJ: Transaction Books.

Lipsky, D. K., & Gartner, A. (1989). *Beyond separate education.* Baltimore, MD: Brookes.

Lockheed, M. E. (1985). Women, girls, and computers: A first look at the evidence. *Sex Roles, 13,* 115–122.

Locust, C. (1988). Wounding the spirit: Discrimination and traditional American Indian belief systems. *Harvard Educational Review, 58,* 315–330.

Lonetto, R. (1980). *Children's conceptions of death.* New York: Springer.

Long, T., & Long, L. (1983). *Latchkey children.* New York: Penguin.

Looney, J. G., & Blotcky, M. J. (1989). Adolescent psychological development revisited. In A. H. Esman (Ed.), *International Annals of Adolescent Psychiatry.* Chicago: University of Chicago Press.

Lorenz, K. Z. (1965). *Evolution and the modification of behavior.* Chicago: University of Chicago Press.

Lozoff, B. (1989). Nutrition and Behavior. *American Psychologist, 44,* 231–236.

Ludtke, M. (1988, August 6). Bianca. *Time, 132* (6), 49–51.

Ludtke, M. (1988, August 8). Josh. *Time,* pp. 55–57.

Ludtke, M. (1988, August 8). John David. *Time,* pp. 44–48.

Ludtke, M. (August 8, 1988). Katie, Age 8, Seattle. *Time,* p. 36.

Luria, A., & Herzog, E. (1985, April). *Gender segregation across and within settings.* Paper presented at the biennial meeting of the Society for Research in Child Development, Toronto.

Lyle, J., & Hoffman, H. R. (1972). Children's use of television and other media. In E. A. Rubenstein, G. A. Comstock, & J. P. Murray (Eds.), *Television and social behavior,* (Vol. 4). Washington, DC: U.S. Government Printing Office.

Lynch, M. A., & Roberts, J. (1982). *The consequences of child abuse.* New York: Academic Press.

Maccoby, E. E. (1980). *Social development.* San Diego: Harcourt Brace Jovanovich.

Maccoby, E E. (1984). Middle childhood in the context of the family. In *Development during middle childhood.* Washington, DC: National Academy Press.

Maccoby, E. E. (1987). The varied meanings of "masculine" and "feminine." In J. M. Reinisch, L. A. Rosenblum, & S. A. Sanders (Eds.), *Masculinity/femininity.* New York: Oxford University Press.

Maccoby, E. E. (1987, November). Interview with Elizabeth Hall: All in the family. *Psychology Today,* pp. 54–60.

Maccoby, E. E. (1989, August). *Gender and relationships: A developmental account.* Paper presented at the meeting of the American Psychological Association, New Orleans.

Maccoby, E. E., & Jacklin, C. N. (1974). *The psychology of sex differences.* Palo Alto, CA: Stanford University Press.

Maccoby, E. E., & Jacklin, C. N. (in press). Gender segregation in childhood. In H. Reese (Ed.), *Advances in child development and behavior,* (Vol. 20). New York: Academic Press.

Maccoby, E. E., & Martin, J. A. (1983). Socialization in the context of the family: Parent-child interaction. In P. H. Mussen (Ed.), *Handbook of child psychology* (4th ed., Vol. 4). New York: Wiley.

Maccoby, E. E. & Mnookin, R. (1989, April). *Custody, conflict, and family processes following divorce.* Paper presented at the biennial meeting of the Society for Research in Child Development, Kansas City.

MacDonald, K. (1987). Parent-child physical play with rejected, neglected and popular boys. *Developmental Psychology, 23,* 705–711.

MacFarlane, J. A. (1975). Olfaction in the development of social preferences in the human neonate. In *Parent-infant interaction,* Ciba Foundation Symposium, 33. Amsterdam: Elsevier.

MacPherson, S. (1987). *Five hundred million children.* New York: St. Martin's Press.

Maddux, J. E., Roberts, M. C., Sledden, E. A., & Wright, L. (1986). Developmental issues in child health psychology. *American Psychologist, 41,* 24–34.

Mahler, M. (1979). *Separation-individuation* (Vol. 2). London: Jason Aronson.

Maltsberger, J. T. (1988). *Suicide risk.* New York: Human Sciences Press.

Mandler, J. M. (1983). Representation. In P. H. Mussen (Ed.) (4th ed., Vol. 3). *Handbook of child psychology.* New York: Wiley.

Maratsos, M. (1983). Some current issues in the study of the acquisition of grammar. In P. H. Mussen (Ed.), *Handbook of child psychology* (4th ed., Vol. 3). New York: Wiley.

Marcia, J. (1966). Identity six years after: A follow-up study. *Journal of Youth and Adolescence, 5,* 145–160.

Marcia, J. (1980). Ego identity development. In J. Adelson (Ed.), *Handbook of adolescent psychology.* New York: Wiley.

Marcia, J. (1987). The identity status approach to the study of ego identity development. In T. Honess & K. Yardley (Eds.), *Self and identity: Perspectives across the lifespan.* London: Routledge & Kegan Paul.

Martin, C. L. (1989, April). *Beyond knowledge-based conceptions of gender schematic processing.* Paper presented at the biennial meeting of the Society for Research in Child Development, Kansas City.

Martin, J. (1976). *The education of adolescents.* Washington, DC: U.S. Office of Education.

Masters, J. C., Burish, T. G., Hollow, S. D., & Rimm, D. C. (1988). *Behavior therapy.* San Diego: Harcourt Brace Jovanovich.

Matarazzo, J. D. (1979). Health psychology: APA's newest division. *The Health Psychologist, 1,* 1.

Matas, L., Arend, R. A., & Sroufe, L. A. (1978). Continuity in adaptation: Quality of attachment and later competence. *Child Development, 49,* 547–556.

Matheny, A. P., Dolan, R. S., & Wilson, R. S. (1976). Relation between twins's similarity: Testing an assumption. *Behavior Genetics, 6,* 343–351.

McAdoo, H. P. (Ed.) (1988). *Black families.* Newsbury Park, CA: Sage.

McAdoo, H. P., & McAdoo, J. L. (Eds.). (1985). *Black children: Social, educational, and parental environments*. Beverly Hills, CA: Sage.

McCandless, B. R. (1973). *Male caregivers in day care: Demonstration Project*. Atlanta, GA: Emory University.

McCarley, R. W. (1989). The biology of dreaming sleep. In M. H. Kryger, T. Roth, & W. C. Dement (Eds.), *Principles and practices of sleep medicine*. San Diego: Harcourt Brace Jovanovich.

McClelland, D. C. (1955). Some social consequences of achievement motivation. In M. R. Jones (Ed.), *The Nebraska Symposium on Motivation*. Lincoln: University of Nebraska Press.

McClelland, D. C., Atkinson, J. W., Clark, R. W., & Lowell, E. L. (1953). *The achievement motive*. New York: Appleton-Century-Crofts.

McCue, M., & Bouchard, T. J. (in press). Genetic and environmental determinants of information processing and special mental abilities. In R. J. Sternberg (Ed.), *Advances in the psychology of human intelligence*. Hillsdale, NJ: Erlbaum.

McDaniel, M. A., & Pressley, M. (1987). *Imagery and related mnemonic processes*. New York: Springer-Verlag.

McGilly, K., & Siegler, R. S. (1989). How children choose among serial recall strategies. *Child Development, 60,* 172–182.

McLoyd, V. C. (1989, April). *Facing the future in hard times: Choices, perceptions, and behavior of black adolescents*. Paper presented at the biennial meeting of the Society for Research in Child Development, Kansas City.

McNeil, D. (1970). *The acquisition of language*. New York: Harper & Row.

Medrich, E. A., Rossen, J., Rubin, V., & Buckley, S. (1982). *The serious business of growing up*. Berkeley, CA: University of California Press.

Melson, G. F., & Fogel, A. (1988, March). The development of nurturance in young children. *Young Children,* pp. 57–65.

Meltzoff, A., & Kuhl, P. (1989). Infants' perceptions of faces and speech sounds: challenges to developmental theory. In P. R. Zelazo & R. Barr (Eds.), Challenges to developmental paradigms. Hillsdale, NJ: Erlbaum.

Meltzoff, A. N. (1987, April). *Imitation by nine-month olds in immediate and deferred tests*. Paper presented at the biennial meeting of the Society for Research in Child Development, Baltimore.

Meltzoff, A. N. (1988). Infant imitation and memory: Nine-month-old infants in immediate and deferred tests. *Child Development, 59,* 217–225.

Meltzoff, A. N., & Moore, M. K. (1977). Interpreting "imitative" responses in early infancy. *Science, 205,* 217–219.

Menolacino, F. (in press). The nature and types of mental illness in the mentally retarded. In M. Lewis & S. Miller (Eds.), *Handbook of developmental psychopathology*. New York: Plenum.

Meredith, H. V. (1978). Research between 1960 and 1970 on the standing height of young children in different parts of the world. In H. W. Reece & L. P. Lipsitt (Eds.), *Advances in child development and behavior* (Vol. 12). New York: Academic Press.

Meyerhoff, M. K., & White, B. L. (1986). Making the grade as parents. *Psychology Today.* September, 38–45.

Michel, G. L. (1981). Right-handedness: A consequence of infant supine head-orientation preference? *Science, 212,* 685–687.

Milham, J., Widmayer, S., Bauer, C. R., & Peterson, L. (1983, April), *Predictory cognitive deficits for pre-term, low birthweight infants*. Paper presented at the biennial meeting of the Society for Research in Child Development, Detroit.

Miller, G. (1981). *Language and speech*. New York: W. H. Freeman.

Miller, G. (1989). Foreward. In J. T. Gibbs & L. N. Huang (Eds.), *Children of color*. San Francisco: Jossey-Bass.

Miller, P. H. (1989). Developmental theories of adolescence. In J. Worrell & F. Danner (Eds.), *The adolescent as decision maker*. New York: Academic Press.

Minnett, A. M., Vandell, D. L., & Santrock, J. W. (1983). The effects of sibling status on sibling interaction: Influence of birth order, age spacing, sex of the child, and sex of the sibling. *Child Development, 54,* 1064–1072.

Minuchin, P. P., & Shapiro, E. K. (1983). The school as a context for social development. In P. H. Mussen (Ed.), *Handbook of child psychology* (4th ed., Vol. 4). New York: Wiley.

Mischel, W. (1973). Toward a cognitive social learning reconceptualization of personality. *Psychological Review, 80,* 252–283.

Mischel, W. (1984). Convergences and challenges in the search for consistency. *American Pyschologist, 39,* 351–364.

Mischel, W., & Patterson, C. J. (1976). Substantive and structural elements of effective plans for self-control. *Journal of Personality and Social Psychology, 34,* 942–950.

Moely, B. E., Olson, F. A., Halwes, T. G., & Flavell, J. H. (1969). Production deficiency in young children's clustered recall. *Developmental Psychology, 1,* 26–34.

Money, J. (1987). Propaedeutics of Diecious G-I/R: Theoretical foundations for understanding dimorphic gender-identity role. In J. M. Reinisch, L. A. Rosenblum, & S. A. Sanders (Eds.). *Masculinity/femininity*. New York: Oxford University Press.

Money, J., & Ehrhardt, A. A. (1972). *Man and woman, boy and girl*. Baltimore: Johns Hopkins Press.

Monroe, R. (1988). *Creative brainstorms*. New York: Irvington.

Montemayor, R., & Hanson, E. (1985). A naturalistic view of conflict between adolescents and their parents and siblings. *Journal of Early Adolescence, 5,* 23–30.

Morrison, D. M. (1985). Adolescent contraceptive behavior: A review. *Psychological Bulletin, 98,* 538–568.

Morrow, L. (1988, August 8). Through the eyes of children. *Time,* pp. 32–33.

Mott, F. L., & Marsiglio, W. (1985, September/October). Early childbearing and completion of high school. *Family Planning Perspectives,* p. 234.

Moyer, J., Egertson, H., & Isenberg, J. (1987). The child-centered kindergarten. *Childhood Education, 63,* 235–242.

Munroe, R. H., Himmin, H. S., & Munroe, R. L. (1984). Gender understanding and sex role preference in four cultures. *Developmental Psychology, 20,* 673–682.

Murphy, J. (1987). Educational influences. In B. B. Van Hasselt & M. Hersen (Eds.), *Handbook of adolescent psychology*. New York: Pergamon.

Murray, F. B. (1978, August). *Generation of educational practice from*

Murray, F. B. (1978, August). *Generation of educational practice from developmental theory*. Paper presented at the meeting of the American Psychological Association, Toronto.

NAEYC (1988). NAEYC position statement on developmentally appropriate practices in the primary grades, serving 5- through 8-year-olds. *Young Children, 43,* 64–83.

National Assessment of Educational Progress. (1976). *Adult work skills and knowledge.* (Report No. 35. COD 01). Denver, CO: Author.

National Research Council (1987). *Risking the future: Adolescent sexuality, pregnancy, and childbearing.* Washington, DC: National Academy Press.

Neiger, B. L., & Hopkins, R. W. (1988). Adolescent suicide: Character traits of high-risk teenagers. *Adolescence, 23,* 469–475.

Neimark, E. D. (1982). Adolescent thought: Transition to formal operations. In B. B. Wolman (Ed.), *Handbook of developmental psychology*. Englewood Cliffs, NJ: Prentice-Hall.

Newcomb, M. D., & Bentler, P. M. (1988). Impact of adolescent drug use and social support on problems of young adults: A longitudinal study. *Journal of Abnormal Psychology, 97,* 64–75.

Newcomb, M. D., & Bentler, P. M. (1989). Substance use and abuse among children and teenagers. *American Psychologist, 44,* 242–248.

Nicholls, J. G. (1984). Conceptions of ability and achievement motivation. In R. E. Ames & C. Ames (Eds.), *Motivation in education*. New York: Academic Press.

Nichtern, S. (1989). Introduction: The world within the adolescent. In A. H. Esman (Ed.), *International Annals of Adolescent Psychiatry*. Chicago: University of Chicago Press.

Nottelman, E D., Susman, E. J., Blue, J. H., Inoff-Germain, G., Dorn, L. D., Loriaux, D. L., Cutler, G. B., & Chrousos, G. P. (1987). Gonadal and adrenal hormone correlates of adjustment in early adolescence. In R. M. Lerner & T. T. Foch (Eds.), *Biological-psychological interactions in early adolescence*. Hillsdale, NJ: Erlbaum.

Novick, B. (1989). Pediatric AIDS: A medical overview. In J. M. Seibert & R. A. Olson (Eds.), *Children, adolescents, and AIDS*. Lincoln: University of Nebraska Press.

Odlin, T. (1989). *Language transfer.* New York: Cambridge University Press.

Oetting, E. R., Beauvais, F. & Edwards, R. (1988). Alcohol and Indian youth: Social and psychological correlates and prevention. *Journal of Drug Issues, 18,* 87–101.

Offer, D., Ostrov, E., Howard, K. I., & Atkinson, R. (1988). *The teenage world: Adolescents' self-image in ten countries*. New York: Plenum.

Olweus, D. (1980). Bullying among schoolboys. In R. Barnen (Ed.), *Children and violence*. Stockholm: Adaemic Litteratur.

Olweus, D. (1989, April). Peer relationships problems: *Conceptual issues and a successful intervention program against bully/victim problems*. Paper presented at the biennial meeting of the Society for Research in Child Development, Kansas City.

Oppenheimer, M. (1982, October). What you should know about herpes. *Seventeen Magazine,* pp. 154–155, 170.

Osofsky, J. D. (1989, April). *Affective relationships in adolescent mothers and their infants*. Paper presented at the biennial meeting of the Society for Research in Child Development, Kansas City.

Ostrov, E., Offer, D., Howard, K. I., Kaufman, B., & Meyer, H. (1985). Adolescent sexual behavior. *Medical Aspects of Human Sexuality, 19,* 28, 30–31, 34–36.

Ottinger, D. R., & Simmons, J. E. (1964). Behavior of human neonates and prenatal maternal anxiety. *Psychological Reports, 14,* 391–394.

Ourselves and our children (1978). New York: Random House.

Oyama, S. (1973). *A sensitive period for the acquisition of a second language.* Unpublished doctoral dissertation, Harvard University.

Page, D. C., Mosher, R., Simpson, E. M., Fisher, E. M. C., Mardon, G., Pollack, J., & Brown, L. G. (1987). The sex-determining region of the human Y chromosome encodes a finger protein. *Cell, 51,* 1091–1104.

Papini, D., Barnett, J., Clark, S., & Micka, J. C. (1989, April). Family influences and individual concomitants of adolescent ego identity statuses. Paper presented at the biennial meeting of the Society for Research in Child Development, Kansas City.

Parcel, G. S., Simons-Morton, G. G., O'Hara, N. M., Baranowski, T., Kolbe, L. J., & Bee, D. E. (1987). School promotion of healthful diet and exercise behavior: An integration of organizational change and social learning theory interventions. *Journal of School Health, 57,* 150–156.

Parcel, G. S., Tiernan, K., Nadar, P. R., & Gottlob, D. (1979). Health education and kindergarten children. *Journal of School Health, 49,* 129–131.

Paris, S. C., & Lindauer, B. K. (1982). The development of cognitive skills during childhood. In B. B. Wolman (Ed.), *Handbook of developmental psychology*. Englewood Cliffs, NJ: Prentice-Hall.

Parish, T. S. (1988). Evaluations of family as a function of one's family structure and sex. *Perceptual and Motor Skills, 66,* 25–26.

Parish, T. S., & Osterberg, J. (1985). Evaluations of self, parents, and family: Variations caused by family structure and personal stress. *Journal of Psychology, 119,* 231–233.

Parke, R. D. (1988). Families in life-span perspective: A multilevel developmental approach. In E. M. Hetherington, R. M. Lerner, & M. Perlmutter (Eds.), *Child development in life-span perspective*. Hillsdale, NJ: Erlbaum.

Parke, R. D. (in press). In search of fathers: A narrative of an empirical journey. In I. E. Sigel & G. Brody (Eds.), *Methods of family research* (Vol. 1). Hillsdale, NJ: Erlbaum.

Parke, R. D., MacDonald, K., Beitel, A., & Bhavangri, N. (1988). The interrelationships among families, fathers, and peers. In R. D. Peters (Ed.), *New approaches in family research*. New York: Bruner/Mazel.

Parke, R. D., & Sawin, D. B. (1980). The family in early infancy. In F. Pedersen (Ed.), *The father-infant relationship: Observational studies in family context*. New York: Praeger.

Parke, R. D., & Suomi, S. (1981). Adult male-infant relationships: Human and non-human primate evidence. In K. Immelmann, G. W. Barlow, L. Petrinovithc, & M. Main (Eds.), *Behavioral development: The Bielefeld Interdisciplinary Project*. New York: Cambridge University Press.

Parker, J. G., & Asher, S. R. (1987). Peer relations and later personal adjustment: Are low accepted children at risk? *Psychological Bulletin, 102,* 357–389.

Parker, J. G., and Gottman, J. M. (1989). Social and emotional development in a relational context: Friendship interaction from early childhood to adolescence. In T. J. Berndt & G. W. Ladd (Eds.), *Peer relations in child development*. New York: Wiley.

Parmalee, A., Wenner, W., & Schulz, H. (1964). Infant sleep patterns from birth to 16 weeks of age. *Journal of Pediatrics, 65,* 576–572.

Parmalee, A. H. (1986). Children's illnesses: Their beneficial effects on behavioral development. *Child Development, 57,* 1–10.

Parten, M. (1932). Social play among preschool children. *Journal of Abnormal and Social Psychology, 27,* 243–269.

Pasley, K., & Ihinger-Tallman, M. (Eds.). (1987). *Remarriage and stepparenting*. New York: Guilford.

Patterson, G. R. (1986). Performance models for antisocial boys. *American Psychologist, 41,* 432–444.

Patterson, G. R., DeBarsyshe, B. D., & Ramsey, E. (1989). A developmental perspective on antisocial behavior. *American Psychologist, 44,* 329–335.

Patterson, G. R., & Stouthamer-Loeber, M. (1984). The correlation of family management practices and delinquency. *Child Development, 55,* 1299–1307.

Pawson, M., & Morris, N. (1972). The role of the father in pregnancy and labor. In N. Morris (Ed.), *Psychological medicine in obstetrics and gynecology*. Basel: Karger.

Pederson, D. R., Moran, G., Sitko, C., Cambpell, K., Ghesquire, K., & Acton, H. (1989, April). *Maternal sensitivity and the security of infant-mother attachment*. Paper presented at the biennial meeting of the Society for Research in Child Development, Kansas City.

Pellegrini, A. (1987). Rough-and-tumble play: Developmental and educational significance. *Educational Psychology, 22,* 23–43.

Pellegrini, A. D., & Perlmutter, J. C. (1988, January). Rough-and-tumble play on the elementary school playground, *Young Children,* 14–17.

Penner, S. G. (1987). Parental responses to grammatical and ungramatical child utterances. *Child Development, 58,* 376–384.

Perry, I. (1988). A black student's reflection on public and private schools. *Harvard Educational Review, 58,* 332–336.

Peskin, H. (1967). Pubertal onset and ego functioning. *Journal of Abnormal Psychology, 72,* 1–15.

Petersen, A. C. (1979, January). Can puberty come any faster? *Psychology Today,* pp. 45–56.

Petersen, A. C., & Taylor, B. (1980). The biological approach to adolescence: Biological change and psychological adaptation. In J. Adelson (Ed.), *Handbook of adolescent psychology*. New York: John Wiley.

Peterson, P. L. (1977). Interactive effects of student anxiety, achievement orientation, and teacher behavior on student achievement and attitude. *Journal of Educational Psychology, 69,* 779–792.

Pettit, G. S., Dodge, K. A., & Brown, M. M. (1988). Early family experience, social problem solving patterns, and children's social competence. *Child Development, 59,* 107–120.

Phares, E. J. (1984). *Personality*. Columbus, OH: Charles E. Merrill.

Phillips, D. (in press). Future directions and needs for child care in the United States. In J. Lande, S. Scarr, & N. Gunzenhauer (Eds.), *Caring for children: Challenge to America*. Hillsdale, NJ: Erlbaum.

Phinney, J. S. (1989). Stages of ethnic identity development in minority group adolescents. *Journal of Early Adolescence, 9,* 34–49.

Piaget, J. (1932). *The moral judgment of the child*. New York: Harcourt Brace Jovanovich.

Piaget, J. (1936). *The origins of intelligence in children*. New York: Norton.

Piaget, J. (1952). *The origins of intelligence in children*. New York: International Universities Press.

Piaget, J. (1954). *The construction of reality in the child*. New York: Basic Books.

Piaget, J. (1962). *Play, dreams, and imitation in childhood*. New York: Norton.

Piaget, J. (1967). *The child's conception of the world*. Totowa, NJ: Littlefield, Adams, & Co.

Piaget, J. (1967). *The child's construction of the world*. Totowa, NJ: Littlefield, Adams & Co.

Piaget, J., & Inhelder, B. (1969). *The child's conception of space*. (F. J. Langdon & J. L. Lunzer, Trans.). New York: Norton.

Pines, M. (1981, March). Only isn't lonely (or spoiled or selfish). *Psychology Today,* pp. 15–19.

Pipes, P. (1988). Nutrition during infancy. In S. R. Williams and B. S. Worthington-Roberts (Eds.), *Nutrition through the life cycle*. St. Louis: Times Mirror/Mosby.

Pipes, P. (1988). Nutrition in childhood. In S. R. Williams & B. S. Worthington (Eds.), *Nutrition throughout the life cycle*. St. Louis: Times Mirror/Mosby.

Pipp, S., Fischer, K. W., & Jennings, S. (1987). Acquisition of self- and mother knowledge in infancy. *Developmental Psychology, 23,* 86–96.

Pleck, J. H. (1984). *Working wives and family well-being*. Beverly Hills, CA: Sage.

Plomin, R. (1989). Environment and genes: Determinants of behavior. *American Psychologist, 44,* 105–111.

Plomin, R., DeFries, J. C., & McClearn, G. E. (in press). *Behavioral genetics: A primer*. New York: W. H. Freeman.

Plomin, R., DeFries, J. C., & Fulker, D. W. (1988). *Nature and nurture during infancy*. New York: Cambridge University Press.

Plomin, R., & Thompson, L. (1987). Life-span developmental behavior genetics. In P. B. Baltes, D. L. Featherman, & R. M. Lerner (Eds.), *Life-span development and behavior* (Vol. 7). Hillsdale, NJ: Erlbaum.

Polier, J. W. (in press). *Juvenile justice in double jeopardy*. Hillsdale, NJ: Erlbaum.

Polivy, J., & Thomsen, L. (1987). Eating, dieting, and body image. In E. A. Blechman & K. D. Brownell (Eds.), *Handbook of behavioral medicine for women*. Elmsford, NY: Pergamon.

Porter, F. L., Porges, S. W., & Marshall, R. E. (1988). Newborn pain cries and vagal tone: Parallel changes in response to circumcision. *Child Development, 59*, 495–515.

Powers, S. I., Hauser, S. T., & Kilner, L. A. (1989). Adolescent mental health. *American Psychologist, 44*, 200–208.

Premack, A. J., & Premack, D. (1972). Teaching language to an ape. *Scientific American, 227*, 92–98.

Price, J., & Feshbach, S. (1982, August). *Emotional adjustment correlates of television viewing in children*. Paper presented at the meeting of the American Psychological Association, Washington, DC.

Price, J. M., & Dodge, K. A. (in press). Reactive and proactive aggression among young children: Relations to peer status and social context dimensions. *Journal of Abnormal Child Psychology*.

Prinsky, L. E., & Rosenbaum, J. L. (1987). Leer-ics or lyrics? *Youth and Society, 18*, 384–394.

Prothrow-Stith, D. (1989). Excerpts from address to the Massachusetts Department of Public Health. *Journal of Adolescent Health Care, 10*, 5–7.

Puffer, J. C. (1987, September). *Risky sports for young children*. Paper presented at the annual meeting of the American Academy of Family Physicians, San Francisco.

Puka, B. (in press). Toward the redevelopment of Kohlberg's theory: Preserving the essential structure, removing controversial content. In W. M. Kurtines & J. Gewirtz (Eds.), *Moral behavior and development*. Hillsdale, NJ: Erlbaum.

Ramirez, O. (1989). Mexican American children and adolescents. In J. T. Gibbs & L. N. Huang (Eds.), *Children of color*. San Francisco: Jossey-Bass.

Ramsay, D. S. (1980). Onset of unimanual handedness in infants. *Infant Behavior and Development, 3*, 377–385.

Rand Youth Poll (1988). New York: The Rand Corporation.

Rauh, V. A. Achenbach, T. M., Nurcombe, B., Howell, C. T., & Teti, D. M. (1988). Minimizing adverse effects of low birthweight: Four-year results of an early intervention program. *Child Development, 49*, 544–553.

Read, M. (1968). *Children of their fathers: Growing up among the Ngoni of Malawi*. New York: Holt, Rinehart & Winston.

Reid, D. K. (1988). *Teaching the learning disabled*. Boston, MA: Allyn & Bacon.

Reilly, R. (1988, August 15). Here no one is spared. *Sports Illustrated, 69* (7), 70–77.

Resnick, L. (Ed.). (1989). *Knowing, learning, and instruction: Essays in honor of Robert Glaser*. Hillsdale, NJ: Erlbaum.

Rice, F. P. (1989). *Human sexuality*. Dubuque, IA: Wm. C. Brown.

Rice, M. L. (1989). Children's language acquisition. *American Psychologist, 44*, 149–156.

Rich, C. L., Young, D., & Fowler, R. C. (1986). San Diego suicide study. *Archives of General Psychiatry, 43*, 577–582.

Riddle, D. B., & Prinz, R. (1984, August). *Sugar consumption in young children*. Paper presented at the Meeting of The American Psychological Association, Toronto.

Risser, W. L. (1989). Exercise for children. *Pediatrics in Review, 10*, 131–140.

Robinson, D. P., & Greene, J. W. (1988). The adolescent alcohol and drug problem: A practical approach. *Pediatric Nursing, 14*, 305–310.

Robinson, N. M. (1987). Psychology and mental retardation. *American Psychologist, 42*, 791.

Roche, A. F. (1977). Secular trends in stature, weight and maturation. *Monographs of the Society for Research in Child Development, 44*, (Serial No. 179).

Rode, S. S., Chang, P., Fisch, R. O., & Sroufe, L. A. (1981). Attachment patterns of infants separated at birth. *Developmental Psychology, 17*, 188–191.

Rodman, H., Pratto, D. J., & Nelson, R. S. (1988). Toward a definition of self-care children: A commentary on Steinberg (1986). *Developmental Psychology, 24*, 292–294.

Rodriguez-Haynes, M., & Crittenden, P. M. (1988). *Ethnic differences among abusing, neglecting, and non-maltreating families*. Paper presented at the Southeastern Conference on Human Development, Charleston, SC.

Rogers, C. R. (1961). *On becoming a person*. Boston: Houghton Mifflin.

Rogers, C. R. (1963). The actualizing tendency in relation to "motives" and consciousness. In M. R. Jones (Ed.), *Nebraska Symposium on Motivation*. Lincoln: University of Nebraska Press.

Rogers, C. R. (1967). Carl R. Rogers. In E. G. Boring & G. Lindzey (Eds.), *A history of psychology in autobiography*. New York: Macmillan.

Rogers, C. R. (1974). In retrospect: Forty-six years. *American Psychologist, 29*, 115–123.

Rogers, C. R. (1980). *A way of being*. Boston: Houghton Mifflin.

Rogers, C. S., & Morris, S. S. (1986, July). Reducing sugar in children diets: Why? How? *Young Children*, 11–16.

Rogers, T., Kuiper, N., & Kirker, W. (1977). Self-reference and the encoding of personal information. *Journal of Personality and Social Psychology, 35*, 677–688.

Rogoff, B. (in press). Peer influences on cognitive development: Piagetian versus Vygotskian perspectives. In M. H. Bornstein & J. S. Bruner (Eds.), *Interaction in human development*. Hillsdale, NJ: Erlbaum.

Rogoff, B., & Morelli, G. (1989). Perspectives on children's development from cultural psychology. *American Psychologist, 44*, 343–348.

Rogoff, B., & Mistry J. J. (in press). Memory development in cultural context. In M. Pressley & C. Brainerd (Eds.), *Progress in cognitive development*. New York: Springer-Verlag.

Rogoff, B., & Morelli, G. (1989). Perspectives on children's development from cultural psychology. *American Psychologist, 44*, 343–348.

Romaine, S. (1989). *Bilingualism*. New York: Basil Blackwell.

Rose, S. A. (1989). Measuring infant intelligence: New perspectives. In M. H. Bornstein & N. A. Krasnegor (Eds.), *Stability and continuity in mental development*. Hillsdale, NJ: Erlbaum.

Rose, S. A., Feldman, J. F., McCarton, C. M., & Wolfson, J. (1988). Information processing in seven-month-old infants as a function of risk status. *Child Development, 59,* 489–603.

Rose, S. A., & Ruff, H. A. (1987). Cross-modal abilities in human infants. In J. D. Osofsky (Ed.), *Handbook of infant development* (2nd ed.). New York: Wiley.

Rosenblith, J. F., & Sims-Knight, J. E. (1985). *In the beginning*. Monterey, CA: Brooks/Cole.

Rosenblith, J. F., & Sims-Knight, J. E. (1985). *In the beginning: Development in the first two years*. Monterey, CA: Brooks/Cole.

Rosenthal, R. (1985). *Lyric cognition and the potential for protest among punk rockers*. Unpublished manuscript, University of Hartford, Hartford, CT.

Rosenthal, R. (1987). Pygmalion effects: Existence, magnitude, and social importance. *Educational Researcher, 16,* 37–41.

Rosenthal, R., & Jacobsen, L. (1968). *Pygmalian in the classroom*. New York: Holt, Rinehart & Winston.

Rothbart, M. K. (in press). Temperament and the development of inhibited approach. *Child Development.*

Rothbart, M. L. K. (1971). Birth order and mother-child interaction. *Dissertation Abstracts, 27,* 45–57.

Rotter, J. B. (1989, August). *Internal versus external locus of control of reinforcement: A case history of a variable*. Paper presented at the meeting of the American Psychological Association, New Orleans.

Rovee-Collier, C. (1987). Learning and memory in children. In J. D. Osofsky (Ed.), *Handbook of infant development* (2nd ed.). New York: Wiley.

Rowe, D. C., & Rodgers, J. E. (1989). Behavioral genetics, adolescent deviance, and "d" contributions and issues. In G. R. Adams, R. Montemayor, & T. P. Gulotta (Eds.), *Biology of adolescent behavior and development*. Newburg, CA: Sage.

Rubin, K. H. (1978). Role-taking in childhood: Some methodological considerations. *Child Development, 49,* 428–433.

Rubin, R. R., & Fisher, J. J. (1982). *Your preschooler*. London: Collier Books.

Ruble, D. N. (1987). The acquisition of self-knowledge: A self-socialization perspective. In N. Eisenberg (Ed.), *Contemporary topics in developmental psychology*. New York: Wiley.

Ruebenstein, J., Heeren, T., Housman, D., Rubin, C., & Stechler, G. (1989). Suicidal behavior in "normal" adolescents: Risk and protective factors. *American Journal of Orthopsychiatry, 59,* 59–71.

Rumbaugh, D. M. (1988, August). *Comparative psychology and the great apes: Their competency in learning, language, and numbers*. Paper presented at the meeting of the American Psychological Association, Atlanta.

Rumberger, R. W. (1983). Dropping out of high school: The influence of race, sex, and family background. *American Educational Research Journal, 20,* 199–220.

Rumberger, R. W. (1987). High school dropouts: A review of the issues and evidence. *Review of Educational Research, 57,* 101–121.

Rutter, M. (1979). Protective factors in children's response to stress and disadvantage. In M. W. Kent & J. E. Rolf (Eds.), *Primary prevention in psychopathology* (Vol. 3). Hanover, NH: University Press of New England.

Rutter, M. (1983, April). *Influences from family and school*. Paper presented at the meeting of the Society for Research in Child Development, Detroit.

Rutter, M., & Garmezy, N. (1983). Developmental psychopathology. In P. H. Mussen (Ed.), *Handbook of child psychology* (4th ed., Vol. 4). New York: Wiley.

Rutter, M. M., & Schopler, E. (1987). Autism and pervasive developmental disorders: Concepts and diagnostic issues. *Journal of Autism and Developmental Disorders, 17,* 159–186.

Sachdev, P. (1988). Abortion trends: An international review. In P. Sachdev (Ed.), *International handbook on abortion*. New York: Greenwood Press.

Santrock, J. W. (1989). *Life-span development* (3rd ed.). Dubuque, IA: Wm. C. Brown.

Santrock, J. W. (1990). *Adolescence* (4th ed.). Dubuque, IA: Wm. C. Brown.

Santrock, J. W., & Bartlett, J. C. (1986). *Developmental psychology*. Dubuque, IA: Wm. C. Brown.

Santrock, J. W., & Sitterle, K. A. (1987). Parent-child relationships in stepmother families. In K. Pasley & M. Ihinger-Tallman (Eds.), *Remarriage and stepparenting*. New York: Guilford.

Santrock, J. W., Sitterle, K. A., & Warshak, R. A. (1988). Parent-child relationships in stepfather families. In P. Bronstein & C. Cowan (Eds.), *The father's role today: Men's changing roles in the family*. New York: Wiley.

Santrock, J. W., & Warshak, R. A. (1979). Father custody and social development in boys and girls. *Journal of Social Issues, 35,* 112–125.

Santrock, J. W., & Warshak, R. A. (1986). Development, relationships, and legal/clinical considerations in father custody families. In M. E. Lamb (Ed.), *The father's role: Applied perspectives*. New York: Wiley.

Santrock, J. W., & Yussen, S. R. (1989). *Child development* (4th ed.). Dubuque, IA: Wm. C. Brown.

Sax, G. (1989). *Principles of educational and psychological measurement* (3rd ed.). Belmont, CA: Wadsworth.

Saxe, G. B., Guberman, S. R., & Gearhart, M. (1987). Social processes in early number development. *Monographs of the Society for Research in Child Development, 52* (2, Serial No. 216).

Scardamalia, M., Bereiter, C., & Goelman, H. (1982). The role of production factors in writing ability. In M. Nystrand (Ed.), *What writers know: The language process and structure of written discourse*. New York: Academic Press.

Scarr, S. (1984, May). Interview. *Psychology Today*, pp. 59–63.

Scarr, S. (1984). *Mother care/ Other care*. New York: Basic Books.

Scarr, S. (1989, April). *Transracial adoption*. Discussion at the biennial meeting of the Society for Research in Child Development, Kansas City.

Scarr, S. (1989, August). *The legitimate role of psychology in public policy*. Paper presented at the meeting of the American Psychological Association, New Orleans.

Scarr, S., & Kidd, K. K. (1983). Developmental behavior genetics. In P. H. Mussen (Ed.), *Handbook of child psychology* (4th ed., Vol. 2). New York: Wiley.

Scarr, S., Lande, J., & McCartney, K. (1989). Child care and the family: Complements and interactions. In J. Lande, S. Scarr, & N. Gunzenhauser, (Eds.), *Caring for children: Challenge to America*. Hillsdale, NJ: Erlbaum.

Scarr, S., & Weinberg, R. A. (1980). Calling all camps! The war is over. *American Sociological Review, 45*, 859–865.

Schaffer, H. R. (1977). *Mothering*. Cambridge, MA: Harvard University Press.

Schaffer, H. R., & Emerson, P. E. (1964). The development of social attachments in infancy. *Monographs of the Society for Research in Child Development, 29* (3, Serial No. 94).

Schaie, K. W. (1965). A general model for the study of developmental problems. *Psychological Bulletin, 64*, 92–107.

Schaie, K. W. (1988). Sampling and generalizability: Adult development and aging research issues examined within the general methodological framework of selection. In K. W. Schaie, R. T. Campbell, W. M. Meredith, & S. C. Rawlings (Eds.), *Methodological issues in aging research*. New York: Springer.

Schank, R., & Abelson, R. (1977). *Scripts, plans, goals, and understanding*. Hillsdale, NJ: Erlbaum.

Schegloff, E. A. (1989). Reflections on language, development, and the interactional character of talk-in-interaction. In M. H. Bornstein & J. S. Bruner (Eds.), *Interaction in human development*. Hillsdale, NJ: Erlbaum.

Schlundt, D. G., & Johnson, W. G., (1990). *Assessment and treatment of anorexia nervosa and bulimia nervosa*. Needham Heights, MA: Allyn & Bacon.

Schneidman, E. S. (1971). Suicide among the gifted. *Suicide and Life-threatening Behavior I*, 23–45.

Schorr, L. B. (1989, April). *Within our reach: Breaking the cycle of disadvantage*. Paper presented at the biennial meeting of the Society for Research for Child Development, Kansas City.

Schulenberg, J. E., Shimizu, K., Vondracek, F. W., & Hostetler, M. (1988). Factorial invariance of career indecision dimensions across junior high and high school male and females. *Journal of Vocational Behavior, 33*, 63–81.

Schunk, D. H. (1983). Developing children's self-efficacy and skills: The roles of social comparative information and goal-setting. *Contemporary Educational Psychology, 8*, 76–86.

Schuster, C. S. (1986). Biophysical development of the school-ager and the pubescent. In S. S. Schuster & S. S. Ashburn (Eds.), *The process of human development* (2nd ed.). Boston: Little, Brown.

Schwartz, D., & Mayaux, M. J. (1982). Female fecundity as a function of age: Results of artificial insemination in nullparous women with azoospermic husbands. *New England Journal of Medicine, 306*, 304–406.

Scott, D. K. (1985, May). Child safety seats—They work! *Young Children*, 13–17.

Seibert, J. M. & Olson, R. A. (Eds.). (1989). *Children, adolescents, and AIDS*. Lincoln, NE: University of Nebraska Press.

Selman, R. L. (1980). *The growth of interpersonal understanding*. New York: Academic Press.

Selye, H. (1974). *Stress without distress*. Philadelphia: W. B. Saunders.

Selye, H. (1983). The stress concept: Past, present, and future. In C. L. Cooper (Ed.), *Stress research*. New York: Wiley.

Senn, M. J. (1975). Insights on the child development movement in the United States. *Monographs of the Society for Research in Child Development, No. 161* (40), 3–4.

Serbin, L. A., Tonick, I. J., & Sternglanz, S. (1977). Shaping cooperative cross-sex play. *Child Development, 48*, 924–929.

Sexton, M., & Hebel, J. R. (1984). A clinical trial of change in maternal smoking and its effects on birth weight. *Journal of the American Medical Association, 251*, 911–915.

Shantz, C. O. (1988). Conflicts between children. *Child Development, 58*, 283–305.

Shantz, C. U. (1983). Social cognition. In P. H. Mussen (Ed.), *Handbook of child psychology* (4th ed., Vol. 3). New York: Wiley.

Shapiro, E. R., & Freedman, J. (1989). Family dynamics of adolescent suicide. In A. H. Esman (Ed.), *International Annals of Adolescent Psychiatry*. Chicago: University of Chicago Press.

Shatz, M., & Gelman, R. (1973). The development of communication skills: Modifications in the speech of young children as a function of the listener. *Monographs of the Society for Research in Child Development, 38*, (Serial No. 152).

Sheingold, K., & Tenney, Y. J. (1982). Memory for a salient childhood event. In U. Neisser (Ed.), *Memory observed*. San Francisco: W. H. Freeman.

Sheldon, A. (1989, April). *Socialization of gender in preschool children through conversations with peers*. Paper presented at the biennial meeting of the Society for Research in Child Development, Kansas City.

Siegel, L. S. (1988). Definitional and theoretical issues and research on learning disabilities. *Journal of Learning Disabilities, 21*, 264–266.

Siegel, L. S., & Ryan, E. B. (1989). The development of working memory in normally achieving and subtypes of learning disabled children. *Child Development, 69*, 973–980.

Siegel, L. S. (1989, April). *Perceptual-motor, cognitive, and language skills as predictors of cognitive abilities at school age*. Paper presented at the biennial meeting of the Society for Research in Children, Kansas City.

Siegler, R. S. (1987, April). *Some general conclusions about children's strategy choice procedures.* Paper presented at the biennial meeting of the Society for Research in Child Development, Baltimore.

Siegler, R. S. (1989). How domain-general and domain-specific knowledge interact to produce strategy choices. *Merrill-Palmer Quarterly, 35,* 1–26.

Siegman, A. W. (1989). The role of hostility, neuroticism, and speech style in coronary-prone behavior. In A. W. Siegman & T. Dembrowski (Eds.), *In search of coronary-prone behavior: Beyond Type A.* Hillsdale, NJ: Erlbaum.

Sigman, M., Asarnow, R., Cohen, S., & Parmalee, A. H. (1989, April). *Infant attention as a measure of information processing.* Paper presented at the biennial meeting of the Society for Research in Child Development, Kansas City.

Silver, L. B. (1987). *Attention deficit disorders.* Summit, NJ: CIBA.

Silver, L. B. (1989). Learning disabilities. *Journal of the American Academy of Child and Adolescent Psychiatry, 28,* 309.

Simmons, R. G., & Blyth, D. A. (1987). *Moving into adolescence.* Hawthorne, NY: Aldine.

Simmons, R. G., Brown, L., Bush, D. M., & Blyth, D. A. (1978). Self-esteem and achievement of Black and White adolescents. *Social Problems, 26,* 86–96.

Simmons, R. G., Burgeson, R., Carton-Ford, S., & Blyth, D. A. (1987). The impact of cumulative change in early adolescence. *Child Development, 58,* 1235–1243.

Simons, R. L., & Gray, P. A. (1989). Perceived blocked opportunity as an explanation of delinquency among lowerclass black males: A research note. *Journal of Research in Crime and Delinquency, 26,* 90–101.

Singer, D. (1972, June). Piglet, Pooh, & Piaget. *Psychology Today,* pp. 70–74.

Singer, J. L. (1984). *The human personality.* San Diego: Harcourt Brace Jovanovich.

Sizer, T. R. (1984). *Horace's compromise: The dilemma of the American high school today.* Boston: Houghton Mifflin.

Skinner, B. F. (1938). *The behavior of organisms: An experimental analysis.* New York: Appleton-Century-Crofts.

Skinner, B. F. (1948). *Walden two.* New York: Macmillan.

Skinner, B. F. (1957). *Verbal behavior.* New York: Appleton-Century-Crofts.

Slavin, R. (1989). Cooperative learning and student achievement. In R. E. Slavin (Ed.), *School and classroom organization.* Hillsdale, NJ: Erlbaum.

Slavin, R. E. (1987). Developmental and motivational perspectives on cooperative learning: A reconciliation. *Child Development, 58,* 1161–1167.

Slobin, D. (1972, July). Children and language: They learn the same all around the world, *Psychology Today,* 71–76.

Small, M. (1990). *Cognitive development.* San Diego: Harcourt Brace Jovanovich.

Smith, D. E. (1986). Cocaine-alcohol abuse: Epidemiological, diagnostic, and treatment considerations. *Journal of Psychoactive Drugs, 18,* 117–129.

Smith, P. K. (1989, April). *Rough-and-tumble play and its relationship to serious fighting.* Paper presented at the biennial meeting of the Society for Research in Child Development, Kansas City.

Smith, P. K., & Hagen, T. (1980). Effects of deprivation on excessive play in nursery school children. *Animal Behavior, 28,* 922–928.

Smolucha, F. (1989, April). *Vygotsky's theory of creative imagination and its relevance for research on play.* Paper presented at the biennial meeting of the Society for Research on Child Development, Kansas City.

Snarey, J. (1987, June). A question of morality. *Psychology Today,* pp. 6–8.

Snedeker, B. (1982). *Hard knocks.* Baltimore, MD: Johns Hopkins University Press.

Snidman, N., & Kagan, J. (1989, April). *Infant predictors of behaviorally inhibited and uninhibited children.* Paper presented at the biennial meeting of the Society for Research in Child Development, Kansas City.

Snow, C. E. (1989a). Understanding social interaction in language interaction: Sentences are not enough. In M. H. Bornstein & J. S. Bruner (Eds.), *Interaction in human development.* Hillsdale, NJ: Erlbaum.

Snow, C. E. (1989b, April). Imitation as one path to language acquisition. Paper presented at the biennial meeting of the Society for Research in Child Development, Kansas City.

Solberg, V. S. (1989, August). *Maximizing the benefits of prevention research with Mexican-American families.* Paper presented at the meeting of the American Psychological Association, New Orleans.

Sommer, B. B. (1978). *Puberty and adolescence.* New York: Oxford University Press.

Sorenson, R. C. (1973). *Adolescent sexuality in contemporary America.* New York: World.

Sowers, S. (1987). Six questions teachers ask about invented spelling. In T. Newkirk & N. Atwell (Eds.), *Understanding writing.* Portsmouth, NH: Heinemann.

Sowers-Hoag, K. W., Thyer, B. A., & Bailey, J. S. (1987). Promoting automobile safety belt use by young children. *Journal of Applied Behavior Analysis, 20,* 133–138.

Spearman, C. E. (1927). *The abilities of man.* New York: Macmillan.

Spelke, E. S. (1979). Perceiving bimodally specified events in infancy. *Developmental Psychology, 5,* 626–636.

Spence, J. T., & Helmreich, R. L. (1978). *Masculinity and femininity: Their psychological dimensions.* Austin, TX: University of Texas Press.

Spence, M., & DeCasper, A. J. (1982). *Human fetuses perceive human speech.* Paper presented at the International Conference on Infant Studies, Austin, TX.

Sroufe, L. A. (1985). Attachment classification from the perspective of infant-caregiver relationships and infant temperament. *Child Development, 56,* 1–14.

Sroufe, L. A. (1987). *The role of infant-caregiver attachment in development.* Unpublished manuscript, Institute of Child Development, University of Minnesota.

Sroufe, L. A. (in press). Pathways to adaptation and maladaptation: Psychopatholgy as developmental deviation. In D. Cicchetti (Ed.), *Developmental psychopathology: Past, present, and future.* Hillsdale, NJ: Erlbaum.

Sroufe, L. A., & Waters, E. (1976). The ontogenesis of smiling and laughter: A perspective on the organization of development in infancy. *Psychological Review, 83,* 173–189.

Stallings, J. (1975). Implementation and child effects of teaching practices in Follow Through classrooms. *Monographs of the Society for Research in Child Development, 40* (Serial No. 163).

Steinberg, L. (1986). Latchkey children and susceptibility to peer pressure: An ecological analysis. *Developmental Psychology, 22,* 433–439.

Steinberg, L. (1986). Stability (and instability) of Type A behavior from childhood to young adulthood. *Developmental Psychology, 22,* 393–402.

Steinberg, L. (1987). Impact of puberty on family relations: Effects of pubertal status and pubertal timing. *Developmental Psychology, 23,* 451–460.

Steinberg, L. (1988). Simple solutions to a complex problem: A response to Rodman, Pratto, and Nelson (1988). *Development Psychology, 24,* 295–296.

Steinberg, L. D. (1981). Transformations in family relations at puberty. *Developmental Psychology, 17,* 833–840.

Steinberg, L. D. (1988). Reciprocal relation between parent-child distance and pubertal maturation. *Developmental Psychology, 24,* 122–128.

Steiner, J. E. (1979). Human facial expressions in response to taste and smell stimulation. In H. Reese & L. Lipsitt (Eds.), *Advances in child development and behavior* (Vol. 13). New York: Academic Press.

Stern, D. N., Beebe, B., Jaffe, J., & Bennett, S. L. (1977). The infant's stimulus world during social interaction: A study of caregiver behaviors with particular reference to repetition and timing. In H. R. Schaffer (Ed.), *Studies in mother-infant interaction.* London: Academic Press.

Stern, S. L., Dixon, K. N., Jones, D., Lake, M., Nemzer, E., & Sansone, R. (1989). Family environment in anorexia nervosa and bulimia. *International Journal of Eating Disorders, 8,* 25–31.

Sternberg, R. J. (1988). *The triarchic mind.* New York: Viking.

Sternberg, R. J. (1989). Introduction. In R. J. Sternberg (Ed.), *Advances in the psychology of human intelligence* (Vol. 5). Hillsdale, NJ: Erlbaum.

Stevenson, H. W., Stigler, J. W., & Lee, S. (1986). Achievement in mathematics. In H. W. Stevenson, H. Azuma, & K. Hakuta (Eds.), *Child development and education in Japan.* San Francisco: W. H. Freeman.

Stine, E. L., & Bohannon, J. N. (1984). Imitations, interactions, and language acquisition. *Journal of Child Language, 10,* 589–603.

Stipek, D. J., & Hoffman, J. M. (1980). Children's achievement-related expectancies as a function of academic performance histories and sex. *Journal of Educational Psychology, 72,* 861–865.

Streissguth, A. P., Martin, D. C., Barr, H. M., Sandman, B. M., Kirshner, G. L., & Darby, B. L. (1984). Intrauterine alcohol and nicotine exposure: Attention and reaction time in 4-year-old children. *Developmental Pscyhology, 20,* 533–541.

Stunkard, A. J. (1987). The regulation of body weight and the treatment of obesity. In H. Weiner & A. Baum (Eds.), *Eating regulation and discontrol.* Hillsdale, NJ: Erlbaum.

Stunkard, A. J. (1989). Perspectives on human obesity. In A. J. Stunkard & A. Baum (Eds.), *Perspectives on behavioral medicine: Eating, sleeping, and sex.* Hillsdale, NJ: Erlbaum.

Sugarman, S. (1989). *Piaget's construction of the child's reality.* New York: Cambridge University Press.

Sullivan, H. S. (1953). *The interpersonal theory of psychiatry.* New York: Norton.

Sullivan, K., & Sullivan, A. (1980). Adolescent-parent separation. *Developmental Psychology, 16,* 93–99.

Suomi, S. (1987, April). *Individual differences in rhesus monkey behavioral and adrenocortical responses to social challenge: Correlations with measures of heart rate variability.* Paper presented at the biennial meeting of the Society for Research in Child Development, Baltimore.

Suomi, S. J., Harlow, H. F., & Domek, C. J. (1970). Effect of repetitive infant-infant separations of young monkeys. *Journal of Abnormal Psychology, 76,* 161–172.

Susman, E. J., & Chrousos, G. P. (1988, March). *Physiological reactivity and emotional development in young adolescents.* Paper presented at the meeting of the Society for Research in Adolescence, Alexandria, VA.

Sutton-Smith, B. (1973). *Child psychology.* New York: Appleton-Century-Crofts.

Sutton-Smith, B. (1985, October). The child at play. *Psychology Today,* pp. 64–65.

Swope, G. (1980). Kids and cults: Who joins and why? *Media and Methods, 16,* 18–21.

Tager-Flusberg, H. (in press). A psycholinguistic perspective on language development in autistic children. In G. Dawson (Ed.), *Autism: New directions on diagnosis, nature, and treatment.* New York: Guilford.

Tamis-LeMonda, C. S., & Bornstein, M. H. (1989). Habituation and maternal encouragement of attention in infancy as predictors of toddler language, play, and representational competence. *Child Development, 60,* 738–751.

Tangney, J. P. (1988). Aspects of the family and children's television viewing content preferences. *Child Development, 59,* 1070–1079.

Tanner, J. M. (1970). Physical growth. In P. H. Mussen (Ed.), *Manual of child psychology* (3rd. ed., Vol. 1). New York: Wiley.

Tanner J. M. (1978). *Fetus into man: Physical growth from conception into maturity.* Cambridge, MA: Harvard University Press.

Task Force on Pediatric AIDS (1989). Pediatric AIDS and human immunodeficiency virus infection. *American Psychologist, 44,* 248–264.

Tchibinda, J., & Mayetela, N. (1983). The rights of the child in the People's Republic of the Congo. In A. Pappas (Ed.), *Law and the status of the child.* New York: United Nations Institute for Training and Research.

Tellegen, A., Lykken, D. T., Bouchard, T. J., Wilcox, K. J., Segal, N. L., & Rich, S. (1988). Journal of Personality and Social Psychology.

Terman, L. (1925). *Genetic studies of genius: Vol. 1. Mental and physical traits of a thousand gifted children.* Stanford, CA: Stanford University Press.

Terrace, H. (1979). *Nim.* New York: Knopf.

Tharp, R. G. (1989). Psychocultural variables and constants: Effects on teaching and learning in schools. *American Psychologist, 44,* 349–359.

Tharp, R. G., & Gallimore, R. G. (1989). *Rousing minds to life.* New York: Cambridge University Press.

Thelen, E. (1981). Rhythmical behavior in infancy: An ethological perspective. *Developmental Psychology, 17,* 237–257.

Thelen, E. (1987). *Order, adaptation, and change: A synergetic approach to development.* Paper presented at the 22nd Annual Minnesota Symposium on Child Psychology, Minneapolis.

Thomas, A., & Chess, S. (1987). Commentary. In H. H. Goldsmith, A. H. Buss, R. Plomin, M. K. Rothbart, A. Thomas, A. Chess, R. R. Hinde, & R. B. McCall. Roundtable: What is temperament? Four approaches. *Child Development, 58,* 505–529.

Thomas, A., Chess, S., & Birch, H. G. (1970). The origin of personality. *Scientific American, 233,* 102–109.

Thompson, C. E. (1989. August). *Providing benefits to racial and ethnic minorities in research on counseling process and outcome.* Paper presented at the meeting of the American Psychological Association, New Orleans.

Thoresen, C. E., Eagleston, J. R. Kirmil-Gray, K., & Bracke, P. E. (1985, August). *Exploring the Type A behavior pattern in children and adolescents.* Paper presented at the meeting of the American Psychological Association, Los Angeles, CA.

Thorndike, R. L., Hagen, E. P., & Sattler, J. M. (1985). *Stanford-Binet* (4th ed.). Chicago: Riverside Publishing.

Thorpy, M. J., & Glovinsky, P. B. (1989). Headbanging (*Jactatio capitis nocturna*). In M. H. Kryger, T. Roth, & W. C. Dement (Eds.), *Principles and practices of sleep medicine.* San Diego: Harcourt Brace Jovanovich.

Timberlake, B., Fox, R. A., Baisch, M. J., & Goldberg, B. D. (1987). Prenatal education for pregnant adolescents. *Journal of School Health, 57,* 105–108.

Tittle, C. K. (1988). Validity, gender research, and studies of the effects of career development interventions. *Applied Psychology: An International Review, 37,* 121–131.

Tomlinson-Keasey, C., Warren, L. W., & Elliott, J. E. (1986). Suicide among gifted women: A prospective study. *Journal of Abnormal Psychology, 95,* 123–130.

Trimble, J. E. (1989, August). *The enculturation of contemporary psychology.* Paper presented at the meeting of the American Psychological Association, New Orleans.

Trotter, R. J. (1987, December). Project Day-Care. *Psychology Today,* pp. 32–38.

Tucker, L. A. (1987). Television, teenagers, and health. *Journal of Youth and Adolescence, 16,* 415–425.

Tuckman, B. W., & Hinkle, J. S. (1988). An experimental study of the physical and psychological effects of aerobic exercise on school children. In B. G. Melamed, K. A. Matthews, D. K. Routh, B. Stabler, & N. Schneiderman (Eds.), *Child health psychology.* Hillsdale, NJ: Erlbaum.

Tulkin, S. R., & Kagan, J. (1971). Mother-child interaction in the first year of life. *Child Development, 43,* 31–41.

Turkle, S. (1984). *The second self.* Cambridge, MA: Harvard University Press.

Tyack, D. (1976). Ways of seeing: An essay on the history of compulsory schooling. *Harvard Educational Review, 46,* 355–389.

UNICEF (1986). *The state of the world's children 1987: A summary,* New York: UNICEF.

U.S. Bureau of the Census (1986). Statistical Abstract of the United States. Washington, DC: U.S. Government Printing Office.

U.S. Department of Health and Human Services (1981). *The prevalence of dental caries in U.S. children, 1979–1980* (NIH Publication No. 82–2245).

United States Public Health Service (1988). *Moratorium on certain fetal tissue research.* Washington, D.C.: U.S. Government Printing Office.

Vaillant, G. E. (1977). *Adaptation to life.* Boston: Little, Brown.

Valsiner, J. (Ed.). (1988). *Child development in cultural context.* Toronto: C. J. Hogrefe.

Vandell, D. L. (1987). Baby sister/Baby brother: Reactions to the birth of a sibling and patterns of early sibling relations. In F. F. Schachter & R. K. Stone (Eds.). *Practical concerns about siblings.* New York: The Haworth Press.

Vandell, D. L., & Corasaniti, M. A. (1988). Variations in early child care: Do they predict subsequent social, emotional, and cognitive differences? *Child Development, 59,* 176–186.

Vandell, D. L., Henderson, V. K., & Wilson, K. S. (1988). A longitudinal study of day-care experiences of varying quality. *Child Development, 59,* 1286–1292.

Vandell, D. L., & Wilson, K. S. (1988). Infants' interactions with mother, sibling, and peer: Contrasts and relations between interaction systems. *Child Development, 48,* 176–186.

Van Deusen-Henkel, J., & Argondizza, M. (1987). Early elementary education: Curriculum planning for the primary grades. In: *A framework for curriculum design.* Augusta, ME: Division of Curriculum, Maine Department of Educational and Cultural Services.

Vaughn, B. E., Lefever, G. B., Seifer, R., & Barglow, P. (in press). Attachment behavior, attachment security, and temperament during infancy. *Child Development.*

von Tetzchner, S., & Siegel, L. S. (1989). *The social and cognitive aspects of normal and atypical language development.* New York: Springer-Verlag.

Vorhees, C. V., & Mollnow, E. (1987). Behavioral teratogenesis: Long-term influences in behavior from early exposure to environmental agents. In J. D. Osofsky (Ed.), *Handbook of infant development.* New York: Wiley.

Vurpillot, E. (1968). The development of scanning strategies and their relation to visual differentiation. *Journal of Experimental Child Psychology, 6,* 632–650.

Vygotsky, L. S. (1962). *Thought and language.* Cambridge, MA: MIT Press.

Waddington, C. H. (1957). *The strategy of the genes.* London: Allen & Son.

Wallace, H. M., & Vienonen, M. (1989). Teenage pregnancy in Sweden and Finland: Implications for the United States. *Journal of Adolescent Health Care, 10,* 231–236.

Wallach, M. A. (1985). Creative testing and giftedness. In F. D. Horowitz & M. O'Brien (Eds.), *The gifted and the talented.* Washington, DC: American Psychological Association.

Wallach, M. A., & Kogan, N. (1965). *Modes of thinking in young children.* New York: Holt, Rinehart & Winston.

Wallerstein, J., Corbin, S. B., & Lewis, J. M. (1988). Children of divorce: A ten-year study. In E. M. Hetherington & J. Arasteh (Eds.), *Impact of divorce, single-parenting, and stepparenting on children.* Hillsdale, NJ: Erlbaum.

Wallerstein, J. S., & Kelly, J. B. (1980). *Surviving the breakup: How children actually cope with divorce.* New York: Basic Books.

Wallis, C. (1985, December 9). Children having children. *Time,* pp. 78–88.

Walter, C. A. (1986). *The timing of motherhood.* Lexington, MA: D. C. Heath.

Walton, M. D., & Vallelunga, L. R. (1989, April). *The role of breastfeeding in establishing early mother-infant interactions.* Paper presented at the biennial meeting of the Society for Research in Child Development, Kansas City.

Waters, E., & Sroufe, L. A. (1983). Social competence as a developmental construct. *Developmental Review, 3,* 79–97.

Watson, J. B. (1928). *Psychological care of infant and child.* New York: W. W. Norton.

Watts, T. D., & Lewis, R. G. (1988). Alcoholism and native American youth: An overview. *Journal of Drug Issues. 18,* 69, 86.

Wechsler, D. (1949). *Wechsler Intelligence Scale for Children.* New York: The Psychological Corporation.

Wechsler, D. (1955). *Wechsler Adult Intelligence Scale.* New York: The Psychological Corporation.

Wechsler, D. (1967). *Wechsler Preschool and Primary Scale For Intelligence.* New York: The Psychological Corporation.

Wechsler, D. (1974). *Wechsler Intelligence Scale for Children-Revised.* New York: The Psychological Corporation.

Wechsler, D. (1981). *Wechsler Adult Intelligence Scale-Revised.* New York: The Psychological Corporation.

Wehlage, G. G., & Rutter, R. A. (1986). Dropping out: How much do schools contribute to the problem? *Teachers College Record, 87,* 374–392.

Weidner, G., Sexton, G., Matarazzo, J. D., Pereira, C., & Friend, R. (1988). Type-A behavior in children, adolescents, and their parents. *Developmental Psychology, 24,* 118–121.

Weinberg, R. A. (1989). Intelligence and IQ: Landmark issues and great debates. *American Psychologist, 44,* 98–104.

Weiner, I. B. (1980). Psychopathology in adolescence. In J. Adleson (Ed.), *Handbook of adolescent psychology.* New York: Wiley.

Weinstein, N. D. (1984). Reducing unrealistic optimism about illness susceptibility. *Health Psychology, 3,* 431–457.

Weisberg, R. P., Caplan, M. Z., & Sivo, P. J. (1989). A new conceptual framework for establishing school-based social competence promotion programs. In L. A. Bond, B. E. Compas, & C. Swift (Eds.), *Prevention in the schools.* Menlo Park, CA: Sage.

Weiss, G., & Hechtman, L. T. (1986). *Hyperactive children grown up.* New York: Guilford Press.

Wender, P. H., Kety, S. S., Rosenthal, D., Schulsinger, F., Ortmann, J., & Lunde, I. (1986). Psychiatric disorders in the biological and adoptive families of adopted individuals with affective disorders. *Archives of General Psychiatry, 43,* 923–929.

Werner, E. E. (1979). *Cross-cultural child development: A view from planet earth.* Monerey, CA: Brooks/Cole.

Werner, E. E., & Smith, R. S. (1982). *Vulnerable but invincible: A longitudinal study of resilient children and youth.* New York: McGraw-Hill.

Wertlieb, D. (1989, August). *Coping processes in middle childhood.* Paper presented at the meeting of the American Psychological Association, New Orleans.

Whaley, L., & Wong, D. L. (1989). *Essentials of pediatric nursing* (3rd ed.). St. Louis, MO: Mosby.

Whaley, L. F., & Wong, D. L. (1989). *Essentials of pediatric nursing.* St. Louis, MO: Mosby.

White, B. L. (1988). *Educating the infant and toddler.* Lexington, MA: Lexington Books.

White, M. A. (Ed.). (in press). *What curriculum for the information age?* Hillsdale, NJ: Erlbaum.

White, R. W. (1959). Motivation reconsidered: The concept of competence. *Psychological Review, 66,* 297–333.

White, S. H. (1985, April). *Risings and fallings of developmental psychology.* Paper presented at the biennial meeting of the Society for Research in Child Development, Toronto.

Whitehurst, G. J., & Valdez-Menchaca, M. C. (1988). What is the role of reinforcement in early language acquisition? *Child Development, 59,* 430–440.

Whiting, B. B. (1989, April). *Culture and interpersonal behavior.* Paper presented at the biennial meeting of the Society for Research in Child Development, Kansas City.

Widmayer, S., & Field, T. (1980). Effects of Brazelton demonstrations on early patterns of preterm infants and their teenage mothers. *Infant Behavior and Development, 3,* 79–89.

Wilks, Y. (Ed.) (in press). Theoretical issues in natural language processing. Hillsdale, NJ: Erlbaum.

William T. Grant Foundation Commission on Work, Family, and Citizenship (1988). *The forgotten half: Non-college youth in America.* New York: The William T. Grant Foundation.

Williams, J. (1979). Reading instruction today. *American Psychologist, 34,* 917–922.

Williams, M. F., & Condry, J. (1989, April). *Living color: Minority portrayals and cross-racial interactions on television.* Paper presented at the biennial meeting of the Society for Research in Child Development, Kansas City.

Williams, R. B. (1989). Biological mechanisms mediating the relation between behavior and coronary heart disease. In A. W. Siegman & T. Dembrowski (Eds.), *In search of coronary-prone behavior: Beyond Type A.* Hillsdale, NJ: Erlbaum.

Williams, R. B., Barefoot, J. C., & Haney, T. L. (1986, March). *Type A behavior and angiographically documented atherosclerosis in a sample of 2,289 patients.* Paper presented at the meeting of the American Psychosomatic Association, Baltimore, MD.

Wilson, A. B. (1989). Dreams and aspirations in the status attainment model. In D. Stern & D. Eichorn (Eds.), *Adolescence and work.* Hillsdale, NJ: Erlbaum.

Wilson, M. N. (1989). Child development in the context of the extended family. *American Psychologist, 44,* 380–385.

Wilson, W. J. (1978). *The declining significance of race.* Chicago: University of Chicago Press.

Windle, W. F. (1940). *Physiology of the human fetus.* Philadelphia: Saunders.

Winner, E. (1986, August). Where pelicans kiss seals. *Psychology Today,* pp. 24–35.

Winner, E. (1989). Development in the visual arts. In W. Damon (Ed.), *Child development today and tomorrow.* San Francisco: W. H. Freeman.

Winner, E., & Gardner, H. (1988). Creating a world with words. In F. Kessel (Ed.), *The development of language and language researchers.* Hillsdale, NJ: Erlbaum.

Witkin, H. A., Mednick, S. A., Schulsinger, R., Bakkestrom, E., Christiansen, K. O., Goodenbough, D. R., Hirchhorn, K., Lunsteen, C., Owen, D. R., Philip, J., Ruben, D. B., & Stocking, M. (1976). Criminality in XYY and XXY men. *Science, 193,* 547–555.

Wolf, D. (1989, Spring). Novelty, creativity, and child development. *SRCD Newsletter,* pp. 1–2.

Wolff, P. H. (1987). *The development of behavioral states and the expression of emotions in early infancy.* Chicago, IL: University of Chicago Press.

Wood, F. H. (1988). Learners at risk. *Teaching Exceptional Children, 20,* 4–9.

Worobey, J. & Belsky, J. (1982). Employing the Brazelton Scale to influence mothering: An experimental comparison of three strategies. *Developmental Psychology, 18,* 736–743.

Worthington, B. S. (1988). Maternal nutrition and the course and outcome of pregnancy. In S. R. Williams & B. S. Worthington (Eds.), *Nutrition throughout the life cycle.* St. Louis: Times Mirror/Mosby.

Worthington-Roberts, B. S. (1988). Lactation and human milk. In S. R. Williams & B. S. Worthington-Roberts (Eds.), *Nutrition through the life cycle.* St. Louis: Times Mirror/ Mosby.

Wright, M. R. (1989). Body image satisfaction in adolescent girls and boys: A longitudinal study. *Journal of Youth and Adolescence, 18,* 71–84.

Wylie, R. C. (1979). *The self-concept* (Vol. 2). Lincoln, NE: University of Nebraska Press.

Youniss, J., & Smollar, J. (1985). *Adolescent relations with mothers, fathers, and friends.* Chicago: University of Chicago Press.

Zahn-Waxler, C., Radke-Yarrow, M., & King, R. M. (1979). Child rearing and children's prosocial initiations toward victims of distress. *Child Development, 50,* 319–330.

Zelnik, M., & Kantner, J. F. (1980). Sexual activity, contraceptive use and pregnancy among metropolitan-area teenagers: 1971–1979. *Family Planning Perspectives, 12,* 230–237.

Zembar, M. J., & Naus, M. J. (1985, April). *The combined effect of knowledge base and mnemonic strategies on children's memory.* Paper presented at the biennial meeting of the Society for Research in Child Development, Toronto.

Zeskind, P. S., & Marshall, T. R. (1988). The relation between variations in pitch and maternal perception of infant crying. *Child Development, 59,* 193–196.

Zigler, E. (1987, April). *Child care for parents who work outside the home: Problems and solutions.* Paper presented at the biennial meeting of the Society for Research in Child Development, Baltimore.

Zigler, E. F. (1987, August). *Issues in mental retardation research.* Paper presented at the meeting of the American Psychological Association, New York City.

Zigler, E. F., & Farber, E. A. (1985). Commonalities between the intellectual extremes: Giftedness and mental retardation. In F. D. Horowitz & M. O'Brien (Eds.), *The gifted and the talented.* Washington, DC: American Psychological Association.

Zukow, P. G. (Ed.). (1989). Sibling interaction across cultures. New York: Springer-Verlag.

Credits

G. White; **5.3:** DREAMSTAGE Scientific catalog, © 1977, J. Allen Hobson, Hoffman-LaRoche, Inc.; **page 146:** © Julie O'Neill; **page 145:** © John G. Ross/Photo Researchers, Inc.; **page 146:** © Ray Ellis/Photo Researchers, Inc.; **page 148:** © Bob Daemmerich/The Image Works; **5.7:** J. L. Conel: Postnatal Development of the Human Cerebral Cortex, Cambridge: Harvard University Press, vols. I-VI, 1937–1963; **page 151 (left):** © Joyce Photographics/Photo Researchers, Inc.; **page 151 (right):** © Mark Antman/The Image Works; **page 152:** © Will McIntyre/Photo Researchers; **5.8:** © Richard Anderson; **page 154:** © Allan Stuart Frank/Photo Researchers, Inc.; **5.9:** © David Linton; **5.11:** © Enrico Ferorelli/Dot Inc.; **page 159:** © Michael Siluk.

Chapter 6

Chapter Opener: © Jim Tuten/Black Star; **page 171(a):** © Cleo Photography; **page 171(b):** © C & W Shields, Inc.; **page 171(c):** © Gabor Demjen/Stock Boston; **page 171(d):** © Elizabeth Crews/The Image Works; **page 171(e):** © William Hopkins; **page 171(f):** © Patricia Agre/Photo Researchers, Inc.; **page 172:** © Elizabeth Crews/The Image Works; **page 173 (both):** © James L. Shaffer; **page 175 (both):** © Cleo Photography; **6.1:** © Dr. Carolyn K. Rovee-Collier, Rutgers University; **page 177:** © Suzanne Arms/Jeroboam, Inc.; **6.3 (all):** *Discrimination and Imitation of Facial Expressions* by Neonates by T. M. Field, et al SCIENCE, Fig. 2, Vol. 218 (8 Oct 1982) © by the AAAS; **6.5:** © Patrick Donehue/Photo Researchers, Inc.; **6.7:** The Bettmann Archives; **page 185:** © Charles Mahaux/The Image Bank, Chicago; **6A:** © R. A. and B. T. Gardner; **6B:** © Susan Kuklin; **page 191:** © Jean-Claude Lejeune.

Chapter 7

Chapter Opener: © Elyse Lewin/The Image Bank, Chicago; **7.1a:** © Leonard Lee Rue III/Photo Researchers, Inc.; **7.1b:** © Mitch Reardon/Photo Researchers, Inc.; **7.1c:** © Allen Green/Photo Researchers, Inc.; **7.3a:** © Anthony Bannister/Animals Animals/Earth Scenes; **7.3b:** © Chagnon/Anthro Photo; **page 205:** © Anthony A. Boccaccio/The Image Bank, Chicago; **page 206(a):** © James L. Shaffer; **page 206(b), (c), page 209:** © James G. White; **7.5:** © Martin Rogers/Stock Boston; **page 210 (left):** © Alan Carey/The Image Works; **page 210 (right):** © Scott Blackman/Tom Stack and Associates; **page 213:** © Richard

Anderson; **page 215 (left):** © Kathy Tarantola; **page 215 (right):** © Dr. Barry Hewlett; **page 216:** © Alan Carey/The Image Works; **page 217:** © Cesar Lucas/The Image Bank, Chicago; **page 220:** © Michel Tcherevkoff/The Image Bank, Chicago; **7.8a, b, d, e, g, h:** © Erika Stone; **7.8c, f:** © Nancy Anne Dawe; **page 223:** © D. E. Cox; **page 225:** © Howard Dratch/The Image Works.

Chapter 8

Chapter Opener: © Suzanne Szasz/Photo Researchers, Inc.; **page 241:** © Owen Franken/Stock Boston; **page 244:** © Mel DiGiacomo/The Image Bank, Dallas; **page 245:** © Suzanne Szasz/Photo Researchers, Inc.; **page 246:** © Bryan Peterson; **8.3a:** © Elizabeth Crews/The Image Works; **8.3b:** © Larry Voight/Photo Researchers, Inc.; **8.3c:** © Ulrike Welsch/Photo Researchers, Inc.; **8.3d:** © Alan Carey/The Image Works; **page 251:** © Richard Anderson; **page 255:** © James L. Shaffer; **page 256:** © William Campbell/Time Magazine; **page 259:** © Alan Carey/The Image Works; **page 260:** © Bob Daemmrich/The Image Works.

Chapter 9

Chapter Opener: © Elizabeth Crews/The Image Works; **page 275:** © Mark M. Walker; **page 277:** © Skjold Photographs; **page 283:** © Cleo Photography; **page 284:** © James G. White; **page 289:** © George E. Jones III/Photo Researchers, Inc.; **page 291:** © 1984 Robert Knowles/Black Star; **page 292:** © Joy Hendry.

Chapter 10

Chapter Opener: © Bill Carter/The Image Bank, Chicago; **page 300:** © Eastcott/Momatiuk/The Image Works; **page 301:** © Shelley Gazin/The Image Works; **page 304:** © Bob Daemmrich/The Image Works; **page 306(a):** © Suzanne Szasz/Photo Researchers, Inc.; **page 306(b):** © Blair Seitz/Photo Researchers, Inc.; **page 307:** © Larry Mulvehill/Photo Researchers, Inc.; **page 308:** © Elyse Lewin/The Image Bank, Chicago; **page 312:** © Richard Anderson; **10.2:** The Kunthistoriaches Museum, Vienna; **page 318:** © Bryan Peterson; **page 320:** © Larry Kolvoord/The Image Works; **page 321:** © 1989 Sesame Street, Inc. Used courtesy of Children's Television Workshop; **page 326:** © James G. White; **page 330:** © Suzanne Szasz/Photo Researchers, Inc.; **page 334:** © Richard Anderson.

Chapter 11

Chapter Opener: © Pat LaCroix/The Image Bank, Dallas; **11.1:** © Joe McNally/Sports Illustrated; **page 348:** © Mel DiGiacomo/The Image Bank, Dallas; **page 353:** © James L. Shaffer; **page 356:** © Michael Garland/The Image Bank, Chicago; **page 359:** © Cleo Photography; **page 360:** © Norman Prince; **page 361:** © Jan Doyle; **page 363 (both):** © Mel DiGiacomo/The Image Bank, Dallas; **page 367:** © Bob Daemmerich/The Image Works; **page 369 (left):** © Deborah K. Smith/Apple Photography; **page 369 (right):** © Skjold Photographs.

Chapter 12

Chapter Opener: © Mel DiGiacomo/The Image Bank, Dallas; **page 381:** © Jordan Information Bureau/Frost Publishing Group; **page 382:** © Art Attack/Photo Researchers, Inc.; **page 385:** © Culver Pictures, Inc.; **page 391 (left):** © UPI/Bettmann Newsphotos; **page 391 (right):** Historical Pictures Service, Chicago; **page 394:** © Julie O'Neil; **12.8:** © Jill Cannefax/EKM-Nepenthe; **page 397:** © Mark Antman/The Image Works; **page 400:** © A. Hans-Jorg/The Image Bank, Chicago; **page 403:** © Blair Seitz/Photo Researchers, Inc.; **page 407:** © Elyse Lewin/The Image Bank, Chicago; **page 408:** © Andre Gallant/The Image Bank, Chicago.

Chapter 13

Chapter Opener: © Don Klumpp/The Image Bank, Chicago; **page 417:** © Tim Bieber/The Image Bank, Chicago; **page 421:** © Richard Hutchings/Photo Researchers, Inc.; **page 423:** © Bryan Peterson; **page 425:** © Jan Doyle; **page 426:** Stephanie Dinkins/Photo Researchers, Inc.; **page 429:** © Bob Daemmrich/The Image Works; **page 432(a):** © David de Lossy/The Image Bank, Dallas; **page 432(b):** © Stephen Marks/The Image Bank, Dallas; **page 432(c):** © Don Klumpp/The Image Bank, Dallas; **page 432(d):** © Jack Ward/The Image Bank, Chicago; **page 436(a)** © Lorraine Rorke/The Image Works; **page 436(b):** © Jan Doyle; **page 438:** © Bernard Pierre Wolff/Photo Researchers, Inc.; **page 445:** © Bob Coyle.

Chapter 14

Chapter Opener: © Ellis Herwig/Stock Boston; **page 458:** © Kaz Mori/The Image Bank, Chicago; **page 462:** © Donald Dietz/Stock Boston; **page 464:** © Lawrence Migdale/Photo Researchers,

Inc.; **page 467:** © Abigail Heyman; **page 470:** © Richard Anderson; **page 472:** © Mark Antman/The Image Works; **page 475:** © Bob Daemmerich/The Image Works; **page 478:** © Alan Carey/The Image Works; **page 481:** © Richard Anderson; **page 483:** © Barbara Burnes/Photo Researchers, Inc.; **page 485:** © Andrew Sacks/Time Magazine; **page 487:** © Susan Rosenberg/Photo Researchers, Inc.

Chapter 15

Chapter Opener: © Patsy Davidson/The Image Works; **15.1:** © Michael Siluk; **page 497:** © Bob Daemmerich/The Image Works; **page 499:** © William Hopkins; **page 500:** © Richard Anderson; **page 502:** © Bob Daemmerich/The Image Works; **page 503:** © Catherine Ursillo/Photo Researchers, Inc.; **page 506:** © Don Carl Steffen/Photo Researchers, Inc.; **page 507:** © Bob Daemmerich/The Image Works; **page 508:** © James G. White; **page 512:** © Richard Anderson; **pages 514, 516:** © Bob Daemmerich/The Image Works; **page 519:** © James G. White; **page 522:** © Richard Anderson.

Chapter 16

Chapter Opener: © Lanpher Productions, Inc.; **page 531:** © Blair Seitz/Photo Researchers, Inc.; **page 533:** © John Kelly/The Image Bank, Chicago; **page 534:** © Richard Hutchings/Photo Researchers, Inc.; **page 538(a):** © Cleo Photography; **page 538(b):** © Larry Mulvehill/Photo Researchers, Inc.; **page 542 (top):** © Nancy Brown/The Image Bank, Dallas; **page 542 (bottom):** © James L. Shaffer; **pages 543, 546 (left):** © Bob Daemmrich/The Image Works; **page 546 (right):** © James G. White; **page 549:** © Bob Daemmrich/The Image Works; **page 550:** © Dianne Carter; **page 551:** © Eddie Adams/Time Magazine; **page 552:** © Alan Carey/The Image Works; **page 553:** © Franke Keating/Photo Researchers, Inc.; **page 555:** © Daniele Pellegrini/Photo Researchers, Inc.; **page 556:** © Eddie Adams/Time Magazine

Epilogue
© Jay Maisel

LINE ART, EXCERPTS

Chapter 2

Figure 2.1: From *Psychology: A Scientific Study of Human Behavior, Fifth Edition,* by L. S. Wrightsman, C. K. Sigelman and F. H. Sanford. Copyright © 1961, 1965, 1970, 1975, 1979 by Wadsworth Publishing Company, Inc. Reprinted by permission of the publisher.
Illustration, page 54: Courtesy of Multimedia Entertainment Inc.
Excerpt, page 41: From "Desert Places" by Robert Frost. Copyright 1936 by Robert Frost and renewed 1964 by Lesley Frost Ballantine. Reprinted from *The Poetry of Robert Frost* edited by Edward Connery Lathem, by permission of Henry Holt and Company, Inc.

Chapter 3

Figure 3.7: From I. Gottesman, "Genetic Aspects of Intellectual Behavior" in *Handbook of Mental Deficiency,* Norman R. Ellis, Ed. Copyright © McGraw-Hill Book Company. Reprinted by permission of Norman R. Ellis.
Excerpt, page 83: From *Verses From 1929 On* by Ogden Nash. Copyright © 1945, 1959 by Ogden Nash. By permission of Little, Brown and Company, Boston, Massachusetts, and Curtis Brown, Ltd., New York, New York.

Chapter 4

Figure 4.4: From Moore, K. L.: *The Developing Human. Clinically Oriented Embryology,* 3rd ed, 1982. Courtesy, W. B. Saunders Company, Philadelphia, Pennsylvania. Reprinted by permission.

Chapter 5

Excerpt, pages 142–143: Reprinted from "States in Newborn Infants" in *Merrill-Palmer Quarterly,* Volume 10, No. 4. (1964), pp. 313–327 by J. L. Brown by permission of the Wayne State University Press. Copyright © 1964 Wayne State University Press, Detroit, Michigan.
Figure 5.6: From Esther Thelen, "Rhythmical Behavior in Infancy: An Ethological Perspective" in *Developmental Psychology,* 1981. © 1981 American Psychological Association. Reprinted by permission of the author.
Figure 5.10: From R.L. Frantz, "Pattern Discrimination and Selective Attention as Determinants in Infancy" in Aline H. Kidd and Jeanne L. Rivoire: *Perceptual Development in Children.* © 1966 International Universities Press, Inc., New York.
Figure 5.12: Data from M. R. Gunnar, et al., "The Psychology of Stress and Coping in the Human Neonate: Studies of Adrenocortical Activity in Response to Stress in the First Week of Life" in T. Field, et al., eds., *Stress and Coping.* Copyright © Lawrence Erlbaum Associates, Inc., Hillsdale, NJ. Reprinted by permission.

Chapter 6

Excerpt, page 166: Source: Walt Whitman, *Leaves of Grass,* 1945. Random House Modern Library, New York.
Figure 6.2: From K. Scheingold and Y. J. Tenney, "Memory of a Salient Childhood Event" in *Memory Observed: Remembering in Natural Contexts* by Ulric Neisser. © 1982 W.H. Freeman and Company, New York. Adapted by permission.
Figure 6.4: From T. M. Field, et al., "Discrimination and Imitation of Facial Expressions by Neonates" in *Science,* Vol. 218, No. 4568, 179–181, 8 October 1982. Copyright 1982 by the American Association for the Advancement of Science. Reprinted by permission.
Figure 6.8: From R. Brown, et al., *Minnesota Symposium on Child Psychology,* Vol. 2, J. P. Hill, ed., 1969. Reprinted by permission.

Chapter 7

Figure 7.2: J. Garbarino from Kopp/Krakow, THE CHILD, 1982 fig. 12.1, p. 648.
Figure 7.4: From Jay Belsky, "Early Human Experience: A Family Perspective" in *Developmental Psychology,* 17, 3–23, 1981. © 1981 American Psychological Association. Reprinted by permission of the author.
Figure 7.6: From Harry F. Harlow, et al., "Affectional Responses in the Infant Monkey" in *Science,* Vol. 130, #3373, pp. 421–432, 21 August 1959. Copyright 1959 by the American Association for the Advancement of Science, Washington, DC. Reprinted by permission.
Figure 7.7: From L. Matas, et al., "Continuity in Adaptation: Quality of Attachment and Later Competence" in *Child Development,* 49, 547–556, 1978. © 1978 by The Society for Research in Child Development. Reprinted by permission.
Figure 7.9: From M. Lewis and J. Brooks-Gunn, *Social Cognition and the Acquisition of the Self.* Copyright © 1979 Plenum Publishing Corporation, New York. Reprinted by permission.

Chapter 8

Figure 8.2: Adapted from *Human Biology and Ecology,* Albert Damon, by permission of W. W. Norton & Company, Inc. Copyright © 1977 by W. W. Norton & Company, Inc.
Figure 8.4: From R. Kellogg, *Understanding Children's Art: Readings*

in Developmental Psychology Today, 1970. Copyright © McGraw-Hill Book Company, New York, New York.

Figure 8.5: From Goodman, *You and Your Child.* Copyright © 1979 Mitchell Beazley Publishers, Ltd., London, England.

Chapter 9

Figure 9.B: Courtesy Dr. Ellen Winner, Project Zero.

Figure 9.C: From Claire Golomb, *The Child's Invention of a Pictorial World: Studies in the Psychology of Child Art* (book in preparation).

Figure 9.D: Courtesy Dr. Ellen Winner, Project Zero.

Figure 9.E: Courtesy Dr. Ellen Winner, Project Zero.

Figure 9.6: From Daniel R. Anderson, et al., "Television Viewing at Home: Age Trends in Visual Attention and Time with TV." Paper presented at the meeting of the Society for Research in Child Development. Copyright © Daniel R. Anderson. Reprinted by permission.

Figure 9.7: From Frank N. Dempster, "Memory Span: Sources of Individual and Developmental Differences" in *Psychological Bulletin,* 89, 63–100, 1981. © 1981 American Psychological Association. Reprinted by permission of the author.

Figure 9.8: From Jean Berko, "The Child's Learning of English Morphology" in *Word,* 14, 150–177, 361, 1958. © 1958 International Linguistic Association. Reprinted by permission.

Figure 9.9: Courtesy of Katie Hueneke, Michelle Salow, and Jason Obra.

Chapter 10

Figure 10.3: From K. E. Barnes, "Preschool Play Norms: A Replication" in *Developmental Psychology,* 5, 99–103, 1971. Copyright © 1971 American Psychological Association. Reprinted by permission of the author.

Excerpt, page 313: Source: Dylan Thomas, 1954.

Chapter 11

Figure 11.2: From *The Process of Human Development,* 2/e by Clara Shaw Schuster and Shirley Smith Ashburn. Copyright © 1986 by Clara Shaw Schuster and Shirley Smith Ashburn. Reprinted by permission of Scott, Foresman and Company.

Excerpt, page 350: From R. Hubbard, "Allow Children's Individuality to Emerge in Their Writing: Let Their Voices Through" in *Young Children,* 43, pp. 33–38, 1988. Copyright © 1988 by the National Association for the Education of Young Children. Reprinted by permission.

Figure 11.A: From R. Hubbard, "Allow Children's Individuality to Emerge in Their Writing: Let Their Voices Through" in *Young Children,* 43, pp. 33–38, 1988. Copyright © 1988 by the National Association for the Education of Young Children. Reprinted by permission.

Chapter 12

Figure 12.2: From Joel Levin, et al., "The Keyword Method in the Classroom" in *Elementary School Journal,* 80, 4, 1980. Copyright © 1980 The University of Chicago Press. Reprinted by permission.

Figure 12.3: From Jerome M. Sattler, *Assessment of Children's Intelligence and Special Abilities,* 2d ed. Copyright © 1982 Allyn & Bacon, Inc., Needham Heights, MA. Reprinted by permission of the author.

Figure 12.6: From Raven's *Standard Progressive Matrices.* Reprinted by permission of J. C. Raven, Limited.

Figure 12.10: From Goodman, *You and Your Child.* Copyright © 1979 Mitchell Beazley Publishers, Ltd., London, England.

Figure 12.11 (top): From Mark R. Lepper, "Microcomputers in Education" in *American Psychologist,* 40, 1–9, 1985. Copyright © 1985 American Psychological Association. Reprinted by permission of the author.

Figure 12.11 (bottom): Designed by Sharon Dugdale and David Kibbey. Copyright © 1973 by the University of Illinois.

Figure 12.12: From M. R. Lepper, et al., "Undermining Children's Intrinsic Interest with Extrinsic Rewards" in *Journal of Personality and Social Psychology,* 28, 129–137, 1973. Reprinted with permission of the Helen Dwight Reid Educational Foundation.

Chapter 13

Excerpt, page 429: From Perry, Imani, "A Black Student's Reflection on Public and Private Schools," in *Harvard Educational Review,* 58:3, 332–336. Copyright © 1988 by the President and Fellows of Harvard College. All rights reserved.

Figure 13.5: From T. Achenbach and C. S. Edelbrock, "Behavioral Problems and Competencies Reported by Parents of Normal and Disturbed Children Aged Four Through Sixteen" in *Monographs of the Society for Research in Child Development,* Serial No. 188, Vol. 46, No. 1, 1981. Reprinted by permission.

Excerpt, page 433: From *Now We Are Six* by A. A. Milne. Copyright 1927 by E.P. Dutton, renewed 1955 by A. A. Milne. Reprinted by permission of the publisher, Dutton Children's Books, a division of Penguin Books USA, Inc.

Chapter 14

Figure 14.1: From A. F. Roche, "Secular Trends in Stature, Weight and Maturation" in *Monographs of the Society for Research in Child Development,* 44, Serial No. 179, 1977. © 1977 by The Society for Research in Child Development. Reprinted by permission.

Figure 14.2: From J. M. Tanner, et al., "Standards from Birth to Maturity for Height, Weight, Height Velocity, and Weight Velocity: British Children 1965" in *Archives of Diseases in Childhood,* 41, 1966. Copyright © 1966 British Medical Association, London, England. Reprinted by permission.

Figure 14.5: From D. A. Blythe, et al., "The Impact of Puberty on Adolescence: A Longitudinal Study" in *Girls in Puberty* by Jeanne Brooks Gunn. Copyright © 1981 Plenum Publishing Corporation, New York, NY. Reprinted by permission.

Figure 14.6: From C. A. Darling, et al., "Sex in Transition: 1900–1984" in *Journal of Youth and Adolescence,* 13:385–399, 1984. Copyright © 1984 Plenum Publishing Corporation, New York. Reprinted by permission.

Figure 14.7: From Elise F. Jones, et al., "Teenage Pregnancy in Developed Countries: Determinants & Policy Implications" in *Family Planning Perspectives,* Vol. 17, No. 2 (March/April 1985), Fig. 3, p. 55. © The Alan Guttmacher Institute.

Chapter 15

Figure 15.2: Data collected by The Higher Education Research Institute, Graduate School of Education, University of California, Los Angeles. Copyright © 1987. Reprinted by permission.

Excerpt, page 519: I AM WOMAN. Words by Helen Reddy. Music by Ray Burton © 1971 IRVING MUSIC, INC. (BMI) & BUGGERLUGS MUSIC CO. (BMI) All Rights Reserved. International Copyright Secured.

Chapter 16

Figure 16.1: From D. C. Dunphy, "The Social Structure of Peer Groups" in *Sociometry,* 26, fig. 1, p. 263, 1963. © 1963 American Sociological Association. Reprinted by permission.

Name Index

Bloom, B. S., 397
Bloome, D., 283, 506
Blos, P., 49, 535
Blotcky, M. J., 41
Blue, J. H., 460, 461
Blum, R. W., 112
Blumenfeld, P. C., 425
Blumenthal, S. J., 486
Blyth, D. A., 464, 465, 508
Bobrow, N. A., 465
Bogin, B., 153
Bohannon, J. N., III, 190
Bolter, J. D., 440
Bornstein, M. H., 66, 158, 175, 226, 276
Bornstein, M. W., 22, 181, 213
Borovsky, D., 176
Borstelmann, L. J., 13, 14
Bouchard, T. J., 80
Bower, G., 250
Bowlby, J., 142, 209
Boxer, A. M., 471
Brackbill, Y., 119
Bracke, P. E., 366
Brady, M. P., 352
Bransford, J. D., 381
Bray, J. H., 419
Brazelton, T. B., 124, 125, 126, 140, 145
Bredekamp, S., 289
Bremer, M., 319, 323
Brenner, A., 362, 366, 368, 369, 370
Brent, D. A., 486
Bresolin, L. B., 322
Bretherton, I., 220
Brody, L., 520
Bronfenbrenner, U., 26, 201, 443
Brooks-Gunn, J., 291, 462, 463, 465, 475, 477, 487
Brown, A. L., 381, 495
Brown, B. B., 538
Brown, F., 280, 505
Brown, J. L., 142, 154
Brown, J. V., 127
Brown, L. G., 27, 88
Brown, M. M., 313
Brown, R., 188, 190, 193, 294, 335, 430
Brumberg, J. J., 487
Bruner, J., 205, 288
Bryant, B., 26
Buckley, S., 421
Buckley, W. E., 481
Bugbee, N. M., 149
Buhrmester, D., 424
Bulcroft, R., 464, 465
Bullock, M., 271
Burgeson, R., 508
Burish, T. G., 59
Burkett, C. L., 325
Burtchaell, J., 109
Buss, A. H., 93, 95
Byrnes, J. P., 496

Cairns, B. D., 26
Cairns, R. B., 14, 15, 26
Calhoun, J. A., 484
Callan, J. W., 422
Camara, K. A., 309
Campbell, K., 210
Campione, J. C., 381
Campos, J. J., 122, 158, 220
Camreon, D., 426
Caplan, M. Z., 422
Carbo, M., 400
Carey, S., 282
Carpenter, C. J., 329
Carper, L., 331
Carroll, J. B., 389
Carskadon, G., 143
Carter, D. B., 328
Carter-Saltzman, L., 251
Carton, B., 530
Carton-Ford, S., 508
Case, R., 279
Casper, R., 487
Caspi, A., 457
Cassell, C., 469, 470
Cassidy, D. J., 329
Cavett, D., 539
Chalfant, J. C., 354
Chard, S., 349, 426
Charlesworth, R., 289
Charnov, E. L., 212
Chase-Lansdale, P. L., 309, 475
Chasnoff, I. J., 114
Chen, C., 409
Chesney-Lind, M., 484
Chess, S., 93, 95
Chi, M. T., 381
Chinsky, J. M., 380
Chivian, E., 9
Chomsky, N., 185, 187, 195
Christiansen, K. O., 86
Chrousos, G. P., 27, 460, 461
Cicirelli, V., 305
Clark, E. V., 191, 192
Clark, H. H., 191
Clark, R. W., 404
Clark, S., 545
Clark, S. D., 469
Clarke-Stewart, K. A., 208, 218
Clifford, E., 353
Cobb, P. A., 382
Cohen, D., 178
Cohen, P., 124
Cohen, S., 181
Cohn, J. F., 205
Colby, A., 440, 442
Cole, S., 521
Coleman, J., 537
Coleman, J. S., 505

Coles, R., 49, 502, 543
Colletta, N. D., 309
Collins, P. A., 277
Collins, W. A., 533
Colombo, J., 142
Compas, B., 363
Comtois, J. H., 255
Conant, J. B., 505
Condon, S. M., 535
Condry, J., 319, 322
Conger, R., 477, 498, 500, 548
Cool, V. A., 286
Coons, S., 143
Cooper, B. A., 120
Cooper, C. R., 535, 544
Coopersmith, S., 433, 549
Corasaniti, M. A., 216
Corbin, S. B., 309, 310
Corrigan, R., 173
Corter, C., 306
Corwin, V., 321
Cowan, C., 204
Cowan, P., 204
Cox, M., 309
Cox, R., 309
Cratty, B., 248
Crimmins, D. B., 230
Crites, J. O., 518
Crittenden, P., 227, 228
Crnic, K. A., 123
Croft, K., 326
Cronbach, L., 428
Cross, P., 506
Crowder, R., 400
Csapo, M., 353
Cuban, L., 10
Curtiss, S., 189
Cutler, G. B., 27, 460, 461
Czajkowski, S. M., 365

Damon, W., 243
Dann, S., 312
Danner, F., 496
Darby, B. L., 113, 356
Darling, C. A., 468
Darlington, R., 291
Daro, D., 228
Darwin, C., 14, 15
Dawson, G., 229
deArmas, A., 422
DeBarsyshe, B. D., 24, 25, 484
DeCasper, A. J., 159
Deci, E. L., 406
DeFries, J. C., 92, 95
DeLoache, J. S., 329
Dembrowski, T., 365
Dement, W. C., 143
Demorest, A., 495
DeMoss, V., 254

Gearhart, B. R., 286, 352
Gelman, R., 275, 283, 376
Gesell, A., 15, 16, 146, 179, 180, 182
Gewirtz, J., 142, 331, 443
Ghesquire, K., 210
Gibbs, J., 390, 442
Gibbs, J. T., 12, 428, 539, 548, 553
Gibson, E. J., 157, 158, 161, 162
Gibson, J. J., 161, 162
Gilgun, J. F., 469, 470, 471
Gill, S., 436, 437
Gilligan, C., 443, 444
Ginsburg, H., 169
Gjerde, P. F., 309
Glasser, R., 11
Glazer, R., 383
Gleason, J. B., 282
Glick, J., 378
Glovinsky, P. B., 143
Goelman, H., 495
Gold, M., 484, 532
Gold, M. S., 479
Goldberg, J., 279
Goldening, J., 9
Goldhagen, J., 112
Golding, E., 214
Goldman, J. A., 255
Goldman, N., 474
Goldman-Rakic, P. S., 149
Goldsmith, H. H., 95, 123
Goodchilds, J. D., 470
Goodenbough, D. R., 86
Goodlad, J. I., 506
Goodman, R. A., 479
Goodman, S., 247, 250, 272
Gordon, S., 469, 470, 471
Gore, T., 546
Gorlitz, D., 315
Gorski, P. A., 126
Gotowiec, A., 141
Gottesman, I. I., 95
Gottfried, A. W., 181
Gottlieb, D., 428
Gottlob, D., 261
Gottman, J. M., 423
Graddol, D., 328
Graham, D., 112
Graham, S., 407
Granrud, C. E., 158
Grant, J. P., 153, 254, 257, 258
Graubard, P., 59
Graves, D., 350
Gray, P. A., 484
Green, J. A., 141
Green, K. C., 498, 500
Green, T. M., 535
Greenberg, M. T., 123
Greenberg, R., 178
Greenberger, E., 521, 522
Greene, B., 456
Greene, J. W., 406, 477
Greenfield, P., 547
Grieser, D. L., 190

Griffing, P., 300
Grobel, J., 21
Grossman, F. K., 214
Grotevant, H. D., 518, 535, 544
Grubb, W. N., 523
Guberman, S. R., 286
Guilford, J. P., 397
Guilleminault, C., 143
Gunnar, M. R., 160
Gurtner, J., 11, 405
Gustafson, G. E., 141
Gutek, B. A., 518
Gyurke, J. S., 120

H

Hagan, E. P., 286
Hagan, M. S., 309, 310, 419, 420
Hagen, T., 246
Hahn, A., 511
Haith, M. M., 140
Hake, J. L., 159
Hakuta, K., 403
Hall, G. S., 14, 15, 400, 457, 466
Hallahan, D. P., 353
Halwes, T. G., 380
Hankins, C. A., 472
Hans, S., 114
Hanson, E., 533
Hardy, J. B., 469
Hardyck, C., 251
Harlow, H., 209, 312
Harmon, R. 142
Harris, L., 420
Harter, S., 228, 406, 433
Hartshorne, H., 333
Hartsough, C. S., 356
Hartup, W., 207, 311, 312, 313, 421
Harvard Medical School Newsletter, 472
Haskins, R., 291, 292
Hathaway, B., 389
Haugard, J. J., 227
Hauser, S. T., 433, 544
Havighurst, R. J., 548, 553
Hawkins, J. A., 508
Hayden-Thomson, L., 330
Hayes, C., 186
Hayes, K. J., 186
Heath, S. B., 203, 322, 548
Hebel, J. R., 114
Hechtman, L. T., 356
Heeren, T., 486
Heft, L., 366
Hein, K., 473
Helmreich, R., 435
Helson, R., 521
Hendry, J., 192, 292
Henker, B., 356
Hennessey, B. A., 397
Henshaw, S. K., 474
Herdt, G. H., 471
Hertzig, M., 229

Herzog, E., 330
Hess, R. D., 226
Heston, L., 80
Hetherington, E. M., 20, 309, 310, 419, 420
Hewlitt, B. S., 215
Hiebert, E. H., 495
Higgens-Trenk, A., 405
Higgins, A., 440
Hill, C. R., 416
Hill, J. P., 458, 462, 507, 532, 535
Hill, W., 176
Himmin, H. S., 438
Hinde, R. A., 21, 65, 66, 69, 95, 328
Hinkle, J. S., 361
Hirchhorn, K., 86
Hirsch, B. J., 508
Hirsch, E. D., 402
Ho, D. Y. F., 215
Hobbs, N., 354
Hoffman, H. R., 319
Hoffman, J. M., 520
Hoffman, L., 308
Hoge, R. D., 396
Hollow, S. D., 59
Holmbeck, G. N., 532, 535
Holmes, D. L., 120
Holtzmann, W. H., 304
Holzman, M., 399
Honig, A. S., 363
Hopkins, R. W., 486
Horne, M. D., 354
Horowitz, F. D., 142
Housman, D., 486
Howard, J., 350
Howard, K. I., 458
Howell, C. T., 123
Howes, C., 218, 316
Hoyt, J. D., 381
Huang, L. N., 12, 307, 390, 428, 539, 552, 553
Hubbard, R., 350, 351
Humphreys, A., 246
Hunt, J. V., 120
Hunt, M., 471
Hurley, L. S., 112
Hurrelmann, K., 362
Hurt, B., 328
Huston, A. C., 319, 320, 323, 328, 329
Huston-Stein, A., 405
Hutchings, B., 114, 227
Hwang, C. P., 215
Hyde, J., 439
Hymel, S., 330
Hynd, G. W., 354

I

Ianni, F. A. J., 11
Iannotti, R. J., 335
Idol, L., 383
Iheanacho, S. O., 549

Pellegrino, J. W., 376
Penner, S. G., 190
Pepler, D. J., 306
Perkins, D., 398
Perlmutter, M., 20, 177, 246
Perret, Y. M., 357
Perry, T. B., 424, 429, 537
Peskin, H., 464
Petersen, A. C., 460
Peterson, L., 261
Peterson, P. L., 428
Petrinovich, L. F., 251
Pettit, G. S., 313
Phares, E. J., 45
Phelps, E., 495
Philip, J., 86
Phillips, D., 216
Phinney, J. S., 548
Piaget, J., 17, 50, 51, 52, 53, 57, 67, 146,
    161, 168, 169, 170, 173, 174, 175,
    267, 268, 271, 273, 314, 332, 376,
    377, 379, 384, 504
Pines, M., 307
Pintrich, P. R., 425
Pipes, P., 150, 253, 255
Pipp, S., 224
Pizer, H. F., 154
Pleck, J., 213
Plomin, R., 21, 92, 93, 95
Polier, J. W., 484
Poling, D., 502, 503, 504
Polit, D. F., 307
Polivy, J., 487
Pollack, J., 27, 88, 214
Pomeroy, W. B., 471
Pomrehn, P. R., 359
Porges, S. W., 160
Porter, F. L., 160
Pottebaum, S. M., 286
Powers, S. I., 433, 544
Pratt, C., 283
Pratto, D. J., 420
Premack, A. J., 186
Premack, D., 186
Pressley, M., 380
Price, C. G., 226
Price, J., 323
Price, J. M., 422
Prinsky, L. E., 547
Prinz, R., 255
Prothrow-Stith, D., 473
Psychology Today, 494
Puffer, J. C., 361
Puka, B., 443
Pyke, S. W., 26

Quintana, S., 325
Quisenberry, N. L., 313

Radford, J. L., 472
Radke-Yarrow, M., 153, 335
Ramey, C. T., 395
Ramirez, M., 550
Ramsay, D. S., 251
Ramsey, E., 24, 25, 484
Rand Youth Poll, 530
Rapkin, B. D., 508
Rauh, V. A., 122
Raynor, I. O., 405
Read, M., 117
Rebelsky, F. G., 191
Reich, J., 120
Reilly, R., 346
Resnick, S., 80, 309, 383
Reuman, D., 508
Rice, F. P., 110, 190
Rich, C. L., 486
Rich, S., 80
Riddle, D. B., 255
Ridgeway, D., 220
Rimm, D. C., 59
Rinaldi, R. C., 322
Risser, D., 361
Roberts, M. C., 227, 258
Robertson, A. S., 472
Robinson, D. P., 477
Robinson, N. M., 395, 397
Roche, A. F., 460
Rode, S. S., 127
Rodgers, J. E., 98
Rodman, H., 420
Rodriguez-Haynes, M., 228
Rogers, C. R., 40, 61, 62, 63, 64, 69, 325,
    326
Rogers, C. S., 255
Rogers, T., 325
Rogoff, B., 145, 286, 287, 378
Romaine, S., 403
Rose, S., 121, 161
Rose, S. A., 181
Rosenbaum, J. L., 547
Rosenberg, H., 59
Rosenberg, M. L., 479
Rosenblith, J. F., 104, 116, 119, 176
Rosenman, R., 365
Rosenthal, D., 486
Rosenthal, R., 394, 547
Rosoff, J. I., 474
Rossen, J., 421
Rothbart, R., 95, 306
Rotter, J. B., 406
Rovee-Collier, C., 175, 176
Rovine, M., 207
Rowe, D. C., 98
Ruben, D. B., 86
Rubenstein, J., 486
Rubin, C., 486
Rubin, D. N., 271
Rubin, K. M., 330

Rubin, R. R., 317
Rubin, V., 421
Ruble, D. N., 325, 328, 366
Rudes, B., 511
Rudy, J. W., 175
Ruff, H. A., 161
Rumbaugh, D. M., 187
Rumberger, R. W., 511, 512
Rutter, M., 229, 230, 309, 363, 369, 512
Ryan, E. B., 354

Sachdev, P., 108
Sackett, G. P., 114
Salapatek, P., 140, 157
Sandman, B. M., 113, 356
Sanger, C., 223
Sansone, R., 487
Santrock, J. W., 20, 55, 306, 309, 400,
    419, 420, 532
Sattler, J. M., 286
Sawin, D. B., 214
Sax, G., 26
Saxe, G. B., 286
Scardamalia, M., 495
Scarr, S., 11, 17, 89, 96, 98, 218, 389,
    460
Schaffer, H. R., 190, 208
Schaie, K. W., 33
Schank, R., 381
Schegloff, E. A., 189
Schiebe, C., 322
Schlundt, D. G., 487
Schnur, E., 291
Schopler, E., 229, 230
Schorr, L. B., 548
Schulenberg, J. E., 518
Schulsinger, F., 486
Schulsinger, R., 86
Schulz, H., 143
Schunk, D. H., 406
Schuster, C. S., 349, 359
Schwartz, D., 112
Schwartz, M. L., 149
Schwarz, P. M., 438
Scott, D. K., 260
Segal, N. L., 80
Seibert, J. M., 111
Seidman, E., 427
Seidner, L. B., 316
Seifer, R., 207
Seigle, J., 319, 323
Selman, R., 424
Selye, H., 362
Senn, M. J., 15
Serbin, L. A., 330
Serlin, R. C., 457
Sexton, M., 114, 366
Shantz, C. U., 271, 422
Shapiro, E. K., 428, 482
Shapiro, E. R., 486

Walton, M. D., 150
Warren, L. W., 486
Warren, M. P., 461, 463
Warren, W. K., 472
Warshak, R. A., 309, 419, 420
Waters, E., 142, 434
Watkins, B. A., 320
Watson, J. B., 16, 58, 141, 151, 301
Watts, T. D., 480
Wechsler, D., 286
Wehlage, G. G., 512
Weidemann, C., 383
Weidner, G., 366
Weinberg, M. S., 471
Weinberg, R. A., 96
Weinberger, D. A., 364
Weiner, I. B., 445
Weinstein, N. D., 359
Weisberg, R. P., 422
Weishahn, M. W., 352
Weiskopf, F., 177
Weiss, G., 356
Weiss, M., 223
Weiss-Perry, B., 433
Wellman, H. M., 381
Wender, P. H., 486
Wenner, W., 143
Werner, E. E., 112, 227
Werner, J. S., 175
Wertlieb, D., 363
Wessles, K., 425
Westoff, C. G., 474

Whalen, C. K., 356
Whaley, L., 84, 347
Whiren, A., 318
White, B. L., 143, 146, 172, 303
White, L. J., 286
White, M. A., 382
White, R. W., 406
White, S. H., 17
Whitehurst, G. J., 190
Whiting, B. B., 546
Widmayer, S., 126
Wiedenfield, S. A., 366
Wigfield, A., 508
Wilcox, K. J., 80
Wilks, Y., 185
Williams, J., 400
Williams, M. F., 319
Williams, R. B., 365
Williams, S., 436, 437
William T. Grant Foundation, 11, 459,
    511, 513, 523
Wilson, J., 548
Wilson, K., 205
Wilson, M. N., 309, 523, 548
Wilson, R. S., 95
Windle, W. F., 158
Winner, E., 269, 282, 397, 495
Witkin, H. A., 86
Wohlwill, J. F., 315
Wolf, D., 268, 398
Wolfson, J., 121
Wong, D. L., 84, 347
Wood, F. H., 354

Woodson, R., 178
Worobey, J., 126
Wortham, S. C., 259
Worthington, B. S., 112
Worthington-Roberts, B. S., 150
Wright, H. F., 420
Wright, J. E., 481
Wright, L., 258
Wright, M. R., 463
Wulf, G., 474
Wylie, R. C., 325

Yanof, D. S., 532
Yesalis, C. E., 359, 481
Young, D., 486
Youniss, J., 458
Yussen, S. R., 11, 400

Zabin, L. S., 469
Zahn-Waxler, C., 220, 335
Zeigler, S., 283
Zellman, G. L., 470
Zelnik, M., 468
Zembar, M., 393
Zeskind, P. S., 141
Zigler, E., 12, 218, 395, 396
Zimmerman, R., 208, 209
Zukow, P. G., 305

Subject Index

industry versus inferiority, 46
initiative versus guilt, 46
integrity versus despair, 47
intimacy versus isolation, 47
trust versus mistrust, 46
See also specific stages.
Ethical issues
fetal tissue, medical use issue, 109
research studies, 33–34
Ethnicity and adolescence, 548–554
Asian-American adolescents, 552
black adolescents, 548–549
Hispanic adolescents, 550–551
Native American adolescents, 553
Ethnic stereotypes, television, 319
Ethological theories, 64–67
of attachment, 209–210
evaluation of, 67
Lorenz's theory, 64–65
neo-ethological theory, 65–66
Eustress, 362
Exercise
family influences, 361
infants and, 148
injuries from, 361
poor condition of American children,
360–361
preterm infants and, 123
Exosystem, 202
Expanding, language development, 190
Experiential intelligence, 393
Experimental strategy, 29–31
cause and effect, investigation of,
29–30
compared to correlational strategy, 31
control groups in, 30
dependent/independent variables in,
30
experimental group in, 30
random assignment in, 30
Expressive orientation, gender roles, 437,
439
Extrinsic motivation, 406

F

Families
autonomy and adolescence, 523–533
birth order, 305–307
child abuse and, 228
coregulation period, 418
cross-cultural view, 304
current issues, 11
delayed childbearing trend, 536
discipline, 418
gender role development and, 329–330
identity of adolescent and, 544
labeling of parents/children, 418
life changes and, 418
maturation of children/parents, 535
parent-adolescent conflicts, 533–535
parent-child issues, 417–418

parenting styles, 301–304
sibling relationships, 305
socialization and, 205–207
societal changes and
divorce, 308–310
latchkey children, 420
stepfamilies, 419–420
working mothers, 308
transition to parenthood, 204
Fathers
as caretakers, 214
changing role of, 213–214
childbirth participation, 118
paternal interactions, 214
Swedish study, 214–215
Femininity, 435, 437
Fetal period, 106–107
Fine motor skills, 146
early childhood, 245–250
middle childhood, 349
First words, 191–192
Formal operational thought, 52, 494–496
age of, 494
criticisms of, 496
cross-cultural view, 497
hypothetical deductive reasoning in,
495
idealism in, 495
language and, 495
metaphor, 495
satire, 495
writing ability, 495–496
Freud's theory, 41–45
of attachment, 208
defense mechanisms, 42–43
dreams, 54
ego in, 41–42
erogenous zones in, 43
id in, 41–42
pleasure principle in, 41
reality principle in, 41
stages of development
anal stage, 44
fixation and, 44
genital stage, 44
latency stage, 44
Oedipus complex in, 44
oral stage, 44
phallic stage, 44
superego in, 42
Friendships, 423–424
developmental model, 424
functions of, 423–424
intimacy, 424
Fully-functioning person, 62

G

Games, of socialization, 206
Gang membership, 484, 485
Gender differences
careers and, 518–520

classic study of, 439
computer ability and, 440
disappearance of, 439–440
math and, 440
reactions to divorce, 309
Gender roles
androgyny, 435–436
biographical influences, 327–328
cognitive influences, 328–329
cross-cultural view, 438
development of, 331
environmental influences, 329–331
expressive orientation, 437, 439
gender schema, 328
historical view of, 18
instrumental orientation, 437, 439
interactionist position, 328
masculinity/femininity, definitional
issues, 435–437
parental influences, 329–330
personality development, 434–440
same-sex play, 330–331
school influences, 330
undifferentiated gender role, 435, 437
Generativity versus stagnation, 47
Genetic counseling, 87
Genetic disorders, 96, 98
Down syndrome, 84
incidence of, 86
Klinefelter's syndrome, 86
PKU (phenylketonuria), 84
sickle-cell anemia, 84
Turner's syndrome, 86
XYY syndrome, 86
Genetics
behavior genetics, 90–91
dominant-recessive genes, 86
genetic codes, 80–81
genotype, 88–90
phenotype, 89–90
polygenic inheritance, 88
reaction range and, 89
sexual differentiation, 88
structure of, 81
testis determining factor, 88
transmission of genes, 81, 83
See also Heredity and development.
Genetic testing
amniocentesis, 87
chorionic villus test, 87
ultrasound sonography, 87
Genital herpes, and prenatal development,
110
Genital stage, 44
Genotype, 88–90
Germinal period, 104
Giftedness, 396–397
definition of, 396
development of, 397
social/mental maladjustment myth,
396–397
Terman study, 396

structure-process dilemma, 392–393
tacit knowledge as, 394
triarchic theory, 393
two-factor theory, 389
Intelligence tests
Binet tests, 385–386
cross-cultural view, 389
culture fair tests, 390–391
infant intelligence tests, 179–181
intelligence quotient (IQ), 385
normal distribution and, 385
use and misuse of, 394
Wechsler scales, 386–389
Internalization of schemes, sensorimotor
stage, 173
Interviews, 26
problems of, 26
Intimacy, 424
Intimacy versus isolation, 47
Intrinsic motivation, 406
Intuitive thought substage, preoperational
thought, 272
In vitro fertilization, 83

Jigsaw classroom, 430
Justice perspective, moral development,
443
Juvenile delinquency, 482–484
causes of, 484
definition of, 483
drug-related violence, 485
gang membership, 484, 485
incidence of, 483–484
lower-class culture and, 484

Kilogram babies, 122
Kindergarten, child-centered
kindergarten, 289
Klinefelter's syndrome, 86
Kohlberg's theory of moral development,
440–443
age sequence, 442
conventional reasoning, 441
criticisms of, 443, 444
Kohlberg dilemma, 440–441, 442, 444
postconventional reasoning, 441
preconventional reasoning, 441

Labeling, language development, 190
Labor, childbirth, 118–119
Laboratory observation, 25–26
Lamaze method, 116–117, 118

Language
creative aspects of, 183
definition of, 183
displacement, 183
gender based language, 328–329
human evolution and, 186–187
rule systems, 183–184
grammar, 184
morphology, 183–184, 280–281
overgeneralizations of rules, 280
phonology, 183
pragmatics, 184, 282–283
semantics, 184, 282
syntax, 184, 281–282
Language development
adolescence, 495–496
babbling, 191
behavioral view, 188–189
bilingualism, 402–403
conversation, 496
critical period in, 188
early childhood, 280–283
environmental influences, 189–190
echoing, 190
expanding, 190
labeling, 190
motherese, 190
recasting, 190
first words, 191–192
grammar, 399
language acquisition device, 185–187
language learning by chimpanzees,
186–187
lateralization of brain and, 188
mean length of utterance (MLU),
193–194
metaphor, 495
middle childhood, 399–403
overextensions/underextensions of
word meaning, 192
satire, 495
social isolation and, 189
telegraphic speech, 193
two-word statements, 192–193
vocabulary, 399
writing ability, 495–496
Latchkey children, 420
Latency stage, 44
Lazy eye, 243–244
Learning disabilities
characteristics of, 354–355
needs of learning disabled, 354
Least restrictive environment, 352
Leboyer method, 116
Left-handedness, 250
Literacy
cross-cultural view, 513
program for preschoolers, 283–284
Longitudinal approach, 32
Long-term memory, 380

Lorenz's theory, 64–65
critical period in, 65
geese experiments, 64–65
imprinting in, 65
Low-birthweight infants, 120
See also Preterm infants.

Macrosystem, 202
Mainstreaming, 352–353
Malnutrition
effects of, 153
hunger in America, 154
marasmus, 153
prenatal development and, 112
Marital satisfaction, parenthood and, 204
Masculinity, 435, 437
Massage, preterm infants and, 123
Maternal age, and prenatal development,
111–112
Maternal disease, and prenatal
development, 110–111
Maternal employment, 308
Math
Americans compared to Japanese, 409
gender differences, 440
Mean length of utterance (MLU),
193–194
Memory, 176–177
control processes, 380–381
early childhood, 278–279
elaboration and, 383
imagery strategies, 180
infancy, 176–177
infantile amnesia, 177
memory acquisition, 177
influence of child characteristics, 381
keyword method, 380
long-term memory, 380
meta memory, 381
middle childhood, 380–381
rehearsal, 278, 380
short-term memory, 278
speed of processing/retention and,
278–279
Mental age (MA), 385
Mental retardation
categories of, 395
cultural-familial retardation, 395
current issues, 12
definition of, 395
organic retardation, 395
Mesosystem, 201
Meta memory, 381
Metaphor, 495
Microsystem, 201
Middle Ages, view of children, 14

Recasting, language development, 190
Reciprocal socialization, 205–207
Reflexes of infant, 51, 138–142
  changes over time, 139–140
  grasping reflex, 139–140
  Moro reflex, 139
  reflexive smile, 142
  rooting reflex, 138–139
  simple reflexes, 170
  sucking reflex, 138, 140–141
Reflexive smile, 142
Regression, 42
Rehearsal, memory, 278, 380
Rejected children, and popularity, 422
Religious beliefs
  adolescence, 501–502
  development of, 501
  individual-reflective faith, 501
  spiritual interest, 501–502
REM sleep, infancy, 143–144
Renaissance, view of children, 14
Repression, 42
Reproduction
  in vitro fertilization, 83
  moment of conception, 81
  process of, 83
  sperm/ovum in, 83
Research methods
  case studies, 26
  ethical issues, 33–34
  interviews, 26
  multimeasure/multisource/
    multicontext approach, 27, 29
  observation, 25–26
  physiological research, 26
  questionnaires, 26
  standardized tests, 26
Research strategies
  correlational strategy, 29
  cross-sectional approach, 31–32
  experimental strategy, 29–31
  longitudinal approach, 32
  sequential approach, 33
Reversible mental actions, in concrete
    operational thought, 377
Rhythmic motor behavior
  infancy, 146–148
  theories of, 146–147
Rites of passage
  adult status and, 556
  American adolescents, 555–556
  primitive cultures, 554–555
Rock music, 546–547
Roger's theory, 62–63
  fully-functioning person in, 62
  self-actualization in, 63–64
  self-concept in, 325
  self in, 62
  unconditional positive regard in, 62
Rooting reflex, 138–139

Rough-and-tumble play, 246
Rubella, and prenatal development, 110
Rule systems. *See* Language

S

Satanism, 503
Satire, 495
Scaffolding, 205
Scheduled feeding schedule, 151
Schemata
  in information processing, 381
  in Piaget's theory, 169
Scholastic Aptitude Test (SAT), 383
Schools
  achievement and, 425, 428
  aptitude-treatment interaction, 428
  back-to-basics movement, 505
  best middle schools, characteristics of,
    509, 510
  cooperative learning approach, 430
  cross-cultural view, 426
  dropouts, 511–515
  drug prevention programs, 482
  gender roles and, 330
  jigsaw classroom, 430
  learning area approach, 426–427
  minority-group students and, 428–430
  secondary schools, issues related to,
    505–506
  teacher's influence, 427–428
  top-dog phenomenon, 508
  transition to middle/junior high
    school, 506–507
  transition to school, 425
Scientific method
  hypothesis in, 24
  steps in, 24–25
  theories in, 24
Scientific thinking, 495, 497
Scripts, in information processing,
    381–382
Seat belts, 260
Secondary circular reactions, sensorimotor
    stage, 170
Secure attachment, 210–211
Self
  "I" and "me" and, 325
  initiative versus guilt, 324–325
  inner/outer self, 326–327
  parental attributes related to high self-
    esteem, 433
  personality development, 431–434
  in Roger's theory, 62
  self-concept, 433
  self-concept measure, 433
  self-esteem, 325–326, 433
  social competence and, 434
  See also Identity.

Self-actualization, 63–64
Semantics, 184, 282
Sensation, 156
Sensitive period, 65, 66
Sensorimotor stage, 51, 146, 169–175
  coordination of secondary reactions,
    171
  internalization of schemes, 173
  object permanence, 173–174
  primary circular reactions, 170
  secondary circular reactions, 170
  simple reflexes, 170
  tertiary circular reactions, 171, 173
Separation anxiety, 207–208
Sequential approach, 33
Seven intelligences concept, 390
Sex education, cross-cultural view, 476
Sexual abuse, 229
Sexual differentiation, 88
Sexuality, 466–477
  adolescent pregnancy, 473–477
  cross-cultural view, 476
  double standard, 470–471
  homosexuality, 471
  new norm, 469–470
  sexual scripts, 469
  trends related to sexual behavior,
    468–469
Sexually transmitted diseases
  AIDS, 472–473
  chlamydia, 471–472
  herpes simplex virus II, 472
Short-term memory, 278
Shyness
  consistency over time, 97
  modification of, 97
Sibling relationships
  and birth order, 306
  socialization and, 305
Sickle-cell anemia, 84
Simple reflexes, sensorimotor stage, 170
Sleep in infancy
  REM sleep, 143–144
  sleep-waking cycles, 143
  types of sleep, 142
Smell, development in infancy, 158
Smiling in infancy, 220
  reflexive smile, 142
  social smile, 142
Social cognition
  adolescence, 496, 498
  egocentrism, 496
  imaginary audience, 496
  and middle childhood, 422–423
  personal fable, 496, 498
  personality, understanding of, 498
  social monitoring, 498
Social competence
  dimensions of, 434
  industry versus inferiority, 434

Visual perception
    depth perception, 157–158
    development in infancy, 156–158
    early childhood, 243
    functional amblyopia, 243–244
    research methods, 156–157
    vision problems, signs of, 244
Visual problems, middle childhood, 359
Vocabulary, development in middle
        childhood, 399
Vygotsky's theory
    play, 314
    sociological aspects, 287–288
    thought and language in, 287
    zone of proximal development,
        286–287

Wechsler scales, 386–389
Weight, early childhood, 240–242
Whole word method, reading, 399, 400
Winnie-the-Pooh, relationship to Piaget's
        concepts, 275
Wolf children, 28
Work
    part-time work, 521–522
    sociohistorical view, 520–521
    transition to, 522–523
Writing
    in adolescence, 495–496
    process approach, 350

XYY syndrome, 86

Zone of proximal development,
        Vygotsky's theory, 286–287